Wonders

McGraw Hill

Also Available from McGraw Hill

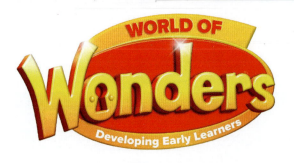 

mheducation.com/prek-12

Send all inquiries to:
McGraw Hill
1325 Avenue of the Americas.
New York, NY 10019

ISBN: 978-1-26-575864-6
MHID: 1-26-575864-6

Printed in China

7 8 9 10 11 DSS 27 26 25 24 23

D

Welcome to *Wonders*

Designed to support teachers and empower students.

You want all your students to build knowledge while fostering exploration of our world through literacy. Literacy is the key to understanding – across time, across borders, across cultures – and will help students realize the role they play in the world they are creating.

The result: an evidence-based K–5 ELA program, aligned with standards and based on the Science of Reading, that empowers students to take an active role in learning and exploration. Your students will enjoy unparalleled opportunities for student-friendly self-assessments and self-expression through reading, writing, and speaking. By experiencing diverse perspectives and sharing their own, students will expand their learning. Best-in-class differentiation ensures that all your students have opportunities to become strong readers, writers, and critical thinkers.

We're excited for you to get to know *Wonders* and honored to join you and your students on your pathways to success!

Authors and Consultants

With unmatched expertise in English Language Arts, supporting English language learners, intervention, and more, the *Wonders* team of authors is composed of scholars, researchers, and teachers from across the country. From managing ELA research centers, to creating evidence-based classroom practices for teachers, this highly qualified team of professionals is fully invested in improving student and district outcomes.

Authors

Dr. Douglas Fisher
Close Reading and Writing,
Writing to Sources,
Text Complexity

Dr. Diane August
English Language Learners,
Dual Language

Kathy Bumgardner
Instructional Best Practices,
Multi-Sensory Teaching,
Student Engagement

Dr. Vicki Gibson
Small Group Instruction,
Social Emotional Learning,
Foundational Skills

Dr. Josefina V. Tinajero
English Language Learners,
Dual Language

Dr. Timothy Shanahan
Text Complexity,
Reading and Writing,
Oral Reading Fluency,
Close Reading,
Disciplinary Literacy

Dr. Donald Bear
Word Study, Vocabulary,
Foundational Skills

Dr. Jana Echevarria
English Language Learners,
Oral Language Development

Dr. Jan Hasbrouck
Oral Reading Fluency,
Foundational Skills,
Response to Intervention

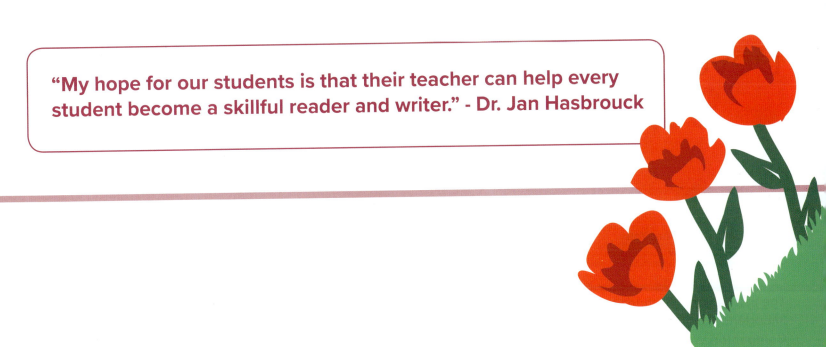

"My hope for our students is that their teacher can help every student become a skillful reader and writer." - Dr. Jan Hasbrouck

Consultants

Dr. Doris Walker-Dalhouse
Multicultural Literature

Dr. David J. Francis
Assessment, English Language
Learners Research

Jay McTighe
Understanding by Design

Dr. Tracy Spinrad
Social Emotional Learning

Dinah Zike
Professional Development,
Multi-Sensory Teaching

"My hope for our students including English Learners, is that they will receive outstanding English language arts and reading instruction to allow them to reach their full academic potential and excel in school and in life." - Dr. Josefina V. Tinajero

Developing **Student Ownership** of Learning

| Reflect on What You Know | Monitor Learning | Choose Learning Resources | Reflect on Progress | Set Learning Goals |

The instructional routines in *Wonders* guide students to understand the importance of taking ownership of their own learning. The **Reading/Writing Companion** Welcome pages introduce students to routines they will be using throughout the year.

AUTHOR INSIGHT

Learning how to identify what they are learning, talk about what they know, figure out what they need more help with, and figure out next steps are all important aspects of taking ownership of learning that students develop in *Wonders*.

- Dr. Douglas Fisher

Reflect on What You Know

Text Set Goals

Students are introduced to three overarching goals for each text set. Students first evaluate what they know before instruction begins.

Reading and Writing

Students evaluate what they know about reading in a particular genre and writing in response to texts using text evidence.

Build Knowledge Goals

Each text set is focused on building knowledge through investigation of an Essential Question. After an introduction to the Essential Question, students self-evaluate how much they already know about the topic.

Extended Writing Goals

Students also think about their ability to write in a particular genre before instruction begins.

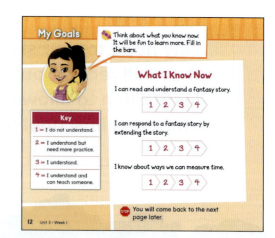

Courtesy of Douglas Fisher

Monitor Learning

Lesson Learning Goals

The journey through a text set and extended writing is made up of a sequence of lessons. The learning goals of these lessons build toward achieving the overarching goals. At the start of each lesson, a targeted learning goal, presented as a "We Can" statement, is introduced to students.

The learning goals are shared with students and parents so that they can track their learning as they work through the lessons.

Check-In Routine

At the end of each lesson, students are asked to self-assess how well they understood the lesson learning goal.

At the end of the lesson, students conference with a partner. They review the lesson learning goal "We Can" statement.

Review

CHECK-IN ROUTINE

Review the lesson learning goal.
Reflect on the activity.
Self-Assess by
- filling in the bars in the Reading/Writing Companion
- holding up 1, 2, 3, or 4 fingers

Share with your teacher.

Reflect

Students take turns self-reflecting on how well they understood the learning goal.

TEACHING TIP

As students develop their ability to reflect on their work, provide sentence frames to support them.

Ask yourself:

Can I _____?
Respond:
I can almost _____.
I am having trouble_____.
I need to work on _____.

Share

Students share their self-assessments with you by holding up their fingers and sharing the filled-in bars. This lets you know how students think they are doing.

TEACHING TIP

Valuing students' self-assessments is important to enabling students to take ownership of their learning. As students progress throughout the year, they become more adept at self-assessing what they know and what help they need moving forward.

Self Assess

Students hold up 1, 2, 3 or 4 fingers to self-assess how well they understood the learning goal. When appropriate, they will fill in the bars in the Reading/Writing Companion as well. At the start of the year, review the ratings with students emphasizing that we all learn differently and at a different pace. It is okay to score a 1 or 2. Understanding what they do not know will help students figure out what to do next.

TEACHING TIP

1 I did not understand the learning goal.

2 I understood some things about the learning goal. I need more explanation.

3 I understood how to do the lesson, but I need more practice.

4 I understood the learning goal really well. I think I can teach someone how to do it.

Developing **Student Ownership** of Learning

| Reflect on What You Know | Monitor Learning | Choose Learning Resources | Reflect on Progress | Set Learning Goals |

Choose Learning Resources

Student-Teacher Conferencing

As students evaluate what they understand, the next step is to think about whether they need more teaching or more practice. The **Reading/Writing Companion** can serve as a powerful conferencing tool. Reviewing their filled-in bars while conferring with each student provides you the opportunity to guide students into identifying what they should do next to improve their understanding.

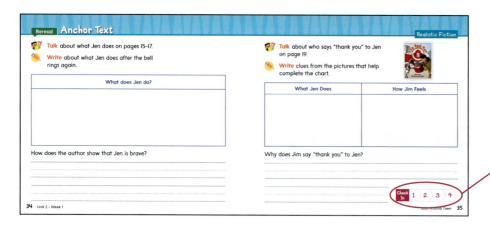

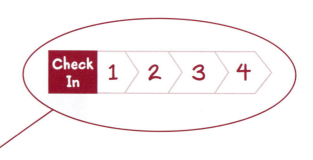

Small Group Teacher-Led Instruction

You and the student may decide that they need more teaching. Student Check-Ins and your observations at the end of each lesson provide timely data that informs the focus for teacher-led small group instruction. Teachers can choose from the small group differentiated lessons provided.

Small Group Independent/Collaborative Work

While meeting with small groups, other students can practice the skills and concepts they have determined they need practice with.

My Weekly Work lists options for collaborative and independent practice. Based on student input and your informal observations, you identify "Must Do" activities to be completed. Students then choose activities focused on areas of need and interests they have identified—promoting student choice and voice.

Reflect on Progress

After completing the lessons in the text set and extended writing, students reflect on their overall progress. They share this information during teacher conferences. The focus of the conversations is on progress made and figuring out next steps to continued progress.

TEACHING TIP

As students discuss their progress, ask them to reflect on the following:

- In what areas did you feel that you made a lot of progress?
- What are some examples?
- What areas do you still need to work on?
- What things can you do to make more progress in these areas?

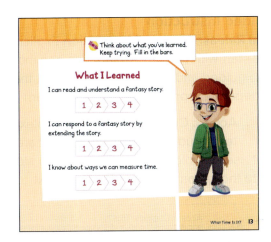

Set Learning Goals

At the end of the unit, students continue to reflect on their learning. They are also asked to set their own learning goals as they move into the next unit of instruction.

See additional guidance online for supporting students in evaluating work, working toward meeting learning goals, and reflecting on progress.

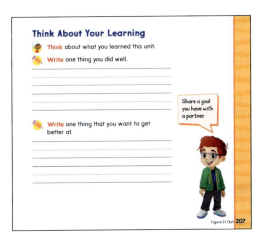

Equity and Access

Differentiated Resources

Every student deserves high-quality instruction. *Wonders* provides high-quality, rigorous instruction that supports access to grade-level content and ELA Skills through equitable, differentiated instruction and resources.

Scaffolded Instruction

Gradual Release Model of Instruction Explicit skills lessons start with teacher explanation and modeling, then move to guided and collaborative practice, then culminate with independent practice with the Your Turn activities.

Access Complex Text The complex features of texts students are asked to read are highlighted. Point-of-use scaffolds are provided to help students to attend to those complex aspects of the text.

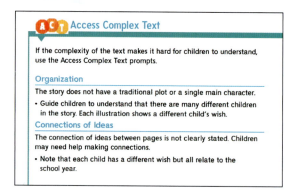

Differentiated Small Group Time

Teacher-Led Instruction Key skills and concepts are supported with explicit differentiated lessons. The Differentiated Genre Passages and Leveled Readers provide a variety of differentiated texts. Literature Small group lessons guide teachers in scaffolding support so all students have access to the same text.

Tier 2 instruction is incorporated into the Approaching level lessons. Additional Tier 2 instruction is available online.

Gifted and Talented activities are also provided for those students who are ready to extend their learning.

Independent/Collaborative Work

A range of choices for practice and extension are provided to support the key skills and concepts taught. Students use this time to work on their independent reading and writing. Resources include the Center Activity Cards, online games, Practice Book, and Content Area Reading blackline masters.

Data Informed Instruction *Wonders* offers frequent opportunities for informal and formative assessment. The student Check-Ins and teacher Check for Success features provide daily input allowing adjustments for instruction and student practice. The Data Dashboard collects data from online games and activities and the Progress Monitoring assessments.

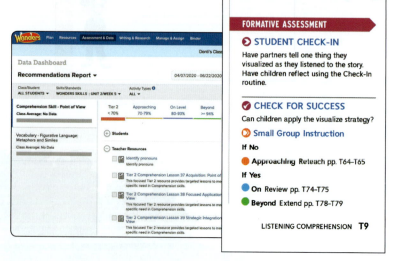

 English Language Learners

Access to Grade Level Lessons

English Language Proficiency Levels Targeted support addressing the different English Language Proficiency Levels allows all students to participate.

Spotlight on Language Point-of-use support that highlights English phrases and vocabulary that may be particularly difficult for English Language Learners.

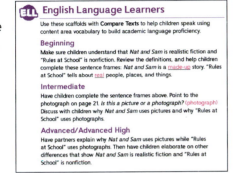

Multilingual Resources

Home Language Support The following features are available in Spanish, Haitian-Creole, Portuguese, Vietnamese, French, Arabic, Chinese, Russian, Tagalog, and Urdu:

- Summaries of the Shared Read and Anchor Texts.
- School–to-Home Letters that help families support students in their learning goals.
- Multilingual Glossary of key content words with definitions from grade-level texts.
- Spanish and Haitian-Creole Leveled Readers available online.

Strategic Support

A separate resource is available for small group instruction focused specifically on English Language Learners. The lessons are carefully designed to support the language development, grade level skills, and content. The instruction and resources are differentiated to address all levels of English Language Proficiency and carefully align with the instruction in Reading and Writing.

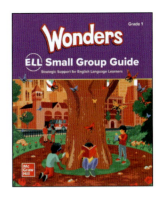

Additional Resources for Differentiation

Newcomer Kit Instructional cards and practice focused on access to basic, high-utility vocabulary.

Language Development Kit Differentiated instruction and practice for key English grammar concepts.

Collection of Diverse Literature

The literature in *Wonders* provides a diverse representation of various individuals and cultures. The texts give students the opportunity to see themselves and others within and outside of their communities. As students read, listen to, discuss, and write about texts, they are able to make real-life connections to themselves and the world around them.

Culturally Responsive Teaching

Drawing from the research, there are a number of factors that support classroom equity and enable the underpinnings of culturally responsive teaching: high academic expectations for all students; a socially and emotionally positive classroom; a safe school climate; authentic and rigorous tasks; inclusive, relevant, and meaningful content; open and accepting communication; drawing from students' strengths, knowledge, culture, and competence; critically and socially aware inquiry practices; strong teaching; and school staff professional support and learning about equity and inclusion (Aronson & Laughter, 2016; Gay, 2010; Krasnoff, 2016; Ladson-Billings, 2006; Morrison, Robbins, & Rose, 2008; NYSED, 2019; Saphier, 2017; Snyder, Trowery & McGrath, 2019; Waddell, 2014). It is important to note the emphasis on developing classrooms and instructional practices that support all students, rather than focusing solely on who the students are and what they bring to school.

Through the high-quality content and research-based best practices of the instructional routines embedded in the program, the *Wonders* curriculum supports all important aspects of culturally responsive teaching.

The Learning Community: providing avenues for the development of a classroom community grounded in collaboration, risk-taking, responsibility, perseverance, and communication. This allows all learners to find a pathway to deep learning and academic success.

Wonders promotes classroom practices that best support meaningful learning and collaboration among peers. Valuing students' voices on what they think about the world around them and what they know allows teachers to build on students' funds of knowledge and adapt instruction and application opportunities. Starting in Kindergarten and progressing through the grades, students develop their ability to engage in focused academic discussions, assisting each other in deep understanding of the texts they read and building knowledge on various topics.

Authentic and Rigorous Learning Tasks: providing multiple methods to learn new material, challenging content for all levels of learners, opportunities to discuss, grapple with, and critique ideas, and space to personally connect to the content. This allows all learners to develop enthusiasm and dedication in their academic endeavors.

In *Wonders*, many of the texts center on relevant issues, examples, and real-world problems, along with prompts and questions that encourage students to engage and think critically about how they would address a similar problem or issue. The Essential Question for each text set introduces the topic that will be explored, culminating in a Show Your Knowledge activity. This allows students to synthesize information they learned analyzing all the texts. Extended writing tasks allow additional opportunities for flexible connections, elaboration of student thinking, and original expression.

Differentiation Opportunities: providing instructional pathways to meet the individual needs of all learners, which creates a more equitable learning experience.

In *Wonders*, clarity around differentiation of instruction, flexibility, adaptability, and choice are some of the key guiding principles on which the resources have been built. In addition to providing a range of differentiated leveled texts, *Wonders* is designed to ensure all students have access to rich, authentic grade-level informational and literary texts. A variety of print and digital resources are provided as options for differentiating practice opportunities.

FatCamera/Getty Images

Evidence of Learning: providing continuous opportunities to gather information about each learner's academic progress through a variety of assessment methods. This allows for timely feedback to learners and supports differentiation for meeting the needs of all learners.

In *Wonders*, students' self-evaluation of their own learning and progress over time is integral to student success. Student Check-In Routines assist students in documenting how well they understand leaning goals and encourage them to reflect on what may have been difficult to understand. Resources such as the Learning Goals Blackline Masters and features in the Reading/Writing Companion assist students in monitoring their progress. Teachers use the results of the Student Check-Ins and their informal observations of students with the Check for Success features in the Teacher's Edition to inform decisions about small group differentiated instruction. A range of innovative tools equip the teacher for assessment-informed instructional decision making, and ensure students are equipped to fully participate in responsive, engaging instruction. This Data Dashboard uses student results from assessments and activities to provide instructional recommendations tailored to the individual needs.

Relevant, Respectful, and Meaningful Content: providing content that represents the lives and experiences of a range of individuals who belong to different racial, ethnic, religious, age, gender, linguistic, socio-economic, and ability groups in equitable, positive, and non-stereotypical ways. This allows all learners to see themselves reflected in the content they are learning.

In *Wonders*, resources have been created and curated to promote literacy and deepen understanding for every student. A commitment to multicultural education and our nation's diverse population is evident in the literature selections and themes found throughout every grade. *Wonders* depicts people from various ethnic backgrounds in all types of environments, avoiding stereotypes. Students of all backgrounds will be able to relate to the texts. The authors of the texts in *Wonders* are also diverse and represent a rich range of backgrounds and cultures, which they bring to their writing.

Supporting Family Communication: providing open communication avenues for families by developing regular and varied interactions about program content. This provides opportunities for all families to be involved in the academic progress of their learner.

In *Wonders*, the School to Home tab on the ConnectEd Student Workspace provides information to families about what students are learning. The letters introduce the Essential Questions that the students will be investigating in each text set, as well as the key skills and skills. Activities that families can complete with students at home are provided. Access to texts that students are reading is also available through the Student Workspace. Home-to-school letters and audio summaries of student texts are available in multiple languages, including English, Spanish, Haitian-Creole, Portuguese, Vietnamese, French, Arabic, Chinese (Cantonese and Mandarin), Russian, Tagalog, and Urdu.

Professional Learning: providing instructional guidance for administrators and teachers that supports enacting culturally responsive and sustaining pedagogical practices and focuses on asset-based approaches, bias surfacing, cultural awareness, and connections to learner communities, cultures, and resources.

In *Wonders*, a comprehensive set of resources assists administrators and teachers in a successful implementation of the program to ensure teacher and student success. Information embedded in the Teacher's Edition, and targeted components such as the Instructional Routines Handbook, as well as online Professional Learning Videos and resources, provide a wide range of support. Resources focused on helping teachers reflect on their understanding of the different cultures of their students, as well as assisting teachers in facilitating meaningful conversations about texts, are also provided.

Teaching the
Whole Child

Your students are learning so much more than reading from you. They're learning how to learn, how to master new content areas, and how to handle themselves in and out of the classroom. Research shows that this leads to increased academic success. *Wonders* resources have been developed to support you in teaching the whole child, for success this year and throughout your students' lives.

Habits of Learning

prepare students to master skills and to be lifelong learners.

Social Emotional Learning

grounds students in the classroom and teaches self-mastery.

Classroom Culture

sets the stage for collaboration, focus, and a love of reading.

DEVELOPING CRITICAL THINKERS

- Mastery of reading, writing, speaking, and listening
- Knowledge that spans content areas
- College and career readiness
- Strong results this year and beyond

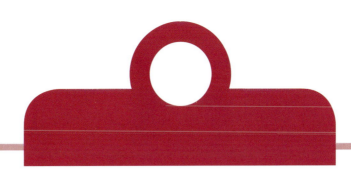

Habits of Learning

I am part of a community of learners.

- ☐ I listen actively to others to learn new ideas.
- ☐ I build upon others' ideas in a conversation.
- ☐ I work with others to understand my learning goals.
- ☐ I stay on topic during discussion.
- ☐ I use words that will make my ideas clear.
- ☐ I share what I know.
- ☐ I gather information to support my thinking.

I use a variety of strategies when I read.

- ☐ I make predictions.
- ☐ I take notes.
- ☐ I think about how a text is organized.
- ☐ I visualize what I'm reading.
- ☐ I think about the author's purpose.

I think critically about what I read.

- ☐ I ask questions.
- ☐ I look for text evidence.
- ☐ I make inferences based on evidence.
- ☐ I connect new ideas to what I already know.

I write to communicate.

- ☐ I think about what I read as models for my writing.
- ☐ I talk with my peers to help make my writing better.
- ☐ I use rubrics to analyze my own writing.
- ☐ I use different tools when I write and present.

I believe I can succeed.

- ☐ I try different ways to learn things that are difficult for me.
- ☐ I ask for help when I need it.
- ☐ I challenge myself to do better.
- ☐ I work to complete my tasks.
- ☐ I read independently.

I am a problem solver.

- ☐ I analyze the problem.
- ☐ I try different ways.

Classroom Culture

We respect and value each other's experiences.

- ☐ We value what each of us brings from home.
- ☐ We work together to understand each other's perspectives.
- ☐ We work with our peers in pairs and in small groups.
- ☐ We use new academic vocabulary we learn when we speak and write.
- ☐ We share our work and learn from others.

We promote student ownership of learning.

- ☐ We understand what our learning goals are.
- ☐ We evaluate how well we understand each learning goal.
- ☐ We find different ways to learn what is difficult.

We learn through modeling and practice.

- ☐ We practice together to make sure we understand.
- ☐ We access many different resources to get information.
- ☐ We use many different tools when we share what we learn.

We foster a love of reading.

- ☐ We create inviting places to sit and read.
- ☐ We read for enjoyment.
- ☐ We read to understand ourselves and our world.

We build knowledge.

- ☐ We investigate what we want to know more about.
- ☐ We read many different types of texts to gain information.
- ☐ We build on what we know.

We inspire confident writers.

- ☐ We analyze the connection between reading and writing.
- ☐ We understand the purpose and audience for our writing.
- ☐ We revise our writing to make it stronger.

Social EMOTIONAL Learning

Positive social emotional learning **(SEL) gives young learners the critical foundation to experience success in school and life** with understanding, flexibility, support, and resiliency. Research shows that children's ability to regulate their own emotions and behaviors affects their ability to build and maintain relationships with others, which in turn has a direct impact on their academic success.

The SEL Curriculum

We are proud to partner with Sesame Workshop to provide an integrated approach to SEL skills within the *Wonders* curriculum. Key SEL foundations are sequenced through three interrelated strands:

- **Approaches to learning:** The skills and behaviors that children use to engage in learning.
- **Social and emotional development:** The experiences, expressions, and management of emotions, as well as the ability to establish positive and rewarding relationships with others.
- **Executive function and self-regulation skills:** Cognitive processes that enable us to plan, focus attention, remember instructions, and attend to tasks successfully. Self-regulation and executive function skills help children learn how to learn!

The SEL Lesson Plan

Each SEL lesson is built on active engagement, carefully **crafted to bolster each week's targeted literacy skills.** Through the research-based Sesame Workshop media and engaging learning experiences, we offer strategies for rich teacher/child interactions that are developmentally appropriate and, of course, joyful!

Child-Centered Media
Each resource has been carefully selected to support a specific SEL competency. Additional instruction helps guide learning before and after viewing.

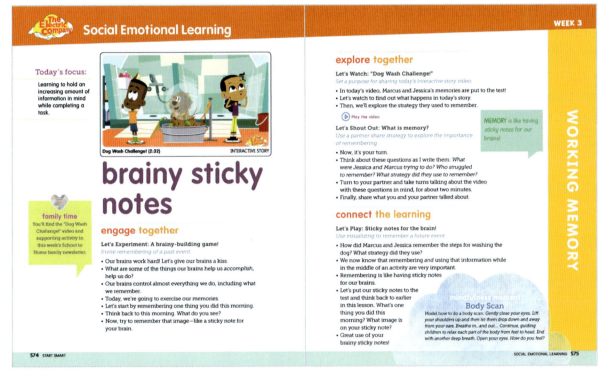

Engage Together
Active learning that bridges children's prior knowledge and skills to the next concept.

Explore Together
A "view and do" experience that combines a media-based investigation with collaborative learning.

Connect the Learning
Language-rich interactions that transfer children's developing understandings to everyday moments and learning at home.

Family Time

Research highlights a consistent relationship between family engagement and student achievement. We engage families in their children's education and development through a powerful home-school partnership that strengthens SEL skills enriching media and supporting hands-on learning experiences each week.

About Sesame Workshop
Sesame Workshop is the nonprofit media and educational organization behind *Sesame Street*, *The Electric Company*, and much more. Since 1969, our programs have helped kids everywhere grow smarter, stronger, and kinder. Today, Sesame Workshop is an innovative force for change, serving vulnerable children in 150+ countries with media, philanthropically-funded social impact initiatives, and formal education programs, all grounded in rigorous research. Visit www.sesameworkshop.org to learn more.

Wonders and the Science of Reading

Dr. Timothy Shanahan

Wonders supports the delivery of high-quality literacy instruction aligned to the science of reading. It provides a comprehensive, integrated plan for meeting the needs of all students. Carefully monitoring advances in literacy research, the program is developed to ensure that lessons focus on teaching the right content at the right time. The right content refers to teaching sufficient amounts of the content that has been proven to deliver learning advantages to students. The right time refers to a carefully structured scope and sequence within a grade and across grades. This ensures that teaching is presented in the most effective and efficient manner, with sound guidance to better support diverse learners.

Foundational Skills

English is an alphabetic language; developing readers must learn to translate letters and spelling patterns to sounds and pronunciations, and to read text accurately, automatically, and with proper expression. When students learn to manage these foundational skills with a minimum of conscious attention, they will have the cognitive resources available to comprehend what they read.

Research shows that the explicit teaching of phonemic awareness, phonics, and text reading fluency are the most successful ways to succeed in foundational skills. *Wonders* presents a sequence of research-aligned learning activities in its grade-level placements, sequences of instruction, and instructional guidance across the following areas:

- Phonemic Awareness
- Phonics/Decoding
- Text Reading Fluency

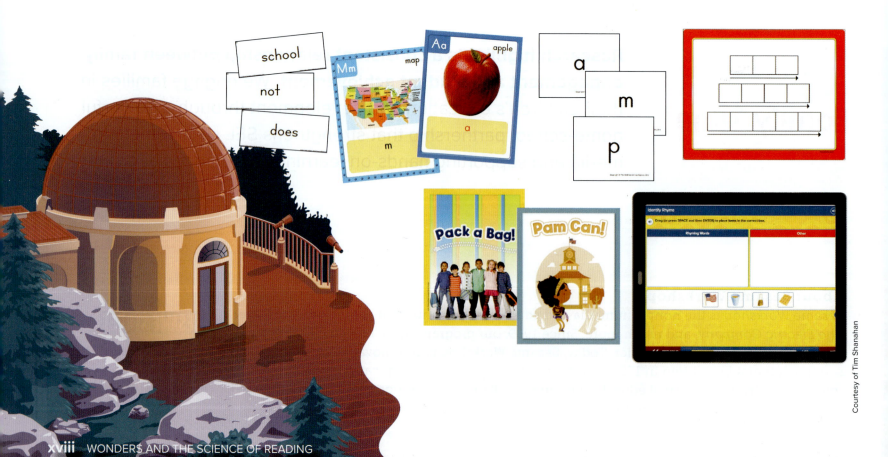

Courtesy of Tim Shanahan

Reading Comprehension

Reading comprehension requires that students extract and construct meaning from text. To comprehend, students must learn to apply the prior knowledge they bring to the text to the information expressed through written language in the text. To accomplish this successfully, readers must do three things. They must:

- expand their knowledge through the reading of high-quality informative texts;
- learn to negotiate increasingly sophisticated and complex written language;
- develop the cognitive abilities to manage and monitor these processes.

Wonders provides lessons built around a high-quality collection of complex literary and informational texts, focused on both the natural and social worlds. Teachers using *Wonders* will find explicit, research-based lessons in vocabulary and other language skills, guidance for high-level, high-quality discussions, and well-designed lessons aimed at building the executive processes that can shift reading comprehension into high gear, including:

- Building Knowledge/Using Knowledge
- Vocabulary and other aspects of written language
- Text complexity
- Executive processes and comprehension strategies

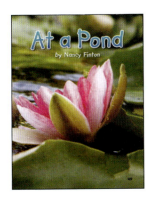
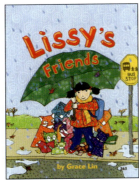

Writing

In the 21st century, it is not enough to be able to read, understand, and learn from the writing of others. Being able to communicate one's own ideas logically and effectively is necessary, too. As with reading, writing includes foundational skills (like spelling and handwriting), as well as higher-order abilities (composition and communication) and the executive processes required to manage the accomplishment of successful writing. Research shows that reading and writing strengthen one another. Focusing writing instruction in the following areas will help students improve their reading:

- Writing foundations
- Quality writing for multiple purposes
- The writing processes
- Writing to enhance reading

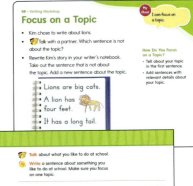

Quality of Instruction

The science of reading is dependent upon the sciences of teaching and learning, as well as on reading research. Reading research has identified specific best practices for teaching particular aspects of literacy. However, research has also revealed other important features of quality instruction that have implications for all learners and that may better support certain student populations. *Wonders* lessons reflect these quality issues in teaching:

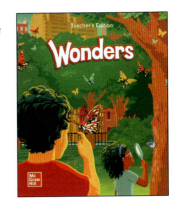

- Lessons with explicit and appropriate purposes
- High-challenge levels
- Appropriate opportunities for review
- Quality discussions promoted by high DOK-level questions
- Ongoing monitoring of learning
- Supports for English language learners
- Connections to social emotional learning

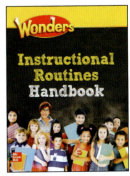

Build Critical Readers, Writers, Communicators, and Thinkers

LISTENING

SPEAKING

COLLABORATING

READING

Build Knowledge Through a Text Set

- **Investigate** an Essential Question.
- **Read** a variety of texts.
- **Closely read** texts for deeper meaning.
- **Respond** to texts using text evidence.
- **Conduct** research.
- **Share** your knowledge.
- **Inspire** action.

WRITING

Communicate Effectively Through Writing

- **Analyze** mentor texts and student models.
- **Understand** purpose and audience.
- **Plan** writing, using sources as needed.
- **Conference** with peers and teachers.
- **Evaluate** work against a rubric.
- **Improve** writing continuously.
- **Share** your writing.

SMALL GROUP

EXTEND CONNECT

ASSESS

Instruction Aligned to the **Science of Reading**

Reading

Explicit instruction supports students in building knowledge.

- Foundational Reading Skills
  - Phonics/Word Analysis
  - Fluency
- Reading Literature
- Reading Informational Texts
- Comparing Texts
- Vocabulary
- Researching

Writing

Skills-based minilessons support students in developing their writing.

- Writing
  - Narrative
  - Argumentative
  - Expository
- Handwriting
- Speaking and Listening
- Conventions
- Creating and Collaborating

Differentiation

Differentiate resources, instruction, and level of scaffolds.

Small Group Teacher-Led Instruction

- Choose from small group skills lesson options to target instruction to meet students' needs.
- Read texts with scaffolded support.

Independent/Collaborative Work

- Students transfer knowledge of skills to independent reading and practice.
- Students transfer skills to their writing.

Extend, Connect, and Assess

At the end of the unit, students transfer and apply knowledge gained to new contexts.

Demonstrate Understanding

- Extend knowledge through online reading and Reader's Theater.
- Connect ELA skills to content area reading with science and social studies texts.
- Assess learning with program assessments.

Grade 1
Resources

The resources in *Wonders* support skills mastery, differentiated instruction, and the transfer and application of knowledge to new contexts. Teachers will find ways to enhance student learning and ownership through multimodal supports, a strong focus on foundational skills, opportunities to build knowledge, and fostering of expression through writing. All of your *Wonders*-created print resources are available digitally to support a variety of learning environments. The resources shown represent the key instructional elements of your *Wonders* classroom and are a portion of the supports available to you and your students. Login to your **Teacher Workspace** to explore multimedia resources, professional learning, and thousands of resources to meet your students where they are.

Component		Differentiate	Extend, Connect, Assess	Available Digitally
Teacher's Edition		●	●	●
Reading/Writing Companion			●	●
Literature Anthology				●
Literature Big Books		●		●
Classroom Library		●		

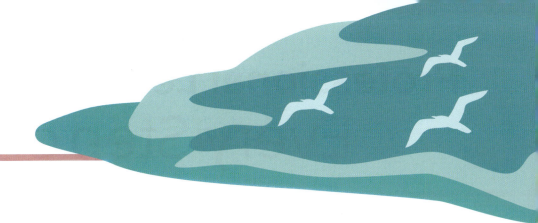

Component	Differentiate	Extend, Connect, Assess	Available Digitally
Classroom Library Lessons	●		●
Leveled Readers & Lesson Cards	●	●	●
Center Activity Cards	●	●	●
ELL Small Group Guide	●		●
Data Dashboard	●	●	●
Progress Monitoring Assessment		●	●
Unit Assessment		●	●
Benchmark Assessments		●	●
Practice Book Blackline Masters		●	●
Foundational Skills Resources: multimodal manipulatives, cards, activities, and games to build key skills	●	●	●
Skills-Based Online Games	●	●	●
Differentiated Genre Passages	●	●	●
Content Area Reading Blackline Masters		●	●

Professional Learning
Every Step of the Way

Get Started Using *Wonders*. Every day of instruction is based on evidence-based classroom best practices, which are embedded into the daily routines to strengthen your teaching and enhance students' learning. Throughout *Wonders*, you'll find support for employing these new routines and making the most of your literacy block.

Use this checklist to access support resources to help you get started with *Wonders* during the first weeks of school. Then refer to this list during the year for ongoing implementation support and to get the most from *Wonders*.

Beginning the Year

We encourage you to review these resources before the first day of school and then use them to support your first weeks of instruction.

In Your Teacher's Edition: Support pages for planning and teaching are embedded throughout your Teacher's Edition to support your big-picture understanding and help you teach effectively.

- ☐ **StartSmart:** In Unit 1 of your Teacher's Edition, the first three weeks of instruction are the StartSmart weeks. They will introduce you to your instructional routines with on-page supports and guide you through placement testing to get ready for small group lessons.

- ☐ **Text Set Support:** Each text set is accompanied by an introduction that supports your understanding of the content and simplifies instructional planning. These pages include a daily planner, differentiated learning support, guidance for developing student ownership and building knowledge, and more.

- ☐ **Progress Monitoring and Assessment:** Use data to track progress toward mastery of skills-based content, lesson objectives, and student goals.
The **My Goals Routine** supports continuous self-monitoring and student feedback.

Online Resources: The digital Teacher Dashboard is your access point for key resources to get you up and running with *Wonders*. From the Teacher Dashboard, select *Resources > Professional Development > Overview*

- ☐ ***Wonders* Basics Module:** Set up your classroom, get to know your materials, learn about the structure of *Wonders*, and receive support for placement testing and grouping students for small group learning.
  - ▶ Select *Learn to Use Wonders*

- ☐ **Placement and Diagnostic Assessment:** Access assessments, testing instructions, and placement charts that can be used at the beginning of the year to assess and place students in small groups.
  - ▶ Select *Assessment & Data*

Ongoing Support

Your online **Teacher Workspace** also includes a wide range of additional resources. Use them throughout the year for ongoing support and professional learning. From the Teacher Dashboard, select *Resources > Professional Development*

☐ **Instructional Routines Handbook:** Reference this handbook throughout the year for support implementing the *Wonders* evidence-based routines and understanding the research behind them, and for guidance on what student success looks like.
  ▶ Select *Overview > Instructional Routines*

☐ **Small Group Differentiated Learning Guide:** Use the first few weeks of small group time to teach and model routines and establish small group rules and procedures.
  ▶ Select *Overview > Instructional Routines > Managing Small Groups: A How-to Guide PDF*

☐ **Suggested Lesson Plans and Pacing Guides:** Adjust your instruction to your literacy block and meet the needs of your classroom with flexible lesson plans and pacing.
  ▶ Select *Overview > Instructional Routines*

☐ **Classroom Videos:** Watch *Wonders* teachers model classroom lessons in reading, writing, collaboration, and teaching English language learners.
  ▶ Select *Classroom Videos*

☐ **Small Group Classroom Videos:** Watch *Wonders* teachers model small group instruction and share tips and strategies for effective differentiated lessons.
  ▶ Select *Classroom Videos > Small Group Instruction*

☐ **Author & Coach Videos:** Watch Dr. Douglas Fisher, Dr. Timothy Shanahan, and other *Wonders* authors as they provide short explanations of best practices and classroom coaching. Also provided are videos from Dr. Sheldon Eakins, founder of the Leading Equity Center, that focus on important aspects of educational equity and cultural responsive teaching.
  ▶ Select *Author & Coach Videos*

☐ **Assessment Handbook:** Review your assessment options and find support for managing multiple assessments, interpreting their results, and using data to inform your instructional planning.
  ▶ Select *Overview > Assessment & Data*

☐ **Assessment & Data Guides:** Review your assessment resources and get to know your reporting tools.
  ▶ Select *Overview > Assessment & Data*

☐ **Digital Help:** Access video tutorials and printable PDFs to support planning, assessment, writing and research, assignments, and connecting school to home.
  ▶ Select *Digital Help*

Explore the Professional Development section in your Teacher Workspace for more videos, resources, and printable guides. Select *Resources > Professional Development*

Notes

UNIT 3 Contents

Unit Overview

English Language Arts is not a discrete set of skills. Skills work together to help children analyze the meaningful texts. In *Wonders*, skills are not taught in isolation, rather they are purposefully combined to support student learning of texts they read.

	Week 1	Week 2	Week 3	Week 4
	Essential Question: How do we measure time?	**Essential Question:** How do plants change as they grow?	**Essential Question:** What is a folktale?	**Essential Question:** How is life different than it was long ago?

Reading

Week 1

Print Concepts
Locate Title, Author, Illustrator

Phonological Awareness
✓ Phoneme Identity, Addition, Substitution
Phoneme Blending/Segmentation

Phonics and Word Analysis
✓ Long *a*: *a_e*
✓ Contractions with *Not*

Fluency
Accuracy and Automaticity
✓ High-Frequency Words

Reading Literature
✓ Events: Beginning, Middle, End
Retell

Reading Informational Text
Text Feature: Bold Print

Compare Texts
Compare and Contrast

Vocabulary
Academic Vocabulary

Researching
Interview a Classmate

Week 2

Print Concepts
Locate Title, Author

Phonological Awareness
✓ Alliteration
✓ Phoneme Deletion, Segmentation
Phoneme Blending

Phonics and Word Analysis
✓ Long *i*: *i_e*
✓ Plurals (with CVCe words)

Fluency
Accuracy and Automaticity
✓ High-Frequency Words

Reading Literature
✓ Sequence of Events
Retell

Reading Informational Text
✓ Text Feature: Diagrams

Compare Texts
Compare and Contrast

Vocabulary
Academic Vocabulary

Researching
Research What a Plant Needs

Week 3

Print Concepts
Locate Title, Author

Phonological Awareness
✓ Identify and Produce Rhyme
✓ Phoneme Segmentation, Blending

Phonics and Word Analysis
✓ Soft *c*, Soft *g/dge*
✓ Inflectional Endings *-ed*, *-ing*

Fluency
Accuracy and Automaticity
✓ High-Frequency Words

Reading Literature
✓ Moral
✓ Descriptive Words and Phrases
Retell

Compare Texts
Compare and Contrast

Vocabulary
Academic Vocabulary

Researching
Learn Storytelling Technique

Week 4

Print Concepts
Locate Title, Author, Illustrator

Phonological Awareness
✓ Phoneme Isolation, Segmentation, Blending

Phonics and Word Analysis
✓ Long *o*: *o_e*; Long *u*: *u_e*; Long *e*: *e_e*
✓ CVCe Syllables

Fluency
Accuracy and Automaticity
✓ High-Frequency Words

Reading Informational Text
Text Feature: Captions
✓ Details: Compare and Contrast
Retell

Compare Texts
Compare and Contrast

Vocabulary
Academic Vocabulary

Researching
Interview an Older Person at School

Writing

Week 1

Writing
Handwriting
Narrative Writing
Improving Writing

Conventions
✓ Grammar: Verbs

Week 2

Writing
Handwriting
Narrative Writing
Improving Writing

Conventions
✓ Grammar: Present-Tense Verbs

Week 3

Writing
Handwriting
Narrative Writing
Improving Writing

Conventions
✓ Grammar: Past- and Future-Tense Verbs

Week 4

Writing
Handwriting
Opinion Writing
Extended Writing: Expository
Improving Writing

Conventions
✓ Grammar: Irregular Verbs *is, are*

Key
✓ Tested in *Wonders* Assessments

Week 5	Extend, Connect, and Assess	Key Skills Trace

Week 5

Essential Question: How do we get our food?

Print Concepts
Locate Title, Author

Phonological Awareness
✓ Phoneme Deletion, Segmentation, Blending

Phonics and Word Analysis
✓ Variant Vowel Spellings with Digraphs *oo, u*
✓ Inflectional Endings *-ed, -ing*

Fluency
Accuracy and Automaticity
✓ High-Frequency Words

Reading Informational Text
✓ Text Feature: Diagrams
✓ Details: Time-Order
Retell

Compare Texts
Compare and Contrast

Vocabulary
Academic Vocabulary

Researching
Trace the Steps of a Food Item

Writing
Handwriting
Opinion Writing
Extended Writing: Expository
Improving Writing

Conventions
✓ Grammar: Contractions with *Not*

Extend, Connect, and Assess

Extend previously taught skills and connect to new content.

Extend

Reading Informational Text
Reading Digitally

Text Features
Retell

Conduct Research
Use a Multimedia Event

Fluency
Reader's Theater

Phrasing and Expression

Connect

Connect to Science
Organization and Development of Living Organisms

Assess

Academic Vocabulary
Expository Writing

Read Grade-Level Texts
Collaborate

Unit Assessment
Unit 3 Test

Fluency Assessment

Key Skills Trace

Print Concepts/Phonological Awareness
The Print Concepts and Phonological Awareness standards are taught throughout the text sets of each unit.

Phonics and Word Analysis
Long Vowels
Introduce: Unit 3 Week 1
Review: Unit 3, Week 2, Week 4; Unit 4 Week 1, Week 2, Week 3, Week 4, Week 5
Assess: Unit 3, Unit 4

Vowel Digraphs
Introduce: Unit 3 Week 5
Review: Unit 6 Week 1, Week 2
Assess: Unit 3, Unit 6

Reading Literature
Events: Beginning, Middle, End
Introduce: Unit 3 Week 1
Assess: Unit 3

Sequence of Events
Introduce: Unit 3 Week 2
Review: Unit 4 Week 1; Unit 5 Week 1
Assess: Unit 3, Unit 4

Moral
Introduce: Unit 3 Week 3
Assess: Unit 3

Literary Element: Descriptive Words and Phrases
Introduce: Unit 3 Week 3
Review: Unit 5 Week 2, Week 3
Assess: Unit 5

Reading Informational Text
Text Features
Introduce: Unit 1 Week 1
Review: Unit 1 Week 2, Week 3, Week 5; Unit 2 Week 1, Week 2, Week 4, Week 5; Unit 3 Week 1, Week 2, Week 4, Week 5; Unit 4 Week 1, Week 2, Week 4, Week 5; Unit 5 Week 1, Week 2, Week 4, Week 5; Unit 6 Week 1, Week 3, Week 4, Week 5
Assess: Unit 1, Unit 2, Unit 3, Unit 4, Unit 5, Unit 6

Compare and Contrast
Introduce: Unit 3 Week 4
Review: Unit 4 Week 2
Assess: Unit 3

Details: Time-Order
Introduce: Unit 3 Week 5
Review: Unit 4 Week 5; Unit 5 Week 3
Assess: Unit 3, Unit 4

Grammar
Verbs
Introduce: Unit 3 Week 1
Review: Unit 3 Week 2, Week 3, Week 4, Week 5; Unit 4 Week 2, Week 3, Week 4, Week 5
Assess: Unit 3, Unit 4

Extended Writing
Unit 1: Expository: Personal Narrative
Unit 2: Narrative: Fantasy
Unit 3: Expository Text
Unit 4: Poetry
Unit 5: Expository: Procedural Text
Unit 6: Opinion Text

Independent Reading and Read Alouds

Additional Reading Options

Classroom Library

Online Lessons Available

Independent Reading

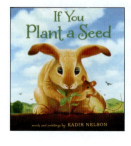

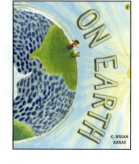

If You Plant a Seed
By Kadir Nelson
Fantasy
Lexile AD340L

On Earth
By G. Brian Karas
Informational Text
Lexile AD540L

Read Aloud

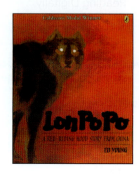

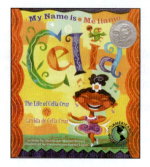

Lon Po Po
By Ed Young
Fiction
Lexile 670L

My Name Is Celia/Me llamo Celia
By Monica Brown and Rafael López
Informational Text
Lexile AD850L

Genre Read-Aloud Anthology

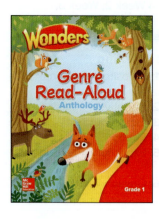

More Leveled Readers to Explore

 Search the **Online Leveled Reader Library** to provide children with texts at various levels to apply skills or to learn about various topics.

Unit Bibliography

Choose titles from the online Unit Bibliography to read aloud to children, or ask children to self-select titles. For more titles to choose from each week, see the online Unit Bibliography.

Week 1	Henkes, Kevin. *A Good Day.* Greenwillow, 2007.
Week 2	Bulla, Clyde Robert. Illustrated by Stacey Schuett. *A Tree Is a Plant.* Collins, 2001.
Week 3	Ziefert, Harriet. *The Turnip.* Viking, 1996.
Week 4	Williams, Rozanne Lanczak. Illustrated by Meryl Treatner. *Long Ago and Today.* Creative Teaching Press, 1996.
Week 5	Dickmann, Nancy. *Food from Farms.* Heinemann-Raintree, 2010.

UNIT 3

Teach the Whole Child

Foster student academic success in English Language Arts and Content Knowledge by creating a Classroom Culture that supports children in growing their Social-Emotional Learning and developing strong Habits of Learning.

CLASSROOM CULTURE

ELA AND CONTENT KNOWLEDGE

SOCIAL-EMOTIONAL LEARNING

HABITS OF LEARNING

 ## Classroom Culture

Focus: We learn through modeling and practice.

Develop the mindset in your classroom that children can learn from models. Explain that watching someone perform a skill or complete a task is a helpful way to learn because it provides an example, or model, of what to do. It gives children an example of what success looks like. Encourage children to ask any questions they have about the example or model so they are clear on their task. Then emphasize that practicing a skill is part of the learning process.

 ## Habits of Learning

Focus: I believe I can succeed.

The goal of this Habit of Learning is to help children develop a positive attitude about learning. When children are encouraged to find the learning strategies and tools that work best for them, they develop a sense of agency and see that their actions make a difference. Share the following statements with children, and then discuss their reactions.

- I stay on task until I complete it.
- I read independently.
- I choose the right book.

Social Emotional Learning

A Classroom of Confidence!

The Social Emotional Learning (SEL) competencies of this unit help your children **develop skills, knowledge, and dispositions needed to investigate the here and now as well as other worlds, near and far.** As children collaborate, self-confidence strengthens their abilities to share ideas and tolerate challenges.

Each SEL lesson provides opportunities to deepen the skills children need to feel more confident to take academic risks:

Week 1 • Prosocial Behavior & Self-Regulation
Exploring self-regulation and prosocial skills.
Video: "Turtle Investigation"

Week 4 • Self-Confidence
Developing resilience and confidence as learners.
Video: "I'm a Superstar"

Weeks 2, 3, and 5 • Teachable Moments
Select from your library of Social Emotional Learning resources.

family time!

At this mid-year point, engage families by supporting their efforts to **acknowledge and celebrate the process of learning, not just the end results.** It's effort, hard work, and practice, practice, practice that allow children to achieve their potential and build the confidence and joy that fuel learning.

Invite families to celebrate the different ways they engage with their children around the weekly Social Emotional Learning video and activity found in the **School to Home** newsletter.

Introduce the Unit

Reading/Writing Companion, pp. 8–9

The Big Idea: *What can happen over time?*

Talk About It

Have children read the Big Idea aloud. Ask them how they have changed since they were babies. Then ask how parents are different from children. Children may point out changes in size, maturity, abilities, education, and occupation.

Ask: *How does nature change over time?* Have children discuss with partners or in groups and then share their ideas with the class. Remind children to listen actively to partners or group members. Let children know they will discuss the Big Idea throughout the unit. Each week they will talk, read, and write about an Essential Question related to the Big Idea.

Read the Poem: "Changes, Changes"

Display pages 8–9 in the **Reading/Writing Companion.** Read aloud "Changes, Changes."

Ask children questions about the poem.

- What things in the poem change?
- How do birds change?
- How can the speaker tell he or she has grown?

Changes, Changes

Little by little, day by day,
Things grow and change in every way.

Trees get taller and touch the sky,
Eggs hatch new birds who learn to fly.

A puppy born in spring is small,
But he'll be bigger when it's fall.

I'm also growing, bit by bit,
Just see—my clothes no longer fit!

—George Samos

Guide children to complete the activities on **Reading/Writing Companion** page 9.

Listen Ask children to listen actively to the poem, thinking about its meaning as they listen.

Talk Have partners talk about the girl in the picture and discuss what she can do now that she could not do when she was younger.

READING/ WRITING

WEEK 1

Essential Question

How do we measure time?

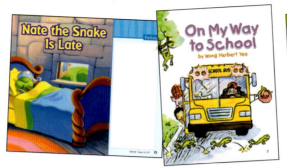

WEEK 2

Essential Question

How do plants change as they grow?

WEEK 3

Essential Question

What is a folktale?

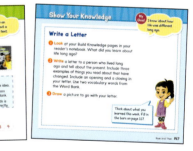

WEEK 4

Essential Question

How is life different than it was long ago?

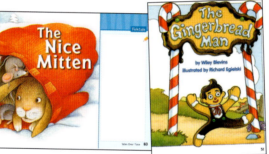

WEEK 5

Essential Question

How do we get our food?

FOUNDATIONAL SKILLS

Print Concepts
- Locate title, author, illustrator

Phonological Awareness
- ✓ Phoneme Identity
- ✓ Phoneme Addition
- ✓ Phoneme Substitution
- Phoneme Segmentation
- Phoneme Blending

Phonics and Word Analysis
- ✓ Long *a: a_e*
- ✓ Contractions with *not*

Fluency
- Read with accuracy and automaticity
- ✓ High-Frequency Words
- *away   now   some   today   way   why*

READING

Reading Literature
- ✓ Identify and describe the main story elements in a story
- Retell a story to enhance comprehension
- Read prose and poetry appropriately complex for grade 1

Reading Informational Text
- Use text features including bold print to locate key facts or information
- Read informational texts appropriately complex for grade 1

Compare Texts
- Compare and contrast two texts on the same topic

COMMUNICATION

Writing
- Handwriting: *Dd*
- Write narratives that retell two or more appropriately sequenced events, including relevant details and a sense of closure
- Focus on a topic, respond to suggestions from peers, and add details to strengthen writing

Speaking and Listening
- Participate in collaborative conversations
- Ask and answer questions to gather or clarify information
- Present information orally using complete sentences

Conventions
- ✓ **Grammar:** Identify and use verbs
- **Mechanics:** Use commas in series
- **Spelling:** Spell words with Long *a: a_e*

Researching
- Participate in shared research and writing projects

Creating and Collaborating
- Add drawings and visual displays to descriptions
- Use digital tools to produce and publish writing

VOCABULARY

Academic Vocabulary
- Acquire and use grade-appropriate academic vocabulary
- Identify real-life connections between words and their use

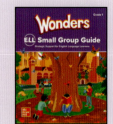

ELL Scaffolded supports for English Language Learners are embedded throughout the lessons, enabling children to communicate information, ideas, and concepts in English Language Arts and for social and instructional purposes within the school setting.

See the **ELL Small Group Guide** for additional support of the skills for the text set.

FORMATIVE ASSESSMENT

For assessment throughout the text set, use children's self-assessments and your observations.

Use the Data Dashboard to filter class, group, or individual student data to guide group placement decisions. It provides recommendations to enhance learning for gifted and talented children and offers extra support for children needing remediation.

DATA DASHBOARD

Develop Student Ownership

To build student ownership, children need to know what they are learning, why they are learning it, and determine how well they understood it.

Students Discuss Their Goals

TEXT SET GOALS

- I can read and understand a fantasy story.
- I can respond to a fantasy story by extending the story.
- I know about ways we can measure time.

Have children think about what they know and fill in the bars on **Reading/Writing Companion** page 12.

Students Monitor Their Learning

LEARNING GOALS

Specific learning goals identified in every lesson make clear what children will be learning and why. These smaller goals provide stepping stones to help children meet their Text Set Goals.

CHECK-IN ROUTINE

The Check-In Routine at the close of each lesson guides children to self-reflect on how well they understood each learning goal.

Review the lesson learning goal.
Reflect on the activity.
Self-Assess by
- filling in the bars in the **Reading/Writing Companion**
- holding up 1, 2, 3, or 4 fingers

Share with your teacher.

Students Reflect on Their Progress

TEXT SET GOALS

After completing the Show Your Knowledge task for the text set, children reflect on their understanding of the Text Set Goals by filling in the bars on **Reading/Writing Companion** page 13.

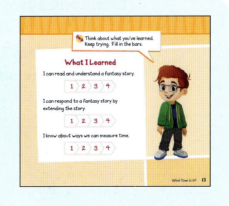

Build Knowledge

Literature Big Book

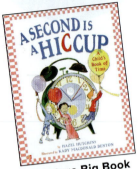
Shared Read
Reading/Writing Companion p. 14

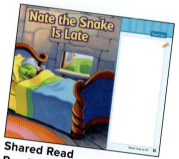
Anchor Text
Literature Anthology p. 6

Paired Selection
Literature Anthology p. 24

Essential Question
How do we measure time?

 Video We do different activities at different times of the day. For example, we have breakfast and go to school in the morning. At night, we read and go to sleep.

Literature Big Book Time can be measured in seconds, minutes, hours, days, weeks, months, and years. A lot can happen during each time period.

Shared Read We use clocks to help us stay on time. Nate the snake watches the clock so he's not late for story time, but he gets distracted.

Interactive Read Aloud Many things help us measure time. Clocks tell us hours, minutes, and seconds. The days of the week help us plan. Calendars help us track days, weeks, and months. The four seasons make up one year.

Anchor Text A boy tries to get to school on time. He comes up with many reasons for being late.

Paired Selection Today, numbers on a clock tell us the time. Long ago, people used sundials to tell time.

 Poem Birds can let people know when it's time to wake up.

Differentiated Sources

Leveled Readers 🔊

🟠 Busy the dog loves his watch. It tells him when it's time to do different things during the day.

🔵🟣 Kate the mouse uses a calendar to figure out when her friend Amy will arrive.

🟢 Skip the skunk watches the clock until it's time for Uncle George to visit.

Build Knowledge Routine

After reading each text, ask children to document facts and details they learned that help them answer the Essential Question of the text set.

 Talk about the source.

 Write about the source.

 Add to the class Anchor Chart

• Add to the Word Bank.

Show Your Knowledge

Write Tips for Being on Time

Have children think about what they learned about measuring time. Guide them to write a list of tips for being on time that includes text evidence, vocabulary words, and a picture to illustrate the tips.

Social Emotional Learning

Turtle Investigation   (2:35)

Prosocial Behavior & Self-Regulation

SEL Focus: Engage in rich social conversations in support of children exploring self-regulation and prosocial skills.

Invite children to share a time they helped a friend, family member, or neighbor as a way to introduce the lesson titled "Helping Others," pp. T4–T5.

Family Time • Share the video and activity in the **School to Home** newsletter.

Explore the Texts

Essential Question: How do we measure time?

Literature Big Book	Interactive Read Aloud	Reading/Writing Companion	Literature Anthology
	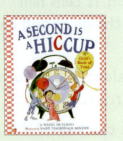		
A Second Is a Hiccup Poetry	**"Measuring Time"** Informational Text	**"Nate the Snake Is Late"** Shared Read pp. 14–23 Fantasy	***On My Way to School*** Anchor Text pp. 6–23 Fantasy

Qualitative

Meaning/Purpose: Moderate Complexity **Structure:** Moderate Complexity **Language:** Moderate Complexity **Knowledge Demands:** Moderate Complexity	**Meaning/Purpose:** Moderate Complexity **Structure:** Moderate Complexity **Language:** High Complexity **Knowledge Demands:** Moderate Complexity	**Meaning/Purpose:** Low Complexity **Structure:** Low Complexity **Language:** Low Complexity **Knowledge Demands:** Moderate Complexity	**Meaning/Purpose:** Moderate Complexity **Structure:** Low Complexity **Language:** Low Complexity **Knowledge Demands:** Low Complexity

Quantitative

Lexile NP	Lexile 630L	Lexile 460L	Lexile 330L

Reader and Task Considerations

Reader Children may need support understanding the measurements of time, as well as the story's lyrical, poetic format.	**Reader** Children may need support in understanding units of time and the use of clocks and calendars for keeping track of time.	**Reader** Children will need to use their knowledge of sound-spelling correspondences and high-frequency words to read the text.	**Reader** Children should be able to connect with the story by recalling instances when they were running late for an appointment or event.

Task The questions for the Interactive Read Aloud are supported by teacher modeling. The tasks provide a variety of ways for students to begin to build knowledge and vocabulary about the text set topic. The questions and tasks provided for the other texts are at various levels of complexity, ensuring that all students can interact with the text in meaningful ways.

Additional Texts

Classroom Library
Lon Po Po: A Red-Riding Hood Story from China
Genre: Fiction
Lexile: 670L

If You Plant a Seed
Genre: Fiction
Lexile: 340L

See **Classroom Library Lessons.**

Content Area Reading BLMs
Additional online texts related to grade-level Science, Social Studies, and Arts content.

Literature Anthology

"It's About Time!"
Paired Selection
pp. 24–27
Informational Text

Qualitative

Meaning/Purpose: Low Complexity
Structure: Low Complexity
Language: Moderate Complexity
Knowledge Demands: Low Complexity

Quantitative

Lexile 270L

Reader and Task Considerations

Reader Children might need background information about the different timepieces that have been used throughout history and how these have evolved.

Task The questions and tasks provided for this text are at various levels of complexity, ensuring that all students can interact with the text in meaningful ways.

Leveled Readers (All Leveled Readers are provided in eBook format with audio support.)

(A)
Busy's Watch
Fantasy

(O)
Kate Saves the Date!
Fantasy

(B)
Uncle George Is Coming!
Fantasy

(ELL)
Kate Saves the Date!
Fantasy

Qualitative

Meaning/Purpose: Low Complexity	**Meaning/Purpose:** Low Complexity	**Meaning/Purpose:** Moderate Complexity	**Meaning/Purpose:** Low Complexity
Structure: Low Complexity	**Structure:** Low Complexity	**Structure:** Moderate Complexity	**Structure:** Low Complexity
Language: Low Complexity	**Language:** Low Complexity	**Language:** Moderate Complexity	**Language:** Low Complexity
Knowledge Demands: Low Complexity	**Knowledge Demands:** Moderate Complexity	**Knowledge Demands:** Moderate Complexity	**Knowledge Demands:** Moderate Complexity

Quantitative

Lexile 40L	Lexile 220L	Lexile 320L	Lexile 330L

Reader and Task Considerations

Reader Children should be able to relate to the story by recalling how they keep to individual schedules to do different things, such as a dance class or soccer practice.	**Reader** Children should be able to relate to the story by recalling instances when they've counted down the days to a special event or occasion.	**Reader** Children should be able to relate to the story by recalling instances when they've waited for someone to arrive at a specific time and what waiting feels like.	**Reader** Children should be able to relate to the story by recalling instances when they've counted down the days to a special event or occasion.

Task The questions and tasks provided for the Leveled Readers are at various levels of complexity, ensuring that all students can interact with the text in meaningful ways.

Focus on Word Work

Build Foundational Skills with Multimodal Learning

MULTIMODAL

Phonemic Awareness Activities

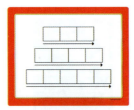
Response Board

Sound-Spelling Cards

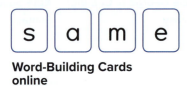
s a m e
Word-Building Cards online

t a n
Phonics Activities

Practice Book

make | take
came | game
gate | late
Spelling Cards online

away
High-Frequency Word Cards

High-Frequency Word Activities

Visual Vocabulary Cards

Phonemic Awareness

- Identify, add, substitute, blend, and segment phonemes

Phonics: Long *a*: *a_e*

- Introduce/review sound-spellings
- Blend/build words with sound-spellings
- Practice handwriting
- Structural Analysis: Build reading word bank
- Decode and encode in connected texts

Spelling: Long *a*: *a_e*

- Differentiated spelling instruction
- Encode with sound-spellings
- Explore relationships with word sorts and word families

High-Frequency Words

- Read/Spell/Write routine

See Word Work, pages T10–T13, T20–T23, T30–T33, T52–T53, T58–T59.

Nate the Snake Is Late
Shared Read

Is It Late?
Dave Was Late
Decodable Readers

Whale at the Lake
Take-Home Story

Apply Skills to Read

- Children apply foundational skills as they read decodable texts.
- Children practice fluency to develop word automaticity.

PHONICS SKILLS TRACE

Initial Consonants ⟩ Short Vowels ⟩ Consonant Blends and Digraphs ⟩ Long Vowels ⟩ Vowel Digraphs ⟩ r-Controlled Vowels ⟩ Diphthongs ⟩ Variant Vowels ⟩ Silent Letters and 3-Letter Blends

Explicit Systematic Instruction

Word Work instruction expands foundational skills to enable children to become proficient readers.

Daily Routine

- Use the In a Flash: Sound-Spelling routine and the In a Flash: High-Frequency Word routine to build fluency.
- Set Learning Goal.

Explicit Minilessons and Practice

Use daily instruction in both whole and small groups to model, practice, and apply key foundational skills. Opportunities include:

- Multimodal engagement.
- Corrective feedback.
- Supports for English Language Learners in each lesson.
- Peer collaboration.

Formative Assessment

Check-In

- Children reflect on their learning.
- Children show their progress by holding up 1 to 4 fingers in a Check-In routine.

Check for Success

- Teacher monitors children's achievement and differentiates for Small Group instruction.

Differentiated Instruction

To strengthen skills, provide targeted review and reteaching lessons and multimodal activities to meet children's diverse needs.

🟠🟣 **Approaching Level, ELL**
- Includes Tier 2 **2**

🔵 **On Level**

🟢 **Beyond Level**
- Includes Gifted and Talented

Independent Practice

Provide additional practice as needed. Have children work individually or with partners.

Center Activity Cards

Digital Activities

Word-Building Cards online

Decodable Readers

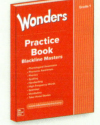

Practice Book

Inspire Early Writers

Build Writing Skills and Conventions

Practice Book

Handwriting Video

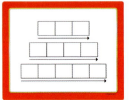

Reading/Writing Companion

Write Letters

- Learn to write letters
- Practice writing

Response Board

Practice Book

High-Frequency Word Activities

Write Words

- Write words with long *a*: *a_e*
- Write spelling words
- Write high-frequency words

Reading/Writing Companion

Practice Book

Write Sentences

- Write sentences with contractions with *not*
- Write sentences to respond to text

Follow Conventions

- Use verbs
- Use commas in a series

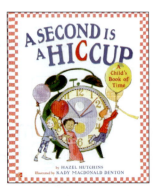

A Second Is a Hiccup
Literature Big Book

Writing Fluency

To increase children's writing fluency, have them write as much as they can in response to the **Literature Big Book f**or five minutes. Tell children to write about how we measure time.

For lessons, see pages T10–T13, T16–T17, T20–T23, T26–T27, T44–T45, T54–55, T59, T60–T61.

Write About Texts

**Reading/Writing Companion,
pp. 24–25, 30–31**

Modeled Writing

Write About the Shared Read "Nate the Snake Is Late"

- Prompt: Write about a new activity that makes Nate late.

Interactive Writing

- Prompt: Write what might happen next in "Nate the Snake Is Late."

**Reading/Writing
Companion, p. 36**

Independent Writing

Write About the Anchor Text *On My Way to School*
Literature Anthology, pp. 6–21

- Prompt: Write four more pages of the story. Tell the excuses the boy might give his mom for getting home late.

- Have children follow the steps of the writing process: draft, revise, edit/proofread, share.

Additional Lessons

Writing Skill Lesson Bank To provide differentiated support for writing skills, see pages T420–T429.

Extended Writing Minilessons For a full set of lessons that support the writing process and writing in a specific genre, see pages T402–T413.

Self-Selected Writing

Children can explore different writing modes.

 Picture Spark

 Letter Writing

 Storyboard

Planner

Customize your own lesson plans at
my.mheducation.com

 Select from your Social Emotional Learning resources.

 LESSON 1

 **LESSON 2**

Reading

Lesson 1

Introduce the Concept, T6–T7
Build Knowledge: What Time Is It?

Listening Comprehension, T8–T9
A Second Is a Hiccup

Word Work, T10–T13
Phonemic Awareness: Phoneme Identify
Phonics/Spelling: Long *a: a_e*
High-Frequency Words: *away, now, some, today, way, why*

Shared Read, T14–T15
Read "Nate the Snake Is Late"

Lesson 2

Build the Concept, T18
Oral Language

Listening Comprehension, T19
"Measuring Time"

Word Work, T20–T23
Phonemic Awareness: Phoneme Addition
Phonics/Spelling: Long *a: a_e*
Structural Analysis: Contractions with *not*
High-Frequency Words: *away, now, some, today, way, why*

Shared Read, T24–T25
Reread "Nate the Snake Is Late"

Writing

Lesson 1

Modeled Writing, T16
Write About the Shared Read
Grammar, T17
Verbs

Lesson 2

Interactive Writing, T26
Write About the Shared Read
Grammar, T27
Verbs

 SMALL GROUP

Teacher-Led Instruction

Differentiated Reading
Leveled Readers
- 🔴 *Busy's Watch,* T64–T65
- 🔵 *Kate Saves the Date!,* T74–T75
- 🟢 *Uncle George Is Coming!,* T78–T79

Differentiated Skills Practice, T66–T81
🔴 **Approaching Level, T66–T73**
Phonological/Phonemic Awareness
- Phoneme Identity, T66 **TIER 2**
- Phoneme Segmentation, T66 **TIER 2**
- Phoneme Addition, T67
- Phoneme Substitution, T67

Phonics
- Connect *a_e* to /ā/, T68 **TIER 2**
- Blend Words with Long *a: a_e*, T68 **TIER 2**
- Build Words with Long *a: a_e*, T69
- Read Words with Long *a: a_e*, T69
- Build Fluency with Phonics, T69

Structural Analysis
- Review Contractions with *not*, T70
- Reteach Contractions with *not*, T70

Independent/Collaborative Work See pages T3K–T3L

Reading
Comprehension
- Fantasy
- Make and Confirm Prediction
- Main Story Elements: Events: Beginning, Middle, End

Independent Reading

Word Work
Phonics/Spelling
- Long *a: a_e*

High-Frequency Words
- *away, now, some, today, way, why*

Writing
Self-Selected Writing
Grammar
- Verbs

Handwriting
- Upper and lowercase *Dd*

ORAL VOCABULARY
immediately, schedule, weekend, calendar, occasion

SPELLING
make, take, came, game, gate, late, chin, graph, some, today
See page T12 for Differentiated Spelling Lists.

 LESSON 3

 LESSON 4

 LESSON 5

Reading

Lesson 3

Build the Concept, T28
Oral Language
Take Notes About Text

Listening Comprehension, T29
A Second Is a Hiccup

 **Word Work, T30–T33**
Phonemic Awareness: Phoneme Substitution
Phonics/Spelling: Long *a: a_e*
Structural Analysis: Contractions with *not*
High-Frequency Words: *away, now, some, today, way, why*

Anchor Text, T34–T43
Read *On My Way to School*

Lesson 4

Extend the Concept, T46–T47
Oral Language

Paired Selection, T48–T51
Read "It's About Time!"

Word Work, T52–T53
Phonemic Awareness: Phoneme Identity
Phonics/Spelling: Long *a: a_e*
Structural Analysis: Contractions with *not*
High-Frequency Words: *away, now, some, today, way, why*

Research and Inquiry, T56–T57
Research and Inquiry: Interview

Lesson 5

Word Work, T58–T59
Phonemic Awareness: Phoneme Blending and Segmentation
Phonics/Spelling: Long *a: a_e*
Phonics: Read the Decodable Reader
Structural Analysis: Contractions with *not*
High-Frequency Words: *away, now, some, today, way, why*

Integrate Ideas, T62
Make Connections

Culminating Task, T63
Show Your Knowledge

Writing

Lesson 3

Independent Writing, T44
Write About the Anchor Text
Grammar, T45
Verbs
Mechanics, T45
Commas in a Series

Lesson 4

Independent Writing, T54
Write About the Anchor Text
Grammar, T55
Verbs
Mechanics, T55
Commas in a Series

Lesson 5

Self-Selected Writing, T60
Grammar, T61
Verbs
Mechanics, T61
Commas in a Series

High-Frequency Words
- Review/Reteach/Cumulative Review, T71
Comprehension
- Read for Fluency, T72 **TIER 2**
- Identify Character, T72 **TIER 2**
- Review Beginning, Middle, End, T73
- Self-Selected Reading, T73

● **On Level, T76–T77**
Phonics
- Read and Build Words with Long *a: a_e*, T76
High-Frequency Words
- Review Words, T76
Comprehension
- Review Beginning, Middle, End, T77
- Self-Selected Reading, T77

● **Beyond Level, T80–T81**
Vocabulary
- Oral Vocabulary: Synonyms, T80
Comprehension
- Review Beginning, Middle, End, T81
- Self-Selected Reading, T81 **GIFTED and TALENTED**

 ● **English Language Learners**
See ELL Small Group Guide, pp. 106–115.

Content Area Connections
Content Area Reading
- Science, Social Studies, and the Arts
Research and Inquiry
- Interview

 ● **English Language Learners**
See ELL Small Group Guide, pp. 107, 109, 111.

Independent and Collaborative Work

As you meet with small groups, have the rest of the class complete activities and projects to practice and apply the skills they have been working on.

Student Choice and Student Voice

- Review My Weekly Work blackline master with children and identify the "Must Do" activities.
- Have children choose some additional activities that provide the practice they need.
- Remind children to reflect on their learning each day.

My Weekly Work BLMs

Reading

Text Options

Children can choose a **Center Activity Card** to use while they listen to a text or read independently.

Classroom Library
Read Aloud
Lon Po Po: A Red-Riding Hood Story from China
Genre: Fiction
Lexile: 670L

Classroom Library
If You Plant a Seed
Genre: Fantasy
Lexile: 340L

Unit Bibliography
See the online bibliography. Children can select independent reading texts about how we measure time.

Leveled Texts Online
All **Leveled Readers** are provided in eBook format with audio support.
- **Differentiated Texts** provide English Language Learners with passages at different proficiency levels.

Literature Big Book e-Book
A Second Is a Hiccup
Genre: Poetry

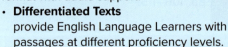

Center Activity Cards

Make and Confirm Predictions Card 3

Fantasy Story Card 28

Events: Beginning, Middle, End Card 7

Digital Activities

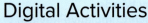

Comprehension

Word Work

Center Activity Cards

Long *a*: *a_e* Card 81

Word-Building Cards

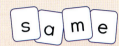

Practice Book BLMs

Phonological Awareness: pp. 161, 162

Phonics: pp. 163, 164

Spelling: pp. 165–167

Structural Analysis: pp. 169, 170

High-Frequency Words: p. 171

Take-Home Story: pp. 175–176

Decodable Readers

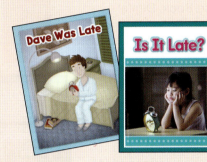

Unit 3, pp. 1–12

Digital Activities

Phonemic Awareness

Phonics

Spelling

High-Frequency Words

Writing

Center Activity Cards

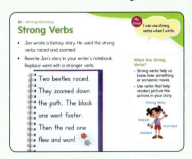

Strong Verbs Card 62

Practice Book BLMs

Handwriting: p. 168

Grammar: pp. 172–173

Mechanics: p. 174

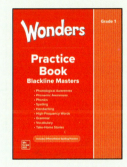

Self-Selected Writing

- Write about how you measure time.
- What are some different ways you measure time?
- Write about a time you were late.

Digital Activities

Grammar

Grammar: Mechanics

Content Area Connections

Content Area Reading BLMs
- Additional texts related to Science, Social Studies, Health, and the Arts.

Research and Inquiry
- Complete Interview project

Progress Monitoring
Moving Toward Mastery

FORMATIVE ASSESSMENT

➤ STUDENT CHECK-IN

✔ CHECK FOR SUCCESS

For ongoing formative assessment, use children's self-assessments at the end of each lesson along with your own observations.

Assessing skills along the way . . .

SKILLS	HOW ASSESSED	
Phonological/Phonemic Awareness **Phonics** **Structural Analysis** **High-Frequency Words**	Practice Book, Digital Activities, Online Rubrics	
Comprehension	Digital Activities, Graphic Organizers, Online Rubrics	
Text-Based Writing **Handwriting** **Grammar** **Spelling**	Reading/Writing Companion: Independent Writing, Practice Book, Digital Activities, Spelling Word Sorts	
Listening/Presenting/Research	Reading/Writing Companion: Share and Evaluate; Research: Online Student Checklists	
Oral Reading Fluency (ORF) Conduct group fluency assessments using the **Letter Naming, Phoneme Segmentation**, and **Sight Word Fluency** assessments.	Fluency Assessment	

At the end of the text set . . .

SKILLS	HOW ASSESSED
Events: Beginning, Middle, End	
Phoneme Identity **Phoneme Addition** **Phoneme Substitution**	Progress Monitoring
Long *a*: *a_e*	
Contractions with *not*	
away, now, some, today, way, why	

Making the Most of Assessment Results

Make data-based grouping decisions by using the following reports to verify assessment results. For additional support options for children, refer to the reteaching and enrichment opportunities.

ONLINE ASSESSMENT CENTER
- *Gradebook*

DATA DASHBOARD
- *Recommendations Report*
- *Activity Report*
- *Skills Report*
- *Progress Report*
- *Grade Card Report*

Reteaching Opportunities with Intervention Online PDFs

IF CHILDREN ANSWER . . .	THEN ASSIGN . . .
0–3 **comprehension** items correctly . . .	lessons 22–24 on Beginning, Middle, End from the **Comprehension PDF.**
0–2 **phonological/phonemic** items correctly . . .	lessons 14–15 on Phoneme Identity, lessons 98–99 on Phoneme Addition, and lessons 84–85 on Phoneme Substitution from the **Phonemic Awareness PDF.**
0–5 **phonics/structural analysis/HFW** items correctly . . .	lesson 59 on Long *a*: *a_e* and lesson 69–70 on Contractions with *not* from the **Phonics/Word Study PDF** and lessons from Section 3 of the **Fluency PDF.**

Enrichment Opportunities

Beyond Level small-group lessons and resources include suggestions for additional activities in these areas to extend learning opportunities for gifted and talented children:

- *Leveled Reader*
- *Vocabulary*
- *Comprehension*
- *Leveled Reader Library Online*
- *Center Activity Cards*

Today's focus:

Exploring self-regulation and prosocial skills.

Turtle Investigation (2:35)   INTERACTIVE STORY

helping others

family time

You'll find the "Turtle Investigation" video and supporting activity in this week's School to Home family newsletter.

engage together

Let's Talk: We love to help each other!

Think aloud to model prosocial behaviors that support community building.

- We are a classroom community that works well together!
- We are a community that cares about other people.
- One way we can help a new friend feel welcome in our classroom is by _____.
- Let's role play welcoming a new friend. Who would like to start?
- How does it feel to be helpful?

explore together

Let's Watch: "Turtle Investigation"

Set a purpose for sharing today's interactive story video.

- Izzy has a problem. She is worried about something.
- First, let's watch the video and think about how a friend can help us solve our problem.
- Then, let's explore what it means to show care by trying to help someone.

 **Play the video**

Let's Shout Out: How can we be a helpful friend?

Develop a shared definition of being helpful.

- As members of the Pet Planet Crew, what do you think Dibble needed?
- Let's think about what it means to be a helpful friend.
- Hey you guys! How do we work together and care for one another?
- Yes! Things like solving problems together and listening to each other are ways you can be a helpful classmate.

> **A HELPFUL FRIEND...**
> - Is respectful.
> - Listens to ideas of others.
> - Shares resources.
> - Offers to help.

connect the learning

Let's Play: Flash forward to problem solve!

Think aloud to model the strategy.

- In the video, Marcus and Izzy "flash forward" to think about how best to help to Dribble *before* they act.
- Thinking ahead can help us plan and be more thoughtful.
- Turn to a partner. Ask: *What problem can we solve? How can we "flash forward" to come up with a solution together?*

mindfulness moment
Belly Breathe

Working together requires us to manage our actions. Practice belly breathing when children are calm. *Let's do our belly breathing. Close your eyes. Breathe in deeply through your nose, and out through your mouth. To keep our breathing slow, we'll count to four as we breathe in and again as we breathe out. Put one hand on your belly: "In 1– 2 – 3 – 4. Out 1– 2 – 3 – 4..."*

PROSOCIAL BEHAVIOR & SELF-REGULATION

LESSON 1

OBJECTIVES

Follow agreed-upon rules for discussions.

Build on others' talk in conversations by responding to the comments of others through multiple exchanges.

Build background knowledge.

Discuss the Essential Question.

ELA ACADEMIC LANGUAGE

• *theme*
• Cognate: *tema*

DIGITAL TOOLS

To enhance the class discussion, use these additional components.

Discuss Concept

Watch Video

Discuss Images

Collaborative Conversation Video

LESSON FOCUS

READING
Introduce the Essential Question
Read Literature Big Book:
A Second Is a Hiccup
• Make Predictions
Word Work
• Introduce Long *a*: *a_e*
Read Shared Read: "Nate the Snake Is Late"
• Introduce Genre

WRITING
Modeled Writing
• Introduce Grammar

Reading/Writing Companion, pp. 14–23

---

5 mins

Build Knowledge

MULTIMODAL

 ### Essential Question
How do we measure time?

Tell children that this week they will be talking and reading about time and how we measure it. Discuss the Essential Question. Children can share different ways they know to tell time.

Watch the Video Play the video without sound first and have partners narrate what they see. Then replay the video with sound and have children listen.

Talk About the Video Have partners share one thing they saw that reminded them of different ways to measure time.

 Anchor Chart Create a Build Knowledge anchor chart with the Essential Question and have volunteers share what they learned. Record their ideas on the chart.

Oral Vocabulary Words

Use the Define/Example/Ask routine on the print or digital **Visual Vocabulary Cards** to introduce the oral vocabulary words *immediately* and *schedule*. Children can use the words to discuss measuring time.

Oral Vocabulary Routine

Visual Vocabulary Cards

Define: When you do something **immediately**, you do it right away, without waiting.

Example: When the mouse saw the hungry cat, it immediately ran into its hole.

Ask: What do you do immediately after you wake up?

Define: A **schedule** is a timetable showing when things will happen.

Example: According to the bus schedule, the last bus leaves at midnight.

Ask: According to our school schedule, what do we do after we eat lunch?

Reading/Writing Companion, pp. 10–11

Build Knowledge

Review how to be open to all ideas using the Collaborative Conversations box. Then have children turn to pages 10–11 of their **Reading/Writing Companion.** Guide them to discuss the photo. Ask:

- *What are the kids holding?*
- *What are the kids learning to do? How do you know?*

Build Vocabulary

Talk Have partners talk about words we use for measuring time.
Write Have children write words about measuring time on page 11.
Create a Word Bank Create a separate section of the Word Bank for words about measuring time. Have children suggest words to add.

English Language Learners

Use the following scaffolds with **Build Knowledge.**

Beginning

Point to one of the clocks in the photo. *This is a clock. What is this?* Have children point to the photo and respond: This is a clock. *The children use the clock to tell what time it is.*

Intermediate

Have children tell what they see in the photo. *What are the children learning?* The children are learning to tell time. *What do the children use to tell time?* The children use a clock.

Advanced/Advanced High

Why do you look at a clock? (to see what time it is) Have partners find a way to tell time in your classroom and then talk about other ways to tell time. Provide vocabulary as needed.

COLLABORATIVE CONVERSATIONS

Be Open to All Ideas As children engage in partner, small-group, and whole-group discussions, remind them:

- that everyone's ideas are important and should be heard.
- not to be afraid to ask a question if something is unclear.
- to respect the opinions of others.

ELL NEWCOMERS

To help children develop oral language and build vocabulary, use **Newcomer Cards** 5–9 and the accompanying lessons in the **Newcomer Teacher's Guide.** For additional practice, have children complete the online **Newcomer Activities.**

MY GOALS ROUTINE

What I Know Now

Read Goals Read goals with children on **Reading/Writing Companion** page 12.

Reflect Ask children to reflect on each goal and fill in the bars to show what they know now. Explain that they will fill in the bars on page 13 at the end of the week to show their progress.

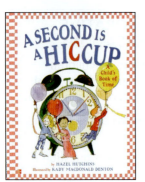

Literature Big Book

LEARNING GOALS

We can make and confirm predictions about measuring time as we listen to a story.

OBJECTIVES

Retell stories, including key details, and demonstrate understanding of their central message or lesson.

Demonstrate understanding of the organization and basic features of print.

ELA ACADEMIC LANGUAGE

• *capitalization*

Close Reading Routine

Read   DOK 1–2

• Identify important ideas and details.
• Take notes and retell.
• Use prompts as needed.

Reread   DOK 2–3

• Analyze the text, craft, and structure.
• Use the Reread minilessons.

Integrate   DOK 3–4

• Integrate knowledge and ideas.
• Make text-to-text connections.
• Complete the Show Your Knowledge task.
• Inspire action.

Read

15 mins

A Second Is a Hiccup

Connect to Concept: What Time Is It? Tell children that they will listen to a poem about words we use to talk about and measure time, such as *minute* and *month*.

Genre: Poem Explain that this selection is a poem. Say: *A poem is writing with short lines and line breaks.*

Anchor Chart Review the Make and Confirm Predictions anchor chart.

Make and Confirm Predictions Review that we use text and illustrations to make a prediction. We continue reading to confirm or correct it.

Read the Selection

Display the Big Book. Have children point to the title, and the author and illustrator names as you read them aloud.

Set Purpose Say: *Let's read to find words we use to talk about time.*

As you read, model making and confirming predictions. Review the anchor chart, as necessary.

> **Think Aloud** The first pages cover what happens in a second. The next pages cover what happens in a minute. I predict the next pages will cover what happens in an hour. Let's see if my prediction is correct.

Correct or confirm your prediction as you continue reading. Remind children to make, confirm, and correct their own predictions as you read.

A C T Access Complex Text

If the complexity of the text makes it hard for children to understand, use the Access Complex Text prompts.

Purpose

The purpose of the selection is to explain units of time. Identifying details about time in each section is important for understanding.

• Guide children to see that the author wants to explain units of time, so she gives examples of what can be done in different units of time.

Organization

Time units grow increasingly longer throughout the selection.

• Help children recognize that the selection is organized from the shortest unit of time to the longest.

Concepts of Print: Capitalization and Punctuation As you read *A Second Is a Hiccup,* point out the capital letter at the beginning of each line and the end punctuation. Explain that in poems, the first letter of each line is capitalized, even if it is not the first word in the sentence. Have children find the capital letters and end punctuation. See prompts in the Big Book for modeling concepts of print.

Respond to the Text

After reading, prompt children to share what they learned about different measurements of time. Discuss the predictions they made as they read and whether their predictions were correct.

Model Retelling

Pause to retell portions of the selection. Say: *I can describe the text and illustrations in my own words. I read that a second is just enough time to hiccup, kiss somebody, jump over a rope, or turn around.*

Continue to model retelling the selection, using your own words to tell the important facts and details in the correct order. Have children practice retelling a page or two.

Writing Fluency

To increase children's writing fluency, have them write as much as they can about the poem for five minutes. Have partners share.

English Language Learners

Make and Confirm Predictions Display pages 6–7. *The story talks about things you can do in one second. A second is a way to measure time.* Have children repeat *second.* Say, *What time measurement do you think will come next in the poem? Make a prediction.* Use a sentence frame to help children form their predictions: I predict the story will be about minutes next. *Let's turn the page to find out if our prediction is correct.*

For additional support, see the **ELL Small Group Guide,** pp. 112–113.

MODEL FLUENCY

Intonation Turn to page 5 of the selection. Point to the question mark. Explain that a question mark signals that the sentence asks something. Say: *When you read a question, your voice should rise. It sounds like you are wondering something.* Read aloud page 5 with slightly exaggerated intonation. Have children identify other questions.

DIGITAL TOOLS

Retell

❯ STUDENT CHECK-IN

Have partners tell one prediction they made as they listened to the story. Have children reflect using the Check-In Routine.

✔ CHECK FOR SUCCESS

Can children make and confirm predictions about a story?

❯❯ Small Group Instruction

If No

🟠 **Approaching** Reteach pp. T64–T65

If Yes

🔵 **On** Review pp. T74–T75

🟢 **Beyond** Extend pp. T78–T79

LESSON 1

In a Flash: Sound-Spellings

Display the Sound-Spelling Card *cheese*.
Point to the letters ch.

1. **Teacher:** What are the letters?   **Children:** ch
2. **Teacher:** What's the sound?   **Children:** /ch/
3. **Teacher:** What's the word?   **Children:** cheese

Continue the routine for previously taught sounds.

⏱ 5 mins Phonemic Awareness

Phoneme Identity

1 **Model** Say: *I will say three words. One sound will be the same in all three words. Listen:* late, make, gave. *I hear the same middle sound in* late, make, *and* gave. *Listen:* /lāāāt/, /māāāk/, /gāāāv/. *The middle sound is /ā/. Say the sound with me: /āāā/.*

2 **Guided Practice/Practice** Have children practice identifying the middle sound in words. Do the first set together. Say: *Listen as I say three words. Tell me the middle sound you hear in all three words. Let's do the first one together. Listen:* /tāāāk/, /vāāās/, /nāāām/.

take, vase, name	gate, tape, bake	fan, bag, mad
wave, game, cape	bug, pup, sun	safe, cape, tale
pen, net, web	date, fake, vase	top, log, not

If children need additional practice identifying phonemes, see **Practice Book** page 161 or the online activity.

⏱ 5 mins Phonics

MULTIMODAL

Introduce Long *a*: *a_e*

1 **Model** Display the *train* **Sound-Spelling Card.** Teach /ā/ spelled *a_e* using the words *ate* and *made*. Model writing the word *at* and adding an *e* to make *ate*. Say: *This is the* train *Sound-Spelling Card. The sound is /ā/. Today we will learn one spelling for the /ā/ sound. Look at this word:* at. *This word has the short a sound /a/. I'll add an e to the end. The new word is* ate. *The letters* a *and* e *work together to make the sound /ā/. Listen as I say the word: /āt/. I'll say /āāāt/ as I write the word* ate *several times.* Continue to model using the word *made*.

Sound-Spelling Card

2 **Guided Practice/Practice** Have children practice connecting the letters *a_e* to the sound /ā/ by writing words with the sound-spelling. Say: *Now do it with me. Say /āāāp/ as I write the word* ape. *This time, write the word* ape *five times as you say /āāāp/. Now write the word* mad. *Add an* e *to the end to make the word* made.

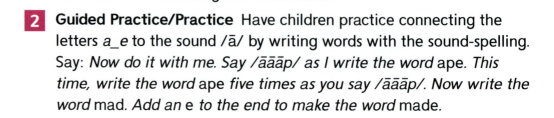

Blend Words with Long *a: a_e*

1 **Model** Display the Word-Building Cards *m, a, k, e.* Model how to blend the sounds. Say: *This is the letter* m. *It stands for /m/. These are the letters* a *and* e. *Together they stand for /ā/. This is the letter* k. *It stands for /k/. Listen as I blend these sounds together: /mmmāāāk/.* Continue by modeling the words *bake, game, sale,* and *grape.*

2 **Guided Practice/Practice** Display the Lesson 1 Phonics Practice Activity. Read each word in the first row, blending the sounds; for example, say: */lllāāāt/. The word is* late. Have children blend each word with you. Prompt children to read the connected text, sounding out the decodable words.

late	take	lake	wade	wake	gaze
lane	gate	cave	fade	save	tame
tap	tape	rat	rate	snack	snake
whale	skate	shade	chase	grape	phase

Nate and Kate like to wade in the lake.

Brave Dave gave the whale a snack.

Can a snake bake you a cake?

Lesson 1 Phonics Practice Activity

If children need additional practice blending words with long *a,* see **Practice Book** page 163 or the online activity.

Corrective Feedback

Sound Error Model the sound that children missed, then have them repeat the sound. Say: *My turn.* Tap under the letter and say: *Sound? /a/. What's the sound?* Return to the beginning of the word. Say: *Let's start over.* Blend the word again.

 Daily Handwriting

Throughout the week, teach uppercase and lowercase letters *Dd* using the online Handwriting models. Model writing the letters using the strokes as shown. Children can practice *Dd* using Practice Book page 168. For more support, use the models at the back of the **Reading/Writing Companion.**

ELL ENGLISH LANGUAGE LEARNERS

Phonemic Awareness, Model Focus on articulation. Say /ā/ and note your mouth position. Have children repeat. Repeat for /a/. Have children say the sounds and notice the difference between the long and short sounds. Have children practice identifying each sound with the words *can/cane, hat/hate, man/mane.*

Phonics Refer to pages 8–9 in the **Language Transfers Handbook.** In Cantonese, Vietnamese, and Hmong, there is only an approximate transfer for the long *a* sound. Emphasize /ā/, and show correct mouth position.

DIGITAL TOOLS

To differentiate instruction for key skills, use the results of this activity.

Phonics: Practice

For more practice, use these activities.

Word Work

Phonemic Awareness

❯ STUDENT CHECK-IN

Phonics Have partners read a long *a* word to each other. Have children reflect using the Check-In Routine.

LEARNING GOALS

- We can spell words with long *a*.
- We can read the words *away, now, some, today, way,* and *why*.

OBJECTIVES

Spell untaught words phonetically, drawing on phonemic awareness and spelling conventions.

Decode regularly spelled one-syllable words.

Recognize and read grade-appropriate irregularly spelled words.

Spell words with long *a*.

ELA ACADEMIC LANGUAGE

- *dictation*

DIGITAL TOOLS

To differentiate instruction for key skills, use the results of this activity.

High-Frequency Words: Practice

For more practice, use this activity.

Spelling

Spelling: Page 165

Spelling

5 mins

Words with Long *a*: *a_e*

Dictation Follow the Spelling Dictation routine to help children transfer their growing knowledge of sound-spellings to writing. After dictation, give the spelling pretest in the **Practice Book** on page 165.

Pretest Say each spelling word. Read each sentence and say the word again. Ask children to say each word, stretching the sounds, before writing it. Then display the spelling words, and write each word as you say the letters. Have children check their words using the Practice Book page.

make	Let's **make** a birthday cake.
take	**Take** me to the store, please.
came	Grandma **came** to visit yesterday.
game	What **game** would you like to play?
gate	Don't forget to close the **gate.**
late	Are you ever **late** for school?
chin	You have soup on your **chin**!
graph	We made a bar **graph** in math class.
some	Would you like **some** grapes?
today	What are you doing **today**?

English Language Learners should use this list for their spelling pretest.

⊙ DIFFERENTIATED SPELLING LISTS

Approaching Level came, game, make, take

Beyond Level came, game, gate, late, make, page, space, take

English Language Learners

Spelling, Dictation Before dictation, review the meanings of words using images or gestures when possible. Pantomime stirring, and say: *I make a cake.* Have children repeat. Act out taking a book from a desk or shelf, and say: *I take the book.* Have children repeat. Point to your chin. Say: *This is my chin.* Have children point to their chins and repeat the sentence.

In a Flash: High-Frequency Words

around

1. **Teacher:** Read the word.   **Children:** around
2. **Teacher:** Spell the word.   **Children:** a-r-o-u-n-d
3. **Teacher:** Write the word.   **Children write the word.**

Repeat with *place, by, walk, many* from last week.

MULTIMODAL

⏱ 5 mins

High-Frequency Words

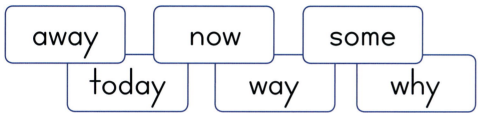

away	now	some
today	way	why

1 **Model** Display the **High-Frequency Word Cards** *away, now, some, today, way,* and *why.* Use the Read/Spell/Write routine to teach each word.

- **Read** Point to and say the word *away.* Say: *This is the word* away. *Say it with me:* away. *He rode* away *on his bike.*

- **Spell** *The word* away *is spelled* a-w-a-y. *Spell it with me.*

- **Write** *Now write the word on your Response Board as we say each letter:* a-w-a-y.

- Follow the same steps to introduce *now, some, today, way,* and *why.*

- As children spell each word, point out sound-spellings children have already learned as well as any irregular sound-spellings, such as /u/ spelled *o_e* in *some.*

COLLABORATE

- Have partners say sentences using each word.

2 **Guided Practice** Have children read the sentences. Prompt them to identify the high-frequency words in connected text and to blend the decodable words.

1. My dog ran **away,** but he came back.
2. Can we play the game **now**?
3. I see **some** snakes in the grass.
4. I had fun at camp **today.**
5. Is this the **way** to school?
6. **Why** are the ducks quacking at me?

3 **Practice** Display the High-Frequency Word Cards. Have children use a pointer to highlight specific words. Have them say each highlighted word.

For additional practice with high-frequency words, have children complete the online activities.

ELL **ENGLISH LANGUAGE LEARNERS**

High-Frequency Words, Model Tell children that *why* is a question word. Provide examples: *Why are you late? Why did you wear a raincoat today? Why is blue your favorite color?* Have children suggest questions they know that begin with *why,* and list them on the board. Then have partners ask and answer *why* questions, using the questions on the board as necessary.

FORMATIVE ASSESSMENT

❯ STUDENT CHECK-IN

Spelling Have partners dictate one long *a* word from the list for each other to write.

High-Frequency Words Have partners take turns reading the high-frequency words.

Have children reflect using the Check-In Routine.

✔ CHECK FOR SUCCESS

Rubric Use your online rubric to record children's progress.

Can children read and decode words with long *a: a_e*?

Can children recognize and read high-frequency words?

❯ Small Group Instruction

If No

🟠 **Approaching** Reteach pp. T66–T71

🟣 **ELL** Develop pp. T66–T71

If Yes

🔵 **On** Review pp. T74–T76

🟢 **Beyond** Extend pp. T78–T79

LEARNING GOALS

We can read and understand a fantasy story.

OBJECTIVES

Decode regularly spelled one-syllable words.

Recognize and read grade-appropriate irregularly spelled words.

With prompting and support, read prose and poetry of appropriate complexity for grade 1.

Understand the fantasy genre.

ELA ACADEMIC LANGUAGE

• fantasy, predict

• Cognates: fantasía, predecir

Close Reading Routine

Read   DOK 1–2

• Identify important ideas and details.

• Take notes and retell.

• Use **A C T** prompts as needed.

Reread   DOK 2–3

• Analyze the text, craft, and structure.

• Use the Reread minilessons.

Integrate   DOK 3–4

• Integrate knowledge and ideas.

• Make text-to-text connections.

• Complete the Show Your Knowledge task.

• Inspire action.

 Read

10 mins

"Nate the Snake Is Late"

Focus on Foundational Skills

• Review the high-frequency words: *away, now, some, today, way, why.*

• Review that the long *a* sound can be spelled *a_e.*

• Display the words *wait, time, say, hear, story, there,* and *spare.* Spell the words and model reading them. Tell children they will be reading the words in the selection. Have children read the words as you point to them. Include definitions for words children may not be familiar with.

Read the Shared Read

 Anchor Chart Review the Fantasy anchor chart.

Genre: Fantasy Tell children that "Nate the Snake Is Late" is a fantasy story. It can be told in the first person, using the words *I, me, my,* and *we.* Add this to the chart.

Make and Confirm Predictions

Explain Tell children that as they read they can make predictions about what might happen and confirm whether their predictions were correct as they read. Children can correct inaccurate predictions.

Connect to Concept: What Time Is It?

Explain that this week, they are reading about time and how to measure time. Children can describe how to tell what time it is.

Take Notes As children read the selection, you may wish to have them take notes in the boxes provided. Children may take notes by:

• writing a word with *long a: a_e* or a high-frequency word

Have children read each page, pointing to each word as they read. Have them sound out or say the words in each sentence. Then read aloud the prompts.

Reading/Writing Companion, pp. 14–15

SET PURPOSE

Say: *Let's read to find out why Nate is late.*

PHONICS

Have children read and circle words with the same middle sound as *cake.*

Reading/Writing Companion, pp. 16–17

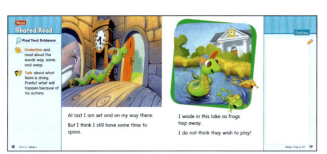

Reading/Writing Companion, pp. 18–19

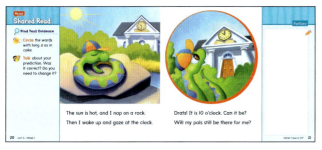

Reading/Writing Companion, pp. 20–21

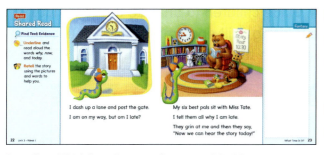

Reading/Writing Companion, pp. 22–23

Respond to the Text

Have partners discuss why Nate is late for school. Use a sentence starter to begin: *Nate is late because . . . .*

COMPREHENSION

Have partners tell why Nate doesn't want to be late. What does this tell them about him?

COMPREHENSION

Have partners discuss why Nate isn't worried about the time on page 17.

HIGH-FREQUENCY WORDS

Have children underline and read aloud *way*, *some*, and *away*.

MAKE AND CONFIRM PREDICTIONS

Have partners tell what Nate does. Say: *Predict what happens because of his actions.*

PHONICS

Have children circle words with the long *a* sound as in *cake*.

MAKE AND CONFIRM PREDICTIONS

Have partners discuss their last prediction. Were they right? Do they need to correct it?

HIGH-FREQUENCY WORDS

Have children underline and read aloud *why*, *now*, and *today*.

RETELL

Have partners use the words and pictures to retell the story. Then have partners act out their favorite part of the story.

 ### SPOTLIGHT ON LANGUAGE

Page 18 Read the phrase *time to spare*. Have children repeat. Explain that *time to spare* is an expression that means "more time than you need to do something." Time to spare is *extra time*. Say, *Does Nate the snake have time to spare?* (yes) Turn and talk to your partner about what you like to do when you have time to spare.

FOCUS ON FLUENCY

 With partners, have children reread "Nate the Snake Is Late" to develop fluency. Children should focus on their accuracy, trying to say each word correctly. Then have them reread the story so it sounds like speech. Remind children the goal is to keep practicing until they can read the words automatically.

DIFFERENTIATED READING

● **English Language Learners**
Before reading, have children listen to a summary of the selection, available in multiple languages.

STUDENT CHECK-IN

Have children reflect on their retelling using the Check-In Routine.

LEARNING GOALS

- We can learn how to write a sentence with strong verbs.
- We can identify the verbs in sentences.

OBJECTIVES

Write narratives in which they recount two or more appropriately sequenced events, include some details regarding what happened, use temporal words to signal event order, and provide some sense of closure.

Use verbs to convey a sense of past, present, and future.

ELA ACADEMIC LANGUAGE

- *verb*
- Cognate: *verbo*

COLLABORATIVE CONVERSATIONS

Turn and Talk Use this routine.

Child 1: Nate plays with a ball.

Child 2: Why do you think that?

Child 1: He likes to play with toys.

Display speech bubbles "Why do you think that?" and "What do you mean?" Have partners use them to practice collaborating.

DIFFERENTIATED WRITING

● **English Language Learners** For more writing support, see the **ELL Small Group Guide,** p. 114.

 5 mins

Modeled Writing

Write About the Shared Read

 Build Oral Language Read aloud the prompt. Say: *Write about a new activity that makes Nate late.* Have partners use the Turn and Talk routine to discuss ideas.

Model Writing Sentences Say: *I will write about another activity that makes Nate late for school.* Display page 19. *I see that Nate likes to swim. I will write about him doing something else in the water.*

Sample Teacher Talk

- Listen to my sentences: *Nate floats down the river in a sailboat. Now he is really late for school!* Nate has the /ā/ sound in the middle. I'll use *a_e* to write *Nate.* PHONICS

- The next word is *floats. Floats* is a strong verb. It helps us know how Nate's boat moves in the water. I'll write *floats.* TRAIT: WORD CHOICE

- I look at the Word Bank to find *down.* It's spelled d-o-w-n. I'll write *down.* HIGH-FREQUENCY WORDS

- As I write the word *the,* I start on the left and move to the right. When I get to the end of the line, I move down to the next line. WRITING SKILL

Continue modeling writing the remaining words in your sentences.

Write about a new activity that makes Nate late.

Nate floats down the river in a sailboat. Now he is really late for school!

Writing Practice

Analyze and Write Sentences Have children turn to page 24 in their **Reading/Writing Companion.** Guide children to analyze the sentences using the prompts. Review the Writing Skill and Trait boxes, as necessary. Then have children write and analyze their own sentences.

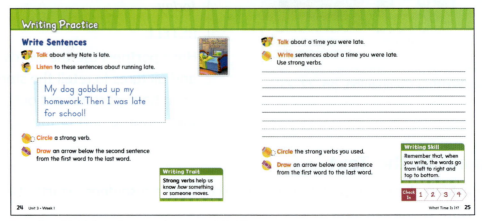

Reading/Writing Companion, pp. 24–25

Stephen Coburn/Shutterstock

5 mins

Grammar

Verbs

1 **Model** Tell children that a word that shows action is called a *verb*. Explain that writers use many different verbs to show action. Display the following sentences:

Frogs hop in the lake.

Nate naps on a rock.

Explain that *hop* and *naps* are verbs. To illustrate that a verb shows action, have children act out these verbs: *smile, write, stand, sit, laugh, eat, sleep.*

2 **Guided Practice/Practice** Display these sentences and read them aloud. Prompt children to chorally reread them with you. Have partners identify the verbs.

The wet dog shakes. (shakes)

Jake kicks the ball and then runs. (kicks, runs)

 Talk About It Have partners orally generate sentences with different verbs. Challenge them to act out each sentence.

Link to Writing Review the Modeled Writing for the correct use of verbs.

 ## English Language Learners

Use the following with **Grammar, Guided Practice/Practice.**

Beginning

Read the first sentence. *Is* dog *a verb?* (no) *Is* shakes *a verb?* (yes) *How do you know? What does a verb show?* (action) Ask children to demonstrate *shakes.*

Intermediate

Display the first sentence, and ask children to circle the verb. *How do you know* shakes *is a verb?* *Shakes* is a word that shows <u>action</u>. Repeat with the second sentence.

Advanced/Advanced High

Ask children to identify the verbs in the sentences. Then have them extend their thinking by forming new sentences with the verbs. (He shakes the toy. She kicks the ball. I run fast.)

DIGITAL TOOLS
Use these activities to practice grammar.

 Grammar

 Grammar Song

 Grammar Video

FORMATIVE ASSESSMENT

⊗ STUDENT CHECK-IN

Writing Have partners read each other their writing. Have children reflect using the Check-In Routine to fill in the bars.

Grammar Have partners share one verb they identified from the sentences. Have children reflect using the Check-In routine.

LEARNING GOALS

We can learn and use new vocabulary words.

OBJECTIVES

Identify real-life connections between words and their use.

Discuss the Essential Question.

Develop oral language.

ELA ACADEMIC LANGUAGE

• *define, discuss*
• Cognates: *definir, discutir*

TEACH IN SMALL GROUP

🟣 **ELL** See the Teacher Talk on the back of the **Visual Vocabulary Cards** for additional support.

🟠 **Approaching** Group children with students in a higher level to practice saying the words. Then children can draw their own picture of the word.

🔵🟢 **On Level** and **Beyond Level** Have children look up each word in the online **Visual Glossary.**

FORMATIVE ASSESSMENT

STUDENT CHECK-IN

Have partners use a vocabulary word in a sentence. Have children reflect using the Check-In Routine.

LESSON FOCUS

READING
Revisit the Essential Question
Read Interactive Read Aloud:
"Measuring Time"
• Use Antonyms
Word Work
• Review Long *a*: *a_e*

Reread Shared Read:
"Nate the Snake Is Late"
• Review Genre
• Introduce Skill
WRITING
• Interactive Writing
• Review Grammar

Reading/Writing Companion, pp. 14–23

🕐 5 mins

Oral Language

MULTIMODAL

❓ Essential Question
How do we measure time?

Remind children that this week you have been talking and reading about time and how it is measured. Remind them of the children's clocks and how Nate kept track of time.

Oral Vocabulary Words

Review the oral vocabulary words *immediately* and *schedule* from Lesson 1. Use the Define/Example/Ask routine on the print or digital **Visual Vocabulary Cards** to introduce the oral vocabulary words *calendar, occasion,* and *weekend.* Prompt children to use the words as they discuss how we measure time.

Visual Vocabulary Cards

Oral Vocabulary Routine

Define: A **calendar** is a chart that shows the days, weeks, and months in a year.

Example: Juan looks at the calendar to count the days until Thanksgiving.

Ask: How might you use a calendar?

Define: An **occasion** is a special time or event.

Example: Sometimes we celebrate a special occasion with a party.

Ask: What is your favorite special occasion?

Define: The **weekend** is Saturday and Sunday.

Example: There is no school on the weekend, so the children stay home and play.

Ask: What do you do on the weekend?

OPTION
10 mins

Read the Interactive Read Aloud

Connect to Concept

Tell children that you will be reading aloud a nonfiction text about days and months in a year. Display the **Interactive Read Aloud Cards.** Read aloud the title "Measuring Time."

Set Purpose Say: *Let's read to learn about different ways to measure and track time.* Read or play the selection aloud as you display the cards. Remind children to listen carefully.

Oral Vocabulary Use the Oral Vocabulary prompts as you read the selection to provide more practice with the words in context.

Antonyms Tell children that as you read, they can use antonyms to help them understand the meaning of unfamiliar words. Explain that antonyms are words that have the opposite meaning. Model the strategy using a sentence at the bottom of Card 2.

Teacher Think Aloud I read "Other families take trips to the zoo, ride bikes, or just stay home and play games together." I know that the word *together* means "in a group," so I thought of a word with the opposite meaning. The word *alone* is the antonym for *together*. This helped me understand that family members spend time with each other doing fun things on the weekend.

Continue reading the story. Model the strategy as needed.

Student Think Along After you read Card 4, stop and say: *The word* warmer *means "a little bit of heat." What are some antonyms for* warmer*? How does this help you understand how people feel in the spring?* The word *colder* is an antonym for *warmer*. Now I know what the air feels like for many people in spring.

Build Knowledge: Make Connections

Talk About the Text Have partners discuss how clocks, days, months, years, calendars, and seasons help people measure time.

Add to the Anchor Chart Record any new ideas on the Build Knowledge anchor chart.

Add to the Word Bank Then add words related to measuring time to a separate section of the Word Bank.

"Measuring Time"

OBJECTIVES

Determine or clarify the meaning of unknown and multiple-meaning words and phrases based on *grade 1 reading and content*, choosing flexibly from an array of strategies.

ELA ACADEMIC LANGUAGE

• *antonym*

• Cognate: *antónimo*

DIGITAL TOOLS

MULTIMODAL

Interactive
Read Aloud

ELL SPOTLIGHT ON LANGUAGE

Card 1 *Clocks are divided into equal parts. There are sixty lines on this clock. Each line is the same size and represents one minute. How many minutes are there in an hour?* (sixty)

FORMATIVE ASSESSMENT

❯ **STUDENT CHECK-IN**

Have partners share one thing they learned about seasons in a year. Have children reflect using the Check-In Routine.

LESSON **2**

OBJECTIVES

Demonstrate understanding of spoken words, syllables, and sounds (phonemes).

Know final -e and common vowel team conventions for representing long vowel sounds.

Use apostrophes to form contractions.

ELA ACADEMIC LANGUAGE

• addition, contraction

• Cognate: *contracción*

TEACH IN SMALL GROUP

Word Work lessons can be taught in small groups.

Phonemic Awareness: Page 162

OPTION **5 mins**

Phonemic Awareness

Phoneme Addition

1 **Model** Say: *Listen as I say this word:* ape. *Now listen as I add the /k/ sound to the beginning:* ape, /k/ /k/ /kāp/. *I made a new word:* cape. Continue modeling phoneme addition with the following word sets:

ace/face   age/page   take/steak

2 **Guided Practice/Practice** Have children practice adding phonemes. Say: *I am going to say more sounds and words. Add the sound to the beginning of the word to get a new word. Tell me the word. Listen:* aim. *Let's add /n/ to the beginning of* aim. *Aim with /n/ at the beginning is* name. Guide practice and provide feedback as needed.

aim/name	ache/make	ace/race	ate/date
aid/fade	late/plate	ape/shape	age/stage

If children need additional practice adding phonemes, see **Practice Book** page 162 or the online activity.

5 mins

Phonics

MULTIMODAL

Review Long *a: a_e*

1 **Model** Display the *train* Sound-Spelling Card. Say: *The sound /ā/ can be spelled* a-consonant-e. *You can hear the /ā/ sound at the beginning of a word such as* ape *and in the middle of the word* gave.

2 **Guided Practice/Practice** Point to the *a_e* spelling on the Sound-Spelling Card. Ask: *What are these letters? What sound do they stand for?* Provide corrective feedback as needed.

Sound-Spelling Card

Blend Words with Long *a: a_e*

1 **Model** Display **Word-Building Cards** *s, a, m, e*. Model blending the sounds. *This is the letter* s. *It stands for /s/. These are the letters* a *and* e. *Together they stand for /ā/. This is the letter* m. *It stands for /m/. Listen as I blend these sounds: /sssāāāmmm/.* Next, model the words *late, snake,* and *whale.*

s   a   m   e

2 **Guided Practice/Practice** Say: *Now let's do some together.* Display the **Word-Building Cards** for the letters *l, a, t, e. Let's blend these sounds together: /l/ /ā/ /t/, /lllāāāt/,* late. Repeat the routine with children with the words *game, gave, ate, cane, tale, tape, fame, date, skate, grade,* and *chase.* Guide practice and provide corrective feedback as needed.

Build Words with Long *a: a_e*

Provide children with Word-Building Cards *a–z.* Have children put the letters in alphabetical order as quickly as possible.

1 **Model** Display the Word-Building Cards *g, a, v, e.* Blend: /g/ /ā/ /v/, /gāāāvvv/, *gave.* Replace *g* with *s* and repeat with *save.* Change *v* to *l* and repeat with *sale.*

2 **Guided Practice/Practice** Continue building the words: *male, make, lake, lane, plane, plate, late, rate, gate, gape, grape, shape, shave, wave, wade,* and *shade.* Guide children to build and blend each word. Then dictate the words and have children write the words.

For additional practice decoding long *a* in connected text, see Build Words with Long *a* lessons on T69 and T76.

Structural Analysis

Contractions with *not*

1 **Model** Write and read aloud *is not* and *isn't.* Explain to children that *isn't* is a contraction, which is a word made by putting two words together. Then point out that *isn't* is a shorter way of saying *is not.* Underline the *n't.* Explain that the apostrophe (') stands for the letter *o* in *not.* This letter was removed when the contraction was formed.

Repeat for *are not* and *aren't.* Then write *can not* and *can't.* Explain that in *can't,* the apostrophe (') stands for the letters *n* and *o.* Use each word in a sentence.

2 **Guided Practice/Practice** Write *was not, were not, has not,* and *have not* on the board. Help children write the contractions for the words, and then have them use the contractions in sentences. Guide practice and provide corrective feedback as needed.

Blend Words with Long *a: a_e,* Guided Practice/Practice Review the meanings of example words that can be explained or demonstrated in a concrete way. For example, ask children to point to the *tape* or a *game* in the classroom. Model the actions for *gave* and *take* as you say: *I gave you a pencil. Now I take it back.* Have children repeat. Provide sentence frames such as: I *ate* lunch. I am in first grade. Correct grammar and pronunciation as needed.

DIGITAL TOOLS

To differentiate instruction for key skills, use the results of this activity.

Phonics: Practice

For more practice, use these activities.

Phonemic Awareness Structural Analysis

❯ STUDENT CHECK-IN

Phonics Have partners build a word with the long *a* sound.

Structural Analysis Have partners read one contraction they wrote and use it in a sentence.

Have children reflect using the Check-In Routine.

LESSON 2

LEARNING GOALS

- We can sort and spell words with long *a*.
- We can read and write the words *away, now, some, today, way,* and *why*.

OBJECTIVES

Use conventional spelling for words with common spelling patterns and for frequently occurring irregular words.

Recognize and read grade-appropriate irregularly spelled words.

Sort words with long *a*.

ELA ACADEMIC LANGUAGE

- *pattern*

DIGITAL TOOLS

To differentiate instruction for key skills, use the results of this activity.

High-Frequency Words: Practice

For more practice, use this activity.

Word Work   **Spelling**

Spelling: On Level, Page 166
Approaching, Page 166A
Beyond, Page 166B
High-Frequency Words: Page 171

---

5 mins

Spelling

MULTIMODAL

Word Sort with *-ake, -ame, -ate*

1 **Model** Display the online **Spelling Word Cards** for Unit 3 Week 1, one at a time. Have children read each word, listening for the long *a* sound and the ending sound.

Use cards with the endings *-ake, -ame,* and *-ate* to create a three-column chart. Then model sorting the words *lake, same,* and *date*. Say each word and pronounce the sounds: /l/ /ā/ /k/; /s/ /ā/ /m/; /d/ /ā/ /t/. Say each word again, emphasizing the long *a* plus final consonant sound. Ask children to chorally spell each word.

2 **Guided Practice/Practice** Have children place each Spelling Word Card in the column with the word containing the same sound-spelling patterns.

When completed, have children chorally read the words in each column. Then call out a word. Have a child find the word card and point to it as the class chorally spells the word.

If children need additional practice spelling words with long *a*, see differentiated **Practice Book** pages 166–166B or the online activity.

-ake	-ame
-ate	make
take	came
game	gate
late	

Spelling Word Cards   *Unit 3 • Week 1*

Analyze Errors/Articulation Support

Use children's pretest errors to analyze spelling problems and provide corrective feedback. For example, some children will leave off the final letter *e*.

Work with children to recognize the difference in vowel sound and spelling in minimal contrast pairs such as *mad/made, rat/rate, tap/tape, hat/hate,* and *plan/plane*.

Say each word. Have children repeat. Focus on the medial vowel sound and how the mouth forms that sound. Then have children write the words. Emphasize that when they hear the long *a* sound, they use the *a_e* spelling pattern. Tell children they will learn other long *a* spellings in upcoming weeks.

OPTION
5 mins

High-Frequency Words

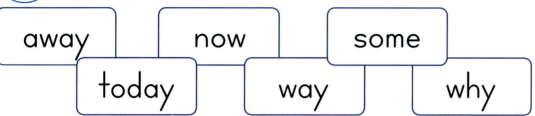

away   now   some
today   way   why

1 **Guided Practice** Say each word and have children Read/Spell/Write it.

- Point out irregularities in sound-spellings, such as the /u/ sound in *some*. Connect the *o_e* spelling pattern in *some* to the previously taught high-frequency word *come*.

2 **Practice** Add the high-frequency words *away, now, some, today, way,* and *why* to the cumulative Word Bank.

- Have children work with a partner to create sentences using the words.

- Have children look at the words and compare their sounds and spellings with words from previous weeks.

- Suggest that children write one sentence about measuring time or getting to places on time.

Cumulative Review Review last week's words *(around, by, many, place,* and *walk)* by displaying each word and having children read it with automaticity.

Have children independently practice identifying, spelling, and reading high-frequency words using **Practice Book** page 171 or the online activity.

 ENGLISH LANGUAGE LEARNERS

Use the following scaffolds with **High-Frequency Words, Practice.**

Beginning
Provide sentence frames to help partners create sentences: I drink some <u>water</u>. Today is <u>Monday</u>.

Intermediate
Provide additional sentence frames: Do you know the way to the <u>park</u>? Now it is time to <u>read</u>.

Advanced/Advanced High
Challenge partners to use two high-frequency words in the same sentence. Model: *Today, I am going away.* Have them share their sentences with the class.

FORMATIVE ASSESSMENT

STUDENT CHECK-IN

Spelling Have partners share one column of words they sorted.

High-Frequency Words Have partners quiz each other using the High-Frequency Word Cards.

Have children reflect using the Check-In Routine.

CHECK FOR SUCCESS

Rubric Use your online rubric to record children's progress.

Can children read and decode words with long *a: a_e*?

Can children recognize and read high-frequency words?

Small Group Instruction

If No

● **Approaching** Reteach pp. T66–T71

● **ELL** Develop pp. T66–T71

If Yes

● **On** Review pp. T74–T76

● **Beyond** Extend pp. T78–T79

LESSON 2

LEARNING GOALS

- We can tell what makes a story a fantasy story.
- We can identify events at the beginning, middle, and end of a story.

OBJECTIVES

Describe major events in a story, using key details.

Explain major differences between books that tell stories and books that give information.

Identify who is telling the story at various points in a text.

Understand fantasy genre.

ELA ACADEMIC LANGUAGE

- *fantasy, events*
- Cognates: *fantasía, eventos*

▶ TEACH IN SMALL GROUP

🟠 **Approaching** Have partners work together to complete the chart.

🔵🟢 **On Level** and **Beyond Level** Have children write their responses independently and then discuss them.

🟣 **ELL** For specific comprehension support in reading "Nate the Snake Is Late," see the **ELL Small Group Guide**, pp. 108-109.

DIGITAL TOOLS

To differentiate instruction for key skills, use the results of this activity.

Events: Beginning, Middle, End

Reread

10 mins

"Nate the Snake Is Late"

Genre: Fantasy

1 **Model** Tell children they will now reread the fantasy story "Nate the Snake Is Late." Remind them that books that tell stories and books that give information have major difference. Have children discuss a few characteristics of fiction. Then have them turn to page 26 in their **Reading/Writing Companion**. Review the characteristics of a fantasy story. Fantasy:

- has made-up characters.
- can be told in first person using the words *I, me, my,* and *we.*

Display the story "Nate the Snake Is Late" in the Reading/Writing Companion. Say: *On page 16, Nate's alarm clock wakes him up. Nate says, "It is 8 o'clock, and I can not be late." Nate uses the word* I. *Nate's telling the story and he's a character in the story.* Model filling in the first box of the graphic organizer on page 27 by writing *I,* the word Nate uses to tell the story.

Reading/Writing Companion, pp. 26–27

2 **Guided Practice/Practice** Have children copy what you wrote in the graphic organizer on page 27 of their Reading/Writing Companion. Have them continue by rereading page 18 of the story. Have children share with a partner who is telling the story and how they know. Ask: *Who is telling the story?* (Nate) *What words does Nate use to show he is telling the story?* (I, my)

Guide children to write the words in the graphic organizer. Then ask children to find a word on page 23 that shows who is telling the story and how they know. They can add this information to the graphic organizer, and draw a picture of Nate. Offer help as needed.

Events: Beginning, Middle, End

 Anchor Chart Create a Beginning, Middle, End anchor chart. Say: *Events are the most important things that happen in a story. Events take place in the beginning, middle, and end of the story. We read the text to find the most important events.* Write this information on the chart.

1 **Model** Display page 28 of the **Reading/Writing Companion.** Have children talk about the most important thing that happens in the beginning of the story. Model filling in the first box on page 29. Say: *On page 16, we read that Nate wakes up. He doesn't want to be late. This is an important event at the beginning of the story.* Write this event in the first box.

Reading/Writing Companion, pp. 28–29

2 **Guided Practice/Practice** Guide children to copy what you wrote in the graphic organizer on page 29 of their own Reading/Writing Companion. Then have children reread pages 17-20 and talk with a partner about the important events that happen in the middle of the story. Ask: *What important things is Nate doing on these pages?* (Nate takes a bath. He wades in a lake. He takes a nap.) Guide children to write these events in the second box.

Have children identify important events on the last page of the story and add them to the last box. Offer help as needed.

For more practice, have children complete the online activity.

 ## English Language Learners

Events: Beginning, Middle, End, Guided Practice Say, *Let's talk about the middle of the story.* Point to the illustration on page 17. *What important event is happening on this page?* Nate is taking a bath. Provide more sentence frames for children to talk about important events on pages 18-20.

BUILD KNOWLEDGE: MAKE CONNECTIONS

Talk About the Text Have partners discuss how Nate thinks about and measures time during his day.

Write About the Text Then have children add their ideas to the Build Knowledge page of their reader's notebook.

Add to the Anchor Chart Record any new ideas on the Build Knowledge anchor chart.

Add to the Word Bank Then add words related to measuring time to a separate section of the Word Bank.

FORMATIVE ASSESSMENT

❯ STUDENT CHECK-IN

Genre Have partners take turns telling why this is a fantasy story.

Skill Have children identify one important event from the beginning, middle, or end of the story.

Have children reflect using the Check-In Routine to fill in the bars.

✓ CHECK FOR SUCCESS

Rubric Use your online rubric to record children's progress.

Can children identify events at the beginning, middle, and end of "Nate the Snake Is Late"?

❯ Small Group Instruction

If No

🔴 **Approaching** Reteach pp. T64–T65, T72–T73

If Yes

🔵 **On** Review pp. T74–T75, T77

🟢 **Beyond** Extend pp. T78–T81

LESSON 2

- We can read and write about a Student Model.
- We can identify verbs and act them out.

OBJECTIVES

Write narratives in which they recount two or more appropriately sequenced events, include some details regarding what happened, use temporal words to signal event order, and provide some sense of closure.

Use verbs to convey a sense of past, present, and future.

ELA ACADEMIC LANGUAGE

- *text evidence, verb*
- Cognate: *verbo*

COLLABORATIVE CONVERSATIONS

Circulate as partners talk about the prompt. Notice who is not asking questions. Remind them to use the speech bubbles to help generate questions. As you listen in to children's conversations, you may choose to write down your observations on children's language development.

DIFFERENTIATED WRITING

🟣 **English Language Learners**
For more writing support, see **ELL Small Group Guide,** p. 114.

5 mins

Interactive Writing

Write About the Shared Read

Analyze the Prompt Read aloud a new prompt: *Write what might happen next in "Nate the Snake Is Late."* Have partners talk about it.

Find Text Evidence Guide children to find text evidence to respond to the prompt. Display page 23. Say: *Nate likes hearing a story. What do you think happens next?* Use a volunteer's response and the sample teacher talk below to write sentences, such as: *Nate grabs a different book. He reads in the corner. Soon he exclaims, "Oh no, I am late for snack!"*

Sample Teacher Talk: Share the Pen

- Who knows the middle sound in *Nate?* That's right, /ā/. Have a volunteer write *Nate.* Phonics

- *Grabs* is a strong verb. It means Nate took the book quickly. Have a volunteer write *grabs.* Trait: Word Choice

- Who can find *a* on the Word Bank and spell it? That's right. *a.* Have a volunteer write *a.* High-Frequency Words

- Continue sharing the pen to complete the sentences. Then ask: Who can show where the sentences begin and end? Writing Skill

Analyze the Student Model

Say: *Let's read how another child responded to the prompt.* Have children turn to page 30 of the **Reading/Writing Companion.** Guide them to analyze Luke's writing using the prompts on page 31. Then have children write what they notice. Review the Grammar box, as necessary. Use the Quick Tip box for support.

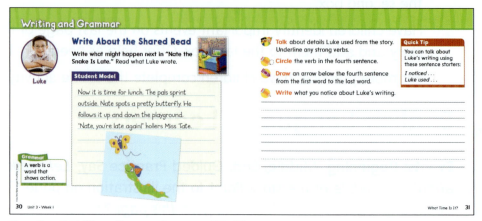

Reading/Writing Companion, pp. 30–31

Stephen Coburn/Shutterstock

5 mins

Grammar

Verbs

1 **Review** Remind children that a verb shows action. *Some verbs are* drop, jump, *and* mix. *These words show something you can do.* Write the sentences below.

> The ape hangs on a branch.
>
> Dale and Jane play a game.

Read the sentences aloud and have children chorally repeat. Guide children to circle the verb in each sentence. (hangs, play)

2 **Practice** Once children identify the verbs above, they can act them out. Then children can work with partners to act out other verbs, such as *jump, hop, skip, dance, wiggle, smile.*

For additional practice with verbs, see **Practice Book** page 172 or the online activity.

Talk About It

 COLLABORATE

Have partners work together to orally generate sentences with different verbs. Challenge them to use more than one verb in a sentence.

 ELL # English Language Learners

Grammar, Practice Help children learn the meaning of each verb by saying the word and having children repeat it. For example, say *jump,* and have children repeat. Then demonstrate the verb by jumping into the air. Have children jump as well. Use the other Practice verbs, and repeat the process by having children say each verb and then show its action.

DIGITAL TOOLS

Use this activity to practice grammar.

I see a fish.

Grammar

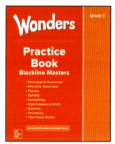
Wonders
Practice Book
Blackline Masters

Grammar: Page 172

FORMATIVE ASSESSMENT

STUDENT CHECK-IN

Writing Have partners share one thing they noticed about the Student Model.

Grammar Have children choose a verb and act it out.

Have children reflect using the Check-In Routine.

LEARNING GOALS

We can learn and use new vocabulary words.

OBJECTIVES

Identify real-life connections between words and their use.

Discuss the Essential Question.

Develop oral language.

ELA ACADEMIC LANGUAGE

• *discuss*

• Cognate: *discutir*

LESSON FOCUS

READING

Revisit the Essential Question

Reread Literature Big Book:
A Second Is a Hiccup
• Use Antonyms
• Analyze Author's Craft

Word Work
• Blend Words with Long *a: a_e*

Read and Reread Anchor Text: *On My Way to School*
• Review Genre
• Make Predictions
• Review Skill

WRITING
• Independent Writing
• Review Grammar and Introduce Mechanics

Literature Anthology, pp. 6–23

---

 5 mins

Oral Language

 MULTIMODAL

 Essential Question

How do we measure time?

Remind children that this week they are talking and reading about how we measure time. Remind them of the units of time they read about in *A Second Is a Hiccup*, the way Nate the Snake lost track of time, and the different ways to tell time that they read about.

Review Oral Vocabulary

Review the oral vocabulary words *immediately, schedule, weekend, calendar,* and *occasion* using the Define/Example/Ask routine on the print or digital **Visual Vocabulary Cards.** Encourage children to discuss measuring time when coming up with examples for each word.

Visual Vocabulary Cards

FORMATIVE ASSESSMENT

❯ STUDENT CHECK-IN

Have partners use a vocabulary word in a sentence. Have children reflect using the Check-In Routine.

A Second Is a Hiccup

As you reread the book *A Second Is a Hiccup,* model using text evidence to respond to questions about author's craft. Also model using antonyms to help children understand the meaning of unfamiliar words.

Author's Purpose Authors have a purpose or reason for organizing the text in a certain way. Point out the questions that appear on pages 5 and 8. Why does the author ask a question at the beginning of each section?

Think Aloud On page 5, the author asks "How long is a second?" The pages that follow this question show the answer, so I can make an inference that asking the question helps the reader to focus on the things that can happen during that length of time.

Antonyms Review that some words have opposite meanings. These words are called antonyms. Tell children that thinking of antonyms can help them understand the meaning of words.

Model the strategy. Reread page 19. Point to *melt.* Say: Melt *means that something, such as ice, changes from solid to liquid. The opposite of* melt *is* freeze. *Thinking about words with opposite meanings helps us understand what happens to snow and ice when winter turns to spring.*

Continue modeling the strategy for additional words as needed.

Author's Purpose Make an inference about why the author begins with explaining a second and ends with explaining a year. (I know that a second is a short amount of time, so the author began with that. I know that a year is a long amount of time, so the author ended with that. I can make an inference that the author wrote the story this way to show how a second grows and grows, until a year has gone by.)

Build Knowledge: Make Connections

Talk About the Text Have partners discuss the different ways the characters measure time in the text.

Add to the Anchor Chart Record any new ideas on the Build Knowledge anchor chart.

Add to the Word Bank Then add words related to measuring time to a separate section of the Word Bank.

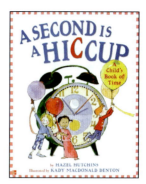

Literature Big Book

LEARNING GOALS

We can think about the choices an author makes when writing a text.

OBJECTIVES

With guidance and support from adults, demonstrate understanding of word relationships and nuances in word meanings.

ELA ACADEMIC LANGUAGE

• *antonym*
• Cognate: *antónimo*

ELL ENGLISH LANGUAGE LEARNERS

Antonyms Provide children with additional practice identifying antonyms. Write two lists of words for children: *long, hot, sad; cold, happy, short.* Have them work with partners. Tell each partner to say a word from the list, and have the other partner say the antonym. Have partners switch roles and repeat until all words have been used. Help children identify antonyms if necessary.

FORMATIVE ASSESSMENT

❯ STUDENT CHECK-IN

Have partners name one choice the author made. Have children reflect using the Check-In Routine.

LEARNING GOALS

- We can change the first sound in a word to make a new word.
- We can read words with long *a*.
- We can read contractions with *not*.

OBJECTIVES

Isolate and pronounce initial sounds (phonemes) in spoken single-syllable words.

Decode regularly spelled one-syllable words.

Use apostrophes to form contractions.

ELA ACADEMIC LANGUAGE

- *contraction, apostrophe*
- Cognates: *contracción, apóstrofo*

▶ TEACH IN SMALL GROUP

Word Work lessons can be taught in small groups.

Phonics: Page 164
Structural Analysis: Page 169

Phonemic Awareness

5 mins

Phoneme Substitution

1 **Model** Say: *I am going to say a word. Listen:* cane, */k/ /k/ /kān/. I will change the /k/ to /l/ to make a new word. Listen: /l/ /l/ /lān/. The new word is* lane.

2 **Guided Practice/Practice** Say: *Let's do some together. I will say a word. Then I will say a sound. We will change the first sound in the word to make a new word. The word is* pale. *Say it with me: /p/ /p/ /pāl/. We will change the /p/ to /s/. Let's say the new word together: /s/ /s/ /sāl/,* sale. Continue to guide practice and provide corrective feedback as needed with the following words:

date/late	lake/bake	save/cave	name/game
case/chase	rain/mane	whale/pale	cape/tape

Phonics

OPTION 5 mins

Blend Words with Long *a: a_e*

1 **Model** Display **Word-Building Cards** *t, a, k, e.* Model how to blend the sounds. *This is the letter* t. *It stands for /t/. These are the letters* a *and* e. *Together they stand for /ā/. This is the letter* k. *It stands for /k/. Let's blend all three sounds: /tāāāk/. The word is* take. Continue by modeling the words *fake, blame, crate,* and *shade.*

2 **Guided Practice/Practice** Display the Lesson 3 Phonics Practice Activity. Say: *Let's blend the letter sounds to read each word: /w/ /ā/ /k/; /wāāāk/. The word is* wake. Have children blend each word with you.

wake	late	gaze	Nate	take	tape
apes	lane	game	gate	date	make
plan	plane	van	vane	chase	shape
isn't	hasn't	aren't	wasn't	weren't	can't
haven't	it's	he's	she's	let's	here's

Jane chases Tate to the lake.

Dave ate some grapes for lunch.

Lesson 3 Phonics Practice Activity

Prompt children to read the connected text, sounding out the decodable words. Provide corrective feedback as needed.

If children need additional practice blending words with long *a*, see **Practice Book** page 164 or the online activity.

Corrective Feedback

Sound Error Help children with any sounds they missed. Say: *My turn. This sound says* (make the correct sound). Then blend the word. Say: *Do it with me.* Blend the word aloud with children. Say: *Your turn. Blend this word.* Have children chorally blend. Say. *Let's do it again.* Follow these steps until children are confidently producing the sound.

Decodable Reader

Have children read "Dave Was Late" to practice decoding words in connected text. If children need support reading words with long *a*, see page T69 or T76 for instruction and support for "Dave Was Late."

Structural Analysis

Contractions with *not*

1. **Model** Write the words *is not* and *isn't.* Model decoding each word and ask children to listen closely to hear what is different. Point out that *isn't* is a shortened way to say the words *is not.* Write the contraction *isn't.* Circle the *n't* at the end. Tell children that the *n't* at the end shows that *isn't* is a contraction. When the base words *is* and *not* were put together to make one word, the letter *o* in *not* was replaced with an apostrophe. Write *is not.* Model how to form the contraction *isn't.*

2. **Practice/Apply** Help children read the contractions *aren't, wasn't, weren't, hasn't, haven't,* and *can't.* Have them look for the base words they know plus the *n't* ending. Have children tell what words the contractions stand for. Have children practice decoding words with contractions using Practice Book page 169 or the online activity.

DIGITAL TOOLS

For more practice, use these activities.

Word Work

Phonemic Awareness
Phonics
Structural Analysis

ELL ENGLISH LANGUAGE LEARNERS

Structural Analysis, Practice/Apply Help children distinguish between endings with contractions and those without. Say *aren't,* and have children repeat. Then say each of the Practice/Apply words and their noncontracted forms, such as *aren't* and *are not.* Have children raise their hand when they hear the contracted form. Then reread each contraction, and have children repeat.

FORMATIVE ASSESSMENT

❯ STUDENT CHECK-IN

Phonics Have partners read a long *a* word to each other.

Structural Analysis Have partners read one contraction aloud and tell which two words it stands for.

Have children reflect using the Check-In Routine.

LEARNING GOALS

- We can sort words by word families.
- We can read and write the words *away, now, some, today, way,* and *why.*

OBJECTIVES

Use conventional spelling for words with common spelling patterns and for frequently occurring irregular words.

Recognize and read grade-appropriate irregularly spelled words.

Sort words with long *a.*

ELA ACADEMIC LANGUAGE

- *pattern, rhyme*
- Cognate: *rima*

OPTION 5 mins

Spelling

MULTIMODAL

Word Families: *-ake, -ame, -ate*

1 **Model** Make index cards for *-ake, -ame, -ate* and form three columns in a pocket chart. Blend the sounds with children.

Hold up the online **Spelling Word Card** for *make.* Say and spell *make.* Pronounce each sound clearly: /m/ /ā/ /k/. Blend the sounds, stretching the vowel sound to emphasize it: /māāāk/. Repeat this step with *take.* Place both words below the *-ake* card. Read and spell *make* and *take.* Ask: *What do you notice about these spelling words? They have the /ā/ sound, and they rhyme because they both end with /ā ke/ spelled* a-k-e.

-ake	-ame
-ate	make
take	came
game	gate
late	

Spelling Word Cards   Unit 3 • Week I   106

2 **Guided Practice/Practice** Provide children with the Spelling Word Cards. Have children say and spell *-ake* and each word in the word family. Repeat the process with the *-ame* and *-ate* words.

Display the words *chin, graph, some,* and *to* in a separate column. Read and spell the words together with children. Point out that these spelling words do not contain the /ā/ sound spelled *a_e.*

Conclude by asking children to orally generate additional words that rhyme with each word. Write the additional words on the board. Underline the common spelling patterns in the additional words. If necessary, point out the differences and explain why they are unusual.

If children need additional practice spelling words with long *a,* see **Practice Book** page 167 or the online activity.

ELL English Language Learners

Spelling, Model Hold up the **Spelling Word Card** for *make.* Blend the word slowly. Ask children to tell what letters they see on the card. (*m, a, k, e*) Pronounce each sound clearly: /m/ /ā/ /k/. Have children repeat the sounds and then blend the word. *When I said the word, did you hear the* e *at the end?* (no) *When we have an* e *at the end of these word families, we don't hear it, but the* a *is pronounced* /ā/. Review mouth position to form long *a,* and have children repeat.

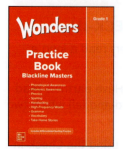

Spelling: Page 167

High-Frequency Words

5 mins

1 **Guided Practice** Say each high-frequency word: *away, now, some, today, way,* and *why.* Have children Read/Spell/Write it. As children spell each word with you, guide them to spell one syllable at a time in the multisyllabic words *away* and *today.*

Display the print or digital **Visual Vocabulary Cards** to review this week's high-frequency words.

2 **Practice** Repeat the activity with last week's words. Children can practice reading the high-frequency words independently using the online activity.

Build Fluency: Word Automaticity

Have children read the following sentences aloud together at the same pace. Repeat several times until children can read the words automatically.

Why are you going **away now,** Duck?

I have **some** things to do **today** with Frog.

I am on my **way** to the pond.

Word Bank

Review the current and previous words in the Word Bank. Discuss with children which words should be removed, or added back, from previous high-frequency word lists. Remind children that the Word Bank should change as the class needs it to.

DIGITAL TOOLS

For more practice, use these activities.

Spelling
High-Frequency Words

❯ STUDENT CHECK-IN

Spelling Have partners think of another word to go with one of the word families.

High-Frequency Words Have partners point to one high-frequency word and read it aloud to each other.

Have children reflect using the Check-In Routine.

✔ CHECK FOR SUCCESS

Rubric Use your online rubric to record children's progress.

Can children read and decode words with long *a: a_e?*

Can children recognize and read high-frequency words?

❯ Small Group Instruction

If No

🔴 **Approaching** Reteach pp. T66–T71

🟣 **ELL** Develop pp. T66–T71

If Yes

🔵 **On** Review pp. T74–T76

🟢 **Beyond** Extend pp. T78–T79

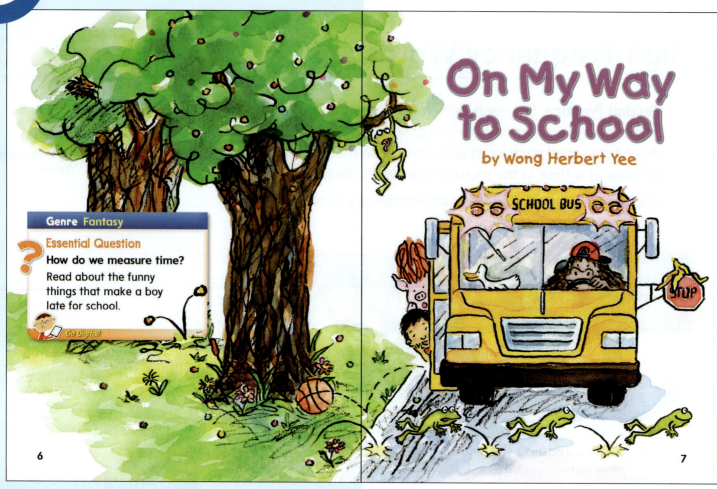

On My Way to School

Read We can understand the important ideas and details in a story.

Reread We can name the choices an author made when writing a story.

Have children apply what they learned as they read.

Close Reading Routine

Read DOK 1–2

• Identify important ideas and details.
• Take notes and retell.
• Use **A C T** prompts as needed.

Reread DOK 2–3

• Analyze text, craft, and structure.
• Use the Reread minilessons.

Integrate DOK 3–4

• Integrate knowledge and ideas.
• Make text-to-text connections.
• Complete the Show Your Knowledge task.
• Inspire action.

Read

Celebratory Read You may wish to read the full selection aloud once with minimal stopping before you begin using the Read prompts.

Set Purpose

Say: *Let's read to find out what happens to a little boy on his way to school.*

▶▶ DIFFERENTIATED READING

Approaching Level Have children listen to the selection summary. Use the Reread prompts during Small Group time.

On Level and **Beyond Level** Pair children or have them independently complete the Reread prompts on **Reading/Writing Companion** pages 33–35.

English Language Learners Before reading, have children listen to a summary of the selection. See the **ELL Small Group Guide,** pp. 110-111 for more support.

On my way to school today,
a pig asks me to come and play. **1**

8

It's not just a pig.
It's a pig in a wig!
We run for the bus,
just the two of us. **2**

9

Literature Anthology, pp. 8–9

Story Words Read and spell the words *tree, pool,* and *crocodile.* Review word meaning as needed.

Glossary Have children locate the glossary on **Literature Anthology** page 106. Read the page aloud. Children can look up the word *lake* when they read page 17.

Note Taking: Graphic Organizer

Have children fill in the online Beginning, Middle, End Graphic Organizer 5 as they read.

1 Make and Confirm Predictions DOK 2

Teacher Think Aloud I use clues in the text and illustrations to guess what happens next. I see a boy and a pig. I predict the boy meets other animals. As I read, I will check my predictions.

Build Vocabulary page 9
wig: fake hair

2 Events: Beginning, Middle, End DOK 1

Teacher Think Aloud Events are the important things that happen in a story. I read the text to find events at the beginning, middle, and end of the story. The boy meets a pig. This is an event at the beginning of the story. I will write this in the chart.

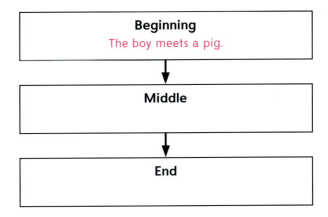

Beginning
The boy meets a pig.

↓

Middle

↓

End

Pig and I run fast, fast, fast!
We get on the bus at last.
Huff, puff! The bus zips **away**.
Pig makes me late for school today! ③

10

On my way to school, we pass
a trash truck that ran out of gas.
On top of that truck,
sit two apes and a duck!

11

Literature Anthology, pp. 10–11

Read

❸ Events: Beginning, Middle, End DOK 2

Name another event at the beginning of the story.
(They run for the bus.) Let's add that to the chart.

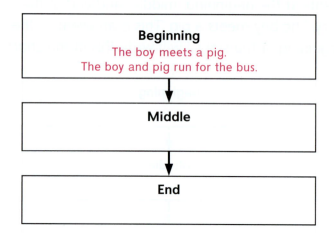

Beginning
The boy meets a pig.
The boy and pig run for the bus.

↓

Middle

↓

End

Build Vocabulary page 10
at last: finally
zips: moves fast

❹ Make and Confirm Predictions DOK 2

Teacher Think Aloud We predicted the boy would meet other animals. Did he? Yes, our prediction was correct. What do you think happens next?

Student Think Aloud On page 10, the boy and a pig get on the bus. On page 12, apes and a duck get on. I predict that another animal gets on next!

Apes and a duck hop in the bus.
They sit down with the rest of us.

12

Slip, flip! The bus zips away.
Apes make me late for school today!

13

Literature Anthology, pp. 12–13

Reread

Author's Craft DOK 2

Reading/Writing Companion, 33

How does the author let you know who is telling the story? (The author uses pictures and the word "I," so I know the boy is telling the story.)

Use clues to make an inference. I know that a fantasy story can be told in first-person using the word *I*. When I see the picture of the boy running to the bus, I can infer that he's the one telling the story. DOK 2

 Spotlight on Language

Page 12 Point to the words *hop in*. Say, Hop *can mean "to jump up and down." But* hop *in this sentence means "to get into something quickly." What are the apes and duck getting into quickly?* (the bus) Have partners turn and talk about something they can hop in, like the apes and duck.

Reread

Word Choice DOK 2

Reading/Writing Companion, 34

What feeling does the story have because of the rhyming words? (The story feels silly and funny because of the rhyming words.)

On my way to school, I see **some** frogs in a gumdrop tree. **5**

14

Plip, plop! The gumdrops drop. **6**
Two frogs cut. Two frogs mop.

15

Literature Anthology, pp. 14–15

Read

5 **Genre: Fantasy** DOK 2

Remember, this is a fantasy story. Fantasies can be told in the first person, using the words *I, me, my,* and *we.* Look at page 14. Who is telling the story? (the boy) How do you know? (He uses the words *my* and *I* to tell what happens.)

Build Vocabulary page 15
mop: to wipe or clean

6 **Make and Confirm Predictions** DOK 2

Check the last prediction you made. Was it correct? If not, correct it. Then make a new one. Look at the picture on page 15 and reread the text. Tell your partner what the frogs will do next.

 Spotlight on Language

Page 14 Point to the words *gumdrop tree. What grows on this tree?* (gumdrops) *What two words do you hear in the word* gumdrop? (gum, drop) Drop *means "a small bit," like a drop of water. Also, gumdrops are not chewing gum, but chewy candy. So gumdrops are small bits of chewy candy.* Explain that gumdrop trees are not real. Have partners talk about whether they'd like to have such a tree.

7 Frogs hop in the bus.
They sit down with the rest of us.
Hip! Hop! The bus zips away.
Frogs make me late for school today!

16

Here we go, just one last stop.
Frogs hop in the lake. Plip, plop!

17

Literature Anthology, pp. 16–17

7 **Make and Confirm Predictions** DOK 2

Turn to a partner and discuss the predictions you've made so far. Were your predictions correct? How do you know? Look at the illustrations. Then make a prediction together about what you think will happen next.

Build Vocabulary page 17
lake: a small body of water

ELL **Spotlight on Language**

Page 16 Read the first two lines on the page: *Frogs hop in the bus. They sit down with the rest of us.* Say: Rest *can mean "to relax or take a break."* The phrase rest of us *means something different. Here,* rest of us *refers to a group of living beings that doesn't include the frogs.* Demonstrate by having half of the children sit in one area and the other half sit in another area. Provide a sentence frame to help the children in one group use the expression: Come sit with the ! Have all of the children sit together. *In the story, who is the* rest of us*? Who is on the bus?* (the boy and all the animals)

Duck is off to get some gas.
Apes fish and nap in the grass. **8**

18

Tick, tock! The bus zips away.
It looks like I am late today! **9**

19

Literature Anthology, pp. 18–19

Read

8 **Events: Beginning, Middle, End** DOK 2

A lot has happened on this bus ride. Let's look at our chart and name important events we can include about the middle of the story.

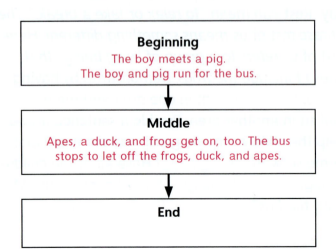

Beginning
The boy meets a pig.
The boy and pig run for the bus.

↓

Middle
Apes, a duck, and frogs get on, too. The bus stops to let off the frogs, duck, and apes.

↓

End

9 **Make and Confirm Predictions** DOK 2

How do you think the story will end? Let's make some predictions. Think about what has happened so far to make a prediction about what will happen next. After we read the rest of the story, we can use the evidence in the text to check our predictions.

 **English Language Learners**

Seek Clarification Some children may be confused by complex syntax. Encourage children to always seek clarification when they encounter a word or phrase that does not make sense to them. For example, *This sentence does not make sense to me.*

Now the bus drops me off at school.
I see a crocodile slink out of a pool!

20

I think it slid under the gate.
And that, Miss Blake, is **why** I am late!

21

Literature Anthology, pp. 20–21

Events: Beginning, Middle, End DOK 2

Guide children to review the information recorded in the chart and add important events that happened at the end of the story.

Beginning
The boy meets a pig.
The boy and pig run for the bus.

↓

Middle
Apes, a duck, and frogs get on, too.
The bus stops to let off the frogs, duck, and apes.

↓

End
The bus gets to school. The boy sees a crocodile. The boy tells the teacher the animals made him late.

Reread

Author's Craft DOK 3

Reading/Writing Companion, 35

Why did the boy say these things happened? (The boy made these things up because he wants to find an excuse for being late.)

Make Inferences

If necessary, remind children how to make an inference as they read. He said that silly things happened on the way to school. These things can't happen in real life, so I can infer that he hopes his silly story will be a good excuse for being late. DOK 3

Meet Wong Herbert Yee

Wong Herbert Yee says, "No bus picked me up at the corner. I walked a mile to get to school! When I write, I use things that really happened. My imagination fills in the rest. Remember what you see, read, and hear. You may write a funny story, too!"

Author's Purpose

Wong Herbert Yee wanted to write a funny story about getting to school. Draw how you get to school. Write about it.

22

Literature Anthology, p. 22

Return to Purposes

Have partners discuss what happened on the boy's way to school. Remind them to use evidence from the story.

Meet the Author

Wong Herbert Yee

Read aloud page 22 with children. Ask them how Wong Herbert Yee gets some of his funny ideas. Then ask: *What things in this story do you think really happened? Why does Wong Herbert Yee think it's important to remember things?*

Author's Purpose

Have children draw a picture of how they get to school. Provide a sentence frame they can use to tell about their picture: *I _____ to school.*

AUTHOR'S CRAFT   DOK 2

Focus on Rhyme and Humor

Wong Herbert Yee uses rhyme to tell what happens to the boy on his way to school. Discuss how rhyme adds humor to the story:

- *Rhyme helps make the words flow. They add rhythm, like a poem. This makes the story easy to read or listen to. For example: "It's not just a pig. It's a pig in a wig!"*

- Help children find other examples of rhyming lines that add humor, such as "On top of that truck . . . " (page 11)

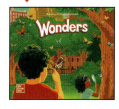

Read

Retell

Have children turn to page 32 in their **Reading/Writing Companion.** Remind them that as they read the story, they paid attention to the events that happened in the beginning, middle, and end. Have children use what they recorded on their chart to retell the story.

Use Text Evidence Guide children to use text evidence to respond to the questions on page 32.

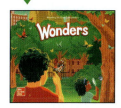

Reread

Analyze the Text

After children read and retell the selection, have them reread *On My Way to School* to develop a deeper understanding of the text by answering the questions on pages 33–35 in the Reading/Writing Companion. For children who need support finding text evidence to support their responses, use the scaffolded instruction from the Reread prompts on pages T35–T41.

Integrate

Build Knowledge: Make Connections

Talk About the Text Have partners discuss how the boy in the story thinks about and measures time.

Write About the Text Then have children add their ideas to their Build Knowledge page of their reader's notebook.

Add to the Anchor Chart Record any new ideas on the Build Knowledge anchor chart.

Add to the Word Bank Then add words related to measuring time to a separate section of the Word Bank.

Compare Texts   DOK 4

Guide children to compare two stories. Share the prompt: How are the boy and Nate the same in the stories we read this week? Say: *Think about the stories* On My Way to School *and "Nate the Snake is Late." What is the same about their experiences?* (Both the boy and Nate were late to school because silly things happened to them on the way.)

Ask children to identify other ways that the boy and Nate are the same. You can use a two-column chart to show the similarities.

ENGLISH LANGUAGE LEARNERS

Retell Help children retell the story using the illustrations. Have them look at each page, and then prompt them with questions and sentence frames. For example, *What animal does the boy see first?* The boy sees a pig. *What do the animals do?* They make the bus late.

FORMATIVE ASSESSMENT

❯ STUDENT CHECK-IN

Read Have partners tell each other an important detail from the story.

Reread Have partners tell one choice the author made when writing this story.

Have children reflect using the Check-In Routine to fill in the bars.

LEARNING GOALS

- We can respond to a fantasy story by extending the story.
- We can write new sentences and circle the verbs.

OBJECTIVES

Write narratives in which they recount two or more appropriately sequenced events, include some details regarding what happened, use temporal words to signal event order, and provide some sense of closure.

Use verbs to convey a sense of past, present, and future.

Use commas in dates and to separate single words in a series.

Produce complete sentences when appropriate to task and situation.

ELA ACADEMIC LANGUAGE

- *evidence, comma*
- Cognates: *evidencia, oma*

TEACH IN SMALL GROUP

Choose from these options to enable all children to complete the writing activity:

- Drawing and labeling a picture
- Completing sentence frames
- Writing one sentence
- Writing multiple sentences

Additionally, to provide differentiated support for children, see Writing Skills mini lessons on pages T420–T429. These can be used throughout the year.

5 mins — Independent Writing

Write About the Anchor Text   DOK 3

 Analyze the Prompt Read the prompt: *Write four more pages of the story. Tell the excuses the boy might give his mom for getting home late.* Have partners turn and talk about excuses the boy might make up.

- Explain that the prompt is asking them to imagine what the boy might tell his mother if he gets home late from school. Explain that they will create their own continuation of the story. Tell children that the next step is to find text evidence about the kinds of excuses the boy tells in the story.

Find Text Evidence Say: *To answer the prompt, we need to find evidence in the text and the illustrations in the* **Literature Anthology**.

- *Look at page 10. What excuse does the boy give for being late to school?* (A pig makes him late for school.)

- Point out that this is a silly excuse and does not explain what really made him late.

Have children continue finding text evidence, as needed, to respond to the prompt. You may choose to take notes on a chart or have children take notes in their writer's notebook.

 Write a Response Tell children to turn to page 36 in their **Reading/ Writing Companion**. Guide children to use the text evidence to create a list of silly excuses the boy might make up. They can then decide which ones to write about.

- **Writing Checklist:** Read the checklist with children. Remind them to use strong verbs, turn the line as they write, and use verbs correctly.

- **Writing Support:** If needed, provide sentence starters. Model completing one, as necessary.

After school, the boy _____.
He tells his mom _____.

Tell children they will finalize and present their writing the next day.

Reading/Writing Companion, p. 36

Grammar

5 mins

Verbs

1 **Review** Have children look at pages 10–11 in the **Literature Anthology.** Remind them that a verb shows action. Have children identify the verbs on those pages. Say: *Name the verb in this sentence:*

> Pig and I run fast, fast, fast!

Which word tells something you do? Yes, run *is the verb. It tells something you can do.*

2 **Guided Practice/Practice** Guide children to identify other verbs in the story. Remind children that every sentence has at least one verb, but some have more than one. Have children work with partners to write new sentences and circle the verbs.

Talk About It

Have partners orally generate sentences with different verbs. Challenge them to include three or more verbs in a sentence.

Mechanics: Commas in a Series

1 **Model** Tell children that when a writer uses three or more verbs in a row, there is a comma after all but the last verb. Display the following sentence:

> I run, catch, and pitch at the game.

Point out the list of three verbs and circle the commas after the first two verbs.

2 **Guided Practice** Prompt children to complete the sentence frame: I can ____, ____, and ____.

ELL English Language Learners

Independent Writing, Analyze the Prompt Review the concept of excuses. Say: *We give excuses when we want to explain why something happened. Is the boy early or late for school?* (late) *Why?* (animals made him late.) Provide sentence frames: The pig asks the boy to play. Next, the boy sees apes and a duck on a garbage truck. Then the boy sees frogs in a gumdrop tree. The frogs hop on the bus, too.

For additional support, see the **ELL Small Group Guide,** p. 115.

DIGITAL TOOLS

Use these activities to practice grammar and mechanics.

Grammar

Mechanics

Grammar Song

Grammar Video

FORMATIVE ASSESSMENT

> **STUDENT CHECK-IN**

Writing Have partners share their responses to the prompt. Have children reflect using the Check-In Routine to fill in the bars.

Grammar Have partners read one of their sentences and identify the verb. Have children reflect using the Check-In routine.

LEARNING GOALS

We can learn and use new vocabulary words.

OBJECTIVES

Identify real-life connections between words and their use.

Discuss the Essential Question.

Develop oral language.

ELA ACADEMIC LANGUAGE

• *vocabulary*
• Cognate: *vocabulario*

DIGITAL TOOLS

Visual Vocabulary Cards

LESSON FOCUS

READING
Revisit the Essential Question
Read and Reread Paired Selection:
"It's About Time"
• Introduce Text Feature
• Make Predictions
Word Work
• Build Words with Long *a*: *a_e*

WRITING
• Independent Writing
• Review Grammar and Mechanics

Literature Anthology, pp. 24–27

 15 mins

Oral Language

 MULTIMODAL

 Essential Question

How do we measure time?

Remind children that this week they have been learning about how we measure time. Guide children to discuss the Essential Question using information from what they have read and discussed. Use the online or print **Visual Vocabulary Cards** and the Define/Example/Ask routine to review the oral vocabulary words *calendar, immediately, occasion, schedule,* and *weekend*.

Guide children to use each word as they talk about what they have read and learned about measuring time. Prompt children by asking questions.

• What are some good things to write on a *calendar*?

• What do you do *immediately* after you get home from school?

• What is your favorite special *occasion*?

• What is your *schedule* after school?

• Which *weekend* day is your favorite—Saturday or Sunday? Why?

Review last week's oral vocabulary words: *locate, route, height, model,* and *separate*.

FORMATIVE ASSESSMENT

 **STUDENT CHECK-IN**

Have partners use a vocabulary word in a sentence. Have children reflect using the Check-In Routine.

Text Features

Bold Print

1 **Explain** Tell children they can use nonfiction texts to find facts about time. Explain that nonfiction text often has bold print—words that are darker than the others. Authors use bold print to point out important information.

Online Teaching Chart

2 **Model** Display **Online Teaching Chart** for Text Features: Bold Print. Point to the drawing on the right and read the text underneath it. Say: *The word* night *is in bold print. The word is darker than the other words. The illustration shows a scene at night. The text tells us it is night and then tells us what happens at night. The author put the word* night *in bold print to show us it is the most important idea of the illustration and the text.*

3 **Guided Practice/Practice** Read together the text underneath the first illustration. Guide children to identify the word in bold print. Ask: *Why did the author put this word in bold print? What is the most important idea?* Repeat for the second illustration. Tell children to look for bold print in nonfiction selections they read.

 ## English Language Learners

Use the scaffolds with **Text Features, Guided Practice/Practice.**

Beginning

Point to the text under the first image. *Which word looks different? Morning looks different. What is this type of text called?* (bold)

Intermediate

Point to the text under the first image. *What is the most important word?* (morning) *Why is it important?* It is in bold. It shows that morning is an important idea.

Advanced/Advanced High

Point to all three parts of the poster. *What words did the author put in bold?* (morning, noon, night) *Why?* (to show that those are the most important ideas)

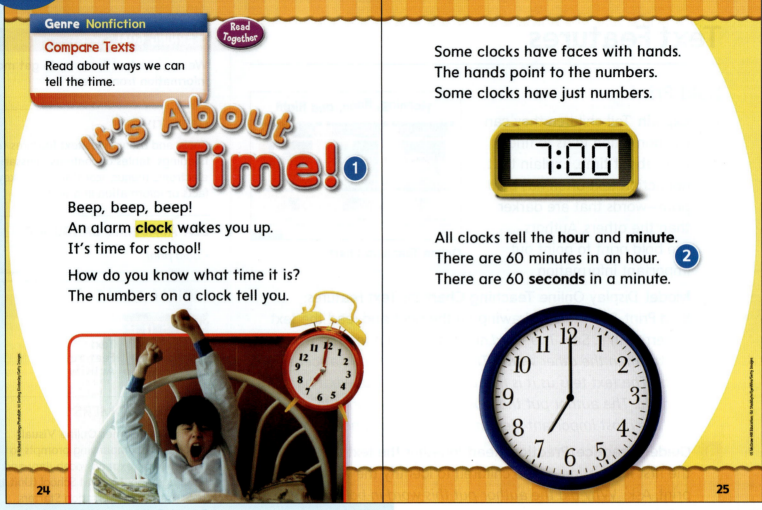

Genre Nonfiction

Compare Texts

Read about ways we can tell the time.

Read Together

It's About Time! ①

Beep, beep, beep!
An alarm **clock** wakes you up.
It's time for school!

How do you know what time it is?
The numbers on a clock tell you.

Some clocks have faces with hands.
The hands point to the numbers.
Some clocks have just numbers.

All clocks tell the **hour** and **minute**. ②
There are 60 minutes in an hour.
There are 60 **seconds** in a minute.

24

25

Literature Anthology, pp. 24–25
Lexile 270

"It's About Time!"

LEARNING GOAL

Read We can understand the important ideas and details in a text.

Reread We can name the choices an author makes when writing a text.

Compare Texts

As children read and reread "It's About Time!" encourage them to think about the Essential Question. Have children think about how the ways to tell time in this text are the same as and different from the ways in *On My Way to School*. Review the words *clock, sundials,* and *shadow* for children.

Genre Focus Tell children that this is a nonfiction text, so it will tell about real people, places, things, or events by presenting facts and information about them. Review that nonfiction texts may have bold print, which authors use to highlight important information.

Read

❶ Make and Confirm Predictions DOK 2

Teacher Think Aloud After reading the title and seeing the photos, I predict this selection will be about clocks, watches, and other kinds of devices that measure time. Let's read on to see if my prediction is correct.

❷ Text Feature: Bold Print DOK 2

Teacher Think Aloud Words in bold are important. The words *hour, minute,* and *seconds* are in bold. When I read the page carefully, I learn there are 60 minutes in an hour and 60 seconds in a minute.

Reread

Author's Craft DOK 3

Reading/Writing Companion, 37

Set Purpose Let's reread to find out about telling time.

What sentence explains how all clocks are the same? Underline the sentence in the text. (All clocks tell the hour and minute.)

Talk with a partner about why the author included two different photos. (Possible answer: The two photos show different clocks for telling time.)

 # English Language Learners

Use the following scaffolds with **Compare Texts.**

Beginning

Review that *On My Way to School* is fantasy, and "It's About Time!" is nonfiction. *Which story tells facts about real people, places, or things?* ("It's About Time!") *Why?* Have children respond: It is <u>nonfiction.</u>

Intermediate

Have children use the above sentence frame to talk about "It's About Time!" Then ask: *Is* On My Way to School *about real people, places, or things? Could it happen in real life?* (no) *Why not?* It is a <u>fantasy</u>.

Advanced/Advanced High

Have partners compare and contrast the selections. Ask one partner to focus on ways the selections are the same, while the other partner focuses on the ways they are different. To get the discussion started, ask: *How are the genres of the texts different?* Provide vocabulary as needed.

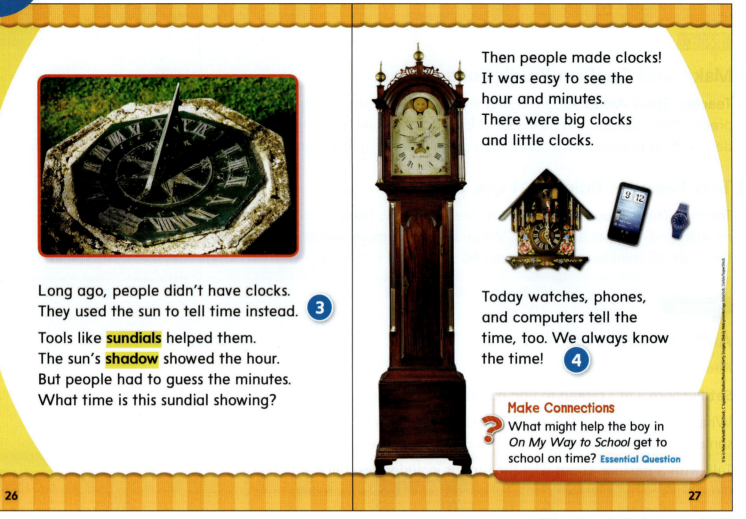

Long ago, people didn't have clocks. They used the sun to tell time instead. **3**

Tools like **sundials** helped them. The sun's **shadow** showed the hour. But people had to guess the minutes. What time is this sundial showing?

26

Then people made clocks! It was easy to see the hour and minutes. There were big clocks and little clocks.

Today watches, phones, and computers tell the time, too. We always know the time! **4**

Make Connections
? What might help the boy in *On My Way to School* get to school on time? **Essential Question**

27

Literature Anthology, pp. 26-27

Read

❸ Text Feature: Bold Print DOK 2

What words are bold on page 26? (*sundials* and *shadow*) Why are these words bold? (They're important words in the text.) What relevant detail do we learn about sundials? (They help us use the sun to tell time.) Why is *shadow* an important word? (The sun's shadow shows the hour on a sundial.)

❹ Make and Confirm Predictions DOK 2

I predicted this selection would be about clocks, watches, and other devices that measure time. Use the text and photos to confirm if I was correct. (Yes. The text tells about clocks and sundials. It also has pictures of different clocks.)

Reread

Author's Craft DOK 3

Reading/Writing Companion, 38

What word in the text tells what people used before clocks? Underline it. (Sun)

What is needed for a sundial to work? Circle the answer in the text. (Sun's shadow)

Talk with a partner about why the author included information about sundials. How is this information different from what you learned on page 37? (Possible answer: The author wants us to know that people had a way to tell time before we had clocks. A sundial is different from clocks because clocks show the hour and minutes. A sundial only shows the hour.)

You can use the Quick Tip box to support children as they work.

Author's Craft DOK 3

Reading/Writing Companion, 39

Talk with a partner about the information in this selection. Why is "It's About Time!" a good title for this text? (The text tells about clocks and how people tell time.)

Talk About It What does the author want you to know after reading this text? (Possible answer: There are different tools we can use to tell time.)

Read

Retell

Guide children to use important details to retell the selection. Have partners talk about the different ways to tell time.

Reread

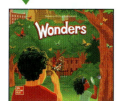

Analyze the Text

After children retell the selection, have them reread to develop a deeper understanding of the text. Have children annotate the text and answer the questions on **Reading/ Writing Companion** pages 37–39. For children who need support citing text evidence, use the Reread prompts on pages T49–T51.

Integrate

Build Knowledge: Make Connections

Talk About the Text Have partners discuss the different devices in this text that people use to measure time.

Write About the Text Then have children add their ideas to the Build Knowledge page of their reader's notebook.

Add to the Anchor Chart Record any new ideas on the Build Knowledge anchor chart.

Add to the Word Bank Then add words related to measuring time to a separate section of the Word Bank.

ELL SPOTLIGHT ON LANGUAGE

Page 26 Read the first two lines aloud. Emphasize *instead* at the end of the second line. Say it again, and have children repeat. *We use* instead *to talk about something we do in the place of something else. Long ago, did people have clocks?* (no) *Long ago, did they tell time?* (yes) *What did they use to tell time* instead *of clocks?* Instead of clocks, they used the sun to tell time. *Have partners answer this question using the word* instead: *What would you like to do instead of cleaning your room?* Instead of cleaning my room, I would like to play.

CONNECT TO CONTENT

Remind children that they have been learning about ways to tell and track time. Say: *In this selection, you learned about different clocks we use and that we use clocks to help us plan our days. We know a clock is important for waking up in the morning. Now think about how a calendar is another important tool for planning.* Display a simple calendar. Ask how a calendar can help us plan a party for next week or a summer vacation.

FORMATIVE ASSESSMENT

❯ STUDENT CHECK-IN

Read Have partners tell each other one important detail from the text. Have children reflect using the Check-In Routine.

Reread Have partners tell one choice the author made when creating this text. Have children reflect using the Check-In Routine to fill in the bars.

READING • WORD WORK

Display the Sound-Spelling Card *train*. Point to the letters a_e.

1. **Teacher:** What are the letters? **Children:** a, e
2. **Teacher:** What's the sound? **Children:** /ā/

Continue the routine for previously taught sounds.

LEARNING GOALS

- We can name the same sound in a group of words.
- We can build words with long *a*.
- We can write sentences with contractions with *not*.
- We can spell and sort words with long *a*.
- We can read the words *away, now, some, today, way,* and *why.*

OBJECTIVES

Demonstrate understanding of spoken words, syllables, and sounds (phonemes).

Know final -e and common vowel team conventions for representing long vowel sounds.

Use conventional spelling for words with common spelling patterns and for frequently occurring irregular words.

Recognize and read grade-appropriate irregularly spelled words.

ELA ACADEMIC LANGUAGE

- *contraction, apostrophe*

◯ TEACH IN SMALL GROUP

Word Work lessons can be taught in small groups.

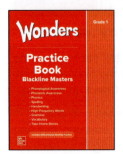

Structural Analysis: Page 170

OPTION 5 mins

Phonemic Awareness

Phoneme Identity

1 **Model** Say: *We are going to listen for the same sound in words. Listen carefully as I say three words:* gaze, take, cape. *What sound is the same in /gāāāz/, /tāāāk/, and /kāāāp/? That's right. The middle sound is /ā/.*

2 **Guided Practice/Practice** Have children practice identifying the same phoneme in a group of words. Then have children practice identifying the same sounds in the remaining words. Guide practice and provide corrective feedback as needed.

made, take, cave	bake, name, date	van, hat, pack
wave, mane, case	pup, fun, bug	hot, mop, sock

5 mins

Phonics

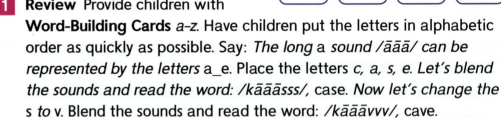

MULTIMODAL

Build Words with Long *a: a_e*

1 **Review** Provide children with **Word-Building Cards** *a–z*. Have children put the letters in alphabetic order as quickly as possible. Say: *The long* a *sound /āāā/ can be represented by the letters* a_e. *Place the letters* c, a, s, e. *Let's blend the sounds and read the word:* /kāāāsss/, case. *Now let's change the* s *to* v. *Blend the sounds and read the word:* /kāāāvvv/, cave.

2 **Practice** Continue with *pave, pale, tale, tame, same, shame, lame, lake, flake, flame, fame, faze, maze, made, mad, mat, mate, male, whale.* Once children have finished building the words, dictate the words in the list and have children write out the word-building list. Have partners exchange and check the written lists for spelling. Listen in and provide corrective feedback as needed.

Color Coding After each dictation, reveal the secret color-coding letter(s) for children to find on their **Response Board.** Have them say the sound(s) as they trace each letter in color. Use one or two of the phonics skills of the week for color coding.

Decodable Reader

Have children read "Is It Late?" to practice decoding words in connected text. If children need support, turn to Small Group, pages T69 and T76 for instruction on "Is It Late?"

Structural Analysis

5 mins

Contractions with *not*

Review Write the words *has not* and *hasn't* on the board and read them with children. Remind children that when two words are put together to make a contraction, the letters that are left out are replaced with an apostrophe.

Write the following words: *is not, are not, was not, have not, can not*. Have children work in pairs to construct contractions. Then have them write a sentence for each contraction.

If children need additional practice identifying and reading contractions, see **Practice Book** page 170 or the online activity.

Spelling

5 mins

MULTIMODAL

Word Sort with *-ake, -ame, -ate*

Review Provide pairs of children with copies of the online **Spelling Word Cards.** While one partner reads the words one at a time, the other partner should orally segment the word and then write the word. After reading all the words, partners should switch roles.

Have children correct their own papers. Then have them sort the words by ending spelling pattern: *-ake, -ame, -ate,* or no *a_e* ending.

High-Frequency Words

OPTION
5 mins

away, now, some, today, way, why

Review Display online **Visual Vocabulary Cards** for high-frequency words *away, now, some, today, way, why*. Have children Read/Spell/Write each word.

- Point to a word and call on a child to use it in a sentence.
- Review last week's words using the same procedure.

DIGITAL TOOLS

For more practice, use these activities.

Word Work

Phonemic Awareness
Phonics
Structural Analysis
Spelling
High-Frequency Words

FORMATIVE ASSESSMENT

❯ STUDENT CHECK-IN

Phonics/Spelling Have children spell words with the long *a* sound.

Structural Analysis Have partners read a sentence that includes a contraction with *not.*

High-Frequency Words Have partners share a sentence using a high-frequency word.

Have children reflect using the Check-In Routine.

✓ CHECK FOR SUCCESS

Rubric Use your online rubric to record children's progress.

Can children read and decode words with long *a: a_e*?

Can children recognize and read high-frequency words?

❯ Small Group Instruction

If No

🟠 **Approaching** Reteach pp. T66–T71

🟣 **ELL** Develop pp. T66–T71

If Yes

🔵 **On** Review pp. T74–T76

🟢 **Beyond** Extend pp. T78–T79

Independent Writing

5 mins

Write About the Anchor Text

Revise

Reread the prompt about *On My Way to School: Write four more pages of the story. Tell the excuses the boy might give his mom for getting home late.*

- Have children read their drafts in their **Reading/Writing Companion.** Ask them to check that they responded to the prompt. Then have them review the checklist to confirm that they used strong verbs, turned the line as they wrote, and used verbs correctly.

Peer Review Have pairs take notes about what they liked most, questions they have for the author, and additional ideas the author could include. Have partners discuss these topics. Provide time for revisions.

Edit/Proofread

Review the online proofreading marks with children. Model how to use each mark. Then have children edit for the following:

- High-frequency words are spelled correctly.
- Commas in a series are used correctly.

Write Final Draft

Have children create their final draft in their writer's notebook by:

- writing it neatly, or using digital tools to produce and publish it.
- adding details and drawings that will help make their ideas clear.

Teacher Conference As children work, conference with them to provide guidance. Make sure children used strong verbs, turned the line as they wrote, and used verbs correctly in sentences. Have children make changes based on your feedback.

Share and Evaluate

After children have finalized their draft, have them:

- work with a partner to practice presenting their writing to each other.
- share their final drafts with the class.
- ask and answer questions about each other's work.

If possible, record children as they share so that they can self-evaluate. After children share, display their final papers on a bulletin board.

Have children add their work to their writing folder. Invite them to look at their previous writing and discuss with a partner how it has improved.

Grammar

OPTION 5 mins

Verbs

1 **Review** Review that verbs are words that tell about actions. Ask: *What are some actions that you can do?* (run, jump, hop)

2 **Guided Practice** Remind children that every sentence has at least one verb. Guide children to identify the verb, or verbs, as you say some sentences: *Chan sees pancakes on a plate. Can you help my mom rake?* Have children suggest a replacement verb for each sentence.

3 **Practice** Display the following words: *run, grab, lunch, shake, vase, make, catch, grape.* Have children identify the verbs.

For additional practice with editing using verbs, see **Practice Book** page 173 or the online activity.

Talk About It

Have partners work together to orally generate sentences with the verbs in the Practice section above. Challenge them to make sentences that rhyme.

Mechanics: Commas in a Series

1 **Review** Remind children that when a writer uses three or more verbs in a list, there is a comma after all but the last verb.

2 **Practice** Display sentences with punctuation errors. Read each aloud. Have children work together to fix the sentences.

We hop skip and jump. (We hop, skip, and jump.)

A duck can quack swim, and sit. (A duck can quack, swim, and sit.)

For additional practice with commas in a series, see Practice Book page 174 or the online activity.

English Language Learners

Independent Writing, Revise Read: *Apes and a duck hop on a bus.* Say, Hop *is a strong verb. A strong verb describes actions better than a verb such as* get *or* go. Create a word bank of strong verbs children can use as they revise their writing, such as *leap, fly, bounce,* and *trot.* Assist children with revising verbs in their writing.

For additional support, see the **ELL Small Group Guide**, p. 115.

DIGITAL TOOLS

Use these resources with the lessons.

Proofreading Marks

Grammar

Mechanics

Grammar Song

Grammar Video

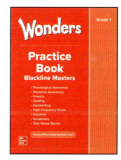

Grammar: Page 173
Mechanics: Page 174

STUDENT CHECK-IN

Writing Have children reflect on one way they revised their writing.

Grammar Have children share two verbs they identified from the list.

Have children reflect using the Check-In Routine.

LESSON 4

LEARNING GOALS

We can interview classmates to gather information about their day.

OBJECTIVES

Participate in shared research and writing projects.

With guidance and support from adults, recall information from experiences or gather information from provided sources to answer a question.

Add drawings or other visual displays to descriptions when appropriate to clarify ideas, thoughts, and feelings.

Build on others' talk in conversations by responding to the comments of others through multiple exchanges.

ELA ACADEMIC LANGUAGE

- *interview, present*
- Cognate: *presentar*

COLLABORATIVE CONVERSATIONS

Be Open to All Ideas
Review with children that as they engage in partner, small-group, and whole-class discussions, they should remember:

- that everyone's ideas are important and should be heard
- to work collaboratively, making contributions to the conversation and listening to other's contributions
- to respect the opinions of others

Integrate

Interview

10 mins

Model

Tell children that today they will interview a classmate about what he or she does during a usual day. Display pages 40–41 in the **Reading/Writing Companion** and model filling them in, reviewing the steps in the research process below.

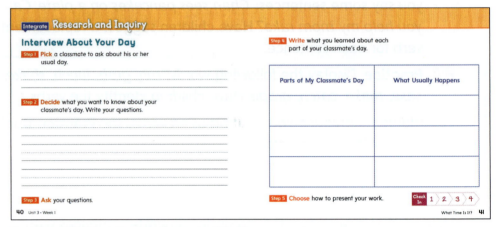

Reading/Writing Companion, pp. 40–41

STEP 1 **Pick a Classmate to Interview**

The project is to interview someone about what happens during a usual day. First I need to choose a person to talk to. I will choose John, a student from another class.

STEP 2 **Write Your Questions**

Now I need to decide what I want to know about John's day. I will ask him what happens in the morning, afternoon, and evening on a usual day.

STEP 3 **Interview the Person**

I talked to John and asked him my questions. He told me that in the morning, he eats breakfast and gets dressed for school. In the afternoon, he takes music lessons or goes to the park with his older brother. In the evening, he eats dinner with his family.

STEP 4 **Write What You Learned**

I will fill in the chart to show the different times of John's day and what usually happens. John has a busy day!

STEP 5 **Choose How to Present**

I can decide the best way to present the information I learned. I will create a timeline of John's day. I will label the three different times of day and draw pictures of him doing his activities.

Apply

Have children turn to pages 40–41 in their **Reading/Writing Companion.**

Guide them through the steps of the research process. In Step 1, help them choose a classmate to interview. In Step 2, guide them to formulate their questions. Encourage children to make sure their questions are appropriate to the conversation. When they ask their questions in Step 3, remind children to always use the agreed-upon rules of collaborative conversation.

Before they write what they learned during their interview in Step 4, they can discuss it with a partner.

After children have completed their interviews, guide them to fill out the Research Process Checklist on the online Student Checklist. This checklist helps children decide if they've completed all of the necessary parts of the research process.

Choose the Presentation Format

Have children turn to pages 40–41 in their Reading/Writing Companion to review their research and consider what they learned about the classmate they interviewed. Tell them that today they are going to take the next step by creating a way to present their findings. This will be their final product.

Options include:

- create a timeline showing different times and pictures, with events and times of day labeled
- create a drawing of the classmate doing a daily activity, and include a sentence that tells what the classmate is doing
- write a journal entry of the classmate's day using word-processing software, including drawings and labels

Create the Presentation

Have children develop their presentation. Remind children of the rules of working with others.

Gather Materials Have children gather the materials they'll need to create their finished product. Most of the materials should be available in the classroom or can be brought from home.

Make the Presentation Once children have gathered the materials they need for their presentation, provide time for them to create it. Have children review their research before they begin. Then support children as they work on their presentation.

You may wish to have children collaborate on projects.

ELL ENGLISH LANGUAGE LEARNERS

Apply, Step 2 Provide sentence frames to guide children in creating questions for their partner interviews. For example: What time do you wake up? Then model how to complete the frames for children: I wake up at 7:00. Provide additional examples of question and answer frames and how to complete them, as needed.

TEACH IN SMALL GROUP

You may wish to have children create their presentation during Small Group time. Group children of varying abilities together, or group children together if they are doing similar projects.

RESEARCH AND INQUIRY: SHARING FINAL PROJECTS

As children get ready to wrap up the week, have them share their Research and Inquiry projects. Then have children self-evaluate.

Prepare Have children gather materials they need to present their projects. Then partners can take turns practicing their presentations.

Share Guide children to present their Research and Inquiry projects. Encourage children to ask questions to clarify when something is unclear.

Evaluate Have children discuss and evaluate their own presentations. You may wish to have them fill out the Presentation Checklist on the online Student Checklist.

FORMATIVE ASSESSMENT

STUDENT CHECK-IN

Have partners share one thing they learned from interviewing a classmate. Have children reflect using the Check-In Routine to fill in the bars.

LESSON 5

LEARNING GOALS

- We can blend and segment sounds in words.
- We can build long *a* words.
- We can write and read contractions with *not*.
- We can write long *a* words.
- We can write the words *away, now, some, today, way,* and *why.*

OBJECTIVES

Orally produce single-syllable words by blending sounds (phonemes), including consonant blends.

Segment spoken single-syllable words into their complete sequence of individual sounds (phonemes).

Decode regularly spelled one-syllable words.

Use conventional spelling for words with common spelling patterns and for frequently occurring irregular words.

Recognize and read grade-appropriate irregularly spelled words.

ELA ACADEMIC LANGUAGE

- *contractions, apostrophe*
- Cognate: *contracciones*

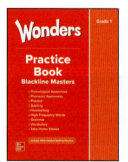

Take-Home Story: Pages 175–176
Spelling: Posttest, Page 165

LESSON FOCUS

READING
Word Work
- Review Long *a: a_e*

Make Connections
- Connect the poem to the Essential Question
- Show Your Knowledge

WRITING
- Self-Selected Writing
- Review Grammar and Mechanics

Reading/Writing Companion, pp. 42–43

Phonemic Awareness
5 mins

Phoneme Blending

Review Guide children to blend phonemes to form words. Say: *Listen as I say a group of sounds. Then blend those sounds to form a word.*

/m/ /ā/ /n/   /b/ /ā/ /k/   /l/ /ā/ /k/   /f/ /l/ /ā/ /k/

Phoneme Segmentation

Review Guide children to segment phonemes in words. Say: *Now I am going to say a word. I want you to say each sound in the word.*

safe   game   plate   brave   snake   crate

Phonics
5 mins

MULTIMODAL

Blend and Build Words with Long *a: a_e*

Review Have children read and say the words *make, sale, shade,* and *plate.* Then have children follow the word-building routine with **Word-Building Cards** to build *rat, rate, hate, hat, fat, fate, fame, same, shame, shade, made, mad, man, mane, pane, plane, plate, late, lake, flake.*

Word Automaticity Help children practice word automaticity. Display decodable words and point to each word as children chorally read it. Test how many words children can read in one minute. Model blending words children miss.

Read the Decodable Reader

If children need extra practice decoding words in context, have them read "Dave Was Late" and "Is It Late?" If children need additional support for these stories, turn to Small Group, pages T69 and T76 for instruction and support.

In a Flash: Sound-Spellings

Display the Sound-Spelling Card *train*. Point to the letters a_e.

1. **Teacher:** What are the letters? **Children:** a, e
2. **Teacher:** What's the sound? **Children:** /ā/

Continue the routine for previously taught sounds.

Structural Analysis

Contractions with *not*

Review Have children explain how to form a contraction using the word *not*. Then have children practice writing and reading the contractions for *is not, are not, was not, were not, has not, have not,* and *can not*.

Spelling

MULTIMODAL

Word Sort with *-ake, -ame, -ate*

Review Have children use the online **Spelling Word Cards** to sort the weekly words by vowel and ending sounds. Remind children that four of the words do not have the long *a* sound spelled *a_e*.

Assess Test children on their abilities to spell words in the *-ake, -ame,* and *-ate* word families. Say each word and provide a sentence so that children can hear the words used in a correct context. Then allow them time to write down the words. Remind children to write their answers legibly, leaving space between words as they write. As a challenge, provide more words that follow the same spelling pattern. Have children complete the spelling posttest using **Practice Book** page 165.

High-Frequency Words

away, now, some, today, way, why

Review Display **Visual Vocabulary Cards** *away, now, some, today, way, why.* Have children Read/Spell/Write each word. Have children write a sentence with each word.

If children need assistance reading high-frequency words, they can practice reading independently using the Take-Home Story in the Practice Book on pages 175–176 or use online resources.

DIGITAL TOOLS

For more practice, use these activities.

Word Work

- Phonemic Awareness
- Phonics
- Structural Analysis
- Spelling
- High-Frequency Words

FORMATIVE ASSESSMENT

❯ STUDENT CHECK-IN

Phonics/Spelling Have children spell words with the long *a* sound.

Structural Analysis Have partners read some of the contractions they wrote.

High-Frequency Words Have partners share sentences using the high-frequency words.

Have children reflect using the Check-In Routine.

✓ CHECK FOR SUCCESS

Rubric Use your online rubric to record children's progress.

Can children read and decode words with long *a*: *a_e*?

Can children recognize and read high-frequency words?

❯ Small Group Instruction

If No

🔴 **Approaching** Reteach pp. T66–T71

🟣 **ELL** Develop pp. T66–T71

If Yes

🔵 **On** Review pp. T74–T76

🟢 **Beyond** Extend pp. T78–T79

Self-Selected Writing

5 mins

Talk About the Topic

Remind children of the Essential Question: *How do we measure time?* Have partners talk about the Essential Question and encourage them to ask each other questions about how they measure time.

Choose a Writing Activity

Tell children they will select, or choose, a type of writing they would like to do. Children may choose to write about the theme of the week or write about a different topic that is important to them. Children may choose from the following modes of writing.

 Picture Spark Display several photographs or illustrations of calendars and different types of clocks. Explain that a picture can "spark" an idea about what to write about. Have children write about what they see.

 Storyboard Review that a storyboard is a series of three or four pictures with labels or sentences that tell a story. Have children create a storyboard to tells a story related to time or another topic. Remind children to include sentences.

 Letter Writing Tell children that a letter is a written message that is often sent through the mail. Have children write a letter to a friend about a time they were late or another topic. Model how to write the greeting, the body of the letter, and the closing.

Use Digital Tools You may wish to work with children to explore a variety of digital tools to produce or publish their writing.

Share Your Writing

 Review the speaking and listening strategies with children. Then have children share their writing with a partner or small group. You may wish to display their work on a bulletin board or in a classroom writing area.

SPEAKING STRATEGIES	LISTENING STRATEGIES
✓ Speak in complete sentences.	✓ Listen actively and politely.
	✓ Face the presenter.

Grammar

OPTION 5 mins

Verbs

1 **Review** Have children describe what verbs are and how they are used. Write the following sentence and have children identify the verbs: The big dog jumps in the pond and fetches a stick. (jumps, fetches)

2 **Practice** Ask: *How do I know which word in a sentence is the verb?* Write sentence frames. Have children provide one or more verbs to complete each sentence. We _____ at school today. I don't _____ at school. I can't _____ very well. I can _____ very well! Have children read their completed sentences to the class. Have them choose one verb to act out.

Mechanics: Commas in a Series

1 **Review** Remind children that when three or more verbs are in a list, there is a comma after each verb but the last one.

2 **Practice** Write the following sentences. Read each aloud. Have children fix the errors. My dog Rex tosses catches, and chomps the red sock. (My dog Rex tosses, catches, and chomps the red sock.) I like to pet hug and rub my little cat. (I like to pet, hug, and rub my little cat.) Mom will pin mend and stitch, the rip in my pants. (Mom will pin, mend, and stitch the rip in my pants.)

ELL English Language Learners

Self-Selected Writing, Choose a Writing Activity Present the writing activities, and tell the children that they will vote on one of the activities. Then, you will work on the writing as a group. Make sure to do the activity on chart paper as you will revise and publish it during small group time. Provide sentence frames and starters as you talk through the writing together. For example, if children choose Picture Spark, possible frames and starters are: The clock has/is _____. The hands are _____. The calendar shows _____.

For additional support, see the **ELL Small Group Guide,** p. 115.

For additional support, see the **ELL Small Group Guide,** p. 115.

DIGITAL TOOLS

For more practice, use these activities.

Grammar

Mechanics

Grammar Song

Grammar Video

How to Give a Presentation

⏵ TEACH IN SMALL GROUP

🔴 **Approaching** Provide more opportunities for children to identify verbs in sentences before they complete sentences with verbs and act them out.

🔵 🟢 **On Level** and **Beyond** Children can do the Practice sections only.

🟣 **ELL** Use the chart in the **Language Transfers Handbook** to identify grammatical forms that may cause difficulty.

FORMATIVE ASSESSMENT

⏵ STUDENT CHECK-IN

Writing: Have partners share one sentence or label they wrote.

Grammar: Have partners share one sentence they completed.

Have children reflect using the Check-In Routine.

LESSON 5

LEARNING GOALS

We can compare a text we've read to a poem.

OBJECTIVES

Compare and contrast the adventures and experiences of characters in stories.

ELA ACADEMIC LANGUAGE

• *compare*
• Cognate: *comparar*

Close Reading Routine

Read   DOK 1–2

• Identify important ideas and details.
• Take notes and retell.
• Use prompts as needed.

Reread   DOK 2–3

• Analyze the text, craft, and structure.
• Use the Reread minilessons.

Integrate   DOK 3–4

• Integrate knowledge and ideas.
• Make text-to-text connections.
• Complete the Show Your Knowledge task.
• Inspire action.

Integrate

5 mins

Make Connections

Connect to the Essential Question   DOK 4

COLLABORATE Turn to page 42 in the **Reading/Writing Companion.** Help partners discuss the poem. Use the first prompt as a guide.

Reading/Writing Companion, p. 42

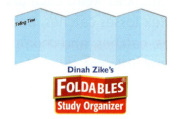

Find Text Evidence Read aloud the second prompt. Guide children to discuss the connections between the poem and *On My Way to School.* Use the Quick Tip box for support.

Compare Texts Guide partners to compare the ideas in the poem with those in "Nate the Snake Is Late." Children can record their notes using a Foldable® like the one shown. Guide them to record details that help them answer the Essential Question.

Build Knowledge: Make Connections

Talk About the Text Have partners discuss how the bird in the poem thinks and measures about time.

Add to the Anchor Chart Record any new ideas on the Build Knowledge anchor chart.

Add to the Word Bank Then add words related to measuring time to a separate section of the Word Bank.

FORMATIVE ASSESSMENT

❯ STUDENT CHECK-IN

Have partners share how they compared the poem and the text. Have children reflect using the Check-In Routine to fill in the bars.

Integrate

10 mins

Show Your Knowledge

Write Tips For Being on Time   DOK 4

Display the Build Knowledge anchor chart about measuring time. Have children lead a discussion about what they have learned. Then have children turn to page 43 in their **Reading/Writing Companion**. Guide children through the steps below to draw and write about tips for being on time.

Reading/Writing Companion, p. 43

Step 1 Have children read through the Build Knowledge pages of their reader's notebook to review what they have learned about ways to measure time.

Step 2 Ask children to think about two of the characters they read about and why they were late. Then have children write a list of tips that might help the characters be on time in the future. Remind them to use text evidence to explain why they were late. Have children use two vocabulary words from the Word Bank.

Step 3 Have children draw a picture to go with their tips.

Inspire Action

You may choose to extend the learning with the activities below.

Classroom Calendar Create a calendar showing the schedule for each day, including classroom work, specials, lunch, and recess. Have volunteers check off items and events as they are completed.

Books About Time Invite children to read another book about measuring time or being late.

Choose Your Own Action Have children talk about the texts they read this week. Ask: *What do these texts inspire you to do?*

We can show what we have learned about ways to measure time.

OBJECTIVES

Add drawings or other visual displays to descriptions when appropriate to clarify ideas, thoughts, and feelings.

Use words and phrases acquired through conversations, reading and being read to, and responding to texts.

ELA ACADEMIC LANGUAGE

• *evidence*

ELL ENGLISH LANGUAGE LEARNERS

Show Your Knowledge, Step 2 Provide and model sentence frames and/or starters to help children write tips for being on time. Examples are: Leave ___. Check the ___. Have ___. Use a ___ to ___.

DIGITAL TOOLS

RUBRIC   Show Your Knowledge Rubric

What I Learned

Review Goals Have children turn back to page 13 of the **Reading/ Writing Companion** and review the goals for the week.

Reflect Have children think about the progress they've made towards the goals. Review the key, if needed. Have children fill in the bars.

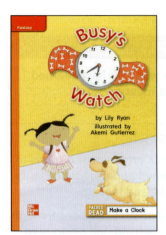

Lexile 40

OBJECTIVES

Describe major events in a story, using key details.

Read grade-level text orally with accuracy, appropriate rate, and expression on successive readings.

Retell stories, including key details, and demonstrate understanding of their central message or lesson.

Make and confirm predictions.

ELA ACADEMIC LANGUAGE

• *predict, events*

• Cognates: *predicción, eventos,*

●Approaching Level

Leveled Reader: *Busy's Watch*

Preview and Predict

Have children turn to the title page. Read the title and the author's name, and have children repeat. Preview the selection's illustrations. Prompt children to predict what the selection might be about.

Review Genre: Fantasy

Have children recall that a fantasy is a story that has made-up characters that could not exist in real life.

Set Purpose

Remind children of the Essential Question. Set a purpose for reading: *Let's read to find out what Busy uses his watch for.* Remind children that as they read a selection, they can seek clarification by asking questions about what they do not understand or want to know more about.

Guided Comprehension

As children whisper read *Busy's Watch* independently or with a partner, monitor and provide guidance. Correct blending and model the key strategies and skills as needed. As needed, provide definitions for words unfamiliar to children.

Make and Confirm Predictions

Model making and confirming predictions: *On page 3, we read that Busy uses his watch to tell Kay it is time to get up. I predict he uses it to tell time for other events.* Confirm the prediction on pages 4 and 5. Remind children that they can use words and illustrations to predict story events. Then they can read on to correct or confirm their predictions.

Events: Beginning, Middle, End

Hand out Graphic Organizer 5 to children. Remind children that events are the most important things that happen in a story. Events take place in the beginning, middle, and end of the story. We can find the most important events by reading the text. While reading, ask: *What events happen in the beginning? What happens in the middle and end of the story?* Display a Beginning, Middle, End chart 5 for children to copy.

Model recording children's answers in the beginning, middle, and end boxes. Have children copy the answers into their own charts.

Think Aloud On pages 2 and 3, Kay is waking up. Busy is looking at his watch. The text tells me that Busy tells Kay it is 6:00 and time to get up. I'll write this event in the beginning of my chart.

Guide children to complete the chart.

Respond to Reading Have children complete the Respond to Reading on page 12 after reading.

Retell Have children take turns retelling the selection using the **Retelling Cards** as a guide. Help children make a connection by asking: *What are times that you need to know? How can knowing the time help you?*

Fluency: Accuracy and Rate

Model Model reading page 2 with accuracy and an appropriate rate. Read aloud. Have children read along with you.

Apply Have children practice reading the text with a partner. Correct any errors, as needed.

Paired Read: "Make a Clock"

 Make Connections: Write About It

Before reading, ask children to note that the genre of this text is nonfiction. Read the Compare Texts direction in the **Leveled Reader**.

Ask children to tell how what they learned about time and watches in *Busy's Watch* is connected to what they read about in "Make a Clock."

Leveled Reader

Build Knowledge: Make Connections

 Talk About the Texts Have partners discuss the different ways time is measured in these texts.

Write About the Texts Then have children add their ideas to the Build Knowledge page of their reader's notebook.

LITERATURE CIRCLES

Lead children in conducting a literature circle using the Thinkmark questions to guide the discussion. You may wish to discuss what children have learned about time from both selections in the **Leveled Reader**.

ANALYTICAL WRITING

Compare Texts

Have children identify characteristics of each genre in each text. Then have them use text evidence to tell how the selections are similar to and different from each other.

LEVEL UP

IF children can read the Approaching Level fluently and answer the questions,

THEN tell children that they will read another story about time.

- Have children read the selection, checking their comprehension by using the graphic organizer.

●Approaching Level

Phonological/Phonemic Awareness

PHONEME IDENTITY

OBJECTIVES

Demonstrate understanding of spoken words, syllables, and sounds (phonemes).

Identify medial phonemes.

I Do Explain to children that they will identify the same sound in words. *Listen as I say three words:* came, made, gate. *I hear the /ā/ sound in the middle of these words. Listen: /kāāām/, /māāād/, /gāāāt/. The middle sound is /ā/.*

We Do *Listen as I say three words:* cake, shade, name. *Repeat the words:* cake, shade, name. *What sound do you hear in the middle of /kāāāk/, /shāāād/, /nāāām/?* (The middle sound is /ā/.)

Repeat this routine with the following words:

game, save, tale   ate, cane, pane   rake, shape, tame

You Do *It's your turn. What sound do you hear in the middle of each set of words?*

date, cape, maze   mane, shake, safe   pat, sap, Jack   bake, late, train

Repeat the identity routine with additional long *a* words.

PHONEME SEGMENTATION

OBJECTIVES

Segment spoken single-syllable words into their complete sequence of individual sounds (phonemes).

I Do Explain to children that they will be separating words into sounds. *Listen as I say a word:* ate. *I hear two sounds: /ā/ and /t/. There are two sounds in the word* ate: */āāā/ and /t/.*

We Do *Let's do some together. I am going to say a word:* lake. *How many sounds do you hear?* (three) *The sounds in* lake *are /lll/ /āāā/ and /k/.*

Repeat this routine with the following words:

ape (2)   save (3)   cape (3)   chase (3)   brake (4)   snake (4)

You Do *I'll say a word. Tell me how many sounds you hear. Then tell me the sounds.*

date (3)   wave (3)   cane (3)   safe (3)   skate (4)   brave (4)   shave (3)

Repeat the segmentation routine with additional long *a* words.

PHONEME ADDITION

OBJECTIVES

Demonstrate understanding of spoken words, syllables, and sounds (phonemes).

Add initial phonemes to make new words.

I Do Explain to children that they will add sounds to make new words. *Listen as I say this word:* ate. *I will add /d/ to the beginning of* ate *to make a new word. Listen:* ate, date. Ate *with /d/ at the beginning is* date.

We Do *Listen as I say this word:* ace. *Say it with me:* ace. *Let's add /f/ to the beginning of* ace. *Say it with me: /fff/ /āāāsss/. What word do we make when we add /f/ to* ace? *We get* face.

Repeat this routine with the following words:

ape/tape	ache/bake	aim/same	take/stake

You Do *It's your turn. Add the sound I say to make a new word.*

age/page	aid/wade	lane/plane	ace/chase

Repeat the addition routine with additional long *a* words.

PHONEME SUBSTITUTION

OBJECTIVES

Isolate and pronounce initial sounds (phonemes) in spoken single-syllable words.

Substitute initial phonemes to make new words.

I Do Explain to children that they will be changing the first sounds in words. *Listen as I say a word:* cake. *I will change the /k/ to /b/ to make a new word. Listen: /b/ /b/ /bāk/. The new word is* bake.

We Do *Let's do some together. Listen to this word:* name. *Say it with me: /nnnām/. We will change the /n/ to /g/. Say the new word with me: /gāāām/,* game.

Repeat this routine with the following words:

lace/race	cane/mane	tape/shape	pale/male

You Do *It's your turn. I'll say a word. Then I'll say a sound. Change the first sound in the word to the new sound to make a new word.*

cave/save	made/shade	rake/take	base/chase

Repeat the substitution routine with additional long *a* words.

ELL You may wish to review phonological/phonemic awareness, phonics, and fluency using this section. Use scaffolding methods as necessary to ensure children understand the meanings of the words. Refer to the **Language Transfers Handbook** for phonics elements that may not transfer in children's native languages.

Approaching Level

Phonics

CONNECT a_e TO /ā/

OBJECTIVES

Know and apply grade-level phonics and word analysis skills in decoding words.

Recognize spelling-sound correspondences for long *a*.

I Do Display the **Word-Building Card** *a_e*. *These letters are lowercase* a *and* e. *They stand for the sound /āāā/.* Write the word *ate* on the board. *I am going to trace the letters while I say the sound: /āāāt/.* Trace the letters while saying /āāāt/ five times.

We Do *Now do it with me.* Have children take turns saying /āāāt/ while using their fingers to trace the word *ate* on paper. Then have them say /āāāt/ as they write the letters *ate* five more times on paper.

You Do Have children connect the letters *a_e* to the sound /ā/ by saying /āāāt/ as they trace *ate* on paper five to ten times. Then ask them to write the letters *a-t-e* while saying /āāāt/ five to ten times.

Repeat, connecting the letters *a_e* to the sound /āāā/ by tracing and writing the letters *a_e* throughout the week.

BLEND WORDS WITH LONG a: a_e

OBJECTIVES

Decode regularly spelled one-syllable words.

I Do Display Word-Building Cards *n, a, m, e*. *This is the letter* n. *It stands for /n/. Say it with me: /n/. These are the letters* a *and* e. *Together they stand for /ā/. Let's say it together: /ā/. This is the letter* m. *It stands for /m/. I'll blend the sounds together: /nnnāāāmmm/,* name.

We Do Use the same routine and guide children to blend the sounds and read: *ape, cave, safe, skate, whale.*

You Do Have children use Word-Building Cards to blend and read *sale, base, rake, date, maze, tale, same, grade, shade, plate.*

Repeat, blending additional long *a_e* words.

You may wish to practice reading and decoding with **ELL** using this section.

BUILD WORDS WITH LONG *a: a_e*

OBJECTIVES

Decode regularly spelled one-syllable words.

Build and decode words with long *a*.

 I Do Display **Word-Building Cards** *a, t, e. These are the letters* a, t, *and* e. *They stand for* /āāā/ *and* /t/. *I will blend* /āāā/ *and* /t/ *together:* /āāāt/, ate.

 We Do *Now let's do one together.* Place the letter *g* in front of *ate. Let's blend:* /g/ /āāāt/, /gāāāt/, gate. *I am going to change the letter* t *in* gate *to the letter* v. *Change* t *to* v. *Let's blend and read the new word:* /g/ /āāā/ /v/, /gāāāv/, gave.

 You Do Have children build and read the words *save, same, tame, tale, take, stake, shake, wave, shade.* **Repeat,** building more words with long *a: a_e*.

READ WORDS WITH LONG *a: a_e*

OBJECTIVES

Read grade-level text orally with accuracy, appropriate rate, and expression on successive readings.

Unit 3 Decodable Reader pages 1-12

Focus on Foundational Skills

Review the high-frequency words *away, now, some, today, way,* and *why* with children. Review that the long *a* sound can be spelled *a_e.* Guide children to blend the sounds to read the words.

Read the Decodable Readers

Guide children to read "Dave Was Late" and "Is It Late?" Point out the high-frequency words and words in which *a_e* stands for the long *a* sound. If children struggle sounding out words, model blending.

Focus on Fluency

With partners, have children reread "Dave Was Late" and "Is It Late?" As children read the text, guide them to focus on their accuracy, rate, and automaticity. Children can provide feedback to their partners.

BUILD FLUENCY WITH PHONICS

Sound-Spellings Fluency

Display the following Word-Building Cards: *a_e, ch, tch, wh, ph, th, sh, ng, mp, sk, st, nt, nk, nd, u, e, ea, sp, sn, sl, cr, fr, tr, o, pl, fl.* Have children chorally say the sounds. Repeat, and vary the pace.

Fluency in Connected Text

Have children review the **Decodable Reader** selections. Identify words with long *a: a_e,* and blend words as needed. Have partners reread the selections for fluency.

● Approaching Level

Structural Analysis

REVIEW CONTRACTIONS WITH *not*

OBJECTIVES

Demonstrate command of the conventions of standard English grammar and usage when writing or speaking.

Read and use contractions with *not*.

I Do Write *isn't.* Read the word: /izint/. *I look at the word* isn't, *and I see a word I know:* is. *The* n't *tells me this word is a contraction.* Isn't *is a shorter way of saying* is not. *I'm going to use* is not *and* isn't *in sentences: Paul is not here. Paul isn't here.*

We Do Write *hasn't. Let's read this word:* /hazint/. *If we look at* hasn't, *we see the word* has. *We know that* n't *tells us* hasn't *is a contraction. The contraction* hasn't *stands for* has not. *Let's use* has not *and* hasn't *in sentences.*

You Do Write *aren't, wasn't, weren't, haven't, can't.* Ask partners to identify the two base words each contraction stands for.

Repeat Have partners use the contractions. One partner says a sentence with the two words. The other says the sentence with a contraction.

RETEACH CONTRACTIONS WITH *not*

OBJECTIVES

Demonstrate command of the conventions of standard English grammar and usage when writing or speaking.

Use apostrophes to form contractions.

I Do Write *is not* and *isn't.* Read the words. Circle the *n't* in *isn't. When I see* n't *at the end of the word* is, *I know the word is a contraction.* Isn't *is a short way of saying* is not. *Listen: The dog is not big. The dog isn't big.*

We Do Write *are. Let's add* n't. *Say* aren't. *What two words does* aren't *stand for?* Write *are not. Let's use* are not *and* aren't *in sentences. Say a sentence for* are not. Have children substitute *aren't* for *are not* in the sentence.

Repeat this routine with *was not/wasn't* and *can not/can't.*

You Do Have children match the contractions *isn't, aren't, wasn't, weren't, hasn't, haven't,* and *can't* with the words they stand for and use the contractions in sentences. Guide children as needed.

Repeat Have children write the contractions for *is not, are not, was not, were not, has not, have not,* and *can not.*

You may wish to review structural analysis and high-frequency words with **ELL** using this section.

High-Frequency Words

REVIEW

OBJECTIVES

Recognize and read grade-appropriate irregularly spelled words.

I Do Use **High-Frequency Word Cards** to Read/Spell/Write *away, now, some, today, way,* and *why.* Use each word orally in a sentence.

We Do Guide children to Read/Spell/Write each word on their **Response Boards.** Help them generate oral sentences for the words.

You Do Have partners work together to Read/Spell/Write the words *away, now, some, today, way,* and *why.* Ask them to say sentences for the words.

RETEACH

OBJECTIVES

Recognize and read grade-appropriate irregularly spelled words.

I Do Review the high-frequency words using the Read/Spell/Write routine. Write and read a sentence for each word.

We Do Guide children in using the Read/Spell/Write routine. Ask them to complete sentence starters: *(1) I go away when ____. (2) Now we can ____. (3) I will eat some ____. (4) Today my pals and I will ____. (4) This is the way to ____. (5) Why do you ____?*

You Do Ask children to close their eyes, picture the word, and write it as they see it. Have children self-correct as needed. Provide feedback as needed.

CUMULATIVE REVIEW

OBJECTIVES

Recognize and read grade-appropriate irregularly spelled words.

I Do Display the High-Frequency Word Cards from the previous weeks. Use the Read/Spell/Write routine to review each word.

We Do Guide children as they Read/Spell/Write the words on their Response Boards. Complete sentence frames for each word. *I like to walk around ____.*

You Do Have partners take turns reading and using each word in a sentence.

Fluency Display the High-Frequency Word Cards. Point to words in random order. Have children chorally read each word. Repeat at a faster pace.

● Approaching Level

Comprehension

READ FOR FLUENCY

TIER 2

OBJECTIVES
Read grade-level text orally with accuracy, appropriate rate, and expression on successive readings.

Set Purpose Tell children that they will now focus on reading *Busy's Watch*. Remind them that this story is fiction and that they will be reading it for enjoyment. Tell children that they need to read with accuracy and at an appropriate rate.

I Do Read the first sentence of **Leveled Reader** *Busy's Watch* aloud. Model reading at the appropriate rate. Tell children that as they read, it should sound like speech. Also explain to children that they need to read each word accurately.

We Do Read the next two sentences and have children repeat each sentence after you. Point out how you read the words accurately and at the appropriate rate. Provide corrective feedback as needed.

You Do Have children read the rest of the story aloud. Remind them to read each word accurately and to read so that it sounds like speech. Have children self-correct, as needed.

IDENTIFY MAIN STORY ELEMENTS: CHARACTER

TIER 2

OBJECTIVES
Describe characters in a story, using key details.

I Do Remind children that they have been reading a fantasy story. Say: *When I read a fantasy story, I look for information about the characters. The characters are the people or animals in a story. We can use the text and illustrations to help us learn what a character does, thinks, and feels.*

We Do Read the first two sentences of Leveled Reader *Busy's Watch* aloud. Pause to describe a character. *Busy is a dog. He is a character in the story. He wakes up Kay. He is excited about his watch. I know this because he smiles as he points to it.*

You Do Guide children as they read the rest of the story. Prompt them to describe another character in the story. Provide feedback as needed.

REVIEW EVENTS: BEGINNING, MIDDLE, END

OBJECTIVES

Describe major events in a story, using key details.

I Do Remind children that events are the most important things that happen in the story. Events happen at the beginning, middle, and end of the story. We can read the text to help us learn about the events.

We Do Read the first two pages of **Leveled Reader** *Busy's Watch* together. Pause to tell events in the beginning of the story. Ask: *What does Busy do? Yes, he wakes up Kay. This is an event at the beginning of the story.* Help children record this information on a Beginning, Middle, End chart.

You Do Have children read the rest of the story. Ask: *What important events happen in the middle of the story? At the end?* Remind children to read the text to learn about the events. Guide children to complete their charts.

SELF-SELECTED READING

OBJECTIVES

Describe major events in a story, using key details.

Read grade-level text with purpose and understanding.

Independent Reading

Have children select a fantasy story for independent reading. Children may use the **Classroom Library,** the **Leveled Reader Library,** the online **Unit Bibliography,** or other books for their independent reading. Encourage them to read for at least fifteen minutes.

Guide children to transfer what they have learned in this week as they read. Remind children that events are things that happen in a story, and events take place in the beginning, middle, and end of a story. Have children record information about events: beginning, middle, end on **Graphic Organizer 5.**

After reading, guide children to participate in a group discussion about the story they read. In addition, children can choose activities from the Reading **Center Activity Cards** to help them apply skills to the text as they read. Offer assistance and guidance with self-selected assignments.

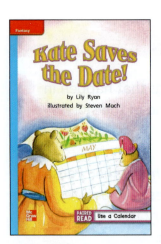

Lexile 220

OBJECTIVES

Describe major events in a story, using key details.

Read grade-level text orally with accuracy, appropriate rate, and expression on successive readings.

Retell stories, including key details, and demonstrate understanding of their central message or lesson.

Make and confirm predictions.

ELA ACADEMIC LANGUAGE

• *confirm, events*
• Cognates: *confirmar, eventos*

●On Level

Leveled Reader: *Kate Saves the Date!*

Preview and Predict

Have children turn to the title page. Read the title and the author's name, and have children repeat. Preview the selection's illustrations. Prompt children to predict what the selection might be about.

Review Genre: Fantasy

Have children recall that a fantasy is a made-up story that has characters that could not exist in real life.

Set Purpose

Remind children of the Essential Question. Set a purpose for reading: *Let's read to find out why Kate needs to save the date.* Remind children that as they read a selection, they can ask questions about what they do not understand or what they want to know more about.

Guided Comprehension

As children whisper read *Kate Saves the Date!* independently or with a partner, monitor and provide guidance. Correct blending and model the key strategies and skills as needed. As needed, provide definitions for words unfamiliar to children.

Make and Confirm Predictions

Model making and confirming predictions: *On page 4, the words tell me that today is Tuesday. I know Kate is waiting for Amy to come, but I predict she will not come today.* Read page 5 and confirm the prediction. Remind children that they can make and correct or confirm predictions as they read.

Events: Beginning, Middle, End

Hand out Graphic Organizer 5 to children. Review that events are the most important things that happen in a story. Events take place in the beginning, middle, and end of the story. We can find the most important events by reading the text. While reading, ask: *What happens in the beginning? What happens in the middle and end?*

Display a Beginning, Middle, End chart 5 for children to copy. Model recording children's answers in the beginning, middle, and end boxes. Have children copy the answers into their own charts.

Think Aloud On page 2, I read that Kate is waiting for Amy to come to a party. This is the beginning of the story, and it's not the day of the party yet. I will write that event in the beginning part of my chart.

Guide children to complete the chart.

Respond to Reading Have children complete the Respond to Reading on page 12.

Retell Have children take turns retelling the selection using the **Retelling Cards** as a guide. Help children make a connection by asking: *What are some dates you know? When is your birthday? How can a calendar help you know how long you must wait for your birthday?*

Fluency: Accuracy and Rate

Model Model reading page 2 with accuracy and an appropriate rate. Read aloud. Have children read along with you.

Apply Have children practice reading the text with a partner. Correct any errors, as needed.

Paired Read: "Use a Calendar"

 Make Connections: Write About It

Before reading, ask children to note that the genre of this text is nonfiction. Then read the Compare Texts direction in the **Leveled Reader**.

After reading the selection, ask children how the calendar in *Kate Saves the Date!* and the calendar in "Use a Calendar" are alike.

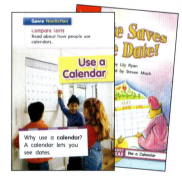

Leveled Reader

Build Knowledge: Make Connections

 Talk About the Texts Have partners discuss the different ways time is measured in these texts.

 Write About the Texts Then have children add their ideas to the Build Knowledge page of their reader's notebook.

LITERATURE CIRCLES

Lead children in conducting a literature circle using the Thinkmark questions to guide the discussion. You may wish to discuss what children have learned about calendars from both selections in the **Leveled Reader.**

ANALYTICAL WRITING

Compare Texts

Have children use text evidence to compare fantasy with informational text.

 **LEVEL** UP

IF children can read *Kate Saves the Date!* **On Level** with fluency and correctly answer the questions,

THEN tell children that they will read another story about time.

• Have children read the selection, checking their comprehension by using the graphic organizer.

●On Level

Phonics

READ AND BUILD WORDS WITH LONG *a: a_e*

OBJECTIVES

Decode regularly spelled one-syllable words.

Read grade-level text orally with accuracy, appropriate rate, and expression on successive readings.

Unit 3 Decodable Reader pages 2–3

I Do Display **Word-Building Cards** *t, a, p, e.* These are the letters t, a, p, *and* e. *They stand for* /t/ /āāā/ *and* /p/. *Remember that the* a *and* e *act together to stand for the long* a *sound* /ā /. *I will blend* /t/ /āāā/ *and* /p/ *together:* /tāāāp/, tape. *The word is* tape.

We Do *Now let's build a new word together.* Change the letter *t* to *c. Let's blend and read the new word:* /k/ /āāā/ /p/, /kāāāp/, cape. *The new word is* cape.

You Do Have children build and blend these words: *cake, make, male, sale, save, shave, shade, made, mane, pane, plane.*

Read the Decodable Readers

Guide children to read "Dave Was Late" and "Is It Late?" Point out the high-frequency words and words in which the spelling a_e stands for the long a sound. Model blending sound by sound as needed.

Focus on Fluency With partners, have children reread "Dave Was Late" and "Is It Late?" As children read the text, guide them to focus on accuracy, rate, and automaticity. They can provide feedback to their partners.

High-Frequency Words

REVIEW WORDS

OBJECTIVES

Recognize and read grade-appropriate irregularly spelled words.

I Do Use the Read/Spell/Write routine to review *away, now, some, today, way,* and *why.* Use each word orally in a sentence.

We Do Guide children to Read/Spell/Write each word using their **Response Boards.** Then work with the group to generate oral sentences for the words.

You Do Have partners use the Read/Spell/Write routine with the words *away, now, some, today, way,* and *why.* Ask them to write sentences about the stories they have read this week, using the high-frequency words.

Comprehension

REVIEW EVENTS: BEGINNING, MIDDLE, END

OBJECTIVES

Describe major events in a story, using key details.

I Do Remind children that events are important things that happen in a story. We can learn about events at the beginning, middle, and end of the story by reading the text.

We Do Read the first two pages of **Leveled Reader** *Kate Saves the Date!* aloud. Pause to discuss an important event that happens at the beginning of the story. Ask: *What happens in the kitchen with Kate and Mommy?*

You Do Guide children to read the rest of *Kate Saves the Date!* Invite children to describe what happens in the middle and end of the story. Provide feedback as needed.

SELF-SELECTED READING

OBJECTIVES

Describe major events in a story, using key details.

Read grade-level text with purpose and understanding.

Independent Reading

Have children select a fantasy story to read for independent reading. Children may use the **Classroom Library,** the **Leveled Reader Library,** the online **Unit Bibliography,** or other books for their independent reading. Encourage them to read for at least fifteen minutes.

Guide children to transfer what they have learned in this week as they read. Remind children that events are things that happen in a story, and events take place in the beginning, middle, and end of a story. Have children record information about events: beginning, middle, end on **Graphic Organizer 5.**

After reading, guide children to participate in a group discussion about the story they read. In addition, children can choose activities from the Reading **Center Activity Cards** to help them apply skills to the text as they read. Offer assistance and guidance with self-selected assignments.

You may wish to review Comprehension with **ELL** using this section.

Lexile 320

OBJECTIVES

Describe major events in a story, using key details.

Retell stories, including key details, and demonstrate understanding of their central message or lesson.

Make and confirm predictions.

ELA ACADEMIC LANGUAGE

• confirm, retell
• Cognate: confirmar

●Beyond Level

Leveled Reader:
Uncle George Is Coming!

Preview and Predict

Read the title and the author's name. Have children preview the title page and the illustrations. Ask: *What do you think this book will be about?*

Review Genre: Fantasy

Have children recall that a fantasy is a story that has made-up characters that could not exist in real life.

Set Purpose

Remind children of the Essential Question. Set a purpose for reading: *What do you want to find out about Uncle George? As you get ready to read this fluently, think about the purpose.*

Guided Comprehension

Have children whisper read *Uncle George Is Coming!* independently or with a partner. Have them place self-stick notes next to difficult words. Monitor and provide guidance. Correct blending and model the key strategies and skills, as needed.

Monitor children's reading. Stop periodically and ask open-ended questions to facilitate rich discussion, such as *What does the author want us to know about Skip? His dad? Uncle George?* Build on children's responses to develop deeper understanding of the text.

Make and Confirm Predictions

Model making and confirming predictions: *On page 5, we see Skip and his dad eating a snack after school. I predict that it is almost time for them to go meet Uncle George. I can read on to see if my prediction is right.* Remind children that making and correcting or confirming predictions as they read can help them better understand a selection.

Events: Beginning, Middle, End

Hand out Graphic Organizer 5 to children. Ask children to define events and when they happen in a story. While reading, ask: *What events take place in the beginning, middle, and end?* Display the Beginning, Middle, End chart 5. Model how to record the information. Have children fill in their chart.

Think Aloud As I read page 2, I learn that Skip and his dad are waiting for Uncle George to come at 4:45. This is an important event at the beginning of the story. I will write this in the beginning box.

Respond to Reading Have children complete the Respond to Reading on page 12.

Retell Have children take turns retelling the story. Help children make a personal connection by writing about a time they had to wait. *Write about a time when you had to wait for someone or something. How did you feel while you were waiting? How did you feel after you waited?*

Paired Read: "So Many Clocks!"

 Make Connections: Write About It

Before reading, ask children to preview the title page and prompt them to identify the genre as nonfiction text. Then read the Compare Texts direction in the **Leveled Reader.**

After reading the selection, have children work with a partner to discuss how the information they learned in *Uncle George Is Coming!* is similar to what they learned in "So Many Clocks!"

Leveled Reader

Build Knowledge: Make Connections

 Talk About the Text Have partners discuss the different ways time is measured in these texts.

 Write About the Text Then have children add their ideas to the Build Knowledge page of their reader's notebook.

LITERATURE CIRCLES

Lead children in conducting a literature circle using the Thinkmark questions to guide the discussion. You may wish to discuss what children have learned about different kinds of clocks from both selections in the **Leveled Reader.**

⭐ GIFTED AND TALENTED

Synthesize Challenge children to think of the various ways we keep track of time. Children should write about what they use to plan and stay organized. Encourage them to consider how clocks are helpful to our lives.

Extend Have children use facts they learned from this week's readings or do additional research to find out more about clocks.

ANALYTICAL WRITING

Compare Texts

Have children use text evidence to compare fantasy with informational text.

Beyond Level

Vocabulary

ORAL VOCABULARY: SYNONYMS

OBJECTIVES

With guidance and support from adults, demonstrate understanding of word relationships and nuances in word meanings.

I Do Review with children the meaning of the oral vocabulary word *immediately*. Write the sentence *We will leave immediately*. Read the sentence aloud and have children repeat it. Discuss what *immediately* means.

Remind children that a synonym is a word that means almost the same thing as another word. *When you do something immediately, you do it right away.* Right away, now, *and* pronto *are synonyms for* immediately.

We Do Collaborate with children to use the words *right away, now*, and *pronto* in sentences about important things they must do.

You Do Have partners use the words to act out a short scene about a friend needing something right away.

⭐ **GIFTED and TALENTED** **Extend** Have children work with partners to tell each other a story that involves having to do something right away, using the word *immediately* and its synonyms *right away, now*, and *pronto* as many times as possible.

Comprehension

REVIEW EVENTS: BEGINNING, MIDDLE, END

OBJECTIVES
Describe major events in a story, using key details.

I Do Discuss with children what events are. Prompt them to explain that important events happen at the beginning, middle, and end of a story.

We Do Guide children in reading the first page of **Leveled Reader** *Uncle George Is Coming!* aloud. Pause to prompt children to describe what happens at the beginning of the story. *What important thing happens with Skip and his dad at the beginning?*

You Do Have children read the rest of the selection independently. Then invite children to describe what happens in the middle and end of the story. Provide feedback as needed.

SELF-SELECTED READING

OBJECTIVES
Describe major events in a story, using key details.

Read grade-level text with purpose and understanding.

Independent Reading

Have children select a fantasy story for independent reading. Children may use the **Classroom Library,** the **Leveled Reader Library,** the online **Unit Bibliography,** or other books for their independent reading. Encourage them to read for at least fifteen minutes.

Guide children to transfer what they have learned in this week as they read by reminding them that events are things that happen in a story, and events take place in the beginning, middle, and end of a story. Have children record information about events: beginning, middle, end on **Graphic Organizer 5.**

After reading, guide children to participate in a group discussion about the story they read. In addition, children can choose activities from the Reading **Center Activity Cards** to help them apply skills to the text as they read. Offer assistance and guidance with self-selected assignments.

 Independent Study Have children write a paragraph discussing why they did or did not like their self-selected reading. Have them create book posters that illustrate what happens in their story.

Student Outcomes

✓ Tested in *Wonders* Assessments

FOUNDATIONAL SKILLS

Print Concepts
- Locate title, author

Phonological Awareness
- Alliteration
- Phoneme Deletion
- Phoneme Segmentation
- Phoneme Blending

Phonics and Word Analysis
- ✓ Long *i: i_e*
- ✓ Plurals with CVCe words

Fluency
- Read with accuracy and automaticity
- ✓ High-Frequency Words
- *green   grow   pretty   should   together   water*

READING

Reading Literature
- ✓ Identify and describe the sequence of events in a story
- Retell a text to enhance comprehension
- Read prose and poetry appropriately complex for grade 1

Reading Informational Text
- ✓ Use text features including diagrams to locate key facts or information
- Read informational texts appropriately complex for grade 1

Compare Texts
- Compare and contrast two texts on the same topic

COMMUNICATION

Writing
- Handwriting: *Vv*
- Write narratives that retell two or more appropriately sequenced events, including relevant details and a sense of closure
- Focus on a topic, respond to suggestions from peers, and add details to strengthen writing

Speaking and Listening
- Participate in collaborative conversations
- Ask and answer questions to gather or clarify information
- Present information orally using complete sentences

Conventions
- ✓ **Grammar:** Identify and use present-tense verbs
- **Mechanics:** Capitalize and underline titles of plays
- **Spelling:** Spell words with Long *i: i_e*

Researching
- Recall or gather information to answer a question
- Participate in shared research and writing projects

Creating and Collaborating
- Add drawings and visual displays to descriptions
- Use digital tools to produce and publish writing

VOCABULARY

Academic Vocabulary
- Acquire and use grade-appropriate academic vocabulary
- Identify real-life connections between words and their use

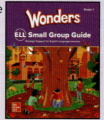

ELL Scaffolded supports for English Language Learners are embedded throughout the lessons, enabling children to communicate information, ideas, and concepts in English Language Arts and for social and instructional purposes within the school setting.

See the **ELL Small Group Guide** for additional support of the skills for the text set.

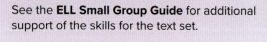

FORMATIVE ASSESSMENT

For assessment throughout the text set, use children's self-assessments and your observations.

Use the Data Dashboard to filter class, group, or individual student data to guide group placement decisions. It provides recommendations to enhance learning for gifted and talented children and offers extra support for children needing remediation.

DATA DASHBOARD

Develop Student Ownership

To build student ownership, children need to know what they are learning, why they are learning it, and determine how well they understood it.

Students Discuss Their Goals

TEXT SET GOALS

- I can read and understand a play.
- I can respond to a play by extending the play.
- I know about how plants change as they grow.

Have children think about what they know and fill in the bars on **Reading/Writing Companion** page 46.

Students Monitor Their Learning

LEARNING GOALS

Specific learning goals identified in every lesson make clear what children will be learning and why. These smaller goals provide stepping stones to help children meet their Text Set Goals.

CHECK-IN ROUTINE

The Check-In routine at the close of each lesson guides children to self-reflect on how well they understood each learning goal.

Review the lesson learning goal.
Reflect on the activity.
Self-Assess by
- filling in the bars in the **Reading/Writing Companion.**
- holding up 1, 2, 3, or 4 fingers.

Share with your teacher.

Students Reflect on Their Progress

TEXT SET GOALS

After completing the Show Your Knowledge task for the text set, children reflect on their understanding of the Text Set Goals by filling in the bars on **Reading/Writing Companion** page 47.

Build Knowledge

Literature Big Book

Shared Read
Reading/Writing Companion p. 48

Anchor Text
Literature Anthology p. 28

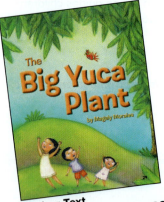
Paired Selection
Literature Anthology p. 46

Essential Question
How do plants change as they grow?

 Video Most plants change in size as they grow. Some vegetables and fruits change color as they grow. Some plants bloom with flowers as they grow.

Literature Big Book Fruits and vegetables start as seeds. The seeds sprout from the ground. The plants grow, and some bloom flowers. Pumpkins grow slowly on special vines.

Shared Read A family plants a vegetable garden. It needs sun and water to grow. Soon, the vines have buds. They grow into big vegetables.

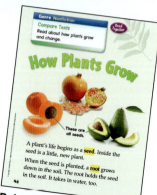 **Interactive Read Aloud** A man plants a seed that grows into a huge turnip. His whole family and some animals pull it from the ground.

Anchor Text When a sister plants a seed, it grows into a huge yucca plant. The whole family and some animals pull it from the ground.

Paired Selection When a seed is planted, roots grow in the soil. Then a stem sprouts from the soil. Green leaves grow. Blossoms grow into fruit. Inside the fruits are more seeds.

 Art Pomegranates grow on trees. The trees have colorful blossoms. They turn into the fruit.

Differentiated Sources

Leveled Readers 🔊

🟠 Two boys plant corn seeds and watch them grow. The corn plants grow tall and change from green to golden yellow.

🔵🟣 Lily waits for strawberries to grow on her strawberry plants. When they finally grow, she has a picnic.

🟢 A family watches an apple tree grow and change. In winter, it loses its leaves. In spring, it grows pretty flowers.

Build Knowledge Routine

After reading each text, ask children to document facts and details they learned that help them answer the Essential Question of the text set.

 Talk about the source.

 Write about the source.

 Add to the class Anchor Chart

• Add to the Word Bank.

Show Your Knowledge

Draw Growing Plants

Have children think of the types of plants they read about. Guide them to draw and write about how plants change as they grow. Encourage children to include vocabulary words in their writing.

Social Emotional Learning

Teachable Moment

Take a moment to reflect on children's developing skills on assessed or previously-taught SEL competencies. Then, select an SEL lesson from your library of resources to meet children's individualized needs, and integrate it into your weekly plan.

Family Time • Share your selected SEL lesson's video and activity in the **School to Home** newsletter.

Explore the Texts

Essential Question: How do plants change as they grow?

Literature Big Book	Interactive Read Aloud	Reading/Writing Companion	Literature Anthology

  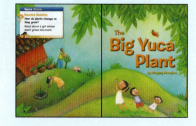

Literature Big Book	Interactive Read Aloud	Reading/Writing Companion	Literature Anthology
Mystery Vine Realistic Fiction	"The Great Big Gigantic Turnip" Folktale	"Time to Plant!" Shared Read pp. 48–57 Play	*The Big Yuca Plant* Anchor Text pp. 28–45 Play

Qualitative

Meaning/Purpose: Moderate Complexity **Structure:** Moderate Complexity **Language:** Moderate Complexity **Knowledge Demands:** Moderate Complexity	**Meaning/Purpose:** Moderate Complexity **Structure:** Low Complexity **Language:** High Complexity **Knowledge Demands:** Moderate Complexity	**Meaning/Purpose:** Moderate Complexity **Structure:** Low Complexity **Language:** Low Complexity **Knowledge Demands:** Moderate Complexity	**Meaning/Purpose:** Moderate Complexity **Structure:** Low Complexity **Language:** Low Complexity **Knowledge Demands:** Moderate Complexity

Quantitative

Lexile 480L	Lexile 760L	Lexile NP	Lexile NP

Reader and Task Considerations

Reader Children may need prior knowledge about caring for a garden and basic concepts of how plants grow.	**Reader** Children may need prior knowledge on the function of folktales, as well as support with the characters and dialogue in the story.	**Reader** Children will need to use their knowledge of sound-spelling correspondences and high-frequency words to read the text.	**Reader** Children might need prior knowledge on how plays are written and performed. Information about the yuca plant might also be helpful.

Task The questions for the Interactive Read Aloud are supported by teacher modeling. The tasks provide a variety of ways for students to begin to build knowledge and vocabulary about the text set topic. The questions and tasks provided for the other texts are at various levels of complexity, ensuring that all students can interact with the text in meaningful ways.

Additional Texts

Classroom Library
Lon Po Po: A Red-Riding Hood Story from China
Genre: Fiction
Lexile: 670L

If You Plant a Seed
Genre: Fiction
Lexile: 340L

See **Classroom Library Lessons.**

Content Area Reading BLMs
Additional online texts related to grade-level Science, Social Studies, and Arts content.

A C T

Access Complex Text (ACT) boxes provide scaffolded instruction for seven different elements that may make the **Literature Big Book** complex.

Literature Anthology

"How Plants Grow"
Paired Selection
pp. 46–49
Informational Text

Qualitative

Meaning/Purpose: Low Complexity
Structure: Moderate Complexity
Language: Moderate Complexity
Knowledge Demands: Low Complexity

Quantitative

Lexile 400L

Reader and Task Considerations

Reader Children might need background information on the plants and fruits shown, including pomegranate, avocado, pumpkin and apricot.

Task The questions and tasks provided for this text are at various levels of complexity, ensuring that all students can interact with the text in meaningful ways.

Leveled Readers 🔊 (All Leveled Readers are provided in eBook format with audio support.)

(A)	(O)	(B)	(ELL)

Corn Fun	**Yum, Strawberries!**	**A Tree's Life**	**Yum, Strawberries!**
Play	Play	Play	Play

Qualitative

Meaning/Purpose: Low Complexity	**Meaning/Purpose:** Low Complexity	**Meaning/Purpose:** High Complexity	**Meaning/Purpose:** Low Complexity
Structure: Moderate Complexity	**Structure:** Moderate Complexity	**Structure:** Moderate Complexity	**Structure:** Moderate Complexity
Language: Low Complexity	**Language:** Low Complexity	**Language:** Moderate Complexity	**Language:** Low Complexity
Knowledge Demands: Low Complexity	**Knowledge Demands:** Moderate Complexity	**Knowledge Demands:** Moerate Complexity	**Knowledge Demands:** Moderate Complexity

Quantitative

Lexile NP	Lexile NP	Lexile NP	Lexile NP

Reader and Task Considerations

Reader Children might need familiarity with some of the farming vocabulary used in the story, including *rake, crop,* and *water.*	**Reader** Children may need background knowledge on what strawberry plants look like and how they grow.	**Reader** Children may need background knowledge on how trees grow from seeds and how it changes during each season.	**Reader** Children may need background knowledge on what strawberry plants look like and how they grow.

Task The questions and tasks provided for the Leveled Readers are at various levels of complexity, ensuring that all students can interact with the text in meaningful ways.

WEEK 2

Focus on Word Work

Build Foundational Skills with Multimodal Learning

MULTIMODAL

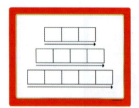
Response Board

Phonemic Awareness Activities

Sound-Spelling Cards

Word-Building Cards online

Phonics Activities

Practice Book

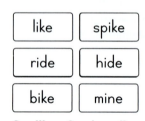
Spelling Cards online

High-Frequency Word Cards

High-Frequency Word Activities

Visual Vocabulary Cards

Shared Read

Decodable Readers

Take-Home Story

Phonological/Phonemic Awareness

- Identify and produce alliteration
- Delete, segment, and blend phonemes

Phonics: Long *i*: *i_e*

- Introduce/review sound-spellings
- Blend/build words with sound-spellings
- Practice handwriting
- Structural Analysis: Build reading word bank
- Decode and encode in connected texts

Spelling: Long *i*: *i_e*

- Differentiated spelling instruction
- Encode with sound-spellings
- Explore relationships with word sorts and word families

High-Frequency Words

- Read/Spell/Write routine

See Word Work, pages T90–T93, T100–T103, T110–T113, T132–T133, T138–T139.

Apply Skills to Read

- Children apply foundational skills as they read decodable texts.
- Children practice fluency to develop word automaticity.

PHONICS SKILLS TRACE

Initial Consonants ▸ Short Vowels ▸ Consonant Blends and Digraphs ▸ Long Vowels ▸ Vowel Digraphs ▸ *r*-Controlled Vowels ▸ Diphthongs ▸ Variant Vowels ▸ Silent Letters and 3-Letter Blends

Explicit Systematic Instruction

Word Work instruction expands foundational skills to enable children to become proficient readers.

Daily Routine

- Use the In a Flash: Sound-Spelling routine and the In a Flash: High-Frequency Word routine to build fluency.
- Set Learning Goal.

Explicit Minilessons and Practice

Use daily instruction in both whole and small groups to model, practice, and apply key foundational skills. Opportunities include:

- Multimodal engagement.
- Corrective feedback.
- Supports for English Language Learners in each lesson.
- Peer collaboration.

Formative Assessment

Check-In

- Children reflect on their learning.
- Children show their progress by holding up 1 to 4 fingers in a Check-In routine.

Check for Success

- Teacher monitors children's achievement and differentiates for Small Group instruction.

Differentiated Instruction

To strengthen skills, provide targeted review and reteaching lessons and multimodal activities to meet children's diverse needs.

🟠🟣 **Approaching Level, ELL**
- Includes Tier 2 ②

🔵 **On Level**

🟢 **Beyond Level**
- Includes Gifted and Talented ★GIFTED and TALENTED

Independent Practice

Provide additional practice as needed. Have children work individually or with partners.

Center Activity Cards

Digital Activities

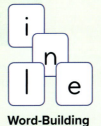
Word-Building Cards online

Decodable Readers

Practice Book

Inspire Early Writers

Build Writing Skills and Conventions

Practice Book

Handwriting Video

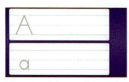

Reading/Writing Companion

Write Letters

- Learn to write letters
- Practice writing

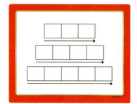

Response Board

Practice Book

High-Frequency Word Activities

Write Words

- Write words with long *i*: *i_e*
- Write spelling words
- Write high-frequency words

Reading/Writing Companion

Practice Book

Write Sentences

- Write sentences with plurals
- Write sentences to respond to text

Follow Conventions

- Form and use present-tense verbs
- Capitalize and underline titles of plays

Mystery Vine
Literature Big Book

Writing Fluency

To increase children's writing fluency, have them write as much as they can in response to the **Literature Big Book** for five minutes. Tell children to write about how things grow.

For lessons, see pages **T90–T93, T96–T97, T100–T103, T106–T107, T124–T125, T133, T134–135, T139, T140–T141.**

Write About Texts

**Reading/Writing Companion,
pp. 58–59, 64–65**

Modeled Writing

Write About the Shared Read "Time to Plant"

- Prompt: Which vegetables might the family plant next. Add a page to the play.

Interactive Writing

- Prompt: Write a scene about what Mike and Beth might make with their vegetables.

**Reading/Writing
Companion, p. 70**

Independent Writing

Write About the Anchor Text *The Big Yuca Plant*
Literature Anthology, pp. 28–45

- Prompt: Think of a different animal that might have been able to get the yuca plant out. Write a scene where he/she helps out.

- Have children follow the steps of the writing process: draft, revise, edit/proofread, share.

Additional Lessons

Writing Skill Lesson Bank To provide differentiated support for writing skills, see pages T420–T429.

Extended Writing Minilessons For a full set of lessons that support the writing process and writing in a specific genre, see pages T402–T413.

Self-Selected Writing

Children can explore different writing modes.

 Journal Writing

 Squiggle Writing

 Comic Strip

 Select from your Social Emotional Learning resources.

 LESSON 1

 LESSON 2

TEXT SET GOALS

- **We can read and understand a play.**
- **I can respond to a play by extending the play.**
- **I know about how plants change as they grow.**

 90+ mins **Reading Suggested Daily Time Includes Small Group**

SMALL GROUP OPTIONS
The designated lessons can be taught in small groups. To determine how to differentiate instruction for small groups, use Formative Assessment and Data Dashboard.

30+ mins **Writing Suggested Daily Time**

Reading

Lesson 1

Introduce the Concept, T86–T87
Build Knowledge: Watch It Grow!

Listening Comprehension, T88–T89
Mystery Vine

▶ **Word Work, T90–T93**
Phonological Awareness: Alliteration
Phonics/Spelling: Long *i: i_e*
High-Frequency Words: *green, grow, pretty, should, together, water*

Shared Read, T94–T95
Read "Time to Plant!"

Lesson 2

▶ **Build the Concept, T98**
Oral Language

Listening Comprehension, T99
"The Great Big, Gigantic Turnip"

▶ **Word Work, T100–T103**
Phonemic Awareness: Phoneme Deletion
Phonics/Spelling: Long *i: i_e*
Structural Analysis: Plurals
High-Frequency Words: *green, grow, pretty, should, together, water*

▶ **Shared Read, T104–T105**
Reread "Time to Plant!"

Writing

Modeled Writing, T96
Write About the Shared Read
Grammar, T97
Present-Tense Verbs

▶ **Interactive Writing, T106**
Write About the Shared Read
Grammar, T107
Present-Tense Verbs

Teacher-Led Instruction

 SMALL GROUP

Differentiated Reading
Leveled Readers
- 🔴 *Corn Fun,* T144–T145
- 🔵 *Yum, Strawberries!,* T154–T155
- 🟢 *A Tree's Life,* T158–T159

Differentiated Skills Practice, T146–T161
🔴 **Approaching Level, T146–T153**
Phonological/Phonemic Awareness
- Phoneme Segmentation, T146 **TIER 2**
- Phoneme Blending, T146 **TIER 2**
- Recognize and Generate Alliteration, T147
- Phoneme Deletion, T147

Phonics
- Connect *i_e* to /ī/, T148 **TIER 2**
- Blend Words with Long *i: i_e,* T148 **TIER 2**
- Build Words with Long *i: i_e,* T149
- Read Words with Long *i: i_e,* T149
- Build Fluency with Phonics, T149

Structural Analysis
- Review Plurals, T150
- Reteach Plurals, T150

Independent/Collaborative Work See pages T85I–85J

Reading
Comprehension
- Drama: Play
- Make and Confirm Predictions
- Main Story Elements: Sequence of Events
Independent Reading

Word Work
Phonics/Spelling
- Long *i: i_e*
High-Frequency Words
- *green, grow, pretty, should, together, water*

Writing
Self-Selected Writing
Grammar
- Present-Tense Verbs
Handwriting
- Upper and lowercase *Vv*

LESSON 3

LESSON 4

LESSON 5

Reading

Build the Concept, T108
Oral Language
Take Notes About Text

Listening Comprehension, T109
Mystery Vine

▶ **Word Work, T110–T113**
Phonemic Awareness: Phoneme Segmentation
Phonics/Spelling: Long *i: i_e*
Structural Analysis: Plurals
High-Frequency Words: *green, grow, pretty, should, together, water*

Anchor Text, T114–T123
Read *The Big Yuca Plant*

Extend the Concept, T126–T127
Oral Language

Paired Selection, T128–T131
Read "How Plants Grow"

▶ **Word Work, T132–T133**
Phonemic Awareness: Phoneme Deletion
Phonics/Spelling: Long *i: i_e*
Structural Analysis: Plurals
High-Frequency Words: *green, grow, pretty, should, together, water*

▶ **Research and Inquiry, T136–T137**
Research and Inquiry: Plants Grow

▶ **Word Work, T138–T139**
Phonemic Awareness: Phoneme Blending and Segmentation
Phonics/Spelling: Long *i: i_e*
Phonics: Read the Decodable Reader
Structural Analysis: Plurals
High-Frequency Words: *green, grow, pretty, should, together, water*

Integrate Ideas, T142
Make Connections

Culminating Task, T143
Show Your Knowledge

Writing

Independent Writing, T124
Write About the Anchor Text
Grammar, T125
Present-Tense Verbs
Mechanics, T125
Capitalize and Underline Titles of Plays

Independent Writing, T134
Write About the Anchor Text
Grammar, T135
Present-Tense Verbs
Mechanics, T135
Capitalize and Underline Titles of Plays

▶ **Self-Selected Writing, T140**
Grammar, T141
Present-Tense Verbs
Mechanics, T141
Capitalize and Underline Titles of Plays

High-Frequency Words
• Review/Reteach/Cumulative Review, T151
Comprehension
• Read for Fluency, T152 ②
• Identify Character, T152 ②
• Review Sequence of Events, T153
• Self-Selected Reading, T153

● **On Level, T156–T157**
Phonics
• Read and Build Words with Long *i: i_e*, T156
High-Frequency Words
• Review Words, T156
Comprehension
• Review Sequence of Events, T157
• Self-Selected Reading, T157

● **Beyond Level, T160–T161**
Vocabulary
• Oral Vocabulary: Antonyms, T160
Comprehension
• Review Sequence of Events, T161
• Self-Selected Reading, T161 🏅GIFTED and TALENTED

 ● **English Language Learners**
See ELL Small Group Guide, pp. 116–125.

Content Area Connections
Content Area Reading
• Science, Social Studies, and the Arts
Research and Inquiry
• Plants Grow

 ● **English Language Learners**
See ELL Small Group Guide, pp. 117, 119, 121.

Independent and Collaborative Work

As you meet with small groups, have the rest of the class complete activities and projects to practice and apply the skills they have been working on.

Student Choice and Student Voice

- Review My Weekly Work blackline master with children and identify the "Must Do" activities.
- Have children choose some additional activities that provide the practice they need.
- Remind children to reflect on their learning each day.

Online Contract BLMs

Reading

Text Options

Children can choose a **Center Activity Card** to use while they listen to a text or read independently.

Classroom Library Read Aloud
Lon Po Po: A Red-Riding Hood Story from China
Genre: Fiction
Lexile: 670L

Classroom Library
If You Plant a Seed
Genre: Fantasy
Lexile: 340L

Unit Bibliography
See the online bibliography. Children can select independent reading texts about how plants change as they grow.

Leveled Texts Online
All **Leveled Readers** are provided in eBook format with audio support.

- **Differentiated Texts** provide English Language Learners with passages at different proficiency levels.

Literature Big Book e-Book
Mystery Vine
Genre: Realistic Fiction

Center Activity Cards

Make and Confirm Predictions Card 3

Play Card 30

Sequence of Events Card 8

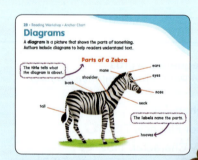

Diagrams with Labels Card 23

Digital Activities

Comprehension

Word Work

Center Activity Cards

Long i: i_e Card 82

Word-Building Cards

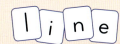

Practice Book BLMs

Phonological Awareness:
pp. 177, 178

Phonics: pp. 179, 180

Spelling: pp. 181–183

Structural Analysis: pp. 185, 186

High-Frequency Words: p. 187

Take-Home Story: pp. 191–192

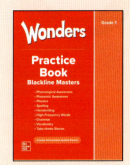

Decodable Readers

 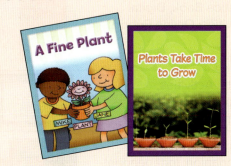

Unit 3, pp. 13–24

Digital Activities

Phonemic Awareness

Phonics

Spelling

High-Frequency Words

Writing

Center Activity Cards

Sensory Details Card 63

Practice Book BLMs

Handwriting: p. 184

Grammar: pp. 188–189

Mechanics: p. 190

Self-Selected Writing

- How do you think plants grow?
- Write about how a plant changes as it grows.
- What do plants need as they grow?

Digital Activities

Grammar

Grammar: Mechanics

Content Area Connections

Content Area Reading BLMs
- Additional texts related to Science, Social Studies, Health, and the Arts.

Research and Inquiry
- Complete Plants Grow project

Progress Monitoring
Moving Toward Mastery

> **FORMATIVE ASSESSMENT**
> ➤ **STUDENT CHECK-IN**
> ✓ **CHECK FOR SUCCESS**

For ongoing formative assessment, use children's self-assessments at the end of each lesson along with your own observations.

Assessing skills along the way . . .

SKILLS	HOW ASSESSED	
Phonological/Phonemic Awareness **Phonics** **Structural Analysis** **High-Frequency Words**	Practice Book, Digital Activities, Online Rubrics	
Comprehension	Digital Activities, Graphic Organizers, Online Rubrics	
Text-Based Writing **Handwriting** **Grammar** **Spelling**	Reading/Writing Companion: Independent Writing, Practice Book, Digital Activities, Spelling Word Sorts	
Listening/Presenting/Research	Reading/Writing Companion: Share and Evaluate; Research: Online Student Checklists	
Oral Reading Fluency (ORF) Conduct group fluency assessments using the **Letter Naming, Phoneme Segmentation**, and **Sight Word Fluency** assessments.	Fluency Assessment	

At the end of the text set . . .

SKILLS	HOW ASSESSED
Main Story Elements: Sequence of Events **Text Features: Diagrams**	Progress Monitoring
Alliteration **Phoneme Deletion** **Phoneme Segmentation**	
Long *i*: *i_e*	
Plurals with CVCe words	
green, grow, pretty, should, together, water	

Making the Most of Assessment Results

Make data-based grouping decisions by using the following reports to verify assessment results. For additional support options for children, refer to the reteaching and enrichment opportunities.

ONLINE ASSESSMENT CENTER
- *Gradebook*

DATA DASHBOARD
- *Recommendations Report*
- *Activity Report*
- *Skills Report*
- *Progress Report*
- *Grade Card Report*

Reteaching Opportunities with Intervention Online PDFs

IF CHILDREN ANSWER . . .	THEN ASSIGN . . .
0–3 **comprehension** items correctly . . .	lessons 25–27 on Sequence of Events and/or lesson 135 on Text Features: Diagrams from the **Comprehension PDF.**
0–2 **phonological/phonemic** items correctly . . .	lessons 18–19 on Alliteration, lessons 102–103 on Phoneme Deletion, and lessons 67–71 on Phoneme Segmentation from the **Phonemic Awareness PDF.**
0–5 **phonics/structural analysis/HFW** items correctly . . .	lesson 60 on Long *i*: *i_e* and lesson 54 on Plurals from the **Phonics/Word Study PDF** and lessons from Section 3 of the **Fluency PDF.**

Enrichment Opportunities

Beyond Level small-group lessons and resources include suggestions for additional activities in these areas to extend learning opportunities for gifted and talented children:

- *Leveled Reader*
- *Vocabulary*
- *Comprehension*

- *Leveled Reader Library Online*
- *Center Activity Cards*

OBJECTIVES

Build on others' talk in conversations by responding to the comments of others through multiple exchanges.

Ask questions to clear up any confusion about the topics and texts under discussion.

Build background knowledge.

Discuss the Essential Question.

ELA ACADEMIC LANGUAGE

• *discuss, video*
• Cognates: *discutir, vídeo*

DIGITAL TOOLS

To enhance the class discussion, use these additional components.

Watch Video

Discuss Images

Discuss Concept

LESSON FOCUS

READING
Introduce the Essential Question
Read Literature Big Book:
Mystery Vine
• Make Predictions
Word Work
• Introduce Long *i: i_e*
Read Shared Read: "Time to Plant"
• Introduce Genre

WRITING
Modeled Writing
• Introduce Grammar

Reading/Writing Companion, pp. 48–57

---

5 mins

Build Knowledge

MULTIMODAL

 Essential Question
How do plants change as they grow?

Tell children that this week they will be talking and reading about plants and how they grow. Discuss the Essential Question. Children can describe what they know about how plants change as they grow.

Watch the Video Play the video without sound first and have partners narrate what they see. Then replay the video with sound and have children listen.

Talk About the Video Have partners share one thing they saw that reminded them of their school.

 Anchor Chart Create a Build Knowledge anchor chart with the Essential Question and have volunteers share what they learned. Record their ideas on the chart.

Oral Vocabulary Words

Use the Define/Example/Ask Routine on the print or digital **Visual Vocabulary Cards** to introduce the oral vocabulary words *bloom* and *sprout*. Prompt children to use the words as they answer the question.

Oral Vocabulary Routine

Visual Vocabulary Cards

<u>Define:</u> When flower buds open, they **bloom.**

<u>Example:</u> In spring, the flowers bloom and show their pink petals.

<u>Ask:</u> What do flowers look like before they bloom?

<u>Define:</u> When seeds **sprout**, they begin to grow.

<u>Example:</u> Tiny leaves start to grow after the seed sprouts.

<u>Ask:</u> What does a seed need in order to sprout?

Reading/Writing Companion, pp. 44–45

Build Knowledge

Review how to add new ideas using the Collaborative Conversations box. Then have children turn to pages 44–45 of their **Reading/Writing Companion.** Guide them to discuss the photo. Then ask:

- *What clues in the photo tell you what the boy is looking at?*
- *Describe to your partner what the sprout will become.*

Build Vocabulary

Talk Have partners talk about words they know about plants.

Write Have children write words about plants on page 45.

Create a Word Bank Create a separate section of the Word Bank for words about plants. Have children suggest words to add.

English Language Learners

Use the scaffolds to help children complete **Build Knowledge.**

Beginning

Point to the sprout. *This is a sprout. Have children say sprout. What is this?* Have children point to the photo and respond: This is a <u>sprout</u>.

Intermediate

Provide a sentence frame to help children respond: The boy is looking at a <u>sprout</u>. *What will the sprout become?* Have children respond: The sprout will become a <u>plant</u>.

Advanced/Advanced High

As partners share questions about the photo, provide vocabulary as necessary. Model sharing a question about the photo: *How will this sprout change as it grows?*

COLLABORATIVE CONVERSATIONS

Add New Ideas As children engage in partner, small-group, and whole-group discussions, encourage them to:

- stay on topic.
- connect their own ideas to the comments of others.
- look for ways to connect their experiences to the conversation.

ELL NEWCOMERS

To help children develop oral language and build vocabulary, continue using **Newcomer Cards** 5–9 and the accompanying lessons in the **Newcomer Teacher's Guide.** For thematic connections, use Newcomer Card 22. For additional practice, have children complete the online **Newcomer Activities.**

MY GOALS ROUTINE

What I Know Now

Read Goals Read goals with children on **Reading/Writing Companion** page 46.

Reflect Ask children to reflect on each goal and fill in the bars to show what they know now. Explain that they will fill in the bars on page 47 at the end of the week to show their progress.

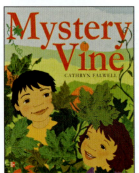

Literature Big Book

OBJECTIVES

Retell stories, including key details, and demonstrate understanding of their central message or lesson.

Make and confirm predictions.

ELA ACADEMIC LANGUAGE

- *ellipses*
- Cognate: *elipsis*

Close Reading Routine

Read DOK 1–2

- Identify important ideas and details.
- Take notes and retell.
- Use prompts as needed.

Reread DOK 2–3

- Analyze the text, craft, and structure.
- Use the Reread minilessons.

Integrate DOK 3–4

- Integrate knowledge and ideas.
- Make text-to-text connections.
- Complete the Show Your Knowledge task.
- Inspire action.

Read

Mystery Vine

Connect to Concept: Watch It Grow! Tell children that they will now listen to a story about a family that finds a mysterious vine growing in their garden.

Genre: Realistic Fiction Explain that this story is realistic fiction. Say: *Realistic fiction stories are made-up stories that have characters, settings, and events that could happen in real life.*

Anchor Chart Review the Make and Confirm Predictions anchor chart.

Make and Confirm Predictions Review that we can use text features, such as illustrations, to predict what will happen next. We can also use text features to help us correct or confirm our predictions.

> **Think Aloud** I will use the illustration on the cover to make a prediction before I read. I see leaves. I predict this story will be about plants. I will continue reading to see if my prediction is correct.

Read the Selection

Display the Big Book. Have children point to the title and author name as you read them aloud. Note that the author is also the illustrator. Review the Make and Confirm Predictions anchor chart.

Set Purpose Say: *Let's read to find out what grew on the mystery vine.*

As you read, confirm or correct the prediction you made above. Encourage children to make and confirm their own predictions as they listen.

A C T Access Complex Text

If the complexity of the text makes it hard for children to understand, use the Access Complex Text prompts.

Prior Knowledge

Children may not be familiar with caring for a garden.

- Explain what the family is doing in the garden, the purpose of the tools and trellis, and the steps required to plant a garden.

Vocabulary

The text contains garden-related words that children may not know, such as *vine* and *blossom*.

- Point out the vine and blossoms in the illustrations and define the words for children.

Concepts of Print: Punctuation Within Sentences Point out the ellipses on page 27 of *Mystery Vine*. Explain that ellipses fall in the middle of a sentence and indicate that the reader should pause. Explain that commas also fall within a sentence and mean that the reader should pause briefly. Have children identify commas in the text. See prompts in the Big Book for modeling concepts of print.

Focus on Narrator Review that the narrator can be a speaker outside the story. Then say: *We've also learned that the narrator can be a person in the story. Words such as* my, we, *and* I *tell you the narrator is a person in the story.* Read aloud page 11. *What words tell you the narrator is a person in the story?*

Respond to the Text

After reading, prompt children to share what they learned about the Mystery Vine and how the plant changed as it grew. Discuss children's predictions and whether they were correct.

Model Retelling

Pause to model retelling portions of the selection. Say: *I can put story details and events into my own words. I read that the family planted seeds in the springtime. They pulled the weeds and watched as the plants sprouted.* Continue to model retelling the entire story, using your own words to tell the important events and details in the correct order. Have children practice retelling a page or two.

Writing Fluency

To increase children's writing fluency, have them write as much as they can about the story for five minutes. Then have partners share.

English Language Learners

Make and Confirm Predictions Display pages 20 and 21. Point to the pumpkins. *These are pumpkins.* Have children point as they repeat *pumpkins. Will the family eat the pumpkins? Let's make a prediction.* Provide a sentence frame: I predict the family will eat the pumpkins. *Let's keep reading to check our prediction.*

For additional support, see the **ELL Small Group Guide,** pp. 122-123.

MODEL FLUENCY

Phrasing Turn to page 11 of *Mystery Vine*. Point out the commas. Say: *When you come to a comma in a sentence, you should pause briefly before continuing to read.* Read aloud page 11 with slightly exaggerated phrasing. Have children identify other sentences they see with commas.

DIGITAL TOOLS

Retell

❯ STUDENT CHECK-IN

Have partners tell one prediction they made as they listened to the story. Have children reflect using the Check-In Routine.

✔ CHECK FOR SUCCESS

Can children make and confirm predictions about a story?

❯ Small Group Instruction

If No

🔴 **Approaching** Reteach pp. T144–T45

If Yes

🔵 **On** Review pp. T154–T155

🟢 **Beyond** Extend pp. T158–T159

Display the Sound-Spelling Card *train*. Point to the letters a_e.

1. **Teacher:** What are the letters?   **Children:** a, e
2. **Teacher:** What's the sound?   **Children:** /ā/

Continue the routine for previously taught sounds.

LEARNING GOALS

- We can say words that have the same beginning sound.
- We can read and blend words with long *i*.

OBJECTIVES

Demonstrate understanding of spoken words, syllables, and sounds (phonemes).

Know final -e and common vowel team conventions for representing long vowel sounds.

Decode regularly spelled one-syllable words.

Print all upper- and lowercase letters.

Recognize and generate alliteration.

ELA ACADEMIC LANGUAGE

- *alliteration*
- Cognate: *aliteración*

 **TEACH IN SMALL GROUP**

Word Work lessons can be taught in small groups.

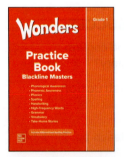

**Phonological Awareness:
Page 177
Phonics: Page 179
Handwriting: Page 184**

---

 5 mins

Phonological Awareness

Recognize and Generate Alliteration

1 **Model** Say: *The same sound repeated in several words is called alliteration. Listen as I say a sentence:* Len likes limes. *I hear the same sound, the /l/ sound, at the beginning of* Len, likes, *and* limes. *I can change the name* Len *to another name that begins with /l/ to make a new sentence. Listen:* Lisa likes limes.

2 **Guided Practice/Practice** Have children practice identifying initial sounds and then generating a new alliterative sentence. *I am going to say some sentences. Tell me the sound you hear at the beginning of most words. Then change the name to another name that begins with that sound. Say the new sentence.* Guide practice and provide corrective feedback as needed.

Dale dives deep.	Ted told a tale.	Hannah hiked up a hill.
Bob built a barn.	Cate can clap.	Rob ran in a race.

If children need additional practice recognizing alliteration, see **Practice Book** page 177 or the online activity.

---

5 mins

Phonics

MULTIMODAL

Introduce Long *i: i_e*

1 **Model** Display the *five* Sound-Spelling Card. Teach /ī/ spelled *i_e* using *ride* and *bike*. *This is the* five *Sound-Spelling Card. The sound is /ī/ . Today we will learn a spelling for the /ī/ sound. Write* rid. *Then say: This word has the short* i *sound, /i/. I'll add an* e *to the end. The new word is* ride. *The letters* i *and* e *act together to make the long* i *sound, /ī/. Listen as I say the word: /rīd/. I'll say /ī/ as I write* ride *several times.*

5
i y i_e
igh ie
five

**Sound-Spelling
Card**

2 **Guided Practice/Practice** Have children practice connecting the letters *i_e* to the sound /ī/ by writing it. *Now do it with me. Say /ī/ as I write* ride *and say /r ī ī īd/. This time, write the word five times as you say the /ī/ sound. Now write the word* bit. *Add an* e *to the end to make* bite.

Blend Words with Long *i: i_e*

| l | i | n | e |

1 Model Display the **Word-Building Cards** *l, i, n, e.* Model how to blend the sounds. *This is* l. *It stands for /l/. These are the letters* i *and* e. *Together they stand for /ī/. This is* n. *It stands for /n/. Listen as I blend these sounds together: /līīīn/. Say it with me:* line. Continue by modeling the words *nine, wide, prize,* and *white.*

2 Guided Practice/Practice Display the Lesson 1 Phonics Practice Activity. Read each word in the first row, blending the sounds; for example: */pīīīn/. The word is* pine. Have children blend each word with you. Prompt children to read the connected text, sounding out the decodable words.

pine	pile	mile	like	life	ripe
vine	shine	smile	while	dime	yikes
bit	bite	rid	ride	kit	kite
take	skate	slide	trash	thing	drive

Mike likes to ride his bike fast.

Kate got quite a big prize.

Clive and Jake will hike for a mile.

Lesson 1 Phonics Practice Activity

If children need additional practice blending words with long *i*, see **Practice Book** page 179 or the online activity.

Corrective Feedback

Sound Error Model the sound that children missed, then have them repeat the sound. Say: *My turn.* Tap under the letter and say: *Sound? /ī/. What's the sound?* Return to the beginning of the word. Say: *Let's start over.* Blend the word with children.

Daily Handwriting

Throughout the week, teach uppercase and lowercase *Vv* using the online Handwriting models. Model writing the letters, using the strokes as shown. Children can practice *Vv* using Practice Book page 184. For additional support, use the models in the **Reading/Writing Companion.**

ELL ENGLISH LANGUAGE LEARNERS

Phonological Awareness, Model Model another example. Say: *Listen for the /s/ sound that repeats at the beginning of these words. Sam sits still.* Emphasize the /s/ sound as you say the sentence. Have children repeat the sentence and sound. Change the name to Sara, and repeat.

Phonics See pages 8-9 of the **Language Transfers Handbook.** In Cantonese, there is only an approximate transfer for /i/. Emphasize /i/, and show correct mouth position.

DIGITAL TOOLS

To differentiate instruction for key skills, use the results of this activity.

Phonics: Practice

For more practice, use these activities.

Word Work

Phonological Awareness

Handwriting

FORMATIVE ASSESSMENT

STUDENT CHECK-IN

Phonics Have partners read a long *i* word to each other. Have children reflect using the Check-In Routine.

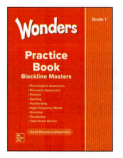

5 mins

Spelling

Words with Long *i: i_e*

Dictation Follow the Spelling Dictation routine to help children transfer their growing knowledge of sound-spellings to writing. After dictation, give the spelling pretest in the **Practice Book** on page 181.

Pretest After dictation, pronounce each spelling word. Read the sentence and pronounce the word again. Ask children to say each word softly, stretching the sounds, before writing it. After the pretest, display the spelling words and write each word as you say the letter names. Have children check their words using the Practice Book page.

like	Do you **like** to paint?
spike	He pounded the **spike** into the fence.
ride	I will go for a **ride** on the bus.
hide	Where did you **hide** my toy?
bike	He rode his **bike** uphill.
mine	This book is **mine**.
make	Look what a great cake I can **make**!
came	My friends **came** to my party.
water	May I have a drink of **water**?
should	You **should** read this book.

English Language Learners should use this list for their spelling pretest.

▶▶ DIFFERENTIATED SPELLING LISTS

Approaching Level bike, hide, like, ride

Beyond Level bike, hide, like, mine, ride, shine, spike, twice

English Language Learners

Spelling, Dictation Review the meanings of the spelling words. Pantomime riding a bike. *I ride a bike.* Have children pretend to ride a bike as they repeat the sentence. Point to your shoes. *These shoes are mine.* Point to a child's shoes. *Those shoes are not mine.* Have children point to their own shoes and another child's shoes and repeat both sentences.

In a Flash: High-Frequency Words

today

1. **Teacher:** Read the word.   **Children:** today
2. **Teacher:** Spell the word.   **Children:** t-o-d-a-y
3. **Teacher:** Write the word.   **Children write the word.**

Repeat with *away, now, some, why, way* from last week.

High-Frequency Words

MULTIMODAL

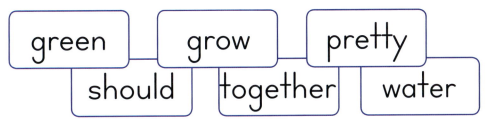

green   grow   pretty

should   together   water

1 **Model** Display the **High-Frequency Word Cards** *green, grow, pretty, should, together,* and *water.* Use the Read/Spell/Write routine to teach each word.

- **Read** Point to and say the word *green. This is the word* green. *Say it with me:* green. *The grass is green.*

- **Spell** *The word* green *is spelled* g-r-e-e-n. *Spell it with me.*

- **Write** *Now write the word on your Response Board as we say each letter:* g-r-e-e-n.

- Follow the same steps to introduce *grow, pretty, should, together,* and *water.*

- As children spell each word, point out *-ould* in *should* and compare to the previously taught high-frequency word *could.*

- Have partners say sentences using each word.

2 **Guided Practice** Have children read the sentences. Prompt them to identify the high-frequency words in connected text and to blend the decodable words.

1. My new bike is **green** and white.
2. The grass will **grow.**
3. This is a **pretty** dress.
4. When **should** I come to see you?
5. We can play **together.**
6. Do you want a drink of **water**?

3 **Practice** Display the High-Frequency Word Cards. Have children use a pointer to highlight specific words. Have them say each highlighted word.

For additional practice with high-frequency words, have children complete the online activities.

ELL **ENGLISH LANGUAGE LEARNERS**

High-Frequency Words, Model Say: *We can use* should *to talk about choices. What should I eat? Should I eat an apple or a cookie? I should eat an apple.* Repeat with another choice, such as, *Should I wear a green shirt or a red shirt?* Then have partners practice using the word *should* to talk about choices. Provide sentence frames: Should I drink water or juice? I should drink water.

FORMATIVE ASSESSMENT

◆ STUDENT CHECK-IN

Spelling Have partners dictate one long *i* word from the list for each other to write.

High-Frequency Words Have partners take turns reading the high-frequency words.

Have children reflect using the Check-In Routine.

✔ CHECK FOR SUCCESS

Rubric Use your online rubric to record children's progress.

Can children read and decode words with long *i: i_e?*

Can children recognize and read high-frequency words?

◆ Small Group Instruction

If No

● **Approaching** Reteach pp. T146–T151

● **ELL** Develop pp. T146–T151

If Yes

● **On** Review pp. T154–T156

● **Beyond** Extend pp. T158–T159

LEARNING GOALS

We can read and understand a play.

OBJECTIVES

Decode regularly spelled one-syllable words.

Know final -e and common vowel team conventions for representing long vowel sounds.

Recognize and read grade-appropriate irregularly spelled words.

With prompting and support, read prose and poetry of appropriate complexity for grade 1.

ELA ACADEMIC LANGUAGE

• prediction, play

• Cognate: predicción

Close Reading Routine

Read   DOK 1–2

• Identify important ideas and details.

• Take notes and retell.

• Use prompts as needed.

Reread   DOK 2–3

• Analyze the text, craft, and structure.

• Use the Reread minilessons.

Integrate   DOK 3–4

• Integrate knowledge and ideas.

• Make text-to-text connections.

• Complete the Show Your Knowledge task.

• Inspire action.

Read

 10 mins

"Time to Plant!"

Focus on Foundational Skills

• Review: *green, grow, pretty, should, together,* and *water.*

• Review that the long *i* sound can be spelled *i_e.*

• Display: *narrator, garden, vegetables, seeds,* and *rain.* Spell and model reading them. Have children read the words as you point to them.

Read the Shared Read

Anchor Chart Create a Play anchor chart.

Genre: Drama: Play Tell children "Time to Plant!" is a play. A play is a story intended to be performed. It often has a narrator telling the story, and a setting. It has dialogue spoken by each character. Write these features on the chart. Have volunteers share a play they know.

Make and Confirm Predictions

Explain Tell children that as they read they can make predictions about what they think will happen. Children can use characteristics of the genre, such as dialogue, to confirm whether their predictions were correct. Remind children that they can correct their predictions as needed.

Connect to Concept: Watch It Grow!

Explain that this week, they are reading about how things change as they grow. Children can describe how living things change.

Take Notes As children read the selection, you may wish to have them take notes in the boxes provided. Children may take notes by:

• writing the letters *i* and *e*

• writing a word spelled with the *i_e* pattern or a high-frequency word

Have children read each page. Then read the prompts one at a time.

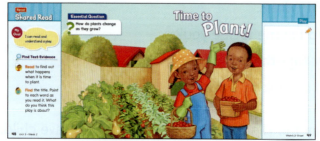

Reading/Writing Companion, pp. 48–49

SET PURPOSE

Say: *Let's read to find out what happens when it's time to plant.*

MAKE AND CONFIRM PREDICTIONS

Have children use the title to make a prediction about the play.

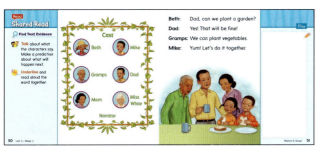

Reading/Writing Companion, pp. 50–51

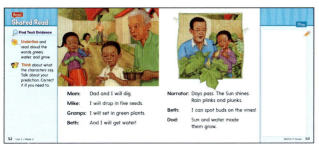

Reading/Writing Companion, pp. 52–53

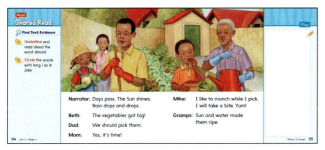

Reading/Writing Companion, pp. 54–55

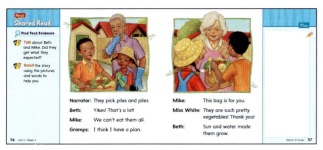

Reading/Writing Companion, pp. 56–57

Respond to the Text

Have partners discuss what Beth and her family do when they have picked too many vegetables. Use this sentence starter: *Beth and her family . . . .*

MAKE AND CONFIRM PREDICTIONS

Have partners discuss what the characters say. Have them predict what happens next.

HIGH-FREQUENCY WORDS

Have children underline and read aloud the word *together*.

HIGH-FREQUENCY WORDS

Have children underline and read aloud *green, water,* and *grow*.

MAKE AND CONFIRM PREDICTIONS

Have children think about what the characters say. Partners can discuss their prediction and correct it, as needed.

HIGH-FREQUENCY WORDS

Have children underline and read aloud the word *should*.

PHONICS

Have children circle and read aloud the words with long *i* as in *bike*.

COMPREHENSION

Have partners discuss Beth and Mike. Did they get what they expected? How do they know?

RETELL

Have partners use the pictures and any new words they learned to retell "Time to Plant!"

SPOTLIGHT ON LANGUAGE

Page 51 Point to *yum* on page 51. Read the word with expression, and have children repeat. Explain that we say *yum* when something tastes really good. Pretend to take a bite of something. Say: *Yum! That was good!* while rubbing your stomach. *What made Mike say* yum? (He took a bite of a vegetable from the garden.) *Talk to your partner about a food that makes you say* yum.

FOCUS ON FLUENCY

With partners, have children reread "Time to Plant!" to develop fluency. Children should focus on their accuracy, trying to say each word correctly. Then have them reread the story so it sounds like speech. Remind children the goal is to keep practicing until they can read the words automatically.

DIFFERENTIATED READING

● **English Language Learners**
Before reading, have children listen to a summary of the selection, available in multiple languages.

❯ STUDENT CHECK-IN

Have children reflect on their retelling using the Check-In Routine.

LEARNING GOALS

- We can learn to write sentences with sensory details.
- We can identify present-tense verbs.

OBJECTIVES

Write narratives in which they recount two or more appropriately sequenced events, include some details regarding what happened, use temporal words to signal event order, and provide some sense of closure.

Use verbs to convey a sense of past, present, and future.

Use singular and plural nouns with matching verbs in basic sentences.

ELA ACADEMIC LANGUAGE

- *sensory, present tense*
- Cognates: *sensorial, presente*

COLLABORATIVE CONVERSATIONS

Turn and Talk Review this routine.

Child 1: They will plant peppers next.
Child 2: Why do you think that?
Child 1: They didn't have peppers in their basket.

Display the speech bubbles "What do you mean?" and "Why do you think that?" Have partners use them to practice collaborating.

DIFFERENTIATED WRITING

● **English Language Learners** For more writing support, see **ELL Small Group Guide**, p. 124.

Modeled Writing

5 mins

Write About the Shared Read

Build Oral Language Read aloud the prompt. Ask: *Which vegetables might the family plant next? Add a page to the play.* Have partners use the Turn and Talk routine to discuss vegetables the family might plant.

Model Writing Sentences Say: *I will write new lines about vegetables the family plants next.* Point to the picture on page 56. *I don't see any corn in this basket of vegetables. I think the family might plant corn next.*

Sample Teacher Talk

- Listen to my lines: Mike: I want to plant big, tall corn plants. Beth: Yes, I like sweet, crunchy corn too! My first word is *Mike*. *Mike* has the /ī/ sound in the middle. I'll write *Mike*. PHONICS

- The next word is *I*. I know I need to capitalize the letter *i* when it's a word. I'll write *I*. WRITING SKILL

- The next word is *want*. I look at the Word Bank to find *want*. It's spelled *w-a-n-t*. I'll write *want*. HIGH-FREQUENCY WORDS

- Continue writing the remaining words. Then point to *big* and *tall* and say: These are sensory details that tell what the plant looks like. Repeat for *sweet* and *crunchy*. TRAIT: WORD CHOICE

> Which vegetables might the family plant next? Add a page to the play.
>
> Mike: I want to plant big, tall corn plants.
>
> Beth: Yes, I like sweet, crunchy corn too!

Writing Practice

Analyze and Write Sentences Have children turn to page 58 in their **Reading/Writing Companion**. Guide children to analyze the sentences using the prompts. Review the Writing Skill and Trait boxes, as necessary. Then have children write and analyze their own sentences.

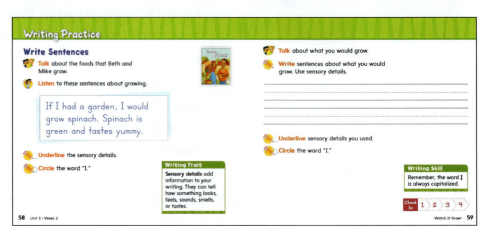

Reading/Writing Companion, pp. 58–59

5 mins

Grammar

Present-Tense Verbs

1 **Model** Review that a verb is an action word. Explain that a present-tense verb tells about an action happening now. Display and read: Spike <u>hikes</u> up the hill. *When a present-tense verb tells about one noun, it ends in -s.* Display the sentences: Jan and Dave <u>wipe</u> off the plates. I <u>ride</u> my bike. You <u>ride</u> your bike.

Explain when a present-tense verb tells about more than one noun, like *Jan and Dave*, it does not end in -s. When the naming word is *I* or *you*, the present-tense verb does not end in -s.

2 **Guided Practice/Practice** Write and read aloud these sentences. Guide children to identify present-tense verbs and explain why they do or do not have an -s at the end.

They swim in the lake. (swim; *they* is more than one)

Ike thumps the drum. (thumps; *Ike* is one)

The kids wave on the bus. (wave; *kids* is more than one)

 Talk About It Have partners orally generate a sentence using a present-tense verb and one noun.

Link to Writing Review the Modeled Writing to identify present-tense verbs. Have children point out the present-tense verbs.

 # English Language Learners

Use the following scaffolds with **Grammar, Model.**

Beginning

Read and point to *hikes* in the first example. Say: Hikes *is the verb.* Have children repeat. Explain why it is a present-tense verb. Then ask: *What is the present-tense verb?* (hikes)

Intermediate

Have children identify the verb. *Does* hikes *tell about an action that is happening now?* Help children respond as needed.

Advanced/Advanced High

How do you know hikes *is a verb?* (It shows action.) Have partners discuss how they can tell *hikes* is a present-tense verb and why there is an -s at the end of *hikes.*

DIGITAL TOOLS

Use these activities to practice grammar.

 Grammar

 Grammar Song

 Grammar Video

LEARNING GOALS

We can learn and use new vocabulary words.

OBJECTIVES

Identify real-life connections between words and their use.

Discuss the Essential Question.

Develop oral language.

ELA ACADEMIC LANGUAGE

- *example*
- Cognate: *ejemplo*

TEACH IN SMALL GROUP

🟣 **ELL** See the Teacher Talk on the back of the **Visual Vocabulary Cards** for additional support.

🟠 **Approaching** Group children with students in a higher level to practice saying the words. Then children can draw their own picture of the word.

🔵🟢 **On Level** and **Beyond Level** Have children look up each word in the online **Visual Glossary.**

FORMATIVE ASSESSMENT

❯ STUDENT CHECK-IN

Have partners use a vocabulary word in a sentence. Have children reflect using the Check-In Routine.

LESSON FOCUS

READING
Revisit the Essential Question
Read Interactive Read Aloud:
"The Great Big Gigantic Turnip"
- Use Context Clues
Word Work
- Review Long *i: i_e*

Reread Shared Read:
"Time to Plant!"
- Review Genre
- Introduce Skill
WRITING
- Interactive Writing
- Review Grammar

Reading/Writing Companion, pp. 44–53

 5 mins

Oral Language

 MULTIMODAL

 ### Essential Question
How do plants change as they grow?

Remind children that this week you have been talking and reading about how plants change as they grow. Say: *We talked about the little sprout and how the family grew vegetables in their garden.*

Oral Vocabulary Words

Review the oral vocabulary words *bloom* and *sprout* from Lesson 1. Use the Define/Example/Ask routine on the print or digital **Visual Vocabulary Cards** to introduce the oral vocabulary words *assist, grasped,* and *spied.* Prompt children to use the words as they discuss how plants grow.

Oral Vocabulary Routine

Define: Assist means "to help."

Example: Max assists his teacher by handing back papers to the class.

Ask: How can you assist the teacher?

Define: Grasped means "held tightly."

Example: Maya grasped the string of the kite so it would not blow away.

Ask: What is something you grasp when you write?

Define: Spied means "noticed" or "saw."

Example: The cat spied a mouse sneaking across the table.

Ask: What would you do if you spied a mouse?

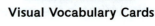

Visual Vocabulary Cards

OPTION
10 mins

Read the Interactive Read Aloud

Connect to Concept

Tell children that you will be reading a story about a turnip that grows very, very big. Display the **Interactive Read-Aloud Cards.**

Read the title "The Great Big, Gigantic Turnip."

Set Purpose Read or play the selection as you display the cards. *Let's read to find out how the turnip changes as it grows.* Remind children to listen carefully as you read aloud the text.

Oral Vocabulary Use the Oral Vocabulary prompts as you read the selection to provide more practice with the words in context.

Context Clues: Sentence Clues Tell children that as you read, they can use clues in the sentence and what they already know to help them understand the meaning of unfamiliar words. Model the strategy using a sentence on Card 1.

Teacher Think Aloud When I read "May this small seed sprout and grow a turnip…," I wondered what the word *turnip* meant. I looked for clues in the sentence to help me. The word *feast* helps me understand that a turnip is something you eat.

Continue reading aloud the selection, stopping to ask children to use context clues to figure out the meaning of unfamiliar words.

Student Think Along After you read the top of Card 2, stop and ask: What clues in the sentence help you understand the meaning of the word *yanked*? The sentence says that the man also *tugged* and *pulled* at the turnip. That helps me understand that *yanked* means he tried to move the turnip out of the ground.

Build Knowledge: Make Connections

Talk About the Text Have partners discuss how the turnip plant in the story changes as it grows.

Add to the Anchor Chart Record any new ideas on the Build Knowledge anchor chart.

Add to the Word Bank Then add words related to the way plants change as they grow to a separate section of the Word Bank.

"The Great Big, Gigantic Turnip"

five

Display the Sound-Spelling Card *five.*
Point to the letters i_e.

1. **Teacher:** What are the letters?   **Children:** i, e
2. **Teacher:** What's the sound?   **Children:** /ī/
3. **Teacher:** What's the word?   **Children:** five

Continue the routine for previously taught sounds.

LEARNING GOALS

- We can delete the first sound in a word to make a new word.
- We can read and build words with long *i.*
- We can make nouns plural by adding *-s.*

OBJECTIVES

Orally produce single-syllable words by blending sounds (phonemes), including consonant blends.

Know final -e and common vowel team conventions for representing long vowel sounds.

Decode regularly spelled one-syllable words.

Read words with inflectional endings.

Delete initial phonemes to form new words.

ELA ACADEMIC LANGUAGE

- *plurals, noun*
- Cognate: *plurales*

 **TEACH IN SMALL GROUP**

Word Work lessons can be taught in small groups.

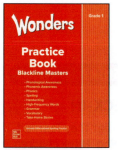

Phonemic Awareness: Page 178

OPTION
5 mins

Phonemic Awareness

Phoneme Deletion

1 **Model** Say: *Listen carefully as I say a word:* smile. *The word* smile *has four sounds* /s/ /m/ /ī/ /l/. *I'll take away the first sound,* /s/, *and make a new word with three sounds:* /m/ /ī/ /l/, *mile.*

Continue modeling phoneme deletion with the following word sets.

bride/ride   gripe/ripe   slime/lime   spike/pike

2 **Guided Practice/Practice** Have children practice deleting phonemes to create new words. Say: *Listen as I say a word. The word is* spine, /s/ /p/ /ī/ /n/. *Now I'll say the word without the first sound to make a new word:* /p/ /ī/ /n/, *pine.* Provide corrective feedback as needed.

spine	swipe	stale	Fred	flake
slime	pride	plane	crate	brake

If children need additional practice adding phonemes, see **Practice Book** page 178 or the online activity.

5 mins

Phonics

MULTIMODAL

Review Long *i*: *i_e*

1 **Model** Display the *five* **Sound-Spelling Card**. Say: *This is the* five *Sound-Spelling Card. The sound* /ī/ *can be spelled* i-consonant-e. *You can hear the* /ī/ *sound in the middle of words such as* life *and* time.

five

Sound-Spelling Card

2 **Guided Practice/Practice** Have children practice connecting the letters and sound. Point to the *i_e* spelling on the Sound-Spelling Card. *What are these letters? What sound do they stand for?* Provide corrective feedback as needed.

Blend Words with Long *i*: *i_e*

1 **Model** Display **Word-Building Cards** *r, i, d, e* to form the word *ride.* Model how to blend the sounds to say the word. *The letter* r *stands for* /r/. *The letters* i *and* e *together stand for* /ī/. *This is the letter* d. *It stands for* /d/. *Listen as I blend:* /rīīīd/. Continue by modeling the words *like, while, swipe,* and *slide.*

2 **Guided Practice/Practice** Display the **Word-Building Cards** for the letters *f, i, v, e. Let's blend these sounds together: /f/ /ī/ /v/, /fffīīīv/,* five. Repeat the routine with the words *nine, ripe, size, hike, dive, drive, glide, pride, spike, lime, wide, smile,* and *tile.* Guide practice and provide corrective feedback as needed.

Build Words with Long *i*: *i_e*

Provide children with Word-Building Cards *a–z*. Have children put the letters in alphabetic order as quickly as possible.

1 **Model** Display the Word-Building Cards *d, i, m, e.* Blend: /d/ /ī/ /m/, /dīīīmmm/, *dime.* Replace *m* with *n* and repeat with *dine.* Change *n* to *v* and repeat with *dive.*

2 **Guided Practice/Practice** Continue building the words: *drive, five, file, fine, nine, pine, pipe, ripe, ride,* and *bride.* Guide children to build and blend each word. Then dictate the words and have children write the words.

For additional practice decoding long *i* in connected text, see Build Words with Long *i* lessons on T149 and T156.

Structural Analysis

Plurals

1 **Model** Write and read aloud *bike* and *bikes.* Underline the inflectional ending *-s.* Tell children that adding *-s* to a noun, or naming word, makes the noun tell about more than one.

Say *bike* and *bikes* again. Use each word in a sentence to show that adding *-s* to *bike* means more than one bike: *I ride my bike. I see three more bikes.* Then write and say *bite, bites; hive, hives;* and *case, cases.* Point out that the letter *-s* at the end of a final *-e* word can stand for /s/ as in *bites,* /z/ as in *hives,* or /ez/ as in *cases.* Use each word in a sentence.

2 **Guided Practice/Practice** Write the following words on the board: *dime, cape, kite, lake, vine, snake, plate.* Have children add *-s* to each word and then use each word in a sentence. Guide practice and provide corrective feedback as needed.

ELL **ENGLISH LANGUAGE LEARNERS**

Blend Words with Long *i*: *i_e*, Guided Practice/Practice Review the meanings of example words that can be explained or demonstrated in a concrete way. For example, hold up the number of fingers to show *nine.* Model the actions for *hike* and *dive* saying, *I can hike up a hill and dive into the water.* Provide sentence frames: I have nine books. I dive into the pool. Correct grammar and pronunciation as needed.

DIGITAL TOOLS

To differentiate instruction for key skills, use the results of this activity.

Phonics: Practice

For more practice, use these activities.

Phonemic Awareness
Structural Analysis

FORMATIVE ASSESSMENT

● STUDENT CHECK-IN

Phonics Have partners build a word with the long *i* sound.

Structural Analysis Have partners share a sentence using a plural noun.

Have children reflect using the Check-In Routine.

LESSON 2

OBJECTIVES

Use conventional spelling for words with common spelling patterns and for frequently occurring irregular words.

Recognize and read grade-appropriate irregularly spelled words.

Sort words with long *i.*

ELA ACADEMIC LANGUAGE

- *patterns*

DIGITAL TOOLS

To differentiate instruction for key skills, use the results of this activity.

High-Frequency Words: Practice

For more practice, use this activity.

Word Work

Spelling

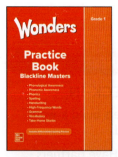

Spelling: On Level, Page 182
Approaching, Page 182A
Beyond, Page 182B
High-Frequency Words: Page 187

Spelling

5 mins

MULTIMODAL

Word Sort with *-ike, -ide, -ine*

1 **Model** Display the online **Spelling Word Cards** for Unit 3 Week 2, one at a time. Have children read each word, listening for the long *i* and ending sound.

Use cards with the endings *-ike, -ide,* and *-ine* to create a three-column chart. Then model sorting words *hike, side,* and *fine* below the correct word endings. Say each word and pronounce the sounds: /h/ /ī/ /k/; /s/ /ī/ /d/; /f/ /ī/ /n/. Say each word again, emphasizing the long *i* plus final consonant sound. Ask children to chorally spell each word.

2 **Guided Practice/Practice** Have children place each Spelling Word Card in the column with the words containing the same sound-spelling patterns.

When completed, have children chorally read the words in each column. Then call out a word. Have a child find the word card and point to it as the class chorally spells the word.

If children need additional practice spelling words with long *i,* see differentiated **Practice Book** pages 182–182B or the online activity.

-ike	-ide
-ine	like
spike	ride
hide	bike
mine	

Unit 3 • Week 2   Spelling Word Cards

Analyze Errors/Articulation Support

Use children's pretest errors to analyze spelling problems and provide corrective feedback. For example, some children will leave off the final letter *e.*

Work with children to recognize the difference in vowel sound and spelling in minimal contrast pairs such as *bit/bite, hid/hide, rid/ride, kit/kite,* and *rip/ripe.*

Say each word. Have children repeat. Focus on the medial vowel sound and how the mouth forms that sound. Then have children write the words. Emphasize that when they hear the long *i* sound, they use the *i_e* spelling pattern. Tell children they will learn other long *i* spellings in upcoming weeks.

OPTION 5 mins

High-Frequency Words

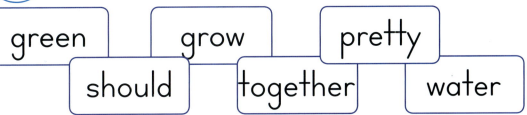

green   grow   pretty   should   together   water

1 **Guided Practice** Say each word and have children Read/Spell/Write it.

- Point out irregularities in sound-spellings, such as the /i/ sound spelled with the letter *e* in *pretty*.

2 **Practice** Add the high-frequency words *green, grow, pretty, should, together,* and *water* to the cumulative Word Bank.

- Have children work with a partner to create sentences using the words.

- Have children look at the words and compare their sounds and spellings with words from previous weeks.

- Suggest that they write one sentence about how plants grow.

Cumulative Review Review last week's words *(away, now, some, today, way,* and *why)* by displaying each word and having children read it with automaticity.

Have children independently practice identifying, spelling, and reading high-frequency words using **Practice Book** page 187 or the online activity.

ELL ENGLISH LANGUAGE LEARNERS

Use these scaffolds with **High-Frequency Words, Practice.**

Beginning
Provide a sentence frame to help children write about how plants grow: Plants need water.

Intermediate
Have children add a detail to their sentence: Some plants grow tall.

Advanced/Advanced High
Have partners write their own sentence about how plants grow. Point out that they may want to use the words *should, water, grow* and *green* in their sentence.

FORMATIVE ASSESSMENT

› STUDENT CHECK-IN

Spelling Have partners share one column of words they sorted.

High-Frequency Words Have partners quiz each other using the High-Frequency Word Cards.

Have children reflect using the Check-In Routine.

✔ CHECK FOR SUCCESS

Rubric Use your online rubric to record children's progress.

Can children read and decode words with long *i: i_e?*

Can children recognize and read high-frequency words?

› Small Group Instruction

If No

🔴 **Approaching** Reteach pp. T146–T151

🟣 **ELL** Develop pp. T146–T151

If Yes

🔵 **On** Review pp. T154–T156

🟢 **Beyond** Extend pp. T158–T159

LESSON 2

- We can tell what makes a story a play.
- We can identify the sequence of events in a play.

OBJECTIVES

Describe characters and major events in a story, using key details.

Identify who is telling the story at various points in a text.

Understand drama genre.

ELA ACADEMIC LANGUAGE

- *play, event, sequence*
- Cognates: *evento, secuencia*

 **TEACH IN SMALL GROUP**

🔴 **Approaching** Have partners work together to complete the chart.

🔵🟢 **On Level** and **Beyond Level** Have children write their responses independently and then discuss them.

🟣 **ELL** For specific comprehension support in reading "Time to Plant!" see **ELL Small Group Guide**, pp. 118-119.

DIGITAL TOOLS

To differentiate instruction for key skills, use the results of this activity.

 Main Story Elements: Sequence of Events

---

Reread

 10 mins

"Time to Plant!"

Genre: Play

1 **Model** Tell children they will now reread the play "Time to Plant!" Have children turn to page 60 in their **Reading/Writing Companion**. Review the characteristics of a play. A play:

- is a story that is meant to be performed.
- has dialogue that is spoken by each character.
- has a setting.
- often has a narrator who tells the story.

Explain that dialogue is words the characters speak. Dialogue appears after each character's name so the reader knows who is speaking.

Display "Time to Plant!" in the Reading/Writing Companion. Say: *On page 52, we see Beth behind her house, helping to start the garden. She is a character in the play and the garden is the setting. On page 52 she says, "And I will get water!" This is dialogue spoken by Beth. It shows she is excited about the garden.* Model filling in the first row on page 61 by writing Beth's name and what we learn from the dialogue.

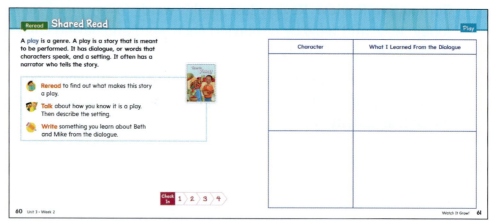

Reading/Writing Companion, pp. 60–61

2 **Guided Practice/Practice** Guide children to copy the information on page 61 of their Reading/Writing Companion. As they continue to reread, have children talk about how they know this is a play. They can describe the characters and setting. Then turn to page 55. Ask: *Who takes a bite?* (Mike) *What does he say?* (Yum)

Guide children to write the character's name in the graphic organizer. Ask children what they learned about Mike from his dialogue on that page. They can add this information to the graphic organizer. Offer help as needed.

Main Story Elements: Sequence of Events

 Anchor Chart Create a Sequence of Events anchor chart. Say: *The sequence of events is the order in which events appear in a story. Think about what happens* first, next, then, *and* last *to understand the sequence of events.* Write this information on the chart.

1 **Model** Display page 62 of the **Reading/Writing Companion.** Have children talk about the order of events in the play. Then model filling in the first box on page 63 by finding the first main event. Say: *On page 51, Beth asks if they can plant a garden. Dad says yes. On page 52, the family plants a garden. So planting a garden is the first main event in the story.* Write this event in the first box.

Reading/Writing Companion, pp. 62–63

2 **Guided Practice/Practice** Guide children to copy what you wrote in the graphic organizer on page 63 of their own Reading/Writing Companion. Then display page 54. Have children reread the page and talk with a partner about what happens next. Then ask: *What is the next main event?* (The plants get big and grow.) Guide children to write this in the second box.

Ask children to find the next two main events in the play and add them to the third and fourth boxes. Offer help as needed.

For more practice, have children complete the online activity.

ELL English Language Learners

Main Story Elements: Sequence of Events, Guided Practice/ Practice Have children point to the word *next* in the graphic organizer. *What happens after the family plants a garden?* The plants grow. Repeat with the word *then.* *What happens then?* The family picks the vegetables. Repeat with the last box. They share.

🗒 BUILD KNOWLEDGE: MAKE CONNECTIONS

Talk About the Text Have partners discuss how the vegetable plants in the play change as they grow.

Write About the Text Then have children add their ideas to their Build Knowledge page of their reader's notebook.

Add to the Anchor Chart Record any new ideas on the Build Knowledge anchor chart.

Add to the Word Bank Then add words related to plants the ways plants change as they grow to a separate section of the Word Bank.

FORMATIVE ASSESSMENT

❯ STUDENT CHECK-IN

Genre Have partners take turns telling why this story is a play.

Skill Have children identify the last two events in the story in the order they happened.

Have children reflect using the Check-In Routine to fill in the bars.

✓ CHECK FOR SUCCESS

Rubric Use your online rubric to record children's progress.

Can children identify the sequence in "Time to Plant!"?

❯ Small Group Instruction

If No

🔶 **Approaching** Reteach pp. T144–T145, T152–T153

If Yes

🔵 **On** Review pp. T154–T155, T157

🟢 **Beyond** Extend pp. T158–T161

OBJECTIVES

Write narratives in which they recount two or more appropriately sequenced events, include some details regarding what happened, use temporal words to signal event order, and provide some sense of closure.

Use verbs to convey a sense of past, present, and future.

Use singular and plural nouns with matching verbs in basic sentences.

ELA ACADEMIC LANGUAGE

- *scene, verb*
- Cognates: *escena, verbo*

COLLABORATIVE CONVERSATIONS

Circulate as partners discuss the prompt. Notice who is not asking questions. Remind them to use the speech bubbles to help generate questions. As you listen to children's conversations, you may write down your observations on children's language development.

DIFFERENTIATED WRITING

⬤ **English Language Learners**
For more writing support, see **ELL Small Group Guide,** p. 124.

---

 5 mins # Interactive Writing

Write About the Shared Read

 Analyze the Prompt Read aloud a new prompt: *Write a scene about what Mike and Beth might make with their vegetables.* Have partners turn and talk about the prompt.

Find Text Evidence Guide children to find text evidence to respond to the prompt. Point to the vegetables on page 56. Ask: *What might they make with these vegetables?* Use a volunteer's response and the sample teacher talk below to write a scene, such as: *Beth: I like spicy vegetable soup. Mike: I will wash the peas. Dad: I can chop the tomatoes and hot peppers.*

Sample Teacher Talk: Share the Pen

- Who knows the ending sound in *Beth*? That's right, /th/. Have a volunteer write *Beth*. PHONICS

- When we use *I* as a word, it is capitalized. Have a volunteer write *I*. WRITING SKILL

- Who can find *like* on the Word Bank and spell it? That's right. *l-i-k-e*. HIGH-FREQUENCY WORDS

- *Spicy* is a sensory detail. It tells how the soup tastes. Have a volunteer write *spicy*. TRAIT: WORD CHOICE

Continue sharing the pen to complete the scene.

> Write a scene about what Mike and Beth might make with their vegetables.
> Beth: I like spicy vegetable soup.
> Mike: I will wash the peas.
> Dad: I can chop the tomatoes and hot peppers.

Analyze the Student Model

Say: *Let's read how another child responded to the prompt.* Have children turn to page 64 of the **Reading/Writing Companion.** Guide them to analyze Elizabeth's writing using the prompts on page 65. Then have children write what they notice. Review the Grammar box, as necessary. Use the Quick Tip box for support.

Reading/Writing Companion, pp. 64–65

5 mins

Grammar

Present-Tense Verbs

1 **Review** Remind children that present-tense verbs tell about an action that is happening right now. Review that when a present-tense verb tells about one noun, it ends in -s. Say: *When it tells about more than one noun or* I *or* you, *it does not end in -s.*

2 **Guided Practice** Write and read the sample sentences. Have partners circle each verb. Then have them create a new sentence using each verb with the words in parentheses.

Jane hides in the bush. (I)

Nate eats lunch. (Nate and Tess)

3 **Practice** Once children have changed the sentences, have them act out each sentence either singly or in pairs and repeat the sentence as they are acting.

For additional practice with present-tense verbs, see **Practice Book** pages 188 or the online activity.

Talk About It

Have partners work together to create more oral sentences that have present-tense verbs.

 # English Language Learners

Grammar, Guided Practice To help children build academic language proficiency, ask them to point to the verb in the first example. *The verb is* hides. *What is the verb?* The verb is <u>hides</u>. Say: Hides *tells something that is happening right now. That makes it a present-tense verb. What kind of verb is* hides*?* It is a <u>present-tense</u> verb. Write three more present-tense verbs on the board: *runs, eats, reads.* Read the words, and have children repeat. Have partners turn and use each verb in a sentence. Provide sentence frames: The boy <u>reads</u>. The dog <u>runs</u>.

DIGITAL TOOLS

Use this activity to practice grammar.

Grammar

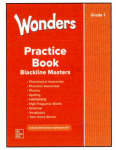
Grammar: Page 188

FORMATIVE ASSESSMENT

⊙ STUDENT CHECK-IN

Writing Have partners share one thing they noticed about the Student Model.

Grammar Have children identify the plural noun in the sentence his or her partner is acting out.

Have children reflect using the Check-In Routine.

OBJECTIVES

Identify real-life connections between words and their use.

Discuss the Essential Question.

Develop oral language.

ELA ACADEMIC LANGUAGE

• *define, example*
• Cognates: *definir, ejemplo*

LESSON FOCUS

READING
Revisit the Essential Question
Reread Literature Big Book:
Mystery Vine
• Use Context Clues
• Analyze Author's Craft
Word Work
• Blend Words with Long *i: i_e*

Read and reread the Anchor Text: *The Big Yuca Plant*
• Review Genre
• Make Predictions
• Review Skill
WRITING
• Independent Writing
• Review Grammar and Introduce Mechanics

Literature Anthology, pp. 28–45

---

5 mins # Oral Language

 MULTIMODAL

 ## Essential Question
How do plants change as they grow?

Remind children that this week you are talking and reading about how plants change while they grow. Remind them of the little boy and the sprout, the pumpkins on the mystery vine, and the family's plants.

Review Oral Vocabulary

Review the oral vocabulary words *bloom, sprout, grasped, assist,* and *spied* using the Define/Example/Ask routine on the print or digital **Visual Vocabulary Cards.** Encourage children to discuss how plants grow when coming up with examples for each word.

Visual Vocabulary Cards

▶ STUDENT CHECK-IN

Have partners use a vocabulary word in a sentence. Have children reflect using the Check-In Routine.

Reread

Mystery Vine

As you reread *Mystery Vine,* have children focus on using text evidence to respond to questions about author's craft. Also model using sentence clues to help children understand the meaning of unfamiliar words.

Author's/Illustrator's Craft Reread pages 6–7. Why might the author use words like *crisp, crunching, bright green,* and *munching* to tell about plants?

Think Aloud When I look at the illustration, I see lettuce. I think the author uses words like *crunching* to help me understand the sound lettuce makes as the children eat it. The words appeal to the senses and make the story more interesting. I notice that the children enjoy eating the vegetables from the garden because they are smiling.

Author's/Illustrator's Craft Reread page 11. The author says that the children "...watched the creeping Mystery Vine." What clues help you understand what the word *creeping* means? (The picture shows the vine growing over the fence. So I can understand that *creeping* means to grow up and over something.)

Context Clues: Sentence Clues Explain to children that they can use other words in a sentence and what they already know to figure out the meaning of an unfamiliar word. Point to the word *blossoms* on page 12.

Model the strategy with this sentence: *The vine grew on, and overnight came yellow blossoms, big and bright.* Say: *I'm not sure what blossoms are. The words* yellow *and* bright *in the sentence are clues. I think* blossoms *are flowers, since I know that flowers can be both yellow and bright.* Continue modeling the strategy for additional words as needed.

Build Knowledge: Make Connections

Talk About the Text Have partners discuss how the vegetable plants in the story, especially the mystery vine, change as they grow.

Add to the Anchor Chart Record any new ideas on the Build Knowledge anchor chart.

Add to the Word Bank Then add words related to how plants change as they grow to a separate section of the Word Bank.

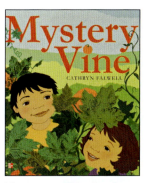

Literature Big Book

We can think about the choices an author makes when writing and illustrating a text.

OBJECTIVES

Use illustrations and details in a story to describe its characters, setting, or events.

Use sentence-level context as a clue to the meaning of a word or phrase.

ELA ACADEMIC LANGUAGE

• *clues, illustration*

• Cognate: *ilustración*

ELL ENGLISH LANGUAGE LEARNERS

Context Clues: Sentence Clues Remind children that in addition to using the words on the page as context clues, they can use the illustrations to help them understand unfamiliar words. Display page 11. Say: *The picture helps me understand the word* creeping *because I can see how the vine is slowly spreading across the garden.* Display page 12. Have children use a sentence frame: The picture of the flowers helps me understand the word blossoms.

FORMATIVE ASSESSMENT

❯ **STUDENT CHECK-IN**

Have partners name one choice the author made. Have children reflect using the Check-In Routine.

In a Flash: Sound-Spellings

Display the Sound-Spelling Card *five*. Point to the letters i_e.

1. **Teacher:** What are the letters?   **Children:** i, e
2. **Teacher:** What's the sound?   **Children:** /ī/
3. **Teacher:** What's the word?   **Children:** five

Continue the routine for previously taught sounds.

LEARNING GOALS

- We can segment sounds in words.
- We can read words with long *i*.
- We can read plural nouns.

OBJECTIVES

Segment spoken single-syllable words into their complete sequence of individual sounds (phonemes).

Know final -e and common vowel team conventions for representing long vowel sounds.

Decode regularly spelled one-syllable words.

Read words with inflectional endings.

ELA ACADEMIC LANGUAGE

- *plurals*
- Cognate: *plurales*

▶ TEACH IN SMALL GROUP

Word Work lessons can be taught in small groups.

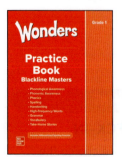

Phonics: Page 180
Structural Analysis: Page 185

---

 5 mins

Phonemic Awareness

MULTIMODAL

Phoneme Segmentation

1 **Model** Use the **Response Board** to show children how to segment the individual sounds in words. Say: *I am going to say the sounds in the word* slide: /s/ /l/ /ī/ /d/. *The first sound is* /s/. *The second sound is* /l/. *The next sound is* /ī/. *The last sound is* /d/. *I'll place a marker in a box on the Response Board for each sound I hear. This word has four sounds:* /s/ /l/ /ī/ /d/, slide.

2 **Guided Practice/Practice** Say: *Let's do some together using your own Response Board. I'm going to say some words. Place a marker in a box to stand for each sound. The word is* bride. *Listen:* /b/ /r/ /ī/ /d/. *Place a marker in the box to stand for each sound. This word has four sounds. Say the word and sounds with me:* bride, /b/ /r/ /ī/ /d/.

ride	mine	mile	smile	prize
time	spike	like	slide	tribe

OPTION **5 mins**

Phonics

Blend Words with Long *i: i_e*

1 **Model** Display the **Word-Building Cards** *g, l, i, d, e*. Model how to blend the sounds. *This is* g. *It stands for* /g/. *This is* l. *It stands for* /l/. *These are the letters* i *and* e. *Together they stand for* /ī/. *This is* d. *It stands for* /d/. *Let's blend all four sounds:* /glīīd/. *The word is* glide. Continue by modeling the words *wipe, size, shine,* and *spine.*

bite	dine	five	hide	lime	mine
pipe	quite	ripe	vine	inside	sunshine
piles	rides	bikes	sides	smiles	lives
dimes	gates	bites	skates	spikes	cakes
slid	slide	slim	slime	white	while

Mike likes ripe red grapes.

We will skate and then ride bikes.

Lesson 3 Phonics Practice Activity

2 **Guided Practice/Practice** Display the Lesson 3 Phonics Practice Activity. Say: *Let's blend the letter sounds to read each word: /b/ /ī/ /t/, /bīīīt/. The word is* bite. Have children blend each word with you.

Prompt children to read the connected text, sounding out the decodable words. Provide corrective feedback as needed.

If children need additional practice blending words with long *i*, see **Practice Book** page 180 or the online activity.

DIGITAL TOOLS

For more practice, use these activities.

Word Work   **Phonemic Awareness**
Phonics
Structural Analysis

Corrective Feedback

Sound Error Help children with any sounds they missed. Say: *My turn. This sound says* (make the correct sound). Then blend the word. Say: *Do it with me.* Blend the word aloud with children. Say: *Your turn. Blend this word.* Have children chorally blend. Say: *Let's do it again.* Follow these steps until children are confidently producing the sound.

Decodable Reader

Have children read "A Fine Plant" to practice decoding words in connected text. If children need support reading words with long *i*, see page T149 or T156 for instruction and support for "A Fine Plant."

Structural Analysis

Plurals

1 **Model** Say the words *dime* and *dimes*. Ask children to listen closely to hear what is different. Point out the /z/ sound at the end of *dimes*.

Write the words *dime* and *dimes*. Model decoding each word and have children repeat. Underline the letter -*s* at the end. Tell children that the letter -*s* at the end of *dimes* means that there is more than one dime. Remind children that the word *dime* is a noun. Because of this, we add the letter -*s* to the end. It makes the word *dime* plural.

2 **Practice/Apply** Help children decode and blend the words *cape, capes, mile, miles, base, bases, crate, crates, line, lines*. Point out that the letter -*s* at the end of a final -*e* word can stand for /s/ as in *capes*, /z/ as in *miles*, or /ez/ as in *bases*.

Have children practice identifying and reading plural nouns using Practice Book page 185 or the online activity.

ELL ENGLISH LANGUAGE LEARNERS

Structural Analysis, Practice/Apply Point to the -*s* at the end of *capes*. Say: *The s means there is more than one cape.* Capes *is plural.* Say the word *capes*, emphasizing the /s/. Have children repeat the word and say the /s/. Point to the -*s* at the end of *mines*. Ask: *What does the -s mean?* Mines is plural. Then say *mines*, emphasizing the /z/. Have children repeat the word and the sound. Tell children to listen to the sound at the end of *crates*. Ask: *Do you hear the /s/ or the /z/?* (/s/) Repeat with *miles*. (/z/) Have children use the sentence frame to tell that both *crates* and *miles* are plural.

FORMATIVE ASSESSMENT

⊙ STUDENT CHECK-IN

Phonics Have partners read a long *i* word to each other.

Structural Analysis Have partners use a plural noun in a sentence.

Have children reflect using the Check-In Routine.

MULTIMODAL

LEARNING GOALS

- We can sort words by word families.
- We can read and write the words *green, grow, pretty, should, together,* and *water.*

OBJECTIVES

Use conventional spelling for words with common spelling patterns and for frequently occurring irregular words.

Recognize and read grade-appropriate irregularly spelled words.

Sort words with long *i.*

ELA ACADEMIC LANGUAGE

- *patterns, rhyme*
- Cognate: *rima*

OPTION
5 mins

Spelling

MULTIMODAL

Word Families: *-ike, -ide, -ine*

1 **Model** Make index cards for *-ike, -ide, -ine* and form three columns in a pocket chart. Blend the sounds with children.

Hold up the online **Spelling Word Card** for *like.* Say and spell *like.* Pronounce each sound clearly: /l/ /ī/ /k/. Blend the sounds, stretching the vowel sound to emphasize it: /līīīk/. Repeat this step with *spike* and *bike.* Place all three words below the *-ike* card. Read and spell each spelling word. *What do you notice about these spelling words? They have the /ī/ sound, and they rhyme because they end in /īk/ spelled* i-k-e.

-ike	-ide
-ine	like
spike	ride
hide	bike
mine	

106 Unit 3 • Week 2   Spelling Word Cards

2 **Guided Practice/Practice** Provide children with the Spelling Word Cards. Have children say and spell *-ike* and each word in the word family. Repeat the process with the *-ide* and *-ine* words.

Display the words *make, came, water,* and *should* in a separate column. Read and spell the words together with children. Point out that these spelling words do not contain the /ī/ sound spelled *i_e.*

Conclude by asking children to orally generate additional words that rhyme with each word. Write the additional words on the board. Underline the common spelling patterns in the additional words. If necessary, point out the differences and explain why they are unusual.

If children need additional practice spelling words with long *i,* see **Practice Book** page 183 or the online activity.

 # English Language Learners

Spelling, Guided Practice/Practice Help children generate more words with long *i: i_e* spelling patterns that rhyme with the spelling words. Provide clues: *Think of a word that starts with* h *and rhymes with* ride. Write the word, and have children practice reading it. Correct pronunciation as needed. Repeat with additional clues: *Think of a word that starts with* f *and rhymes with* mine; *and think of a word that starts with* h *and rhymes with* bike.

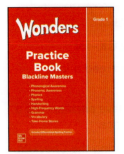

Spelling: Page 183

High-Frequency Words

5 mins

DIGITAL TOOLS

For more practice, use these activities.

Word Work

Spelling
High-Frequency Words

1 **Guided Practice** Say each high-frequency word: *green, grow, pretty, should, together,* and *water.* Have children Read/Spell/Write it. As children spell each word with you, point out irregularities in sound-spellings, such as the /ô/ sound spelled *a* in *water.*

Display the print or digital **Visual Vocabulary Cards** to review this week's high-frequency words.

2 **Practice** Repeat the activity with last week's words. Children can practice reading the high-frequency words independently using the online activity.

Build Fluency: Word Automaticity

Have children read the following sentences aloud together at the same pace. Repeat several times until children can read the words automatically.

We **should** put **water** on the grass **together.**

Then **green** grass should **grow.**

The grass will be thick and **pretty.**

Word Bank

Review the current and previous words in the Word Bank. Discuss with children which words should be removed, or added back, from previous high-frequency word lists. Remind children that the Word Bank should change as the class needs it to.

FORMATIVE ASSESSMENT

STUDENT CHECK-IN

Spelling Have partners think of another word to go with one of the word families.

High-Frequency Words Have partners point to one high-frequency word and read it aloud to each other.

Have children reflect using the Check-In Routine.

CHECK FOR SUCCESS

Rubric Use your online rubric to record children's progress.

Can children read and decode words with long *i: i_e?*

Can children recognize and read high-frequency words?

Small Group Instruction

If No

● **Approaching** Reteach pp. T146–T151

● **ELL** Develop pp. T146–T151

If Yes

● **On** Review pp. T154–T156

● **Beyond** Extend pp. T158–T159

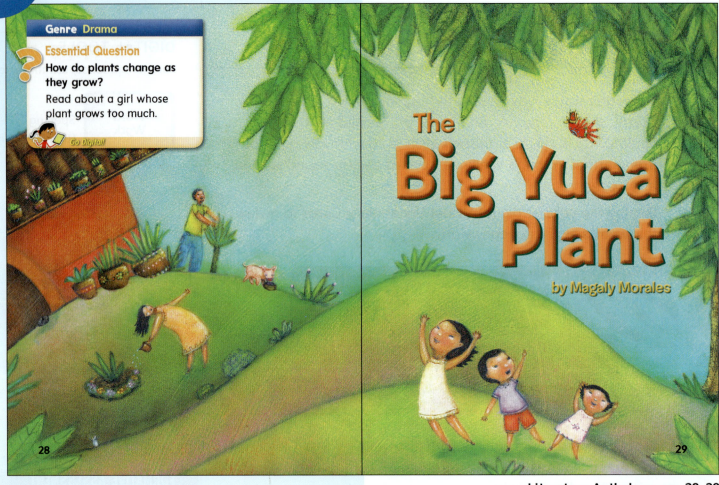

Literature Anthology, pp. 28–29
Lexile NP

The Big Yuca Plant

Read We can understand the important ideas and details in a play.

Reread We can name the choices an author made when writing a play.

Have children apply what they learned as they read.

Close Reading Routine

Read   DOK 1–2

• Identify important ideas and details.
• Take notes and retell.
• Use **A C T** prompts as needed.

Reread   DOK 2–3

• Analyze the text, craft, and structure.
• Use the Reread minilessons.

Integrate   DOK 3–4

• Integrate knowledge and ideas.
• Make text-to-text connections.
• Complete the Show Your Knowledge task.
• Inspire action.

Read

Celebratory Read You may wish to read the full selection aloud once with minimal stopping before you begin using the Read prompts.

Set Purpose

Say: *Let's read to find out how one family deals with a huge plant.*

⊙ DIFFERENTIATED READING

Approaching Level Have children listen to the selection summary. Use the Reread prompts during Small Group time.

On Level and **Beyond Level** Pair children or have them independently complete the Reread prompts on **Reading/Writing Companion** pp. 67–69.

🎧 **English Language Learners** Before reading, have children listen to a summary of the selection. See the **ELL Small Group Guide,** pp. 120–121.

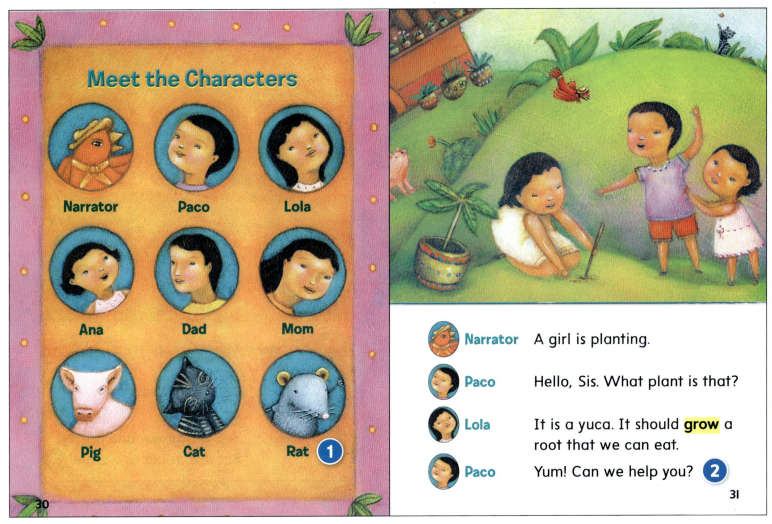

Literature Anthology, pp. 30–31

Story Words Read and spell the words *yuca, hello,* and *root.* Tell children that a yuca is a plant with roots we can eat. Review word meanings as needed.

Note Taking: Graphic Organizer

As children read the selection, guide them to fill in the online Sequence of Events Graphic Organizer 6 as they read.

❶ Make and Confirm Predictions DOK 2

Teacher Think Aloud On page 30, I see a list of all the characters in the play. I will make a prediction. I predict the characters who are children will get help from the adults to do something. I will read the play to find out what the children and adults do.

Build Vocabulary page 31
root: the part of a plant that grows underground

❷ Main Story Elements: Sequence of Events DOK 1

Teacher Think Aloud The sequence of events is the order events appear in a story. Think about what happens *first, next, then,* and *last* to understand the sequence. First, they plant a yuca. Let's write it.

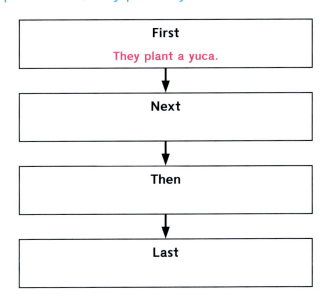

First
They plant a yuca.

↓

Next

↓

Then

↓

Last

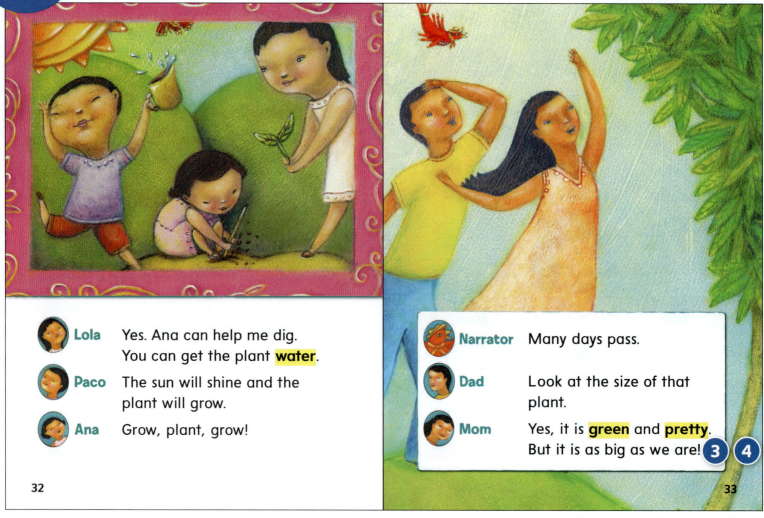

Lola Yes. Ana can help me dig. You can get the plant **water**.

Paco The sun will shine and the plant will grow.

Ana Grow, plant, grow!

32

Narrator Many days pass.

Dad Look at the size of that plant.

Mom Yes, it is **green** and **pretty**. But it is as big as we are! ❸ ❹

33

Literature Anthology, pp. 32–33

Read

❸ Genre: Drama: Play DOK 2

This is a play. Remember that a play is a story meant to be performed. It has a narrator that tells the story. It has a setting. It also has dialogue spoken by each character. Look at pages 32-33. Then turn to a partner and name some things on these pages that tell you this is a play.

❹ Retelling DOK 1

Teacher Think Aloud We can retell what has happened so far in the play by reading the characters' words and looking at the illustrations. So far, Lola, Paco, and Ana have planted a yuca. After many days have passed, the plant has grown big.

Connect to Content

Plants Grow and Change Remind children they have been learning about how plants grow and change over time. Prompt them to describe how the yuca plant has changed and grown so far in the play. What do they think will happen to the plant next?

STEM

Lola	My yuca did grow! It is time to pull it up.	
Narrator	She tugs and tugs.	
Lola	I can't get it. It is too big!	
Paco	I will help. I will grab you. You grab the plant. ⑤	

34

Lola	This plant is stuck!	
Ana	I can tug. Come up, yuca!	
Dad	That is quite a plant! Let us help.	
Narrator	Mom and Dad tug. But the plant does not come up.	

35

Literature Anthology, pp. 34–35

⑤ **Make and Confirm Predictions** DOK 2

I predicted that the children would get help from adults to do something. They did! They got help from the adults to pull up the plant. Let's make another prediction. A lot of people are already helping, so let's predict that no one else will help pull up the plant.

Build Vocabulary pages 34–35
grab: take hold of firmly
stuck: not able to move or to be moved

Reread

Author's Craft DOK 3

Reading/Writing Companion, 67

How does the author help you know the characters' feelings? (The author uses exclamation marks to show that Ana and Mom are excited and surprised.)

ELL Spotlight on Language

Page 34 Point to the dialogue: "I can't get it. It is too big." Say: It *is a word that takes the place of other words. What word is* it *taking place of here? What is too big?* (the yuca) Read the sentence, replacing *it: I can't get the yuca. The yuca is too big.* Have partners turn and talk, using *it* to replace another word. Provide sentence frames: I like my bike. It is green.

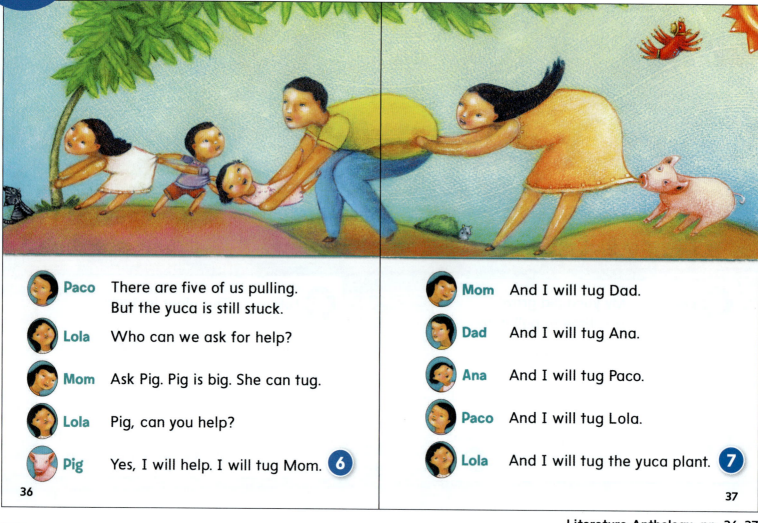

	Paco	There are five of us pulling. But the yuca is still stuck.
	Lola	Who can we ask for help?
	Mom	Ask Pig. Pig is big. She can tug.
	Lola	Pig, can you help?
	Pig	Yes, I will help. I will tug Mom. ⑥

36

	Mom	And I will tug Dad.
	Dad	And I will tug Ana.
	Ana	And I will tug Paco.
	Paco	And I will tug Lola.
	Lola	And I will tug the yuca plant. ⑦

37

Literature Anthology, pp. 36–37

Read

⑥ Make and Confirm Predictions DOK 2

Teacher Think Aloud We predicted that no one would help the family pull up the yuca plant. But Pig helps! Our prediction was not correct. Let's make new predictions. What is your prediction?

Student Think Aloud There is another character: Cat. I predict that Cat will help with the plant.

⑦ Main Story Elements: Sequence of Events DOK 1

Think about what has already happened. What main event happens next? (The family works together to pull up the yuca plant.) Let's add that to the chart.

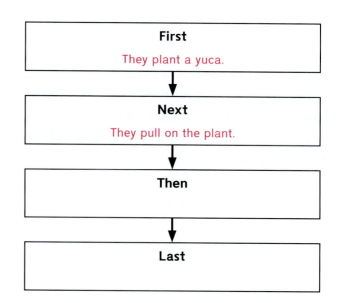

First
They plant a yuca.

↓

Next
They pull on the plant.

↓

Then

↓

Last

	Narrator	But the plant does not move a bit.
	Ana	This plant can't be picked.
	Lola	Yes, it can! There must be a way. We can ask Cat.
	Paco	Cat, will you help?

38

	Cat	But I am not big like Pig.
	Lola	You can still help. **Together** we can get the yuca out.
	Cat	I will do my best. **8**

39

Literature Anthology, pp. 38–39

Reread

Author's Craft DOK 2

Reading/Writing Companion, 68

What does Lola like to do? (She likes to work with others.)

Make Inferences

Remind children that we can use clues to make an inference. I notice that Lola isn't afraid to ask for help if she has trouble doing something. I can look at the pictures of everyone working together and think of what Lola says to make the inference that she thinks it is important for everyone to work together. **DOK 2**

8 Make and Confirm Predictions DOK 2

Let's confirm predictions. You predicted that Cat helps. Cat says he will help. Your prediction is correct! Let's make new predictions. Let's predict that everyone will pull up the yuca plant.

ELL Spotlight on Language

Page 38 Point to the phrase *a bit.* Read it and have children repeat. Hold your fingers close together. *A bit is a small amount. What will not move a bit?* (the plant) *This means that the plant will not move even a small amount. Use your fingers to show me the size of a bit. What size is a bit?* Provide a sentence frame: A bit is small. Have partners turn and talk about whether they would rather have a bit of a tasty treat or a lot. Have them explain why.

Narrator	They all tug. But the plant is still stuck.	
Lola	**Should** we ask that rat to help?	
Paco	A rat? A rat is little. He can't help.	
Rat	Yes, I can.	

40

Rat	Take this vine. Tie it to the plant. We all must tug on the vine.
Lola	Yes, do as Rat said!
Narrator	They get in a line.
Lola	Grab the vine and tug! **9** **10**

41

Literature Anthology, pp. 40–41

Read

9 Make and Confirm Predictions DOK 2

 Turn to a partner and discuss the predictions you made as you read the play. Work together to use the text to see if they were correct.

10 Main Story Elements: Sequence of Events DOK 1

The last event is that the family worked together to pull up the yuca. Then what happened? (The family and all of the animals try to pull the plant out of the ground.) Let's add this event to the chart.

Build Vocabulary page 41

vine: a plant that grows in a long, thin rope shape

Main Story Elements: Sequence of Events DOK 1

Read pages 42-43 with a partner. Let's add what happens last to the chart.

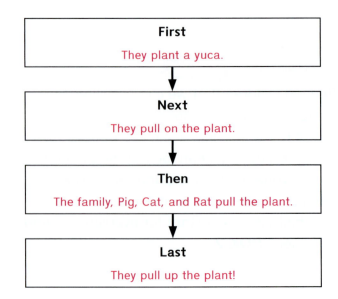

First
They plant a yuca.

↓

Next
They pull on the plant.

↓

Then
The family, Pig, Cat, and Rat pull the plant.

↓

Last
They pull up the plant!

Dad	It is out at last!	
Ana	What a fine yuca.	
Pig	It could win a prize.	

42

Mom	We all must thank Rat.
Lola	You are little, but you are wise.
All	Thank you!

43

Literature Anthology, pp. 42–43

Reread

Author's Craft DOK 3

Reading/Writing Companion, 69

Remember that plays have dialogue that is spoken by each character. How does the dialogue help you learn about the characters? (The dialogue tells me what the characters think.)

Make Inferences

If necessary, remind children how to make an inference. Lola says that if they listen to Rat, they can pull out the yuca. I know that sometimes great things happen when we listen to the advice of others. So I can infer from her dialogue that she thinks everyone has value, even the smallest animal. **DOK 2**

ELL English Language Learners

Seek Clarification Some children may be confused by complex syntax. Encourage them to always seek clarification when they encounter a word or phrase that does not make sense to them. For example, *The word* fine *does not make sense to me.*

Return to Purposes

Have partners discuss how Lola and her family were finally able to pull out their huge yuca plant. Remind them to use evidence from the play.

Literature Anthology, p. 44

Meet the Author

Magaly Morales

Read aloud page 44 with children. Ask them why they think Magaly Morales wrote about a family like hers. *What is Magaly's family like? How do they get along? How is Lola's family like Magaly's family?*

Author's Purpose

Have children write in their reader's notebook about one way they can help a family member or a friend. Encourage them to write dialogue in play format. Challenge them to include a narrator, too.

AUTHOR'S CRAFT   DOK 2

Focus on Narrator

Remind children that *The Big Yuca Plant* is a play. It is written for actors to perform, and the text only lists what each character says. Magaly Morales uses the narrator to give information readers need that characters do not say. *What important information does the narrator give on page 31?* (what is happening: a girl is planting) *What information does the narrator give on page 33?* (Many days have passed.) Tell children they can include a narrator when they write plays.

Read

Retell

Have children turn to page 66 in their **Reading/Writing Companion.** Remind them that as they read the story, they made and confirmed predictions and paid attention to the sequence of events. Have children use the information they recorded on their Sequence charts to help them retell the story.

Use Text Evidence Guide children to use text evidence to respond to the questions on page 66.

Reread

Analyze the Text

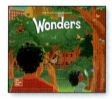

After children read and retell the selection, have them reread it to develop a deeper understanding of the text by answering the questions on pages 67–69 in their Reading/Writing Companion. For children who need support finding text evidence to support their responses, use the scaffolded instruction from the Reread prompts on pages T115–T121.

Integrate

Build Knowledge: Make Connections

Talk About the Text Have partners discuss how the yuca plant in the play changes as it grows.

Write About the Text Then have children add their ideas to their Build Knowledge page of their reader's notebook.

Add to the Anchor Chart Record any new ideas on the Build Knowledge anchor chart.

Add to the Word Bank Then add words related to how plants change as they grow to a separate section of the Word Bank.

Compare Texts   DOK 4

Guide children to compare two plays. Share the prompt: How are Lola and Beth both surprised in the plays we read this week? Say: *Think about* The Big Yuca Plant *and "Time to Plant." How did plants surprise both Lola and Beth?* (Lola was surprised by how big the yuca was. Beth was surprised by how many vegetables they picked in their garden.) You can use a two-column chart to show the similarities.

ENGLISH LANGUAGE LEARNERS

Retell Help children retell the events in the play in order. Ask questions, such as: *What happens first in the play? What happens next? Then what do the characters do? What happens last?* Provide sentence frames with time-order words: First, the family <u>plants</u> a yuca. Then, they <u>pull</u> on it. Next, everyone <u>pulls</u>. Last, they pull it <u>up</u>.

CONNECT TO CONTENT

Plants Grow and Change Review how plants grow and change. Children read about a plant with roots people eat. On page 42, they finally see the yuca root. Have children review the illustrations and describe how the yuca plant grew and changed throughout the play.

STEM

FORMATIVE ASSESSMENT

❯ STUDENT CHECK-IN

Read Have partners tell each other an important detail from the play.

Reread Have partners tell one choice the author made when writing this play.

Have children reflect using the Check-In Routine to fill in the bars.

LESSON 3

LEARNING GOALS

- We can respond to a play by extending the play.
- We can add present-tense verbs to sentences.

OBJECTIVES

Write narratives in which they recount two or more appropriately sequenced events, include some details regarding what happened, use temporal words to signal event order, and provide some sense of closure.

Use verbs to convey a sense of past, present, and future.

Use singular and plural nouns with matching verbs in basic sentences.

Capitalize and underline a title.

ELA ACADEMIC LANGUAGE

- *inference, title*
- Cognates: *inferencia, titular*

 TEACH IN SMALL GROUP

Choose from these options to enable all children to complete the writing activity:

- Drawing and labeling a picture
- Completing sentence frames
- Writing one sentence
- Writing multiple sentences

Additionally, to provide differentiated support for children, see Writing Skills mini lessons on pages T420-T429. These can be used throughout the year.

---

5 mins # Independent Writing

Write About the Anchor Text   DOK 3

Analyze the Prompt Read the prompt: *Think of a different animal that might have been able to help get the yuca plant out. Write a scene where he/she helps out.* Have partners turn and talk about how hard it was to get the yuca plant out of the ground.

- Tell children that they will create their own scene, so they must think about how other animals helped, and that the final helper had a clever idea. This will help them think about a new animal that helps. Explain that the next step in answering the prompt is to find text evidence and make inferences.

Find Text Evidence Say: *To add a scene to the play, we need to look for clues in the text and illustrations about other animals that helped. The clues can help us figure out a different animal that could help.* Tell children they can use text evidence to make inferences about what is not stated in the text. Say: *Look at the text on pages 40-41 in the* **Literature Anthology**. Then ask:

- *What is Rat's idea?* (He says to pull out the plant with a vine.)
- *Why do you think his idea worked?* (It gave the family something to hold on to.)

Have children continue finding text evidence, as necessary, to respond to the prompt. You may choose to take notes on a chart or have children take notes in their writer's notebook.

 Write a Response Tell children to turn to page 70 in their **Reading/Writing Companion.** Guide children to use the text evidence to draft a response. Tell them to write the title of the play. Remind them to include a narrator and to write the name of each character that speaks.

- **Writing Checklist:** Read the checklist with children. Remind them to use sensory details, capitalize the word *I*, and use present-tense verbs correctly.

- **Writing Support:** If needed, provide sentence frames. Model completing one, as necessary.

Lola: This yuca _____.

Narrator: Then _____.

Tell children they will finalize and present their writing the next day.

Writing and Grammar

My Goal: I can respond to a play by extending the play.

Write About the Anchor Text

Think of a different animal that might have been able to help get the yuca plant out. Write a scene where he/she helps out.

Talk about the question.

Write your answer below.

Remember:
- ☐ Use sensory details.
- ☐ Capitalize the word *I*.
- ☐ Use present-tense verbs correctly.

Check In 1 2 3 4

70 Unit 3 · Week 2

Reading/Writing Companion, p. 70

Grammar

Present-Tense Verbs

1 **Review** Remind children that when a present-tense verb tells about one noun, it ends in *-s.* When it tells about more than one noun or *I* or *you,* it does not end in *-s.* Have children identify the present-tense verb in the model sentence below.

Name the verb in this sentence: I like fresh peas. *Why doesn't* like *end in s? The subject is* I. *We do not end present-tense verbs with -s with the pronoun* I.

2 **Guided Practice/Practice** Guide children to identify the present-tense verb in this sentence: *These vegetables look ripe and delicious.* Provide children with new subjects: *This tomato, The beans,* and *The watermelon.* Have partners work together to write the correct present-tense verb.

Talk About It

Have partners create sentences with present-tense verbs, using one noun and more than one noun.

Mechanics: Titles of Plays

1 **Model** Tell children we start the name of a play with a capital letter. All the important words in the title are also capitalized. Little words, like *the, a, an, and, of,* and *in,* are not capitalized unless they are the first or last words in the title. The title of a play is underlined. Display the following sentence: I read <u>Time to Plant!</u> Point out the capitalized words and the underlined title.

2 **Guided Practice** Prompt children to correct each title. I like the play a day in the park. <u>(A Day in the Park)</u> Did you see the play Frog in the water? <u>(Frog in the Water)</u>

ELL English Language Learners

Independent Writing, Analyze the Text To help children talk to a partner about how hard it was to get the yuca plant out, say, *Think about all the animals who helped the family.* Allow children to refer to the illustrations in the story. Provide sentence frames for their discussion, such as, The family had to ask _____ to help them. But even then, they couldn't ___.

For additional support, see the **ELL Small Group Guide,** p. 125.

DIGITAL TOOLS
Use these activities to practice grammar and mechanics.

Grammar

Mechanics

Grammar Song

Grammar Video

FORMATIVE ASSESSMENT

 **STUDENT CHECK-IN**

Writing Have partners share their responses to the prompt. Have children reflect using the Check-In Routine to fill in the bars.

Grammar Have partners read a sentence with a present-tense verb to each other. Have children reflect using the Check-In routine.

LEARNING GOALS

We can learn and use new vocabulary words.

OBJECTIVES

Identify real-life connections between words and their use.

ELA ACADEMIC LANGUAGE

• *vocabulary*
• Cognate: *vocabulario*

DIGITAL TOOLS

Visual Vocabulary Cards

LESSON FOCUS

READING
Revisit the Essential Question
Read and Reread Paired Selection:
"How Plants Grow"
• Introduce Text Feature
• Make Predictions
Word Work
• Build Words with Long *i: i_e*

WRITING
• Independent Writing
• Review Grammar and Mechanics

Literature Anthology, pp. 46–49

 15 mins

Oral Language

 MULTIMODAL

 Essential Question

How do plants change as they grow?

Remind children that this week they have been learning about how plants change as they grow. Guide children to discuss the question using information from what they have read and discussed. Use the **Visual Vocabulary Cards** and the Define/Example/Ask routine to review the oral vocabulary words *assist, bloom, grasped, spied,* and *sprout*.

Guide children to use each word as they talk about what they have read and learned about how plants change and grow. Prompt children by asking questions.

• How could someone *assist* you with tying your shoes?

• What does a flower look like when it *blooms*?

• Which would you rather *grasp*—a cotton ball or a cactus? Why?

• If you *spied* on a pet dog during the day, what do you think you would see?

• What can you see when a plant is a *sprout*?

Review last week's oral vocabulary words: *schedule, immediately, weekend, calendar,* and *occasion*.

FORMATIVE ASSESSMENT

❯ STUDENT CHECK-IN

Have partners use a vocabulary word in a sentence. Have children reflect using the Check-In Routine.

Text Features

Diagram

1 **Explain** Review that nonfiction texts have facts and details. Explain that nonfiction can also have diagrams—pictures that show the parts of something and help us locate information. Diagrams usually have labels that name the parts.

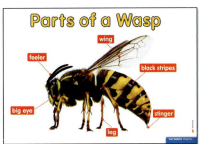
Online Teaching Chart

2 **Model** Display **Online Teaching Chart** for Text Features: Diagram. Point to the wing and read the label aloud. Say: *The illustration shows the parts of a wasp. The labels tell the names of the parts. This part of the wasp is the wing.*

3 **Guided Practice/Practice** Read together the other labels as you point to the corresponding parts. Guide children to discuss the information the diagram gives. *What information do we learn from the illustration? What information do we learn from the labels?* Tell children to look for diagrams as they read nonfiction texts.

English Language Learners

Use with **Text Features, Guided Practice/Practice.**

Beginning

Use sentence frames to help children discuss the diagram. Point to the label *leg*. Say: *This is a label. What is this?* (a label) Point to and read each label, and have children repeat.

Intermediate

Point to the label *feeler*. Ask: *What is this part of a wasp called?* It is a <u>feeler</u>. *How do you know?* The label says <u>feeler</u>. Repeat with the label *stinger*.

Advanced/Advanced High

Point out the word *big* in the label *big eye* and the word *black* in the label *black stripes*. Explain that these words tell more about each part of the wasp. Have partners come up with words they can add to the other labels to tell more about a wasp, such as *sharp* for the stinger or *long* for the feeler.

Genre **Nonfiction**

Compare Texts
Read about how plants grow
and change.

Read Together

How Plants Grow

These are all seeds.

A plant's life begins as a **seed**. Inside the seed is a little, new plant.

When the seed is planted, a **root** grows down in the soil. The root holds the seed in the soil. It takes in water, too.

46

The stem grows up from the seed. When it pops out of the soil, it is called a **sprout**. Green leaves grow on the stem.

The leaves have a big job. They make food for the plant to live. The leaves use water, sunlight, and air to make food.

1

47

Literature Anthology, pp. 46–47
Lexile 400

"How Plants Grow"

LEARNING GOAL

Read We can understand the important ideas and details in a text.

Reread We can name the choices an author made when writing a text.

Compare Texts

As children read and reread "How Plants Grow," encourage them to think about the Essential Question. Have children think about how these plants are like the yuca in *The Big Yuca Plant*. Review the words *seed, root,* and *sprout.*

Genre Focus Tell children that this is a nonfiction text, which tells about real people, places, events, or things by presenting facts about them. Explain that nonfiction text sometimes includes a diagram that shows the parts of something. Diagrams can help us locate information.

Read

❶ Make and Confirm Predictions DOK 2

Teacher Think Aloud *I predict that the next step for a tiny plant is growing flowers. Let's continue reading to see if my prediction is correct.*

Reread

Author's Craft DOK 2

Reading/Writing Companion, 71

Set Purpose Let's reread to find out how plants grow.

What are two ways that the root helps a plant? Underline the two ways in the text. (holds the seed in the soil; takes in water)

Talk with a partner about how the photo helps you understand the meaning of the word *sprout*. (Possible answer: The photo shows a plant starting to grow. So now I know that a sprout is like a baby plant.)

ELL English Language Learners

Use the following scaffolds to help children **Compare Texts**.

Beginning

Have children describe the yuca plant that grew in *The Big Yuca Plant*. Provide a sentence frame: The yuca is green. Ask: *How is the plant in the photo on page 47 the same as the yuca?* The plant is green.

Intermediate

Have children describe the yuca plant that grew in *The Big Yuca Plant*. Provide sentence frames: The yuca has leaves. The yuca is green. Ask: *How is the plant in the photo on page 47 the same as the yuca?* The plant is green. The plant has leaves.

Advanced/Advanced High

Have partners discuss how the big yuca is the same as and different from the plant in the photo on page 47. Have one partner focus on ways the plants are the same while the other focuses on ways they are different. Provide vocabulary as needed.

CONNECT TO CONTENT

Plants Grow And Change
Guide children to discuss how plants grow and change over time. Have children draw a diagram of a plant in their home, classroom, or neighborhood. Encourage them to label all the parts they can identify. **STEM**

blossom

fruit

Over time, blossoms pop up on the ❷ plant. These blossoms are the plant's flowers. They can grow into a fruit such as this pumpkin. Many fruits can grow on one plant vine.

Inside the fruit are seeds. These seeds can be used to grow new plants.

48

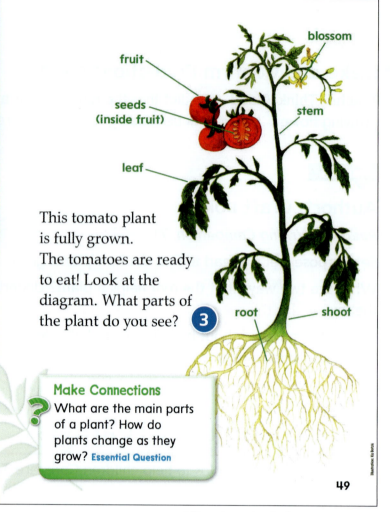

blossom

fruit

seeds (inside fruit)

stem

leaf

root

shoot

This tomato plant is fully grown. The tomatoes are ready to eat! Look at the diagram. What parts of the plant do you see? ❸

Make Connections

? What are the main parts of a plant? How do plants change as they grow? **Essential Question**

49

Literature Anthology, pp. 48-49

Read

❷ Make and Confirm Predictions DOK 2

I predicted that the next step would be for a plant to grow flowers. Use the photo and text on page 48 to confirm if I was correct. (Yes. The text says that blossoms pop up on the plant. These are flowers. The picture also shows flowers on the plant.)

❸ Text Feature: Diagram DOK 2

What parts of a plant does the diagram on page 49 show? (blossom, fruit, seeds, stem, leaf, shoot, root) Talk with a partner about how the diagram helps you understand the meaning of these words.

Reread

Author's Craft DOK 3

Reading/Writing Companion, 72

What word in the selection helps you understand what *blossoms* are? Circle the word in the text. (flowers)

What words in the selection tell what flowers do? Underline the words in the text. (They can grow into a fruit.)

Talk with a partner about the photo and the labels. Why do you think the author included them on this page? (Possible answer: The author included them so that we could find and name the parts of this plant.)

Use the Quick Tip box to support children as they work.

Author's Craft DOK 3

Reading/Writing Companion, 73

Talk with a partner about the sequence of the text. How is the information in this text organized? (The author tells how the plant grows from beginning to end.)

Talk About It What would be another good title for this text? (Possible answer: Another title for this text could be *From Seed to Fruit.*)

Read

Retell

Guide children to use important details to retell the selection. Have partners talk about the different parts of a plant.

Reread

Analyze the Text

After children retell, have them reread to develop a deeper understanding of the text. Have children annotate the text and answer the questions on **Reading/Writing Companion** pages 71–73. For children who need support citing text evidence, use the Reread prompts on pages T129–T131.

Integrate

Build Knowledge: Make Connections

Talk About the Text Have partners discuss how the plants in this text change as they grow from seed to plant to fruit or vegetable.

Write About the Text Then have children add their ideas to their Build Knowledge page of their reader's notebook.

Add to the Anchor Chart Record any new ideas on the Build Knowledge anchor chart.

Add to the Word Bank Then add words related to how plants change as they grow to a separate section of the Word Bank.

SPOTLIGHT ON LANGUAGE

Page 48 Point to the phrase *pop up.* Read it, and have children repeat. Explain that *pop up* can mean "appear suddenly." *I can pop up.* Hide behind your desk or a table and then pop up. *I appeared suddenly. I popped up. What appears suddenly on the plant?* (blossoms or flowers) Let children pop up from their seats they say: I <u>pop up</u>.

FORMATIVE ASSESSMENT

❯ STUDENT CHECK-IN

Read Have partners tell each other one important detail from the text. Have children reflect using the Check-In Routine.

Reread Have partners tell one choice the author made when creating this text. Have children reflect using the Check-In Routine to fill in the bars.

Display the Sound-Spelling Card *five*. Point to the letters i_e.

1. **Teacher:** What are the letters? **Children:** i, e
2. **Teacher:** What's the sound? **Children:** /ī/
3. **Teacher:** What's the word? **Children:** five

Continue the routine for previously taught sounds.

OBJECTIVES

Orally produce single-syllable words by blending sounds (phonemes), including consonant blends.

Know final -e and common vowel team conventions for representing long vowel sounds.

Read words with inflectional endings.

Use conventional spelling for words with common spelling patterns and for frequently occurring irregular words.

Recognize and read grade-appropriate irregularly spelled words.

Delete initial sounds to form new words.

ELA ACADEMIC LANGUAGE

- *blend, nouns*

TEACH IN SMALL GROUP

Word Work lessons can be taught in small groups.

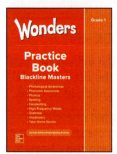

Structural Analysis: Page 186

OPTION 5 mins

Phonemic Awareness

Phoneme Deletion

1 **Model** Say: *Listen carefully as I say a word:* swipe. *The word* swipe *has four sounds: /s/ /w/ /ī/ /p/. I'll take away the first sound and make a new word: /w/ /ī/ /p/,* wipe.

2 **Guided Practice/Practice** Have children practice deleting the initial phoneme in words. Guide practice for the first example. Provide corrective feedback as needed. Then have children practice removing initial sounds from the remaining words.

smile	slime	gripe	price	pride
brace	blast	crush	swell	trash

5 mins

Phonics

MULTIMODAL

Build Words with Long *i: i_e*

1 **Review** Provide children with **Word-Building Cards** *a–z*. Say:
The long i *sound /ī/ can be represented by the letters* i_e. *We'll use Word-Building Cards to build words with long* i *spelled* i_e. *Place the letters* t, i, l, e. *Then say: Let's blend the sounds together and read the word: /tī ī ī l/,* tile. *Now change the* t *to* m. *Blend the sounds and read the word: /mī ī ī l/,* mile.

2 **Practice** Continue with *mine, pine, pin, fin, fine, five, live, hive, hide, hid, rid, ride.* Once children have finished building the words, dictate the words in the list and have children write out the word-building list. Have partners exchange and check the written lists for spelling. Listen in and provide corrective feedback.

Color Coding After each dictation, reveal the secret color-coding letter(s) for children to find on their **Response Board**. Have them say the sound(s) as they trace each letter in color. Use one or two of the phonics skills of the week for color coding.

Decodable Reader

Have children read "Plants Take Time to Grow" to practice decoding words in connected text. If children need support, turn to Small Group, pages T149 and T156 for instruction on "Plants Take Time to Grow."

5 mins Structural Analysis

Plurals

Review Write the words *side* and *sides* on the board and read them with children. Remind children that when *-s* is added to a noun, or naming word, it makes the word plural. The word *sides* means more than one side.

Write the following words: *prize, ride, cake, plane*. Have children work in pairs to construct plural nouns with inflectional endings, then have them write a sentence with each word.

If children need additional practice identifying and reading plural nouns, see **Practice Book** page 186 or the online activity.

5 mins Spelling

MULTIMODAL

Word Sort with *-ike, -ide, -ine*

Review Provide partners with copies of the online **Spelling Word Cards.** While one partner reads the words one at a time, the other orally segments the word and then writes it. After reading all the words, partners switch roles and repeat.

Have children self-correct their papers. Then have partners work together to sort the words by ending spelling pattern: *-ike, -ide, -ine,* or no long *i* ending.

OPTION 5 mins High-Frequency Words

green, grow, pretty, should, together, water

Review Display online **Visual Vocabulary Cards** for the high-frequency words *green, grow, pretty, should, together, water*. Have children Read/Spell/Write each word.

- Point to a word and call on a child to use it in a sentence.
- Review last week's words using the same procedure.

DIGITAL TOOLS

For more practice, use these activities.

Word Work

Phonemic Awareness
Phonics
Structural Analysis
Spelling
High-Frequency Words

FORMATIVE ASSESSMENT

❯ STUDENT CHECK-IN

Phonics/Spelling Have children spell words with the long *i* sound.

Structural Analysis Have partners read a sentence that includes a plural noun ending in *-s*.

High-Frequency Words Have partners share a sentence using a high-frequency word.

Have children reflect using the Check-In routine.

✓ CHECK FOR SUCCESS

Rubric Use your online rubric to record children's progress.

Can children read and decode words with long *i: i_e?*

Can children recognize and read high-frequency words?

❯ Small Group Instruction

If No

🟠 **Approaching** Reteach pp. T146–T151

🟣 **ELL** Develop pp. T146–T151

If Yes

🔵 **On** Review pp. T154–T156

🟢 **Beyond** Extend pp. T158–T159

OPTION
5 mins

Independent Writing

Write About the Anchor Text

Revise

Reread the prompt about *The Big Yuca Plant: Think of a different animal that might have been able to help get the yuca plant out. Write a scene where he/she helps out.*

- Have children read their drafts in their **Reading/Writing Companion.** Ask them to check that they responded to the prompt. Then have them review the checklist to confirm that they used sensory details, capitalized the word *I*, and used present-tense verbs correctly.

Peer Review Have pairs take notes about what they liked most, questions they have for the author, and additional ideas the author could include. Have partners discuss these topics. Provide time for revisions.

Edit/Proofread

Review the online proofreading marks with children. Model how to use each mark. Then have children edit for the following:

- High-frequency words are spelled correctly.
- The title of the play is underlined.

Write Final Draft

Have children create their final draft in their writer's notebook by:

- writing it neatly, or using digital tools to produce and publish it.
- adding details and a drawing.

Teacher Conference As children work, conference with them to provide guidance. Make sure children included sensory details, used present-tense verbs correctly, and capitalized the word *I*. Have children make changes based on your feedback.

Share and Evaluate

After children have finalized their draft, have them:

- work with a partner to practice presenting their writing to each other.
- share their final drafts with the class.
- ask questions about each other's work to clear up any confusion.

If possible, record children as they share so that they can self-evaluate. After children share, display their final papers on a bulletin board.

Have children add their work to their writing folder. Invite them to look at their previous writing and discuss with a partner how it has improved.

Grammar

Present-Tense Verbs

1 **Review** Review with children that when a present-tense verb tells about one noun, it ends in *-s*. When it tells about more than one noun, or *I* or *you*, it does not end in *-s*. Ask: *When does the action of a present-tense verb happen?* (right now)

2 **Guided Practice/Practice** Display the following nouns and verbs: *cat, snakes, naps, slide.* Have children match the nouns and verbs that go together and have them make each pair into a complete sentence. Have children edit their drafts in their writer's notebook for present-tense verbs.

For additional practice editing their writing for present-tense verbs, see **Practice Book** page 189 or the online activity.

 ### Talk About It

Instruct children to create oral sentences with a partner. These sentences should have present-tense verbs that tell about one noun as well as present-tense verbs that tell about more than one noun.

Mechanics: Titles of Plays

1 **Review** Remind children that the title of a play is underlined and the first, last, and all important words are capitalized.

2 **Practice** Have partners fix the following sentences.

I think the big sandwich is a fun play. (I think <u>The Big Sandwich is a fun play.</u>)

We went to see the three little pigs. (We went to see <u>The Three Little Pigs.</u>)

For additional practice with titles of plays, see Practice Book page 190 or the online activity.

 # English Language Learners

Write About the Anchor Text, Peer Review Before children begin their peer review, model how to give feedback. Ask a volunteer to share his or her draft. Read it aloud. Then model giving feedback, such as: *I like how you explain how Crow helps. Could you add a sentence for Lola to say?* Provide two sentence frames for children to use during their peer review discussion: I like the way you <u>underlined the title</u>. Could you add a <u>sensory detail</u>?

For additional support, see the **ELL Small Group Guide,** p. 125.

DIGITAL TOOLS

Use these resources with the lessons.

Proofreading Marks

Grammar

Mechanics

Grammar Song

Grammar Video

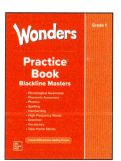

Grammar: Page 189
Mechanics: Page 190

FORMATIVE ASSESSMENT

❯ STUDENT CHECK-IN

Writing Have children reflect on one way they revised their writing.

Grammar Have partners share a sentence with a matching noun and verb pair.

Have children reflect using the Check-In routine.

LESSON 4

OBJECTIVES

Participate in shared research and writing projects.

With guidance and support from adults, recall information from experiences or gather information from provided sources to answer a question.

Add drawings or other visual displays to descriptions when appropriate to clarify ideas, thoughts, and feelings.

Ask and answer questions about what a speaker says in order to gather additional information or clarify something that is not understood.

ELA ACADEMIC LANGUAGE

- *research, diagram*
- Cognate: *diagrama*

COLLABORATIVE CONVERSATIONS

Add New Ideas Review with children that in partner, small-group, and whole-group discussions they should:

- stay on topic.
- connect their own ideas to the comments of others.
- look for ways to connect their experiences to the conversation.

Integrate

10 mins

Plants Grow

Model

Tell children that today they will research how a plant changes as it grows. Display pages 74–75 in the **Reading/Writing Companion** and model filling them in, reviewing the steps in the research process below.

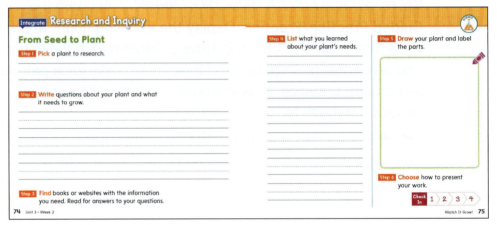

Reading/Writing Companion, pp. 74–75

STEP 1 Pick a Plant

The project is to pick a plant to research and find out what it needs to grow. First, I need to choose a plant I would like to research. I will choose sunflowers because I want to learn more about them.

STEP 2 Write Your Questions

Now I have to decide what I want to know about sunflowers and what they need to grow. I have two questions. I'd like to know how much light a sunflower needs and how often I should water it.

STEP 3 Find Information

I can research by looking at books in the classroom or in the library. I can use the table of contents or index to find the information I am looking for. I will write the materials I will use to answer my questions.

STEP 4 Write What You Learned

I will write the answers to my questions. I learned that a sunflower needs about eight hours of sun a day. It needs water a few times a week.

STEP 5 Draw Your Plant

Now I know more about sunflowers and what they need to grow. I can draw a picture of a sunflower. I can add labels to show what I learned in my research.

STEP 6 Choose How to Present Your Work

Next, I will choose how to present my work and share my findings with my classmates. I will create and label of diagram of a sunflower.

Apply

Have children turn to pages 74–75 in their **Reading/Writing Companion.**

Guide them as they choose a plant to research and formulate their questions. For Step 1, have partners discuss how or why they chose the plant they chose. For Step 2, guide children to write their questions by asking what they hope to learn about their chosen plant. If children are unsure where to do research for Step 3, you can help them gather print or online books. Have them locate the table of contents or index to more quickly find the information they need.

Before they write what they learned in Step 4, they can discuss it with a partner. When children are ready to draw their plant in Step 5, challenge them to create their own labels.

After children have completed their research, guide them to fill out the Research Process Checklist on the online Student Checklist. This checklist helps children decide if they've completed all of the necessary parts of the research process.

Choose the Presentation Format

Have children turn to pages 74–75 in their Reading/Writing Companion to review their research, what they learned about the plant they chose, and their drawing. Tell them that today they are going to take the next step by creating a way to present their findings. This will be their final product. Options include:

- draw and label a diagram of their plant
- create a three-dimensional model of their plant and include a written description
- create a slide show with photographs and drawings of their plant, including labels, using an interactive white board

Create the Presentation

Have children develop their presentation. Remind children of the rules of working with others.

Gather Materials Have children gather the materials they'll need to create their finished product. Most of the materials should be available in the classroom or can be brought from home.

Make the Presentation Once children have gathered the materials they need for their presentation, provide time for them to create it. Have children review their research before they begin. Then support children as they work on their presentation.

You may wish to have children collaborate on research projects.

ENGLISH LANGUAGE LEARNERS

Apply, Step 1 Help children choose a plant to write about. *What plants do you know?* Provide vocabulary support as needed. If children have trouble thinking of a plant, help them find pictures or photographs in books or magazines. Then provide frames for children to complete: I am going to write about <u>ivy</u>. Provide additional examples of question frames and how to complete them as needed.

TEACH IN SMALL GROUP

You may wish to have children create their presentation during Small Group time. Group children of varying abilities together, or group children together if they are doing similar projects.

RESEARCH AND INQUIRY: SHARING FINAL PROJECTS

As children get ready to wrap up the week, have them share their Research and Inquiry projects. Then have children self-evaluate.

Prepare Have children gather materials they need to present their projects. Then partners can take turns practicing their presentations.

Share Guide children to present their Research and Inquiry projects. Encourage children to ask questions to clarify when something is unclear.

Evaluate Have children discuss and evaluate their own presentations. You may wish to have them fill out the Presentation Checklist on the online Student Checklist.

FORMATIVE ASSESSMENT

STUDENT CHECK-IN

Have partners share one piece of information they learned from doing research. Have children reflect using the Check-In Routine to fill in the bars.

OBJECTIVES

Orally produce single-syllable words by blending sounds (phonemes), including consonant blends.

Segment spoken single-syllable words into their complete sequence of individual sounds (phonemes).

Know final -e and common vowel team conventions for representing long vowel sounds.

Read words with inflectional endings.

Use conventional spelling for words with common spelling patterns and for frequently occurring irregular words.

Recognize and read grade-appropriate irregularly spelled words.

ELA ACADEMIC LANGUAGE

- *plurals, sort*

Take-Home Story: Pages 191–192
Spelling: Posttest, Page 181

LESSON FOCUS

READING

Word Work
- Review /e/ *e*

Make Connections
- Connect the painting to the Essential Question
- Show Your Knowledge

WRITING
- Self-Selected Writing
- Review Grammar and Mechanics

Reading/Writing Companion, pp. 76–77

---

5 mins

Phonemic Awareness

Phoneme Blending

Review Guide children to blend phonemes to form words. Say: *Listen as I say a group of sounds. Then blend those sounds to form a word.*

/s/ /ī/ /d/	/s/ /l/ /ī/ /d/	/b/ /ī/ /k/	/b/ /ī/ /t/
/d/ /r/ /ī/ /v/	/p/ /r/ /ī/ /z/	/s/ /m/ /ī/ /l/	/sh/ /ī/ /n/

Phoneme Segmentation

Review Guide children to segment phonemes in words. Say: *Now I am going to say a word. I want you to say each sound in the word.*

mile	smile	ripe	drive	white
rise	prize	life	kite	bride

MULTIMODAL

5 mins

Phonics

Blend and Build Words with Long *i: i_e*

Review Have children read and say the words *like, bite, smile, shine,* and *while*. Then have children follow the word-building routine with **Word-Building Cards** to build *side, tide, tile, mile, pile, pipe, pip, rip, ripe, gripe, wipe, wise, rise, ride, rid, hid, hide.*

Word Automaticity Help children practice word automaticity. Display decodable words and point to each word as children chorally read it. Test how many words children can read in one minute. Model blending words children miss.

Read the Decodable Reader

If children need extra practice decoding words in context, have them read "A Fine Plant" and "Plants Take Time to Grow." If children need additional support for these stories, turn to Small Group, pages T149 and T156 for instruction and support.

In a Flash: Sound-Spellings

Display the Sound-Spelling Card *five*. Point to the letters i_e.

1. **Teacher:** What are the letters?   **Children:** i, e
2. **Teacher:** What's the sound?   **Children:** /ī/
3. **Teacher:** What's the word?   **Children:** five

Continue the routine for previously taught sounds.

DIGITAL TOOLS

For more practice, use these activities.

Word Work

Phonemic Awareness
Phonics
Structural Analysis
Spelling
High-Frequency Words

Structural Analysis

Plurals

Review Have children explain how to form a plural noun when the word ends in a final -e spelling. Then have children practice adding -s to nouns such as *bike, file, wave, mile, maze,* and *shape*.

Spelling

MULTIMODAL

Word Sort with -ike, -ide, -ine

Review Have children use the **Spelling Word Cards** to sort the weekly words by vowel and ending sounds. Remind children that four of the words do not have the long *i* sound spelled *i_e*.

Assess Test children on their ability to spell words in the -ike, -ide, and -ine word families. Say each word and provide a sentence so that children can hear the words used in a correct context. Then allow them time to write down the words. Remind children to write legibly, leaving space between their answers as they write the words. As a challenge, provide more words that follow the same spelling pattern. Have children complete the spelling posttest using **Practice Book** page 181.

High-Frequency Words

green, grow, pretty, should, together, water

Review Display **Visual Vocabulary Cards** *green, grow, pretty, should, together, water.* Have children Read/Spell/Write each word. Have children write a sentence with each word.

If children need assistance reading high-frequency words, they can practice reading independently using the Take-Home Story in the Practice Book on pages 191–192 or use online resources.

FORMATIVE ASSESSMENT

❯ STUDENT CHECK-IN

Phonics/Spelling Have children spell words with the long *i* sound.

Structural Analysis Have partners read a word ending in -s to each other.

High-Frequency Words Have partners share sentences using the high-frequency words.

Have children reflect using the Check-In Routine.

✓ CHECK FOR SUCCESS

Rubric Use your online rubric to record children's progress.

Can children read and decode words with long *i: i_e?*

Can children recognize and read high-frequency words?

❯ Small Group Instruction

If No

● **Approaching** Reteach pp. T146–T151

● **ELL** Develop pp. T146–T151

If Yes

● **On** Review pp. T154–T156

● **Beyond** Extend pp. T158–T159

- We can choose a writing activity and share it.
- We can complete sentences with present-tense verbs.

OBJECTIVES

With guidance and support from adults, use a variety of digital tools to produce and publish writing, including in collaboration with peers.

Ask and answer questions about what a speaker says in order to gather additional information or clarify something that is not understood.

Use verbs to convey a sense of past, present, and future.

Use singular and plural nouns with matching verbs in basic sentences.

Self-select writing activity and topic.

Capitalize and underline a title.

 DIFFERENTIATED WRITING

You may choose to conference with children to provide additional support for the following writing activities.

- Journal Writing: Have partners brainstorm things they know about plants before they write in their journals.
- Comic Strip: Have children talk with a partner about their ideas for each frame of their comic strip, including what to write in their characters' speech bubbles.

 5 mins

Self-Selected Writing

Talk About the Topic

Remind children of the Essential Question: *How do plants change as they grow?* Have partners talk about the Essential Question and encourage them to ask each other questions about growing plants.

Choose a Writing Activity

Tell children they will select, or choose, a type of writing they would like to do. Children may choose to write about the theme of the week or write about a different topic that is important to them. Children may choose from the following modes of writing.

 Journal Writing Remind children that a journal is a place where they can write their thoughts about topics that are important to them. Have children draw and write in their journal about how plants change as they grow or a different topic.

 Squiggle Writing Have children draw a squiggle or shape on a piece of paper and then trade their paper with a partner. Have partners complete a drawing about plants or another topic using the squiggle and write two or three sentences

 Comic Strip Show age-appropriate comic strips to children. Have children draw and write their own comic strip about plants or another topic they choose. Remind them to put their characters' dialogue in speech bubbles.

Use Digital Tools You may wish to work with children to explore a variety of digital tools to produce or publish their writing.

Share Your Writing

 Review the speaking and listening strategies with children. Then have children share their writing with a partner or small group. You may wish to display their work on a bulletin board or in a classroom writing area.

SPEAKING STRATEGIES	LISTENING STRATEGIES
✓ Express ideas clearly.	✓ Face the presenter.
✓ Answer questions about information presented.	✓ Wait until the presenter has finished to ask questions.

OPTION
5 mins

Grammar

Present-Tense Verbs

1 **Review** Have children describe present-tense verbs and how they change with different nouns. Write the following sentences and have children tell why some verbs end in *-s* and others do not: The sun shines on the plant. We water the plants.

2 **Practice** Ask: *How do I know if the action in a sentence is happening right now?* (The verb might end in *-s* or not have any special ending.) Write sentence frames. Have children provide present-tense verbs to complete them. Nate and Chuck ____ with the dog. I ____ down the hill. The rabbit ____ in the grass. Have children read their completed sentences to the class.

Mechanics: Titles of Plays

1 **Review** Remind children that the title of a play is underlined and the first, last, and all important words are capitalized.

2 **Practice** Write the following sentences. Read each aloud. Have children fix the sentences. I think The egg fell is not a good play. (I think <u>The Egg Fell</u> is not a good play.) Chet sings in I see a White crane. (Chet sings in <u>I See a White Crane</u>.)

ELL English Language Learners

Self-Selected Writing, Choose a Writing Activity Present the writing activities and tell children that they will vote on one of the activities. Then, you will work on the writing as a group. Make sure to do the activity on chart paper as you will revise and publish it during small group time. Provide sentence frames and starters as you talk through the writing together. For example, if children have selected Journal Writing, have them talk about how plants grow as they change, and write a few of their thoughts. Possible frames and starters are: First, it is a ____. As it gets bigger, the sprout ____. Then, more leaves ____. The stalk ____.

For additional support, see the **ELL Small Group Guide,** p. 125.

DIGITAL TOOLS

Use these activities to practice grammar and mechanics.

Grammar

Mechanics

Grammar Song

Grammar Video

▶ TEACH IN SMALL GROUP

● **Approaching** Provide more opportunities for children to identify present tense verbs and master subject-verb agreement before they supply present-tense verbs for sentences.

● ● **On Level and Beyond** Children can do the Practice sections only.

● **ELL** Use the chart in the **Language Transfers Handbook** to identify grammatical forms that may cause difficulty.

FORMATIVE ASSESSMENT

▶ STUDENT CHECK-IN

Writing: Have partners share one sentence or speech bubble they wrote.

Grammar: Have partners read a completed sentence to each other.

Have children reflect using the Check-In Routine.

LESSON 5

⏱ 5 mins

Make Connections

LEARNING GOALS

We can compare a text we've read to a painting.

OBJECTIVES

Identify basic similarities in and differences between two texts on the same topic.

Describe people, places, things, and events with relevant details, expressing ideas and feelings clearly.

ELA ACADEMIC LANGUAGE

• compare
• Cognate: comparar

Close Reading Routine

Read DOK 1–2

• Identify important ideas and details.
• Take notes and retell.
• Use **ACT** prompts as needed.

Reread DOK 2–3

• Analyze the text, craft, and structure.
• Use the Reread minilessons.

Integrate DOK 3–4

• Integrate knowledge and ideas.
• Make text-to-text connections.
• Complete the Show Your Knowledge task.
• Inspire action.

Connect to the Essential Question DOK 4

Turn to page 76 in the **Reading/ Writing Companion.** Help partners discuss what they see in the image. Use the first prompt as a guide.

Find Text Evidence Read aloud the second prompt. Guide children to discuss the connections between the painting and "Time to Plant!" Use the Quick Tip box for support.

Reading/Writing Companion, p. 76

Compare Texts Guide partners to compare the pomegranate with the plant in "How Plants Grow." Children can record notes using a Foldable® like the one shown. Guide them to record details that help them answer the Essential Question.

Build Knowledge: Make Connections

Talk About the Text Have partners discuss how the painting of the pomegranate shows the changes a plant goes through, from seeds to plant to fruit.

Add to the Anchor Chart Record any new ideas on the Build Knowledge anchor chart.

Add to the Word Bank Then add words related to how plants change as they grow to a separate section of the Word Bank.

FORMATIVE ASSESSMENT

❯ STUDENT CHECK-IN

Have partners share how they compared the painting and the text. Have children reflect using the Check-In Routine to fill in the bars.

Integrate

Show Your Knowledge

Draw Growing Plants DOK 4

Display the Build Knowledge anchor chart about how plants change as they grow. Have children lead a discussion about what they have learned. Then have children turn to page 77 in their **Reading/Writing Companion**. Guide children through the steps below to draw and write about how plants change as they grow.

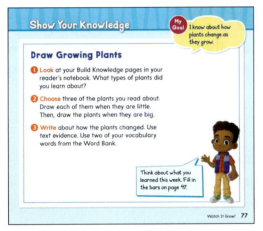

Reading/Writing Companion, p. 77

Step 1 Have children read through the Build Knowledge pages of their reader's notebook to review what they have learned about how plants change as they grow.

Step 2 Ask children to choose three of the plants they read about. Then have children draw pictures of the plants when they are little and when they are big.

Step 3 Have children write how each plant changed over time. Remind them to use text evidence from the texts they read. Have children use two vocabulary words from the Word Bank.

Inspire Action

You may choose to extend the learning with the activities below.

Visit a Garden Take a tour of a community garden or Botanical Center. Have children observe the plants and share what they see.

Growing Plants Have children plant an herb garden in the classroom. Have them draw and write about the changes they observe over time.

Choose Your Own Action Have children talk about the texts they read this week. Ask: *What do these texts inspire you to do?*

We know about how plants change as they grow.

OBJECTIVES

Add drawings or other visual displays to descriptions when appropriate to clarify ideas, thoughts, and feelings.

Use words and phrases acquired through conversations, reading and being read to, and responding to texts.

ELA ACADEMIC LANGUAGE

• *inspire*

• Cognate: *inspirar*

ELL ENGLISH LANGUAGE LEARNERS

Show Your Knowledge, Step 3 Provide and model sentence frames and starters to help children write how each plant changed over time: First, the plant ___. Then, the leaves ___. The stalk also ___. Next, the plant ___.

DIGITAL TOOLS.

RUBRIC Show Your Knowledge Rubric

MY GOALS ROUTINE

What I Learned

Review Goals Have children turn back to page 47 of the **Reading/Writing Companion** and review the goals for the week.

Reflect Have children think about the progress they've made towards the goals. Review the key, if needed. Have children fill in the bars.

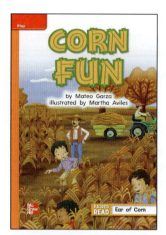

Lexile NP

OBJECTIVES

Describe major events in a story, using key details.

Retell stories, including key details, and demonstrate understanding of their central message or lesson.

Read grade-level text orally with accuracy, appropriate rate, and expression on successive readings.

Make and confirm predictions.

ELA ACADEMIC LANGUAGE

- *confirm, predict, sequence*
- Cognate: *predicción*

●Approaching Level

Leveled Reader: *Corn Fun*

Preview and Predict

Have children turn to the title page. Read the title and the author's name and have children repeat. Preview the selection's illustrations. Prompt children to predict what the selection might be about.

Review Genre: Drama: Play

Remind children that a play is a story that is intended to be performed. It often has a narrator that tells the story, and has a setting. It has dialogue spoken by each character.

Set Purpose

Remind children of the Essential Question. Set a purpose for reading: *Let's read to find out what happens when a family plants corn.* Remind children that as they read a selection, they can ask questions about what they do not understand or what they want to know more about.

Guided Comprehension

As children whisper read *Corn Fun* independently or with a partner, monitor and provide guidance. Correct blending and model the key strategies and skills as needed. As needed, provide definitions for words unfamiliar to children.

Make and Confirm Predictions

Model making and confirming predictions: *On page 3, they plant seeds. I predict we'll see the corn grow.* Read page 4, point to the illustration, and confirm the prediction. Remind children that as they read they can use the words and illustrations to make predictions. They can read on to correct or confirm their predictions.

Main Story Elements: Sequence of Events

Hand out Graphic Organizer 6 to children. Remind children that the sequence of events is the order that events appear in a story. We think about what happens *first, next, then,* and *last* to understand the sequence of events. As you read, ask: *What is the first important event to happen?*

Display a Sequence of Events chart 6 for children to copy. Model recording children's answers in the first box. Have children copy the answers into their own charts.

Think Aloud On page 2, the first important thing that happens is Cole, Dave, and the workers rake the field. I'll write this important event in the first box of my chart.

Guide children to complete the chart.

Respond to Reading Have children complete the Respond to Reading on page 12.

Retell Have children take turns retelling the selection, using the **Retelling Cards** as a guide. Help children make a connection by asking: *What have you ever planted? Where did you plant? What did you do to care for your plant? How did the plant change?*

Fluency: Accuracy and Rate

Model Model reading page 2 with accuracy and an appropriate rate. Read aloud. Have children read along with you.

Apply Have children practice reading the text with a partner. Correct any errors, as needed.

Paired Read: "Ear of Corn"

 Make Connections:
Write About It

Before reading, have children note that the genre is nonfiction text. Read the Compare Texts direction in the **Leveled Reader**.

Leveled Reader

After reading, ask children to tell how the information they learned in "Ear of Corn" adds to their understanding of the setting and events in *Corn Fun*.

Build Knowledge: Make Connections

 Talk About the Texts Have partners discuss how the plants in the texts change as they grow.

 Write About the Texts Then have children add their ideas to their Build Knowledge page of their reader's notebook.

LITERATURE CIRCLES

Lead children in conducting a literature circle using the Thinkmark questions to guide the discussion. You may wish to discuss what children have learned about corn from both selections in the **Leveled Reader**.

 FOCUS ON SCIENCE

Children can extend their knowledge of food we grow by completing the science activity on page 16. **STEM**

 **LEVEL UP**

IF children can read *Corn Fun* **Approaching Level** with fluency and correctly answer the questions,

THEN tell children that they will read another play about planting.

• Have children read the selection, checking their comprehension by using the graphic organizer.

●Approaching Level

Phonemic Awareness

PHONEME SEGMENTATION

OBJECTIVES
Segment spoken single-syllable words into their complete sequence of individual sounds (phonemes).

I Do Explain to children that today they will be listening for the sounds in words. *Listen as I say a word:* ride. *I hear three sounds in* ride: /r/ /ī/ /d/. Repeat with the word *time*.

We Do *Let's do some together. Listen as I say the word* five. *How many sounds do you hear in the word? Yes, three sounds. The sounds in* five *are* /f/ /ī/ /v/.

Repeat this routine with the following words:

bite   fine   pine   wide   drive

You Do *It's your turn. I'll say a word. Tell me how many sounds you hear. Then tell me the sounds.*

brake   kite   flight   pile   prize   ripe   vine   dive

PHONEME BLENDING

OBJECTIVES
Orally produce single-syllable words by blending sounds (phonemes), including consonant blends.

I Do Explain to children that they will be blending sounds to form words. *Listen as I say three sounds:* /l/ /ī/ /m/. *Say the sounds with me:* /l/ /ī/ /m/. *I'm going to blend the sounds together:* /l/ /ī ī ī/ /m/, /lī ī īm/, lime.

We Do *Listen as I say three sounds:* /r/ /ī/ /d/. *Repeat the sounds:* /r/ /ī/ /d/. *Let's blend the sounds:* /r/ /ī ī ī/ /d/, /rī ī īd/, ride. *We made the word* ride.

Repeat this routine with the following words:

/m/ /ī/ /l/   /w/ /ī/ /p/   /l/ /ī/ /f/   /s/ /p/ /ī/ /t/   /d/ /r/ /ī/ /v/

You Do *It's your turn. Listen carefully. Blend the sounds I say together to form a word.*

/h/ /ī/ /v/   /d/ /ī/ /v/   /p/ /ī/ /k/   /s/ /p/ /ī/ /n/

RECOGNIZE AND GENERATE ALLITERATION

OBJECTIVES

Demonstrate understanding of spoken words, syllables, and sounds (phonemes).

Identify and generate words with the same initial sound.

I Do *Listen as I say a sentence: Mike makes a maze. I hear the same sound at the beginning of the words* Mike, makes, *and* maze: /mmm/. *I know two more words that begin with /m/:* may, mouse.

We Do *Let's try some together. Listen as I say another sentence: Luke likes limes. I hear the /l/ sound at the beginning of each word. What other names do you know that begin with /l/ that we could use in this sentence?*

Repeat this routine with the following sentences:

Beth bakes buns.   Trips take time.

You Do *It's your turn. Tell me what sound you hear at the beginning of each word in these sentences. Then say two more words that begin with the same sound.*

Five fish fry.   Wes will wave.   Seth sells skates.

PHONEME DELETION

OBJECTIVES

Orally produce single-syllable words by blending sounds (phonemes), including consonant blends.

Delete initial sounds to form new words.

I Do *Listen carefully as I say a word:* spine. *The word* spine *has four sounds: /s/ /p/ / ī/ /n/. I'll take away the first sound, /s/, and make a new word:* pine.

We Do *Let's do some together. Listen as I say the word. The word is* pride. */p/ /r/ /ī/ /d/. Say the sounds with me: /p/ /r/ / ī / /d/. Now, let's take away the first sound, /p/. Let's say the new word together:* ride.

Repeat this routine with the following words:

price   smile   spike   trace

You Do *It's your turn. Repeat the word I say. Then say the new word without the first sound.*

swipe   gripe   plate   brake

ELL You may wish to review phonemic awareness, phonics, decoding, and fluency using this section. Use scaffolding methods as necessary to ensure children understand the meaning of the words. Refer to the **Language Transfers Handbook** for phonics elements that may not transfer in children's native languages.

Approaching Level

Phonics

CONNECT *i_e* TO /ī/

OBJECTIVES

Know final -e and common vowel team conventions for representing long vowel sounds.

I Do Display the **Word-Building Card** *i_e. These are the letters lowercase* i *and lowercase* e. *I am going to trace the letters* i_e *while I say* /ī ī ī/. Trace the letters *i_e* in the air while saying /ī ī ī/ five times. Remind children that you will not say a sound for the *e* because the *e* at the end of a word is silent.

We Do *Now do it with me.* Have children trace the lowercase *i_e* with their finger while saying /ī ī ī/. Trace the letters *i_e* five times and say /ī ī ī/ with children.

You Do Have children connect the letters *i_e* to the sound /ī/ by tracing lowercase *i_e* on paper while saying /ī ī ī/. Once children have traced on paper five to ten times, they should then write the letters *i_e* while saying /ī ī ī/ five to ten times.

Repeat, connecting the letters *i_e* to the sound /ī/ by tracing and writing the letters *i_e* throughout the week.

BLEND WORDS WITH LONG *i: i_e*

OBJECTIVES

Know final -e and common vowel team conventions for representing long vowel sounds.

Decode regularly spelled one-syllable words.

I Do Display Word-Building Cards *t, i, m, e. This is the letter* t. *It stands for* /t/. *Say it with me:* /t/. *These are the letters* i *and* e. *Together they stand for the sound* /ī/. *Let's say it together:* /ī/. *This is the letter* m. *It stands for* /m/. *I'll blend the sounds together:* /tī ī īm/, time.

We Do Guide children to blend the sounds and read: *ride, wife, pile, mine, kite.* Provide help as needed.

You Do Have children use the Word-Building cards to blend and read: *bike, dime, five, hide, like, bride, wise, drive, fine, bite, dine, spine, wide, size.*

Repeat, blending additional *i_e* words.

You may wish to practice reading and decoding with **ELL** using this section.

BUILD WORDS WITH LONG *i: i_e*

OBJECTIVES

Know final -e and common vowel team conventions for representing long vowel sounds.

Decode regularly spelled one-syllable words.

I Do Display **Word-Building Cards** *f, i, n, e. These are the letters* f, i, n, *and* e. *They stand for /f/, /ī /, and /n/. The* i *and* e *together stand for /ī /. I will blend /f/, /ī /, and /n/ together: /fīn/,* fine. *The word is* fine.

We Do *Let's build a new word together.* Change the letter *n* in *fine* to *v. Let's blend and read the new word: /fīv/,* five.

You Do Have children continue building and blending words: *file, mile, mine, nine, pine, pipe, ripe, rise, ride, side, tide, tile.*

READ WORDS WITH LONG *i: i_e*

OBJECTIVES

Read grade-level text orally with accuracy, appropriate rate, and expression on successive readings.

Unit 3 Decodable
Reader pages 13-24

Focus on Foundational Skills

Review the high-frequency words *green, grow, pretty, should, together,* and *water* with children. Review that the long *i* sound can be spelled *i_e.* Guide children to blend the sounds to read the words.

Read the Decodable Readers

Guide children to read "A Fine Plant" and "Plants Take Time to Grow." Point out the high-frequency words and words in which *i_e* stands for the long *i* sound. If children struggle sounding out words, model blending.

Focus on Fluency

With partners, have children reread "A Fine Plant" and "Plants Take Time to Grow." As children read the text, guide them to focus on their accuracy, rate, and automaticity. Children can provide feedback to their partners.

BUILD FLUENCY WITH PHONICS

Sound/Spellings Fluency

Display the following Word-Building Cards: *i_e, a_e, ch, tch, wh, ph, th, sh, ng, mp, sk, st, nt, nk, nd, u, e, ea, sp, sn, sl, cr, fr, tr, o, pl.* Have children chorally say the sounds. Repeat, and vary the pace.

Fluency in Connected Text

Have children review the **Decodable Reader** selections. Identify words with long *i: i_e,* and blend words as needed. Have partners reread the selections for fluency.

●Approaching Level

Structural Analysis

REVIEW PLURALS

OBJECTIVES

Read words with inflectional endings.

Form and use plural nouns.

I Do Write *miles*. Read the word: */mīlz/. I look at the word* miles *and I see a word I know,* mile. *The -s ending tells me that it means more than one mile. I'm going to use* mile *and* miles *in sentences. I walked one mile yesterday. Today I will walk two miles.*

We Do Write *lines. Let's read this word: /līnz/. If we look at* lines, *is there a word we know? Yes,* line. *We know that -s at the end tells us that* lines *means more than one line.* Remind children that -s at the end of a final -e word can stand for /z/, as in *lines. Let's use* line *and* lines *in sentences.*

You Do Have children work with partners. Write several final -e nouns on the board. Children can work together to add inflectional ending -s and create sentences that use each form of the word correctly.

Repeat Have children create additional sentences with plural nouns.

RETEACH PLURALS

OBJECTIVES

Read words with inflectional endings.

Form and use plural nouns.

I Do Write *kite* and *kites*. Read the word: */kīts/. This is the word* kites. Underline the inflectional ending -s. *When -s is added to a noun, it makes the word tell about more than one. If I buy some kites, I buy more than one kite.*

We Do Write *plane* and *bride. Let's add* -s. *Say* planes: */plānz/. Say* brides: */brīdz/.* Point out that -s at the end of a final -e word can stand for /z/, as in these words. Have the group come up with sentences for the words.

Repeat the routine with the following words.

lake   shape   prize   slide   pipe   case

You Do Have children add -s to more nouns. Guide children to repeat the words as needed. *Now it's your turn. Add -s to each word, then say each word and use it in a sentence.* Provide feedback as needed.

chime   cane   vase   hive   file   crime

Repeat Have children add -s to the ends of additional final -e nouns.

You may wish to review structural analysis and high-frequency words with **ELL** using this section.

High-Frequency Words

REVIEW

OBJECTIVES

Recognize and read grade-appropriate irregularly spelled words.

I Do Use **High-Frequency Word Cards** to Read/Spell/Write *green, grow, pretty, should, together,* and *water.* Use each word orally in a sentence.

We Do Guide children to Read/Spell/Write each word on their **Response Boards.** Work together to generate oral sentences using the words.

You Do Have children work with a partner to Read/Spell/Write on their own, using the words *green, grow, pretty, should, together,* and *water.* Ask them to use each word in a complete sentence. Provide feedback as needed.

RETEACH

OBJECTIVES

Recognize and read grade-appropriate irregularly spelled words.

I Do Review the high-frequency words using the Read/Spell/Write routine. Write a sentence on the board for each high-frequency word.

We Do Guide children to use the Read/Spell/Write routine. Use sentence starters: *(1) I have a green ____. (2) Mike likes to grow ____. (3) What a pretty ____! (4) Do you think we should ____? (5) We went together to ____. (6) The water in the pond is ____.*

You Do Ask children to close their eyes, picture the word, and write it as they see it. Have children self-correct. Provide feedback as needed.

CUMULATIVE REVIEW

OBJECTIVES

Recognize and read grade-appropriate irregularly spelled words.

I Do Display the High-Frequency Word Cards from the previous weeks. Review each word using the Read/Spell/Write routine.

We Do Have children write the words on their **Response Boards.** Complete sentences for each, such as: *The men could ____. She only has one ____.*

You Do Show each card and have children chorally read. Mix and repeat.

Fluency Display the High-Frequency Word Cards. Point to the words in random order. Have children chorally read. Repeat at a faster pace.

Approaching Level

Comprehension

READ FOR FLUENCY

OBJECTIVES

Read grade-level text orally with accuracy, appropriate rate, and expression on successive readings.

Set Purpose Tell children that they will now focus on reading *Corn Fun*. Remind them that this story is fiction and that they will be reading it for enjoyment. Tell children that they need to read with accuracy and at an appropriate rate.

I Do Read the first two sentences of **Leveled Reader** *Corn Fun*. Model reading at the appropriate rate. Tell children as they read it should sound like speech. Also explain that they need to read each word accurately.

We Do Read the rest of Leveled Reader *Corn Fun* and have children repeat each sentence after you. Point out how you read the words accurately and at the appropriate rate. Provide corrective feedback as needed.

You Do Have children work with a partner and take turns rereading passages aloud. Remind them to read each word accurately and to read so that it sounds like speech. Have children self-correct, as needed.

IDENTIFY MAIN STORY ELEMENTS: CHARACTER

OBJECTIVES

Describe characters in a story, using key details.

I Do Remind children that the characters are the people or animals in a story. Tell them that readers use text and illustrations to help them describe what a character looks like, does, thinks, and feels.

We Do Read the first few lines of Leveled Reader *Corn Fun* aloud. Model identifying and describing one of the characters. Say: *We read about Cole. He is one of the characters. He is a boy. He is helping to rake the cornfield. So now we know who Cole is and what he is doing.*

You Do Guide children to read the rest of Leveled Reader *Corn Fun*. Prompt them to tell more about what Cole does, thinks, and feels. Remind them to use the text and illustrations to help. Provide feedback as needed.

REVIEW MAIN STORY ELEMENTS: SEQUENCE OF EVENTS

OBJECTIVES

Describe major events, in a story, using key details.

I Do Remind children that the sequence of events is the order that events appear in a story. We think about what happens *first, next, then,* and *last* to understand the sequence of events.

We Do Read the first few sentences of **Leveled Reader** *Corn Fun* together. Pause to point out the first important event. Say: *We read that Cole, Dave, and the workers raked the field. This is the first event.*

You Do Have partners reread the selection together. Have them work together as you guide them to complete a Sequence of Events chart.

SELF-SELECTED READING

OBJECTIVES

Describe major events in a story, using key details.

Read grade-level text with purpose and understanding.

Independent Reading

Have children select a play for independent reading. Children may use the **Classroom Library,** the **Leveled Reader Library,** the online **Unit Bibliography,** or other books for their independent reading. Encourage them to read for at least fifteen minutes.

Guide children to transfer what they have learned in this week as they read. Remind children that sequence of events is the order in which the events appear in a story. Tell them to think about what happens first, next, then, and last to understand the sequence of events. Have children record information about sequence of events on **Graphic Organizer 6.**

After reading, guide children to participate in a group discussion about the story they read. In addition, children can choose activities from the Reading **Center Activity Cards** to help them apply skills to the text as they read. Offer assistance and guidance with self-selected assignments.

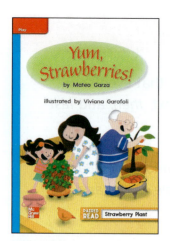

Lexile NP

OBJECTIVES

Describe major events in a story, using key details.

Retell stories, including key details, and demonstrate understanding of their central message or lesson.

Read grade-level text orally with accuracy, appropriate rate, and expression on successive readings.

Make and confirm predictions.

ELA ACADEMIC LANGUAGE

• *confirm, predict, sequence*
• Cognate: *prediccíon*

●On Level

Leveled Reader: *Yum, Strawberries!*

Preview and Predict

Have children turn to the title page. Read the title and the author's name and have children repeat. Preview the selection's illustrations. Prompt children to predict what the selection might be about.

Review Genre: Drama: Play

Have children recall that a play is a story that is intended to be performed. It often has a narrator that tells the story, and has a setting. It has dialogue spoken by each character.

Set Purpose

Remind children of the Essential Question. Set a purpose for reading: *Let's read to find out about a special place to plant a garden.* Remind children that as they read a selection, they can ask questions about what they do not understand or what they want to know more about.

Guided Comprehension

As children whisper read *Yum, Strawberries!* independently or with a partner, monitor and provide guidance. Correct blending and model the key strategies and skills as needed. As needed, provide definitions for words unfamiliar to children.

Make and Confirm Predictions

Model making and confirming predictions: *On page 2, the words tell me Lily likes strawberries. The picture shows a pot, dirt, and shovels. I predict Lily will use the pot and dirt to plant.* Read page 3, point to the picture, and confirm the prediction. Remind children that they can use details from the text and illustrations to make and correct or confirm predictions.

Main Story Elements: Sequence of Events

Hand out Graphic Organizer 6 to children. Review that the sequence of events is the order that events appear in a story. We think about what happens *first, next, then,* and *last* to understand the sequence of events. As you read, ask: *What is the first important event in the play?*

Display a Sequence of Events chart 6 for children to copy. Model recording children's answers in the first box. Have children copy the answers into their own charts.

Think Aloud As I read pages 2 and 3, I learn that Lily and her mom plant and water nine plants. This is the main event that happens first. I will write this in the first box of my chart.

As children read, have them complete their Sequence of Events chart.

Respond to Reading Have children complete the Respond to Reading on page 12.

Retell Have children take turns retelling the selection using the **Retelling Cards** as a guide. Help children make a connection by asking: *What have you planted? Where did you plant? What did you do to care for your plant? How did the plant change?*

Fluency: Accuracy and Rate

Model Model reading page 2 with accuracy and an appropriate rate. Read aloud. Have children read along with you.

Apply Have children practice reading the text with a partner. Correct any errors, as needed.

Paired Read: "Strawberry Plant"

 Make Connections: Write About It

Before reading, ask children to note that the genre of this text is nonfiction. Then read the Compare Texts direction in the **Leveled Reader.**

After reading, ask children how the information in "Strawberry Plant" adds to their understanding of the play *Yum, Strawberries!*

Leveled Reader

Build Knowledge: Make Connections

Talk About the Texts Have partners discuss how the plants in the texts change as they grow.

Write About the Texts Then have children add their ideas to the Build Knowledge page of their reader's notebook.

LITERATURE CIRCLES

Lead children in conducting a literature circle using the Thinkmark questions to guide the discussion. You may wish to discuss what children have learned about strawberries from both selections in the **Leveled Reader.**

 FOCUS ON SCIENCE

Children can extend their knowledge of foods we grow by completing the science activity on page 16. **STEM**

IF children can read *Yum, Strawberries!* On Level with fluency and correctly answer the questions,

THEN tell children that they will read another play about things that grow.

• Have children read the selection, checking their comprehension by using the graphic organizer.

● On Level

Phonics

READ AND BUILD WORDS WITH LONG *i: i_e*

OBJECTIVES

Know final -e and common vowel team conventions for representing long vowel sounds.

Decode regularly spelled one-syllable words.

Unit 3 Decodable Reader pages 13–24

I Do Display **Word-Building Cards** *t, i, l, e. These are letters* t, i, l, *and* e. *They stand for* /t/ /ī/ *and* /l/. *Remember the* i *and* e *together stand for the sound* /ī/. *I will blend* /t/, /ī/, *and* /l/ *together:* /tīīīl/, tile. *The word is* tile.

We Do *Now let's build a new word together.* Make the word *tile* using Word-Building Cards. Place the letter *s* at the end of *tile. Let's blend:* /tīīīl/ /z/, /tīīīlz/, tiles. *Now there is a new word*, tiles. *I am going to change the letter* t *to* f. Change the letter *t* to *f. Let's blend and read the new word:* /f/ /ī/ /l/ /z/, /fīīīlz/, files. *The new word is* files.

You Do Have children build and blend the words: *miles, mile, mine, line, fine, pine, pipe, ripe, ride, side*, and *size*.

Read the Decodable Readers

Guide children to read "A Fine Plant" and "Plants Take Time to Grow." Identify the high-frequency words and words in which the spelling *i_e* stands for the long *i* sound. Model blending sound by sound as needed.

Focus on Fluency With partners, have children reread "A Fine Plant" and "Plants Take Time to Grow." As children read the text, guide them to focus on accuracy, rate, and automaticity. Partners can provide feedback.

High-Frequency Words

REVIEW WORDS

OBJECTIVES

Recognize and read grade-appropriate irregularly spelled words.

I Do Use the Read/Spell/Write routine to review *green, grow, pretty, should, together,* and *water*. Use each word orally in a sentence.

We Do Guide children to Read/Spell/Write each word using their **Response Boards.** Work together to create oral sentences using the words.

You Do Have partners work together using the Read/Spell/Write routine with the words *green, grow, pretty, should, together,* and *water*. Have partners then write sentences about this week's stories. Each sentence must contain at least one high-frequency word. Provide feedback as needed.

Comprehension

REVIEW MAIN STORY ELEMENTS: SEQUENCE OF EVENTS

OBJECTIVES
Describe major events, in a story, using key details.

I Do Remind children that the sequence of events is the order that events appear in a story. We think about what happens *first, next, then,* and *last* to understand the sequence of events.

We Do Read the first two pages of **Leveled Reader** *Yum, Strawberries!* aloud. Pause to discuss event that happens first. *Mom and Lily are in their rooftop garden. What are they doing there? This is the event that happens first.*

You Do Guide children to read the rest of Leveled Reader *Yum, Strawberries!* Have them discuss with a partner other important events in the order they happen. Provide feedback as needed.

SELF-SELECTED READING

OBJECTIVES
Describe major events in a story, using key details.

Read grade-level text with purpose and understanding.

Independent Reading

Have children select a play for independent reading. Children may use the **Classroom Library,** the **Leveled Reader Library,** the online **Unit Bibliography,** or other books for their independent reading. Encourage them to read for at least fifteen minutes.

Guide children to transfer what they have learned in this week as they read. Remind children that sequence of events is the order in which the events appear in a story. Tell them to think about what happens first, next, then, and last to understand the sequence of events. Have children record information about sequence of events on **Graphic Organizer 6.**

After reading, guide children to participate in a group discussion about the story they read. In addition, children can choose activities from the Reading **Center Activity Cards** to help them apply skills to the text as they read. Offer assistance and guidance with self-selected assignments.

You may wish to review Comprehension with **ELL** using this section.

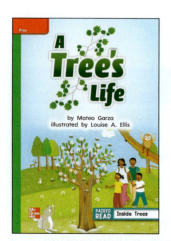

Lexile NP

OBJECTIVES

Describe major events in a story, using key details.

Retell stories, including key details, and demonstrate understanding of their central message or lesson.

Identify basic similarities in and differences between two texts on the same topic.

Make and confirm predictions.

ELA ACADEMIC LANGUAGE

• *confirm, prediction*

• Cognate: *predicción*

●Beyond Level

Leveled Reader: *A Tree's Life*

Preview and Predict

Read the title and the author's name. Have children preview the title page and the illustrations. Ask: *What do you think this book will be about?*

Review Genre: Drama: Play

Have children recall that a play is a story that is intended to be performed. It often has a narrator that tells the story, and has a setting. It has dialogue spoken by each character.

Set Purpose

Remind children of the Essential Question. Set a purpose for reading: *What do you want to find out about a tree's life? As you get ready to read this fluently, think about the purpose.*

Guided Comprehension

Have children whisper read *A Tree's Life* independently or with a partner. Have them place self-stick notes next to difficult words. Monitor and provide guidance. Correct blending and model the key strategies and skills, as needed.

Monitor children's reading. Stop periodically and ask open-ended questions to facilitate rich discussion, such as *What does the author want us to know about the life of a tree?* Build on children's responses to develop deeper understanding.

Make and Confirm Predictions

Model making and confirming a prediction: *After reading page 3 and looking at the illustrations, I predict that the squirrel is hoping the Cash family left some food behind.* Read page 4 to confirm the prediction. Remind children that making and correcting or confirming predictions about what they read can help them read actively and understand a selection.

Main Story Elements: Sequence of Events

Hand out Graphic Organizer 6 to children. Remind children that the sequence of events is the order that events appear in a story. Ask children what we think about to understand the sequence of events. As you read, ask: *What event happens first?* Display a Sequence of Events chart 6 for children to copy. Model recording the first event. Have children fill in their charts.

Think Aloud As I read pages 2 and 3, I learn that the Cash family went on a picnic in the woods. This is event that happens first. I will write this in the first box in my chart.

Have children fill in the rest of their charts in order.

Respond to Reading Have children complete the Respond to Reading on page 12 after reading.

Retell Have children take turns retelling the selection. Help children make a personal connection by writing about the different kinds of trees they have seen. *Write about two different trees you have seen. What kind of trees are they? What seasonal changes have you seen in the trees?*

Paired Read: "Inside Trees"

 Make Connections: Write About It

Ask children to preview the title page and prompt them to identify the genre as nonfiction text. Then read the Compare Texts direction in the **Leveled Reader.**

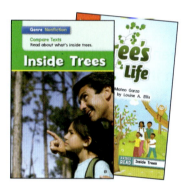
Leveled Reader

After reading, have children work with a partner to discuss how the information they learned in *A Tree's Life* is similar to what they learned in "Inside Trees."

Build Knowledge: Make Connections

 Talk About the Text Have partners discuss how the plants in the texts change as they grow.

 Write About the Text Then have children add their ideas to the Build Knowledge page of their reader's notebook.

LITERATURE CIRCLES

Lead children in conducting a literature circle using the Thinkmark questions to guide the discussion. You may wish to discuss what children have learned about trees from both selections in the **Leveled Reader.**

FOCUS ON SCIENCE

Children can extend their knowledge about what we grow by completing the science activity on page 16. **STEM**

GIFTED AND TALENTED

Synthesize Challenge children to think about how trees are important to people and animals. Have them use the selections they read to support their responses.

Extend Have children use facts they learned from the week or do additional research to find out more about trees.

Beyond Level

Vocabulary

ORAL VOCABULARY: ANTONYMS

OBJECTIVES

With guidance and support from adults, demonstrate understanding of word relationships and nuances in word meanings.

Determine the meaning of antonyms and use them in sentences.

I Do Review the meaning of the oral vocabulary word *bloom.* Remind children that an antonym is a word that has the opposite meaning of another word.

Bloom *means to produce, or grow, flowers. When flowers start to die, they wilt, or lose their leaves and droop.* Wilt *is an antonym of* bloom.

Continue with: *When you assist someone, you help them do something. If you purposely do not help, you hinder, or prevent, that person from doing something.* Hinder *means the opposite of* assist.

We Do Help children orally fill in the sentence frame: Flowers _____ in the spring and _____ in the winter. Then have them think of examples of assisting someone and preventing someone from getting something done.

You Do Have partners create a new sentence for *bloom* and *wilt,* and another for *assist* and *hinder.* Remind them that their sentences should show how the words are antonyms.

GIFTED and TALENTED **Extend** Have children come up with an oral list of ways people can assist growing plants in a garden and things people do that might hinder flowers from growing. Encourage them to share their ideas with the class.

Comprehension

REVIEW MAIN STORY ELEMENTS: SEQUENCE OF EVENTS

OBJECTIVES

Describe major events in a story, using key details.

I Do Remind children that the sequence of events is the order that events appear in a story. We think about what happens *first, next, then,* and *last* to understand the sequence of events.

We Do Guide children in reading the first two pages of **Leveled Reader** *A Tree's Life* aloud. Prompt them to discuss events. Ask: *What important event happens first? What happens next?*

You Do Have children read the rest of the selection independently. Remind them to talk to a partner about the events in the order they happen. Provide feedback as needed.

SELF-SELECTED READING

OBJECTIVES

Describe major events in a story, using key details.

Read grade-level text with purpose and understanding.

Independent Reading

Have children select a play for independent reading. Children may use the **Classroom Library,** the **Leveled Reader Library,** the online **Unit Bibliography,** or other books for their independent reading. Encourage them to read for at least fifteen minutes.

Guide children to transfer what they have learned in this week as they read by reminding them that sequence of events is the order in which the events appear in a story. Tell them to think about what happens first, next, then, and last to understand the sequence of events. Have children record information about sequence of events on **Graphic Organizer 6.**

After reading, guide children to participate in a group discussion about the story they read. In addition, children can choose activities from the Reading **Center Activity Cards** to help them apply skills to the text as they read. Offer assistance and guidance with self-selected assignments.

GIFTED and TALENTED Independent Study Have partners or small groups write a play about growing a plant. Remind them to include the words *first, next, then,* and *last* as they describe events. Invite them to perform the play for the class.

Student Outcomes

✓ Tested in *Wonders* Assessments

FOUNDATIONAL SKILLS

Print Concepts
- Locate title, author

Phonological Awareness
- ✓ Identify and Produce Rhyme
- ✓ Phoneme Segmentation
- ✓ Phoneme Blending

Phonics and Word Analysis
- ✓ Soft *c* and Soft *g/dge*
- ✓ Inflectional endings *-ed* and *-ing*

Fluency
- Read with accuracy and automaticity
- ✓ High-Frequency Words
- • *any   from   happy   once   so   upon*

READING

Reading Literature
- ✓ Identify and explain the moral of a story
- ✓ Identify and explain descriptive words and phrases in texts
- Retell a text to enhance comprehension
- Read prose and poetry appropriately complex for grade 1

Compare Texts
- Compare and contrast two texts on the same topic

COMMUNICATION

Writing
- Handwriting: *Yy*
- Write narratives that retell two or more appropriately sequenced events, including relevant details and a sense of closure
- Focus on a topic, respond to suggestions from peers, and add details to strengthen writing

Speaking and Listening
- Participate in collaborative conversations
- Ask and answer questions to gather or clarify information
- Present information orally using complete sentences

Conventions
- ✓ **Grammar:** Use past- and future-tense verbs
- **Mechanics:** Use commas in series
- **Spelling:** Spell words with Soft *c, g, dge*

Researching
- Recall or gather information to answer a question
- Participate in shared research and writing projects

Creating and Collaborating
- Add drawings and visual displays to descriptions
- Use digital tools to produce and publish writing

VOCABULARY

Academic Vocabulary
- Acquire and use grade-appropriate academic vocabulary
- Identify real-life connections between words and their use

ELL Scaffolded supports for English Language Learners are embedded throughout the lessons, enabling children to communicate information, ideas, and concepts in English Language Arts and for social and instructional purposes within the school setting.

See the **ELL Small Group Guide** for additional support of the skills for the text set.

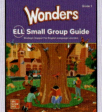

FORMATIVE ASSESSMENT

For assessment throughout the text set, use children's self-assessments and your observations.

Use the Data Dashboard to filter class, group, or individual student data to guide group placement decisions. It provides recommendations to enhance learning for gifted and talented children and offers extra support for children needing remediation.

DATA DASHBOARD

Develop Student Ownership

To build student ownership, children need to know what they are learning, why they are learning it, and determine how well they understood it.

Students Discuss Their Goals

TEXT SET GOALS

- I can read and understand a folktale.
- I can respond to a folktale by writing a new ending.
- I know about different folktales.

Have children think about what they know and fill in the bars on **Reading/Writing Companion** page 80.

Students Monitor Their Learning

LEARNING GOALS

Specific learning goals identified in every lesson make clear what children will be learning and why. These smaller goals provide stepping stones to help children meet their Text Set Goals.

CHECK-IN ROUTINE

The Check-In routine at the close of each lesson guides children to self-reflect on how well they understood each learning goal.

Review the lesson learning goal.
Reflect on the activity.
Self-Assess by
- filling in the bars in the **Reading/Writing Companion.**
- holding up 1, 2, 3, or 4 fingers.

Share with your teacher.

Students Reflect on Their Progress

TEXT SET GOALS

After completing the Show Your Knowledge task for the text set, children reflect on their understanding of the Text Set Goals by filling in the bars on **Reading/Writing Companion** page 81.

Literature Big Book

Shared Read
Reading/Writing Companion p. 82

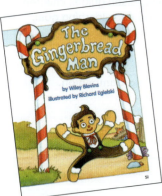

Anchor Text
Literature Anthology p. 50

Paired Selection
Literature Anthology p. 68

Essential Question
What is a folktale?

 Video Folktales are told again and again, from one generation to the next. They teach us lessons. People from many cultures tell folktales. Some examples are *The Squeaky Bed* and *The Magic Paintbrush*.

Literature Big Book An excited little chicken listens as her father reads her folktales, such as *Hansel and Gretel* and *Little Red Riding Hood*.

Shared Read In this folktale, a boy loses his mitten, and many animals creep into it to rest and hide. They cause the mitten to pop.

Interactive Read Aloud In this folktale, a rabbit thinks the Earth is breaking up. He causes a panic among the other animals.

Anchor Text In this folktale, Gram and Gramps bake a grandson out of gingerbread. Many animals try to eat him. He outruns all of them, except for a clever fox.

Paired Selection Mother Goose rhymes have been told over time, from one generation to the next.

Art A wolf tries to trick a young girl in the folktale *Little Red Riding Hood*.

Differentiated Sources

Leveled Readers 🔊

🟠 This folktale tells how the coquí got her voice after winning a race in the forest.

🔵 🟣 In this folktale, a young girl's magic paintbrush makes everything she paints become real. She uses it to help others.

🟢 In this folktale, Rabbit tricks Crocodile into helping her cross the water to the mainland.

Build Knowledge Routine

After reading each text, ask children to document facts and details they learned that help them answer the Essential Question of the text set.

 Talk about the source.

 Write about the source.

 Add to the class Anchor Chart

- Add to the Word Bank.

Show Your Knowledge

Write Your Opinion

Have children think about the different folktales they read. Guide them to write an opinion about why people should read folktales. Have them draw a picture and include vocabulary words and text evidence to support their opinion.

Social Emotional Learning

Teachable Moment

Take a moment to reflect on children's developing skills on assessed or previously-taught SEL competencies. Then, select an SEL lesson from your library of resources to meet children's individualized needs, and integrate it into your weekly plan.

Family Time • Share your selected SEL lesson's video and activity in the **School to Home** newsletter.

Explore the Texts

Essential Question: What is a folktale?

Literature Big Book	Interactive Read Aloud	Reading/Writing Companion	Literature Anthology

Interrupting Chicken Fantasy	**"The Foolish, Timid Rabbit"** Folktale	**"The Nice Mitten"** Shared Read pp. 82–91 Folktale	***The Gingerbread Man*** Anchor Text pp. 50–67 Folktale

Qualitative

Meaning/Purpose: High Complexity **Structure:** High Complexity **Language:** Moderate Complexity **Knowledge Demands:** Moderate Complexity	**Meaning/Purpose:** High Complexity **Structure:** Low Complexity **Language:** Moderate Complexity **Knowledge Demands:** Moderate Complexity	**Meaning/Purpose:** Moderate Complexity **Structure:** Moderate Complexity **Language:** Low Complexity **Knowledge Demands:** Low Complexity	**Meaning/Purpose:** Low Complexity **Structure:** Moderate Complexity **Language:** Moderate Complexity **Knowledge Demands:** Low Complexity

Quantitative

Lexile 510L	Lexile 470L	Lexile 460L	Lexile 320L

Reader and Task Considerations

Reader Children may need some familiarity with the fairytales from the story to understand the little chicken's feelings.	**Reader** Children may need background knowledge that folktales often contain a lesson or moral, so they can listen for it as the story progresses.	**Reader** Children will need to use their knowledge of sound-spelling correspondences and high-frequency words to read the text.	**Reader** Children may be familiar with different versions of this folktale. This text allows for discussion about the morals or lessons taught in folktales.

Task The questions for the Interactive Read Aloud are supported by teacher modeling. The tasks provide a variety of ways for students to begin to build knowledge and vocabulary about the text set topic. The questions and tasks provided for the other texts are at various levels of complexity, ensuring that all students can interact with the text in meaningful ways.

Additional Texts

Content Area Reading BLMs
Additional online texts related to grade-level Science, Social Studies, and Arts content.

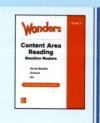

Access Complex Text (ACT) boxes provide scaffolded instruction for seven different elements that may make the **Literature Big Book** complex.

Literature Anthology

"Drakestail"
Paired Selection
pp. 68–75
Folktale

Qualitative

Meaning/Purpose: Low Complexity
Structure: Low Complexity
Language: Moderate Complexity
Knowledge Demands: Moderate Complexity

Quantitative

Lexile 450L

Reader and Task Considerations

Reader Children might be able to recognize the pattern of events in this folktale, as it is similar to that of other folktales.

Task The questions and tasks provided for this text are at various levels of complexity, ensuring that all students can interact with the text in meaningful ways.

Leveled Readers 🔊 (All Leveled Readers are provided in eBook format with audio support.)

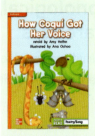  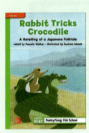 

(A)	**(O)**	**(B)**	**(ELL)**
How Coquí Got Her Voice	***The Magic Paintbrush***	***Rabbit Tricks Crocodile***	***The Magic Paintbrush***
Leveled Reader	Leveled Reader	Leveled Reader	Leveled Reader
Folktale	Folktale	Folktale	Folktale

Qualitative

Meaning/Purpose: Low Complexity	**Meaning/Purpose:** Low Complexity	**Meaning/Purpose:** Low Complexity	**Meaning/Purpose:** Low Complexity
Structure: Moderate Complexity	**Structure:** Moderate Complexity	**Structure:** Moderate Complexity	**Structure:** Moderate Complexity
Language: Moderate Complexity	**Language:** Moderate Complexity	**Language:** Moderate Complexity	**Language:** Low Complexity
Knowledge Demands: Low Complexity	**Knowledge Demands:** Low Complexity	**Knowledge Demands:** Moderate Complexity	**Knowledge Demands:** Low Complexity

Quantitative

Lexile 300L	Lexile 230L	Lexile 420L	Lexile 240L

Reader and Task Considerations

Reader Children may need background information on the coqui, including what it looks like, where it lives and what is sounds like.	**Reader** Children may need background knowledge that folktales often contain a lesson or moral, so they can listen for it as the story progresses.	**Reader** Children may need background knowledge that folktales often contain a lesson or moral, so they can listen for it as the story progresses.	**Reader** Children may need background knowledge that folktales often contain a lesson or moral, so they can listen for it as the story progresses.

Task The questions and tasks provided for the Leveled Readers are at various levels of complexity, ensuring that all students can interact with the text in meaningful ways.

Focus on Word Work

Build Foundational Skills with Multimodal Learning

MULTIMODAL

Response Board

Phonemic Awareness Activities

Sound-Spelling Cards

Word-Building Cards online

Phonics Activities

Practice Book

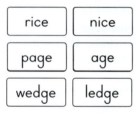

rice	nice
page	age
wedge	ledge

Spelling Cards Online

any

High-Frequency Word Cards

High-Frequency Word Activities

Visual Vocabulary Cards

Shared Read

Decodable Readers

Take-Home Story

Phonological/Phonemic Awareness

- Identify and produce rhyming words
- Blend and segment phonemes

Phonics: Soft *c*, Soft *g*, *dge*

- Introduce/review sound-spellings
- Blend/build words with sound-spellings
- Practice handwriting
- Structural Analysis: Build reading word bank
- Decode and encode in connected texts

Spelling: Soft *c*, Soft *g*, *dge*

- Differentiated spelling instruction
- Encode with sound-spellings
- Explore relationships with word sorts and word families

High-Frequency Words

- Read/Spell/Write routine

See Word Work, pages T170–T173, T180–T183, T190–T193, T214–T215, T220–T221.

Apply Skills to Read

- Children apply foundational skills as they read decodable texts.
- Children practice fluency to develop word automaticity.

PHONICS SKILLS TRACE

Initial Consonants ▸ Short Vowels ▸ Consonant Blends and Digraphs ▸ Long Vowels ▸ Vowel Digraphs ▸ r-Controlled Vowels ▸ Diphthongs ▸ Variant Vowels ▸ Silent Letters and 3-Letter Blends

Explicit Systematic Instruction

Word Work instruction expands foundational skills to enable children to become proficient readers.

Daily Routine

- Use the In a Flash: Sound-Spelling routine and the In a Flash: High-Frequency Word routine to build fluency.
- Set Learning Goal.

Explicit Minilessons and Practice

Use daily instruction in both whole and small groups to model, practice, and apply key foundational skills. Opportunities include:

- Multimodal engagement.
- Corrective feedback.
- Supports for English Language Learners in each lesson.
- Peer collaboration.

Formative Assessment

Check-In

- Children reflect on their learning.
- Children show their progress by holding up 1 to 4 fingers in a Check-In routine.

Check for Success

- Teacher monitors children's achievement and differentiates for Small Group instruction.

Differentiated Instruction

To strengthen skills, provide targeted review and reteaching lessons and multimodal activities to meet children's diverse needs.

🟠 🟣 **Approaching Level, ELL**
- Includes Tier 2 **TIER 2**

🔵 **On Level**

🟢 **Beyond Level**
- Includes Gifted and Talented **GIFTED and TALENTED**

Independent Practice

Provide additional practice as needed. Have children work individually or with partners.

Center Activity Cards

Digital Activities

Word-Building Cards online

Decodable Readers   **Practice Book**

Inspire Early Writers

Build Writing Skills and Conventions

Practice Book

Handwriting Video

Reading/Writing Companion

Write Letters

- Learn to write letters
- Practice writing

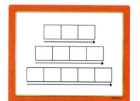

Response Board

Practice Book

High-Frequency Word Activities

Write Words

- Write words with *soft c, soft g; dge*
- Write spelling words
- Write high-frequency words

Reading/Writing Companion

Practice Book

Write Sentences

- Write sentences with inflectional endings
- Write sentences to respond to text

Follow Conventions

- Form and use past- and future-tense verbs
- Use commas in a series

Interrupting Chicken
Literature Big Book

Writing Fluency

To increase children's writing fluency, have them write as much as they can in response to the **Literature Big Book** for five minutes. Tell children to write about different folktales they have heard.

For lessons, see pages T170–T173, T176–T177, T180–T183, T186–T187, T204–T205, T216–T217, T221, T222–T223.

Write About Texts

**Reading/Writing Companion,
pp. 92–93, 98–99**

Modeled Writing

Write About the Shared Read "The Nice Mitten"

- Prompt: Rewrite the ending to "The Nice Mitten."

Interactive Writing

- Prompt: Write a new story about a boy who loses his boot.

**Reading/Writing
Companion, p. 104**

Independent Writing

Write About the Anchor Text *The Gingerbread Man*
Literature Anthology, pp. 50–67

- Prompt: Imagine the Gingerbread Man had chosen to go around the lake. Then write a new ending to the story.

- Have children follow the steps of the writing process: draft, revise, edit/proofread, share.

Additional Lessons

Writing Skill Lesson Bank To provide differentiated support for writing skills, see pages T420–T429.

Extended Writing Minilessons For a full set of lessons that support the writing process and writing in a specific genre, see pages T402–T413.

Self-Selected Writing

Children can explore different writing modes.

 Write an Opinion

 Newspaper Article

 Storyboard

Planner

Customize your own lesson plans at
my.mheducation.com

 Select from your Social Emotional Learning resources.

 LESSON 1

 LESSON 2

TEXT SET GOALS

- I can read and understand a folktale.
- I can respond to a folktale by writing a new ending.
- I know about different folktales.

 90+ mins
Reading Suggested Daily Time Includes Small Group

> **SMALL GROUP OPTIONS**
The designated lessons can be taught in small groups. To determine how to differentiate instruction for small groups, use Formative Assessment and Data Dashboard.

30+ mins
Writing Suggested Daily Time

Reading

Lesson 1

Introduce the Concept, T166–T167
Build Knowledge: Tales Over Time

Listening Comprehension, T168–T169
Interrupting Chicken

> **Word Work, T170–T173**
Phonological Awareness: Identify and Produce Rhyme
Phonics/Spelling: Soft *c*; Soft *g, dge*
High-Frequency Words: *any, from, happy, once, so, upon*

Shared Read, T174–T175
Read "The Nice Mitten"

Lesson 2

> **Build the Concept, T178**
Oral Language

Listening Comprehension, T179
"The Foolish, Timid Rabbit"

> **Word Work, T180–T183**
Phonemic Awareness: Phoneme Segmentation
Phonics/Spelling: Soft *c*; Soft *g, dge*
Structural Analysis: Inflectional Endings -*ed*, -*ing*
High-Frequency Words: *any, from, happy, once, so, upon*

> **Shared Read, T184–T185**
Reread "The Nice Mitten"

Writing

Lesson 1

Modeled Writing, T176
Write About the Shared Read
Grammar, T177
Past- and Future-Tense Verbs

Lesson 2

> **Interactive Writing, T186**
Write About the Shared Read
Grammar, T187
Past- and Future-Tense Verbs

 SMALL GROUP

Teacher-Led Instruction

Differentiated Reading
Leveled Readers

- *How Coquí Got Her Voice*, T226–T227
- *The Magic Paintbrush*, T236–T237
- *Rabbit Tricks Crocodile*, T240–T241

Differentiated Skills Practice, T228–T243
● **Approaching Level, T228–T235**
Phonological/Phonemic Awareness
- Identify Rhyme, T228 **TIER 2**
- Produce Rhyme, T228 **TIER 2**
- Phoneme Blending, T229
- Phoneme Segmentation, T229

Phonics
- Connect *c* to /s/ and *g* to /j/, T230 **TIER 2**
- Blend Words with *c* and *g*, T230 **TIER 2**
- Build Words with soft *c* and *g*, T231
- Read Words with soft *c* and *g*, T231
- Build Fluency with Phonics, T231

Structural Analysis
- Review Inflectional Endings -*ed*, -*ing*, T232
- Reteach Inflectional Endings -*ed*, -*ing*, T232

Independent/Collaborative Work See pages T165I–T165J

Reading
Comprehension
- Folktale
- Make and Confirm Predictions
- Moral
Independent Reading

Word Work
Phonics/Spelling
- Soft *c*; Soft *g, dge*
High-Frequency Words
- *any, from, happy, once, so, upon*

Writing
Self-Selected Writing
Grammar
- Past- and Future-Tense Verbs
Nouns
Handwriting
- Upper and lowercase *Yy*

ORAL VOCABULARY
hero, tale, timid, foolish, eventually

SPELLING
rice, nice, page, age, wedge, ledge, like, ride, from, once
See page T172 for Differentiated Spelling Lists.

 LESSON 3

 LESSON 4

 LESSON 5

Reading

Build the Concept, T188
Oral Language
Take Notes About Text

Listening Comprehension, T189
Interrupting Chicken

▶ Word Work, T190–T193
Phonemic Awareness: Phoneme Blending
Phonics/Spelling: Soft *c*; Soft *g, dge*
Structural Analysis: Inflectional Endings *-ed, -ing*
High-Frequency Words: *any, from, happy, once, so, upon*

Anchor Text, T194–T203
Read *The Gingerbread Man*

Extend the Concept, T206–T207
Oral Language

Paired Selection, T208–T213
Read "Drakestail"

▶ Word Work, T214–T215
Phonemic Awareness: Phoneme Segmentation
Phonics/Spelling: Soft *c*; Soft *g, dge*
Structural Analysis: Inflectional Endings *-ed, -ing*
High-Frequency Words: *any, from, happy, once, so, upon*

▶ Research and Inquiry, T218–T219
Research and Inquiry: Folktales

▶ Word Work, T220–T221
Phonemic Awareness: Phoneme Blending and Segmentation
Phonics/Spelling: Soft *c*; Soft *g, dge*
Phonics: Read the Decodable Reader
Structural Analysis: Inflectional Endings *-ed, -ing*
High-Frequency Words: *any, from, happy, once, so, upon*

Integrate Ideas, T224
Make Connections

Culminating Task, T225
Show Your Knowledge

Writing

Independent Writing, T204
Write About the Anchor Text
Grammar, T205
Past- and Future-Tense Verbs
Mechanics, T205
Commas in a Series

Independent Writing, T216
Write About the Anchor Text
Grammar, T217
Past- and Future-Tense Verbs
Mechanics, T217
Commas in a Series

▶ Self-Selected Writing, T222
Grammar, T223
Past- and Future-Tense Verbs
Mechanics, T223
Commas in a Series

High-Frequency Words
• Review/Reteach/Cumulative Review, T233
Comprehension
• Read for Fluency, T234 ⭕2
• Identify Characters, T234 ⭕2
• Review Moral, T235
• Self-Selected Reading, T235

● **On Level, T238–T239**
Phonics
• Read and Build Words with Soft *c* and *g*, T238
High-Frequency Words
• Review Words, T238
Comprehension
• Review Moral, T239
• Self-Selected Reading, T239

● **Beyond Level, T242–T243**
Vocabulary
• Oral Vocabulary: Synonyms, T242
Comprehension
• Review Moral, T243
• Self-Selected Reading, T243 🌟GIFTED and TALENTED

 ● **English Language Learners**
See ELL Small Group Guide, pp. 126–135.

Content Area Connections
Content Area Reading
• Science, Social Studies, and the Arts
Research and Inquiry
• Folktales

 ● **English Language Learners**
See ELL Small Group Guide, pp. 75, 127, 129, 131.

Independent and Collaborative Work

As you meet with small groups, have the rest of the class complete activities and projects to practice and apply the skills they have been working on.

Student Choice and Student Voice

- Review My Weekly Work blackline master with children and identify the "Must Do" activities.
- Have children choose some additional activities that provide the practice they need.
- Remind children to reflect on their learning each day.

My Weekly Work BLMs

LON PO PO: A RED-RIDING HOOD STORY FROM CHINA by Ed Young, Copyright © 1989. Used by permission of Philomel Books. Nelson, Kadir. If You Plant a Seed. New York, NY: Bolzer + Bray, an imprint of HarperCollins Publishers, 2015. INTERRUPTING CHICKEN. Copyright © 2010 by David Ezra Stein. Reproduced by permission of the publisher, Candlewick Press, Somerville, MA.

Reading

Text Options

Children can choose a **Center Activity Card** to use while they listen to a text or read independently.

Classroom Library Read Aloud
Lon Po Po: A Red-Riding Hood Story from China
Genre: Fiction
Lexile: 670L

Classroom Library
If You Plant a Seed
Genre: Fantasy
Lexile: 340L

Unit Bibliography
See the online bibliography. Children can select independent reading texts about folktales.

Leveled Texts Online
All **Leveled Readers** are provided in eBook format with audio support.

- **Differentiated Texts** provide English Language Learners with passages at different proficiency levels.

Literature Big Book e-Book
Interrupting Chicken
Genre: Fiction

Center Activity Cards

Make and Confirm Predictions Card 3

Folktale Card 31

Moral Card 11

Digital Activities

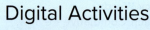

Comprehension

Word Work

Center Activity Cards

Soft c and Soft g Card 83

Word-Building Cards

Practice Book BLMs

Phonological Awareness: pp. 193, 194
Phonics: pp. 195, 196
Spelling: pp. 197–199
Structural Analysis: pp. 201, 202
High-Frequency Words: p. 203
Take-Home Story: pp. 207–208

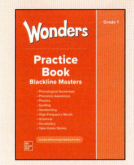

Decodable Readers

Unit 3, pp. 25–36

Digital Activities

Phonemic Awareness
Phonics
Spelling
High-Frequency Words

Writing

Center Activity Cards

Specific Words Card 64

Practice Book BLMs

Handwriting: p. 200
Grammar: pp. 204–205
Mechanics: p. 206

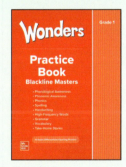

Self-Selected Writing

- Write about your favorite folktale.
- Write about your favorite character in a folktale.
- Name two folktales, and then tell how they are the same and different.

Digital Activities

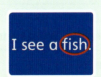

Grammar

Grammar: Mechanics

Content Area Connections

Content Area Reading BLMs
- Additional texts related to Science, Social Studies, Health, and the Arts.

Research and Inquiry
- Complete Folktales project

Progress Monitoring
Moving Toward Mastery

FORMATIVE ASSESSMENT

⊘ STUDENT CHECK-IN

✓ CHECK FOR SUCCESS

For ongoing formative assessment, use children's self-assessments at the end of each lesson along with your own observations.

Assessing skills along the way . . .

SKILLS	HOW ASSESSED
Phonological/Phonemic Awareness **Phonics** **Structural Analysis** **High-Frequency Words**	Practice Book, Digital Activities, Online Rubrics
Comprehension	Digital Activities, Graphic Organizers, Online Rubrics
Text-Based Writing **Handwriting** **Grammar** **Spelling**	Reading/Writing Companion: Independent Writing, Practice Book, Digital Activities, Spelling Word Sorts
Listening/Presenting/Research	Reading/Writing Companion: Share and Evaluate; Research: Online Student Checklists
Oral Reading Fluency (ORF) Conduct group fluency assessments using the **Letter Naming, Phoneme Segmentation**, and **Sight Word Fluency** assessments.	Fluency Assessment

At the end of the text set . . .

SKILLS	HOW ASSESSED
Moral **Folktale: Descriptive Words and Phrases**	Progress Monitoring
Identify Rhyme **Phoneme Segmentation** **Phoneme Blending**	
Soft c; Soft g/dge	
Inflectional Endings -ed, -ing	
any, from, happy, once, so, upon	

Making the Most of Assessment Results

Make data-based grouping decisions by using the following reports to verify assessment results. For additional support options for children, refer to the reteaching and enrichment opportunities.

ONLINE ASSESSMENT CENTER

- *Gradebook*

DATA DASHBOARD

- *Recommendations Report*
- *Activity Report*
- *Skills Report*
- *Progress Report*
- *Grade Card Report*

Reteaching Opportunities with Intervention Online PDFs

IF CHILDREN ANSWER . . .	THEN ASSIGN . . .
0–3 **comprehension** items correctly . . .	lessons 37–39 on Moral and/or lesson 113 on Descriptive Words and Phrases from the **Comprehension PDF.**
0–2 **phonological/phonemic** items correctly . . .	lessons 6–8 on Identify Rhyme, lessons 67–71 on Phoneme Segmentation, and lessons 62–66 on Phoneme Blending from the **Phonemic Awareness PDF.**
0–5 **phonics/structural analysis/HFW** items correctly . . .	lessons 55 on Soft *c*; Soft *g/dge* and lessons 66–67 on on Inflectional Endings *-ed, -ing* from the **Phonics/Word Study PDF** and lessons from Section 3 of the **Fluency PDF.**

Enrichment Opportunities

Beyond Level small-group lessons and resources include suggestions for additional activities in these areas to extend learning opportunities for gifted and talented children:

- *Leveled Reader*
- *Vocabulary*
- *Comprehension*
- *Leveled Reader Library Online*
- *Center Activity Cards*

OBJECTIVES

Follow agreed-upon rules for discussions.

Build on others' talk in conversations by responding to the comments of others through multiple exchanges.

Ask questions to clear up any confusion about the topics and texts under discussion.

Build background knowledge.

Discuss the Essential Question.

ELA ACADEMIC LANGUAGE

• *folktale, define, discuss*
• Cognates: *definir, discutir*

DIGITAL TOOLS

To enhance the class discussion, use these additional components.

Watch Video

Discuss Concept

LESSON FOCUS

READING

Introduce the Essential Question

Read Literature Big Book:
Interrupting Chicken
• Make Predictions

Word Work
• Introduce Soft *c*; Soft *g/dge*

Read Shared Read: "The Nice Mitten"
• Introduce Genre

WRITING
• Modeled Writing
• Introduce Grammar

Reading/Writing Companion, pp. 82–91

---

5 mins

Build Knowledge

MULTIMODAL

 Essential Question

What is a folktale?

Tell children that this week they will be talking and reading about a special kind of story called a folktale. Discuss the Essential Question. Children can discuss different folktales they know.

Watch the Video Play the video without sound first, and have partners narrate what they see. Then replay the video with sound, and have children listen.

Talk About the Video Have partners share one thing they learned from the video about folktales.

 Anchor Chart Create a Build Knowledge anchor chart with the Essential Question, and have volunteers share what they learned. Record their ideas on the chart.

Oral Vocabulary Words

Use the Define/Example/Ask routine on the print or digital **Visual Vocabulary Cards** to introduce the oral vocabulary words *hero* and *tale*. Children can use these words as they discuss folktales.

Oral Vocabulary Routine

Visual Vocabulary Cards

Define: The **hero** of a story is a main character who is brave and good.

Example: The hero saves Little Red Riding Hood from the big, bad wolf.

Ask: Who is the hero of your favorite tale?

Define: A **tale** is a story about exciting imaginary events.

Example: At story time, the teacher told a tale about a princess and a frog.

Ask: What is your favorite tale?

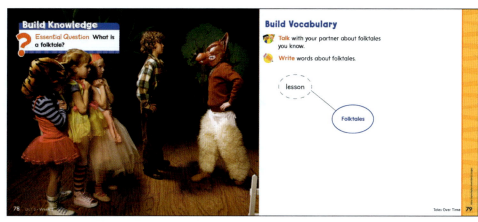

Reading/Writing Companion, pp. 78–79

Build Knowledge

Review how to take turns talking using the Collaborative Conversations box. Then have children turn to pages 78–79 of their **Reading/Writing Companions** and discuss the photo. Then ask:

• *What do you think these children are doing?*

• *Why did the children dress up in costumes?*

Build Vocabulary

Talk Have children talk with a partner about folktales they know.

Write Have children write words about folktales on page 79.

Create a Word Bank Have children suggest words related to folktales to a separate section of the Word Bank.

English Language Learners

Use the scaffolds to help children complete **Build Knowledge.**

Beginning

These children are performing a play. They wear costumes. Have children repeat *play* and *costumes.* Point to the wolf. *This is a wolf costume. What kind of costume is it?* It is a <u>wolf</u> costume.

Intermediate

These children are performing a play. They wear costumes. Have children repeat *play* and *costumes. Why are the children wearing costumes?* The children are in a <u>play</u>. *What is one costume you see?* I see a <u>wolf</u>.

Advanced/Advanced High

Ask partners to elaborate. Create a word bank to support the discussion: *costume, play, farmer, wolf, princess,* and *tiger.* Ask: *What characters are in the children's play? How can you tell?*

COLLABORATIVE CONVERSATIONS

Take Turns Talking As children engage in partner, small-group, and whole-group discussions, encourage them to:

• take turns talking and not speak over others.

• raise their hands if they want to speak.

• ask others to share their ideas and opinions.

ELL NEWCOMERS

To help children develop oral language and build vocabulary, use **Newcomer Cards** 10-14 and the accompanying lessons in the **Newcomer Teacher's Guide.** For additional practice, have children complete the online **Newcomer Activities.**

MY GOALS ROUTINE

What I Know Now

Read Goals Read goals with children on **Reading/Writing Companion** page 80.

Reflect Ask children to reflect on each goal and fill in the bars to show what they know now. Explain that they will fill in the bars on page 81 at the end of the week to show their progress.

Literature Big Book

We can make and confirm predictions when listening to a story.

OBJECTIVES

Retell stories, including key details, and demonstrate understanding of their central message or lesson.

Identify who is telling the story at various point in a text.

ELA ACADEMIC LANGUAGE

• *prediction, quotation marks*

Close Reading Routine

Read   DOK 1–2

• Identify important ideas and details.
• Take notes and retell.
• Use **A C T** prompts as needed.

Reread   DOK 2–3

• Analyze the text, craft, and structure.
• Use the Reread minilessons.

Integrate   DOK 3–4

• Integrate knowledge and ideas.
• Make text-to-text connections.
• Complete the Show Your Knowledge task.
• Inspire action.

Read

 15 mins

Interrupting Chicken

Connect to Concept: Tales Over Time Tell children they will now listen to a story about a little chicken who interrupts when her father reads to her.

Genre: Fantasy Explain that this is a fantasy. Say: *Fantasies are made-up stories with characters, settings, and events that couldn't exist in real life.*

 Anchor Chart Review the Make and Confirm Predictions anchor chart.

Make and Confirm Predictions Review that we can use the text and illustrations to make predictions about what will happen next in a story. We can continue reading to see if our prediction is correct.

Read the Selection

Display the Big Book. Have children point to the title and author's name. Then read them aloud.

Set Purpose Say: *Let's read to find out what happens when the little chicken interrupts during story time.*

As you read, model making and confirming predictions. Review the Make and Confirm Predictions anchor chart as needed.

Think Aloud I predict Chicken will interrupt the story every time because she interrupted the first story. Let's see if my prediction is correct.

Continue to model making and confirming predictions as you read aloud. Ask children to make and confirm their own predictions as they listen.

A C T Access Complex Text

If the complexity of the text makes it hard for children to understand, use the Access Complex Text prompts.

Organization

The text contains stories within a story. Children may be confused as to how the stories fit together.

• Guide children to see where the stories Papa tells begin. Explain that these are stories Papa is trying to read to the little red chicken.

Connection of Ideas

Children may think the little chicken is a character in the stories.

• Make sure children understand that Papa is telling the story, and the little chicken interrupts to tell him what she thinks should happen.

Concepts of Print: Quotation Marks/Text Styles Tell children that quotation marks set off words characters say. Say: *The first quotation mark means a character has started speaking. The second quotation mark means the character is finished speaking.* Point out different text styles. Papa's story on pages 10–11 looks like a storybook. On the next page, the little chicken's interrupting words are in a different style. Pages 30–31 show the story the little chicken writes. See prompts in the Big Book for modeling concepts of print.

Focus on Narrator Remind children that the narrator can be a speaker inside or outside the story. Say: *Words such as* he, she, they, *and characters' names tell you the narrator is someone outside the story. Listen as I read page 6. What character's name do you hear?*

Respond to the Text

After reading, prompt children to share what they learned. Review the folktales in the story, and ask children if they are familiar with them. Discuss predictions children made and whether they were confirmed or corrected.

Model Retelling

Pause to retell portions of the selection. Say: *I can put events of the story into my own words. So far, I have read that the little red chicken wants her father to tell her a story. Papa says he will and reminds her not to interrupt.*

Continue to model retelling the story, using your own words to tell the important events in order. Have children practice retelling a page or two.

Writing Fluency

To increase children's writing fluency, have them write as much as they can about the story for five minutes. Then have partners share.

English Language Learners

Make and Confirm Predictions Display pages 6–7 of *Interrupting Chicken*. Say: *I can look at the illustrations to make predictions about what I will read.* Point to the little chicken and the bed. *What is the little chicken going to do? Make a prediction.* She will go to bed. Point to the books. *Will Papa read a book to her? Make a prediction.* I predict Papa will read a book. Then turn the page. *Look at the illustration. Was your prediction correct?*

For additional support, see the **ELL Small Group Guide,** pp. 132–133.

MODEL FLUENCY

Expression Read aloud page 12 with slightly exaggerated expression. Say: *When reading text inside quotation marks, read it with expression. Speak the way you think the character would. If you see an exclamation mark, you should read the text with strong emotion.* Have children identify the quotation marks and exclamation marks.

DIGITAL TOOLS

Retell

FORMATIVE ASSESSMENT

❯ STUDENT CHECK-IN

Have partners tell one thing they predicted in the story. Have children reflect, using the Check-In routine.

✓ CHECK FOR SUCCESS

Can children make and confirm predictions in a story?

❯❯ **Small Group Instruction**

If No

🟠 **Approaching** Reteach pp. T226–T227

If Yes

🔵 **On** Review pp. T236–T237

🟢 **Beyond** Extend pp. T240–T241

Display the Sound-Spelling Card *five*. Point to the letters i_e.

1. **Teacher:** What are the letters?	**Children:** i, e
2. **Teacher:** What's the sound?	**Children:** /ī/
3. **Teacher:** What's the word?	**Children:** five

Continue the routine for previously taught sounds.

LEARNING GOALS

- We can say rhyming words.
- We can read and blend words with soft *c* and soft *g*.

OBJECTIVES

Demonstrate understanding of spoken words, syllables, and sounds (phonemes).

Know the spelling-sound correspondences for common consonant digraphs.

Print all upper- and lowercase letters.

Identify and produce rhyming words.

ELA ACADEMIC LANGUAGE

- *rhyme, blend*

⊙ TEACH IN SMALL GROUP

Word Work lessons can be taught in small groups.

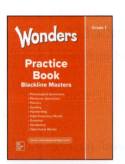

Phonological Awareness: Page 193
Phonics: Page 195
Handwriting: Page 200

⏱ 5 mins # Phonological Awareness

Identify and Produce Rhyme

1 **Model** Say: *I am going to say two words. If the two words rhyme, I'll clap. Listen:* nice, rice. *(clap).* Nice *and* rice *rhyme because they both end in the same sounds:* /īs/. *Listen:* /n/ /īs/, nice; /r/ /īs/, rice.

What is another word that rhymes with nice *and* rice? *I need to think of words that end in* /īs/. *I know one. The word* twice: /tw/ /īs/. *The word* twice *ends in* /is/, *so it rhymes with* nice *and* rice.

2 **Guided Practice/Practice** *Now let's try it together. I'll say a group of words. Tell me which two rhyme. Then think of another rhyming word.* Guide practice, and provide corrective feedback as needed.

trace, trap, place	age, ace, wage	think, twice, blink
lace, late, pace	cane, page, cage	badge, ledge, wedge
fudge, judge, junk	cent, lint, lent	strap, stress, guess

If children need additional practice identifying and producing rhyming words, see **Practice Book** page 193 or the online activity.

⏱ 5 mins # Phonics

MULTIMODAL

Introduce Soft *c*; Soft *g, dge*

1 **Model** Display the *sun* **Sound-Spelling Card.** Teach /s/ spelled *ce* and *ci_*. *This is called soft* c. *The* /s/ *sound can be spelled with* c *when it is followed by* e *or* i. *This is the word* cent. *Listen:* /ssseeennnt/, cent. *This is the word* city. *Listen:* /sssiiitē/, city.

Sound-Spelling Cards

Repeat with the *jump* Sound-Spelling Card. *The* /j/ *sound can be spelled with* g *when it is followed by* e *or* i *as in the words* gem *and* giant. Point out that soft *g* can also be spelled with the trigraph *dge* as long as a short-vowel sound comes before it.

2 **Guided Practice/Practice** Have children practice connecting the letters *ce* to the /s/ sound by writing the word *ice*. *Say* /s/ *as I write the word* ice. *This time, write* ice *five times as you say the* /s/ *sound.* Repeat for *ge* and *dge* and the sound /j/. Use the words *age* and *edge*. As needed, provide handwriting models for children to use.

Blend Words with Soft *c*; Soft *g, dge*

m	i	c	e

1 **Model** Display **Word-Building Cards** *m, i, c,* and *e*. Model blending. *This is the letter* m. *It stands for /m/. These are the letters* i *and* e. *Together they stand for /ī/. This is the letter* c. *It stands for /s/ because of the* e. *Listen as I blend: /mmmīīīsss/. Say it with me:* mice.

Continue by modeling the words *spice, gem, stage,* and *lodge.*

2 **Guided Practice/Practice** Display the Lesson 1 Phonics Practice Activity. Read the first row. Blend the sounds: */f/ /ā/ /s/ /fffāāāsss/,* face. Continue; guide practice and provide corrective feedback with sounding out words and reading connected text.

face	lace	nice	edge	cent	space
slice	raced	gem	chance	place	cage
age	wage	ice	rice	sell	cell
bike	smile	kite	make	shake	can't

Can mice dance?

Lance swam to the bridge.

The nice judge is on stage with a prize.

Lesson 1 Phonics Practice Activity

If children need additional practice blending words with soft *c* and soft *g,* see **Practice Book** page 195 or the online activity.

Corrective Feedback

Sound Error Model the sound children missed, and then have them repeat it. Say: *My turn.* Tap under the letter, and say: *Sound? /s/. What's the sound?* Return to the beginning of the word. Say: *Let's start over.* Blend the word with children again.

✏️ Daily Handwriting

Throughout the week, teach uppercase and lowercase *Yy,* using the online Handwriting models. Use the strokes shown, model writing the letters. Children can practice writing *Yy* using Practice Book page 200. For additional support, use the models in the **Reading/Writing Companion.**

🔵 ENGLISH LANGUAGE LEARNERS

Phonological Awareness, Model Give children more practice listening for rhyming words. This time ask them to clap their hands if the words you say rhyme: *face/lace, make/shake, bike/smile, cage/age, slice/nice.* Have children repeat each rhyming pair after you.

Phonics Refer to pages 6-7 in the **Language Transfers Handbook.** In some languages, including Spanish, Hmong, and Vietnamese, there is no direct transfer for /j/. Emphasize /j/, and show correct mouth position.

DIGITAL TOOLS

For more practice, use these activities.

Word Work

Phonological Awareness
Phonics
Handwriting

FORMATIVE ASSESSMENT

▶ STUDENT CHECK-IN

Phonics Have partners read a soft *c* or soft *g* word to each other. Have children reflect, using the Check-In routine.

LEARNING GOALS

- We can spell words with soft *c* and soft *g*.
- We can read the words *any, from, happy, once, so,* and *upon.*

OBJECTIVES

Spell untaught words phonetically, drawing on phonemic awareness and spelling conventions.

Decode regularly spelled one-syllable words.

Recognize and read grade-appropriate irregularly spelled words.

Spell words with soft *c* and soft *g*.

ELA ACADEMIC LANGUAGE

- *sounds, blend*

DIGITAL TOOLS

To differentiate instruction for key skills, use the results of this activity.

High-Frequency Words: Practice

For more practice, use this activity.

Spelling

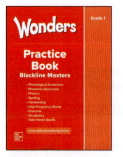

Spelling: Page 197

Spelling

Words with Soft *c;* Soft *g, dge*

Dictation Follow the Spelling Dictation routine to help children transfer their growing knowledge of sound-spellings to writing. After dictation, give the spelling pretest in the **Practice Book** on page 197.

Pretest Pronounce each spelling word. Read the sentence and pronounce the word again. Ask children to say each word softly, stretching the sounds, before writing it. After the pretest, display the spelling words and write each word as you say the letter names. Have children check their words using the Practice Book page.

rice	He likes to eat **rice** and beans.
nice	It's a **nice** day to go to the beach.
page	My story is one **page** long.
age	Your **age** tells how old you are.
wedge	Use this **wedge** to keep the door open.
ledge	Put the plant on the window **ledge**.
like	What kind of food do you **like**?
ride	My sister is learning to **ride** a bike.
from	This letter is **from** my grandma.
once	We **once** lived in that house.

ELLs should use the above list for their spelling pretest.

▶▶ DIFFERENTIATED SPELLING LISTS

Approaching Level age, edge, ice, rice
Beyond Level age, ledge, nice, page, rice, wedge

 # English Language Learners

Spelling, Dictation Before you begin dictation, review the meanings of the words using pictures, pantomime, or gestures when possible. For example, mime eating pizza, and say: *I like pizza.* Have children mimic you and repeat *like.* Open a book. Turn the page and say: *I turn the page.* Have children repeat the sentence.

In a Flash: High-Frequency Words

together

1. **Teacher:** Read the word.   **Children:** together
2. **Teacher:** Spell the word.   **Children:** t-o-g-e-t-h-e-r
3. **Teacher:** Write the word.   **Children write the word.**

Repeat with *green, grow, pretty, should, water* from last week.

High-Frequency Words

⏱ 5 mins

MULTIMODAL

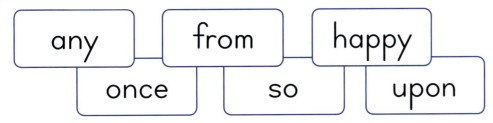

any   from   happy

once   so   upon

1 **Model** Display the **High-Frequency Word Cards** *any, from, happy, once, so,* and *upon*. Use the Read/Spell/Write routine to teach each word.

- **Read** Point to and say the word *any. This is the word* any. *Say it with me:* any. *I don't have any time to play.*

- **Spell** *The word* any *is spelled* a-n-y. *Spell it with me.*

- **Write** *Now write the word* any *on your Response Board as we say each letter:* a-n-y.

- Follow the routine to introduce *from, happy, once, so,* and *upon.*

COLLABORATE

- As children spell each word with you, point out sound-spellings children have already learned as well as any irregular sound-spellings, such as the /u/ sound spelled *o* in *from*.

- Have partners say sentences using each word.

2 **Guided Practice** Have children read the sentences. Prompt them to identify the high-frequency words in connected text and to blend the decodable words.

1. Do you have **any** time to play?

2. The cake came **from** the shop.

3. The dog is **happy** when I pet his face.

4. **Once** I ran a mile.

5. It is hot, **so** I will play inside.

6. **Once upon** a time, a king had a magic stone.

3 **Practice** Using the High-Frequency Word Cards or index cards, create a hopscotch course. Have children toss a marker and hop to the word, saying each word along the way.

For additional practice with high-frequency words, have children complete the online activities for high-frequency words.

ELL ENGLISH LANGUAGE LEARNERS

High-Frequency Words, Model Place a book on another book. Say: *I am placing one book upon another.* Hold the book out, and ask: *Who will take this book from me?* Have children respond and demonstrate: I will take the book <u>from</u> you. Ask: *Do you have any apples?* No, I do not have <u>any</u> apples.

FORMATIVE ASSESSMENT

⊘ STUDENT CHECK-IN

Spelling Have partners dictate one soft *c* or soft *g* word from the list for each other to write.

High-Frequency Words Have partners take turns reading the high-frequency words.

Have children reflect using the Check-In routine.

✓ CHECK FOR SUCCESS

Rubric Use your online rubric to record children's progress.

Can children read and decode words with soft *c* and soft *g*?

Can children recognize and read high-frequency words?

⟩ Small Group Instruction

If No

🔴 **Approaching** Reteach pp. T228–T233

🟣 **ELL** Develop pp. T228–T233

If Yes

🔵 **On** Review pp. T236–T238

🟢 **Beyond** Extend pp. T240–T241

Read

"The Nice Mitten"

Focus on Foundational Skills

• Review the high-frequency words *any, from, happy, once, so,* and *upon.*
• Review that the letter *c* can stand for the /s/ sound and that the letter *g* and the trigraph *dge* can stand for the /j/ sound.
• Display the words *animals, boy, bear, cold, forest, more,* and *warm.* Spell the words, and model reading them. Have children read the words as you point to them.

Read the Shared Read

Anchor Chart Create a Folktale anchor chart.

Genre: Folktale Tell children "The Nice Mitten" is a folktale. A folktale is a story that has been handed down orally from one generation to the next. Folktales often have animal characters that speak and act like humans and they may have a moral, or lesson. Write these features on the chart. Have volunteers share a story they know that is a folktale.

Make and Confirm Predictions

Explain Tell children that as they read, they can make predictions about what they think will happen and confirm whether their predictions were correct as they read. Children should correct predictions as needed.

Connect to Concept: Tales Over Time

Explain that this week children are reading stories that have been told over time. Children can describe what a folktale is.

Take Notes As children read the selection, you may wish to have them take notes in the boxes provided. Children may take notes by:

• writing the letters *c* and *g* and trigraph *dge.*
• writing a word with a soft *c* or *g* sound or a high-frequency word.

Have children read each page. Then read the prompts one at a time.

Reading/Writing Companion, pp. 82–83

SET PURPOSE

Let's read to find out what makes the mitten nice.

CONCEPTS OF PRINT

Have partners point to and read aloud each word in the title.

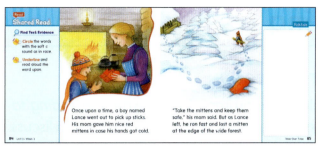

Reading/Writing Companion, pp. 84–85

Reading/Writing Companion, pp. 86–87

Reading/Writing Companion, pp. 88–89

Reading/Writing Companion, pp. 90–91

PHONICS

Have children circle and read aloud the words with the soft *c* sound.

HIGH-FREQUENCY WORDS

Have children underline and read aloud the word *upon*.

HIGH-FREQUENCY WORDS

Have children underline and read aloud the words *so* and *happy*.

COMPREHENSION

Have talk about why the mitten "puffed up a bit."

PHONICS

Have children circle and read aloud the words with the soft *g* sound.

MAKE AND CONFIRM PREDICTIONS

Have partners make a prediction about what will happen to the mitten next.

MAKE AND CONFIRM PREDICTIONS

Have partners talk about what happened to the mitten. Ask them if they predicted this or if they corrected their prediction.

RETELL

Have partners retell the story, using the pictures and words.

 SPOTLIGHT ON LANGUAGE

Pages 86–87 Point to the words *a bit* on each page. Explain that *a bit* means "a small amount" or "a little." *What puffed up a bit as each animal got inside?* (the mitten) Have children crouch down and demonstrate standing "a bit," then "a bit" more, and then as much as they can.

FOCUS ON FLUENCY

With partners, have children reread "The Nice Mitten" to develop fluency. Children should focus on their accuracy, trying to say each word correctly. Then have them reread the story so it sounds like speech. Remind children the goal is to keep practicing until they can read the words automatically.

 DIFFERENTIATED READING

● **English Language Learners**
Before reading, have children listen to a summary of the selection, available in multiple languages.

Respond to the Text

Have children discuss how "The Nice Mitten" is like other folktales they have read. Use this sentence starter to guide discussion: *"The Nice Mitten" is like other folktales because . . .*

 FORMATIVE ASSESSMENT

STUDENT CHECK-IN

Have children reflect on their retelling, using the Check-In routine.

LESSON 1

- We can write a sentence using specific words.
- We can name past- and future-tense verbs.

OBJECTIVES

Write narratives in which they recount two or more appropriately sequenced events, include some details regarding what happened, use temporal words to signal event order, and provide some sense of closure.

Use verbs to convey a sense of past, present, and future.

ELA ACADEMIC LANGUAGE

- *verb*
- Cognate: *verbo*

COLLABORATIVE CONVERSATIONS

Turn and Talk Review this routine.

Child 1: The cricket walked.

Child 2: What do you mean?

Child 1: The cricket walked away from the mitten.

Display speech bubbles "What do you mean?" and "Why do you think that?" Have partners use them to practice collaborating.

DIFFERENTIATED WRITING

● **English Language Learners** For more writing support, see the **ELL Small Group Guide**, p. 134.

---

5 mins

Modeled Writing

Write About the Shared Read

Build Oral Language Read aloud the prompt. Say: *Rewrite the ending to "The Nice Mitten."* Have partners use the Turn and Talk routine to discuss.

Model Writing Sentences Say: *I will write sentences for a new ending.* Point to the text and pictures on pages 90–91. *At the end of the story, the cricket goes into the mitten. If it did not go in, the end would be different.*

Sample Teacher Talk

Rewrite the ending to "The Nice Mitten."

The black cricket walked away from the mitten. Lance gave the cricket the other mitten.

- Listen to my sentences: *The black cricket walked away from the mitten. Lance gave the cricket the other mitten.* I begin my sentence with *The.* I look at the Word Bank to find *the. The* is spelled *t-h-e.* I'll write *The.* HIGH-FREQUENCY WORDS

- The next word is *black.* I choose words that say exactly what I mean. *Black* is a specific word that helps readers picture the cricket. TRAIT: WORD CHOICE

- In the word *cricket,* I hear two sounds blended at the beginning, /kr/. I know the letters *cr* can stand for the /kr/ sound. I'll write *cricket.* PHONICS

- My sentence tells about an action that already happened. I know *-ed* gets added to the end of past-tense verbs. I'll write *walked.* WRITING SKILL

Continue modeling, writing the remaining words in your sentences.

Writing Practice

Analyze and Write Sentences Have children turn to page 92 in their **Reading/Writing Companions.** Guide children to analyze the sentences using the prompts. Review the Writing Skill and Trait boxes as necessary. Then have children write and analyze their own sentences.

Reading/Writing Companion, pp. 92–93

Stephen Coburn/Shutterstock

Grammar

5 mins

Past- and Future-Tense Verbs

1 **Model** Remind children that a verb is an action word. Explain that a past-tense verb tells about an action that has already happened. Display the sentence: **Yesterday Gen danced on a stage.** Say: Danced *is a verb. Many past-tense verbs end in* -ed. Explain that a future-tense verb tells about an action that is going to happen. Display the sentence: **Mike will fix the fence on Monday.** Say: *Adding the verb* will *before the action word shows that something will happen in the future.*

2 **Guided Practice/Practice** Guide children to identify the verbs in the following sentences. Have partners change each verb to past tense by adding *-ed* and to future tense by adding *will.*

> I pick up the slice of bread. (picked; will pick)
>
> I munch on the sandwich. (munched; will munch)

 Talk About It Have partners talk about what they did yesterday. Guide them to generate sentences with past-tense verbs.

Link to Writing Say: *Let's look back at our writing and see what types of verbs we used.* Review Modeled Writing for correct use of verb tenses.

English Language Learners

Use these scaffolds with **Grammar, Model.**

Beginning

Read the first example, and have children point to the verb. Circle the *-ed* ending. Say the sound, and have children repeat. *Does this ending mean the action happened in the past?* (yes)

Intermediate

Ask children to identify the verb in the first example. Point to the *-ed* ending, and ask: *What does this ending tell about when the action happened?* It happened in the past. Repeat with *will.*

Advanced/Advanced High

Ask partners to identify the verbs in each sentence. Have pairs tell whether the verbs indicate actions in the past or the future and explain how they know.

DIGITAL TOOLS

Use these activities to practice grammar.

Grammar

Grammar Song

FORMATIVE ASSESSMENT

❯ STUDENT CHECK-IN

Writing Have partners read each other a sentence they wrote. Have children reflect, using the Check-In routine to fill in the bars.

Grammar Have partners take turns saying a past-tense verb in one of the sentences. Have children reflect, using the Check-In routine.

LEARNING GOALS

We can learn and use new vocabulary words.

OBJECTIVES

Identify real-life connections between words and their use.

Discuss the Essential Question.

Develop oral language.

ELA ACADEMIC LANGUAGE

• *define, discuss*
• Cognates: *definir, discutir*

▶ TEACH IN SMALL GROUP

● **ELL** See the Teacher Talk on the back of the **Visual Vocabulary Cards** for additional support.

● **Approaching** Group children with students in a higher level to practice saying the words. Then children can draw their own pictures of the word.

●● **On Level** and **Beyond Level** Have children look up each word in the online **Visual Glossary.**

FORMATIVE ASSESSMENT

❯ STUDENT CHECK-IN

Have partners use a vocabulary word in a sentence. Have children reflect, using the Check-In routine.

LESSON FOCUS

READING
Revisit the Essential Question
Read Interactive Read Aloud:
"The Foolish, Timid Rabbit"
• Use Compound Words
Word Work
• Review Soft *c*; Soft *g/dge*

Reread Shared Read:
"The Nice Mitten"
• Review Genre
• Introduce Skill
WRITING
• Interactive Writing
• Review Grammar

Reading/Writing Companion, pp. 82–91

---

 5 mins

Oral Language

MULTIMODAL

 ## Essential Question

What is a folktale?

Remind children that this week you have been talking and reading about folktales. Remind children of the photo of children performing the folktale; the story *Interrupting Chicken*; and the story "The Nice Mitten."

Oral Vocabulary Words

Review the oral vocabulary words *hero* and *tale* from Lesson 1. Use the Define/Example/Ask routine on the print or digital **Visual Vocabulary Cards** to introduce the oral vocabulary words *eventually, foolish,* and *timid*. Prompt children to use the words as they discuss folktales.

Visual Vocabulary Cards

Oral Vocabulary Routine

Define: **Eventually** means "finally" or "after a while."

Example: Eventually, the baby will learn to walk and talk.

Ask: What is something you learned to do eventually, after a lot of work?

Define: **Foolish** means "very silly" or "unwise."

Example: It would be foolish to leave your backpack outside in the rain.

Ask: Can you think of story characters who are foolish?

Define: **Timid** means "shy" and "a little bit afraid."

Example: Pete felt timid about knocking on the door of the big, old house.

Ask: Why might a person feel timid on the first day of school?

OPTION
10 mins

Read the Interactive Read Aloud

"The Foolish, Timid Rabbit"

Connect to Concept

Tell children you will be reading aloud a folktale about a rabbit. Display the **Interactive Read Aloud Cards**. Read the title, "The Foolish, Timid Rabbit."

Set Purpose Say: *Let's read to find out what happens with the foolish, timid rabbit.* Read aloud or play the selection as you display the cards. Remind children to listen carefully.

Oral Vocabulary Use the Oral Vocabulary prompts as you read the selection to provide more practice with the words in context.

Compound Words Tell children that a compound word is made when two words are joined to form a new word. Tell them that as you read, they can put together the meanings of the two smaller words to find the meaning of the compound word. Model the strategy as you read Card 2.

Teacher Think Aloud When I read, "I heard it happen myself," I wondered what the word *myself* meant. In *myself*, I see the words *my* and *self*. I can put the meanings of these words together to help me understand *myself*. Both words refer to me, so *myself* is used to emphasize that the rabbit himself heard the earth breaking up.

Continue reading aloud the selection, stopping to have children use the meanings of the two smaller words to determine the meaning of compound words.

Student Think Along After you read the third paragraph on Card 4, ask: *What do you think the word* underneath *means?* Point out that *neath* is short for *beneath*. I can use the meanings of *under* and *beneath* to understand the word *underneath*. Both words mean "below," so I think the lion and rabbit found a coconut below the tree.

Build Knowledge: Make Connections

Talk About the Text Have partners discuss what they think the lesson is in the folktale.

Add to the Anchor Chart Record any new ideas on the Build Knowledge anchor chart.

Add to the Word Bank Add words related to folktales to a separate section of the Word Bank.

LESSON 2

Display the Sound-Spelling Card for *s*.
Point to the letters *ce*.

1. **Teacher:** What are the letters?   **Children:** ce
2. **Teacher:** What's the sound?   **Children:** /s/

Continue the routine for previously taught sounds.

LEARNING GOALS

- We can segment sounds in words.
- We can read and build words with soft *c* and soft *g*.
- We can add the endings *-ed* and *-ing* to make new words.

OBJECTIVES

Segment spoken single-syllable words into their complete sequence of individual sounds (phonemes).

Know the spelling-sound correspondences for common consonant digraphs.

Read words with inflectional endings.

Apply phonics when decoding words with soft *c* and soft *g*.

ELA ACADEMIC LANGUAGE

- *verb, syllable*
- Cognates: *verbo, sílaba*

 **TEACH IN SMALL GROUP**

Word Work lessons can be taught in small groups.

Phonemic Awareness: Page 194

OPTION 5 mins

Phonemic Awareness

 MULTIMODAL

Phoneme Segmentation

1 **Model** Use a **Response Board** to show children how to segment words. *I am going to say the sounds in the word* rice. *Say: Listen: /r/ /ī/ /s/. The first sound is /r/. The second sound is /ī/. The last sound is /s/. I'll place a marker in a box for each sound I hear. This word has three sounds: /r/ /ī/ /s/. Repeat with the three sounds in* line.

2 **Guided Practice/Practice** *Now let's say the sounds in another word. The word is* ledge. *The first sound is /l/. The second is /e/. Ask: What is the last sound?* (/j/) *Repeat them with me: /l/ /e/ /j/. I'll say more words. Place a marker in a box for each sound you hear.* Guide practice using the following examples:

gem (3)   face (3)   dance (4)   cage (3)   bridge (4)   fudge (3)
lodge (3)   lace (3)   cinch (4)   slice (4)   age (2)   dodge (3)

If children need additional practice segmenting phonemes, see **Practice Book** page 194 or the online activity.

5 mins

Phonics

 MULTIMODAL

Review Soft *c*; Soft *g, dge*

1 **Model** Display the *Sun* and *Jump* **Sound-Spelling Cards**. Point to the *ce* and *ci* . Say: *This is called soft* c. *The /s/ sound can be spelled* c *when followed by* e *or* i. *This is the sound at the end of* ice *and the beginning of* cent. Repeat with the *Jump* Sound-Spelling Card. *Soft* g /j/ *can be spelled* g *and as the trigraph* dge.

Sound-Spelling Card

2 **Guided Practice/Practice** Have children practice connecting the letters and sounds. Point to the Sound-Spelling Card. *What are these letters? What sounds do they stand for?* Provide feedback as needed.

Blend Words with Soft *c*; Soft *g, dge*

1 **Model** Display **Word-Building Cards** *r, i, c,* and *e*. Model blending the sounds. *This is* r. *It stands for /r/. These are* i *and* e. *They stand for /ī/. This is* c. *It stands for /s/ because of the* e. *Listen: /rīīīsss/.* Continue, modeling: *slice, age, wedge,* and *hinge*.

| r | i | c | e |

2 **Guided Practice/Practice** Repeat the routine with the words: *cent, ace, nice, space, gel, page, stage, bridge, grudge, dodge,* and *smudge.* Guide practice, and provide corrective feedback as needed.

Build Words with Soft *c;* Soft *g, dge*

Provide children with **Word-Building Cards** *a–z.* Have children put the letters in alphabetical order as quickly as possible.

1 **Model** Display Word-Building Cards *f, a, c,* and *e.* Blend: /f/ /ā/ /s/, /fāāāsss/, face. Replace *f* with *sp,* and repeat with *space.* Replace *sp* with *tr,* and repeat with *trace.*

2 **Guided Practice/Practice** Continue, building the words: *race, rice, nice, mice, lice, lace, pace, face, race, rage, page, wage, cage, sage,* and *stage.* Guide children to build and blend each word. Then dictate the words, and have children write them.

For additional practice decoding words in connected text, see Build Words with soft *c,* soft *g,* and the trigraph *dge* lessons on pages T231 and T238.

Structural Analysis

⏱ 5 mins

Inflectional Endings *-ed, -ing*

1 **Model** Write and read aloud *race, raced,* and *racing.* Underline *-ed* and *-ing.* Explain that when a word ends in final *-e,* you drop the *e* before adding *-ed* or *-ing.* Remind children that when *-ed* is added to a verb, or action word, it tells about something that has already happened; when *-ing* is added to a verb, it tells about something that is happening now.

Say *race* and *raced* again, and have children listen for the /t/ sound at the end of *raced.* Then write and say *cringe* and *cringed.* Point out that the letters *-ed* can also stand for the /d/ sound as in *cringed.* Then write and say *race, racing.* Point out that adding the letters *-ing* at the end of a word adds a syllable, or word part. Use each word in a sentence.

2 **Guided Practice/Practice** Write the following words on the board: *place, slice, rage,* and *plunge.* Have children add *-ed* and *-ing* to each word and then use each word in a sentence. Guide practice, and provide corrective feedback as needed.

FORMATIVE ASSESSMENT

❯ STUDENT CHECK-IN

Phonics Have partners build a word with soft *c* and a word with soft *g.*

Structural Analysis Have partners share their sentences that have words with *-ed* and *-ing.*

Have children reflect, using the Check-In routine.

LEARNING GOALS

- We can sort and spell words with soft *c* and soft *g*.
- We can read and write the words *any, from, happy, once, so,* and *upon.*

OBJECTIVES

Use conventional spelling for words with common spelling patterns and for frequently occurring irregular words.

Recognize and read grade-appropriate irregularly spelled words.

Sort words with soft *c* and soft *g.*

ELA ACADEMIC LANGUAGE

- *pattern, sort*

DIGITAL TOOLS

To differentiate instruction for key skills, use the results of this activity.

High-Frequency Words: Practice

For more practice, use this activity.

Spelling

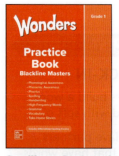

Spelling: On Level, Page 198
Approaching, Page 198A
Beyond, Page 198B
High-Frequency Words: Page 203

5 mins

Spelling

MULTIMODAL

Word Sort with *-ice, -age, -edge*

1. **Model** Display the online **Spelling Word Cards** for Unit 3 Week 3. Have children read each word, listening for the vowel and ending sounds.

   Use cards with the endings *-ice, -age,* and *-edge* to form a three-column chart. Then model sorting the words *mice, cage,* and *hedge* below the correct word ending. Say each word, and pronounce the sounds: /m/ /ī/ /s/; /k/ /ā/ /j/; /h/ /e/ /j/. Say each word again, emphasizing the long- or short-vowel sound and the final consonant sound, and point out the trigraph *dge. (-ice, -age, -edge).* Ask children to chorally spell each word.

2. **Guided Practice/Practice** Have children place each Spelling Word Card in the column with the words containing the same final sounds and spellings *(-ice, -age, -edge).*

   When the chart is complete, have children chorally read the words in each column. Then call out a word. Have a child find the word card and point to it as the class chorally spells the word.

   If children need additional practice spelling words with soft *c,* soft *g,* and the trigraph *dge,* see differentiated **Practice Book** pages 198–198B or the online activity.

-ice	-age
-edge	rice
nice	page
age	wedge
ledge	

Spelling Word Cards   Unit 3 • Week 3   187

Analyze Errors/Articulation Support

Use children's pretest errors to analyze spelling problems and provide corrective feedback. For example, children might use the more common spelling *s* for the /s/ sound in *-ice* and *-ace* words or the more common spelling *j* for the /j/ sound in *-edge* words.

Create word sorts to analyze the /s/ and /j/ spelling patterns. Make index cards for the spelling words. Also make cards for *sun, sad, sick, jump, jet,* and *job.*

Have children sort the spelling words and the six words above into four columns: /s/ spelled *s;* /s/ spelled *c;* /j/ spelled *j;* and /j/ spelled *g, dge.* Then have students chorally read the words in each column.

High-Frequency Words

OPTION
5 mins

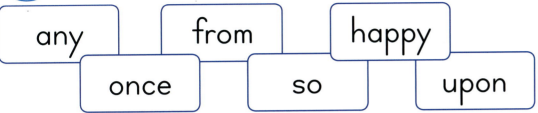

any | from | happy
once | so | upon

1 **Guided Practice** Say each word, and have children Read/Spell/Write it.

- Point out irregularities in sound-spellings, such as the /w/ sound at the beginning of *once*. Compare this to the /w/ sound at the beginning of the previously taught high-frequency word *one*. Also, highlight the soft *c* sound at the end of *once*.

2 **Practice** Add the high-frequency words *any, from, happy, once, so,* and *upon* to the cumulative Word Bank.

- Have children work with a partner to create sentences using the words.
- Have children look at the words and compare their sounds and spellings to words from previous weeks.
- Suggest children write one sentence about a folktale they know.

Cumulative Review Review last week's words (*green, grow, pretty, should, together,* and *water*) by displaying each word and having children read it with automaticity.

Have children independently practice identifying, spelling, and reading high-frequency words, using **Practice Book** page 203 or the online activity.

ELL **ENGLISH LANGUAGE LEARNERS**

Use these scaffolds for **High-Frequency Words, Practice.**

Beginning
Provide a sentence frame to help children write about the folktale "The Nice Mitten": There was not any room left in the <u>mitten</u>.

Intermediate
Have children complete the sentence frame above and then write another sentence: The mitten <u>popped</u>.

Advanced/Advanced High
Have children write their own sentences about folktales, such as "The Nice Mitten." Provide vocabulary as needed.

FORMATIVE ASSESSMENT

> STUDENT CHECK-IN

Spelling Have partners share their word sorts and read words with soft *c* and soft *g*.

High-Frequency Words Have partners quiz each other using the **High-Frequency Word Cards**.

Have children reflect, using the Check-In routine.

✓ CHECK FOR SUCCESS

Rubric Use your online rubric to record children's progress.

Can children read and decode words with soft *c* and soft *g*?

Can children recognize and read high-frequency words?

> Small Group Instruction

If No

🟠 **Approaching** Reteach pp. T228–T233

🟣 **ELL** Develop pp. T228–T233

If Yes

🔵 **On** Review pp. T236–T238

🟢 **Beyond** Extend pp. T240–T241

OBJECTIVES

Retell stories, including key details, and demonstrate understanding of their central message or lesson.

Understand folktale genre.

ELA ACADEMIC LANGUAGE

- *folktale, moral*
- Cognate: *moraleja*

▶ **TEACH IN SMALL GROUP**

🟠 **Approaching** Have partners work together to complete the chart.

🔵🟢 **On Level** and **Beyond Level** Have children write their responses independently and then discuss them.

🟣 **ELL** For specific comprehension support in reading "The Nice Mitten," see the **ELL Small Group Guide,** pp. 128-129.

DIGITAL TOOLS

To differentiate instruction for key skills, use the results of this activity.

Moral

Reread

🕙 10 mins

"The Nice Mitten"

Genre: Folktale

1 **Model** Tell children they will now reread the folktale "The Nice Mitten." Have children turn to page 94 in their **Reading/Writing Companion**. Review the characteristics of a folktale. A folktale:

- is a story handed down orally from one generation to the next.
- has animal characters that speak and act like humans, and can have a moral.

Display the story "The Nice Mitten" in the Reading/Writing Companion. Say: *On pages 82–83, we see animals snuggling in a mitten. Remember that animal characters acting like humans is something we see in folktales. People snuggle under the covers in bed on cold winter mornings. So this picture is a clue that this is a folktale.*

Reading/Writing Companion, pp. 94–95

2 **Guided Practice/Practice** Have partners discuss the words "Once upon a time" and what they think when they read the words. Then have children reread page 86 of the story. Have partners share which details make this a folktale. Ask: *Who is talking?* (the mice) *How does this tell us this is a folktale?* (The animals talk like people.)

Guide children to write this information in the first box of the graphic organizer on page 95. Then have children read pages 87–88 and think about what the animals are doing. In the second box, have them write another clue that shows this is a folktale. Offer help as needed.

Moral

 Anchor Chart Create a Moral anchor chart. Write on the chart: A moral is the lesson of a story. Some stories, such as folktales and fables, have morals.

1 Model Display pages 96–97 of the **Reading/Writing Companion**. Model filling in the first box of the graphic organizer on page 97 by finding a clue about the moral of the story. Say: *We can look for clues in what the characters say and do. On page 87, the illustration shows the mice and the rabbit smiling at each other even though there's not much room.* Write this clue in the top box of the graphic organizer.

Reading/Writing Companion, pp. 96–97

2 Guided Practice Guide children to copy the clue in the graphic organizer on page 97. Then have partners reread pages 88–89, and look for clues about the moral. Ask: *What do the mice and rabbit do on these pages?* (They let the bear and hedgehog come in the mitten.) Guide children to write this clue in the middle box of the graphic organizer.

3 Practice Ask children to use the clues to figure out the folktale's moral and write it in the bottom box of the graphic organizer. For more practice, have children complete the online activity.

English Language Learners

Moral, Guided Practice Say, *The moral of a story is the lesson you learn from the story. The author or storyteller might not tell you what that lesson is. That is why you have to look for clues in the story. The moral usually is about how we can be better people.*

BUILD KNOWLEDGE: MAKE CONNECTIONS

Talk About the Text Have partners discuss the lesson of the story.

Write About the Text Then have children add their ideas to the Build Knowledge page of their reader's notebook.

Add to the Anchor Chart Record any new ideas on the Build Knowledge anchor chart.

Add to the Word Bank Add words related to folktales to a separate section of the Word Bank.

FORMATIVE ASSESSMENT

⟩ STUDENT CHECK-IN

Genre Have partners take turns telling how they know this story is a folktale.

Skill Have children identify the moral of the story.

Have children reflect using the Check-In routine to fill in the bars.

✓ CHECK FOR SUCCESS

Rubric Use your online rubric to record children's progress.

Can children identify the moral of the story?

⟩ Small Group Instruction

If No

🟠 **Approaching** Reteach pp. T226–T227, T234–T235

If Yes

🔵 **On** Review pp. T236–T237, T239

🟢 **Beyond** Extend pp. T240–T243

LEARNING GOALS

- We can read and write about a Student Model.
- We can write past- and future-tense verbs.

OBJECTIVES

Write narratives in which they recount two or more appropriately sequenced events, include some details regarding what happened, use temporal words to signal event order, and provide some sense of closure.

Use verbs to convey a sense of past, present, and future.

ELA ACADEMIC LANGUAGE

- *folktale, verbs*
- Cognate: *verbos*

COLLABORATIVE CONVERSATIONS

Circulate as partners talk about the prompt. Notice who needs to ask questions. Remind them to use the speech bubbles to help them ask clarifying questions. As you listen in to children's conversations, you may write your observations on children's language development.

DIFFERENTIATED WRITING

● **English Language Learners**
For more writing support, see **ELL Small Group Guide**, p. 134.

---

 5 mins # Interactive Writing

Write About the Shared Read

Analyze the Prompt Read aloud a new prompt: *Write a new story about a boy who loses his boot.* Have partners turn and talk about it.

Find Text Evidence Guide children to find text evidence to respond to the prompt. Read the text on page 84. Say: *Your folktale can start with the same sentence as this one.* Use a volunteer's response and the sample teacher talk below to write the next two sentences, such as: *The red boots warmed his feet, so he put them on. Then Lance went outside to play.*

Sample Teacher Talk: Share the Pen

- The first sentence begins with *The*. Who can find *The* on the Word Bank and spell it? That's right. *T-h-e*. HIGH-FREQUENCY WORDS

- Which words help readers know exactly what the sentence will be about? That's right, *red boots*. TRAIT: WORD CHOICE

- The next word tells about something in the past. What should we add to the end of the verb *warm* to show the action already happened? WRITING SKILL

- Who knows the middle sound of the word *his*? That's right, the middle sound is /i/. PHONICS

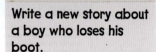

Write a new story about a boy who loses his boot.

The red boots warmed his feet, so he put them on. Then Lance went outside to play.

Continue sharing the pen to complete the sentences.

Analyze the Student Model

Say: *Let's read how another child responded to the prompt.* Have children turn to page 98 of the **Reading/Writing Companion.** Guide them to analyze Anna's writing, using the prompts on page 99. Then have children write what they notice. Review the Grammar box as necessary. Use the Quick Tip box for support.

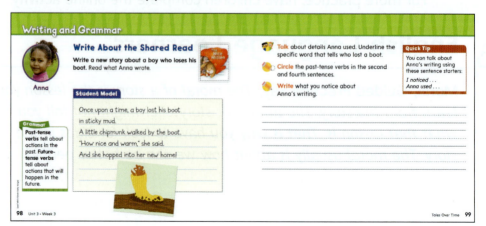

Reading/Writing Companion, pp. 98–99

Stephen Coburn/Shutterstock

Grammar

Past- and Future-Tense Verbs

1 **Review** Remind children that past-tense verbs tell about an action that has already happened. Many past-tense verbs end in *-ed.* Remind children that a future-tense verb tells about an action that is going to happen. Adding *will* before a verb makes it future tense.

2 **Guided Practice** Write and read aloud the following sentences: *Vance sliced the fudge cake. We will play together on Sunday.* Guide children to circle the verb or verbs in each sentence and identify which is past tense and which is future tense.

3 **Practice** Have children rewrite the past-tense sentence to make it future tense, and have them rewrite the future-tense sentence to make it past tense. (Vance will slice the fudge cake. We played together on Sunday.) For additional practice with past- and future-tense verbs, see **Practice Book** page 204 or the online activity.

Talk About It

Have partners talk about something they will do tomorrow. Guide them to orally generate sentences with future-tense verbs.

English Language Learners

Grammar, Guide Practice Read the first sentence aloud, and ask children to repeat it. Have children point to the verb and read it aloud. (sliced) Underline the *-ed* ending. Say: *This is a past-tense verb. It ends in* -ed *and makes the /t/ sound. What kind of verb is this?* Have children respond: It is the past tense.

Read the Review sentence, and have children repeat. *The word* will *tells us this action will happen in the future. When will the action take place?* It will take place in the future.

DIGITAL TOOLS

Use this activity to practice grammar.

Grammar

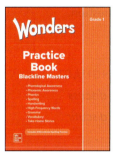

Grammar: Page 204

FORMATIVE ASSESSMENT

❯ STUDENT CHECK-IN

Writing Have partners share one thing they noticed about the Student Model.

Grammar Have partners read a sentence they wrote that contains a past- or future-tense verb.

Have chidlren reflect, using the Check-In routine.

LEARNING GOALS

We can learn and use new vocabulary words.

OBJECTIVES

Identify real-life connections between words and their use.

Discuss the Essential Question.

Develop oral language.

ELA ACADEMIC LANGUAGE

- *folktale, photograph, discuss*
- Cognates: *fotografía, discutir*

LESSON FOCUS

READING
Revisit the Essential Question
Reread Literature Big Book:
Interrupting Chicken
- Use Compound Words
- Analyze Author's Craft
Word Work
- Blend Words with Soft *c*; Soft *g/dge*

Read and Reread
Anchor Text:
The Gingerbread Man
- Review Genre
- Review Make Predictions
- Review Skill
WRITING
- Independent Writing
- Review Grammar and Introduce Mechanics

Literature Anthology,
pp. 50–67

---

 5 mins

Oral Language

MULTIMODAL

Essential Question

What is a folktale?

Remind children that this week you are talking and reading about folktales. Remind them of the photograph of the children putting on a play, the little chicken who could not stop interrupting the stories her father told, and the folktales they read. Guide children to discuss the question, using information from what they have read and talked about throughout the week.

Review Oral Vocabulary

Review the oral vocabulary words *hero, tale, timid, foolish,* and *eventually* using the Define/Example/Ask routine on the print or digital **Visual Vocabulary Cards**. Encourage children to discuss folktales when thinking of examples for each word.

Visual Vocabulary Cards

FORMATIVE ASSESSMENT

▶ STUDENT CHECK-IN

Have partners use a vocabulary word in a sentence.

Have children reflect, using the Check-In routine.

Interrupting Chicken

As you reread *Interrupting Chicken,* have children focus on using text evidence to respond to author's craft questions. Remind children that authors often include features in their stories to grab the reader's attention or make their writing look or sound a certain way. Model using compound words to help children understand the meaning of unfamiliar words.

Compound Words Remind children that a compound word is made when two words are joined to form a new word. Children can put together the meanings of the two smaller words to determine the meaning of the compound word.

Model the strategy. Reread page 5. Point to the compound word *bedtime.* Write the words *bedtime, bed,* and *time.* Explain that children can use the words *bed* and *time* to understand the meaning of the word *bedtime*—the time for bed. Continue modeling the strategy as needed on pages 6, 23, 27, and 31 with the words *something, everyone, without,* and *nothing.*

Author/Illustrator's Craft Display pages 8–11. Why does the author change the style of illustration when Papa tells a story?

Think Aloud On pages 8 and 9, Papa and Chicken are talking, and the illustration is of the two of them speaking. On page 10, Papa begins to tell a story. The author changes the illustration style to show us that Papa is reading a story out of a book.

Author/Illustrator Craft Display pages 12–13. How does the author show us that Chicken interrupts the story? (When Chicken interrupts the story, we can't read the text of the storybook anymore. Instead, we can read only Chicken's large speech bubbles. Lots of capital letters and exclamation points are within the speech bubbles. We know Chicken has interrupted and taken over the story.) Continue asking questions about how the author moves between different characters' perspectives through the art, style, and text.

Build Knowledge: Make Connections

Talk About the Text Have partners discuss the lessons from the folktales that Papa starts to read to Chicken.

Add to the Anchor Chart Record any new ideas on the Build Knowledge anchor chart.

Add to the Word Bank Add words related to folktales to a separate section of the Word Bank.

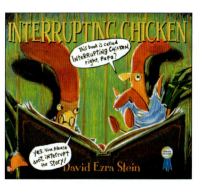
Literature Big Book

We can think about the choices an author makes when writing and illustrating a text.

OBJECTIVES

Determine or clarify the meaning of unknown words based on *grade 1 reading and content,* choosing flexibly from an array of strategies.

Use illustrations and details in a story to describe its characters, setting, or events.

ELA ACADEMIC LANGUAGE

• *text, illustration*
• Cognates: *texto, ilustración*

🅴🅻🅻 ENGLISH LANGUAGE LEARNERS

Compound Words Point to both parts of the compound word *bedtime.* Read each word, and have children repeat. Then read the compound word, and have children repeat. Define *bedtime* using its parts: Bedtime *means "time to go to bed" or "time for bed."* Display page 31. Point to *nothing.* Write *no, thing,* and *nothing* on the board. Have children read and repeat. Help children use the smaller words to understand the meaning of the compound word. Say: Nothing *means "no thing" or "not a thing."*

❯ STUDENT CHECK-IN

Have partners tell one choice the author made. Have children reflect, using the Check-In routine.

In a Flash: Sound-Spellings

Display the Sound-Spelling Card for *s*.
Point to the letters *ce*.
1. **Teacher:** What are the letters?   **Children:** ce
2. **Teacher:** What's the sound?   **Children:** /s/
Continue the routine for previously taught sounds.

LEARNING GOALS

- We can blend sounds in words.
- We can read words with soft *c* and soft *g*.
- We can add the endings *-ed* and *-ing* to make new words.

OBJECTIVES

Orally produce single-syllable words by blending sounds (phonemes), including consonant blend

Know the spelling-sound correspondences for common consonant digraphs.

Read words with inflectional endings.

Apply phonics when decoding words with soft *c* and soft *g*.

ELA ACADEMIC LANGUAGE

- *verb, syllable*
- Cognates: *verbo, sílaba*

TEACH IN SMALL GROUP

Word Work lessons can be taught in small groups.

Phonics: Page 196
Structural Analysis: Page 201

Phonemic Awareness
5 mins

MULTIMODAL

Phoneme Blending

1 Model Place markers in the **Response Board** to show how to orally blend phonemes. Say: *I am going to put one marker in each box as I say each sound. Then I will blend the sounds.* Place a marker for each sound as you say /m/ /ī/ /s/. This word has three sounds: /m/ /ī/ /s/. *Listen as I blend these sounds: /mmmīīīsss/, mice. The word is* mice.

2 Guided Practice/Practice Say: *Using your own boards, place a marker for each sound you hear. I will say one sound at a time. Then blend the sounds to say the word.* Guide practice, and provide corrective feedback as children blend the following sounds:

/s/ /e/ /l/	/e/ /j/	/f/ /ā/ /s/
/n/ /ī/ /s/	/s/ /t/ /ā/ /j/	/s/ /l/ /u/ /j/
/r/ /i/ /j/	/p/ /r/ /a/ /n/ /s/	/p/ /l/ /u/ /n/ /j/

Phonics
OPTION 5 mins

Blend Words with Soft *c*; Soft *g, dge*

1 Model Display **Word-Building Cards** *p, a, g, e*. Model blending the sounds. *This is the letter* p. *It stands for /p/. These are letters* a *and* e. *Together they stand for /ā/. This is letter* g. *It stands for /j/ because it is followed by the letter* e. *Let's blend all three sounds: /pāāāj/. The word is* page. Model the words *cage, badge, spice,* and *grace.*

2 Guided Practice/Practice Display the Lesson 3 Phonics Practice Activity. Say: *Let's blend the sounds to read each word: /e/ /j/, /eeej/. The word is* edge. Have children blend each word with you.

edge	fudge	face	nice	brace	ice
cent	rage	budge	fence	place	fence
raced	piled	placed	making	riding	
slicing	smiled	baked	tracing	liked	
space	spice	dice	cages	states	

Lance raced past the fence.

Madge danced on the stage.

Lesson 3 Phonics Practice Activity

Prompt children to read the connected text, sounding out the decodable words. Provide corrective feedback as needed.

If children need additional practice blending words with soft *c* and soft *g, dge*, see **Practice Book** page 196 or the online activity.

Corrective Feedback

Sound Error Help children with any sounds they missed. Say: *My turn. This sound says* (make the correct sound). Then blend the word. Say: *Do it with me.* Blend the word aloud with children. Say: *Your turn. Blend this word.* Have children chorally blend. Say: *Let's do it again.* Follow these steps until children are confidently producing the sound.

Decodable Reader

Have children read "The King and Five Mice" to practice decoding words in connected text. If children need support reading words with soft *c* and soft *g, dge*, see pages T231 or T238 for instruction and support for "The King and Five Mice."

Structural Analysis

5 mins

Inflectional Endings *-ed, -ing*

1 **Model** Say the words *pledge, pledged,* and *pledging*. Ask children to listen for what is different. Point out the /d/ sound at the end of *pledged* and the /ing/ sound at the end of *pledging*.

Write the words *pledge, pledged,* and *pledging*. Decode each word, and have children repeat. Underline *-ed* and *-ing*. Tell children *pledge* is an action word, or verb. Remind children that the ending *-ed* means the action took place in the past; the ending *-ing* means the action is taking place now. Explain that because the word *pledge* ends in final *-e*, the e in the word *pledge* is dropped before adding *-ed* or *-ing*.

2 **Practice/Apply** Help children decode *race, raced, racing, cringe, cringed, cringing, judge, judged,* and *judging*. Point out that *-ed* at the end of a word can stand for /t/ or /d/. Explain that adding *-ing* to the end of a word adds a syllable, or word part. Have children clap out syllables for two-syllable words.

Have children practice decoding words with inflectional endings *-ed* and *-ing*, using Practice Book page 201 or the online activity.

DIGITAL TOOLS

To differentiate instruction for key skills, use the results of this activity.

Phonics

For more practice, use these activities.

Phonemic Awareness
Structural Analysis

ELL ENGLISH LANGUAGE LEARNERS

Structural Analysis, Practice/Apply Read aloud *cringe, cringed,* and *cringing*. Have children repeat. *I'm going to read the words again. If you hear a word that ends with the inflectional ending -ed that makes the /d/ sound, clap once. If you hear a word that ends with -ing that makes the /ing/ sound clap twice.* Repeat with *judge, judged,* and *judging*. Before you read *race, raced,* and *racing*, tell children to listen for the /t/ sound made by *-ed*.

FORMATIVE ASSESSMENT

STUDENT CHECK-IN

Phonics Have partners read a word with soft *c* and a word with soft *g*.

Structural Analysis Have partners use an *-ed* or *-ing* word in a sentence.

Have children reflect, using the Check-In routine.

OPTION 5 mins

MULTIMODAL

Spelling

- We can sort words by word families.
- We can read and write the words *any, from, happy, once, so,* and *upon.*

OBJECTIVES

Use conventional spelling for words with common spelling patterns and for frequently occurring irregular words.

Recognize and read grade-appropriate irregularly spelled words.

Sort words with soft *c* and soft *g.*

ELA ACADEMIC LANGUAGE

- *pattern, blend*

Word Families: *-ice, -age, -edge*

1 **Model** Display index cards for *-ice, -age,* and *-edge,* and form three columns in a pocket chart. Blend the sounds with children.

Hold up the online **Spelling Word Card** for *rice.* Say and spell *rice.* Pronounce each sound clearly: /r/ /ī/ /s/. Blend the sounds, stretching the ending consonant sounds to emphasize them: /rrrīīīsss/. Repeat this step with *nice.* Place both words below the *-ice* card. Read and spell each spelling word. Ask: *What do you notice about these spelling words? They rhyme because they both end with /īs/ spelled* i-c-e.

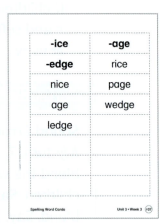

-ice	-age
-edge	rice
nice	page
age	wedge
ledge	

Spelling Word Cards   Unit 3 • Week 3 107

2 **Guided Practice/Practice** Provide children with the Spelling Word Cards. Have children say and spell *-ice* and each word in the word family. Repeat the process with the *-age* and *-edge* words. Have children note the trigraph *dge,* for the words with the *-edge* ending.

Display the words *like, ride, from,* and *once* in a separate column. Read and spell the words together with children. Point out that these spelling words do not end with the /īs/, /āj/, or /ej/ sounds.

Conclude by asking children to orally generate additional words that rhyme with each word. Write the additional words on the board. Underline the common spelling patterns in the additional words. If necessary, point out differences, and explain why they are unusual.

If children need additional practice spelling words with soft *c,* soft *g,* or the trigraph *dge* spelling patterns, see **Practice Book** page 199 or the online activity.

ELL English Language Learners

Spelling, Guided Practice/Practice Help children generate additional rhyming words in the word families. Use the cards from Model: *-ice, -age, -edge.* Create additional index cards with a variety of consonants, such as *l, p, m,* and *w.* Guide children to create words by combining cards. Have children read each word aloud to decide whether it is a real word. For example, say: Wage *is a word, but* wice *is not a word.*

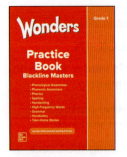

Spelling: Page 199

High-Frequency Words

1 **Guided Practice** Say each high-frequency word: *any, from, happy, once, so* and *upon*. Have children Read/Spell/Write it. As children spell each word with you, point out that the word *upon* is made up of two known words: *up* and *on*.

- Display the **Visual Vocabulary Cards** to review this week's high-frequency words.

2 **Practice** Repeat the activity with last week's words. Children can practice reading the high-frequency words independently, using the online activity.

Build Fluency: Word Automaticity

Have children read the following sentences aloud together at the same pace. Repeat several times until children can read the words automatically.

Can you see **any** ducks **from** the bridge?

I am **happy, so** I smile a lot.

Once upon a time, five mice ran a race.

Word Bank

Review the current and previous words in the Word Bank. Discuss with children which words should be removed or re-added from previous high-frequency word lists. Remind children that the Word Bank should change as the class needs it to.

DIGITAL TOOLS

For more practice, use these activities.

Word Work Spelling
High-Frequency Words

FORMATIVE ASSESSMENT

❯ STUDENT CHECK-IN

Spelling Have partners think of another word to go with one of the word families.

High-Frequency Words Have partners point to one high-frequency word and read it aloud to each other.

Have children reflect, using the Check-In routine.

✔ CHECK FOR SUCCESS

Rubric Use your online rubric to record children's progress.

Can children read and decode words with soft *c* and soft *g*?

Can children recognize and read high-frequency words?

❯❯ Small Group Instruction

If No

🔴 **Approaching** Reteach pp. T228–T233

🟣 **ELL** Develop pp. T228–T233

If Yes

🔵 **On** Review pp. T236–T238

🟢 **Beyond** Extend pp. T240–T241

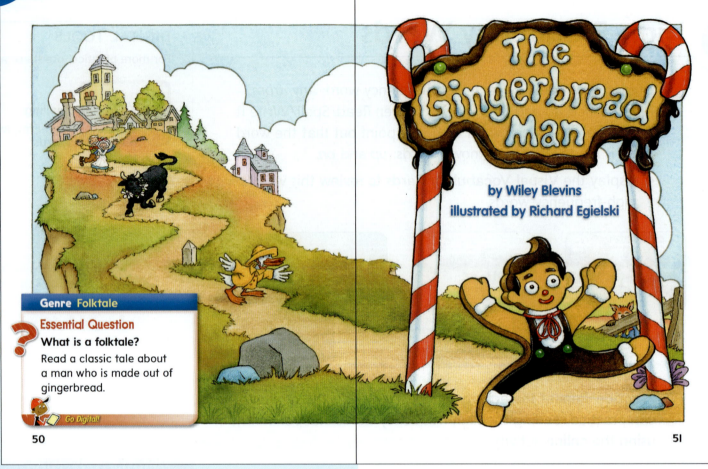

Genre **Folktale**

? Essential Question
What is a folktale?
Read a classic tale about a man who is made out of gingerbread.

Go Digital!

50

51

Literature Anthology, pp. 50–51
Lexile 320

The Gingerbread Man

LEARNING GOAL

Read We can understand the important ideas and details in a story.

Reread We can name the choices an author made when writing a story.

Have children apply what they learned as they read.

Close Reading Routine

Read   DOK 1–2

• Identify important ideas and details.
• Take notes and retell.
• Use **A C T** prompts as needed.

Reread   DOK 2–3

• Analyze the text, craft, and structure.
• Use the Reread minilessons.

Integrate   DOK 3–4

• Integrate knowledge and ideas.
• Make text-to-text connections.
• Complete the Show Your Knowledge task.
• Inspire action.

Read

Celebratory Read You may wish to read the full selection aloud once with minimal stopping before you begin using the Read prompts.

Set Purpose

Say: *Let's read to find out what happens to a man made out of gingerbread.*

DIFFERENTIATED READING

Approaching Level Have children listen to the selection summary. Use the Reread prompts during Small-Group time.

On Level and **Beyond Level** Pair children or have them independently complete the Reread prompts on **Reading/Writing Companion** pages 101–103.

🎧 **English Language Learners** Before reading, have children listen to a summary of the selection. See the **ELL Small Group Guide,** pp. 130-131.

"I will make a grandson out of gingerbread," said Gram.

"That will be nice," said Gramps.

So Gram made a little gingerbread man. Then she placed him in the oven to bake. **2**

Once upon a time there lived a little Gram and a little Gramps. They had a **happy** life. Except for one big thing. They did not have **any** grandkids. **1**

52

53

Literature Anthology, pp. 52–53

Story Words Read and spell the words *gingerbread, oven, cow, hungry,* and *friend.* Review word meanings as needed. Tell children they will read these words in the selection.

Note Taking: Graphic Organizer

Have children fill in online Moral Graphic Organizer 7 as they read.

1 Make and Confirm Predictions DOK 2

Teacher Think Aloud On page 52, the story starts "Once upon a time." Gram and Gramps look realistic, but I predict they will do something that cannot really be done. On page 53 I read Gram made a grandson out of gingerbread. This confirms that my prediction was correct.

Build Vocabulary page 52
except: not including

2 Moral DOK 1

The moral is the lesson of a story. As we read, let's look for clues in what the characters say and do to help us figure out the moral.

At last, it was time to take him out. Gram set him down. She gave him a happy face. She gave him pants made of fudge icing.

Just as she finished, the Gingerbread Man jumped up. Like magic! He looked at Gram and Gramps and smiled. Then he ran away. **4**

54

55

Literature Anthology, pp. 54–55

Read

3 Reread DOK 2

As I read, I stop every few pages to make sure I understand what I have read. If I am not sure I understand something, I go back and reread the parts of the story that are unclear or confusing to me. Are there any details that don't make sense to you so far in the story? Go back and reread the details on the previous pages to make them clear.

4 Make and Confirm Predictions DOK 2

Teacher Think Aloud The story says the Gingerbread Man ran away. I will make a prediction here. I predict that Gram and Gramps will chase the Gingerbread Man and catch him. As we continue reading, let's see if this prediction is confirmed or not.

ELL Spotlight on Language

Page 55 Point to the phrase *Like magic!* Reread the words with excitement, and have children repeat. Explain that this phrase describes how the Gingerbread Man jumped up. *How did the Gingerbread Man jump up?* (like magic) *Look at the illustration. How do Gram and Gramps feel about the way the Gingerbread Man jumped up?* (surprised, shocked) Have partners turn and talk about how they would react if they saw something happen "like magic." Encourage them to make surprised or shocked faces as they talk.

Gram and Gramps raced after him.

"Run, run, run as fast as you can. You can't catch me. I'm the Gingerbread Man," the little man sang.

Gram and Gramps did not catch him.

56

The Gingerbread Man ran on and on. He ran until he met a black cow.

"Stop!" yelled the black cow. "You smell good. I will eat you up. Yum!"

"I ran **from** Gram and Gramps," the Gingerbread Man sang. "I can run from you, too. Yes, I can, can, can!"

57

Literature Anthology, pp. 56–57

⑤ Make and Confirm Predictions DOK 2

Teacher Think Aloud We predicted that Gram and Gramps would chase the Gingerbread Man and catch him. Our prediction was not confirmed. They chased him, but he got away from them.

Build Vocabulary page 56
raced: ran fast

Reread

Author's Purpose DOK 3

Reading/Writing Companion, 101

Remember that authors can organize the text for a certain reason. In this story, the author chose to organize the text around words that repeat. How do the repeating words affect the story? Share your answer. (They make the story exciting to read. I wondered if he would be caught!)

 English Language Learners

Requesting Assistance Remind children of questions they can use to request assistance from the teacher or their partners, such as: *Can you repeat it, please? Can you explain that part?*

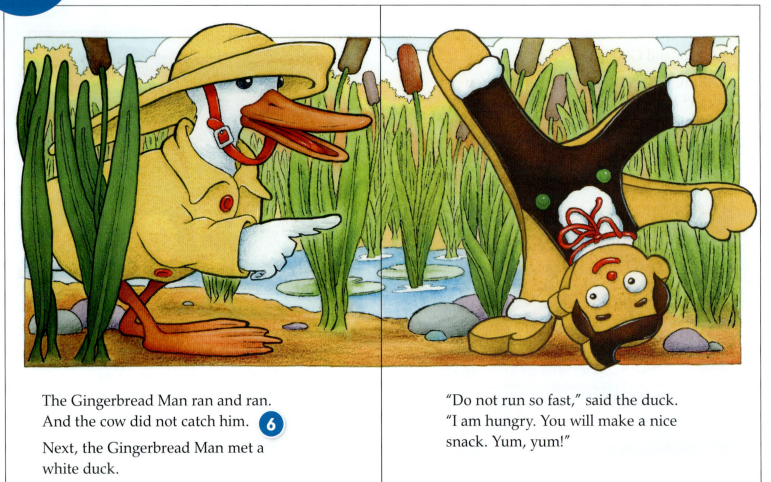

The Gingerbread Man ran and ran. And the cow did not catch him. **6**

Next, the Gingerbread Man met a white duck.

58

"Do not run so fast," said the duck. "I am hungry. You will make a nice snack. Yum, yum!"

59

Literature Anthology, pp. 58–59

6 Moral DOK 2

 Turn to a partner, and discuss what the Gingerbread Man does when he meets the cow. This is a clue to the moral of the story. Let's add this to our Moral chart.

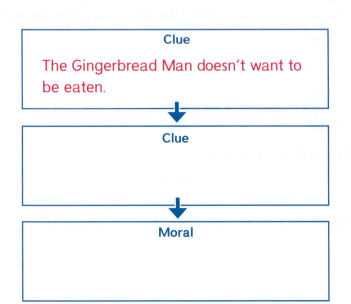

Clue
The Gingerbread Man doesn't want to be eaten.

↓

Clue

↓

Moral

7 Make and Confirm Predictions DOK 2

Think of the pattern or structure in this story. Knowing the pattern, what did you predict would happen when the duck tries to stop the Gingerbread Man? After reading what happens, notice how the author continued the pattern. Did the author confirm or correct your prediction?

Reread

Author's Craft DOK 3

Reading/Writing Companion, 102

What do you notice about the pattern in the story? (The Gingerbread Man runs away from animals that want to eat him.)

"I ran from the cow and Gram and Gramps," yelled the Gingerbread Man. "And I can run from you, too. Yes, I can, can, can!"

And the duck did not catch him.

60

The Gingerbread Man ran on and on and on. He passed a red fox.

"Run, run, run just as fast as you can. You can't catch me. I'm the Gingerbread Man," he sang. **8**

"I do not wish to catch you," said the fox. "I just wish to be a friend."

61

Literature Anthology, pp. 60–61

8 Genre: Folktale DOK 1

In a folktale, phrases or sentences are often repeated. What does the Gingerbread Man say to the fox? ("Run, run, run just as fast as you can. You can't catch me. I'm the Gingerbread Man.") Has the Gingerbread Man said this before? When and to whom? (to Gram and Gramps on page 56)

 Spotlight on Language

Page 61 Point to the words *ran on and on and on.* Explain that by repeating *on* three times, the author is telling us the Gingerbread Man ran for a long time. *What did the Gingerbread Man pass as he ran?* (a red fox) Have partners talk about what the Gingerbread Man should do. *Should he run on and on and on again or talk to the fox?*

Reread

Author's Craft DOK 3

Reading/Writing Companion, 103

How does the pattern in the story change? (The fox says he wants to be a friend. The Gingerbread Man doesn't run away, and he is eaten.)

Build Vocabulary page 61
passed: went by
wish: want

The Gingerbread Man and the fox ran on until they came to the edge of a big lake. **9**

"But I can't swim," said the Gingerbread Man. "What will I do?"

62

"Jump on my back," said the red fox. "I will help."

So, the Gingerbread Man jumped on top of the red fox. The red fox swam and swam and swam. **10**

63

Literature Anthology, pp. 62–63

Read

9 Make and Confirm Predictions DOK 2

The Gingerbread Man believes the fox wants to be his friend. Turn to a partner, and tell what you think will happen next.

10 Moral DOK 2

Teacher Think Aloud The Gingerbread Man ran away from Gram and Gramps, the cow, and the duck, but he trusts the fox. Do you think he should? In stories, foxes tend to be clever and tricky. This is a clue to the moral. Let's add this to our Moral chart.

Build Vocabulary page 62
edge: side

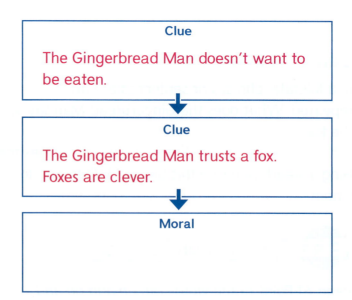

Clue
The Gingerbread Man doesn't want to be eaten.

↓

Clue
The Gingerbread Man trusts a fox. Foxes are clever.

↓

Moral

11 Make and Confirm Predictions DOK 2

What did you predict would happen after the Gingerbread Man met the fox? Was your prediction correct? How do you know?

"Oh, no," said the red fox. "My back is sinking. Jump on my head. Quick! If not, you will get wet."

The Gingerbread Man jumped on the fox's head. The fox tossed the Gingerbread Man up in the air.

64

"Oh, no!" yelled the Gingerbread Man. And then the fox ate him up. **11**

"Run, run, run as fast as you can," said the fox. "This is the last of that Gingerbread Man." **12**

65

Literature Anthology, pp. 64–65

⑫ Moral DOK 3

Display the Moral chart, and read the clues. What is the moral of the story? Let's add this to our chart.

Clue
The Gingerbread Man doesn't want to be eaten.

⬇

Clue
The Gingerbread Man trusts a fox. Foxes are clever.

⬇

Moral
Be careful whom you trust.

ELL Spotlight on Language

Pages 64–65 Point out the two uses of *up*: "up in the air" and "ate him up." Explain that on page 64, *up* means the direction the fox threw the Gingerbread Man. Demonstrate tossing something up in the air. On page 65, *up* is part of the idiom *ate up*, meaning "to eat something completely, or until it is gone." Provide sentence frames for partners to use both meanings of *up*: I walk up the <u>hill</u>. I ate up my <u>lunch</u>.

Return to Purposes

Have partners discuss what happened to the Gingerbread Man. Remind them to use evidence from the story.

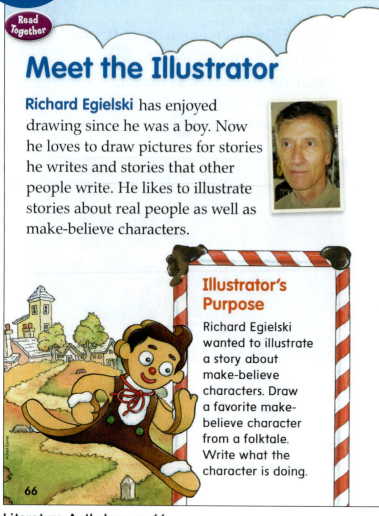

Literature Anthology, p. 66

Meet the Illustrator
Richard Egielski

Have children turn to page 51 and point to the illustrator's name. Read the name aloud. Then read aloud page 66 with children. Ask why they think Richard Egielski enjoyed illustrating *The Gingerbread Man*.

Illustrator's Purpose

Help children brainstorm some characters they know from other folktales. Then have children draw a favorite folktale character in their reader's notebooks. Use sentence starters to help them tell what the character is doing. *This is _____. _____ is _____.* Tell children to include interesting details in their illustrations.

ILLUSTRATOR'S CRAFT   DOK 2
Focus on Details

Authors use words to tell a story. Illustrators use illustrations to help tell the story. The illustrations in *The Gingerbread Man* give us important details that we do not learn from the words. Have children look at page 56. Say: *The words on this page tell us that Gram and Gramps did not catch the Gingerbread Man. The illustrations show us why. Why didn't Gram and Gramps catch the Gingerbread Man?* (He ran away too fast.)

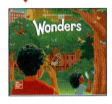

Retell

Have children turn to page 100 in their **Reading/Writing Companions**. Remind children that as they read the story, they made and confirmed predictions and paid attention to clues that helped determine the moral. Have children use the information they recorded on their Moral chart to help them retell the story.

Use Text Evidence Guide children to use text evidence to respond to the questions on page 100.

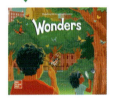

Analyze the Text

After children read and retell the selection, have them reread *The Gingerbread Man* to develop a deeper understanding of the text. Then have them answer the questions on pages 101–103 in their Reading/Writing Companion. For children who need support finding text evidence to support their responses, use the scaffolded instruction from the Reread prompts on pages T197–T199.

Build Knowledge: Make Connections

Talk About the Text Have partners discuss the elements that make *The Gingerbread Man* a folktale.

Write About the Text Have children add their ideas to the Build Knowledge page of their reader's notebooks.

Add to the Anchor Chart Record any new ideas on the Build Knowledge anchor chart.

Add to the Word Bank Add words related to folktales to a separate section of the Word Bank.

Compare Texts DOK 4

Guide children to contrast the lessons in two folktales. Share the prompt: How is the lesson in *The Gingerbread Man* different from the lesson in "The Nice Mitten"? Say: *Think about the characters and the lesson each folktale is trying to teach us. What is different in those lessons?* (*The Gingerbread Man* tries to teach a lesson about being careful about whom you trust. "The Nice Mitten" teaches that it's important to be friendly, even if it causes problems.) Have partners discuss the characters and their experiences in both folktales. Then have partners share their responses with the class. You can use a two-column chart to show the differences.

ENGLISH LANGUAGE LEARNERS

Retell Help children retell by looking at each page in the selection and asking a question, such as: *Who are the characters on this page? What is the Gingerbread Man doing? Why is he doing that?* Provide sentence frames to help children retell the selection, such as: The Gingerbread Man runs away. He meets a duck.

STUDENT CHECK-IN

Read Have partners tell each other an important detail from the story.

Reread Have partners tell one choice the illustrator made when illustrating this story.

Have children reflect, using the Check-In routine to fill in the bars.

LEARNING GOALS

- We can respond to a folktale by writing a new ending.
- We can write sentences with past- and future-tense verbs.

OBJECTIVES

Write narratives in which they recount two or more appropriately sequenced events, include some details regarding what happened, use temporal words to signal event order, and provide some sense of closure.

Use verbs to convey a sense of past, present, and future.

Use commas in dates and to separate single words in a series.

Produce complete sentences when appropriate to task and situation.

ELA ACADEMIC LANGUAGE

- *verbs, past tense, future tense*
- Cognate: *verbos*

 TEACH IN SMALL GROUP

Choose from these options to enable all children to complete the writing activity:

- Drawing and labeling a picture
- Completing sentence frames
- Writing one sentence
- Writing multiple sentences

Additionally, to provide differentiated support for children, see Writing Skills minilessons on pages T420-T429. These can be used throughout the year.

Independent Writing

5 mins

Write About the Anchor Text DOK 3

Analyze the Prompt Read the prompt: *Imagine the Gingerbread Man had chosen to go around the lake. Then write a new ending to the story.* Have partners turn and talk about how the story actually ended and what might happen if the Gingerbread Man had gone around the lake.

- Explain that the prompt is asking children to write a new ending to the story. Children should ask themselves: What would happen if the Gingerbread Man did not accept a ride with the fox?

Find Text Evidence Say: *We need to find clues to help us write a new ending. Look at pages 62–63 in the* **Literature Anthology**. Then ask:

- *What is the Gingerbread Man's problem on these pages?* (He can't swim.)

- *How does the fox help solve this problem?* (He offers the Gingerbread Man a ride on his back to cross the lake.)

- *What happens at the end of the story?* (The fox eats the Gingerbread Man.)

Have children continue finding text evidence, as necessary, to respond to the prompt. You may choose to take notes on a chart or have children take notes in their writer's notebooks.

 Write a Response Tell children to turn to page 104 in their **Reading/Writing Companions**. Guide children to use text evidence to draft a response. Remind them to write an ending that makes sense.

- **Writing Checklist:** Read the checklist with children. Remind them to use specific words, *-ed* and *-ing*, and past-tense verbs correctly.

- **Writing Support:** If needed, provide sentence starters. Model completing one as necessary.

  The Gingerbread Man _____.

  Then the fox _____.

  Tell children they will finalize and present their writing the next day.

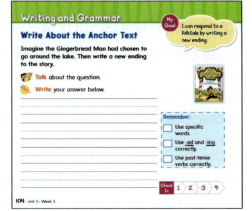

Reading/Writing Companion, p. 104

Grammar

5 mins

Past- and Future-Tense Verbs

1 **Review** Remind children that past-tense verbs tell about an action that has already happened and often end in *-ed*. Remind children that future-tense verbs tell about an action that is going to happen and have *will* before the verbs.

Say: *Let's name the verbs in this sentence:* The animals followed Lance home, and they all lived happily ever after. *How do we know this happened in the past?* Followed *and* lived *are the verbs. They end in* -ed. Next, have children repeat the sentence in future tense.

2 **Guided Practice/Practice** Guide children to identify the past-tense verbs that end in *-ed* on page 55 of *The Gingerbread Man*. Have partners write a new past-tense sentence and circle the verb. Have them rewrite the sentence in future tense.

Talk About It

Have partners orally generate sentences about their stories. Guide them to identify the verbs in their sentences.

Mechanics: Commas in a Series

1 **Model** Tell children that when a writer uses three or more words in a list, the author puts a comma after all but the last word in the list. Display the following sentence: Set out cups, plates, and napkins for lunch. Point out the three words in the list and the comma after all but the last word in the list.

2 **Guided Practice** Prompt children to complete the sentence frame: I ate ____, ____, and ____ for lunch.

ELL English Language Learners

Independent Writing, Analyze the Prompt Be sure children understand the ending they need to write. Have partners look at the illustrations in the **Literature Anthology,** pp. 62-64, to understand how the Gingerbread Man went across the lake. *Show me how the Gingerbread Man could go around the lake. Would the fox run after the Gingerbread Man? Would the fox catch the Gingerbread Man?* Support children's discussions as needed by providing additional vocabulary.

For additional support, see the **ELL Small Group Guide,** p. 135.

DIGITAL TOOLS

Use these activities to practice grammar and mechanics.

Grammar

Mechanics

Grammar Song

FORMATIVE ASSESSMENT

❯ STUDENT CHECK-IN

Writing Have partners share their responses to the prompt. Have children reflect, using the Check-In routine to fill in the bars.

Grammar Have children write another sentence with a past-tense verb. Have children reflect, using the Check-In routine.

LESSON 4

LEARNING GOALS

We can learn and use new vocabulary words.

OBJECTIVES

Identify real-life connections between words and their use.

Discuss the Essential Question.

Develop oral language.

ELA ACADEMIC LANGUAGE

• *poem, rhythm*
• Cognate: *poema*

DIGITAL TOOLS

Visual Vocabulary Cards

LESSON FOCUS

READING

Revisit the Essential Question
Read and Reread Paired Selection:
"Drakestail"
• Introduce Descriptive Words and Phrases
• Make Predictions
Word Work
• Build Words with Soft *c*; Soft *g/dge*

WRITING
• Independent Writing
• Review Grammar and Mechanics

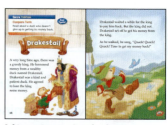

Literature Anthology, pp. 68–75

---

 15 mins

Oral Language

MULTIMODAL

 **Essential Question**
What is a folktale?

Remind children that this week they have been learning about folktales. Guide children to discuss the question, using information from what they have read and discussed. Use the Define/Example/Ask routine to review the oral vocabulary words *eventually, foolish, hero, tale,* and *timid.*

Guide children to use each word as they talk about what they have read and learned about folktales. Prompt children by asking questions.

• What *eventually* happened to the Gingerbread Man?

• Was the Gingerbread Man wise or *foolish*?

• Was the fox a *hero* or a villain?

• How could the *tale* of the Gingerbread Man have ended differently?

• Was the Gingerbread Man *timid* or bold?

Review last week's oral vocabulary words: *assist, bloom, grasped, spied,* and *sprout.*

FORMATIVE ASSESSMENT

⟩ STUDENT CHECK-IN

Have partners use a vocabulary word in a sentence. Have children reflect, using the Check-In routine.

Poetry

Descriptive Words and Phrases

1 **Explain** Tell children that authors use descriptive words and phrases to describe things and actions in interesting ways. Authors may include words that tell about kind, color, shape, size, number, or how things are done. Descriptive words and phrases add meaning to a text.

Jet Plane
A jet plane takes us very far
To places we can't reach by car.
It **rumbles, rattles, roars** up high,
Soaring swiftly in the sky.

Online Teaching Chart

2 **Model** Display **Online Teaching Chart** for Poetry: Alliteration, Descriptive Words and Phrases. Read the text aloud. Then reread the third line, emphasizing the words *rumbles, rattles,* and *roars*. Point out that the author used the words *rumbles, rattles, roars* to help the reader understand how loud and fast the plane flies.

3 **Guided Practice/Practice** Reread the last line of the poem. Help children identify the descriptive phrase and tell how it helps them picture the plane in their minds. Point out that the phrase *Soaring swiftly* describes how the plane moves through the sky. Tell children to look for descriptive words and phrases as they read the folktale.

English Language Learners

Use the scaffolds with **Poetry, Guided Practice/Practice.**

Beginning
Read the third line of the poem. Rumbles, rattles, roars *are words to describe sounds the jet plane makes as it takes off into the sky.* Demonstrate the sounds for each verb, and have children mimic you.

Intermediate
Make sure children know the meanings of *rumbles, rattles,* and *roars.* Then explain that *soaring* in the last line tells how high the plane is flying. Have children tell what else might soar. (eagles)

Advanced/Advanced High
Discuss all the above descriptive words as needed. Then say: Swiftly *adds more detail to the word* soaring. *It means "quickly." The plane not only flies high but also flies quickly.*

OBJECTIVES

Identify words and phrases in stories or poems that suggest feelings or appeal to the senses.

ELA ACADEMIC LANGUAGE

- *descriptive*
- Cognate: *descriptivo*

DIGITAL TOOLS

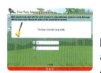

Descriptive Words and Phrases Activity

ELL NEWCOMERS

Use the **Newcomer Online Visuals** and their accompanying prompts to help children expand vocabulary and language about My Family and Me (Unit 2, 10–14). Use the Conversation Starters, Speech Balloons, and Games in the **Newcomer Teacher's Guide** to continue building vocabulary and developing oral and written language.

FORMATIVE ASSESSMENT

STUDENT CHECK-IN

Have partners tell one way that descriptive words and phrases add meaning to a text. Have children reflect, using the Check-In routine.

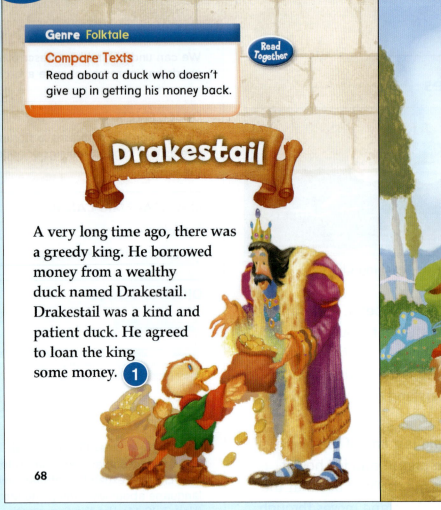

Genre Folktale

Compare Texts
Read about a duck who doesn't give up in getting his money back.

Read Together

Drakestail

A very long time ago, there was a greedy king. He borrowed money from a wealthy duck named Drakestail. Drakestail was a kind and patient duck. He agreed to loan the king some money. **1**

68

Drakestail waited a while for the king to pay him back. But the king did not. Drakestail set off to get his money from the king.

As he walked, he sang, "Quack! Quack! Quack! Time to get my money back!" **2**

69

Literature Anthology, pp. 68–69
Lexile 450L

"Drakestail"

Read We can understand the important ideas and details in a story.

Reread We can name the choices an author made when writing a story.

Compare Texts

As children read and reread "Drakestail," encourage them to think about the Essential Question. Have children think about how this folktale is like *The Gingerbread Man*.

Genre Focus Explain that "Drakestail" is a folktale. Review that a folktale is a story that was handed down orally from one generation to the next. It has animal characters that speak and act like humans and can have a moral. Folktales often include descriptive words and phrases to help readers visualize the story.

Read

❶ Literary Element: Descriptive Words and Phrases DOK 1

Teacher Think Aloud When I read page 68, I noticed descriptive words the author uses to describe the characters. The author describes the king as being greedy. The author describes Drakestail as being wealthy, kind, and patient. These words help us better understand what kind of characters the king and Drakestail are.

❷ Make and Confirm Predictions DOK 2

Teacher Think Aloud We know Drakestail loaned money to the king long ago, and now Drakestail wants his money back. I'm going to make a prediction. I think Drakestail will get his money back. It probably won't be easy, but I think he will get his money back in the end.

Reread

Author's Craft DOK 2

Reading/Writing Companion, 105

Set Purpose Let's reread to find out the moral of this folktale.

Talk with a partner about how the author shows that Drakestail is a kind and patient duck. (The author says Drakestail is kind and patient. Drakestail was kind in loaning the king money and he was patient in waiting for the king to repay him.)

English Language Learners

Use the scaffolds to assist children with **Compare Texts.**

Beginning

Have children look at the illustrations on pages 68-69. *I see a duck wearing clothes. Did the animals in* The Gingerbread Man *wear clothes?* Yes, the animals wore clothes.

Intermediate

Have children complete the above sentence frame. Then point to the title page on page 68. *This is a folktale. Is* The Gingerbread Man *a folktale?* (no) *What kind of story is it?* (a fairy tale)

Advanced/Advanced High

Have partners predict some of the similarities they might see between "Drakestail" and *The Gingerbread Man.* Ask: *What were some of the features of a folktale you noticed in* The Gingerbread Man*?* (animals that act and talk like people) *Do you think you will see this feature in "Drakestail"? Why or why not?* (Yes, because I see a duck wearing clothes.)

"Where are you headed?" asked Fox.

"I'm going to get my money back from the king," Drakestail said.

"Take me," said Fox. "I can help." Drakestail thought it would be best if Fox stayed hidden. So, Fox made himself little and climbed into Drakestail's bag.

70

Pond and Hive heard what Drakestail said to Fox. They asked to come along as well.

Drakestail agreed and opened his bag again. Pond and Hive made themselves small enough to fit into his bag. **3**

71

Literature Anthology, pp. 70–71

Read

3 Make and Confirm Predictions DOK 2

Teacher Think Aloud We predicted Drakestail would get his money back from the king. Can we confirm that prediction yet? What prediction can you make about how Fox, Pond, and Hive might help Drakestail on his journey to the palace?

Student Think Aloud Foxes are clever, so I think Fox will help Drakestail trick the king. Pond is made of water, so I think Pond will help put out a fire. And I think Hive will scare someone.

Reread

Author's Craft DOK 2

Reading/Writing Companion, 106

Why did Fox, Pond, and Hive hop into Drakestail's bag? (They wanted to help Drakestail.)

Look at the picture on page 71. Talk with a partner about what the picture helps you understand about Drakestail's new friends. (They made themselves so small that they could all fit in Drakestail's bag.)

Use the Quick Tip box to support children as they work.

Drakestail walked across the land. After eight days, he made it to the king's palace.

"Quack! Quack! Quack! Can I have my money back?" Drakestail asked the king.

But the king had spent it all! "Stick that duck in the hen pen!" yelled the king.

The hens pecked at Drakestail. "Fox! I am in bad shape! Come and help me!" said Drakestail. Fox sprang out of Drakestail's bag. Fox chased the hens away. Drakestail ran from the hen pen.

The guards caught Drakestail and took him to the king. The king ordered them to cook Drakestail for dinner.

72

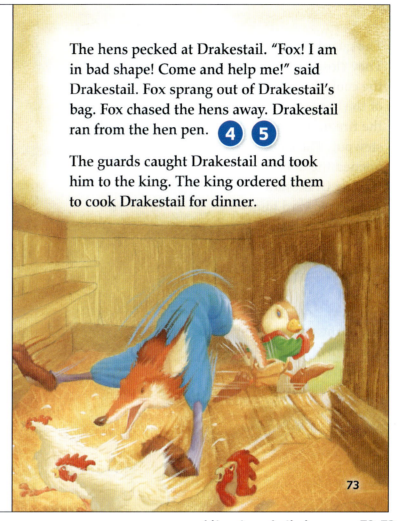

73

Literature Anthology, pp. 72–73

Read

④ Literary Element: Descriptive Words and Phrases DOK 1

Which descriptive words and phrases does the author use in the first paragraph on page 73? (bad, sprang out) How do these words add to the meaning of the folktale? (The word *bad* tells how Drakestail feels. The phrase *sprang out* describes how Fox suddenly jumped out of Drakestail's bag.)

⑤ Make and Confirm Predictions DOK 2

We made a prediction about how each of Drakestail's companions would help him. Was your prediction about Fox confirmed?

Reread

Author's Craft DOK 2

Reading/Writing Companion, 107

What did Fox do to help Drakestail? Underline it in the text. (Fox chased the hens away.) How did the king speak? (the king yelled) What does this tell you about how the king was feeling? (Possible response: The king was angry that Drakestail wanted to get his money back.)

ELL SPOTLIGHT ON LANGUAGE

Page 73 Point to the words *in bad shape.* Read the phrase aloud, and have children repeat. Explain that if someone is in bad shape, he or she is in trouble or hurt. *Who is in bad shape?* (Drakestail) *Why is he in bad shape?* (The hens are pecking at him.) Have partners discuss other characters they have read about that were in bad shape.

The guards threw Drakestail in the kitchen. They closed the door while waiting for the cook. Pond burst out of the bag to put out the fire under the stewpot. The cook opened the door. He saw Drakestail running toward him. "Guards!" he yelled.

Quickly, Hive popped out of the bag! He sent a swarm of bees to chase the guards and the king right out of the palace. ⑥ ⑦

74

Drakestail went back to the throne room. The townsfolk came in. "Drakestail is a duck with brains. Let's make him our king," they said.

Drakestail sang, "I will be the king today, if you say my friends can stay!"

From that day on, Drakestail ruled the kingdom. He had Fox, Pond, and Hive at his side. ⑧

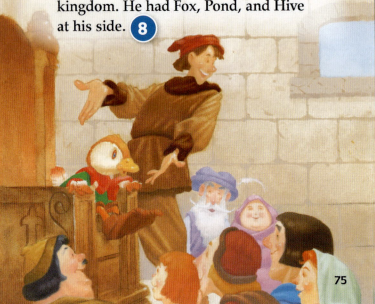

75

Literature Anthology, pp. 74–75

Read

⑥ Make and Confirm Predictions DOK 2

We made a prediction about how Pond and Hive would help Drakestail. Were your predictions confirmed?

⑦ Literary Element: Descriptive Words and Phrases DOK 1

Which descriptive words or phrases did you read on page 74? (burst out, quickly, popped out, swarm) Encourage children to tell how these words help them better understand the events in the folktale.

⑧ Make and Confirm Predictions DOK 2

At the beginning of the story, we made a prediction that Drakestail would get his money back from the king. Was our prediction correct? (No; Drakestail did not get his money back, but he became king.)

Reread

Author's Craft DOK 2

Reading/Writing Companion, 108

What happens to the king? (A swarm of bees chase the king out of the palace.) What does Drakestail say on page 108? Circle it in the text. ("I will be the king today, if you say my friends can stay!") Why does he want his friends to stay? (They helped him when he was in trouble.)

Reread

Author's Craft DOK 3

Reading/Writing Companion, 109

Talk with a partner about what you learned from "Drakestail." What is the moral of this folktale? (The moral of this folktale is that it is important to help friends and to not be greedy.)

Talk About It Talk about how Fox, Pond, and Hive helped Drakestail. (Possible response: They used their special qualities to help Drakestail.) Talk about some ways Drakestail could be a good friend to them in return. (Possible answer: As king, Drakestail will be able to help them when they need it.)

Read

Retell

Guide children to use important details and the illustrations to help them retell the folktale.

Reread

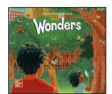

Analyze the Text

After children retell the selection, have them reread to develop a deeper understanding of the text. Have children annotate the text and answer the questions on **Reading/Writing Companion** pages 105–109. For children who need support citing text evidence, use the Reread prompts on pages T209–T213.

Integrate

Build Knowledge: Make Connections

Talk About the Text Have partners discuss how this folktake is similar to and different from other folktales they have read.

Write About the Text Have children add their ideas to the Build Knowledge page of their reader's notebooks.

Add to the Anchor Chart Record any new ideas on the Build Knowledge anchor chart.

Add to the Word Bank Add words related to folktales to a separate section of the Word Bank.

ELL SPOTLIGHT ON LANGUAGE

Page 74 Point out and read the second sentence. Say: *In the story, the word* right *means "immediately, without waiting." This means the bees chased the guards and the king out of the palace immediately, without waiting for anything or for someone to give the bees permission.* Have children complete the sentence frame: Another way of saying "get right to work on your school assignment" is "get to work <u>immediately</u>, or <u>without waiting</u>."

FORMATIVE ASSESSMENT

❯ STUDENT CHECK-IN

Read Have partners tell each other one important detail from the text. Have children reflect, using the Check-In routine.

Reread Have partners tell one choice the author made when creating this text. Have children reflect, using the Check-In routine to fill in the bars.

In a Flash: Sound-Spellings

Display the Sound-Spelling Card for s. Point to the letters ce.

1. **Teacher:** What are the letters? **Children:** ce
2. **Teacher:** What's the sound? **Children:** /s/

Continue the routine for previously taught sounds.

LEARNING GOALS

- We can segment sounds in words.
- We can build words with soft *c* and soft *g*.
- We can add the endings *-ed* and *-ing* to words to make new words.
- We can spell and sort words with soft *c* and soft *g, dge*.
- We can read and write the words *any, from, happy, once, so,* and *upon.*

OBJECTIVES

Segment spoken single-syllable words into their complete sequence of individual sounds (phonemes).

Use conventional spelling for words with common spelling patterns and for frequently occurring irregular words.

Read words with inflectional endings.

Recognize and read grade-appropriate irregularly spelled words.

ELA ACADEMIC LANGUAGE

• verb, syllable

 **TEACH IN SMALL GROUP**

Word Work lessons can be taught in small groups.

Structural Analysis: Page 202

 OPTION 5 mins

Phonemic Awareness

Phoneme Segmentation

1 **Model** Say: *Listen as I say a word:* glance. *The sounds in the word are /g/ /l/ /a/ /n/ /s/. There are five sounds. Let's say them again: /g/ /l/ /a/ /n/ /s/,* glance.

2 **Guided Practice/Practice** Have children practice segmenting words into phonemes. Then have children practice segmenting words using the following words. Say: *I will say a word. Repeat the word, and tell me which sounds you hear. Then tell me how many sounds you hear.* Guide practice, and provide corrective feedback as needed.

ice (2)   cell (3)   stage (4)   fence (4)   pledge (4)   race (3)

chance (4)   face (3)   slice (4)   gel (3)   dodge (3)   page (3)

5 mins # Phonics

Build Words with Soft *c*, Soft *g, dge*

1 **Review** Provide children with **Word-Building Cards** *a–z.* Have children put the letters in alphabetical order as quickly

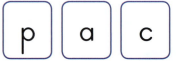

as possible. *The sound /s/ can be represented by the letter* c *when it is followed by* e *or* i. *The sound /j/ can be represented by the letter* g *when it is followed by* e *or* i. *The sound /j/ can also be represented by the trigraph* dge. *Place cards* p, a, c, *and* e. *Let's blend the sounds and read the word: /pāāāsss/. Now let's change the* c *to* g *and read the word:* page.

2 **Practice** Continue with *wage, cage, rage, race, rice, lice, slice, spice, space, race, rice, ridge,* and *bridge.* Point out that in some words, more than one letter will change. After children finish building the words, dictate the list, and have children write the word-building words. Have partners exchange lists and check them for spelling. Guide practice, and provide corrective feedback as needed.

Color Coding After each dictation, reveal the secret color-coding letter(s) for children to find on their **Response Boards**. Have children say the sound(s) as they trace each letter in color. Use one or two of the phonics skills of the week for color coding.

Decodable Reader

Have children read "Tales From a Past Age" to practice decoding words with soft *c* and soft *g, dge* in connected text. If children need support, turn to Small Group pages T231 or T238.

Structural Analysis

5 mins

Inflectional Endings *-ed, -ing*

Review Write the words *dance, danced,* and *dancing* on the board, and read them with children. Remind children that when *-ed* or *-ing* is added to a word that ends in final *-e,* the *e* is dropped before adding the ending.

Write the following words: *trace, change,* and *dodge.* Have children work in pairs to construct words that tell about actions in the past and actions happening now by adding the inflectional endings *-ed* and *-ing.* Then have children write sentences that include each word.

If children need additional practice identifying and reading verbs with inflectional endings *-ed,* and *-ing,* see **Practice Book** page 202 or the online activity.

Spelling

5 mins

MULTIMODAL

Word Sort with *-ice, -age, -edge*

Review Provide pairs of children with copies of the online **Spelling Word Cards**. While one partner reads the words one at a time, the other partner should orally segment the word and then write the word. After reading all the words, partners should switch roles.

Have children correct their own papers. Then have them sort the words by ending spelling pattern: *-ice, -age, -edge* ending or no *-ice, -age, -edge* ending.

High-Frequency Words

OPTION
5 mins

any, from, happy, once, so, upon

Review Display online **Visual Vocabulary Cards** for high-frequency words *any, from, happy, once, so,* and *upon.* Have children Read/Spell/Write each word.

- Point to a word, and call on a child to use it in a sentence.
- Review last week's words using the same procedure.

DIGITAL TOOLS

For more practice, use these activities.

Word Work

Phonemic Awareness
Phonics
Structural Analysis
Spelling
High-Frequency Words

FORMATIVE ASSESSMENT

❯ STUDENT CHECK-IN

Phonics/Spelling Have partners spell words with soft *c* and words with soft *g.*

Structural Analysis Have children write another sentence that includes a word ending in *-ed* or *-ing.*

High-Frequency Words Have partners share a sentence that includes a high-frequency word.

Have children reflect, using the Check-In routine.

✓ CHECK FOR SUCCESS

Rubric Use your online rubric to record children's progress.

Can children read and decode words with soft *c* and soft *g?*

Can children recognize and read high-frequency words?

❯ Small Group Instruction

If No

🔴 **Approaching** Reteach pp. T228–T233

🟣 **ELL** Develop pp. T228–T233

If Yes

🔵 **On** Review pp. T236–T238

🟢 **Beyond** Extend pp. T240–T241

LEARNING GOALS

- We can revise our writing.
- We can use past- and future-tense verbs.

OBJECTIVES

With guidance and support from adults, focus on a topic, respond to questions and suggestions from peers, and add details to strengthen writing as needed.

Ask and answer questions about key details in information presented orally.

Use verbs to convey a sense of past, present, and future.

Use commas in dates and to separate single words in a series.

ELA ACADEMIC LANGUAGE

- *revise, edit, evaluate*
- Cognates: *revisar, editar, evaluar*

Independent Writing

5 mins

Write About the Anchor Text

Revise

Reread the prompt about *The Gingerbread Man: Imagine the Gingerbread Man had chosen to go around the lake. Then write a new ending to the story.*

- Have children read their drafts on page 104 in their **Reading/Writing Companions.** Ask children to check that they responded to the prompt. Then have them review the checklist to confirm that they used specific words, *-ed* and *-ing*, and past-tense verbs correctly.

Peer Review Have pairs take notes about what they liked most, questions they have for the author, and additional ideas the author could include. Have partners discuss these topics. Provide time for revisions.

Edit/Proofread

Review the online proofreading marks with children. Model how to use each mark. Then have children edit for the following:

- Correctly spelled high-frequency words
- Commas used to separate items in a series

Write Final Draft

Have children create their final draft in their writer's notebooks by:

- writing it neatly, or using digital tools to produce and publish it.
- adding details and a drawing that show what happens when the Gingerbread Man goes around the lake.

Teacher Conference As children work, conference with them to provide guidance. Make sure children chose specific words and used verb tenses correctly. Have children make changes based on your feedback.

Share and Evaluate

After children have finalized their drafts, have them:

- work with a partner to practice presenting their writing to each other.
- share their final drafts with the class.
- ask and answer questions about each other's work.

If possible, record children as they share so they can self-evaluate. After children share, display their final papers on a bulletin board.

Have children add their work to their writing folders. Invite children to look at their previous writing and discuss with a partner how it has improved.

5 mins

Grammar

Past- and Future-Tense Verbs

1 **Review** Remind children that past-tense verbs tell about an action that has already happened. Future-tense verbs tell about something that is going to happen. Ask: *What can you do to most verbs to make them past tense?* (add *-ed*) *What can you do to verbs to make them future tense?* (add *will* before the verbs)

2 **Guided Practice** Guide children to identify the past- and future-tense verbs as you say the following sentences. *Yesterday Bob raced Lance down the track.* (raced, past tense) *I will brush my dog on Monday.* (will brush, future tense) *I rested on a nice cot.* (rested, past tense)

3 **Practice** Have pairs work together to edit the past-tense sentences to future-tense and the future-tense sentence to past. For additional practice with editing using past- and future-tense verbs, see **Practice Book** page 205 or the online activity.

 COLLABORATE

Talk About It

Have partners orally generate sentences that include both past-tense and future-tense verbs.

Mechanics: Commas in a Series

1 **Review** Remind children that when a writer uses three or more words in a list, the writer puts a comma after all but the last word.

2 **Practice** Display and read a sentence with punctuation errors. Have pairs fix the sentence. *I will write five nine and six on the slate.* (I will write five, nine, and six on the slate.) For additional practice, see Practice Book page 206 or the online activity.

 ELL # English Language Learners

Independent Writing, Revise *I know past-tense verbs often end in* -ed, *which makes the sound* /d/, /ud/, *or* /t/. *I wrote:* Then the Gingerbread Man looked behind him. *What did I add at the end of* look*?* (-ed) *That's right. I used the past tense correctly because the event had already happened.* Help children with the spelling of any irregular past-tense verbs as needed.

For additional support, see the **ELL Small Group Guide**, p. 135.

DIGITAL TOOLS

Use these resources with the lessons.

Proofreading Marks

Grammar

Mechanics

Grammar Song

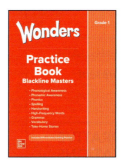

Grammar: Page 205
Mechanics: Page 206

FORMATIVE ASSESSMENT

❯ STUDENT CHECK-IN

Writing Have children reflect on one way they revised their writing.

Grammar Have partners write one of the sentences they said orally.

Have children reflect, using the Check-In routine.

LEARNING GOALS

We can do research to learn about folktales.

OBJECTIVES

Participate in shared research and writing projects.

With guidance and support from adults, recall information from experiences or gather information from provided sources to answer a question.

Add drawings or other visual displays to descriptions when appropriate to clarify ideas, thoughts, and feelings.

Build on others' talk in conversations by responding to the comments of others through multiple exchanges.

ELA ACADEMIC LANGUAGE

• *research, folktales, present*
• Cognate: *presentar*

COLLABORATIVE CONVERSATIONS

Take Turns Talking
Review with children that as they engage in partner, small-group, and whole-group discussions, they should:

• take turns talking and not speak over others.

• raise their hands if they want to speak.

• ask others to share their ideas and opinions.

---

 10 mins

Folktales

Model

Tell children today they will research folktales. Display pages 110–111 of the **Reading/Writing Companion,** and model filling them in, reviewing the steps in the research process below.

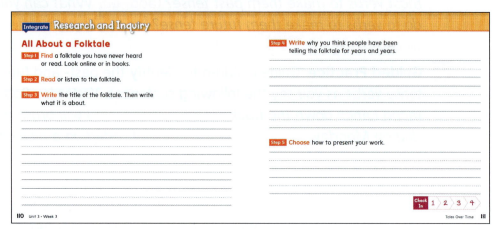

Reading/Writing Companion, pp. 110–111

STEP 1 Find a Folktale

This project is to research a new folktale I have not heard or read before. I will look online or in books to find a folktale I haven't heard or read. I chose The Foolish, Timid Rabbit.

STEP 2 Read or Listen to the Folktale

Now that I have found a folktale I didn't know, I will read it. I will pay attention to the title, the characters, and the story it tells.

STEP 3 Write About the Folktale

I will write about the folktale I read. I will write the title and what the folktale is about. I will also include the country the folktale came from. The Foolish, Timid Rabbit *is a folktale from India.*

STEP 4 Write Your Thoughts

Now I need to think about why people have been telling the folktale for years and years. I think it is because it is a story about the rabbit getting help from his friends and how you shouldn't jump to conclusions.

STEP 5 Choose How to Present What You Learned

I can present my work in different ways. I think I will choose to present my work using colorful pictures. I will draw a storyboard, or pictures in a sequence, of the events in the folktale I read. I will include captions to tell what is happening in each picture.

Apply

Have children turn to pages 110–111 in their **Reading/Writing Companions**. Guide children as they choose a folktale to research and tell about. Help them select books in print or online that might help them find a folktale.

Before children choose how to present their work, they can discuss their folktales with a partner. When children are ready to present their work, challenge them to think about literary elements of folktales and why people tell them for many years.

After children have completed their research, guide them to fill out the Research Process Checklist on the online Student Checklist. This checklist helps children decide whether they've completed the necessary parts of the research process.

Choose the Presentation Format

On pages 110–111 in the Reading/Writing Companion, have children review their research and what they learned about folktales. Tell children that today they are going to take the next step by creating a way to present their findings. This will be their final product. Options include:

- Create a storyboard of the folktale they read, including captions, to explain the story.
- Create a video and a written script, interviewing a character from the folktale.
- Write a news article from the point of view of one of the characters in the folktale.

Create the Presentation

Have children develop their presentations. Remind children of the rules of working with others.

Gather Materials Have children gather the materials they'll need to create their finished product. Most of the materials should be available in the classroom or can be brought from home.

Make the Presentation After children have gathered the materials they need for their presentations, provide time for children to create them. Have children review their research before they begin. Then support children as they work on their presentations.

You may wish to have children collaborate on research projects.

ENGLISH LANGUAGE LEARNERS

Apply, Step 3 Support children as they read or listen to the folktale they found. *What is the title? Who are the characters? What is it about?* Help children respond: The title is "The Ugly Duckling." The characters are ducks. The folktale is about a duck no one likes. Tell children to think about the answers to these questions as they prepare to complete Step 3.

TEACH IN SMALL GROUP

You may wish to have children create their presentations during Small-Group time. Group children of varying abilities, or group children who are doing similar projects.

RESEARCH AND INQUIRY: SHARING FINAL PROJECTS

As children prepare to wrap up the week, have them share their Research and Inquiry projects. Then have children self-evaluate.

Prepare Have children gather materials they need to present their projects. Then partners can take turns practicing their presentations.

Share Guide children to present their Research and Inquiry projects. Encourage children to ask questions to clarify when something is unclear.

Evaluate Have children discuss and evaluate their own presentations. You may wish to have them fill out the Presentation Checklist on the online Student Checklist.

FORMATIVE ASSESSMENT

STUDENT CHECK-IN

Have partners share one thing they learned from their research on folktales. Have children reflect, using the Check-In routine to fill in the bars.

LESSON FOCUS

READING

Word Work
- Review Words with Soft *c*; Soft *g* and Trigraph *dge*

Make Connections
- Connect the Picture to the Essential Question
- Show Your Knowledge

WRITING
- Self-Selected Writing
- Review Grammar and Mechanics

Reading/Writing Companion, pp. 112–113

LEARNING GOALS

- We can blend and segment sounds in words.
- We can build words with soft *c* and soft *g*.
- We can add the endings *-ed* and *-ing* to words to make new words.
- We can write words with soft *c* and soft *g*.
- We can write the words *any, from, happy, once, so,* and *upon.*

OBJECTIVES

Orally produce single-syllable words by blending sounds (phonemes), including consonant blends.

Segment spoken single-syllable words into their complete sequence of individual sounds (phonemes).

Decode regularly spelled one-syllable words.

Use conventional spelling for words with common spelling patterns and for frequently occurring irregular words.

Recognize and read grade-appropriate irregularly spelled words.

ELA ACADEMIC LANGUAGE

- *blend, sort*

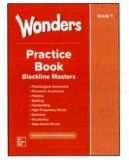

Take-Home Story: Pages 207–208
Spelling: Posttest, Page 197

Phonemic Awareness

Phoneme Blending

Review Guide children to blend phonemes to form words. Say: *Listen as I say a group of sounds. Then blend those sounds to form a word.*

/ī/ /s/	/s/ /l/ /ī/ /s/	/w/ /e/ /j/	/t/ /r/ /ā/ /s/
/ch/ /a/ /n/ /s/	/p/ /l/ /u/ /n/ /j/	/m/ /ī/ /s/	/b/ /a/ /j/

Phoneme Segmentation

Review Guide children to segment phonemes in words. Say: *Now I am going to say a word. I want you to say each sound in the word.*

hinge	dice	wage	smudge	fence	plunge
trace	ledge	cage	twice	lace	sponge

Phonics

MULTIMODAL

Blend and Build with Soft *c*; Soft *g*, *dge*

Review Have children read and say the words *mice, place, cent, gem, stage, edge,* and *lodge.* Then have children follow the word-building routine with **Word-Building Cards** to build *rice, nice, mice, lice, lace, place, pace, race, grace, trace, race, rage, cage, age, edge, wedge, ledge, lodge,* and *dodge.*

Word Automaticity Help children practice word automaticity. Display decodable words, and point to each one as children chorally read it. Test how many words children can read in one minute. Model blending missed words.

Read the Decodable Reader

If children need extra practice decoding words with soft *c*, soft *g*, and the trigraph *dge* in context, have them read "The King and Five Mice" and "Tales From a Past Age." If children need additional support for these stories, turn to pages T231 or T238 for instruction and support.

In a Flash: Sound-Spellings

Display the Sound-Spelling Card for *s*. Point to the letters *ce*.

1. **Teacher:** What are the letters?   **Children:** ce
2. **Teacher:** What's the sound?   **Children:** /s/

Continue the routine for previously taught sounds.

Structural Analysis

Inflectional Endings *-ed, -ing*

Review Have children explain how to add the *-ed* and *-ing* endings to verbs, or action words, that end in final *-e*. Then have children practice adding *-ed* and *-ing* to words such as *place, brace, race, take, make, slice, dodge,* and *judge.*

Spelling

Word Sort with *-ice, -age, -edge*

Review Have children use the online **Spelling Word Cards** to sort the weekly words by vowel and ending sounds. Remind children that four of the words do not end with the /īs/, /āj/, or /ej/ sounds.

Assess Test children on their abilities to spell words in the *-ice, -age,* and *-edge* word families. Say each word, and provide a sentence so children can hear the words used in a correct context. Then allow children time to write the words. Remind children to write legibly, leaving space between the words as they write their answers. As a challenge, provide more words that follow the same spelling pattern. Have children complete the spelling posttest, using **Practice Book** page 197.

High-Frequency Words

any, from, happy, once, so, upon

Review Display **Visual Vocabulary Cards** *any, from, happy, once, so,* and *upon*. Have children Read/Spell/Write each word. Have children write sentences that include each word.

If children need assistance reading high-frequency words, they can practice reading independently using the Take-Home Story in the **Practice Book** on pages 207–208 or use online resources.

DIGITAL TOOLS

For more practice, use these activities.

Word Work

- Phonemic Awareness
- Phonics
- Structural Analysis
- Spelling
- High-Frequency Words

FORMATIVE ASSESSMENT

❯ STUDENT CHECK-IN

Phonics/Spelling Have children spell words with soft *c* and words with soft *g*.

Structural Analysis Have partners tell each other sentences that have words with the endings *-ed* and *-ing*.

High-Frequency Words Have partners share sentences using the high-frequency words.

Have children reflect, using the Check-In routine.

✓ CHECK FOR SUCCESS

Rubric Use your online rubric to record children's progress.

Can children read and decode words with soft *c* and soft *g*?

Can children recognize and read high-frequency words?

❯ Small Group Instruction

If No

🟠 **Approaching** Reteach pp. T228–T233

🟣 **ELL** Develop pp. T228–T233

If Yes

🔵 **On** Review pp. T236–T238

🟢 **Beyond** Extend pp. T240–T241

LEARNING GOALS

- We can choose a writing activity and share it.
- We can use past- and future-tense verbs in sentences.

OBJECTIVES

With guidance and support from adults, focus on a topic, respond to questions and suggestions from peers, and add details to strengthen writing as needed.

Ask and answer questions about what a speaker says in order to gather additional information or clarify something that is not understood.

Use verbs to convey a sense of past, present, and future.

Use commas in dates and to separate single words in a series.

Self-select writing activity and topics.

ELA ACADEMIC LANGUAGE

- *topic, opinion*
- Cognate: *opinión*

 DIFFERENTIATED WRITING

You may choose to conference with children to provide additional support for the following writing activities.

- Newspaper Article: Review the questions typically answered in a newspaper article (*who, what, where, when, why,* and *how*). Have children answer the questions for the topic.
- Storyboard: Have children talk with a partner about their ideas for each picture. Have them tell what happens first, next, and last.

Self-Selected Writing

(10 mins)

Talk About the Topic

Remind children of the Essential Question: *What is a folktale?* Have partners talk about it, and encourage them to ask each other questions.

Choose a Writing Activity

Tell children they will choose a type of writing they would like to do. Children may choose to write about the theme of the week or write about a different topic that is important to them. Children may choose from the following modes of writing.

 Write an Opinion Remind children that an opinion is what they think about a topic. Children can write their opinions about folktales or a topic that is important to them. Tell children to include the reasons they like or don't like folktales or another topic of their choosing.

 Newspaper Article Display several examples of appropriate newspaper articles. Explain that a newspaper article gives facts about a topic. Point out the headline, byline, and other features of the article, such as an accompanying photograph with caption. Children can write a newspaper article to tell what happened to Lance's mitten or about another topic.

 Storyboard Explain that a storyboard is a series of three or four pictures with labels or sentences that tell a story. Have children create a storyboard to tell a folktale or another story. Children can retell a folktale they have read this week or create an original folktale or story.

Use Digital Tools You may wish to work with children to explore a variety of digital tools to produce or publish their writing.

Share Your Writing

 Review the speaking and listening strategies with children. Then have children share their writing with a partner or small group. You may wish to display their work on a bulletin board or in a classroom writing area.

SPEAKING STRATEGIES	LISTENING STRATEGIES
✔ Speak slowly and clearly.	✔ Listen actively and politely.
✔ Speak at an appropriate volume.	✔ Wait until the presenter has finished to ask questions.

OPTION 5 mins

Grammar

Past- and Future-Tense Verbs

1 **Review** Have children describe what past-tense verbs are and how they are used. Write the following sentence, and have children identify the verb: *The sun shined on the class picnic.*

2 **Practice** Ask: *What is one way I would know if the action in a sentence happened in the past?* (The verb might end in *-ed.*) Have children complete these sentences with past-tense verbs: *We _____ at school on Friday. Chad _____ down the hill.*

Ask: *How can you show that an action will happen in the future?* (add *will* before the verb) Have children complete with future-tense verbs. *Tonight, I _____. The frog _____ in the water.*

Have children read their completed sentences to the class.

Mechanics: Commas in a Series

1 **Review** Remind children that when three or more words are in a list, they should put a comma after all but the last word in the list.

2 **Practice** Write the following sentence, and have children fix it. *Miss Nile has capes hats and masks so we can play dress up.* (Miss Nile has capes, hats, and masks so we can play dress up.)

ELL English Language Learners

Self-Selected Writing, Choose a Writing Activity Present the writing activities, and tell children they will vote on one of the activities. Then you will work on the writing as a group. Make sure to do the activity on chart paper as you will revise and publish it during Small-Group time. Provide sentence frames and starters as you talk through the writing together. For example, if children have selected writing a newspaper article to tell what happened to Lance's mitten, have them look at the illustrations in the story and retell the events. Provide frames for the headline, byline, and article, such as: The case of the ___ mitten—A ___ story; A boy named Lance ___. He lost ___. A ___ saw the mitten. It decided to ___. Many more animals ___. But then ___.

For additional support, see the **ELL Small Group Guide,** p. 135.

DIGITAL TOOLS

For more practice, use these activities.

I see a fish.

Grammar

How to Give a Presentation

Grammar Song

Mechanics

◊ TEACH IN SMALL GROUP

● **Approaching** Provide more opportunities for children to add inflectional endings to words before they write sentences.

● ● **On Level and Beyond** Children can do the Practice sections only.

● **ELL** Use the chart in the **Language Transfers Handbook** to identify grammatical forms that may cause difficulty.

FORMATIVE ASSESSMENT

◊ STUDENT CHECK-IN

Writing Have children reflect on how they used the speaking and listening strategies to share their writing.

Grammar Have partners use past- and future-tense verbs in sentences.

Have children reflect, using the Check-In routine.

OBJECTIVES

Compare and contrast the adventures and experiences of characters in stories.

ELA ACADEMIC LANGUAGE

• *compare, connections*
• Cognates: *comparar, conexiones*

Close Reading Routine

Read   DOK 1–2

• Identify important ideas and details.
• Take notes and retell.
• Use prompts as needed.

Reread   DOK 2–3

• Analyze the text, craft, and structure.
• Use the Reread minilessons.

Integrate   DOK 3–4

• Integrate knowledge and ideas.
• Make text-to-text connections.
• Complete the Show Your Knowledge task.
• Inspire action.

Integrate

 5 mins

Make Connections

 MULTIMODAL

Connect to the Essential Question   DOK 4

 COLLABORATE

Turn to page 112 of the **Reading/Writing Companion.** Help partners discuss the image. Use the first prompt as a guide.

Reading/Writing Companion, p. 112

Dinah Zike's
FOLDABLES
Study Organizer

Find Text Evidence Read aloud the second prompt. Guide children to discuss connections between the image and *The Gingerbread Man.* Use the Quick Tip box for support.

Compare Texts Guide partners to compare the image of the Wolf and Red Riding Hood with the characters in "The Nice Mitten." Children can record their notes using a Foldable® like the one shown here. Guide them to record details that help them answer the Essential Question.

Build Knowledge: Make Connections

Talk About the Text Have partners discuss how the picture tells about a folktale and how it relates to other texts they have read this week.

Add to the Anchor Chart Record any new ideas on the Build Knowledge anchor chart.

Add to the Word Bank Add words related to folktales to a separate section of the Word Bank.

Integrate

Show Your Knowledge

10 mins

Write Your Opinion DOK 4

Display the Build Knowledge anchor chart about folktales. Have children lead a discussion about what they have learned. Then have children turn to page 113 in their **Reading/Writing Companions**. Guide children through the steps below to write their opinions about why people should read folktales.

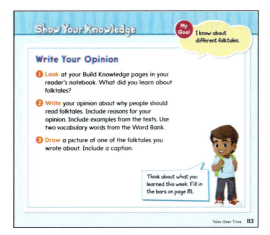

Reading/Writing Companion, p. 113

Step 1 Have children read through the Build Knowledge pages of their reader's notebooks to review what they have learned about folktales. Then have partners talk about the folktales they read.

Step 2 Provide each child with a sheet of paper. Have children write their opinions about why people should read folktales. Remind children to include reasons for their opinions and examples from the texts. Have children use two vocabulary words from the Word Bank.

Step 3 Have children draw a picture of one of the folktales they wrote about. Have children include a caption for their drawings.

Inspire Action

You may choose to extend the learning with the activities below.

Act It Out Have children who wrote about the same folktale get together in a small group to perform a brief play telling the story.

Share a Folktale Have children share the folktale with students from another class. Invite the guests to the classroom. Pair children, and have them share the folktale and their opinions about it.

Choose Your Own Action Have children talk about the texts they read this week. Ask: *What do these texts inspire you to do?*

LEARNING GOALS

We can show what we've learned about different folktales.

OBJECTIVES

Add drawings or other visual displays to descriptions when appropriate to clarify ideas, thoughts, and feelings.

Use words and phrases acquired through conversations, reading and being read to, and responding to texts.

ELA ACADEMIC LANGUAGE

• *opinion*

ELL ENGLISH LANGUAGE LEARNERS

Show Your Knowledge, Step 2 Provide and model sentence frames and/ or starters to help children write. For example: People should read folktales because ___. Another reason is ___. Folktales are ___. They have ___ and ___.

DIGITAL TOOLS

RUBRIC   Show Your Knowledge Rubric

MY GOALS ROUTINE

What I Learned

Review Goals Have children turn to page 81 of the Reading/Writing Companion and review the goals for the week.

Reflect Have children think about the progress they've made toward the goals. Review the key, if needed. Have children fill in the bars.

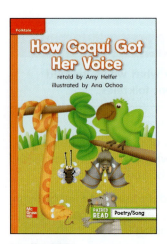

Lexile 300

OBJECTIVES

Read grade-level text orally with accuracy, appropriate rate, and expression on successive readings.

Retell stories, including key details, and demonstrate understanding of their central message or lesson.

Make and confirm predictions.

ELA ACADEMIC LANGUAGE

• *confirm, predict*

• Cognate: *confirmar*

● Approaching Level

Leveled Reader:
How Coquí Got Her Voice

Preview and Predict

Have children turn to the title page. Read the title and the author's and illustrator's names, and have children repeat them. Preview the selection's illustrations. Prompt children to predict what the selection might be about.

Review Genre: Folktale

Have children recall that a folktale is a story that was handed down orally from one generation to the next. A folktale often has animal characters that speak and act like humans, and it can have a moral.

Set Purpose

Remind children of the Essential Question. Set a purpose for reading: *Let's read to find out how Coquí got her voice.* Remind children that as they read a selection, they can ask questions about what they do not understand or what they want to know more about.

Guided Comprehension

As children whisper-read *How Coquí Got Her Voice* independently or with a partner, monitor and provide guidance. Correct blending, and model the key strategies and skills as needed. Also provide definitions for words unfamiliar to children.

Make and Confirm Predictions

Model making and confirming predictions. *On page 3, we learn that Parrot thought the animals were lazy. I predict she will do something so the animals are not so lazy.* Read pages 4 and 5, point to the illustration, and confirm the prediction. Remind children that they can use details from the words and illustrations to make, correct, or confirm predictions as they read.

Moral

Distribute Graphic Organizer 7 to children. Remind them that folktales teach a lesson, and children can use clues to help them identify it. After reading page 2, ask: *What clues help us determine the moral of the story?* Display Moral chart 7 for children to copy.

Model recording children's answers in the boxes. Have children copy the answers into their own charts.

Think Aloud In the illustration on page 6, I see that Tree Frog is thinking about winning. She is focused on that goal, which helps her win the race. I will write that clue in my chart.

Guide children to use the text and illustrations to complete the chart.

Respond to Reading Have children complete Respond to Reading on page 12.

Retell Have children take turns retelling the selection, using the **Retelling Cards** as a guide. Help children make a personal connection by asking: *What story has someone told you? Did you tell it to someone else? What are some reasons people tell each other stories?*

Fluency: Accuracy and Rate

Model Model reading page 2 with accuracy and at an appropriate rate. Read it aloud. Have children read along with you.

Apply Have children practice reading the text with a partner. Correct any errors as needed.

Paired Read: "El Coquí/The Coquí"

 Make Connections: Write About It

Before reading, ask children to note that the genre of this text is poetry. Read the Compare Texts direction in the Leveled Reader.

After they have finished reading, ask children tell how what they learned in "El Coquí/The Coquí" can help them understand *How Coquí Got Her Voice.*

Leveled Reader

Build Knowledge: Make Connections

Talk About the Texts Have partners discuss the lessons in the texts.

Write About the Texts Have children add their ideas to the Build Knowledge page of their reader's notebooks.

LITERATURE CIRCLES

Lead children in conducting a literature circle using the Thinkmark questions to guide the discussion. You may wish to discuss what children have learned about coquís from both selections in the **Leveled Reader**.

ANALYTICAL WRITING

Compare Texts

Have children use text evidence to compare a folktale to poetry.

 **LEVEL** UP

IF children can read *How Coquí Got Her Voice* Approaching Level with fluency and correctly answer the Respond to Reading questions,

THEN tell children they will read another folktale.

- Have children read the selection, checking their comprehension by using the Moral graphic organizer.

Approaching Level

Phonological/Phonemic Awareness

TIER 2

IDENTIFY AND PRODUCE RHYME

OBJECTIVES
Demonstrate understanding of spoken words, syllables, and sounds.

Identify and produce rhyming words.

I Do Explain to children that they will listen for words that rhyme. *Say this word after me: race. Listen as I say another word: case. Say the two words with me: race, case. The words rhyme because they have the same vowel and ending sounds, /ās/.*

We Do *Listen as I say two words. Let's raise our hands if the words rhyme: bit, fit. Yes, the words rhyme because they have the same vowel and ending sounds, /it/.* Continue the routine with these examples:

bug, net   mud, bud   mice, nice   but, nut   vet, men

You Do *Now it's your turn. Raise your hand if the words rhyme. Then say another word that rhymes.*

box, fox   bath, band   ledge, hedge   cost, lost

Repeat the routine with other pairs of words. Provide feedback as needed.

TIER 2

PRODUCE RHYME

OBJECTIVES
Demonstrate understanding of spoken words, syllables, and sounds.

Produce rhyming words.

I Do Explain to children that they will listen for words that rhyme. Display the **Sound-Spelling Card** for *bat. This picture shows a bat. Say the word with me: bat. Now I will say a word that rhymes with bat: sat. Bat and sat rhyme because they have the same vowel and ending sounds: /at/.*

We Do *Listen as I say another word that rhymes with bat and sat: cat. Bat, sat, and cat all have the same vowel and ending sounds. The words rhyme. What is another word that rhymes with bat, sat, and cat?*

Continue this routine with *face, case,* and *lace.*

You Do *Let's say other groups of rhyming words. Ice rhymes with nice. What other rhyming words do you know that rhyme with ice and nice?*

Repeat the routine with other rhyming words. Provide feedback as needed.

PHONEME BLENDING

OBJECTIVES

Orally produce single-syllable words by blending sounds (phonemes), including consonant blends.

I Do Explain that children will blend sounds to form words. *Listen as I say three sounds: /h/ /iii/ /mmm/. Listen as I blend the sounds together: /hiiimmm/,* him. *I blended the word* him. *Say the word with me:* him.

We Do *Listen as I say three sounds: /w/ /e/ /j/. Repeat the sounds with me: /w/ /e/ /j/. Let's blend the sounds together: /weeej/, wedge. We said a word:* wedge.

Repeat the routine with these sounds:

/h/ /a/ /m/   /l/ /ī/ /k/   /l/ /ā/ /s/   /k/ /ā/ /p/

You Do *Are you ready? Blend the sounds together to form a word.*

/j/ /e/ /m/   /s/ /e/ /n/ /t/   /r/ /ī/ /s/   /g/ /l/ /a/ /n/ /s/   /j/ /e/ /l/

Repeat the blending routine with additional soft *c* and soft *g* words.

PHONEME SEGMENTATION

OBJECTIVES

Segment spoken single-syllable words into their complete sequence of individual sounds (phonemes).

I Do Explain to children that they will separate words into sounds. *Listen to this word:* hum. *I hear three sounds: /h/ /u/ and /m/. There are three sounds in* hum.

We Do *Let's try it together. I'll say a word:* ace. *How many sounds do you hear?* (2) *What are the sounds? The two sounds in* ace *are /ā/ and /s/.*

Repeat the routine with these words: *bridge, stuck, that, black, nice, age.*

You Do *Now it's your turn. Tell me how many sounds you hear and what the sounds are in each of the following words:* log, face, chance, cell, spice, gum, fudge, edge, *and* budge. Provide feedback as needed.

ELL You may wish to review phonological/phonemic awareness, phonics, decoding, and fluency using this section. Use scaffolding methods as necessary to ensure children understand the meaning of the words. Refer to the **Language Transfers Handbook** for phonics elements that may not transfer in children's native languages.

Approaching Level

Phonics

CONNECT *c* TO /s/ AND *g* TO /j/

OBJECTIVES

Know and apply grade-level phonics and word analysis skills in decoding words.

Recognize spelling-sound correspondences for soft *c* and soft *g*.

I Do Display **Word-Building Card** *c. This is lowercase* c. *It can stand for different sounds. It can stand for the /k/ sound in* cat. *It can also stand for the /s/ sound in* ice *when it is followed by* e *or* i. *I'm going to write the letter as I say the /s/ sound.* Write the letter *c* on the board as you say /sss/. Repeat for the letter *g* and the /j/ sound.

We Do *Let's do it together.* Have children trace lowercase *c* and *g* while saying /s/ and /j/. Have children trace and say the letters with you several times.

You Do *It's your turn.* Have children connect the letter *c* and the /s/ sound by writing a lowercase *c* on paper while saying /s/. Repeat with the letter *g*. Then have children write the letters as they say the sounds.

Repeat, connecting *c* to /s/ and *g* to /j/ throughout the week.

BLEND WORDS WITH SOFT *c*; SOFT *g, dge*

OBJECTIVES

Decode regularly spelled one-syllable words.

I Do Display Word-Building Cards *c, e, n,* and *t.* Point to the letter *c. This is the letter* c. *It stands for /s/. Say it with me: /s/. This is the letter* e. *It stands for /e/. Let's say it together: /e/.* Point to n, t. *These letters together stand for /nnnt/. I'll blend the sounds together: /ssseeent/. The word is* cent. Repeat with *gem.*

We Do Guide children to blend and read: *cell, face, age, stage, lace,* and *ice.*

You Do Have children use Word-Building Cards to blend and read: *since, cage, gel, gem, mice, space, rage, rice,* and *cent.*

Repeat, blending additional words with soft *c* and soft *g*.

You may wish to practice reading and decoding with **ELL** using this section.

BUILD WORDS WITH SOFT *c*; SOFT *g, dge*

OBJECTIVES

Decode regularly spelled one-syllable words.

Build and decode words with soft *c* and soft *g*.

I Do Display **Word-Building Cards** *e, d, g,* and *e. This is the letter* e. *It stands for /e/. These are the letters* d, g, e. *When you see them together, they stand for the sound /j/. I'll blend these sounds: /e/, /j/,* edge. Repeat with *ice.*

We Do Make the word *edge* with Word-Building Cards. Place the letter *l* in front of *edge. Let's blend: /lll/ /eee/ /j/,* ledge. Repeat with *ice* and *rice.*

You Do *It's your turn.* Have children build and decode: *ledge, hedge, pledge, wedge* and *rice, race, lace, lice, slice,* and *spice.*

Repeat, building additional words with soft *c* and soft *g.*

READ WORDS WITH SOFT *c*; SOFT *g, dge*

OBJECTIVES

Read grade-level text orally with accuracy, appropriate rate, and expression on successive readings.

**Unit 3 Decodable
Reader pages 25–36**

Focus on Foundational Skills

Review the high-frequency words *any, from, happy, once, so,* and *upon* with children. Review that *c* can stand for /s/ and *ge* and *dge* can stand for /j/. Guide children to blend the sounds to read the words.

Read the Decodable Readers

Guide children to read "King and Five Mice" and "Tales from a Past Age." Identify the high-frequency words and words that include soft *c* and soft *g* sounds. If children struggle sounding out words, model blending.

Focus on Fluency

With partners, have children reread "King and Five Mice" and "Tales from a Past Age." As children read, guide them to focus on their accuracy, rate, and automaticity. Children can provide feedback to their partners.

BUILD FLUENCY WITH PHONICS

Sound/Spellings Fluency

Display the following Word-Building Cards: *ce, ge, dge, ie, ae, ch, tch, wh, ph, th, sh, ng, mp, sk, st, nt, nk, nd, e, ea, sp, sn, sl, cr, fr,* and *tr.* Have children chorally say the sounds. Repeat, and vary the pace.

Fluency in Connected Text

Have children review the **Decodable Reader** selections. Identify words with soft *c* and soft *g,* and blend words as needed. Have partners reread the selections for fluency.

● Approaching Level

Structural Analysis

REVIEW INFLECTIONAL ENDINGS -ed AND -ing

OBJECTIVES
Identify frequently occurring root words (e.g., look) and their inflectional forms (e.g., looks, looked, looking).

Read words with inflectional endings.

I Do Write and read *rake*. Use it in a sentence: *I rake the sand.* Then add *d,* and say *raked. The* -ed *ending tells me the action already happened:* I raked the leaves. *Because* rake *ends in* e, *I drop the* e *to add the* -ed.

Erase *d. Now I want to add* -ing. *If a verb ends in* e, *I drop the* e *to add* -ing. Erase *e,* and write *ing. I am raking the leaves.*

We Do Write *dance,* and read it with children. *I dance on a stage. Let's add* -ed *and* -ing. Read the new words together. *Let's use the words in sentences.*

You Do Give partners more decodable verbs that end in *e.* Ask them to add *-ed* and *-ing* endings and write the new words. Provide feedback as needed.

Repeat Have partners create sentences with the words they wrote.

RETEACH INFLECTIONAL ENDINGS -ed AND -ing

OBJECTIVES
Identify frequently occurring root words (e.g., look) and their inflectional forms (e.g., looks, looked, looking).

Read words with inflectional endings.

I Do Write *race, raced,* and *racing. I drop the final* e *to add* -ed *or* -ing *to a word that ends with* e. *The* -ed *ending makes the word tell about something that happened in the past. The* -ing *ending means the action is happening now.*

Use the words *race, raced,* and *racing* in sentences.

We Do Write *slice.* Demonstrate adding *-ed.* Read *sliced* together. *Now let's add* -ing. Demonstrate adding *-ing.* Say *slicing* together. *Let's use* sliced *and* slicing *in sentences.* Have the group create sentences for *sliced* and *slicing.*

Repeat this routine with the following words:

trace   nudge   chase   trade

You Do *Now it's your turn to do it. Add* -ed *and* -ing *to each word, and use each word in a sentence.* Have children repeat the words.

bake   skate   wipe   smudge

Repeat Have children add *-ed* and *-ing* to verbs ending in *e.*

You may wish to review structural analysis and high-frequency words with **ELL** using this section.

High-Frequency Words

REVIEW

OBJECTIVES

Recognize and read grade-appropriate irregularly spelled words.

I Do Use **High-Frequency Word Cards** to Read/Spell/Write *any, from, happy, once, so,* and *upon.* Use each word orally in a sentence.

We Do Guide children to Read/Spell/Write each word on their **Response Boards**. Work together to generate oral sentences using the words.

You Do *It's your turn. Do the Read/Spell/Write routine with a partner. Use the words* any, from, happy, once, so, *and* upon.

RETEACH

OBJECTIVES

Recognize and read grade-appropriate irregularly spelled words.

I Do Review the high-frequency words using the Read/Spell/Write routine. Write a sentence for each high-frequency word.

We Do Guide students to use the Read/Spell/Write routine. Use sentence starters: *(1) Do you have any ____? (2) The gift is from ____. (3) I am happy when ____. (4) Once I ate ____. (5) The cat was so ____! (6) Vance sat upon ____.*

You Do *Now close your eyes, picture the word, and then write it as you see it.* Have children self-correct.

CUMULATIVE REVIEW

OBJECTIVES

Recognize and read grade-appropriate irregularly spelled words.

I Do Display the High-Frequency Word Cards from the previous weeks. Review each word using the Read/Spell/Write routine.

We Do Have children write each word on their **Response Boards**. Complete sentences for each word, such as: *The water is ____. Today we will ____.*

You Do *I will show you a card. Read aloud each word together.* Mix up the cards, and repeat the exercise.

Fluency Display the High-Frequency Word Cards. Point to words randomly. Have children chorally read each word. Repeat at a faster pace.

Approaching Level

Comprehension

READ FOR FLUENCY

OBJECTIVES

Read grade-level text orally with accuracy, appropriate rate, and expression on successive readings.

Set Purpose Tell children they will now focus on reading **Leveled Reader** *How Coquí Got Her Voice*. Remind them that the story is fiction and that they will be reading it for enjoyment. Tell children they need to read with accuracy and at an appropriate rate.

I Do Read aloud the first two pages of *How Coquí Got Her Voice*. Model using appropriate rate and accuracy as you read.

We Do Have children reread the selection with you. Guide children to read with appropriate rate and accuracy.

You Do *Now you read the rest of the selection aloud with a partner.* Children can provide feedback to their partners as they read.

IDENTIFY MAIN STORY ELEMENTS: CHARACTER

OBJECTIVES

Describe characters in a story, using key details.

I Do Remind children that the characters are the people or animals that appear in a story. A story tells what a character does, thinks, and feels.

We Do Ask children to look at the illustrations in *How Coquí Got Her Voice*. Have children describe the characters—what they are doing, thinking, and feeling throughout the story.

You Do *With a partner, read* How Coquí Got Her Voice. *Describe Tree Frog at the beginning of the story and at the end of the story. Tell how she changes.* Provide feedback as needed.

REVIEW MORAL

OBJECTIVES

Retell stories, including key details, and demonstrate understanding of their central message or lesson.

I Do Remind children that the moral is the lesson of the story. Tell them to look for clues in what the characters say and do to figure out the moral. *To understand the moral, I need to look for clues in the characters' words and actions.*

We Do Read **Leveled Reader** *How Coquí Got Her Voice* together. Pause to point out what the characters say and do. *Why was Tree Frog quiet at the beginning of the story? What happened when she won the race?* Record these clues on a Moral chart.

You Do Continue reading the story. Say: *I will stop so you can look for clues that help identify the moral of the story.* Record their responses on the chart.

SELF-SELECTED READING

OBJECTIVES

Retell stories, including key details, and demonstrate understanding of their central message or lesson.

Read grade-level text with purpose and understanding.

Independent Reading

Help children select a folktale for independent reading. Children may use the **Classroom Library**, the **Leveled Reader Library**, the online **Unit Bibliography**, or other books for their independent reading. Encourage children to read for at least ten minutes.

Guide children to transfer what they learned this week as they read. Remind children that a folktale often has animal characters that speak and act like humans, and it can have a moral. Have children record information about character, setting, and events on **Graphic Organizer 7**.

After children read, guide them to participate in a group discussion about the folktale they read. In addition, children can choose activities from the Reading **Center Activity Cards** to help them apply skills to the text as they read. Offer assistance and guidance with self-selected assignments.

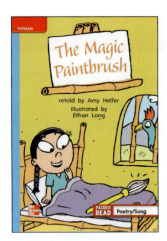

Lexile 230

OBJECTIVES

Read grade-level text orally with accuracy, appropriate rate, and expression on successive readings.

Retell stories, including key details, and demonstrate understanding of their central message or lesson.

Make and confirm predictions.

ELA ACADEMIC LANGUAGE

- *confirm, predict*
- Cognate: *confirmar*

●On Level

Leveled Reader: *The Magic Paintbrush*

Preview and Predict

Have children turn to the title page. Read the title and the author's and illustrator's names, and have children repeat them. Preview the selection's illustrations. Prompt children to predict what the selection might be about.

Review Genre: Folktale

Remind children that a folktale is a story that was handed down orally from one generation to the next. A folktale often has animal characters that speak and act like humans, and it can have a moral.

Set Purpose

Remind children of the Essential Question. Set a purpose for reading: *Let's read to find out what the paintbrush can do.* Remind children that as they read a selection, they can ask questions about what they do not understand or what they want to know more about.

Guided Comprehension

As children whisper-read *The Magic Paintbrush* independently or with a partner, monitor and provide guidance. Correct blending, and model the key strategies and skills as needed. Also provide definitions for words unfamiliar to children.

Make and Confirm Predictions

Model making and confirming predictions: *On page 2, the words tell me Lin-Lin wants a paintbrush badly. I predict she will get one.* Read page 3, point to the illustration, and confirm the prediction. Remind children they can use story details to make, correct, or confirm predictions as they read.

Moral

Distribute Graphic Organizer 7 to children. Remind them that folktales teach a lesson, and they can use clues from what the characters say and do to help them identify the lesson. After reading page 5, ask: *How does Lin-Lin help others with her magic paintbrush?* Display Moral chart 7 for children to copy. Model recording children's answers in the boxes. Have children copy the answers into their own charts.

Think Aloud On page 10, I read that Lin-Lin asked a man to help Chang, even though Chang stole Lin-Lin's magic paintbrush. I think this is a clue that will help us identify the moral. I will write that clue in my chart.

Guide children to use words and pictures to add other clues to their charts.

Respond to Reading Have children complete Respond to Reading on page 12.

Retell Have children take turns retelling the selection, using the **Retelling Cards** as a guide. Help children make a connection by asking: *What would you paint if you had a magic paintbrush?*

Fluency: Accuracy and Rate

Model Model reading page 2 with accuracy and at an appropriate rate. Read aloud. Have children read along with you.

Apply Have children practice reading the text with a partner. Correct any errors as needed.

Paired Read: "Make New Friends"

 Analytical Writing **Make Connections: Write About It**

Before reading, ask children to note that the genre of this text is poetry. Then discuss the Compare Texts direction in the Leveled Reader.

After reading, ask: *How does this poem help you better understand* The Magic Paintbrush?

Leveled Reader

Build Knowledge: Make Connections

Talk About the Texts Have partners discuss the lessons in the texts.

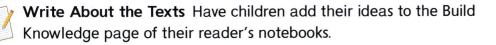 **Write About the Texts** Have children add their ideas to the Build Knowledge page of their reader's notebooks.

LITERATURE CIRCLES

Lead children in conducting a literature circle using the Thinkmark questions to guide the discussion. You may wish to discuss what children have learned about folktales from both selections in the **Leveled Reader**.

ANALYTICAL WRITING

Compare Texts

Have children use text evidence to compare a folktale to a poem.

 **LEVEL** UP

IF children can read *The Magic Paintbrush* On Level with fluency and correctly answer the Respond to Reading questions,

THEN tell children they will read a more detailed selection.

• Have children read the selection, checking their comprehension by using the Moral graphic organizer.

On Level

Phonics

OBJECTIVES

Know the spelling-sound correspondences for common consonant digraphs.

Read grade-level text orally with accuracy, appropriate rate, and expression on successive readings.

Unit 3 Decodable Reader pages 25–36

I Do Display **Word-Building Cards** *a*, *c*, and *e*. Point to the letter *c*. *The letter* c *can stand for the /k/ sound. It can also stand for the /s/ sound when it is followed by an* e *or* i. *I will blend these sounds: /āāāsss/, ace. The word is* ace. Repeat with the word *age*.

We Do *Let's work together.* Make the word *ace* using Word-Building Cards. Place the letter *p* at the beginning. *Let's blend: /p/ /āāāsss/, /pāāāsss/,* pace.

You Do Have children build and blend these words:

pace   place   lace   race   rice   badge   Madge   Midge   ridge   bridge

Read the Decodable Readers

Guide children to read "King and Five Mice" and "Tales from a Past Age." Identify the high-frequency words and words that contain soft *c* and soft *g* sounds. Model blending sound-by-sound as needed.

Focus on Fluency With partners, have children reread "King and Five Mice" and "Tales from a Past Age." As children read, have them focus on accuracy, rate, and automaticity. They can provide feedback to their partners.

High-Frequency Words

OBJECTIVES

Recognize and read grade-appropriate irregularly spelled words.

I Do Use the Read/Spell/Write routine to review *any, from, happy, once, so,* and *upon*. Use each word in a sentence.

We Do Help children Read/Spell/Write each word using their **Response Boards**. Work together to create sentences using each word.

You Do Have partners use the Read/Spell/Write routine with the words *any, from, happy, once, so,* and *upon*. Have partners write sentences about this week's stories, using at least one high-frequency word in each sentence.

Comprehension

REVIEW MORAL

OBJECTIVES

Retell stories, including key details, and demonstrate understanding of their central message or lesson.

I Do Remind children that the moral is the lesson of the story. Tell them to look for clues in what the characters say and do to figure out the moral. *To understand the moral, I need to look for clues in the characters' words and actions.*

We Do Read aloud pages 4–5 of **Leveled Reader** *The Magic Paintbrush.* Ask children to describe what kind of person Lin-Lin is: *By looking at the illustrations and reading these pages, what do we know about Lin-Lin so far?*

You Do Guide children to read the remainder of *The Magic Paintbrush.* Have them use a Moral chart to record the clues and moral of the story. Discuss the completed charts as a group.

SELF-SELECTED READING

OBJECTIVES

Retell stories, including key details, and demonstrate understanding of their central message or lesson.

Read grade-level text with purpose and understanding.

Independent Reading

Help children select a folktale for independent reading. Children may use the **Classroom Library**, the **Leveled Reader Library**, the online **Unit Bibliography,** or other books for their independent reading. Encourage children to read for at least ten minutes.

Guide children to transfer what they learned this week as they read. Remind children that a folktale often has animal characters that speak and act like humans, and it can have a moral. Have children record information about character, setting, and events on **Graphic Organizer 7**.

After children read, guide them to participate in a group discussion about the folktale they read. In addition, children can choose activities from the Reading **Center Activity Cards** to help them apply skills to the text as they read. Offer assistance and guidance with self-selected assignments.

You may wish to review Comprehension with **ELL** using this section.

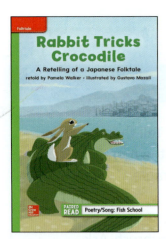

Lexile 420

OBJECTIVES

Retell stories, including key details, and demonstrate understanding of their central message or lesson.

Make and confirm predictions.

ELA ACADEMIC LANGUAGE

• confirm, predict

• Cognate: confirmar

● Beyond Level

Leveled Reader:
Rabbit Tricks Crocodile

Preview and Predict

Read the title and author's and illustrator's names. Have children preview the title page and the illustrations. Ask: *What do you think this book will be about?*

Review Genre: Folktale

Have children recall that a folktale is a story that was handed down orally from one generation to the next. A folktale often has animal characters that speak and act like humans, and it can have a moral.

Set Purpose

Remind children of the Essential Question. Set a purpose for reading: *What do you want to find out about how Rabbit tricks Crocodile? As you prepare to read this story fluently, think about the purpose.*

Guided Comprehension

Have children whisper-read *Rabbit Tricks Crocodile* independently or with a partner. Have them place self-stick notes next to difficult words. Monitor and provide guidance. Correct blending, and model the key strategies and skills as needed.

Monitor children's reading. Stop periodically, and ask open-ended questions to facilitate rich discussion, such as, *What does the author want us to know about folktales?* Build on children's responses to develop deeper understanding.

Make and Confirm Predictions

Model making and confirming predictions: *On page 2, the words say Rabbit wished she could visit the mainland. What prediction can we make? How can we check if it is correct?* Remind children that they can use the words and illustrations to make and confirm predictions about the folktale.

Moral

Distribute Graphic Organizer 7 to children. Remind them that folktales teach a lesson, or moral, and they can use clues to help them identify the moral. After reading page 4, ask: *Why does Crocodile think the island is nicer than the mainland?* Display Moral chart 7 for children to copy. Model how to record the clues. Have children fill in their charts.

Think Aloud As I read pages 10 and 11, I learn what trick Rabbit plays on Crocodile. This is another clue to the moral of the story. I will write this in my chart.

Have children fill in the rest of their charts as they read.

Respond to Reading Have children complete Respond to Reading on page 12.

Retell Have children take turns retelling the selection. Help children make a personal connection by writing about a wish they have. *Write about a wish you have. What is your wish? How can others help you make your wish come true?*

Paired Read: "Fish School"

 Make Connections: Write About It

Before reading, have children preview the title page and identify the genre as poetry. Then have children discuss the Compare Texts direction in the Leveled Reader.

After reading the selection, have partners discuss how Rabbit in *Rabbit Tricks Crocodile* is similar to Fish in "Fish School."

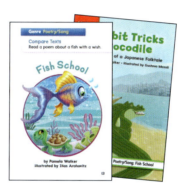

Leveled Reader

Build Knowledge: Make Connections

 Talk About the Texts Have partners discuss the lessons in the texts.

Write About the Texts Have children add their ideas to the Build Knowledge page of their reader's notebooks.

LITERATURE CIRCLES

Lead children in conducting a literature circle using the Thinkmark questions to guide the discussion. You may wish to discuss what children have learned about storytelling from both selections in the **Leveled Reader.**

ANALYTICAL WRITING

Compare Texts

Have children use text evidence to compare a folktale to a poem.

⭐ GIFTED AND TALENTED

Synthesize Challenge children to compare different kinds of stories. Children should write about what they learned about stories from the selections. Encourage children to tell what kinds of stories they like best.

Extend Have children use facts they learned from the week or do additional research to find out more about different kinds of stories, such as myths, legends, and fables.

●Beyond Level

Vocabulary

ORAL VOCABULARY: SYNONYMS

OBJECTIVES
With guidance and support from adults, demonstrate understanding of word relationships and nuances in word meanings.

I Do Review the meanings of the oral vocabulary words *hero* and *timid*. Remind children that a synonym is a word that means almost the same as another word.

A synonym for the word hero *is* champion. *A champion can show courage or strength.*

A synonym for the word timid *is* fearful.

We Do Have partners take turns using the words *champion* and *fearful* in sentences about stories they know.

You Do Ask partners to share their sentences with the group. Encourage children to ask questions about the sentences other pairs wrote.

GIFTED and TALENTED **Extend** Have children perform a funny skit about a fearful champion. Encourage them to use the oral vocabulary words as well as the new words they learned.

Comprehension

REVIEW MORAL

OBJECTIVES

Retell stories, including key details, and demonstrate understanding of their central message or lesson.

I Do Remind children that the moral is the lesson of the story. Look for clues in what the characters say and do to figure out the moral. *To understand the moral, I need to look for clues in the characters' words and actions.*

We Do Have children read the first page of **Leveled Reader** *Rabbit Tricks Crocodile*. Prompt children to identify clues that will help them identify the moral of the story. Ask: *What is Rabbit's wish?*

You Do Have children read the rest of the story independently. Remind them to look for clues in what the characters say and do to figure out the moral of the story. Provide feedback as needed.

SELF-SELECTED READING

OBJECTIVES

Retell stories, including key details, and demonstrate understanding of their central message or lesson.

Read grade-level text with purpose and understanding.

Independent Reading

Help children select a folktale for independent reading. Children may use the **Classroom Library**, the **Leveled Reader Library**, the online **Unit Bibliography**, or other books for their independent reading. Encourage children to read for at least ten minutes.

Guide children to transfer what they learned this week as they read. Remind children that a folktale often has animal characters that speak and act like humans, and it can have a moral. Have children record information about character, setting, and events on **Graphic Organizer 7**.

After children read, guide them to participate in a group discussion about the folktale they read. In addition, children can choose activities from the Reading **Center Activity Cards** to help them apply skills to the text as they read. Offer assistance and guidance with self-selected assignments.

 Independent Study Tell children to draw their favorite scene from the story they read and write a caption explaining what is happening. Challenge them to use details as they share their pictures with the class.

Student Outcomes

✓ Tested in *Wonders* Assessments

FOUNDATIONAL SKILLS

Print Concepts
- Locate title, author, illustrator

Phonological Awareness
- ✓ Phoneme Isolation
- ✓ Phoneme Segmentation
- ✓ Phoneme Blending

Phonics and Word Analysis
- ✓ Long *o: o_e*, Long *u: u_e*, Long *e: e_e*
- ✓ CVCe syllables

Fluency
- Read with accuracy and automaticity
- ✓ High-Frequency Words
- *ago   boy   girl   how   old   people*

READING

Reading Literature
- Read prose and poetry appropriately complex for grade 1

Reading Informational Text
- Use text features including captions to locate key facts or information
- ✓ Identify the topic of and relevant details in a text
- Retell a text to enhance comprehension
- Read informational texts appropriately complex for grade 1

Compare Texts
- Compare and contrast two texts on the same topic

COMMUNICATION

Writing
- Handwriting: *Ww*
- Write opinions about a topic or text with at least one supporting reason from a source and a sense of closure
- Focus on a topic, respond to suggestions from peers, and add details to strengthen writing

Speaking and Listening
- Participate in collaborative conversations
- Ask and answer questions to gather or clarify information
- Present information orally using complete sentences

Conventions
- ✓ **Grammar:** Conjugate regular and irregular verb tenses
- **Mechanics:** Use commas in dates
- **Spelling:** Spell words with *o_e, u_e*

Researching
- Recall or gather information to answer a question
- Participate in shared research and writing projects

Creating and Collaborating
- Add drawings and visual displays to descriptions
- Use digital tools to produce and publish writing

VOCABULARY

Academic Vocabulary
- Acquire and use grade-appropriate academic vocabulary
- Identify real-life connections between words and their use

ELL Scaffolded supports for English Language Learners are embedded throughout the lessons, enabling children to communicate information, ideas, and concepts in English Language Arts and for social and instructional purposes within the school setting.

See the **ELL Small Group Guide** for additional support of the skills for the text set.

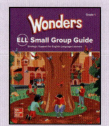

FORMATIVE ASSESSMENT

For assessment throughout the text set, use children's self-assessments and your observations.

Use the Data Dashboard to filter class, group, or individual student data to guide group placement decisions. It provides recommendations to enhance learning for gifted and talented children and offers extra support for children needing remediation.

Develop Student Ownership

To build student ownership, children need to know what they are learning, why they are learning it, and determine how well they understood it.

Students Discuss Their Goals

TEXT SET GOALS

- I can read and understand a nonfiction text.
- I can write an opinion about a nonfiction text.
- I know about how life was different long ago.

Have children think about what they know and fill in the bars on **Reading/Writing Companion** page 116.

EXTENDED WRITING GOALS

- I can write a nonfiction text.

See **Reading/Writing Companion** page 178.

Students Monitor Their Learning

LEARNING GOALS

Specific learning goals identified in every lesson make clear what children will be learning and why. These smaller goals provide stepping stones to help children meet their Text Set Goals.

CHECK-IN ROUTINE

The Check-In routine at the close of each lesson guides children to self-reflect on how well they understood each learning goal.

Review the lesson learning goal.
Reflect on the activity.
Self-Assess by
- filling in the bars in the **Reading/Writing Companion.**
- holding up 1, 2, 3, or 4 fingers.

Share with your teacher.

Students Reflect on Their Progress

TEXT SET GOALS

After completing the Show Your Knowledge task for the text set, children reflect on their understanding of the Text Set Goals by filling in the bars on **Reading/Writing Companion** page 117.

EXTENDED WRITING GOALS

After children complete the evaluation of their writing, they reflect on their ability to write a nonfiction text by filling in the bars on **Reading/Writing Companion** page 197.

Build Knowledge

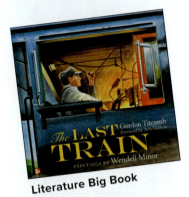

Literature Big Book

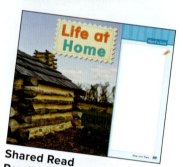

Shared Read
Reading/Writing Companion p. 118

Anchor Text
Literature Anthology p. 76

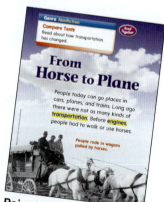

Paired Selection
Literature Anthology p. 92

Essential Question
How is life different than it was long ago?

 Video Some things have changed from the past, but not all. For example, children today go to school, like children in the past, but in today's classrooms, children use computers.

Literature Big Book Long ago, many people rode and worked on trains. There was a little railroad station in one town. Today, this station is closed. There are lots of other ways to travel now.

Shared Read Life at home has changed over time. For example, long ago, people cooked over a fireplace. Today, we use a gas or electric stove.

Interactive Read Aloud Long ago, video games were played in arcades. They were very simple. Today, they can be played on devices anywhere. They are much more advanced and continue to change.

Anchor Text Today, we can get water at home. Long ago, people got water from pumps. Today, we use washing machines. Long ago, people washed clothes by hand. These are some ways life is different today.

Paired Selection Today, we can go places by car, plane, and train. Long ago, people had to walk or use horses to get around.

Photograph Children long ago played on playground equipment, just like today.

Titcomb, Gordon, and Wendell Minor. The Last Train. New York: Roaring Brook Press, 2010.

Differentiated Sources

Leveled Readers 🔊

School long ago was different from school today. For example, long ago, children wrote on slates with chalk. Today, children write using many things, including computers.

Build Knowledge Routine

After reading each text, ask children to document facts and details they learned that help them answer the Essential Question of the text set.

 Talk about the source.

 Write about the source.

 Add to the class Anchor Chart.

- Add to the Word Bank.

Show Your Knowledge

Write a Letter

Have children think about how life was different long ago. Guide them to write a letter to someone who lived in the past, using vocabulary words to describe how things have changed. Have children include an opening and a closing and a picture in their letter.

Social Emotional Learning

Self-Confidence

SEL Focus: Model using the language of respect and appreciation to deepen children's self-confidence.

Invite children to share understandings of the word *confidence*. Then begin the lesson titled "We Are Superstars," pp. T248–249.

I'm a Superstar   (1:36)

Family Time • Share the video and activity in the **School to Home** newsletter.

Explore the Texts

Essential Question: How is life different than it was long ago?

Literature Big Book	Interactive Read Aloud	Reading/Writing Companion	Literature Anthology

The Last Train Song	**"Let's Look at Video Games!"** Informational Text	**"Life at Home"** Shared Read pp. 118–127 Informational Text	***Long Ago and Now*** Anchor Text pp. 76–91 Informational Text

Qualitative

Meaning/Purpose: Moderate Complexity **Structure:** Moderate Complexity **Language:** High Complexity **Knowledge Demands:** Moderate Complexity	**Meaning/Purpose:** Moderate Complexity **Structure:** Moderate Complexity **Language:** High Complexity **Knowledge Demands:** Moderate Complexity	**Meaning/Purpose:** Low Complexity **Structure:** Moderate Complexity **Language:** Low Complexity **Knowledge Demands:** Low Complexity	**Meaning/Purpose:** Low Complexity **Structure:** Low Complexity **Language:** Moderate Complexity **Knowledge Demands:** Low Complexity

Quantitative

Lexile NP	Lexile 770L	Lexile 490L	Lexile 480L

Reader and Task Considerations

Reader Children may need support understanding the structure of the story, showing present day and remembering the past.	**Reader** Children may need information about how technology has advanced and how video games were so simple in the past.	**Reader** Children will need to use their knowledge of sound-spelling correspondences and high-frequency words to read the text.	**Reader** Children may need additional support understanding some practices used in the past, such as horse wagons, ice boxes, pumping water and laundering clothes by hand.

Task The questions for the Interactive Read Aloud are supported by teacher modeling. The tasks provide a variety of ways for students to begin to build knowledge and vocabulary about the text set topic. The questions and tasks provided for the other texts are at various levels of complexity, ensuring that all students can interact with the text in meaningful ways.

Additional Texts

Content Area Reading BLMs
Additional online texts related to grade-level Science, Social Studies, and Arts content.

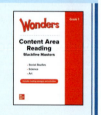

Titcomb, Gordon, and Wendell Minor. The Last Train. New York: Roaring Brook Press, 2010.

Access Complex Text (ACT) boxes provide scaffolded instruction for seven different elements that may make the **Literature Big Book** complex.

Literature Anthology

"From Horse to Plane"
Paired Selection
pp. 92–95
Informational Text

Qualitative

Meaning/Purpose: Low Complexity

Structure: Moderate Complexity

Language: Moderate Complexity

Knowledge Demands: Low Complexity

Quantitative

Lexile 370L

Reader and Task Considerations

Reader Children may need background information on the first airplanes, cars, and steam engines. They can relate their experiences with these modes of transportation.

Task The questions and tasks provided for this text are at various levels of complexity, ensuring that all students can interact with the text in meaningful ways.

Leveled Readers 🔊 (All Leveled Readers are provided in eBook format with audio support.)

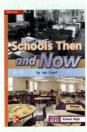

(A)

Schools Then and Now

Informational Text

(O)

Schools Then and Now

Informational Text

(B)

Schools Then and Now

Informational Text

(ELL)

Schools Then and Now

Informational Text

Qualitative

Meaning/Purpose: Low Complexity	**Meaning/Purpose:** Low Complexity	**Meaning/Purpose:** Low Complexity	**Meaning/Purpose:** Low Complexity
Structure: Low Complexity	**Structure:** Low Complexity	**Structure:** Low Complexity	**Structure:** Low Complexity
Language: Low Complexity	**Language:** Moderate Complexity	**Language:** Moderate Complexity	**Language:** Low Complexity
Knowledge Demands: Low Complexity	**Knowledge Demands:** Low Complexity	**Knowledge Demands:** Low Complexity	**Knowledge Demands:** Low Complexity

Quantitative

Lexile 170L	Lexile 220L	Lexile 380L	Lexile 270L

Reader and Task

Reader Children may need additional background information about how schools were set up and how they functioned in the past.	**Reader** Children may need additional background information about how schools were set up and how they functioned in the past.	**Reader** Children may need additional background information about how schools were set up and how they functioned in the past.	**Reader** Children may need additional background information about how schools were set up and how they functioned in the past.

Task The questions and tasks provided for the Leveled Readers are at various levels of complexity, ensuring that all students can interact with the text in meaningful ways.

Focus on Word Work

Build Foundational Skills with Multimodal Learning

MULTIMODAL

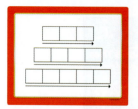
Response Board

Phonemic Awareness Activities

Sound-Spelling Cards

Word-Building Cards online

Phonics Activities

Practice Book

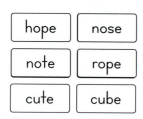
Spelling Cards online

High-Frequency Word Cards

High-Frequency Word Activities

Visual Vocabulary Cards

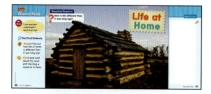
Shared Read

Decodable Readers

Take-Home Story

Phonemic Awareness

- Segment, isolate, and blend phonemes

Phonics: Long *o*: *o_e*; Long *u*: *u_e*; Long *e*: *e_e*

- Introduce/review sound-spellings
- Blend/build words with sound-spellings
- Practice handwriting
- Structural Analysis: Build reading word bank
- Decode and encode in connected texts

Spelling: Long *o*: *o_e*; Long *u*: *u_e*; Long *e*: *e_e*

- Differentiated spelling instruction
- Encode with sound-spellings
- Explore relationships with word sorts and word families

High-Frequency Words

- Read/Spell/Write routine

See Word Work, pages T254–T257, T264–T267, T274–T277, T296–T297, T302–T303.

Apply Skills to Read

- Children apply foundational skills as they read decodable texts.
- Children practice fluency to develop word automaticity.

PHONICS SKILLS TRACE

Initial Consonants > Short Vowels > Consonant Blends and Digraphs > Long Vowels > Vowel Digraphs > r-Controlled Vowels > Diphthongs > Variant Vowels > Silent Letters and 3-Letter Blends

Explicit Systematic Instruction

Word Work instruction expands foundational skills to enable children to become proficient readers.

Daily Routine

- Use the In a Flash: Sound-Spelling routine and the In a Flash: High-Frequency Word routine to build fluency.
- Set Learning Goal.

Explicit Minilessons and Practice

Use daily instruction in both whole and small groups to model, practice, and apply key foundational skills. Opportunities include:

- Multimodal engagement.
- Corrective feedback.
- Supports for English Language Learners in each lesson.
- Peer collaboration.

Formative Assessment

Check-In

- Children reflect on their learning.
- Children show their progress by holding up 1 to 4 fingers in a Check-In routine.

Check for Success

- Teacher monitors children's achievement and differentiates for Small Group instruction.

Differentiated Instruction

To strengthen skills, provide targeted review and reteaching lessons and multimodal activities to meet children's diverse needs.

🟠 🟣 **Approaching Level, ELL**
- Includes Tier 2

🔵 **On Level**

🟢 **Beyond Level**
- Includes Gifted and Talented 🌟 GIFTED and TALENTED

Independent Practice

Provide additional practice as needed. Have children work individually or with partners.

Center Activity Cards

Digital Activities

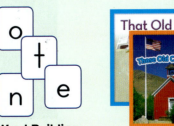

Word-Building Cards online

Decodable Readers

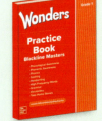

Practice Book

Inspire Early Writers

Build Writing Skills and Conventions

Practice Book

Handwriting Video

Reading/Writing Companion

Write Letters

- Learn to write letters
- Practice writing

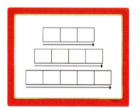

Response Board

Practice Book

High-Frequency Word Activities

Write Words

- Write words with long *o*: *o_e*; long *u*: *u_e*; long *e*: *e_e*
- Write spelling words
- Write high-frequency words

Reading/Writing Companion

Practice Book

Write Sentences

- Write sentences with CVC*e* syllables
- Write sentences to respond to text

Follow Conventions

- Form and use irregular verbs *is* and *are*
- Use commas in dates

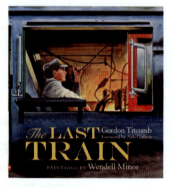

The Last Train
Literature Big Book

Writing Fluency

To increase children's writing fluency, have them write as much as they can in response to the **Literature Big Book** for five minutes. Tell children to write about now and then.

For lessons, see pages T254–T257, T260–T261, T264–T267, T270–T271, T288–T289, T298–T299, T303, T304–T305.

Titcomb, Gordon, and Wendell Minor. *The Last Train*. New York: Roaring Brook Press, 2010.

Write About Texts

WRITING ROUTINE

Analyze the Prompt ▸ Find Text Evidence ▸ Write to the Prompt

**Reading/Writing Companion,
pp. 128–129, 134–135**

Modeled Writing

Write About the Shared Read "Life at Home"

- Prompt: Would you rather cook as we do now or as people did long ago?

Interactive Writing

- Prompt: Based on "Life at Home," do you think home life is better now, or was it better in the past?

**Reading/Writing
Companion, p. 140**

Independent Writing

Write About the Anchor Text *Long Ago and Now*
Literature Anthology, pp. 76–91

- Prompt: Based on *Long Ago and Now*, do you think being a kid is better now, or was it better in the past? Why?

- Have children follow the steps of the writing process: draft, revise, edit/proofread, share.

Additional Lessons

Writing Skill Lesson Bank To provide differentiated support for writing skills, see pages T420–T429.

Extended Writing Minilessons For a full set of lessons that support the writing process and writing in a specific genre, see pages T402–T413.

Self-Selected Writing

Children can explore different writing modes.

 Make a Book

 Comic Strip

 Journal Writing

Planner

Customize your own lesson plans at
my.mheducation.com

Select from your Social Emotional Learning resources.

LESSON 1

LESSON 2

TEXT SET GOALS

- I can read and understand a nonfiction text.
- I can write an opinion about a nonfiction text.
- I know about how life was different long ago.

90+ mins
Reading Suggested Daily Time Includes Small Group

SMALL GROUP OPTIONS
The designated lessons can be taught in small groups. To determine how to differentiate instruction for small groups, use Formative Assessment and Data Dashboard.

30+ mins
Writing Suggested Daily Time

EXTENDED WRITING GOALS

I can write a nonfiction text.

Reading

Introduce the Concept, T250–T251
Build Knowledge: Now and Then

Listening Comprehension, T252–T253
The Last Train

▶ **Word Work, T254–T257**
Phonemic Awareness: Phoneme Segmentation
Phonics/Spelling: Long *o*: o_e; Long *u*: u_e; Long *e*: e_e
High-Frequency Words: *ago, boy, girl, how, old, people*

Shared Read, T258–T259
Read "Life at Home"

▶ **Build the Concept, T262**
Oral Language

Listening Comprehension, T263
"Let's Look at Video Games!"

▶ **Word Work, T264–T267**
Phonemic Awareness: Phoneme Isolation
Phonics/Spelling: Long *o*: o_e; Long *u*: u_e; Long *e*: e_e
Structural Analysis: CVCe Syllables
High-Frequency Words: *ago, boy, girl, how, old, people*

▶ **Shared Read, T268–T269**
Reread "Life at Home"

Writing

Modeled Writing, T260
Write About the Shared Read
Grammar, T261
Irregular Verbs: *Is* and *Are*

Extended Writing: Expository Text, T402–T403
Expert Model
Additional Minilessons, T412–T413, T420–T429

▶ **Interactive Writing, T270**
Write About the Shared Read
Grammar, T271
Irregular Verbs: *Is* and *Are*

Extended Writing: Expository Text, T404–T405
Plan: Choose Your Topic
Additional Minilessons, T412–T413, T420–T429

Teacher-Led Instruction

SMALL GROUP

Differentiated Reading
Leveled Readers
- 🟠 *Schools Then and Now*, T308–T309
- 🔵 *Schools Then and Now*, T318–T319
- 🟢 *Schools Then and Now*, T322–T323

Differentiated Skills Practice, T310–T325
🟠 **Approaching Level, T310–T317**
Phonological/Phonemic Awareness
- Phoneme Isolation, T310 🔲2
- Phoneme Segmentation, T310 🔲2
- Phoneme Blending, T311
- Phoneme Segmentation, T311

Phonics
- Connect /ō/, /ū/, /ē/ to o_e, u_e, e_e, T312 🔲2
- Blend with /ō/ o_e, /ū/ u_e, /ē/ e_e, T312 🔲2
- Build with /ō/ o_e, /ū/ u_e, /ē/ e_e, T313
- Read Words with /ō/ o_e, /ū/ u_e, /ē/ e_e, T313
- Build Fluency with Phonics, T313
Structural Analysis
- Review CVCe Syllables, T314
- Reteach CVCe Syllables, T314

Independent/Collaborative Work See pages T247I–T247J

Reading
Comprehension
- Informational Text: Nonfiction
- Reread
- Details: Compare and Contrast
Independent Reading

Word Work
Phonics/Spelling
- Long *o*: o_e; Long *u*: u_e; Long *e*: e_e
High-Frequency Words
- *ago, boy, girl, how, old, people*

Writing
Self-Selected Writing
Extended Writing: Expository Text
Grammar
- Irregular Verbs: *Is* and *Are*
Handwriting
- Upper and lowercase *Ww*

ORAL VOCABULARY
century, past, present, future, entertainment

SPELLING
hope, nose, note, rope, cute, cube, nice, ledge, ago, people
See page T256 for Differentiated Spelling Lists.

 LESSON 3

 LESSON 4

 LESSON 5

Reading

Build the Concept, T272
Oral Language
Take Notes About Text

Listening Comprehension, T273
The Last Train

▶ **Word Work, T274–T277**
Phonemic Awareness: Phoneme Segmentation
Phonics/Spelling: Long *o: o_e;* Long *u: u_e;* Long *e: e_e*
Structural Analysis: CVCe Syllables
High-Frequency Words: *ago, boy, girl, how, old, people*

Anchor Text, T278–T287
Read *Long Ago and Now*

Extend the Concept, T290–T291
Oral Language

Paired Selection, T292–T295
Read "From Horse to Plane"

▶ **Word Work, T296–T297**
Phonemic Awareness: Phoneme Isolation
Phonics/Spelling: Long *o: o_e;* Long *u: u_e;* Long *e: e_e*
Structural Analysis: CVCe Syllables
High-Frequency Words: *ago, boy, girl, how, old, people*

▶ **Research and Inquiry, T300–T301**
Research and Inquiry: Interview

▶ Word Work, T302–T303
Phonemic Awareness: Phoneme Blending and Segmentation
Phonics/Spelling: Long *o: o_e;* Long *u: u_e;* Long *e: e_e*
Phonics: Read the Decodable Reader
Structural Analysis: CVCe Syllables
High-Frequency Words: *ago, boy, girl, how, old, people*

Integrate Ideas, T306
Make Connections

Culminating Task, T307
Show Your Knowledge

Writing

Independent Writing, T288
Write About the Anchor Text
Grammar, T289
Irregular Verbs: *Is* and *Are*
Mechanics, T289
Commas in Dates

Extended Writing: Expository Text, T406–T407
Draft
Additional Minilessons, T412–T413, T420–T429

Independent Writing, T298
Write About the Anchor Text
Grammar, T299
Irregular Verbs: *Is* and *Are*
Mechanics, T299
Commas in Dates

Extended Writing: Expository Text, T406–T407
Draft
Additional Minilessons, T412–T413, T420–T429

▶ **Self-Selected Writing, T304**
Grammar, T305
Irregular Verbs: *Is* and *Are*
Mechanics, T305
Commas in Dates

Extended Writing: Expository Text, T406–T407
Draft
Additional Minilessons, T412–T413, T420–T429

High-Frequency Words
- Review/Reteach/Cumulative Review, T315

Comprehension
- Read for Fluency, T316 **TIER 2**
- Identify Details, T316 **TIER 2**
- Review Compare and Contrast, T317
- Self-Selected Reading, T317

● **On Level, T320–T321**
Phonics
- Build Words with ō/ *o_e,* /ū/ *u_e,* /ē/ *e_e,* T320

High-Frequency Words
- Review Words, T320

Comprehension
- Review Compare and Contrast, T321
- Self-Selected Reading, T321

● **Beyond Level, T324–T325**
Vocabulary
- Oral Vocabulary: Multiple-Meaning Words, T324

Comprehension
- Review Compare and Contrast, T325
- Self-Selected Reading, T325 **GIFTED and TALENTED**

 ● **English Language Learners**
See ELL Small Group Guide, pp. 136–145.

Content Area Connections
Content Area Reading
- Science, Social Studies, and the Arts
Research and Inquiry
- Interview

 ● **English Language Learners**
See ELL Small Group Guide, pp. 137, 139, 141.

WEEK 4

Independent and Collaborative Work

As you meet with small groups, have the rest of the class complete activities and projects to practice and apply the skills they have been working on.

Student Choice and Student Voice

- Review My Weekly Work blackline master with children and identify the "Must Do" activities.
- Have children choose some additional activities that provide the practice they need.
- Remind children to reflect on their learning each day.

My Weekly Work BLMs

Reading

Text Options

Children can choose a **Center Activity Card** to use while they listen to a text or read independently.

Classroom Library
Read Aloud
On Earth
Genre: Informational Text
Lexile: AD540L

Classroom Library
My Name Is Celia/Me llamo Celia
Genre: Informational Text
Lexile: AD850L

Unit Bibliography
See the online bibliography. Children can select independent reading texts about how life is different than it was long ago.

Leveled Texts Online
 All **Leveled Readers** are provided in eBook format with audio support.

- **Differentiated Texts** provide English Language Learners with passages at different proficiency levels.

Literature Big Book e-Book
The Last Train
Genre: Song

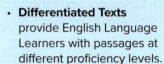

Center Activity Cards

Reread Card 4

Nonfiction Text Card 29

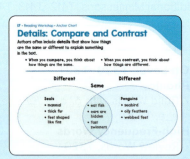

Compare and Contrast Card 17

Digital Activities

Comprehension

Titcomb, Gordon, and Wendell Minor. The Last Train. New York: Roaring Brook Press, 2010.

Word Work

Center Activity Cards

Long *o*: *o_e*; Long *u*: *u_e*;
Long *e*: *e_e* Card 84

Word-Building Cards

Practice Book BLMs

Phonological Awareness:
pp. 209, 210
Phonics: pp. 211, 212
Spelling: pp. 213–215
Structural Analysis: pp. 217, 218
High-Frequency Words: p. 219
Take-Home Story: pp. 223–224

Decodable Readers

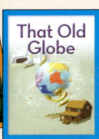

Unit 3, pp. 37–48

Digital Activities

Phonemic Awareness
Phonics
Spelling
High-Frequency Words

Writing

Center Activity Cards

Focus on an Idea Card 52

Nonfiction Text Card 45

Practice Book BLMs

Handwriting: p. 216
Grammar: pp. 220–221
Mechanics: p. 222

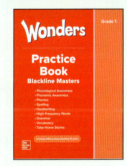

Self-Selected Writing

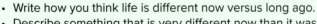

- Write how you think life is different now versus long ago.
- Describe something that is very different now than it was long ago.
- Write about something that is the same now and long ago. Are there any small differences?

Digital Activities

Grammar

Grammar: Mechanics

Content Area Connections

Content Area Reading BLMs
- Additional texts related to Science, Social Studies, Health, and the Arts.

Research and Inquiry
- Complete Interview project

Progress Monitoring
Moving Toward Mastery

FORMATIVE ASSESSMENT

❯ STUDENT CHECK-IN

✓ CHECK FOR SUCCESS

For ongoing formative assessment, use children's self-assessments at the end of each lesson along with your own observations.

Assessing skills along the way . . .

SKILLS	HOW ASSESSED	
Phonological/Phonemic Awareness **Phonics** **Structural Analysis** **High-Frequency Words**	Practice Book, Digital Activities, Online Rubrics	
Comprehension	Digital Activities, Graphic Organizers, Online Rubrics	
Text-Based Writing **Handwriting** **Grammar** **Spelling**	Reading/Writing Companion: Independent Writing, Practice Book, Digital Activities, Spelling Word Sorts	
Listening/Presenting/Research	Reading/Writing Companion: Share and Evaluate; Research: Online Student Checklists	
Oral Reading Fluency (ORF) Conduct group fluency assessments using the **Letter Naming, Phoneme Segmentation,** and **Sight Word Fluency** assessments.	Fluency Assessment	

At the end of the text set . . .

SKILLS	HOW ASSESSED
Details: Compare and Contrast	
Phoneme Segmentation **Phoneme Isolation** **Phoneme Blending**	Progress Monitoring
Long o: *o_e,* ***u:*** *u_e,* ***e:*** *e_e*	
CVCe Syllables	
ago, boy, girl, how, old, people	

Making the Most of Assessment Results

Make data-based grouping decisions by using the following reports to verify assessment results. For additional support options for children, refer to the reteaching and enrichment opportunities.

ONLINE ASSESSMENT CENTER

- *Gradebook*

DATA DASHBOARD

- *Recommendations Report*
- *Activity Report*
- *Skills Report*
- *Progress Report*
- *Grade Card Report*

Reteaching Opportunities with Intervention Online PDFs

IF CHILDREN ANSWER . . .	THEN ASSIGN . . .
0–3 **comprehension** items correctly . . .	lessons 58–60 on Compare and Contrast from the **Comprehension PDF.**
0–2 **phonological/phonemic** items correctly . . .	lessons 67–71 on Phoneme Segmentation, lessons 16–17 on Phoneme Isolation, lessons 62–66 on Phoneme Blending from the **Phonemic Awareness PDF.**
0–5 **phonics/structural analysis/HFW** items correctly . . .	lesson 61-63 on Long *o*: *o_e,* Long *u*: *u_e,* Long *e*: *e_e* and lesson 108 on Final *e* Syllables from the **Phonics/Word Study PDF** and lessons from Section 3 of the **Fluency PDF.**

Enrichment Opportunities

Beyond Level small-group lessons and resources include suggestions for additional activities in these areas to extend learning opportunities for gifted and talented children:

- *Leveled Reader*
- *Vocabulary*
- *Comprehension*
- *Leveled Reader Library Online*
- *Center Activity Cards*

Today's focus:

Developing resilience and confidence as learners.

I'm a Superstar (1:36)

MUSIC VIDEO

family time

You'll find the "I'm a Superstar" video and supporting activity in this week's School to Home family newsletter.

we are superstars

engage together

Let's Share: I can do many things!

Use a partner share strategy to help build confidence.

- There are many things that I can do. I can _____ (write poetry, ride a bike, help my community).
- Take a moment to think: *What things can you do?*
- Now, turn to your partner.
- Take turns saying one thing you can do.
- Keep going until you each say three things.
- Fantastic! Do you know what I think? I think this is a class full of superstars!

explore together

Let's Watch: "I'm a Superstar"
Set a purpose for sharing today's music video.

- Today we're going to watch a music video about being confident in everyday situations.
- Let's watch and listen to how the Pet Planet members turn their nervousness into confidence!
- Now, let's watch again as we sing along.

 **Play the video**

Let's Imagine: I'm a superhero!
Invite children to imagine themselves as superheroes.

- Superheros have confidence in their abilities. Who are your favorite superheroes?
- Close your eyes. Create a picture in your mind of you as a superhero.
- What do you look like? What powers do you have?
- Open your eyes. Who wants to share their mind picture with the class?

> **POSITIVE SELF-TALK:**
> I know, I know, who I am,
> I know, I know, that I can,
> Aiming high to touch
>   the sky,
> I'm a superstar!

connect the learning

Let's Explore: I know I can!
Introduce a strategy to boost confidence.

- Have you ever told yourself, "I can't do this?"
- The next time that happens, remember your superhero mind picture.
- Tell yourself, "I know I can do this!"
- If you fail, that's okay. Superheroes always try and try again! They *persist*, keep going.
- Telling yourself, "I know I can do this," can help give you confidence.
- Later today or this week, we'll draw ourselves as superheroes.

mindfulness moment
Superhero Pose

Our postures can tell a lot about how we feel about ourselves. Help children feel more confident with a simple change in their posture: *Let's put our feet in a wide stance, like a superhero. Place our fists on our hips, fully lengthen our bodies, and widen our elbows. Let's hold this pose for a moment and breathe. We're super confident learners!*

SELF-CONFIDENCE

OBJECTIVES

Build on others' talk in conversations by responding to the comments of others through multiple exchanges.

Ask questions to clear up any confusion about the topics and texts under discussion.

Build background knowledge.

Discuss the Essential Question.

ELA ACADEMIC LANGUAGE
• *chart, photograph*

DIGITAL TOOLS

To enhance the class discussion, use these additional components.

Watch Video

Discuss Concept

LESSON FOCUS

READING

Introduce the Essential Question

Read Literature Big Book:
The Last Train
• Reread Text

Word Work
• Introduce /ō/ o_e, /ū/ u_e, /ē/ e_e

Read Shared Read: "Life at Home"
• Introduce Genre

WRITING
• Modeled Writing
• Introduce Grammar

Reading/Writing Companion, pp. 118–127

MULTIMODAL

⏱ 5 mins

Build Knowledge

? Essential Question

How is life different than it was long ago?

Tell children this week they will be talking and reading about what life was like long ago. Discuss the Essential Question. Have children discuss different ways they think life has changed over time.

Watch the Video Play the video without sound first, and have partners narrate what they see. Then replay the video with sound, and have children listen.

Talk About the Video Have partners share one thing they saw in the video that reminded them of their school.

Anchor Chart Create a Build Knowledge anchor chart with the Essential Question, and have volunteers share what they learned. Record their ideas on the chart.

Oral Vocabulary Words

Use the Define/Example/Ask routine on the print or digital **Visual Vocabulary Cards** to introduce the oral vocabulary words *century* and *past*. Children can use the words to discuss life now and long ago.

Oral Vocabulary Routine

Define: A <mark>century</mark> is one hundred years.

Example: My great-grandfather planted this old tree a century ago.

Visual Vocabulary Cards

Ask: What do you think life might be like a century from now?

Define: The time that has already happened is the <mark>past</mark>.

Example: In the past, there were no telephones; people wrote letters.

Ask: How do you think people traveled long distances in the past?

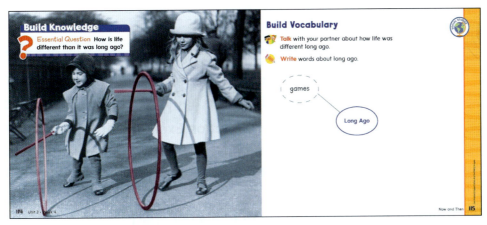

Reading/Writing Companion, pp. 114–115

Build Knowledge

Review how to listen actively using the Collaborative Conversations box. Then have children turn to pages 114–115 of their **Reading/Writing Companions**. Guide children to discuss the photo. Then ask:

- *What are the children playing with?*
- *How is the toy in the photo different from toys you play with? Talk with a partner.*

Build Vocabulary

Talk Have partners talk about how life was different long ago.

Write Have children write words about long ago.

Create a Word Bank Create a separate section of the Word Bank for words related to long ago. Have children suggest words to add.

English Language Learners

Use the following scaffolds with **Build Knowledge**.

Beginning

Point to the children in the picture. *The children are playing.* Have children point to the picture and repeat *playing. What are the children doing?* (playing)

Intermediate

Have children point to the children in the photo. *The children are playing. What are they doing?* The children are playing. *The children are playing with hoops.* Have children point to the hoops. *What are the children playing with?* The children are playing with hoops.

Advanced/Advanced High

As partners describe the photo, have them talk about how these toys are different or the same as their toys. Elicit more details to support children's answers.

COLLABORATIVE CONVERSATIONS

Listen Actively As children engage in partner, small-group, and whole-group discussions, encourage them to:

- always look at the speaker.
- respect others by not interrupting them.
- repeat others' ideas to check understanding.

ELL NEWCOMERS

To help children develop oral language and build vocabulary, use **Newcomer Cards** 10–14 and the accompanying lessons in the **Newcomer Teacher's Guide**. For additional practice, have children complete the online **Newcomer Activities**.

MY GOALS ROUTINE

What I Know Now

Read Goals Read goals with children on Reading/Writing Companion page 116.

Reflect Ask children to reflect on each goal and fill in the bars to show what they know now. Explain that they will fill in the bars on page 117 at the end of the week to show their progress.

LESSON
1

Literature Big Book

Read

The Last Train

15 mins

Connect to Concept: Now and Then Tell children they will now listen to a text about trains that ran long ago and how travel is different today.

Genre: Informational Text: Nonfiction Explain that this is nonfiction text. Say: *A nonfiction text tells about real people, places, things, or events by presenting facts and information about them.* Explain that the author first wrote this nonfiction text as a song.

Anchor Chart Review the Reread anchor chart.

Reread Review that if children do not understand something in the text, they can look at the pictures and ask you to reread parts of it.

Read the Selection

Display the Big Book. Have children point to the title, author's name, and illustrator's name as you read them aloud.

Set Purpose Say: *Let's read to see what happened to the last train.*

Review the Reread anchor chart. Model rereading as you read aloud, and encourage children to ask you to reread for understanding as they listen.

Think Aloud When I read on page 11 that the tracks are now rusty brown, I had to reread to make sure I understood why. I reread page 5 and looked at the picture. Now I understand that the train doesn't come through there anymore. If the train isn't running, the tracks can get rusty.

A C T　Access Complex Text

If the complexity of the text makes it hard for children to understand, use the Access Complex Text prompts.

Lack of Prior Knowledge

The text describes a life built around the railroad. Understanding this culture is key to fully appreciating the author's ideas.

• Explain such concepts as laying pennies on the track to flatten them, the different jobs performed by workers on the train, and the idea of naming certain trains (City of New Orleans, Wabash Cannonball).

Vocabulary

Certain railroad terms may be unfamiliar to children.

• Define the terms *iron horse, tracks, freight train, ticket punch.*

Concepts of Print: Reading Sentences Across Pages Remind children that some pages contain only part of a sentence, and that you must turn the page to read the end of the sentence. Have children identify the beginning and ending of sentences in *The Last Train*. See prompts in the Big Book for modeling concepts of print.

Focus on Narrator Remind children that the narrator of a story can be a speaker outside of the story. Say: *We've also learned that the narrator can be a person in the story. Words such as* my, we, *and* I *tell you the narrator is a person in the story. Listen as I read page 8. Which word tells you the narrator is a person in the story?*

Respond to the Text

After reading, prompt children to share what they learned. Discuss how rereading helped them understand events and details.

Model Retelling

Pause to retell portions of the selection. Say: *I can put details and events into my own words. I read that the town's old train station is boarded up and has holes in the roof. I also read that if you close your eyes, you can imagine the sound of the trains.*

Continue to model retelling the entire selection, using your own words to tell the important events and details in order. Have children practice retelling a page or two.

Writing Fluency

To increase children's writing fluency, have them write as much as they can about the text for five minutes. Then have partners share.

 # English Language Learners

Reread Display pp. 6–7. *On the page before, the station was closed, but on this page, a train is running. Is this a real train? I'm confused. What can I do? I can reread the page.* Reread and say: *Now I know the boy is thinking about what a train would have looked like and sounded like. The train isn't really running. Is this a real train?* The train is <u>not</u> real.

For additional support, see the **ELL Small Group Guide,** pp. 142–143.

MODEL FLUENCY

Phrasing Turn to pages 14–15 of the text. Point to the ellipses, comma, and period. Explain that these marks show where we should pause when reading. Read aloud the pages with slightly exaggerated phrasing. Have children identify the punctuation.

DIGITAL TOOLS

 **Retell**

FORMATIVE ASSESSMENT

❯ **STUDENT CHECK-IN**

Have partners tell one thing they asked to be reread for understanding. Have children reflect, using the Check-In routine.

✔ **CHECK FOR SUCCESS**

Can children reread text for understanding?

❯❯ **Small Group Instruction**

If No

🟠 **Approaching** Reteach pp. T308–T309

If Yes

🔵 **On** Review pp. T318–T319

🟢 **Beyond** Extend pp. T322–T323

LEARNING GOALS

- We can segment sounds in words.
- We can read and blend words with long *o*, long *u*, and long *e*.

OBJECTIVES

Segment spoken single-syllable words into their complete sequence of individual sounds (phonemes).

Know final -e and common vowel team conventions for representing long vowel sounds.

Decode regularly spelled one-syllable words.

Print all upper- and lowercase letters.

ELA ACADEMIC LANGUAGE

- *uppercase, lowercase*

▶ TEACH IN SMALL GROUP

Word Work lessons can be taught in small groups.

Phonemic Awareness: Page 209
Phonics: Page 211
Handwriting: Page 216

---

5 mins

Phonemic Awareness

MULTIMODAL

Phoneme Segmentation

1 **Model** Use the **Response Board** to model how to segment words into phonemes. Say: *Listen carefully as I say a word*: rose. *I will place a marker in a box for each sound I hear: /r/ /ō/ /z/. I will place three markers because I hear three sounds in the word* rose.

2 **Guided Practice/Practice** Have children practice segmenting phonemes in the following words. Say: *Listen carefully as I say some words. Place one marker in a box for each sound you hear. Then tell me how many sounds are in each word.* Guide practice, and provide corrective feedback as needed.

note (3)	hope (3)	stove (4)	smoke (4)	stroke (5)	throne (4)
use (2)	cute (3)	huge (3)	these (3)	strobe (5)	spleen (5)

If children need additional practice segmenting words into phonemes, see **Practice Book** page 209 or the online activity.

---

5 mins

Phonics

MULTIMODAL

Introduce /ō/o_e, /ū/u_e, /ē/e_e

1 **Model** Display the *Boat* Sound-Spelling Card. Teach /ō/ spelled *o_e*, using *hop* and *hope*. Model writing the word *hop* and adding an *e* to make *hope*. Say: *This is the* Boat *Sound-Spelling Card. The sound is /ō /. Today we will learn one of the spellings for /ō/. Look at this word:* hop. *This word has the /o/ sound. I'll add an* e *to the end. The letters* o *and* e *act together to make the long* o *sound: /ō/. Listen: /hōp/,* hope. *I'll say /ō/ as I write the letters* o_e *several times. Repeat with the* Cube *and* Tree *Sound-Spelling Cards.*

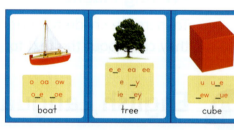

Sound-Spelling Cards

2 **Guided Practice/Practice** Have children practice connecting the letters *o_e* to the sound /ō/ by writing *hope*. Say: *Now do it with me. Say /ō/ as I write the word* hope. *This time, write the word five times as you say the /ō/ sound. Repeat for /ū/ spelled* u_e *and /ē/ spelled* e_e. *As needed, provide handwriting models for children to use.*

Blend Words with /ō/ o_e, /ū/ u_e, /ē/ e_e

1 **Model** Display **Word-Building Cards** n, o, t, and e. Model blending: *This is the letter* n. *It stands for /n/. These are the letters* o *and* e. *Together they stand for /ō/. This is the letter* t. *It stands for /t/. Listen as I blend the sounds together: /nnnōōōt/.* Continue by modeling *hose, mule, fume,* and *eve.*

2 **Guided Practice/Practice** Display the Lesson 1 Phonics Practice Activity. Guide practice, reading each word in the first row with children. Blend the sounds: */h/ /ō/ /m/ /hōōōmmm/. The word is* home. Continue to guide practice as needed with rows 2–7. Provide corrective feedback as children sound out decodable words and read the words in connected text.

home	bone	huge	cute	Pete	Eve
use	nose	stove	cube	those	these
globe	mute	close	hole	vote	smoke
used	hoping	joked	poles	fumes	cones

The rope broke on the flag pole.

Steve woke up when he smelled smoke.

The cute white rat dove down the hole.

Lesson 1 Phonics Practice Activity

For more practice, see **Practice Book** page 211 or the online activity.

Corrective Feedback

Sound Error Model the missed sound, and then have children repeat it. Say: *My turn.* Tap under the letter, and say: *Sound? /ō/ What's the sound?* Return to the beginning of the word. Say: *Let's start over.* Blend the word with children again.

Daily Handwriting

During the week, teach uppercase and lowercase *Ww* using the online Handwriting models. Model writing *Ww,* using the strokes as shown. Children can practice writing *Ww* using Practice Book page 216. For more support, use the models at the back of the **Reading/Writing Companion.**

ENGLISH LANGUAGE LEARNERS

Phonemic Awareness, Guided Practice/ Practice Say the first word slowly, stressing each phoneme. Have children repeat. Ask them to place their markers after saying the word aloud. *How many sounds are in this word?* Provide a sentence frame: There are <u>three</u> sounds.

Phonics, Model Refer to pages 8–9 in the **Language Transfers Handbook.** In some languages, including Hmong, there is no direct transfer for /ō/ or /ū/. Emphasize /ō/, and show correct mouth position. Repeat with /ū/.

DIGITAL TOOLS

To differentiate instruction for key skills, use the results of this activity.

Phonics: Practice

For more practice, use these activities.

Word Work

Phonemic Awareness Handwriting

FORMATIVE ASSESSMENT

❱ STUDENT CHECK-IN

Phonics Have partners read a long *o,* long *u,* or long *e* word to each other. Have children reflect, using the Check-In routine.

LEARNING GOALS

- We can spell words with long *o* and long *u*.
- We can read the words *ago, boy, girl, how, old,* and *people.*

OBJECTIVES

Spell untaught words phonetically, drawing on phonemic awareness and spelling conventions.

Recognize and read grade-appropriate irregularly spelled words.

Spell words with long o and long *u.*

ELA ACADEMIC LANGUAGE

- *sounds*

DIGITAL TOOLS

To differentiate instruction for key skills, use the results of this activity.

High-Frequency Words: Practice

For more practice, use this activity.

Spelling

Spelling: Page 213

---

 5 mins

Spelling

Words with *o_e, u_e*

Dictation Follow the Spelling Dictation routine to help children transfer their growing knowledge of sound-spellings to writing. After dictation, give the spelling pretest in the **Practice Book** on page 213.

Pretest After dictation, pronounce each spelling word. Read the sentence, and pronounce the word again. Ask children to say each word softly, stretching the sounds, before writing it. After the pretest, display the spelling words, and write each word as you say the letter names. Have children check their words using the Practice Book page.

hope	I **hope** it doesn't rain today.
nose	Your **nose** helps you smell things.
note	She wrote a **note** to thank me.
rope	We tied a **rope** around the heavy box.
cute	That **cute** puppy is fun to watch.
cube	An ice **cube** will make the drink cold.
nice	It's **nice** of you to help clean up.
ledge	The window **ledge** is dirty.
ago	My first tooth fell out a year **ago**.
people	How many **people** are in your family?

English Language Learners can use the above list for a spelling pretest.

▷ DIFFERENTIATED SPELLING LISTS

Approaching Level cube, cute, nose, note

Beyond Level close, cube, cute, hope, nose, note, quote, rope

English Language Learners

Spelling, Dictation Use gestures, pantomime, and visual clues to preteach the definitions of the weekly spelling words. For example, point to your nose, and say *nose*. Have children point to their *noses* and say *nose*. Pantomime writing a note, and say: *I write a note*. Have children repeat the pantomime and the word *note*. Reinforce word meaning throughout the week to help build vocabulary.

In a Flash: High-Frequency Words

happy

1. **Teacher:** Read the word.   **Children:** happy
2. **Teacher:** Spell the word.   **Children:** h-a-p-p-y
3. **Teacher:** Write the word.   **Children write the word.**

Repeat with *any, from, once, so,* and *upon* from last week.

High-Frequency Words

MULTIMODAL

5 mins

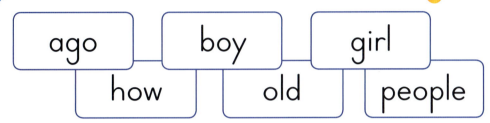

ago | boy | girl
how | old | people

1 Model Display the **High-Frequency Word Cards** *ago, boy, girl, how, old,* and *people.* Use the Read/Spell/Write routine to teach each word.

- **Read** Point to and say the word *ago.* Say: *This is the word* ago. *Say it with me:* ago. *Long* ago *there were no cars.*

- **Spell** *The word* ago *is spelled* a-g-o. *Spell it with me.*

- **Write** *Now write the word* ago *on your* **Response Boards** *as we say each letter:* a-g-o.

- Follow the same steps to introduce *boy, girl, how, old,* and *people.* The word *old* is decodable. Have children blend this word during the Read step.

- For the remaining words, point out sound-spellings children have already learned as well as any irregular sound-spellings, such as the /ə/ sound spelled *a* in *ago.*

COLLABORATE

- Have partners say sentences using each word.

2 Guided Practice Have children read the sentences below. Prompt children to identify the high-frequency words in connected text and to blend the decodable words.

1. The lake froze five days **ago**.

2. Pete is a nice **boy**.

3. A new **girl** is in the class.

4. **How** will you get home?

5. The bridge is **old**.

6. **People** like those games.

3 Practice Write high-frequency words on paper plates. Have children stand or sit in a circle. Play music, and have children pass the plate, face down. When the music stops, have the child who is holding the plate turn it over and read the word.

See the online activities for additional practice.

ELL ENGLISH LANGUAGE LEARNERS

High-Frequency Words, Model Tell children that *how* is a question word. How *asks for more information.* Provide examples: *How do we get to the park? How are you today?* Have partners turn and talk using *how* to ask for more information. Provide sentence frames: How old are you? How do you feel?

FORMATIVE ASSESSMENT

▶ STUDENT CHECK-IN

Spelling Have partners dictate one long *o* or long *u* word from the list to each other to write.

High-Frequency Words Have partners take turns reading the high-frequency words.

Have children reflect, using the Check-In routine.

✓ CHECK FOR SUCCESS

Rubric Use your online rubric to record children's progress.

Can children read and decode words with *o_e, u_e,* and *e_e*?

Can children recognize and read high-frequency words?

▶ Small Group Instruction

If No

🔴 **Approaching** Reteach pp. T310–T315

🟣 **ELL** Develop pp. T310–T315

If Yes

🔵 **On** Review pp. T318–T320

🟢 **Beyond** Extend pp. T322–T323

LESSON 1

OBJECTIVES

Know final -e and common vowel team conventions for representing long vowel sounds.

Decode regularly spelled one-syllable words.

Recognize and read grade-appropriate irregularly spelled words.

With prompting and support, read informational texts appropriately complex for grade 1.

ELA ACADEMIC LANGUAGE

• *information, facts*
• Cognate: *información*

Close Reading Routine

Read DOK 1–2

• Identify important ideas and details.
• Take notes and retell.
• Use prompts as needed.

Reread DOK 2–3

• Analyze the text, craft, and structure.
• Use the Reread minilessons.

Integrate DOK 3–4

• Integrate knowledge and ideas.
• Make text-to-text connections.
• Complete the Show Your Knowledge task.
• Inspire action.

Read

"Life at Home"

Focus on Foundational Skills

• Review the high-frequency words *ago, boy, girl, how, old,* and *people.*

• Review that the long *o* sound can be spelled with o_e; long *u* can be spelled with u_e; and long *e* can be spelled with e_e.

• Display the words *room, cook, fireplace, washed, dishwasher,* and *hard.* Spell the words, and model reading them. Have children read the words as you point to them.

Read the Shared Read

Anchor Chart Review the Nonfiction anchor chart.

Genre: Informational Text: Nonfiction Tell children "Life at Home" is a nonfiction text. Have volunteers share a story they know that is nonfiction.

Reread

Explain Tell children that as they read, they can pause to reread parts of the text and to look at pictures to make sure they understand the details.

Connect to Concept: Now and Then

Explain that this week, children are reading about life in the past. They can describe how life is different now than it was long ago.

Take Notes As children read the selection, you may wish to have them take notes in the boxes provided. Children may take notes by:

• writing the letters *o, u,* and *e.*

• writing a word spelled with *o_e, u_e, or e_e* or a high-frequency word.

Have children read each page. Then read aloud the prompts.

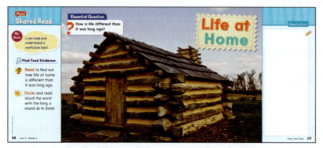

Reading/Writing Companion, pp. 118–119

SET PURPOSE

Let's read to find out how life at home is different than it was long ago.

PHONICS

Have partners circle and read aloud the word with long *o* spelled *o_e,* as in the word *bone.*

Reading/Writing Companion, pp. 120–121

Reading/Writing Companion, pp. 122–123

Reading/Writing Companion, pp. 124–125

Reading/Writing Companion, pp. 126–127

Respond to the Text

Have partners discuss how life at home has changed based on the selection. Provide a sentence starter: *A long time ago, life at home was . . .*

HIGH-FREQUENCY WORDS

Have children underline and read aloud the word *people*.

REREAD

Ask: *Did you understand what you read? If not, reread the page.*

PHONICS

Have children circle and read three words with long *u* spelled *u_e*, as in *cute*.

REREAD

Have partners discuss how people used to cook. Have them look at the picture and reread if they are not sure.

HIGH-FREQUENCY WORDS

Have children underline and read aloud the words *boy* and *girl*.

COMPREHENSION

Have partners talk about helping out long ago and today. Ask: *Which was easier?*

REREAD

Have partners talk about why washing dishes is easier today. Children should reread and use the pictures to make sure they understand.

RETELL

Have partners retell the text using the pictures and new words they learned.

SPOTLIGHT ON LANGUAGE

Page 120 Read the first sentence aloud. Say: Long ago *means "many, many years in the past."* Point to the photo. *Does the photo show life today or long ago?* The picture shows life long ago. Have partners look at the picture and talk about how families cooked, slept, and lived in only one room. Have children use *long ago* in their discussion. Provide a sentence frame: Long ago, families lived in only one room.

FOCUS ON FLUENCY

With partners, have children reread "Life at Home" to develop fluency. Children should focus on their accuracy, trying to say each word correctly. Then have them reread the story so it sounds like speech. Remind children the goal is to keep practicing until they can read the words automatically.

DIFFERENTIATED READING

● **English Language Learners**
Before reading, have children listen to a summary of the selection, which is available in multiple languages.

STUDENT CHECK-IN

Have children reflect on their retelling, using the Check-In routine.

LESSON 1

- We can focus on one idea when we write.
- We can use the present-tense verbs *is* and *are*.

OBJECTIVES

Write opinion pieces in which they introduce the topic or name the book they are writing about, state an opinion, supply a reason for the opinion, and provide some sense of closure.

Use singular and plural nouns with matching verbs in basic sentences.

Use verbs to convey a sense of past, present, and future.

ELA ACADEMIC LANGUAGE

- *verb*
- Cognate: *verbo*

COLLABORATIVE CONVERSATIONS

Turn and Talk Review this routine.

Child 1: Cook now.

Child 2: What do you mean?

Child 1: I want to cook like people now.

Display the speech bubbles "What do you mean?" and "Why do you think that?" Have partners use them to practice collaborating.

DIFFERENTIATED WRITING

● **English Language Learners** For more writing support, see **ELL Small Group Guide**, p. 144.

---

5 mins

Modeled Writing

Write About the Shared Read

Build Oral Language Read aloud the prompt. Ask: *Would you rather cook as we do now or as people did long ago? Why?* Have partners use the Turn and Talk routine to discuss.

Model Writing Sentences Say: *I will write sentences about how I would rather cook.* Point to the text and images on pages 122–123. *The text and image on page 122 helps me understand how people cooked long ago. I can see the huge pot on the pole and the oven to the left.*

Sample Teacher Talk

- Listen to my sentences: *I like how we cook now. I would rather cook that way because it is easier.* I begin my first sentence with *I*. I look at the Word Bank to find *I*. It's spelled *I*. I'll write *I*. HIGH-FREQUENCY WORDS/WRITING SKILL

- The next word is *like*. When I write the word *like*, I think about the sounds. I hear the long *i* sound. I know long *i* can be spelled with the *i*-consonant-*e* pattern. I'll write *like*. PHONICS

- Continue modeling, writing the remaining words in your sentences. I make sure my writing focuses on one idea. My writing focuses on how I would rather cook. TRAIT: IDEAS

> Would you rather cook as we do now or as people did long ago? Why?
>
> I like how we cook now. I would rather cook that way because it is easier.

Writing Practice

Analyze and Write Sentences Have children turn to page 128 in their **Reading/Writing Companions**. Guide children to use the prompts to analyze the sentences. Review the Writing Skill and Trait boxes as necessary. Then have children write and analyze their own sentences.

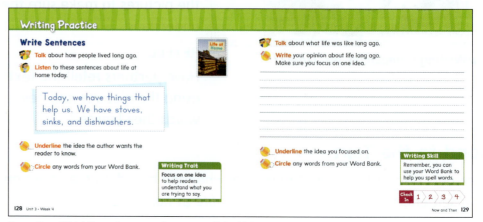

Reading/Writing Companion, pp. 128–129

Stephen Coburn/Shutterstock

Grammar

5 mins

Irregular Verbs: *Is* and *Are*

1 **Model** Tell children *is* and *are* are present-tense verbs. When we talk about the present, we are talking about what is going on right now. Display these sentences: June is cooking. Rose and Lance are riding bikes. Explain that the verb *is* is used when telling about one noun in a sentence. The verb *are* is used when telling about more than one noun in a sentence.

2 **Guided Practice/Practice** Display these sentences, and read them aloud. Have children choose *is* or *are* to complete each.

The sun _____ shining. (is)

Three dogs _____ playing. (are)

They _____ racing to the end. (are)

Talk About It Have partners orally generate sentences that use *is* and *are*. Challenge one partner to create a sentence using *is,* and have the other partner change the sentence to use *are*.

Link to Writing Review the Modeled Writing for correct use of *is* and *are*. If *is* and *are* are not in the Modeled Writing, work with children to add them, and reread the response together.

ELL English Language Learners

Use the following scaffolds with **Grammar, Model.**

Beginning

Point to the first sentence. *Is June one person?* (yes) *We use* is *to talk about one person. Should we use* is *or* are *to talk about June?* Provide a frame: We should use <u>is</u>. Repeat with the second sentence.

Intermediate

Read the first sentence. *Who is the sentence about?* (June) *Is June one person?* (yes) Help children identify the verb. Explain that *is* is used to talk about one person. *What verb is used with one person?* (is) Repeat with the second sentence.

Advanced/Advanced High

Have partners identify the verb in each sentence. *How do the sentences change if Rose and June cook together and Lance rides his bike by himself?*

FORMATIVE ASSESSMENT

❯ STUDENT CHECK-IN

Writing Have partners tell each other the one idea they focused on in their writing. Have children reflect, using the Check-In routine to fill in the bars.

Grammar Have partners use *is* and *are* in sentences. Have children reflect, using the Check-In routine.

WRITING AND CONVENTIONS **T261**

LEARNING GOALS

We can learn and use new vocabulary words.

OBJECTIVES

Identify real-life connections between words and their use.

Discuss the Essential Question.

Develop oral language.

ELA ACADEMIC LANGUAGE

• *routine*

• Cognate: *rutina*

▶ TEACH IN SMALL GROUP

● **ELL** See the Teacher Talk on the back of the **Visual Vocabulary Cards** for additional support.

● **Approaching** Group children with students in a higher level to practice saying the words. Then children can draw their own pictures of the word.

● ● **On Level** and **Beyond Level** Have children look up each word in the online **Visual Glossary.**

FORMATIVE ASSESSMENT

▶ STUDENT CHECK-IN

Have partners use a vocabulary word in a sentence. Have children reflect using the Check-In routine.

LESSON FOCUS

READING
Revisit the Essential Question
Read Interactive Read Aloud:
"Let's Look at Video Games!"
• Reread Text
Word Work
• Review /ō/ o_e, /ū/ u_e, /ē/ e_e

Reread Shared Read:
"Life at Home"
• Review Genre
• Introduce Skill
WRITING
• Interactive Writing
• Review Grammar

Reading/Writing Companion, pp. 118–127

---

5 mins

Oral Language

MULTIMODAL

? ## Essential Question
How is life different than it was long ago?

COLLABORATE

Remind children that this week they have been talking and reading about life long ago and now. Remind them of how children played with hoops long ago and how different life at home was long ago.

Oral Vocabulary Words

Review the oral vocabulary words *century* and *past* from Lesson 1. Use the Define/Example/Ask routine on the print or digital **Visual Vocabulary Cards** to introduce the oral vocabulary words *entertainment, future,* and *present.* Children can use them to discuss how life has changed over time.

Visual Vocabulary Cards

Oral Vocabulary Routine

Define: **Entertainment** is what you do to have fun.

Example: Watching movies is a popular form of entertainment.

Ask: What do you like to do for entertainment?

Define: The **future** is the time that hasn't happened yet.

Example: In the future, you will grow up and have jobs.

Ask: How might school be different in the future?

Define: The **present** is the time that is happening right now.

Example: In the future, cars might be able to fly, but in the present, they can only drive on the road.

Ask: How might school in the present be different than it was in the past?

OPTION
10 mins

Read the Interactive Read Aloud

"Let's Look at Video Games!"

Connect to Concept

Tell children you will be reading aloud a nonfiction text about video games. Display the **Interactive Read Aloud Cards**. Read aloud the title, "Let's Look at Video Games!"

Set Purpose Say: *Let's read to learn how video games changed over time.* Read aloud or play the selection as you display the cards. Remind children to listen carefully.

Oral Vocabulary Use the Oral Vocabulary prompts as you read the selection to provide more practice with the words in context.

Base Words Tell children that as you read, they can use base words to help them figure out the meaning of unfamiliar words. Explain that a base word is a word that can stand alone. You can add to a base word to make a new word. Model the strategy as you read Card 2.

Teacher Think Aloud When I read that "Colorful characters could now move," I wondered what the word *colorful* meant. I can see the base word *color* within the word, and I know that colors include red, blue, green, yellow, and so on. This helps me understand that *colorful* means "full of color."

Continue reading aloud the selection, stopping to ask children to use base words to figure out the meaning of unfamiliar words.

Student Think Along After you read the second paragraph on Card 3, ask: *What base word do you see in the word* reality? *How can the base word help you understand the meaning of the word?* I see the word *real*, which I know means "actual" or "not fake." This helps me understand that *reality* has to do with being real.

Build Knowledge: Make Connections

Talk About the Text Have partners discuss how video games have changed over time.

Add to the Anchor Chart Record any new ideas on the Build Knowledge anchor chart.

Add to the Word Bank Add words related to long ago to a separate section of the Word Bank.

LEARNING GOALS

We can listen actively to learn about the history of video games.

OBJECTIVES

Identify frequently occurring root, or base, words and their inflectional forms.

ELA ACADEMIC LANGUAGE

• base word

DIGITAL TOOLS

MULTIMODAL

Interactive Read Aloud

ELL SPOTLIGHT ON LANGUAGE

Cards 1-2: *How do people travel in the present?* In the present, people <u>drive cars</u>. *How did people travel in the past?* In the past, people <u>rode horses</u>. *What do these people do for entertainment?* These people <u>play games with the family</u> for entertainment.

FORMATIVE ASSESSMENT

❯ STUDENT CHECK-IN

Have children share one thing they learned about video games from the past. Have children reflect, using the Check-In routine.

LESSON 2

In a Flash: Sound-Spellings

boat

Display the Sound-Spelling Card *boat*.
Point to the letters *o_e*.

1. **Teacher:** What are the letters?   **Children:** o, e
2. **Teacher:** What's the sound?   **Children:** /ō/

Continue the routine for previously taught sounds.

LEARNING GOALS

- We can say the middle sounds in words.
- We can read and build words with long *o*, long *u*, and long *e*.
- We can read two-syllable words.

OBJECTIVES

Isolate and pronounce medial vowel sounds (phonemes) in spoken single-syllable words.

Know final -e and common vowel team conventions for representing long vowel sounds.

Use knowledge that every syllable must have a vowel sound to determine the number of syllables in a printed word.

Decode two-syllable words following basic patterns by breaking the words into syllables.

ELA ACADEMIC LANGUAGE

- *syllable, consonant*
- Cognates: *sílaba, consonante*

⟩⟩ TEACH IN SMALL GROUP

Word Work lessons can be taught in small groups.

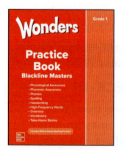

Phonemic Awareness: Page 210

---

 5 mins OPTION

Phonemic Awareness

Phoneme Isolation

1 **Model** Say: *Listen carefully as I say a word:* rope, /r/ /ō/ /p/. *What sound do you hear in the middle of* rope? *That's right. The word* rope *has the /ōōō/ sound in the middle.* Repeat with the word *stone.*

2 **Guided Practice/Practice** Guide children as they practice isolating phonemes. *I'm going to say more words. Say the sound you hear in the middle of each word.* Provide corrective feedback as needed.

rose	these	note	yoke	rice
mule	face	huge	vote	cute

For more practice, see **Practice Book** page 210 or the online activity.

 5 mins

Phonics

MULTIMODAL

Review /ō/ o_e, /ū/ u_e, /ē/ e_e

1 **Model** Display the *Cube* **Sound-Spelling Card.** Review /ū/ spelled *u_e*, using the words *cute* and *mule*. With the *Boat* Sound-Spelling Card, review /ō/ spelled *o_e*, using *rose* and *cone*. With the *Tree* Sound-Spelling Card, review /ē/ spelled *e_e*, using *Eve* and *these*.

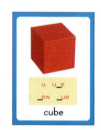
cube
Sound-Spelling Card

2 **Guided Practice/Practice** Guide children to practice connecting the letters with the sounds of the long vowels, providing corrective feedback as needed. Point to the Sound-Spelling Card. Ask: *What are these letters? What sound do they stand for?*

Blend Words with /ō/ o_e, /ū/ u_e, /ē/ e_e

1 **Model** Display **Word-Building Cards** *m, u, t,* and *e* to form *mute*. Model how to generate and blend the sounds to say the word. Say:

This is the letter m. *It stands for /m/. These are the letters* u *and* e. *Together they stand for /ū/. This is the letter* t. *It stands for /t/. Listen as I blend these sounds together: /mmmūūūt/.* Continue by modeling *huge, dome, rope,* and *these.*

m   u   t   e

2 **Guided Practice/Practice** Say: *Now let's do some together.* Display **Word-Building Cards** *b, o, n,* and *e. Let's blend these sounds together: /b/ /ō/ /n/, /bōōōnnn/,* bone. Repeat the routine with *home, rose, close, cube, fume, use, these,* and *Steve.* Guide practice, and provide corrective feedback as needed.

Build Words with /ō/ o_e, /ū/ u_e, /ē/ e_e

Provide children with Word-Building Cards *a–z.* Have children put the letters in alphabetical order as quickly as possible.

1 **Model** Display Word-Building Cards *m, u, l,* and *e.* Blend: /m/ /ū/ /l/, /mūl/, *mule.* Replace *u* with *o,* and repeat with *mole.* Replace *m* with *s,* and repeat with *sole.*

2 **Guided Practice/Practice** Continue building the words: *hole, hope, mope, mole, pole, pose, nose, rose, chose, those,* and *these.* Guide children to build and blend each word. Then dictate the words, and have children write them.

For practice decoding words with long vowels in connected text, see Build Words lessons on T313 and T320.

Structural Analysis

CVC*e* Syllables

1 **Model** Write and read aloud *awake.* Ask children how many syllables they hear. Then draw a line between the syllables. Underline the *a* and *e* in *wake,* and remind children that the letters *a_e* work together to make the long *a* sound. When children see the letter *a* with a silent *e,* they should remember that the letters make only one vowel sound, so they are part of the same syllable. Repeat with *explode.* Use each word in a sentence.

Remind children that when decoding two-syllable words, they will sometimes have to approximate sounds.

2 **Guided Practice/Practice** Write the following words on the board: *bathrobe, inside, cupcake, awoke,* and *compete.* Have children read each word and draw a line to divide it into syllables. Then have children use each word in a sentence. Guide practice, and provide corrective feedback as needed.

DIGITAL TOOLS

To differentiate instruction for key skills, use the results of this activity.

Phonics: Practice

For more practice, use these activities.

Phonemic Awareness
Structural Analysis

LESSON 2

- We can sort and spell words with long *o* and long *u*.
- We can read and write the words *age, boy, girl, how, old,* and *people.*

OBJECTIVES

Use conventional spelling for words with common spelling patterns and for frequently occurring irregular words.

Recognize and read grade-appropriate irregularly spelled words.

Sort words with long *o* and long *u.*

ELA ACADEMIC LANGUAGE

- *pattern*

DIGITAL TOOLS

To differentiate instruction for key skills, use the results of this activity.

High-Frequency Words: Practice

For more practice, use this activity.

Word Work

Spelling

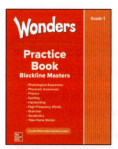

Spelling: On Level, Page 214
Approaching, Page 214A
Beyond, Page 214B
High-Frequency Words: Page 219

Spelling

5 mins

MULTIMODAL

Word Sort with *o_e, u_e*

1 **Model** Display the online **Spelling Word Cards** for Unit 3 Week 4 one at a time. Have children read each word, listening for the vowel sounds.

Use cards with the word parts -*ope, cu,* and *no* to create a three-column chart. Then model sorting the words *node, lope,* and *cute.* Say each word, and pronounce the sounds: /n/ /ō/ /d/, /l/ /ō/ /p/, and /k/ /ū/ /t/. Say each word again, emphasizing the long-vowel sound. Ask children to chorally spell each word.

-ope	cu
no	hope
nose	note
rope	cute
cube	

Unit 3 • Week 4   Spelling Word Cards

2 **Guided Practice/Practice** Have children place each Spelling Word Card in the column with the words containing the same long-vowel sounds and spelling patterns.

When children have completed the chart, have them chorally read the words in each column. Then call out a word. Have a child find the word card and point to it as the class chorally spells the word.

If children need additional practice spelling words with long *u* and long *o,* see differentiated **Practice Book** pages 214–214B or the online activity.

Analyze Errors/Articulation Support

Use children's pretest errors to analyze spelling problems and provide corrective feedback. For example, some children will leave out the final letter *e.*

Work with children to recognize the differences in vowel sounds and spellings in minimal contrast pairs, such as *hop/hope, not/note, cub/cube, rod/rode, rob/robe, hug/huge,* and *cut/cute.*

High-Frequency Words

OPTION
5 mins

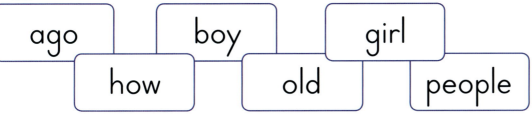

ago boy girl
how old people

COLLABORATE

1 **Guided Practice** Say each word, and have children Read/Spell/Write it.

- Point out irregularities in sound-spellings, such as the /ē/ sound spelled *eo* in *people*.

2 **Practice** Add the high-frequency words *ago, boy, girl, how, old,* and *people* to the cumulative Word Bank.

- Have children work with a partner to create sentences using the words.

- Have children look at the words and compare their sounds and spellings to words from previous weeks.

- Suggest that children write one sentence about life now as compared to long ago.

Cumulative Review Review last week's words *(any, from, happy, once, so,* and *upon)* by displaying each word and having children read it with automaticity.

Have children independently practice identifying, spelling, and reading high-frequency words using **Practice Book** page 219 or the online activity.

ELL ENGLISH LANGUAGE LEARNERS

Use the scaffolds with **High-Frequency Words, Practice.**

Beginning
Provide a sentence frame to help children write about life long ago: Long ago, people got water from a <u>well</u>.

Intermediate
Have children complete the sentence frame above and then write an additional sentence: Now people get water from <u>sinks</u>.

Advanced/Advanced High
Have partners write their own sentences, comparing long ago to now. If necessary, have children review "Life at Home" for ideas.

FORMATIVE ASSESSMENT

❯ STUDENT CHECK-IN

Spelling Have partners share one column of words they sorted.

High-Frequency Words Have partners quiz each other using the **High-Frequency Word Cards**.

Have children reflect, using the Check-In routine.

✔ CHECK FOR SUCCESS

Rubric Use your online rubric to record children's progress.

Can children read and decode words with *o_e, u_e,* and *e_e*?

Can children recognize and read high-frequency words?

❯❯ **Small Group Instruction**

If No

● **Approaching** Reteach pp. T310–T315

● **ELL** Develop pp. T310–T315

If Yes

● **On** Review pp. T318–T320

● **Beyond** Extend pp. T322–T323

LESSON 2

10 mins

"Life at Home"

Genre: Informational Text: Nonfiction

- We can tell what makes a text nonfiction.
- We can compare and contrast what we learn from the text.

OBJECTIVES

Describe the connection between two individuals, events, ideas, or pieces of information in a text.

Use the illustrations and details in a text to describe its key ideas.

Understand nonfiction genre.

ELA ACADEMIC LANGUAGE

- compare, contrast
- Cognates: comparar, contrastar

TEACH IN SMALL GROUP

🟠 **Approaching** Have partners work together to complete the chart.

🔵🟢 **On Level** and **Beyond Level** Have children write their responses independently and then discuss them.

🟣 **ELL** For specific comprehension support in reading "Life at Home," see **ELL Small Group Guide,** pp. 138–139.

DIGITAL TOOLS

To differentiate instruction for key skills, use the results of this activity.

Details: Compare and Contrast

1 **Model** Tell children they will now reread the nonfiction selection "Life at Home." Have children turn to page 130 in their **Reading/ Writing Companions**. Review the characteristics of an informational text: nonfiction. Nonfiction:

- tells about real people, places, things, or events.
- presents facts and information about them.

Display the nonfiction text "Life at Home" in the Reading/Writing Companion. Say: *On pages 120–121, we learn about people's homes from long ago.* Point to the illustration. Say: *This is a real thing in the text. We learned that long ago, people ate and slept in one room.* Model filling in the graphic organizer on page 131 by writing the names of the real things and what we learn about them.

Reading/Writing Companion, pp. 130–131

2 **Guided Practice/Practice** Guide children to copy what you wrote on page 131 of their Reading/Writing Companions. Then have children continue by rereading page 122. Have them share with a partner what real things this text tells about. Ask: *What real thing did you read about on this page?* (cooking and baking long ago)

Guide children to write this information in the first column. Ask children to reread the text and look at the illustration to find something they learned about cooking and baking long ago. They can add this information to the second column. Offer help as needed.

Details: Compare and Contrast

 Anchor Chart Create a Compare and Contrast anchor chart. Say: *Authors often include details that show how things are the same or different to explain something in the text. When you compare things, you think about how they are the same. When you contrast things, you think about how they are different.*

1 **Model** Display page 132 of the **Reading/Writing Companion**. Model filling in the graphic organizer on page 133. Say: *On page 120, we read that homes long ago had one room.* Write this in the Long Ago part. *On page 121, we read that homes today have many rooms.* Write this in the Now part. *That's how they are different. They are the same because people live in homes both long ago and today.* Write this in the "Both" part.

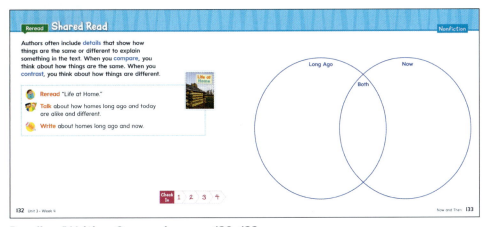

Reading/Writing Companion, pp. 132–133

2 **Guided Practice/Practice** Guide children to copy what you wrote on page 133. Display pages 122–123. Have children reread them and talk with a partner about cooking. Ask: *How did people cook long ago?* (They used fireplaces.) *How do people cook today?* (They use stoves.) Guide children to write these facts in the appropriate circle.

Have children add how cooking long ago and today are alike.

For more practice, have children complete the online activity.

English Language Learners

Details: Compare and Contrast, Guided Practice/Practice Point to the photo on p. 122. *How did people cook long ago?* They used the fireplace. *Look at the photo on p. 123. This photo shows how people cook today. What do you see?* (a pot on a stove) Guide children to fill in their graphic organizers. *What is the same about how people cook then and now?* People use pots to cook.

📋 BUILD KNOWLEDGE: MAKE CONNECTIONS

Talk About the Text Have partners discuss things from the text that would have been harder to do long ago than they are now.

Write About the Text Then have children add their ideas to the Build Knowledge page of their reader's notebooks.

Add to the Anchor Chart Record any new ideas on the Build Knowledge anchor chart.

Add to the Word Bank Add words related to long ago to a separate section of the Word Bank.

FORMATIVE ASSESSMENT

❯ STUDENT CHECK-IN

Genre Have partners take turns telling how they know this text is nonfiction.

Skill Have children compare or contrast a detail from the text between long ago and today.

Have children reflect, using the Check-In routine to fill in the bars.

✅ CHECK FOR SUCCESS

Rubric Use your online rubric to record children's progress.

Can children compare and contrast information in "Life at Home"?

❯ Small Group Instruction

If No

🟠 **Approaching** Reteach pp. T308–T309, T316–T317

If Yes

🔵 **On** Review pp. T318–T319, T321

🟢 **Beyond** Extend pp. T322–T325

LEARNING GOALS

- We can read and write about a Student Model.
- We can read and write the present-tense verbs *is* and *are*.

OBJECTIVES

Write opinion pieces in which they introduce the topic or name the book they are writing about, state an opinion, supply a reason for the opinion, and provide some sense of closure.

Use singular and plural nouns with matching verbs in basic sentences.

Use verbs to convey a sense of past, present, and future.

ELA ACADEMIC LANGUAGE

- text, focus
- Cognates: *texto, foco*

COLLABORATIVE CONVERSATIONS

Circulate as partners talk about the prompt. Notice who needs to ask questions. Remind them to use the speech bubbles to help them ask questions. As you listen in to children's conversations, you may want to write your observations on children's language development.

DIFFERENTIATED WRITING

● **English Language Learners**
For more writing support, see **ELL Small Group Guide**, p. 144.

 5 mins

Interactive Writing

Write About the Shared Read

 COLLABORATE

Analyze the Prompt Read aloud a new prompt: *Based on "Life at Home," do you think home life is better now, or was it better in the past? Why?* Have partners turn and talk about it.

Find Text Evidence Guide children to find text evidence to respond to the prompt. Turn to page 124. Read the text, and point to the photograph. Ask: *How did kids help out at home long ago?* Use a volunteer's response and the sample teacher talk below to write two sentences, such as: *To me, life is better now than long ago. Home life long ago was more work than now.*

Sample Teacher Talk: Share the Pen

- The sentence begins with *To*. Who can find *to* on the Word Bank and spell it? That's right. *T-o.* Have a volunteer write the word *To.* HIGH-FREQUENCY WORDS/WRITING SKILL

- Who knows the first sound of the word *me?* That's right, the first sound is /m/. How do we spell *me?* That's right. *m-e.* PHONICS

- Continue sharing the pen to complete the sentences. Do we focus on one idea? What is that idea? TRAIT: IDEAS

> Based on "Life at Home," do you think home life is better now, or was it better in the past? Why?
>
> To me, life is better now than long ago. Home life long ago was more work than now.

Analyze the Student Model

Say: *Let's read how another child responded to the prompt.* Have children turn to page 134 of the **Reading/Writing Companion.** Guide them to use the prompts on page 135 to analyze Mateo's writing. Then have children write what they notice. Review the Grammar box as necessary. Use the Quick Tip box for support.

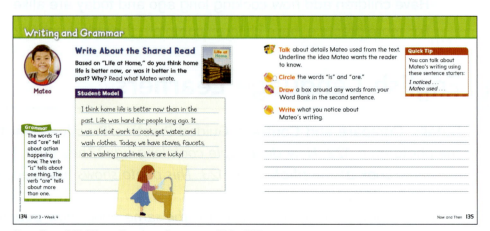

Reading/Writing Companion, pp. 134–135

Stephen Coburn/Shutterstock

Grammar

5 mins

Irregular Verbs: *Is* and *Are*

1 **Review** Remind children that *is* and *are* are present-tense verbs, or verbs that talk about what is happening right now. Remind children that we use the verb *is* when telling about one noun the verb *are* when telling about more than one noun.

2 **Guided Practice** Write sample sentences. Read each sentence aloud. Guide partners to identify *is* or *are* in each sentence.

> My name is Steve. (is)
>
> People are standing on the bridge. (are)
>
> The girl is placing plants in the pots. (is)

3 **Practice** Have children create a new sentence for each verb.

For additional practice with nouns, see **Practice Book** page 220 or the online activity.

Talk About It

Have partners orally generate sentences that use *is* and *are*. Have each child create a sentence that uses either *is* or *are*, and ask his or her partner to change the sentence, this time using the other verb.

English Language Learners

Grammar, Guided Practice Ask children to circle the verb in the first sentence. (is) Read the verb, and have children repeat. Point to *Steve. The author used* is *because Steve is one person.* Have children say *is* and hold up one finger. Read the third sentence. *How many girls?* (one) *Why did the author use* is? *There is* <u>one</u> girl. Go back to the second sentence. *Does* people *mean one or more than one?* (more than one) *The author used* are *because* people *refers to more than one. Why did the author use* are? *People is* <u>more than one</u>.

DIGITAL TOOLS

Use this activity to practice grammar.

Grammar

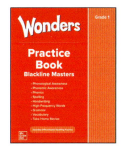

Grammar: Page 220

LESSON 3

LEARNING GOALS

We can learn and use new vocabulary words.

OBJECTIVES

Use real-life connections between words and their use.

Discuss the Essential Question.

Develop oral language.

ELA ACADEMIC LANGUAGE

• *example*
• Cognate: *ejemplo*

LESSON FOCUS

READING
Revisit the Essential Question
Reread Literature Big Book:
The Last Train
• Use Base Words
• Analyze Author's Craft
Word Work
• Blend words with /ō/ *o_e*, /ū/ *u_e*, /ē/ *e_e*

Read and Reread Anchor Text: *Long Ago and Now*
• Review Genre
• Reread Text
• Review Skill
WRITING
• Independent Writing
• Review Grammar and Introduce Mechanics

Literature Anthology, pp. 76–91

 5 mins

Oral Language

MULTIMODAL

 ## Essential Question
How is life different than it was long ago?

Remind children that this week they have been talking and reading about how life has changed over the years. Remind them of the old trains, how home life has changed, and how video games have changed.

Review Oral Vocabulary

Review the oral vocabulary words *century, past, present, future,* and *entertainment* using the Define/Example/Ask routine on the print or digital **Visual Vocabulary Cards.** Encourage children to discuss life in the past when thinking of examples for each word.

Visual Vocabulary Cards

FORMATIVE ASSESSMENT

❯ STUDENT CHECK-IN

Have partners use a vocabulary word in a sentence.

Have children reflect using the Check-In routine.

Reread

The Last Train

As you reread *The Last Train*, model using text evidence to respond to questions about author's craft. Also model using base words to help children understand the meaning of unfamiliar words.

Author's Craft Authors can use words to help readers visualize, or picture in their minds, what is happening in the story. Reread page 11. What does the phrase "tracks that shone like silver" make you picture in your mind?

Think Aloud I can close my eyes and picture in my mind the way the tracks used to be. They were shiny, almost sparkling.

Base Words Remind children that they can look at base words to help them understand what a word means. Tell children that a base word is a word that can stand alone. We can also add a group of letters to the beginning or end of a base word to make a new word.

Model the strategy. Read the third line of text on page 12. Point to the word *thinking*. Say: Think *means to have an idea.* Think *is the base word for* thinking, *so* thinking *must mean the action of having an idea at this very minute.*

Continue modeling the strategy for additional words as needed.

Author's Craft Reread page 30. Why did the author use the word *screamed* to describe the whistle? What picture do you have in your mind when you read this word? Discuss with a partner. Share your answer. (A scream is a really loud sound, and a whistle is a loud sound too. I can close my eyes and visualize a really loud whistle from an old train.)

Build Knowledge: Make Connections

Talk About the Text Have partners discuss how the selection links the past to the present.

Add to the Anchor Chart Record any new ideas on the Build Knowledge anchor chart.

Add to the Word Bank Add words related to long ago to a separate section of the Word Bank.

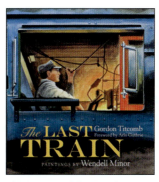

Literature Big Book

READING · WORD WORK

MULTIMODAL

⏱ 5 mins Phonemic Awareness

Phoneme Segmentation

1 **Model** Place markers in the **Response Board** to represent sounds. Say: *I am going to say a word. The word is* cube. *Now I will say the sounds in the word* cube *one at a time. I will place one marker as I say each sound.* Place a marker for each sound as you say: /k/ /ū/ /b/. *The word* cube *has three sounds.* Repeat with *robe* and *please*.

2 **Guided Practice/Practice** Say: *Now it's your turn. I will say a word. Place a counter in each box for each sound you hear.* Guide practice, and provide corrective feedback with the following words:

hose (3)	joke (3)	cute (3)	Eve (2)	stroke (5)
use (2)	pole (3)	smoke (4)	fume (3)	slopes (5)
spoke (4)	theme (3)	huge (3)	globe (4)	stream (5)

⏱ OPTION 5 mins Phonics

Blend Words with /ō/ *o_e*, /ū/ *u_e*, /ē/ *e_e*

1 **Model** Display **Word-Building Cards** *w, o, k,* and *e*. Model blending the sounds. Say: *This is the letter* w. *It stands for* /w/. *These are the letters* o *and* e. *Together they stand for* /ō/. *This is the letter* k. *It stands for* /k/. *I'll blend all three sounds:* /wōōōk/. *The word is* woke. Continue by modeling the words *globe, smoke, cube,* and *Steve*.

2 **Guided Practice/Practice** Display the Lesson 3 Phonics Practice Activity. Say: *Let's blend the letter sounds to read each word:* /th/ /ēēē/ /zzz/; /thēēēzzz/. *The word is* these. Blend each word with children.

these	homes	used	bone	stone	whole
rose	spoke	mule	Pete	phone	clothes
cut	cute	rod	rode	chose	choke
awake		pancake		explode	
inside		complete		bedtime	

Steve smells a rose with his nose.

This cute home can use a new stove.

Lesson 3 Phonics Practice Activity

Prompt children to read the connected text, sounding out the decodable words. Provide corrective feedback as needed.

If children need additional practice blending words with long *o,* long *u,* and long *e,* see **Practice Book** page 212 or the online activity.

Corrective Feedback

Sound Error Help children with any sounds they missed. Say: *My turn. This sound says* (make the correct sound). Then blend the word. Say: *Do it with me.* Blend the word aloud with children. Say: *Your turn. Blend this word.* Have children chorally blend. Say: *Let's do it again.* Follow these steps until children are confidently producing the sound.

Decodable Reader

Have children read "Those Old Classes" to practice decoding words in connected text. If children need support reading words with long vowels, see pages T313 or T320 for instruction and support for the **Decodable Reader**.

Structural Analysis

CVC*e* Syllables

1 **Model** Say the word *pancake.* Ask children to listen closely to hear the vowel sounds. Point out the /a/ sound in *pan* and the /ā/ sound in *cake.* Have children tell how many syllables they hear in *pancake.*

Write the word *pancake.* Draw a line between the syllables. Underline *a* and *e. The letters* a_e *in* cake *act as a team to stand for the* /ā/ *sound. This is a vowel-consonant-*e *syllable.* When decoding two-syllable words, children may have to approximate sounds.

2 **Practice/Apply** Help children blend and decode: *classmate, bedtime, complete, invite, dislike, sunrise, onstage,* and *nickname.* Have children tell how many syllables they hear in each word and divide the word into syllables. Point out that each syllable has one vowel sound even though it may have more than one vowel letter when two vowels act as a team. Have children practice decoding words with CVC*e* syllables using Practice Book page 217 or the online activity.

ENGLISH LANGUAGE LEARNERS

Structural Analysis, Practice/Apply Read each word. Have children clap for each syllable they hear. Then have children echo-read the words and clap as they say each syllable. Ask children to identify the syllable where they find the vowel-consonant-*e* pattern. *What is the first vowel you hear? What is the consonant? Read the whole syllable.* Ask children to point out the vowel in the other syllable. Explain that it has a short vowel sound. Have children say the whole word again.

FORMATIVE ASSESSMENT

❯ STUDENT CHECK-IN

Phonics Have partners read a long-vowel word to each other.

Structural Analysis Have partners share how they divided the words into syllables.

Have children reflect, using the Check-In routine.

LESSON 3

LEARNING GOALS

- We can sort words by families.
- We can read and write the words *ago, boy, girl, how, old,* and *people.*

OBJECTIVES

Use conventional spelling for words with common spelling patterns and for frequently occurring irregular words.

Recognize and read grade-appropriate irregularly spelled words.

Sort words with long *o* and long *u.*

ELA ACADEMIC LANGUAGE

- *pattern*

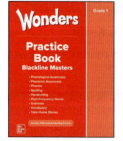

Spelling: Page 215

OPTION **5 mins**

MULTIMODAL

Spelling

Word Sort with *o_e, u_e*

1 **Model** Display cards for *o_e* and *u_e,* and form two columns in a pocket chart. Say the sounds with children.

Hold up the online **Spelling Word Card** for *hope.* Say and spell *hope.* Pronounce each sound clearly: /h/ /ō/ /p/. Blend the sounds, stretching the vowel sound to emphasize it: /hōōōp/. Repeat this step with *nose, note,* and *rope.* Place all four words below the *o_e* card. Read and spell each spelling word. Ask: *What do you notice about these spelling words? They all have the /ō/ sound spelled* o_e.

-ope	cu
no	hope
nose	note
rope	cute
cube	

Unit 3 • Week 4   Spelling Word Cards

2 **Guided Practice/Practice** Provide children with the Spelling Word Cards. Have children say and spell *o*-consonant-*e* and each word in the word family. Repeat the process with the *u_e* words.

Display the words *nice, ledge, ago,* and *people* in a separate column. Read and spell the words together with children. Point out that these spelling words do not have the *o_e* or *u_e* spelling patterns.

Conclude by asking children to orally generate additional words that rhyme with each spelling word. Write the additional words on the board. Underline the common spelling patterns in the additional words. If necessary, point out the differences, and explain why they are unusual.

If children need additional practice spelling words with long *u* and long *o,* see **Practice Book** page 215 or the online activity.

ELL English Language Learners

Spelling, Model Pronounce the spelling word *hope,* and have children repeat it. *This word uses the* o_e *spelling pattern.* Point to the *o.* Have children point. Point to the *e.* Have children point. *What sound do they make together?* Make the long-*o* sound, and have children repeat it. Have children repeat with the remaining spelling words: *nose, note,* and *rope.* Guide children to pronounce the words correctly and identify the *o_e* pattern that creates the sounds.

5 mins

High-Frequency Words

1 **Guided Practice** Say each high-frequency word: *ago, boy, girl, how, old,* and *people.* Have children Read/Spell/Write it. As children spell each word with you, point out the long *o* sound spelled *o* in both *ago* and *old.*

Display the print or digital **Visual Vocabulary Cards** to review this week's high-frequency words.

2 **Practice** Repeat the activity with last week's words. Children can practice reading the high-frequency words independently, using the online activity.

Build Fluency: Word Automaticity

Have children read the following sentences aloud together at the same pace. Repeat several times until children can read the words automatically.

How **old** is that **boy**?

I met a **girl** named Eve five Lessons **ago**.

Lots of **people** went on the hike.

Word Bank

Review the current and previous words in the Word Bank. Discuss with children which words should be removed or added back from previous high-frequency word lists. Remind children that the Word Bank should change as the class needs it to.

DIGITAL TOOLS

For more practice, use these activities.

Word Work

Spelling
High-Frequency Words

FORMATIVE ASSESSMENT

❯ STUDENT CHECK-IN

Spelling Have partners share the additional rhyming words they thought of.

High-Frequency Words Have partners take turns reading a high-frequency word.

Have children reflect, using the Check-In routine.

✔ CHECK FOR SUCCESS

Rubric Use your online rubric to record children's progress.

Can children read and decode words with *o_e, u_e,* and *e_e*?

Can children recognize and read high-frequency words?

❯❯ Small Group Instruction

If No

🟠 **Approaching** Reteach pp. T310–T315

🟣 **ELL** Develop pp. T310–T315

If Yes

🔵 **On** Review pp. T318–T320

🟢 **Beyond** Extend pp. T322–T323

Genre **Nonfiction**

Essential Question
How is life different than it was long ago?
Read about now and long ago.

Go Digital!

Long Ago and Now
by Minda Novek

76   77

Literature Anthology, pp. 76–77
Lexile 480L

Long Ago and Now

LEARNING GOALS

Read We can understand the important ideas and details in a text.

Reread We can name the choices an author made when writing a text.

Have children apply what they learned as they read.

Close Reading Routine

Read   DOK 1–2

• Identify important ideas and details.
• Take notes and retell.
• Use **A C T** prompts as needed.

Reread   DOK 2–3

• Analyze the text, craft, and structure.
• Use the Reread minilessons.

Integrate   DOK 3–4

• Integrate knowledge and ideas.
• Make text-to-text connections.
• Complete the Show Your Knowledge task.
• Inspire action.

Read

Celebratory Read You may wish to read the full selection aloud once with minimal stopping before you use the Read prompts.

Set Purpose

Say: *Let's read to find out how people's lives have changed over time.*

▶ DIFFERENTIATED READING

Approaching Level Have children listen to the selection summary. Use the Reread prompts during Small-Group time.

On Level and **Beyond Level** Pair children or have them independently complete the Reread prompts on **Reading/Writing Companion** pages 137–139.

🎧 **English Language Learners** Before reading, have children listen to a summary of the selection. See the **ELL Small Group Guide,** pp. T140–T141.

What was life like long **ago**?
In some ways it was the same as
today. But in many ways it was not.

Today, we ride in a car. It is a fast
way to go. It is fun to take a trip
with Mom and Dad.

Long ago, **people** rode in wagons. ❶
It could take a long time to get
places. ❷

78

79

Literature Anthology, pp. 78–79

Story Words Read and spell the words *car, cold, clean, clothes, machines,* and *computer.* Review word meanings as needed.

Note Taking: Graphic Organizer

Have children fill in online Compare and Contrast Graphic Organizer 8 as they read.

❶ Reread DOK 2

Teacher Think Aloud I read on page 79 that people used to ride in wagons. It took them a long time to get places. How is that different from today? I will reread page 79 to make sure I understood what I read. Today, people ride in cars. This technology helps us get places fast.

❷ Details: Compare and Contrast DOK 3

Teacher Think Aloud As we read, we can look for connections between the details in the text. On these pages, we learned what people ride in today and what they rode in long ago. The author is comparing life today with life long ago.

Reread

Author's Craft DOK 3

Reading/Writing Companion, 137

How does the author organize the information? (The author organizes the information by telling about life today first. Then the author tells about life long ago.)

Build Vocabulary page 79
wagons: large wooden carts

These days, we have many things to help us at home. This is **how** food is kept fresh. This **boy** can get a snack at any time.

80

In **old** times, people kept things cold in a box filled with ice. Men drove trucks filled with ice to people's homes. This man uses tongs to lift a block of ice. ③ ④

KENNEBEC ICE.
REAT FALLS
ICE
.Y.

81

Literature Anthology, pp. 80–81

Read

③ **Reread** DOK 2

Do you understand why men drove trucks filled with ice to people's homes? If not, we can reread the page. Why did men bring ice to people's homes? (People used the ice in iceboxes to keep food fresh.)

④ **Details: Compare and Contrast** DOK 3

Teacher Think Aloud I read how we keep food fresh today and how people kept food cold long ago. Let's add the information to our chart.

Life Now and Long Ago

Now

We ride in cars.
We use refrigerators.

Both rode places.

Both kept things cold.

Long Ago

They rode in wagons.
They used ice.

⑤ **Genre: Nonfiction** DOK 2

COLLABORATE Nonfiction gives information about real people, places, and things. With a partner, find evidence that this story is nonfiction.

Build Vocabulary page 81
tongs: tool used to pick things up

Today we can get water at home. This **girl** can clean up and take a drink at a sink. **5**

82

Long ago, people used to get water at a pump. This boy pumps water into his bucket. Then, he has to carry the water all the way home! **6**

83

Literature Anthology, pp. 82–83

Read

6 Reread DOK 2

Teacher Think Aloud I read that long ago, people got water at a pump. Where were the pumps? I will reread page 83 and look at the photograph. Now I understand that towns had pumps for people to use to get water.

Reread

Author's Craft DOK 2

Reading/Writing Companion, 138

How do the photos help you understand the information in the text? (The photos show me how food was kept cold long ago and how it is kept cold now.)

Author's Purpose DOK 3

Reading/Writing Companion, 139

Authors have a reason for organizing the text in a certain way. What do you understand because of the way the author organizes the information and details in this story? (I understand how getting water now and long ago is the same and different.)

Combine Information

Remind children how to combine information as they read. Then say: After I looked at page 82, I thought people always got water from a sink. Then I read that people used pumps long ago. Now I know the author organizes the information to show that over time, people have done things in more than one way. DOK 3

LITERATURE ANTHOLOGY **T281**

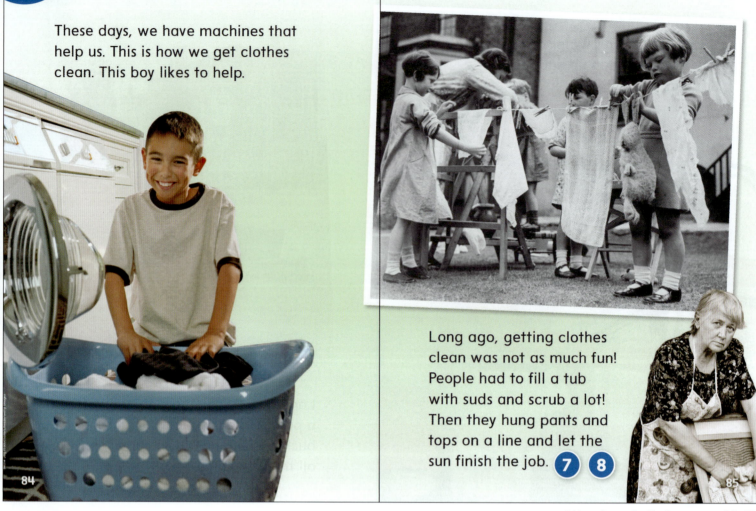

These days, we have machines that help us. This is how we get clothes clean. This boy likes to help.

Long ago, getting clothes clean was not as much fun! People had to fill a tub with suds and scrub a lot! Then they hung pants and tops on a line and let the sun finish the job. 7 8

84

85

Literature Anthology, pp. 84–85

Read

7 Reread DOK 2

Teacher Think Aloud You read that long ago getting clothes clean was not as much fun as it is today. How might rereading help you understand why it was harder to clean clothes long ago?

Student Think Aloud I know that rereading helps me understand and remember what I read. I will reread pages 84 and 85. I read that long ago, people had to fill a tub with suds and scrub a lot. Then they hung the clothes up to dry. That was a lot of work. I think it's much easier to put clothes in a washing machine, the way we do today.

Build Vocabulary page 85
scrub: rub

8 Details: Compare and Contrast DOK 3

COLLABORATE Turn to a partner and talk about getting water and getting clothes clean. Let's add these details to our Compare and Contrast chart.

Life Now and Long Ago

Now

We get water from sinks. We use machines to get clothes clean.

Both used water. Both got clothes clean.

Long Ago

They got water from pumps. They used tubs and scrubbed to get clothes clean.

What do kids today have in common with kids long ago?

Back then, kids went to school just like us. Kids used pencils and paper. They read books in class and used books to look things up.

Today, we still use pencils, paper, and books at school. But there are new things we use in class, too. We can use computers to type. We use the Internet to look things up. **9** **10**

86

87

Literature Anthology, pp. 86–87

9 **Details: Compare and Contrast** DOK 3

COLLABORATE

Turn to a partner, and discuss what you read on pages 86–87. How would you connect the information on these pages? What is different? What is alike? Let's add these ideas to our chart.

Life Now and Long Ago

Now	Both	Long Ago
Kids use the Internet to look things up.	Both looked up information.	Kids used books to look things up.

10 **Genre: Nonfiction** DOK 2

Remind children that nonfiction gives information about real people, places, things, or events. Have children find evidence on pages 86–87 that this story is nonfiction.

ELL Spotlight on Idioms

Pages 86–87 Point to the two uses of the phrase "look things up." Demonstrate the literal meaning of *look up* by directing your eyes upward. Then explain that *look up* can also mean to look in a book or on the Internet to learn about something. *When I look up a word in the dictionary, I find the word to learn its meaning. What is something you would like to look up on the Internet?*

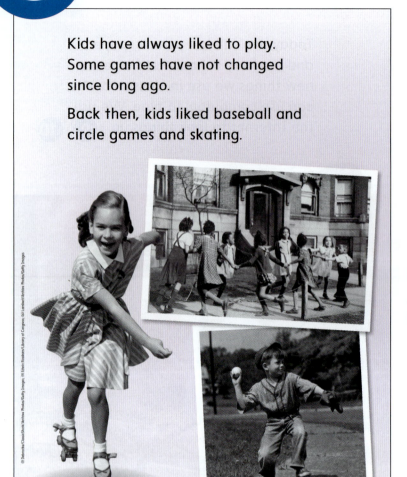

Kids have always liked to play. Some games have not changed since long ago.

Back then, kids liked baseball and circle games and skating.

88

Literature Anthology, p. 88

⑪ **Details: Compare and Contrast** DOK 3

Discuss how to compare and contrast the details in this selection. Let's look at pages 88–89. How did kids play long ago? How do they play today? Let's add these ideas to our chart. Now let's use our chart to connect the ideas in the selection.

Life Now and Long Ago

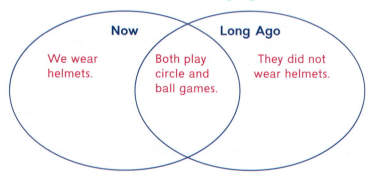

Now — We wear helmets.

Both play circle and ball games.

Long Ago — They did not wear helmets.

ELL Spotlight on Language

Page 88, Paragraph 2 Point to the verb *liked.* Explain that it tells about an action that happened in the past or "back then." Now point to the verb *like* on page 89. Explain that *like* tells about an action that happens in the present, or "today." Model responding to these frames: Last year I liked green. Today I like blue. Ask children to complete the frames with their own ideas.

Kids still like these old-time games today. Which one do you like best? **11**

Literature Anthology, p. 89

Return to Purposes

Guide children to use evidence in the text to tell how people's lives have changed over time. Discuss what children learned from the selection about how life now is different from life long ago.

AUTHOR'S CRAFT DOK 3

Focus on Organization

Explain that authors can organize their work to compare and contrast information.

- Discuss how on pages 78–79, the author compares and contrasts details about traveling. *Comparing traveling long ago and now helps the reader understand how things have changed.*

- Ask children to discuss other comparisons in the selection. Have children tell how the author shows differences between long ago and now.

About Minda Novek

When **Minda Novek** was a little girl, she was already interested in how people lived long ago. She also likes to write about kids today who live in different lands. Minda uses photos for all these projects, so you can learn about real people.

Author's Purpose

Minda Novek wanted to compare life long ago with life today. Draw a picture of something long ago and a picture of something today. Write about each picture.

90

Literature Anthology, p. 90

Meet the Author

Minda Novek

Have children turn to page 77 and point to the author's name. Read the name aloud. Then read aloud page 90 with children. Ask them why they think Minda Novek wrote about life long ago and life now. *Why might Minda Novek have enjoyed writing this book? Why does she use photos for all her projects?*

Author's Purpose

In their reader's notebooks, have children write a sentence to compare how something from long ago is different from something today. *Long ago, _____, but today, _____.*

Read

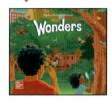

Retell

Have children turn to page 136 in their **Reading/Writing Companions**. Remind them that as they read the text, they compared and contrasted information. Have children use the information they recorded on their Compare and Contrast chart to help them retell the text.

Use Text Evidence Guide children to use text evidence to respond to the questions on page 136.

Reread

Analyze the Text

After children read and retell the selection, have them reread *Long Ago and Now* to develop a deeper understanding of the text. Then have them answer the questions on pages 137–139 of the Reading/Writing Companion. For students who need help finding text evidence to support their responses, use the scaffolded instruction from the Reread prompts on pages T279–T281.

Integrate

Build Knowledge: Make Connections

Talk About the Text Have partners discuss some things that the text mentions that have changed from long ago and some things that are the same.

Write About the Text Have children add their ideas to the Build Knowledge page of their reader's notebooks.

Add to the Anchor Chart Record any new ideas on the Build Knowledge anchor chart.

Add to the Word Bank Add words related to long ago to a separate section of the Word Bank.

Compare Texts DOK 4

Guide children to compare two texts. Share the prompt: What is the same about the author's message in both *Long Ago and Now* and "Life at Home"? Say: *Think about how the authors organized information in each text. What is the same about their messages?* (Both authors show how things were and how they have changed.) Have partners discuss both texts and then share their responses with the class. You can use a two-column chart to show the similarities.

 ENGLISH LANGUAGE LEARNERS

Retell Help children retell the text by turning to each page and prompting with questions and frames, such as, *What are these people doing?* They are riding in a car. *What are these people doing?* They are riding in a wagon. Then supply retelling frames: Now people ride in cars. Long ago they rode in wagons.

 CONNECT TO CONTENT

Life Now and Long Ago Remind children that this week they have been learning about how life now is the same and different from life long ago. Have children choose one example from the selection of how life is the same and one example of how life is different from long ago. Ask partners or small groups to develop a short skit to show the similarities and differences. Then ask children to perform their skits.

FORMATIVE ASSESSMENT

❯ STUDENT CHECK-IN

Read Have partners tell each other an important detail from the text.

Reread Have partners tell one choice the author made when writing this text.

Have children reflect, using the Check-In routine to fill in the bars.

LEARNING GOALS

- We can write an opinion about a nonfiction text.
- We can read and write the present-tense verbs *is* and *are*.

OBJECTIVES

Write opinion pieces in which they introduce the topic or name the book they are writing about, state an opinion, supply a reason for the opinion, and provide some sense of closure.

Use singular and plural nouns with matching verbs in basic sentences.

Use verbs to convey a sense of past, present, and future.

Use commas in dates.

ELA ACADEMIC LANGUAGE

- *inference, opinion, evidence*
- Cognates: *inferencia, opinión, evidencia*

TEACH IN SMALL GROUP

Choose from these options to enable all children to complete the writing activity:

- Drawing and labeling a picture
- Completing sentence frames
- Writing one sentence
- Writing multiple sentences

Additionally, to provide differentiated support for children, see Writing Skills minilessons on pages T420–T429. These can be used throughout the year.

---

 5 mins

Independent Writing

Write About the Anchor Text DOK 3

 COLLABORATE

Analyze the Prompt Read the prompt: *Based on* Long Ago and Now, *do you think being a kid is better now, or was it better in the past? Why?* Have partners turn and talk about what they learned about being a kid long ago.

- Explain that to respond to the prompt, children need to find text evidence and make inferences to form an opinion about whether it was better to be a kid long ago or if it is better to be a kid now.

Find Text Evidence Say: *We need to find evidence in the text and photographs.* Then ask:

- *What can we tell about what it was like to be a kid long ago and what it is like now? Look at the photograph and text on page 86 in the* **Literature Anthology.** *What does this page tell us about life for kids long ago?* (Long ago, kids went to school. They used pencils and paper. They used books to look things up.)

- *Now look at page 87.* Tell children they can use the photograph to make inferences about things that are not stated in the text. Ask: *What are the kids in the photograph doing?* (They are using technology to get information.) Ask: *Which way of working in the classroom do you think is better?*

Have children continue finding text evidence, as necessary, to respond to the prompt. You may choose to take notes on a chart or have children take notes in their writer's notebooks.

 Write a Response Tell children to turn to page 140 in their **Reading/ Writing Companions.** Guide children to use text evidence to draft a response. Remind them to give reasons for their opinions.

- **Writing Checklist:** Read the checklist with children. Remind them to focus on one idea, use words from the Word Bank, and use the words *is* and *are* correctly.

- **Writing Support:** If needed, provide sentence starters. Model completing one as necessary.

  Life today is _____.

  Life long ago was _____.

Tell children they will finalize and present their writing the next day.

Writing and Grammar

My Goal I can write an opinion about a nonfiction text.

Write About the Anchor Text

Based on *Long Ago and Now*, do you think being a kid is better now, or was it better in the past? Why?

Talk about the question.

Write your answer below.

Remember:
- ☐ Focus on one idea.
- ☐ Use words from your Word Bank.
- ☐ Use the words *is* and *are* correctly.

Check In 1 2 3 4

140 Unit 3 • Week 4

Reading/Writing Companion, p. 140

Grammar

5 mins

Irregular Verbs: *Is* and *Are*

1 **Review** Remind children that *is* and *are* tell about action that is happening right now.

Say: *Name the verb in this sentence:* The car is a fast way to travel. Say: *Which word in the beginning of the sentence names a person, place, or thing? The noun is* car. *We use the verb* is *because the noun,* car, *names one thing.* Repeat with examples of a plural noun and the verb *are*.

2 **Guided Practice/Practice** Guide children to find a sentence in *Long Ago and Now* that contains the verb *is* or *are*. Have partners write the verb and then write a new sentence that includes that verb.

Talk About It

Challenge partners to orally generate sentences in dialogue that contain *is* and *are*.

Mechanics: Commas in Dates

1 **Model** Tell children we use commas to separate the day and date and the date and year. Display the following sentence, pointing out the placement of the commas between the date and the year: Today is Sunday, June 6, 20__.

2 **Guided Practice** Prompt children to complete the sentence starter and then correct the sentence.

Today is _____.

The party is on Saturday, October, 5 20 __.

(The party is on Saturday, October 5, 20__.)

ELL English Language Learners

Independent Writing, Analyze the Prompt Review the concept of forming an opinion. Have children look at the illustrations and photographs in *Long Ago and Now,* and then provide sentence frames to help children state their opinions: I think life for kids is better <u>now</u> because we have <u>computers</u>. Clarify children's responses as needed by providing vocabulary.

For additional support, see the **ELL Small Group Guide**, p. 145.

DIGITAL TOOLS

Use these activities to practice grammar and mechanics.

Grammar

Mechanics

FORMATIVE ASSESSMENT

❯ STUDENT CHECK-IN

Writing Have partners share their opinions. Have children reflect, using the Check-In routine to fill in the bars.

Grammar Have partners read their sentences containing *is* and *are*. Have children reflect, using the Check-In routine.

LEARNING GOALS

We can learn and use new vocabulary words.

OBJECTIVES

Use real-life connections between words and their use.

Use words and phrases acquired through conversations, reading and being read to, and responding to texts.

ELA ACADEMIC LANGUAGE

• *selection*
• Cognate: *selección*

DIGITAL TOOLS

Visual Vocabulary Cards

LESSON FOCUS

READING

Revisit the Essential Question

Read and Reread Paired Selection:
"From Horse to Plane"
• Introduce Text Feature
• Reread Text

Word Work
• Build words with /ō/ o_e, /ū/ u_e, /ē/ e_e

WRITING
• Independent Writing
• Review Grammar and Mechanics

Literature Anthology, pp. 92–95

---

 15 mins

Oral Language

MULTIMODAL

 ### Essential Question

How is life different than it was long ago?

Remind children that this week they have been learning about how life has changed from long ago until now. Guide children to discuss the question, using information from what they have read and discussed. Use the online or print **Visual Vocabulary Cards** and the Define/Example/Ask routine to review the oral vocabulary words *century, entertainment, future, past,* and *present*.

Guide children to use each word as they talk about what they have read and learned about how life has changed over time. Prompt children by asking the following questions:

• What *century* are we living in today?

• What is your favorite kind of outdoor *entertainment*?

• What would you like to be in the *future*?

• Who is your favorite hero from the *past*?

• Who is your favorite hero in the *present*?

Review last week's oral vocabulary words *tale, hero, timid, foolish,* and *eventually*.

FORMATIVE ASSESSMENT

▶ STUDENT CHECK-IN

Have partners use a vocabulary word in a sentence. Have children reflect, using the Check-In routine.

Text Features

Captions

1 **Explain** Tell children they can use nonfiction selections to find facts and details. Explain that nonfiction often has photographs with captions, or short descriptions that give information about the photographs.

Online Teaching Chart

2 **Model** Display **Online Teaching Chart** for Text Features: Captions. Read the captions for the top two photographs. *These captions give information about the photographs. The first caption tells about tall buildings. The second tells us what people like to do in parks.*

3 **Guided Practice/Practice** Read the bottom two captions with children. Guide them as they discuss the information. *What information does this caption give us about workers? What do we learn from the caption that we do not learn in the photograph? What does this caption tell us about the city at night?* Tell children to look for and read captions when reading nonfiction.

English Language Learners

Use these scaffolds with **Text Features, Guided Practice/Practice.**

Beginning

Help children explain what the photographs and captions show. *What do you see in the photograph?* I see people <u>working</u>. *Does the caption talk about working?* (yes) *What does it tell you about what workers use to fix the road?* (They use tools.)

Intermediate

Help children explain what they see in the photos and tell what they learn from the captions. In the photograph, I see <u>people working</u>. The caption tells me that <u>the workers use tools to fix the road.</u>

Advanced/Advanced High

Ask partners to work together to explain what they see in the photographs and learn from the captions. Provide vocabulary as needed.

OBJECTIVES

Know and use various text features (e.g., headings, tables of contents, glossaries, electronic menus, icons) to locate key facts or information in a text.

Distinguish between information provided by pictures or other illustrations and information provided by the words in a text.

ELA ACADEMIC LANGUAGE

- *captions, details*
- Cognate: *detalle*

DIGITAL TOOLS

Text Feature Activity

ELL NEWCOMERS

Use the **Newcomer Online Visuals** and their accompanying prompts to help children expand vocabulary and language about My Family and Me (10–14). Use the Conversation Starters, Speech Balloons, and Games in the **Newcomer Teacher's Guide** to continue building vocabulary and developing oral and written language.

FORMATIVE ASSESSMENT

❯ STUDENT CHECK-IN

Have partners tell one thing they learned from the captions. Have children reflect, using the Check-In routine.

Genre Nonfiction

Read Together

Compare Texts
Read about how transportation has changed.

From Horse to Plane

People today can go places in cars, planes, and trains. Long ago there were not as many kinds of ==transportation==. Before ==engines==, people had to walk or use horses.

People rode in wagons pulled by horses.

2 Trains go on rails to and from stations.

Then the train was ==invented==. Steam engines made them go. Now people could go places much faster. It used to take days to go a hundred miles. After the train was invented, it might take hours. 1

92   93

Literature Anthology, pp. 92–93
Lexile 370L

"From Horse to Plane"

LEARNING GOALS

Read We can understand the important ideas and details in a text.

Reread We can name the choices an author made when writing a text.

Compare Texts

As children read and reread "From Horse to Plane," encourage them to think about the Essential Question. Have children think about how this text is the same as and different from *Long Ago and Now* in describing the ways things have changed over time. Review the words *transportation, engines,* and *invented.*

Genre Focus Tell children this is a nonfiction text, which tells about real people, places, events, or things by presenting facts and information about them. Remind children that nonfiction texts often have photographs with captions.

Reread DOK 2

Remind children that if they do not understand something, they can reread the text to help them. Is there anything you do not understand?

❷ Text Feature: Captions DOK 2

Think Aloud When I look at the photograph on page 93, I wonder where the train is stopping. I remember that a caption can give information. The caption explains that trains go on rails to and from stations.

Have partners work together to create another caption for this photo.

Author's Craft DOK 3

Reading/Writing Companion, 141

Set Purpose Let's reread to find out how transportation has changed.

Which words in the selection tell how we can go places today? Circle the words in the text. (cars, planes, trains)

Reread the text, and talk with a partner about why the author included the photo on this page. How does it help you understand the text? (Possible answer: It shows how people used horses for transportation.)

English Language Learners

Use the following scaffolds with **Compare Texts.**

Beginning

What is one way "From Horse to Plane" and Long Ago and Now *are the same?* They both tell facts about life in the past and life now.

Intermediate

Have children complete the above sentence frame. Then have children look at pages 92 and 93. Say: Long Ago and Now *was about the many different ways life is different now than it was in the past. Look at the photos. What do you think "From Horse to Plane" will be about?* It will be about ways people can go places.

Advanced/Advanced High

Have partners compare and contrast the selections. Have one partner focus on telling how they are different. Have the other partner tell how they are the same. Provide vocabulary as needed.

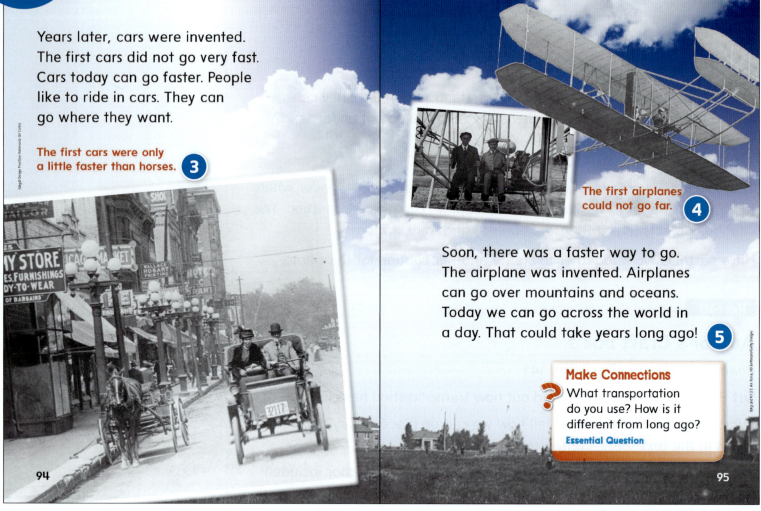

Years later, cars were invented. The first cars did not go very fast. Cars today can go faster. People like to ride in cars. They can go where they want.

The first cars were only a little faster than horses. ③

The first airplanes could not go far. ④

Soon, there was a faster way to go. The airplane was invented. Airplanes can go over mountains and oceans. Today we can go across the world in a day. That could take years long ago! ⑤

Make Connections
? What transportation do you use? How is it different from long ago?
Essential Question

94   95

Literature Anthology, pp. 94–95

Read

③ Text Feature: Captions DOK 1

Teacher Think Aloud A long time ago, people traveled by horse and wagon. Then they traveled by train. The photograph on page 94 shows an old car. The caption tells us the first cars were only a little faster than horses.

④ Text Feature: Captions DOK 1

Look at the photograph on page 95. Then read the caption. What information does this caption give us about the first airplanes? (They could not go far.)

⑤ Reread DOK 2

Teacher Think Aloud The caption says the first planes did not go far, but the text says they were a faster way to go. What were they faster than? I will reread to make sure I understand.

Reread

Author's Craft DOK 3

Reading/Writing Companion, 142

What kinds of transportation came after horses? Circle the kinds of transportation in the text. (train, cars, airplane)

Reread the text and talk with a partner about how the author feels about the invention of airplanes. How do you know? (Possible answer: The author is excited about the invention of airplanes. I know this because he uses an exclamation mark when talking about airplanes.)

Use the Quick Tip box to support children as they work.

Reread

Author's Craft DOK 3

Reading/Writing Companion, 143

Talk with a partner about the information on each page of the selection. Why is "From Horse to Plane" a good title for this text? (The text tells how people went from using horses to using planes to travel.)

Talk About It What does the author want you to learn from reading this text? (Possible answer: The author wants me to learn that transportation has changed over time. People have invented new and faster ways to travel.)

Read

Retell

Guide children to use details to retell the selection. Have partners discuss what it might feel like to ride in a wagon pulled by a horse.

Reread

Analyze the Text

After children retell the selection, have them reread to develop a deeper understanding of the text. Have children annotate the text and answer the questions on **Reading/Writing Companion** pages 141–143. For children who need support citing text evidence, use the Reread prompts on pages T293–T295.

Integrate

Build Knowledge: Make Connections

Talk About the Text Have partners discuss what they learned about how transportation has changed from over time.

Write About the Text Have children add their ideas to the Build Knowledge page of their reader's notebooks.

Add to the Anchor Chart Record any new ideas on the Build Knowledge anchor chart.

Add to the Word Bank Add words related to long ago to a separate section of the Word Bank.

 SPOTLIGHT ON LANGUAGE

Page 94 Point to and read the word *fast.* Demonstrate a fast motion with your hand. Then point to *faster,* and demonstrate an even faster motion. Explain that we add *-er* to words to mean "more." *Faster means "more fast." What can go faster today?* (cars)

CONNECT TO CONTENT

Life Now and Long Ago
Remind children that this week they have been learning about how life now is the same and different from life long ago. Explain that technology is something created by people to make our lives easier or to solve problems. Say: *Think about the transportation changes you learned about. What technology did people invent to make traveling easier now than it was long ago?* Have partners discuss the question and then share with the group.

STEM

❯ STUDENT CHECK-IN

Read Have partners tell each other one important detail from the text. Have children reflect, using the Check-In routine.

Reread Have partners tell one choice the author made when writing this text. Have children reflect, using the Check-In routine to fill in the bars.

LEARNING GOALS

- We can say the middle sounds in words.
- We can build words with long *o*, long *u*, and long *e*.
- We can read and write two-syllable words.
- We can spell and sort words with long *o* and long *u*.
- We can read the words *ago, boy, girl, how, old,* and *people.*

OBJECTIVES

Isolate and pronounce medial vowel sounds (phonemes) in spoken single-syllable words.

Know final -e and common vowel team conventions for representing long vowel sounds.

Decode two-syllable words following basic patterns by breaking the words into syllables.

Use conventional spelling for words with common spelling patterns and for frequently occurring irregular words.

Recognize and read grade-appropriate irregularly spelled words.

ELA ACADEMIC LANGUAGE

- syllable, consonant, pattern
- Cognates: *sílaba, consonante*

 **TEACH IN SMALL GROUP**

Word Work lessons can be taught in small groups.

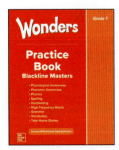

Structural Analysis: Page 218

 OPTION 5 mins

Phonemic Awareness

Phoneme Isolation

1 **Model** Use **Photo Cards** to show children how to isolate the middle sound in words. Say: *Listen as I say the name of each photo:* nose, rope. *I hear the /ō/ sound in the middle of* nose *and* rope. *Listen as I stretch this middle sound: /nōōōz/, /rōōōp/. The middle sound is /ō/.*

2 **Guided Practice/Practice** Have children practice isolating the middle sound in words. Guide practice for the first two words below. Provide corrective feedback as needed. Then have children practice isolating the vowel sound in the remaining words. Say: *Tell me the middle sound you hear in each word. Let's do the first one together.*

boat	phone	dime	leaf	mule	rake
cube	gate	goat	feet	kite	rose

5 mins

Phonics

MULTIMODAL

Build Words with /ō/ o_e, /ū/ u_e, /ē/ e_e

1 **Review** Provide children with **Word-Building Cards** a–z. Say: *The letters o_e can stand for the sound /ō/. The letters u_e can stand for /ū/. The letters e_e can stand for /ē/. We'll use Word-Building Cards to build words with long o, long u, and long e.* Place the letters *t, h, e, s,* and *e.* Say: *Let's blend the sounds together and read the word: /thēēēzzz/. Now let's change the* e *to* o. *Blend the sounds, and read the word.*

2 **Practice** Continue with *chose, broke, poke, hole, mole, mule, mute, cute, cube, theme, Steve,* and *Pete.* After children have finished building the words, dictate them and have children write the word-building list. Have partners exchange lists and check them for spelling. Listen in, and provide corrective feedback.

Color Coding After each dictation, reveal the secret color-coding letter(s) for children to find on their **Response Boards.** Have them say the sound(s) as they trace each letter in color. Use one or two of the phonics skills of the week for color coding.

Decodable Reader

Have children read "That Old Globe" to practice decoding words in connected text. If children need support, turn to Small Group page T313 or T320 for instruction on the **Decodable Reader**.

Structural Analysis

5 mins

CVC*e* Syllables

Review Write the words *update, sunshine,* and *awoke* on the board, and read them with children. Remind children that words are made of smaller parts called syllables and that one vowel sound is heard in each syllable. When children see a vowel-consonant-silent *e* spelling, they should know that this spelling is one syllable and that the letters should be kept together.

Write the following words: *excite, escape, reptile,* and *hopeful.* Have children work in pairs to divide each word into syllables, read the words, and then write sentences that include each word.

If children need additional practice, see **Practice Book** page 218 or the online activity.

Spelling

5 mins

MULTIMODAL

Word Sort with *o_e, u_e*

Review Provide pairs of children with copies of the online **Spelling Word Cards.** While one partner reads the words one at a time, the other partner should orally segment the word and then write it. After reading all the words, partners should switch roles.

Practice Have children correct their own papers. Then have them sort the words by vowel spelling pattern.

High-Frequency Words

OPTION
5 mins

ago, boy, girl, how, old, people

Review Display the print or digital **Visual Vocabulary Cards** for high-frequency words: *ago, boy, girl, how, old,* and *people.* Have children Read/Spell/Write each word.

- Point to a word,, and call on a child to use it in a sentence.
- Review last week's words, using the same procedure.

DIGITAL TOOLS

For more practice, use these activities.

Word Work

Phonemic Awareness
Phonics
Structural Analysis
Spelling
High-Frequency Words

FORMATIVE ASSESSMENT

❯ STUDENT CHECK-IN

Phonics/Spelling Have children spell words with long *o,* long *u,* and long *e.*

Structural Analysis Have partners think of another two-syllable word with a CVC*e* spelling and use the word in a sentence.

High-Frequency Words Have partners share a sentence that includes a high-frequency word.

Have children reflect, using the Check-In routine.

✓ CHECK FOR SUCCESS

Rubric Use your online rubric to record children's progress.

Can children read and decode words with *o_e, u_e,* and *e_e*?

Can children recognize and read high-frequency words?

❯ Small Group Instruction

If No

🔴 **Approaching** Reteach pp. T310–T315

🟣 **ELL** Develop pp. T310–T315

If Yes

🔵 **On** Review pp. T318–T320

🟢 **Beyond** Extend pp. T322–T323

Independent Writing

5 mins

Write About the Anchor Text

Revise

Reread the prompt about *Long Ago and Now: Based on* Long Ago and Now, *do you think being a kid is better now, or was it better in the past? Why?*

• Have children read their drafts in their **Reading/Writing Companions.** Ask them to check that they responded to the prompt. Then have them review the checklist to confirm that they focused on one idea, used words from their word bank, and used the words *is* and *are* correctly.

Peer Review Have pairs take notes about what they liked most, questions they have for the author, and additional ideas the author could include. Have partners discuss these topics. Provide time for revisions.

Edit/Proofread

Review the online proofreading marks with children. Model how to use each mark. Then have children edit for the following:

• Correctly spelled high-frequency words

• Correctly used commas with dates

Write Final Draft

Have children create their final drafts in their writer's notebooks by:

• writing them neatly, or using digital tools to produce and publish them.

• adding details and a drawing that will support their opinions.

Teacher Conference As children work, conference with them to provide guidance. Make sure children focused on one idea, used the words *is* and *are* correctly, and used words from the Word Bank. Have children make changes based on your feedback.

Share and Evaluate

After children have finalized their drafts, have them:

• work with a partner to practice presenting their writing to each other.

• share their final drafts with the class.

• ask and answer questions about each other's work.

If possible, record children as they share so they can self-evaluate. After children share, display their final papers on a bulletin board.

Have children add their work to their writing folders. Invite children to look at their previous writing and discuss with a partner how it has improved.

5 mins

Grammar

Irregular Verbs: *Is* and *Are*

1 **Review** Review that the verb *is* tells about one noun, and *are* tells about more than one noun.

2 **Practice** Display the following sentences. Have children complete the sentences with *is* or *are*.

Grace ___ singing a song. (is)

The girls ___ sliding on ice. (are)

For additional practice with editing using verbs, see **Practice Book** page 221 or the online activity.

 COLLABORATE

Talk About It

Challenge partners to orally create a short story with sentences containing *is* and *are*.

Mechanics: Commas in Dates

1 **Review** Remind children that when we write a date, we put a comma between the day and date number and between the date number and year.

2 **Practice** Display sentences with punctuation errors. Read each aloud. Have children work together to correct the sentences.

Gran will be here on Monday July 3 20 ___ .
(Gran will be here on Monday, July 3, 20__.)

There will be no school on December 4 20__.
(There will be no school on December 4, 20__.)

For additional practice with commas in dates, see **Practice Book** page 222 or the online activity.

 ELL

English Language Learners

Independent Writing, Revise Guide children to edit their writing for correct use of *is* and *are*. As children read their work, have them circle when they used *is* and *are*. Ask: *Why did you use* is/are? Guide children to tell whether the sentence is about one person or thing or more than one person or thing. Have children edit for subject-verb agreement and then check that they have used *is* or *are* correctly. Guide children in correcting errors as they edit their writing.

For additional support, see the **ELL Small Group Guide,** p. 145.

DIGITAL TOOLS

Use these resources with the lessons.

Grammar

Mechanics

Proofreading Marks

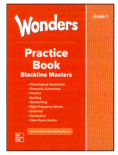

Grammar: Page 221
Mechanics: Page 222

STUDENT CHECK-IN

Writing Have children reflect on one way they revised their writing.

Grammar On their own, have children create a sentence that contains *is* or *are*.

Have children reflect, using the Check-In routine.

WRITING AND CONVENTIONS **T299**

LESSON 4

LEARNING GOALS

We can interview someone to learn about their school life.

OBJECTIVES

Participate in shared research and writing projects.

With guidance and support from adults, recall information from experiences or gather information from provided sources to answer a question.

Add drawings or other visual displays to descriptions when appropriate to clarify ideas, thoughts, and feelings.

Ask and answer questions about what a speaker says in order to gather additional information or clarify something that is not understood.

ELA ACADEMIC LANGUAGE

• *diagram, process*
• Cognates: *diagrama, proceso*

COLLABORATIVE CONVERSATIONS

Listen Carefully Review with children that as they engage in partner, small-group, and whole-group discussions, they should:

• always look at the speaker.
• respect others by not interrupting them.
• repeat others' ideas to check understanding.

Integrate

10 mins

Interview

Model

Tell children that today they will interview a teacher or older person at school about what their school life was like when they were a child. Display pages 144–145 in the **Reading/Writing Companion,** and model filling them in as you review the steps in the research process below.

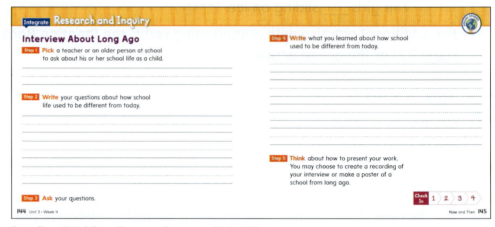

Reading/Writing Companion, pp. 144–145

STEP 1 Choose Someone to Interview

The project is to interview another teacher or older person about what their school life was like when they were a child. First, I need to choose a person to talk to. I will choose another first-grade teacher, Ms. Sherman.

STEP 2 Write Your Questions

I need to decide what I want to know about Ms. Sherman's school life. I will ask her if she sat at a desk or a table, if she ate lunch in the cafeteria, and if she used library books or the Internet to look up information.

STEP 3 Ask Your Questions

I asked Ms. Sherman my questions. She told me she sat at a metal desk with a space inside for her books and pencils. She ate lunch in the cafeteria with her friends. She used library books to look up information.

STEP 4 Write What You Learned

I learned that Ms. Sherman's school life was similar to mine! I sit at a desk and eat in the cafeteria. The one difference is that Ms. Sherman used books to look up information. Today, I can use books and the Internet.

STEP 5 Choose How to Present

I can decide the best way to present the information I learned. I will draw pictures of Ms. Sherman as a child sitting at her desk at school, eating in the cafeteria, and looking at a book. I will write a caption for each picture.

Apply

Have children turn to pages 144–145 in their **Reading/Writing Companions**.

Guide them as they choose a teacher or older person in school to interview and as they formulate their questions. If children are unsure about whom to interview, you can make some suggestions.

Before children write what they learned during their interviews, they can discuss it with a partner.

After children have completed their interviews, guide them to fill out the Research Process Checklist on the online Student Checklist. This checklist helps children decide if they've completed all the necessary parts of the research process.

Choose the Presentation Format

Have children turn to pages 144–145 in their Reading/Writing Companions to review their research and consider what they learned about the person they interviewed. Tell children that today they are going to take the next step by creating a way to present their findings. This will be their final product.

Options include the following:

- Create a Venn diagram showing a comparison between the older person's life at school and the child's current life at school. Children can draw pictures and write labels or sentences for each part of the diagram.

- Create a collage of pictures showing school today compared with school long ago. Write a title for the collage.

- Create a video interview with the person, having them tell about their school life as a child. Include the written questions children asked.

Create the Presentation

Have children develop their presentations. Remind children of the rules of working with others.

Gather Materials Have children gather the materials they'll need to create their finished products. Most of the materials should be available in the classroom or can be brought from home.

Make the Presentation After children have gathered the materials they need for their presentations, provide time for them to create them. Have children review their research before they begin. Then support children as they work on their presentations.

You may wish to have children collaborate on projects.

ELL ENGLISH LANGUAGE LEARNERS

Apply, Step 2 *What topics did you read about?* (transportation, life at home, play) *You can use these topics to help you think of questions.* Provide sentence frames to guide children in creating questions for their interviews. For example: What did you play with when you were a child? Model how to respond: When I was a child, I played with balls outside. Provide additional examples of questions and how to respond to them as needed.

TEACH IN SMALL GROUP

You may wish to have children create their presentations during Small-Group time. Group children of varying abilities or group children who are doing similar projects.

RESEARCH AND INQUIRY: SHARING FINAL PROJECTS

As children prepare to wrap up the week, have them share their Research and Inquiry projects. Then have children self-evaluate.

Prepare Have children gather the materials they need to present their projects. Then partners can take turns practicing their presentations.

Share Guide children to present their Research and Inquiry projects. Encourage children to ask questions to clarify when something is unclear.

Evaluate Have children discuss and evaluate their own presentations. You may wish to have them fill out the Presentation Checklist on the online Student Checklist.

STUDENT CHECK-IN

Have partners share one thing they learned from their interview. Have children reflect, using the Check-In routine to fill in the bars.

OBJECTIVES

Orally produce single-syllable words by blending sounds (phonemes), including consonant blends.

Segment spoken single-syllable words into their complete sequence of individual sounds (phonemes).

Know final -e and common vowel team conventions for representing long vowel sounds.

Decode two-syllable words following basic patterns by breaking the words into syllables.

Use conventional spelling for words with common spelling patterns and for frequently occurring irregular words.

Recognize and read grade-appropriate irregularly spelled words.

ELA ACADEMIC LANGUAGE

- *syllable, pattern*
- Cognate: *sílaba*

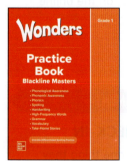

Take-Home Story:
Pages 223–224
Spelling: Posttest, Page 213

LESSON FOCUS

READING

Word Work
- Review Long /ō/ *o_e*, Long /ū/ *u_e*, Long /ē/ *e_e*

Make Connections
- Connect the Photograph to the Essential Question
- Show Your Knowledge

WRITING
- Self-Selected Writing
- Review Grammar and Mechanics

Reading/Writing Companion, pp. 146–147

5 mins

Phonemic Awareness

Phoneme Blending

Review Guide children to blend phonemes to form words. Say: *Now listen as I say a group of sounds. Then blend those sounds to form a word.*

/r/ /ō/ /z/	/ū/ /z/	/b/ /r/ /ō/ /k/	/f/ /ū/ /m/
/n/ /ō/ /t/	/b/ /r/ /ē/ /z/	/f/ /ū/ /z/	/r/ /ō/ /t/

Phoneme Segmentation

Review Guide children to segment phonemes in words. Say: *I am going to say a word. I want you to say each sound in the word.*

bone   robe   muse   phone   huge   smoke   stroke   nose

5 mins

Phonics

MULTIMODAL

Blend and Build Words with /ō/ *o_e*, /ū/ *u_e*, /ē/ *e_e*

Review Have children read and say the words *rose, home, use, cute,* and *Steve.* Then have children follow the word-building routine with **Word-Building Cards** to build *home, dome, dove, wove, woke, joke, poke, pole, mole, mule, mute, cute, cube, Zeke,* and *Eve.*

Word Automaticity Help children practice word automaticity. Display decodable words, and point to each word as children chorally read it. Test how many words children can read in one minute. Model blending words children miss.

Read the Decodable Reader

If children need extra practice decoding words in context, have them read "Those Old Classes" and "That Old Globe." If children need additional support for these stories, turn to Small Group page T313 or T320 for instruction and support.

In a Flash: Sound-Spellings

Display the Sound-Spelling Card *boat*. Point to the letters *o_e*.

1. **Teacher:** What are the letters?   **Children:** o, e
2. **Teacher:** What's the sound?   **Children:** /ō/

Continue the routine for previously taught sounds.

DIGITAL TOOLS

For more practice, use these activities.

Word Work

Phonemic Awareness
Phonics
Structural Analysis
Spelling
High-Frequency Words

5 mins

Structural Analysis

CVC*e* Syllables

Review Have children tell what a syllable is and then tell how many syllables they hear in the word *advice*. Write the word. Have children explain why there are three vowel letters but only two syllables. Then have children practice writing CVCe multisyllabic words such as *unlike, complete, milkshake,* and *expose*.

5 mins

Spelling

MULTIMODAL

Word Sort with *o_e, u_e*

Review Have children use the online **Spelling Word Cards** to sort the weekly words by long-vowel patterns. Remind children that four of the words do not have the *o_e* or *u_e* spelling patterns.

Assess Test children on their abilities to spell words with the *o_e* and *u_e* spelling patterns. Say each word, and provide a sentence so children can hear the words used in a correct context. Then allow children time to write the words. Remind children to write legibly, leaving space between words as they write their answers. As a challenge, provide more words that follow the same spelling patterns. Have children complete the spelling posttest using **Practice Book** page 213.

FORMATIVE ASSESSMENT

❯ STUDENT CHECK-IN

Phonics/Spelling Have children spell words with long *o*, long *u*, and long *e*.

Structural Analysis Have partners use a two-syllable word in a sentence.

High-Frequency Words Have partners share a sentence containing a high-frequency word.

Have children reflect, using the Check-In routine.

5 mins

High-Frequency Words

ago, boy, girl, how, old, people

Review Display the print or digital **Visual Vocabulary Cards** *ago, boy, girl, how, old,* and *people*. Have children Read/Spell/Write each word. Have children write a sentence that contains each word.

If children need assistance reading high-frequency words, they can practice reading independently, using the Take-Home Story in the **Practice Book** on pages 223–224 or use online resources.

✔ CHECK FOR SUCCESS

Rubric Use your online rubric to record children's progress.

Can children read and decode words with *o_e, u_e,* and *e_e*?

Can children recognize and read high-frequency words?

❯ Small Group Instruction

If No

⬤ **Approaching** Reteach pp. T310–T315

⬤ **ELL** Develop pp. T310–T315

If Yes

⬤ **On** Review pp. T318–T320

⬤ **Beyond** Extend pp. T322–T323

LEARNING GOALS

- We can choose a writing activity and share it.
- We can complete sentences with *is* and *are*.

OBJECTIVES

With guidance and support from adults, use a variety of digital tools to produce and publish writing, including in collaboration with peers.

Ask and answer questions about what a speaker says in order to gather additional information or clarify something that is not understood.

Use singular and plural nouns with matching verbs in basic sentences.

Use verbs to convey a sense of past, present, and future.

Use commas in dates.

Self-select writing activity and topics.

ELA ACADEMIC LANGUAGE

- *topic, publish*
- Cognate: *publicar*

 DIFFERENTIATED WRITING

You may choose to conference with children to provide additional support for the following writing activities.

- Make a Book: Have children brainstorm topics they could write their books about.
- Comic Strip: Have partners read the dialogue of several age-appropriate comic strips before writing and drawing their own comic strips.

 10 mins

Self-Selected Writing

Talk About the Topic

Remind children of the Essential Question: *How is life different than it was long ago?* Have partners talk about the Essential Question, and encourage them to ask each other questions.

Choose a Writing Activity

Tell children they will choose a type of writing they would like to do. Children may choose to write about the Essential Question or write about a different topic that is important to them. Children may choose from the following modes of writing.

 **Make a Book** Provide children with paper they can use to make a small book about what life was like in the past or another topic that interests them.

Comic Strip Read a comic strip. Explain that a comic strip is a series of pictures and speech bubbles that tell what the characters are saying. Have partners imagine what people who lived long ago might have talked about. Have them create a comic strip to tell a story that shows this conversation.

 Journal Writing Remind children that a journal is a place where they can write their thoughts about events or topics. Have children write about what they think life was like long ago or about a different topic.

Use Digital Tools You may wish to work with children to explore a variety of digital tools to produce or publish their writing.

Share Your Writing

 COLLABORATE

Review the speaking and listening strategies with children. Then have children share their writing with a partner or small group. You may wish to display their work on a bulletin board or in a classroom writing area.

SPEAKING STRATEGIES	LISTENING STRATEGIES
✔ Answer questions about details in complete sentences.	✔ Raise your hand if you have a question.
✔ Explain drawings as you share your words.	
✔ Ask questions to clarify information.	

Grammar

OPTION 5 mins

Irregular Verbs: *Is* and *Are*

1 **Review** Write the following sentences. Have children identify the verb and tell whether it refers to one or more than one:

Two mice are eating rice. (are, more than one)

A mole is in the hole. (is, one)

2 **Practice** Ask: *Why do we use the verb* are *in the first sentence? Why do we use the verb* is *in the second sentence?*

Have children change the subject of the first sentence to one mouse. Have them identify how the verb will change. Have them change *mole* to *moles* in the second sentence and do the same.

Mechanics: Commas in Dates

1 **Review** Remind children that in a date, commas separate the day and date number and the date number and the year.

2 **Practice** Write and read aloud the following sentences. Have children correct them.

Dave got a new bike on Friday March 27. 20 ___.
(Dave got a new bike on Friday, March 27, 20 ___.)
We are going to France on Thursday June, 30, 20 ___.
(We are going to France on Thursday, June 30, 20 ___.)

English Language Learners

Use with **Self-Selected Writing, Choose a Writing Activity.**

Present the writing activities, and tell children they will vote on one of the activities. Then you will work on the writing as a group. Make sure to do the activity on chart paper as you will revise and publish it during Small-Group time. Provide sentence frames and starters as you talk through the writing together. For example, if children have selected creating a comic strip, create a dialogue together. Then have children create come strips around that dialogue. Sentence frames might include: Let's play ___. I have to ___. I will ___ by candlelight. My friend is ___.

For small group support, see the **ELL Small Group Guide,** p. 145.

DIGITAL TOOLS

For more practice, use these activities.

I see a (fish).

Grammar

Mechanics

▶ TEACH IN SMALL GROUP

● **Approaching** Provide more opportunities for children to decide whether subjects and verbs agree before children change nouns and verbs in different sentences.

●● **On Level** and **Beyond** Children can do the Practice sections only.

● **ELL** Use the chart in the **Language Transfers Handbook** to identify grammatical forms that may cause difficulty.

FORMATIVE ASSESSMENT

▶ STUDENT CHECK-IN

Writing Have children reflect on how they used the speaking and listening strategies to share their writing.

Grammar Have partners tell each other how they know which verb to use in a sentence.

Have children reflect, using the Check-In routine.

LESSON 5

MULTIMODAL

LEARNING GOALS

We can compare a photograph to texts we have read.

OBJECTIVES

Identify basic similarities in and differences between two texts on the same topic.

ELA ACADEMIC LANGUAGE

• *compare, evidence*
• Cognates: *comparar, evidencia*

Close Reading Routine

Read DOK 1–2

• Identify important ideas and details.
• Take notes and retell.
• Use Ⓐ Ⓒ Ⓣ prompts as needed.

Reread DOK 2–3

• Analyze the text, craft, and structure.
• Use the Reread minilessons.

Integrate DOK 3–4

• Integrate knowledge and ideas.
• Make text-to-text connections.
• Complete the Show Your Knowledge task.
• Inspire action.

FORMATIVE ASSESSMENT

❯ STUDENT CHECK-IN

Have partners share how they compared the photograph and the text. Have children reflect, using the Check-In routine to fill in the bars.

Integrate

Make Connections

5 mins

Connect to the Essential Question DOK 4

COLLABORATE

Turn to page 146 in the **Reading/Writing Companion**. Help partners discuss the photograph. Use the first prompt as a guide.

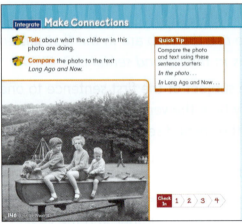

Reading/Writing Companion, p. 146

Dinah Zike's
FOLDABLES®
Study Organizer

Find Text Evidence Read aloud the second prompt. Guide partners to discuss connections between the photograph and pictures in *Long Ago and Now.* Use the Quick Tip box for support.

Compare Texts Guide partners to compare what they see in the photo with any of the photos from "From Horse to Plane." Children can record their notes using a Foldable® like the one shown here. Guide children to record details that help them answer the Essential Question.

Build Knowledge: Make Connections

Talk About the Text Have partners discuss how the photograph tells a story of long ago and how it relates to other texts they read this week.

Add to the Anchor Chart Record any new ideas on the Build Knowledge anchor chart.

Add to the Word Bank Add words related to long ago to a separate section of the Word Bank.

Integrate

Show Your Knowledge

10 mins

Write a Letter DOK 4

Display the Build Knowledge anchor chart about life long ago. Have children lead a discussion about what they have learned. Then have children turn to page 147 in their **Reading/Writing Companions**. Guide children through the steps below to write a letter telling about the present.

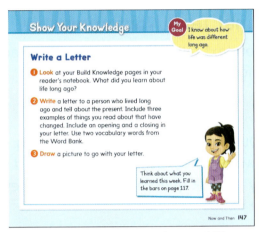

Reading/Writing Companion, p. 147

Step 1 Have children read through the Build Knowledge pages of their reader's notebooks to review what they learned about life long ago. Then have partners talk about how things have changed.

Step 2 Provide each child with a sheet of paper. Have children write a letter to a person who lived long ago and tell them about the present. Have children use three examples of things they read about that have changed. Have children use two vocabulary words from the Word Bank. Remind children to include an opening and a closing in their letters.

Step 3 Have children draw a picture to go with their letters.

Inspire Action

You may choose to extend the learning with the activities below.

Visit a Senior Center With the permission of parents or guardians, organize a trip to a local senior center. Have children think of a question to ask an older person about their early life.

Museum Have children set up a museum in the classroom to display their letters and pictures. Invite other classes and parents. Have children read their letters to the visitors.

Choose Your Own Action Have children talk about the texts they read this week. Ask: *What do these texts inspire you to do?*

LEARNING GOALS

We can show what we've learned about how life was different long ago.

OBJECTIVES

Describe people, places, things, and events with relevant details, expressing ideas and feelings clearly.

Use words and phrases acquired through conversations, reading and being read to, and responding to texts.

ELA ACADEMIC LANGUAGE

• *letter*

ELL ENGLISH LANGUAGE LEARNERS

Show Your Knowledge, Step 2 Provide and model sentence frames and/or starters to help children write their letters. For example: I would like to tell you about ___. One thing that has changed is ___. Another thing is ___. You had ___, but now we have ___.

DIGITAL TOOLS

RUBRIC   Show Your Knowledge Rubric

MY GOALS ROUTINE

What I Learned

Review Goals Have children turn to page 117 of the **Reading/Writing Companion** and review the goals for the week.

Reflect Have children think about the progress they've made toward the goals. Review the key if needed. Have children fill in the bars.

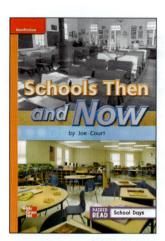

Lexile 170

● Approaching Level

Leveled Reader: *Schools Then and Now*

Preview and Predict

Have children turn to the title page. Read the title and the author's name, and have children repeat them. Preview the selection's photographs. Prompt children to predict what the selection might be about.

Review Genre: Informational Text: Nonfiction

Have children recall that nonfiction text tells about real people, places, things, or events by presenting information and facts about them.

Set Purpose

Remind children of the Essential Question. Set a purpose for reading: *Let's read to find out how schools long ago were like our schools today.* Remind children that as they read a selection, they can ask questions about what they do not understand or want to know more about.

Guided Comprehension

As children whisper-read *Schools Then and Now* independently or with a partner, monitor and provide guidance. Correct blending, and model the key strategies and skills as needed. Also provide definitions for words unfamiliar to children.

Reread

Model rereading: *At the end of page 2, I was confused by reading that some boys and girls used horses. Used horses for what? When I reread the page, I understood that long ago they used horses to get to school.* Remind children that as they read, if they don't understand something, they can reread the page or an earlier section.

Details: Compare and Contrast

Distribute Graphic Organizer 8 to children. Have them label the outer circles *Long Ago* and *Now* and the interlocking circle *Both*. Remind children that they can compare and contrast the details in a selection to help them better understand it. While reading, ask: *How were schools long ago like schools today? How were they different?* Display Compare and Contrast chart 8 for children to copy.

Model recording children's answers in the chart. Have children copy the answers into their own charts.

Think Aloud On page 2, I read that children long ago walked to school or used horses. I can write "by horse" in the *Long Ago* part of the chart. I can read on to fill in the parts labeled *Now* and *Both*.

Guide children to use text and illustrations to complete the chart.

Respond to Reading Have children complete Respond to Reading on page 12.

Retell Have children take turns retelling the selection, using the **Retelling Cards** as a guide. Help children make a personal connection: *What would you have liked about schools long ago? What would you miss about school today?*

Fluency: Accuracy and Rate

Model Model reading page 2 with accuracy and at an appropriate rate. Read aloud. Have children read along with you.

Apply Have children practice reading the text with a partner. Correct any errors as needed.

Paired Read: "School Days"

 Make Connections: Write About It

Before reading, ask children to note that the genre of this text is nonfiction. Discuss the Compare Texts question in the Leveled Reader.

After reading, ask children to tell one thing they learned in both *Schools Then and Now* and "School Days." Then have children tell how the selections are different.

Leveled Reader

Build Knowledge: Make Connections

 Talk About the Texts Have partners discuss how the texts tell about life long ago and today.

 Write About the Texts Have children add their ideas to the Build Knowledge page of their reader's notebooks.

LITERATURE CIRCLES

Lead children in conducting a literature circle using the Thinkmark questions to guide the discussion. You may wish to discuss what children have learned about schools long ago from both selections in the **Leveled Reader**.

FOCUS ON SOCIAL STUDIES

Children can extend their knowledge of how they get to school by completing the social studies activity on page 16.

 LEVEL UP

IF children can read *Schools Then and Now* Approaching Level with fluency and correctly answer the Respond to Reading questions,

THEN tell children they will read a more detailed version of the selection.

• Have children read the selection, checking their comprehension by using the Compare and Contrast graphic organizer.

Approaching Level

Phonemic Awareness

PHONEME ISOLATION

TIER 2

OBJECTIVES
Isolate and pronounce medial vowel sounds (phonemes) in spoken single-syllable words.

I Do *Listen carefully. I'm going to say a word and then say the middle sound in the word: /bōōōnnn/; the middle sound is /ō/. Say the sound with me: /ōōō/. Repeat with cube.*

We Do *Let's do some together. I'll say a word slowly. We'll all repeat the word and then say the middle sound. Here's the word: /kūūūb/. Let's say the middle sound together: /ūūū/.*

Repeat this routine with the following examples:

these   lace   rope   huge   mice   joke

You Do *It's your turn. Tell me the middle sound you hear in each word.*

choke   zone   maze   cute   bean   rise

Repeat the isolation routine with additional long-vowel words.

PHONEME SEGMENTATION

TIER 2

OBJECTIVES
Segment spoken single-syllable words into their complete sequence of individual sounds (phonemes).

I Do *I am going to say a word. I'll say it slowly: /haaammm/. Now I'll say the sounds in the word. I'll raise a finger for each sound: /h/ /aaa/ /mmm/. Ham has three sounds.*

We Do *Let's do some together. I am going to say a word. Then let's repeat the word slowly. Raise a finger for each sound you hear and tell how many sounds.*

ape   such   shell   mule   stone   these   joke

You Do *It's your turn. I'll say a word. Raise a finger for each sound you hear and tell how many sounds.*

fish   prune   rose   clove   tune   bag   glad

Repeat the segmentation routine with additional long-vowel words.

PHONEME BLENDING

OBJECTIVES

Orally produce single-syllable words by blending sounds (phonemes), including consonant blends.

I Do Explain to children that they will blend sounds to form words. *Listen as I say three sounds. The first sound is /h/. The middle sound is /ū/. The ending sound is /j/. I'll put the sounds together to make a word: /h/ /ū/ /j/, /hūūūj/,* huge.

We Do *Listen as I say two sounds. The first sound is /ē/. The second sound is /v/. Let's blend the sounds: /ē/ /v/, /ēēēvvv/,* eve. Repeat the routine with these sounds:

/p/ /ē/ /t/   /t/ /ō/ /n/   /ch/ /a/ /t/   /r/ /ō/ /p/   /k/ /ū/ /t/

You Do *Now it's your turn. Blend the sounds I say to make a word.*

/y/ /e/ /l/   /g/ /r/ /ā/ /t/   /th/ /ō/ /z/   /k/ /ū/ /t/

Repeat the blending routine with additional long-vowel words.

PHONEME SEGMENTATION

OBJECTIVES

Segment spoken single-syllable words into their complete sequence of individual sounds (phonemes).

Count phonemes in spoken words.

I Do Explain to children that they will segment words into sounds. *Listen as I say a word:* late. *I can hear three sounds in the word* late: /lll/ /āāā/ /t/.

We Do *Let's do some together. I'll say a word:* tack. *How many sounds do you hear?* (3) *The sounds in* tack *are /t/ /a/ /k/.*

Repeat the routine with these words:

batch (3)   same (3)   mule (3)   dent (4)   leave (3)   mute (3)

You Do *It's your turn, I'll say a word. You tell me how many sounds you hear and what they are.*

bone (3)   smoke (4)   lodge (3)   muse (3)   whole (3)   luck (3)

ELL You may wish to review phonemic awareness, phonics, decoding, and fluency using this section. Use scaffolding methods as necessary to ensure children understand the meaning of the words. Refer to the **Language Transfers Handbook** for phonics elements that may not transfer in children's native languages.

●Approaching Level

Phonics

CONNECT /ō/, /ū/, /ē/ *to o_e, u_e, e_e*

OBJECTIVES

Know final -e and common vowel team conventions for representing long vowel sounds.

I Do Display **Word-Building Card** o_e. *These are the lowercase letters* o *and* e. *I am going to trace the letters* o_e *while I say /ō/.* Trace the letters o_e while saying /ōōō/. Repeat with u_e and e_e.

We Do *Let's do it together.* Have children trace the lowercase o_e with their fingers while saying /ō/ with you. Repeat with /ū/ u_e and /ē/ e_e.

You Do Have children connect the letters o_e to the sound /ō/ by tracing lowercase o_e with their fingers while saying /ōōō/. After children have traced on paper five times, have them write the letters o_e while saying /ōōō/. Repeat with u_e and e_e. Provide feedback as needed.

Repeat and connect the o_e, u_e, and e_e spellings with their respective long-vowel sounds throughout the week.

BLEND WITH /ō/ *o_e,* /ū/ *u_e,* /ē/ *e_e*

OBJECTIVES

Know final -e and common vowel team conventions for representing long vowel sounds.

Decode regularly spelled one-syllable words.

I Do Display **Word-Building Cards** c, o, n, and e. *This is the letter* c. *It stands for /k/. Say it with me: /k/. These are the letters* o *and* e. *Together they stand for /ō/. Let's say the sound together: /ō/. This is the letter* n. *I'll blend the sounds together: /kōōōnnn/,* cone.

We Do Guide children to blend the sounds and read: *hope, huge, these, chose,* and *theme.*

You Do Help children blend and decode: *vote, mute, cute,* and *Steve.*

Repeat, blending additional o_e, u_e, and e_e words.

You may wish to practice reading and decoding with **ELL** using this section.

BUILD WITH /ō/ o_e, /ū/ u_e, /ē/ e_e

OBJECTIVES

Know final -e and common vowel team conventions for representing long vowel sounds.

Decode regularly spelled one-syllable words.

I Do Display **Word-Building Cards** b, o, n, and e. *These are the letters* b, o, n, e. *They stand for* /b/ /ō/ /n/. *The* o *and* e *together stand for* /ō/. *I will blend* /b/ /ō/ /n/ *together:* /bōōōnnn/, bone. *The word is* bone.

We Do *Now let's do one together.* Point to the cards forming *bone,* and change the letter b to c. *Let's blend and read the new word:* /kōōōnnn/, cone.

You Do Have children build and decode the words: *cope, rope, robe, rose, role, fume, muse,* and *Pete.* Provide feedback as needed.

READ WORDS WITH /ō/ o_e, /ū/ u_e, /ē/ e_e

OBJECTIVES

Read grade-level text orally with accuracy, appropriate rate, and expression on successive readings.

Unit 3 Decodable Reader pages 37–48

Focus on Foundational Skills

Review the high-frequency words *ago, boy, girl, how, old* and *people* with children. Review sounds for each of the long vowels *o, u,* and *e.* Guide children to blend the sounds to read the words.

Read the Decodable Readers

Guide children to read "Those Old Classes" and "That Old Globe." Point out the high-frequency words and words that contain long vowels with VC*e* spellings. If children struggle sounding out words, model blending.

Focus on Fluency

With partners, have children reread the **Decodable Reader** selections. As children read the text, guide them to focus on their accuracy, rate, and automaticity. Children can provide feedback to their partners.

BUILD FLUENCY WITH PHONICS

Sound/Spellings Fluency

Display the following Word-Building Cards: *o_e, u_e, e_e, dge, i_e, a_e, ch, tch, wh, ph, th, sh, ng, mp, sk, st, nt, nk, nd, e, ea, sp, sn, sl, cr,* and *fr.* Have children chorally say the sounds. Repeat, and vary the pace.

Fluency in Connected Text

Have children review the Decodable Reader selections. Identify words with long *o, u, e,* and blend words as needed.

Have partners reread the selections for fluency.

● Approaching Level

Structural Analysis

REVIEW CVCe SYLLABLES

OBJECTIVES

Use knowledge that every syllable must have a vowel sound to determine the number of syllables in a printed word.

Decode two-syllable words following basic patterns by breaking the words into syllables.

I Do Write the word *explode*, and read it. *This word has two vowel sounds and two syllables. The syllables are* ex *and* plode. *I hear the /e/ vowel sound in* ex. Circle *plode. This syllable has an* o *and a silent* e. *They work together to stand for the long* o *vowel sound. The syllable is /*plllōōōd/. *The word is* explode.

We Do Write *awake*, and read the word together. *The word has two syllables,* a *and* wake. Draw a line to divide the syllables. Point out the *a_e.* Have children say *wake*. Then have them read the word. Remind children that they may need to approximate the /a/ sound to sound out the word *awake*.

You Do Have children identify the syllables in these words and say the words: *suppose, amuse, these, complete.* Provide feedback as needed.

Repeat Have partners read and write the above words in sentences.

RETEACH CVCe SYLLABLES

OBJECTIVES

Use knowledge that every syllable must have a vowel sound to determine the number of syllables in a printed word.

Decode two-syllable words following basic patterns by breaking the words into syllables.

I Do Remind children that words have syllables and that a syllable has one vowel sound. Then write *bedtime*. Draw a line between the two syllables. *I hear the /e/ vowel sound in* bed *and the /ī/ sound in* time. Point to the letters *i* and *e. When I see a final* e *spelling in a word, I know that two vowels are working together to stand for one sound. They are in the same syllable.*

We Do *Let's do one together.* Write *pancake. Let's say the word together. How many syllables does it have? What are they? Yes,* pan *and* cake. Draw a line between the syllables. *Let's read the word.*

You Do Write the following words. Have children divide them into syllables. Have them read each word. Provide feedback as needed.

dislike   explode   handshake   sunrise   amuse

Repeat Have children continue to identify and read CVCe syllables.

You may wish to review structural analysis and high-frequency words with **ELL** using this section.

High-Frequency Words

REVIEW

OBJECTIVES
Recognize and read grade-appropriate irregularly spelled words.

I Do Use the **High-Frequency Word Cards** to Read/Spell/Write *ago, boy, girl, how, old,* and *people.* Use each word orally in a sentence.

We Do Guide children to Read/Spell/Write each word on their **Response Boards.** Help children create oral sentences that include the words.

You Do Have partners do the Read/Spell/Write routine on their own, using the words *ago, boy, girl, how, old,* and *people.*

RETEACH

OBJECTIVES
Recognize and read grade-appropriate irregularly spelled words.

I Do Review the high-frequency words using the Read/Spell/Write routine. Write a sentence for each high-frequency word.

We Do Guide children with the Read/Spell/Write routine. Use sentence starters: *(1) Two days ago, we ____. (2) The boy walked ____. (3) The girl moved ____. (4) How did you like ____? (5) How old is ____? (6) The people line up ____.*

You Do *Now close your eyes and picture the word. Open your eyes, and write the word.* Have children self-correct.

CUMULATIVE REVIEW

OBJECTIVES
Recognize and read grade-appropriate irregularly spelled words.

I Do Display the High-Frequency Word Cards from the previous five weeks. Review each word, using the Read/Spell/Write routine.

We Do Have children write each word on their Response Boards. Complete sentences for each word, such as: *The green jacket is ____. Let's walk to ____.*

You Do Show each card. Have children read the word. Mix the cards, and repeat.

Fluency Display the High-Frequency Word Cards. Point to the words randomly. Have children chorally read each word. Repeat at a faster pace.

Approaching Level

Comprehension

READ FOR FLUENCY

TIER 2

OBJECTIVES

Read grade-level text orally with accuracy, appropriate rate, and expression on successive readings.

Set Purpose Tell children they will now focus on reading **Leveled Reader** *Schools Then and Now*. Remind them this story is nonfiction and they will be reading it to learn about the past. Tell children they need to read with accuracy and at an appropriate rate.

I Do Read the first sentence of *Schools Then and Now*. Point out how you read the text so it sounds like speech. Say: *I read each word carefully, and I make sure I don't read too fast or too slow. Listen*. Read the sentence again.

We Do Read the next sentences aloud, and have children repeat them. Remind children to read with accuracy and at an appropriate rate.

You Do *It's your turn*. Have children read the rest of the selection aloud. Provide feedback on accuracy and rate as needed.

IDENTIFY RELEVANT DETAILS

TIER 2

OBJECTIVES

Identify the main topic and retell relevant, or key, details of a text.

I Do Remind children they have been reading a nonfiction text. As they read this type of selection, they can look for relevant, or important, details. *We can find important details in the pictures and in the text.*

We Do Read aloud the first two pages of *Schools Then and Now*. Point out the relevant details in each sentence. Discuss why they are important. Say: *We found out that boys and girls walked far to get to school.* Continue reading. *What did some children use to get to school?*

You Do Guide children to read the rest of the selection. Then ask them to restate relevant details. Provide feedback as needed.

REVIEW DETAILS: COMPARE AND CONTRAST

OBJECTIVES

Describe the connection between two individuals, events, ideas, or pieces of information in a text.

I Do Remind children that they can compare and contrast the details in a nonfiction text to help them better understand it. Say: *Readers can think about how ideas or events are alike and different. Making these connections helps readers understand a selection better.*

We Do Read pages 2–3 of **Leveled Reader** *Schools Then and Now* together. Have children use details to think about how ideas are alike and different. Say: *We read about the ways boys and girls traveled to school long ago and how they travel to school today. In what way are they the same?*

You Do Guide children to finish reading the selection. Pause, and have children ask questions such as: *How are these ideas alike? How are they different?* Help children record the information on a Compare and Contrast chart. Then discuss the similarities and differences they found.

SELF-SELECTED READING

OBJECTIVES

Describe the connection between two individuals, events, ideas, or pieces of information in a text.

Read grade-level text with purpose and understanding.

Independent Reading

Help children select a nonfiction selection for independent reading. Children may use the **Classroom Library,** the **Leveled Reader Library,** the online **Unit Bibliography,** or other books for their independent reading. Encourage children to read for at least ten minutes.

Guide children to transfer what they learned this week as they read. Remind children that they can compare and contrast the details in a selection to help them better understand the text. Tell them to think about how the details in the text are alike and different. Have children record their comparisons and contrasts on **Graphic Organizer 8.**

After children read, guide them to participate in a group discussion about the text they read. In addition, children can choose activities from the Reading **Center Activity Cards** to help them apply skills to the text as they read. Offer assistance and guidance with self-selected assignments.

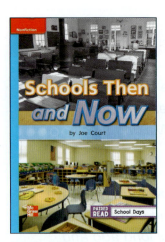

Lexile 220

OBJECTIVES

Describe the connection between two individuals, events, ideas, or pieces of information in a text.

Read grade-level text with purpose and understanding.

Read grade-level text orally with accuracy, appropriate rate, and expression on successive readings.

Identify basic similarities in and differences between two texts on the same topic.

Reread text for understanding.

ELA ACADEMIC LANGUAGE

• *compare, contrast*
• Cognates: *comparar, contrastar*

●On Level

Leveled Reader: *Schools Then and Now*

Preview and Predict

Have children turn to the title page. Read the title and author's name, and have children repeat them. Preview the selection's photographs. Prompt children to predict what the selection might be about.

Review Genre: Informational Text: Nonfiction

Have children recall that nonfiction texts tell about real people, places, things, or events by presenting information and facts about them.

Set Purpose

Remind children of the Essential Question. Set a purpose for reading: *Let's read to see how schools were the same and different long ago and now.* Remind children that as they read a selection, they can ask questions about what they do not understand or want to know more about.

Guided Comprehension

As children read *Schools Then and Now* independently or with a partner, monitor and provide guidance. Correct blending, and model the key strategies and skills as needed. Also provide definitions for words unfamiliar to children.

Reread

Model rereading: *On page 4, I read that the teacher was outside. Is that where she taught the class? I will reread the page.* Reread page 4 aloud. *Now I understand. The teacher waits for the children outside before class.* Remind children that if something doesn't make sense as they read, they can reread a passage.

Details: Compare and Contrast

Distribute Graphic Organizer 8 to children. Have them label the outer circles *Long Ago* and *Now* and the interlocking circle *Both*. Remind children that comparing and contrasting information can help them understand the selection. While reading, ask: *How are schools today like schools of long ago? How are they different?* Display Compare and Contrast chart 8 for children to copy. Model recording children's answers in the chart. Have children copy the answers into their own charts.

Think Aloud On pages 2 and 3 I read about how children traveled to school. I can write "by horse" in the *Long Ago* part of the chart. I can write "by car" in the *Now* part. I can write "walked" in the *Both* part.

Guide children to use the text and pictures to add to their charts.

Respond to Reading Have children complete Respond to Reading on page 12.

Retell Have children take turns retelling the selection, using the **Retelling Cards** as a guide. Help children make a connection by asking: *Do you think you would have liked going to school long ago? Why or why not? What would you miss most from what school is like today?*

Fluency: Accuracy and Rate

Model Model reading page 2 with accuracy and at an appropriate rate. Read aloud. Have children read along with you.

Apply Have children practice reading the text with a partner. Correct any errors as needed.

Paired Read: "School Days"

 Make Connections: Write About It

Before reading, ask children to note that the genre of this text is also nonfiction. Discuss the Compare Texts question in the Leveled Reader.

After reading, ask children to tell one thing they learned in both *Schools Then and Now* and "School Days."

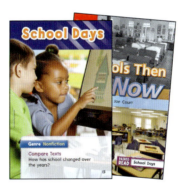

Leveled Reader

Build Knowledge: Make Connections

 Talk About the Texts Have partners discuss how the texts tell about life long ago and today.

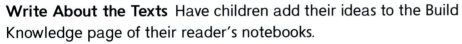 **Write About the Texts** Have children add their ideas to the Build Knowledge page of their reader's notebooks.

LITERATURE CIRCLES

Lead children in conducting a literature circle using the Thinkmark questions to guide the discussion. You may wish to discuss what children have learned about schools from long ago in both selections in the **Leveled Reader**.

 FOCUS ON SOCIAL STUDIES

Children can extend their knowledge of how they get to school by completing the social studies activity on page 16.

 **LEVEL** UP

IF children can read *Schools Then and Now* On Level with fluency and correctly answer the Respond to Reading questions,

THEN tell children they will read a more detailed version of the selection.

- Have children read the selection, checking their comprehension by using the Compare and Contrast graphic organizer.

● On Level

Phonics

BUILD WORDS WITH /ō/ o_e, /ū/ u_e, /ē/ e_e

OBJECTIVES

Know final -e and common vowel team conventions for representing long vowel sounds.

Decode regularly spelled one-syllable words.

Unit 3 Decodable Reader pages 37–48

I Do Display **Word-Building Cards** h, o, l, and e. *These are the letters* h, o, l, e. *The letters* o *and* e *work together to stand for the long* o *sound, so these letters stand for /h/ /ō/ /l/. I will blend these sounds: /hōōōlll/, hole. The word is* hole.

We Do *Let's do it together.* Change *hole* to *role* using Word-Building Cards. Have children blend and say the word.

You Do Have children build and blend these words: *mole, mule, muse, mute, cute.*

Read the Decodable Readers

Guide children to read "Those Old Classes" and "That Old Globe." Identify the high-frequency words and words that contain long vowel sounds with VC*e* spellings. Model blending sound-by-sound as needed.

Focus on Fluency With partners, have children reread the **Decodable Reader** stories. As children read the text, guide them to focus on accuracy, rate, and automaticity. They can provide feedback to their partners.

High-Frequency Words

REVIEW WORDS

OBJECTIVES

Recognize and read grade-appropriate irregularly spelled words.

I Do Use the Read/Spell/Write routine to review *ago, boy, girl, how, old,* and *people.* Use each word orally in a sentence.

We Do Help children Read/Spell/Write each word, using their **Response Boards**. Then work with the group to generate oral sentences using the words.

You Do Have partners do the Read/Spell/Write routine on their own with *ago, boy, girl, how, old,* and *people.* Have them write sentences about this week's selections. Each sentence must contain at least one high-frequency word.

Comprehension

REVIEW DETAILS: COMPARE AND CONTRAST

OBJECTIVES

Describe the connection between two individuals, events, ideas, or pieces of information in a text.

I Do Remind children they can compare and contrast the details in a nonfiction text to help them better understand it. Say: *You can use details to think about how things are alike and different.*

We Do Read aloud the first two pages of **Leveled Reader** *Schools Then and Now.* Ask children to compare and contrast how children went to school long ago with how they go to school today. *How was it different from today? How was it alike?*

You Do *It's your turn.* Guide children to read the remainder of the selection. Then help them compare and contrast the details.

SELF-SELECTED READING

OBJECTIVES

Describe the connection between two individuals, events, ideas, or pieces of information in a text.

Read grade-level text with purpose and understanding.

Independent Reading

Help children select a nonfiction selection for independent reading. Children may use the **Classroom Library,** the **Leveled Reader Library,** the online **Unit Bibliography,** or other books for their independent reading. Encourage children to read for at least ten minutes.

Guide children to transfer what they learned this week as they read. Remind children that they can compare and contrast the details in a selection to help them better understand the text. Tell them to think about how the details in the text are alike and different. Have children record their comparisons and contrasts on **Graphic Organizer 8.**

After children read, guide them to participate in a group discussion about the text they read. In addition, children can choose activities from the Reading **Center Activity Cards** to help them apply skills to the text as they read. Offer assistance and guidance with self-selected assignments.

You may wish to review Comprehension with **ELL** using this section.

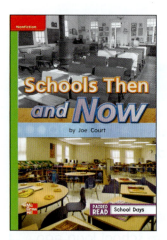

Lexile 380

OBJECTIVES

Describe the connection between two individuals, events, ideas, or pieces of information in a text.

Read grade-level text with purpose and understanding.

Identify basic similarities in and differences between two texts on the same topic.

Reread text for understanding.

ELA ACADEMIC LANGUAGE

• compare, contrast
• Cognates: comparar, contrastar

● Beyond Level

Leveled Reader: *Schools Then and Now*

Preview and Predict

Read the title and author's name. Have children preview the title page and the photographs. Ask: *What do you think this book will be about?*

Review Genre: Informational Text: Nonfiction

Have children recall that nonfiction texts tell about real people, places, things, or events by presenting information and facts about them.

Set Purpose

Remind children of the Essential Question. Set a purpose for reading: *What do you want to find out about schools long ago? As you prepare to read this fluently, think about the purpose.*

Guided Comprehension

Have children whisper-read *Schools Then and Now* independently or with a partner. Have them place self-stick notes next to difficult words. Monitor and provide guidance. Correct blending, and model the key strategies and skills as needed.

Monitor children's reading. Stop periodically, and ask open-ended questions to facilitate rich discussion, such as, *What does the author want us to know about schools long ago?* Build on children's responses to develop deeper understanding.

Reread

Model rereading: *On page 6, we learn what a classroom might have looked like. If I don't understand why the classroom had a stove, I can reread the page. If I still don't understand, I can go back to a previous page to help me.* Remind children to reread if they don't understand something in a selection.

Details: Compare and Contrast

Distribute Graphic Organizer 8 to children. Have them label the outer circles *Long Ago* and *Now* and the interlocking circle *Both*. Remind children that comparing and contrasting information can help them better understand a selection. While reading, ask: *How are schools today like schools of long ago? How are they different?* Display Compare and Contrast chart 8 for children to copy. Model how to record the information. Have children fill in their charts.

Think Aloud On pages 2 and 3, I read about how children traveled to school. I will use this information to fill in the chart.

Have children fill in the chart as they read.

Respond to Reading Have children complete Respond to Reading on page 11 after reading.

Retell Have children take turns retelling the selection. Help them make a personal connection by writing about school long ago. *Write about what you think a school day long ago was like. How would you get to school? What would you do? What would the school look like?*

Paired Read: "School Days"

 Make Connections: Write About It

Before reading, ask children to preview the title page, and prompt them to identify the genre as nonfiction. Then have children discuss the Compare Texts question in the Leveled Reader.

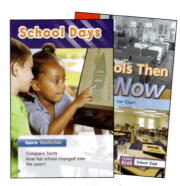

After reading the selection, have partners discuss what they learned from *Schools Then and Now* and "School Days."

Leveled Reader

Build Knowledge: Make Connections

 Talk About the Texts Have partners discuss how the texts tell about life long ago and today.

Write About the Texts Have children add their ideas to the Build Knowledge page of their reader's notebooks.

LITERATURE CIRCLES

Lead children in conducting a literature circle using the Thinkmark questions to guide the discussion. You may wish to discuss what children have learned about schools from both selections in the **Leveled Reader**.

FOCUS ON SOCIAL STUDIES

Children can extend their knowledge about schools today by completing the social studies activity on page 16.

⊕ GIFTED AND TALENTED

Synthesize Challenge children to think of what children long ago learned in school. Encourage them to think of what things might be the same or similar and what things might be different.

Extend Have children use facts from the week's texts and what they have learned from other sources or research to find out about subjects and schoolbooks from long ago. They might find information in books or by asking older family members.

● Beyond Level

Vocabulary

ORAL VOCABULARY: MULTIPLE-MEANING WORDS

OBJECTIVES

Use sentence-level context as a clue to the meaning of a word or phrase.

Understand multiple-meaning words.

I Do Explain that some words have more than one meaning. These words are spelled the same way but can mean different things based on how they are used.

Let's look at the word present. *The word* present *can mean that someone is talking about right now, or it can mean a gift. We know what the word means because of how it's used in a sentence.* With children, create an oral sentence for each meaning of *present*.

Now let's look at the word past. *This week we've been looking at* past *as in a time that has come before now, but* past *has another meaning. You can drive past something in a car. The word* past *can also mean "by and beyond something."*

We Do Help children make sentences for the different meanings of *present* and *past*.

You Do Have partners think of four sentences, one for each meaning of the words *present* and *past*. Ask pairs to share their sentences with the class.

⭐ GIFTED and TALENTED **Extend** Have children plan and perform a short play using the different meanings of the words *present* and *past*.

Comprehension

REVIEW DETAILS: COMPARE AND CONTRAST

OBJECTIVES
Describe the connection between two individuals, events, ideas, or pieces of information in a text.

I Do Discuss how children can use details to compare and contrast information as they read. Children can think about how people, events, and ideas are alike and different.

We Do Ask children to read the first two pages of **Leveled Reader** *Schools Then and Now* aloud. Have them discuss how children traveled to school long ago and today. Talk about how the transportation is alike and different.

You Do Have children read the rest of the selection independently. Ask them to compare and contrast details in the selection. Ask: *How were the insides of the classrooms long ago like the classrooms today? How were they different?*

SELF-SELECTED READING

OBJECTIVES
Describe the connection between two individuals, events, ideas, or pieces of information in a text.

Read grade-level text with purpose and understanding.

Independent Reading

Help children select a nonfiction selection for independent reading. Children may use the **Classroom Library,** the **Leveled Reader Library,** the online **Unit Bibliography,** or other books for their independent reading. Encourage children to read for at least ten minutes.

Guide children to transfer what they learned this week as they read. Remind children that they can compare and contrast the details in a selection to help them better understand the text. Tell them to think about how the details in the text are alike and different. Have children record their comparisons and contrasts on **Graphic Organizer 8.**

After children read, guide them to participate in a group discussion about the text they read. In addition, children can choose activities from the Reading **Center Activity Cards** to help them apply skills to the text as they read. Offer assistance and guidance with self-selected assignments.

GIFTED and TALENTED **Independent Study** Have children discuss their self-selected reading with a partner. Challenge them to compare and contrast their selections with a selection they read this week and write a book report.

Student Outcomes

✓ Tested in *Wonders* Assessments

FOUNDATIONAL SKILLS

Print Concepts
- Locate title, author

Phonological Awareness
✓ Phoneme Segmentation
✓ Phoneme Deletion
✓ Phoneme Blending

Phonics and Word Analysis
✓ Variant vowel spellings with digraphs: *oo, u*
✓ Inflectional endings *-ed, -ing*

Fluency
- Read with accuracy and automaticity
✓ High-Frequency Words
- *after   buy   done   every   soon   work*

READING

Reading Literature
- Read prose and poetry appropriately complex for grade 1

Reading Informational Text
✓ Use text features including diagrams to locate key facts or information
✓ Identify the topic of and relevant details in a text
- Retell a text to enhance comprehension
- Read informational texts appropriately complex for grade 1

Compare Texts
- Compare and contrast two texts on the same topic

COMMUNICATION

Writing
- Handwriting: *Bb*
- Write opinions about a topic or text with at least one supporting reason from a source and a sense of closure
- Focus on a topic, respond to suggestions from peers, and add details to strengthen writing

Speaking and Listening
- Participate in collaborative conversations
- Ask and answer questions to gather or clarify information
- Present information orally using complete sentences

Conventions
✓ **Grammar:** Form contractions with not
- **Mechanics:** Use apostrophes to form contractions
- **Spelling:** Spell words with *ook, ood*

Researching
- Recall or gather information to answer a question
- Participate in shared research and writing projects

Creating and Collaborating
- Add drawings and visual displays to descriptions
- Use digital tools to produce and publish writing

VOCABULARY

Academic Vocabulary
- Acquire and use grade-appropriate academic vocabulary
- Identify real-life connections between words and their use

ELL Scaffolded supports for English Language Learners are embedded throughout the lessons, enabling children to communicate information, ideas, and concepts in English Language Arts and for social and instructional purposes within the school setting.

See the **ELL Small Group Guide** for additional support of the skills for the text set.

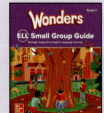

FORMATIVE ASSESSMENT

For assessment throughout the text set, use children's self-assessments and your observations.

Use the Data Dashboard to filter class, group, or individual student data to guide group placement decisions. It provides recommendations to enhance learning for gifted and talented children and offers extra support for children needing remediation.

DATA DASHBOARD

Develop Student Ownership

To build student ownership, children need to know what they are learning, why they are learning it, and determine how well they understood it.

Students Discuss Their Goals

TEXT SET GOALS

- I can read and understand a nonfiction text.
- I can write an opinion about a nonfiction text.
- I know about different ways we get our food.

Have children think about what they know and fill in the bars on **Reading/Writing Companion** page 150.

EXTENDED WRITING GOALS

- I can write a nonfiction text.

See **Reading/Writing Companion** page 178.

Students Monitor Their Learning

LEARNING GOALS

Specific learning goals identified in every lesson make clear what children will be learning and why. These smaller goals provide stepping stones to help children meet their Text Set Goals.

CHECK-IN ROUTINE

The Check-In routine at the close of each lesson guides children to self-reflect on how well they understood each learning goal.

Review the lesson learning goal.
Reflect on the activity.
Self-Assess by
- filling in the bars in the **Reading/Writing Companion.**
- holding up 1, 2, 3, or 4 fingers.

Share with your teacher.

Students Reflect on Their Progress

TEXT SET GOALS

After completing the Show Your Knowledge task for the text set, children reflect on their understanding of the Text Set Goals by filling in the bars on **Reading/Writing Companion** page 151.

EXTENDED WRITING GOALS

After children complete the evaluation of their writing, they reflect on their ability to write a nonfiction text by filling in the bars on **Reading/Writing Companion** page 197.

Build Knowledge

Literature Big Book

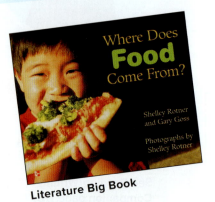
Shared Read
Reading/Writing Companion p. 152

Anchor Text
Literature Anthology p. 96

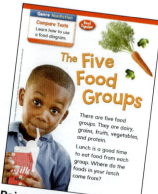
Paired Selection
Literature Anthology p. 104

Essential Question
How do we get our food?

 Video Fruits and vegetables start out as seeds. They are planted and, once they're grown, they're picked and brought to stores for us to buy.

Literature Big Book Foods are made in interesting ways. For example, French fries are made by cutting and cooking potatoes. Peanut butter is made by grinding peanuts.

Shared Read It takes work to make breakfast foods. For example, grape jam starts off as grapes on a vine. The grapes are picked, crushed, and cooked into jam, which is bought in stores.

Interactive Read Aloud A little red hen plants and picks corn alone because no one will help her. When she makes delicious corn tortillas, she enjoys them all herself.

Anchor Text We get milk from cows. Dairy farmers milk the cows. Milk trucks take the milk to dairies. The milk is cooked. Then it is put into cartons or jugs and sent to stores.

Paired Selection We get healthy food from the different food groups: dairy, grains, fruits, vegetables, and protein.

 Art Workers pick olives from olive trees.

Differentiated Sources

Leveled Readers 🔊

Apples start from seeds. The seeds grow into trees. Apples grow on the trees. The apples are picked, washed, waxed, and shipped to stores. Then people can buy and eat them.

Build Knowledge Routine

After reading each text, ask children to document facts and details they learned that help them answer the Essential Question of the text set.

 Talk about the source.

 Write about the source.

 Add to the class Anchor Chart

• Add to the Word Bank.

Show Your Knowledge

Write a Nonfiction Text

Have children think about what they learned regarding how people get food. Guide them to write and illustrate a nonfiction text about workers who provide food. Have children use vocabulary words and text evidence to help them describe how the workers do their jobs.

Social Emotional Learning

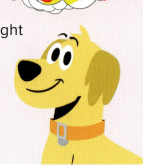

Teachable Moment

Take a moment to reflect on children's developing skills on assessed or previously-taught SEL competencies. Then, select an SEL lesson from your library of resources to meet children's individualized needs, and integrate it into your weekly plan.

Family Time • Share your selected SEL lesson's video and activity in the **School to Home** newsletter.

WEEK 5

Explore the Texts

Essential Question: How do we get our food?

Literature Big Book	Interactive Read Aloud	Reading/Writing Companion	Literature Anthology
		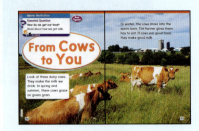	

Where Does Food Come From? Informational Text	**"The Little Red Hen"** Folktale	**"A Look at Breakfast"** Shared Read pp. 152–161 Informational Text	***From Cows to You*** Anchor Text pp. 96–103 Informational Text

Qualitative

Meaning/Purpose: Moderate Complexity **Structure:** High Complexity **Language:** High Complexity **Knowledge Demands:** Moderate Complexity	**Meaning/Purpose:** High Complexity **Structure:** Low Complexity **Language:** High Complexity **Knowledge Demands:** Moderate Complexity	**Meaning/Purpose:** Low Complexity **Structure:** Moderate Complexity **Language:** Low Complexity **Knowledge Demands:** Low Complexity	**Meaning/Purpose:** Low Complexity **Structure:** Moderate Complexity **Language:** Moderate Complexity **Knowledge Demands:** Moderate Complexity

Quantitative

Lexile 770L	Lexile 710L	Lexile 340L	Lexile 500L

Reader and Task Considerations

Reader Children may need basic prior knowledge about how plants grow and how food gets from farm to table.	**Reader** Children should have background knowledge about the purpose of a folktale and the fact that it usually conveys a theme or moral.	**Reader** Children will need to use their knowledge of sound-spelling correspondences and high-frequency words to read the text.	**Reader** Children should be familiar with most of the food products in this text, but may need additional information on a few, such as yogurt.

Task The questions for the Interactive Read Aloud are supported by teacher modeling. The tasks provide a variety of ways for students to begin to build knowledge and vocabulary about the text set topic. The questions and tasks provided for the other texts are at various levels of complexity, ensuring that all students can interact with the text in meaningful ways.

Additional Texts

Classroom Library
On Earth
Genre: Nonfiction
Lexile: 540L

My Name Is Celia/Me llamo Celia
Genre: Nonfiction
Lexile: AD850L

See **Classroom Library Lessons.**

Content Area Reading BLMs

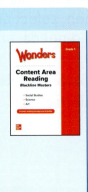

Additional online texts related to grade-level Science, Social Studies, and Arts content.

Where Does Food Come From? by Shelley Rotner and Gary Goss and photographs by Shelley Rotner. Text copyright © 2006 by Shelley Rotner and Gary Goss. Photographs copyright © 2006 by Shelley Rotner. Reprinted.; G. Brian Karas, On Earth, Penguin Group (New York, NY), 2008; From LET'S FIND OUT ABOUT ICE CREAM by Mary Ebeltoft Reid. Photography by John Williams. Scholastic Inc./Scholastic Nonfiction. Text copyright ©1997 by Mary Ebeltoft Reid. Photography copyright ©1997 by John Williams. Reprinted by permission.

Access Complex Text (ACT) boxes provide scaffolded instruction for seven different elements that may make the **Literature Big Book** complex.

Literature Anthology

"The Five Food Groups"
Paired Selection
pp. 104–105
Informational Text

Qualitative

Meaning/Purpose: Low Complexity
Structure: Low Complexity
Language: Moderate Complexity
Knowledge Demands: Low Complexity

Quantitative

Lexile 450L

Reader and Task Considerations

Reader Children should be familiar with most of the food products in this text and ought to relate their experiences with these foods.

Task The questions and tasks provided for this text are at various levels of complexity, ensuring that all students can interact with the text in meaningful ways.

Leveled Readers 🔊 (All Leveled Readers are provided in eBook format with audio support.)

(A)
Apples from Farm to Table
Informational Text

(O)
Apples from Farm to Table
Informational Text

(B)
Apples from Farm to Table
Informational Text

(ELL)
Apples from Farm to Table
Informational Text

Qualitative

Meaning/Purpose: Low Complexity	**Meaning/Purpose:** Low Complexity	**Meaning/Purpose:** Low Complexity	**Meaning/Purpose:** Low Complexity
Structure: Moderate Complexity	**Structure:** Moderate Complexity	**Structure:** Moderate Complexity	**Structure:** Moderate Complexity
Language: Low Complexity	**Language:** Moderate Complexity	**Language:** Moderate Complexity	**Language:** Low Complexity
Knowledge Demands: Low Complexity	**Knowledge Demands:** Low Complexity	**Knowledge Demands:** Low Complexity	**Knowledge Demands:** Moderate Complexity

Quantitative

Lexile 330L	Lexile 550L	Lexile 580L	Lexile 430L

Reader and Task Considerations

Reader Children should be familiar with most of the food products in this text and ought to relate their experiences with these foods.	**Reader** Children should be familiar with most of the food products in this text and ought to relate their experiences with these foods.	**Reader** Children should be familiar with most of the food products in this text and ought to relate their experiences with these foods.	**Reader** Children should be familiar with most of the food products in this text and ought to relate their experiences with these foods.

Task The questions and tasks provided for the Leveled Readers are at various levels of complexity, ensuring that all students can interact with the text in meaningful ways.

Focus on Word Work

Build Foundational Skills with Multimodal Learning

MULTIMODAL

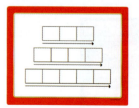

Response Board

Phonemic Awareness Activities

Sound-Spelling Card

Word-Building Cards online

Phonics Activities

Practice Book

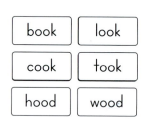

Spelling Cards online

High-Frequency Word Cards

High-Frequency Word Activities

Visual Vocabulary Cards

Shared Read

Decodable Readers

Take-Home Story

Phonological/Phonemic Awareness

- Segment, blend, and delete phonemes

Phonics: /u̇/ oo, u

- Introduce/review sound-spellings
- Blend/build words with sound-spellings
- Practice handwriting
- Structural Analysis: Build reading word bank
- Decode and encode in connected texts

Spelling: Words with oo, u

- Differentiated spelling instruction
- Encode with sound-spellings
- Explore relationships with word sorts and word families

High-Frequency Words

- Read/Spell/Write routine

See Word Work, pages T334–T337, T344–T347, T354–T357, T370–T371, T376–T377.

Apply Skills to Read

- Children apply foundational skills as they read decodable texts.
- Children practice fluency to develop word automaticity.

PHONICS SKILLS TRACE

Initial Consonants › Short Vowels › Consonant Blends and Digraphs › Long Vowels › Vowel Digraphs › r-Controlled Vowels › Diphthongs › Variant Vowels › Silent Letters and 3-Letter Blends

Explicit Systematic Instruction

Word Work instruction expands foundational skills to enable children to become proficient readers.

Daily Routine

- Use the In a Flash: Sound-Spelling routine and the In a Flash: High-Frequency Word routine to build fluency.
- Set Learning Goal.

Explicit Minilessons and Practice

Use daily instruction in both whole and small groups to model, practice, and apply key foundational skills. Opportunities include:

- Multimodal engagement.
- Corrective feedback.
- Supports for English Language Learners in each lesson.
- Peer collaboration.

Formative Assessment

Check-In

- Children reflect on their learning.
- Children show their progress by holding up 1 to 4 fingers in a Check-In routine.

Check for Success

- Teacher monitors children's achievement and differentiates for Small Group instruction.

Differentiated Instruction

To strengthen skills, provide targeted review and reteaching lessons and multimodal activities to meet children's diverse needs.

 Approaching Level, ELL
- Includes Tier 2 **2**

On Level

Beyond Level
- Includes Gifted and Talented **GIFTED and TALENTED**

Independent Practice

Provide additional practice as needed. Have children work individually or with partners.

Center Activity Cards

Digital Activities

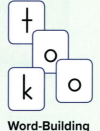
Word-Building Cards online

Decodable Readers

Practice Book

Inspire Early Writers

Build Writing Skills and Conventions

Practice Book

Handwriting Video

Reading/Writing Companion

Write Letters

- Learn to write letters
- Practice writing

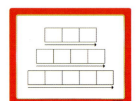

Response Board

Practice Book

High-Frequency Word Activities

Write Words

- Write words with variant vowel /ů/ *oo, u*
- Write spelling words
- Write high-frequency words

Reading/Writing Companion

Practice Book

Write Sentences

- Write sentences with inflectional endings
- Write sentences to respond to text

Follow Conventions

- Form and use contractions with *not*
- Use apostrophes in contractions

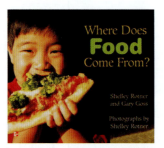

Where Does Food Come From?
Literature Big Book

Writing Fluency

To increase children's writing fluency, have them write as much as they can in response to the **Literature Big Book** for five minutes. Tell children to write about how we get our food.

For lessons, see pages T334–T337, T340–T341, T344–T347, T350–T351, T364–T365, T372–T373, T377, T378–T379.

Write About Texts

WRITING ROUTINE

Analyze the Prompt → Find Text Evidence → Write to the Prompt

**Reading/Writing Companion,
pp. 162–163, 168–169**

Modeled Writing

Write About the Shared Read "A Look at Breakfast"

- Prompt: Which breakfast food in the text is your favorite? Why?

Interactive Writing

- Prompt: What is the hardest breakfast food to make in the text? Why do you think so?

**Reading/Writing
Companion, p. 173**

Independent Writing

Write About the Anchor Text *From Cows to You*
Literature Anthology, pp. 96–102

- Prompt: Based on *From Cows to You,* which job in the milk process would you rather have? Why?

- Have children follow the steps of the writing process: draft, revise, edit/proofread, share.

Additional Lessons

Writing Skill Lesson Bank To provide differentiated support for writing skills, see pages T420–T429.

Extended Writing Minilessons For a full set of lessons that support the writing process and writing in a specific genre, see pages T402–T413.

Self-Selected Writing

Children can explore different writing modes.

 Journal Writing

 Picture Spark

 Book Review

Planner

Customize your own lesson plans at
my.mheducation.com

Select from your Social Emotional
Learning resources.

LESSON 1

LESSON 2

Reading

LESSON 1

Introduce the Concept, T330–T331
Build Knowledge: From Farm to Table

Listening Comprehension, T332–T333
Where Does Food Come From?

▶ **Word Work, T334–T337**
Phonemic Awareness: Phoneme Segmentation
Phonics/Spelling: Variant Vowel Digraphs: *oo, u*
High-Frequency Words: *after, buy, done, every, soon, work*

Shared Read, T338–T339
Read "A Look at Breakfast"

LESSON 2

▶ **Build the Concept, T342**
Oral Language

Listening Comprehension, T343
"The Little Red Hen"

▶ **Word Work, T344–T347**
Phonemic Awareness: Phoneme Blending
Phonics/Spelling: Variant Vowel Digraphs: *oo, u*
Structural Analysis: Inflectional Endings -*ed*, -*ing*
High-Frequency Words: *after, buy, done, every, soon, work*

▶ **Shared Read, T348–T349**
Reread "A Look at Breakfast"

Writing

LESSON 1

Modeled Writing, T340
Write About the Shared Read
Grammar, T341
Contractions with *Not*

Extended Writing: Expository Text, T408–T409
Revise and Edit
Additional Minilessons, T412–T413, T420–T429

LESSON 2

▶ **Interactive Writing, T350**
Write About the Shared Read
Grammar, T351
Contractions with *Not*

Extended Writing: Expository Text, T408–T409
Revise and Edit
Additional Minilessons, T412–T413, T420–T429

Teacher-Led Instruction

SMALL GROUP

Differentiated Reading
Leveled Readers
🔴 *Apples from Farm to Table*, T382–T383
🔵 *Apples from Farm to Table*, T392–T393
🟢 *Apples from Farm to Table*, T396–T397

Differentiated Skills Practice, T384–T399
🔴 **Approaching Level, T384–T391**
Phonological/Phonemic Awareness
- Phoneme Segmentation, T384 🔴
- Phoneme Blending, T384 🔴
- Phoneme Deletion, T385
- Phoneme Segmentation, T385

Phonics
- Connect *oo, u* to /u̇/, T386 🔴
- Blend Words with Variant Vowel /u̇/, T386 🔴
- Build Words with Variant Vowel /u̇/, T387
- Read Words with Variant Vowel /u̇/, T387
- Build Fluency with Phonics, T387

Independent/Collaborative Work See pages T329I–T329J

Reading
Comprehension
- Informational Text: Nonfiction
- Reread
- Details: Time-Order
Independent Reading

Word Work
Phonics/Spelling
- Variant Vowel Digraphs: *oo, u*
High-Frequency Words
- *after, buy, done, every, soon, work*

Writing
Self-Selected Writing
Extended Writing: Expository Text
Grammar
- Contractions with *Not*
Handwriting
- Upper and lowercase *Bb*

ORAL VOCABULARY
delicious, delighted, enormous, nutritious, responsibility

SPELLING
book, look, cook, took, hood, wood, nose, cute, buy, done
See page T336 for Differentiated Spelling Lists.

 LESSON 3

 LESSON 4

 LESSON 5

Reading

Build the Concept, T352
Oral Language
Take Notes About Text

Listening Comprehension, T353
Where Does Food Come From?

Word Work, T354–T357
Phonemic Awareness: Phoneme Deletion
Phonics/Spelling: Variant Vowel Digraphs: *oo, u*
Structural Analysis: Inflectional Endings -*ed*, -*ing*
High-Frequency Words: *after, buy, done, every, soon, work*

Anchor Text, T358–T363
Read *From Cows to You*

Extend the Concept, T366–T367
Oral Language

Paired Selection, T368–T369
Read "The Five Food Groups"

Word Work, T370–T371
Phonemic Awareness: Phoneme Segmentation
Phonics/Spelling: Variant Vowel Digraphs: *oo, u*
Structural Analysis: Inflectional Endings -*ed*, -*ing*
High-Frequency Words: *after, buy, done, every, soon, work*

Research and Inquiry, T374–T375
Research and Inquiry: Foods

Word Work, T376–T377
Phonemic Awareness: Phoneme Blending and Segmentation
Phonics/Spelling: Variant Vowel Digraphs: *oo, u*
Phonics: Read the Decodable Reader
Structural Analysis: Inflectional Endings -*ed*, -*ing*
High-Frequency Words: *after, buy, done, every, soon, work*

Integrate Ideas, T380
Make Connections

Culminating Task, T381
Show Your Knowledge

Writing

Independent Writing, T364
Write About the Anchor Text
Grammar, T365
Contractions with *Not*
Mechanics, T365
Apostrophes in Contractions

Extended Writing: Expository Text, T408–T409
Revise and Edit
Additional Minilessons, T412–T413, T420–T429

Independent Writing, T372
Write About the Anchor Text
Grammar, T373
Contractions with *Not*
Mechanics, T373
Apostrophes in Contractions

Extended Writing: Expository Text, T410–T411
Publish, Present, and Evaluate
Additional Minilessons, T412–T413, T420–T429

Self-Selected Writing, T378
Grammar, T379
Contractions with *Not*
Mechanics, T379
Apostrophes in Contractions

Extended Writing: Expository Text, T410–T411
Publish, Present, and Evaluate
Additional Minilessons, T412–T413, T420–T429

Structural Analysis
• Review Inflectional Endings -*ed*, -*ing*, T388
• Reteach Inflectional Endings -*ed*, -*ing*, T388
High-Frequency Words
• Review/Reteach/Cumulative Review, T389
Comprehension
• Read for Fluency, T390
• Identify Relevant Details, T390
• Review Time Order, T391
• Self-Selected Reading, T391

● **On Level, T394–T395**
Phonics
• Read and Build Words with Variant Vowel /ü/, T394
High-Frequency Words
• Review Words, T394
Comprehension
• Review Time Order, T395
• Self-Selected Reading, T395

● **Beyond Level, T398–T399**
Vocabulary
• Oral Vocabulary: Suffixes, T398
Comprehension
• Review Connections within Text: Sequence, T399
• Self-Selected Reading, T399 ⭐GIFTED and TALENTED

 ● **English Language Learners**
See ELL Small Group Guide, pp. 146–155.

Content Area Connections
Content Area Reading
• Science, Social Studies, and the Arts
Research and Inquiry
• Foods

● **English Language Learners**
See ELL Small Group Guide, pp. 147, 149, 151.

WEEK 5

Independent and Collaborative Work

As you meet with small groups, have the rest of the class complete activities and projects to practice and apply the skills they have been working on.

Student Choice and Student Voice

- Review My Weekly Work blackline master with children and identify the "Must Do" activities.
- Have children choose some additional activities that provide the practice they need.
- Remind children to reflect on their learning each day.

My Weekly Work BLMs

Reading

Text Options

Children can choose a **Center Activity Card** to use while they listen to a text or read independently.

Classroom Library
Read Aloud
On Earth
Genre: Informational Text
Lexile: AD540L

Classroom Library
My Name Is Celia/Me llamo Celia
Genre: Informational Text
Lexile: AD850L

Unit Bibliography
See the online bibliography. Children can select independent reading texts about how we get our food.

Leveled Texts Online
All **Leveled Readers** are provided in eBook format with audio support.

- **Differentiated Texts** provide English Language Learners with passages at different proficiency levels.

Literature Big Book e-Book
Where Does Food Come From?
Genre: Informational Text

Center Activity Cards

Reread Card 4

Folktale Card 31

Time-Order Card 18

Diagrams with Labels Card 23

Digital Activities

Comprehension

Word Work

Center Activity Cards

oo, u Card 85

Word-Building Cards

Practice Book BLMs

Phonological Awareness: pp. 225, 226

Phonics: pp. 227, 228

Spelling: pp. 229–231

Structural Analysis: pp. 233, 234

High-Frequency Words: p. 235

Take-Home Story: pp. 239–240

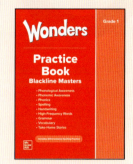

Decodable Readers

Unit 3, pp. 49-60

Digital Activities

Phonemic Awareness

Phonics

Spelling

High-Frequency Words

Writing

Center Activity Cards

Give Reasons for an Opinion Card 53

Nonfiction Text Card 45

Practice Book BLMs

Handwriting: p. 232

Grammar: pp. 236–237

Mechanics: p. 238

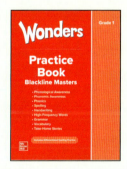

Self-Selected Writing

- How do we get food?
- Pick one type of food. Explain the process it takes to end up on the table.
- What is one new thing you learned about how we get food?

Digital Activities

Grammar

Grammar: Mechanics

Content Area Connections

Content Area Reading BLMs
- Additional texts related to Science, Social Studies, Health, and the Arts.

Research and Inquiry
- Complete Foods project

Progress Monitoring
Moving Toward Mastery

FORMATIVE ASSESSMENT

> **STUDENT CHECK-IN**

✓ **CHECK FOR SUCCESS**

For ongoing formative assessment, use children's self-assessments at the end of each lesson along with your own observations.

Assessing skills along the way . . .

SKILLS	HOW ASSESSED
Phonological/Phonemic Awareness **Phonics** **Structural Analysis** **High-Frequency Words**	Practice Book, Digital Activities, Online Rubrics
Comprehension	Digital Activities, Graphic Organizers, Online Rubrics
Text-Based Writing **Handwriting** **Grammar** **Spelling**	Reading/Writing Companion: Independent Writing, Practice Book, Digital Activities, Spelling Word Sorts
Listening/Presenting/Research	Reading/Writing Companion: Share and Evaluate; Research: Online Student Checklists
Oral Reading Fluency (ORF) Conduct group fluency assessments using the **Letter Naming, Phoneme Segmentation**, and **Sight Word Fluency** assessments.	Fluency Assessment

At the end of the text set . . .

SKILLS	HOW ASSESSED
Text Features: Diagrams **Details: Time-Order**	Progress Monitoring
Phoneme Segmentation **Phoneme Blending** **Phoneme Deletion**	
Variant Vowel Spellings with Digraphs *oo, u*	
Inflectional Endings *-ed, -ing*	
after, buy, done, every, soon, work	

Making the Most of Assessment Results

Make data-based grouping decisions by using the following reports to verify assessment results. For additional support options for children, refer to the reteaching and enrichment opportunities.

ONLINE ASSESSMENT CENTER

- *Gradebook*

DATA DASHBOARD

- *Recommendations Report*
- *Activity Report*
- *Skills Report*
- *Progress Report*
- *Grade Card Report*

Reteaching Opportunities with Intervention Online PDFs

IF CHILDREN ANSWER . . .	THEN ASSIGN . . .
0–3 **comprehension** items correctly . . .	lesson 135 on Text Features: Diagrams and/or lessons 52–54 on Time Order from the **Comprehension PDF.**
0–2 **phonological/phonemic** items correctly . . .	lessons 67–71 on Phoneme Segmentation, lessons 62–66 on Phoneme Blending, and lessons 102–103 on Phoneme Deletion from the **Phonemic Awareness PDF.**
0–5 **phonics/structural analysis/HFW** items correctly . . .	lessons 95 and 99 on Variant Vowel Spellings with Digraphs *oo, u* and lesson 66–67 on Inflectional Endings *-ed, -ing* from the **Phonics/Word Study PDF** and lessons from Section 3 of the **Fluency PDF.**

Enrichment Opportunities

Beyond Level small-group lessons and resources include suggestions for additional activities in these areas to extend learning opportunities for gifted and talented children:

- *Leveled Reader*
- *Vocabulary*
- *Comprehension*
- *Leveled Reader Library Online*
- *Center Activity Cards*

OBJECTIVES

Follow agreed-upon rules for discussions.

Build on others' talk in conversations by responding to the comments of others through multiple exchanges.

Build background knowledge.

Discuss the Essential Question.

ELA ACADEMIC LANGUAGE

• *photo*
• Cognate: *foto*

DIGITAL TOOLS

To enhance the class discussion, use these additional components.

Discuss Concept

Watch Video

LESSON FOCUS

READING
Introduce the Essential Question
Read Literature Big Book:
Where Does Food Come From?
• Reread text for understanding
Word Work
• Introduce /ù/*oo, u*
Read Shared Read: "A Look at Breakfast"
• Introduce Genre

WRITING
• Modeled Writing
• Introduce Grammar

Reading/Writing Companion, pp. 152–161

---

 5 mins # Build Knowledge MULTIMODAL

 ## Essential Question
How do we get our food?

Tell children that this week they will be talking and reading about the food we eat and where it comes from. Discuss the Essential Question. Children can share what they know about where food comes from.

Watch the Video Play the video without sound first and have partners narrate what they see. Then replay the video with sound and have children listen.

Talk About the Video Have partners share one thing they learned from the video about how we get our food.

 Anchor Chart Create a Build Knowledge anchor chart with the Essential Question and have volunteers share what they learned. Record their ideas on the chart.

Oral Vocabulary Words

Use the Define/Example/Ask routine on the print or digital **Visual Vocabulary Cards** to introduce the oral vocabulary words *delicious* and *nutritious*. Children can use these words to discuss different foods that we eat and where the food comes from.

Oral Vocabulary Routine

Visual Vocabulary Cards

Define: **Delicious** means "very tasty."

Example: My dad made a delicious meal.

Ask: What is the most delicious food you have tasted?

Define: A food is **nutritious** if it gives us things our bodies need.

Example: Josie eats a nutritious breakfast of cereal, milk, and fruit each morning.

Ask: What nutritious foods do you like to eat?

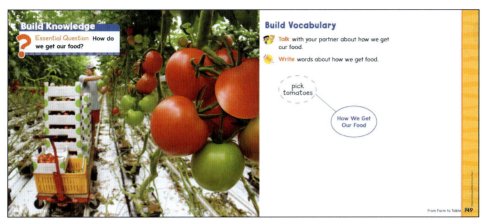

Reading/Writing Companion, pp. 148–149

Build Knowledge

Review how to be open to all ideas in the Collaborative Conversations box. Then have children turn to pages 148–149 of their **Reading/ Writing Companion.** Guide children to discuss the photo.

- *What clues in the photo tell you what the person is doing?*
- *Talk with a partner about what the person might be looking for.*

Build Vocabulary

Talk Have partners talk about words related to how we get food. **Write** Have children write these words on page 149.

Create a Word Bank Create a separate section of the Word Bank for words about how we get food. Have children suggest words.

English Language Learners

Use the following scaffolds with **Build Knowledge.**

Beginning

Point to the tomatoes in the photo. *This is a tomato.* Have children repeat the word *tomato.* Ask: *What is this?* Provide a sentence frame: This is a tomato.

Intermediate

Point to the tomatoes in the photo. *What is this?* Provide a sentence frame: This is a tomato. Point to a red tomato. *What color is this tomato?* This tomato is red. Repeat with a green tomato.

Advanced/Advanced High

Have partners elaborate on the scene. *Why are the tomatoes being put in crates?* (They are ready to eat.) *Where will they go?* (They will go to the store.)

COLLABORATIVE CONVERSATIONS

Be Open to All Ideas As children engage in partner, small-group, and whole-group discussions, remind them:

- that everyone's ideas are important and should be heard.
- that they should not be afraid to ask a question if something is unclear.
- to respect the opinions of others.

ELL NEWCOMERS

To help children develop oral language and build vocabulary, use **Newcomer Cards** 15–19 and the accompanying lessons in the **Newcomer Teacher's Guide.** For thematic connections, use **Newcomer Card** 14. For additional practice, have children complete the online **Newcomer Activities.**

MY GOALS ROUTINE

What I Know Now

Read Goals Read the goals on **Reading/Writing Companion** page 150 with children.

Reflect Ask children to reflect on each goal and fill in the bars to show what they know now. Explain that they will fill in the bars on page 151 at the end of the week to show their progress.

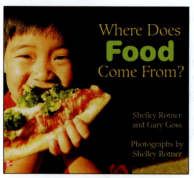

Where Does **Food** Come From?

Shelley Rotner and Gary Goss

Photographs by Shelley Rotner

Literature Big Book

LEARNING GOALS

We can reread to understand where food comes from.

OBJECTIVES

Identify the main topic and retell relevant, or key, details of a text.

Demonstrate understanding of the organization and basic features of print.

ELA ACADEMIC LANGUAGE

• *boldface, print, facts, reread*

Close Reading Routine

Read DOK 1–2

• Identify important ideas and details.
• Take notes and retell.
• Use **ACT** prompts as needed.

Reread DOK 2–3

• Analyze the text, craft, and structure.
• Use the Reread minilessons.

Integrate DOK 3–4

• Integrate knowledge and ideas.
• Make text-to-text connections.
• Complete the Show Your Knowledge task.
• Inspire action.

Read

 15 mins

Where Does Food Come From?

Connect to Concept: From Farm to Table Tell children that they will now listen to a text about where food comes from.

Genre: Informational Text: Nonfiction Explain that this is nonfiction. Say: *It tells about real people, places, things, or events by presenting facts about them. It can also use captions to give more information.*

 Anchor Chart Review the Reread anchor chart.

Reread Review that, if children do not understand something in the text, they can ask you to reread parts of it. They can also use the photos. This will help them monitor their comprehension as they listen to the story.

Read the Selection

Display the Big Book. Have children point to the title and the author names as you read them aloud. Point out the name of the photographer.

Set Purpose Say: *Let's read to find out where food comes from.*

As you read, model applying the strategy. Review the anchor chart.

> **Think Aloud** When I read on page 15 that cornstalks grow corn cobs, I had to reread and look at the photos again to make sure I understood what a stalk is. After rereading the text on page 15 and looking at the picture of the corn growing in the field, I now understand that a stalk is the tall, thick stem of the corn plant.

Continue to model rereading and encourage children to ask you to reread parts of the text when they don't understand it.

ACT Access Complex Text

If the complexity of the text makes it hard for children to understand, use the Access Complex Text prompts.

Purpose

The purpose of the text is to give information on where some common foods come from.

• Help children to identify the important details presented in the text.

Genre

Children may be distracted by the playful use of colored print and the side features.

• Guide children through the facts and details presented in the text.

Concepts of Print: Special Text Treatments Explain that authors can change the size and color of print. Have children point to a few examples, providing guidance as needed. Say: *They can also print some words in boldface, which is heavy, dark type.* As you read *Where Does Food Come From?* point out the words in large, colored print. Explain that even though these words are a different size and color, they are part of the sentences. Say: *The large, colorful print shows readers the most important ideas on the page.* Then, point out the "Did You Know?" side features. Explain that these give additional facts about the main ideas. See prompts in the Big Book for modeling concepts of print.

Respond to the Text

After reading, prompt children to share what they learned about where food comes from. Discuss what parts they wanted to reread and how rereading helped them understand the facts and details.

Model Retelling

Pause to retell portions of the selection. Say: *I can put information into my own words. I have read that the seeds of cocoa trees are called cocoa beans and that they can be ground and cooked to make chocolate.* Continue to model retelling the selection, using your own words to tell the important facts and details in the correct order. Have children practice retelling a page or two.

Writing Fluency

To increase children's writing fluency, have them write about the text as much as they can for five minutes. Then have partners share.

English Language Learners

Reread Support children by using question prompts on each page. Display pages 8 and 9. *I don't understand how french fries are made.* Reread the text. *What are french fries made from?* Provide a sentence frame: French fries are made from <u>potatoes</u>.

For additional support, see the **ELL Small Group Guide,** pp. 152–153.

MODEL FLUENCY

Intonation Turn to page 15 of the text. Point out *corn, cornstalks,* and *popcorn* in gold text. Explain that the authors set these words in colored text to emphasize them. Say: *When you read emphasized words, you can stress them by reading them a little bit louder than the other words.* Read aloud page 11 with slightly exaggerated stress on the words set in colored print.

DIGITAL TOOLS

Retell

FORMATIVE ASSESSMENT

❯ STUDENT CHECK-IN

Have partners tell one thing they reread as they listened to the story.

Have children reflect, using the Check-In routine.

✔ CHECK FOR SUCCESS

Can children reread for understanding?

❯❯ Small Group Instruction

If No

🔴 **Approaching** Reteach pp. T382–T383

If Yes

🔵 **On** Review pp. T392–T393

🟢 **Beyond** Extend pp. T396–T397

In a Flash: Sound-Spellings

Display the Sound-Spelling Card *boat*. Point to the letters o_e.
1. **Teacher:** What are the letters?   **Children:** o, e
2. **Teacher:** What's the sound?   **Children:** /ō/
Continue the routine for previously taught sounds.

LEARNING GOALS

• We can count how many sounds are in a spoken word.

• We can read and blend words with the /u̇/ sound.

OBJECTIVES

Demonstrate understanding of spoken words, syllables, and sounds (phonemes).

Decode regularly spelled one-syllable words.

Segment spoken single-syllable words into their complete sequence of individual sounds (phonemes).

Print all upper- and lowercase letters.

ELA ACADEMIC LANGUAGE

• uppercase, lowercase

 **TEACH IN SMALL GROUP**

Word Work lessons can be taught in small groups.

 Phonemic Awareness MULTIMODAL

Phoneme Segmentation

1 **Model** Use the **Response Board** to model phoneme segmentation. Say: *Listen carefully as I say a word:* good. *I will place a marker in a box for each sound I hear:* /g/ /u̇/ /d/. *I will place three markers because I hear three sounds in the word* good.

2 **Guided Practice/Practice** Have children practice segmenting words using the following. Explain: *Listen carefully as I say some words. Place one marker in a box for each sound you hear. Then tell me how many sounds are in each word.* Guide practice using the following examples and providing corrective feedback as needed.

foot (3)	woods (4)	push (3)	cooks (4)
put (3)	wool (3)	brook (4)	stood (4)
brooks (5)	crooks (5)	books (4)	should (3)

If children need additional practice segmenting words into phonemes, see **Practice Book** page 225 or the online activity.

 Phonics MULTIMODAL

Introduce /u̇/ oo, u

1 **Model** Display the *book* **Sound-Spelling Card.** Teach /u̇/ spelled *oo* and *u* using *book* and *put*. Model writing the letters *oo* and *u*. Use the handwriting models provided. *This is the* book *Sound-Spelling Card. The sound is* /u̇/. *The* /u̇/ *sound can be spelled with the letters* oo. *This is the sound in the middle of the word* book. *Listen:* /b/ /u̇/ /k/, book. *I'll say* /u̇/ *as I write the letters* oo *several times.* Repeat for /u̇/ spelled *u* as in *put*.

Sound-Spelling Card

2 **Guided Practice/Practice** Have children practice connecting the letters *oo* to the sound /u̇/ by writing them. *Now do it with me. Say* /u̇/ *as I write the letters* oo. *This time, write the letters* oo *five times as you say the* /u̇/ *sound.* Repeat for /u̇/ spelled *u* as in *put*. As needed, provide handwriting models for children to use.

Phonemic Awareness: Page 225
Phonics: Page 227
Handwriting: Page 232

Blend Words with /ủ/ *oo, u*

1 **Model** Display **Word-Building Cards** *f, o, o, t.* Say: *This is* f. *It stands for* / f/. *These are* oo. *They stand for* /ủ/. *This is* t. *It stands for* / t/. *Listen as I blend:* /fffủủủt/. Continue by modeling: *hook, good,* and *pull.*

2 **Guided Practice/Practice** Display the Lesson 1 Phonics Practice Activity. Guide practice, reading each word in the first row with children. Blend: /l/ /ủ/ /k/ /lllủủủk/, *look.* Continue to guide practice and provide corrective feedback as needed for rows 2–7.

look	good	full	wool	book	wood
hood	crook	shook	stood	push	pull
top	took	pot	put	cake	cook
home	cage	cute	race	nice	baked

Who took my book?

Put the wood in the box.

He pushed it with his foot.

Lesson 1 Phonics Practice Activity

If children need additional practice blending words with digraphs, see **Practice Book** page 227 or the online activity.

Corrective Feedback

Sound Error Model the sound that children missed; then have them repeat the sound. Say: *My turn.* Tap under the letter and say: *Sound?* /ủ/ *What's the sound?* Return to the beginning of the word. Say: *Let's start over.* Blend the word with children again.

 ## Daily Handwriting

Throughout the week, teach upper- and lowercase *Bb,* using the online handwriting models. Model writing the letters using the strokes as shown. Children can practice using Practice Book page 232. For additional support use the models in the **Reading/Writing Companion.**

ELL ENGLISH LANGUAGE LEARNERS

Phonological Awareness, Model After modeling with markers, have children clap for each separate sound they hear in *good.* Focus on articulation as you say each sound and note your mouth position. Provide corrective feedback as children say *good.*

Phonics Refer to pages 8–9 in the **Language Transfers Handbook.** In some languages, including Spanish and Hmong, there is no direct sound transfer for /ủ/. Emphasize /ủ/ and show correct mouth position.

DIGITAL TOOLS

To differentiate instruction for key skills, use the results of this activity.

Phonics: Practice

FORMATIVE ASSESSMENT

⊙ STUDENT CHECK-IN

Phonics Have partners read a word with the /ủ/ sound to each other. Have children reflect, using the Check-In routine.

LESSON 1

- We can spell words with *oo*.
- We can read the words *after, buy, done, every, soon,* and *work.*

OBJECTIVES

Spell untaught words phonetically, drawing on phonemic awareness and spelling conventions.

Decode regularly spelled one-syllable words.

Recognize and read grade-appropriate irregularly spelled words.

Spell words with the /ʊ/ sound.

ELA ACADEMIC LANGUAGE

- *dictation*

DIGITAL TOOLS

To differentiate instruction for key skills, use the results of this activity.

High-Frequency Words: Practice

For more practice, use this activity.

Word Work

Spelling

Spelling: Page 229

---

 5 mins

Spelling

Words with *-ook, -ood*

Dictation Follow the Spelling Dictation routine to help children transfer their growing knowledge of sound-spellings to writing. After dictation, give the spelling pretest in the **Practice Book** on page 229.

Pretest Pronounce each spelling word. Read the sentence and pronounce the word again. Ask children to say each word softly, stretching the sounds, before writing it. After the pretest, display the spelling words and write each word as you say the letter names. Have children check their words using the practice book page.

book	Let's read a **book**.
look	**Look** at that tall building!
cook	I helped Dad **cook** dinner.
took	She **took** a book from the shelf.
hood	My **hood** keeps my head warm.
wood	The desk is made of **wood**.
nose	Breathe through your **nose**.
cute	What a **cute** puppy!
buy	What did you **buy** at the store?
done	I like to eat steak that is well **done**.

ELLs should use the above list for their spelling pretest.

▶▶ DIFFERENTIATED SPELLING LISTS

> **Approaching Level** book, hood, look, took
>
> **Beyond Level** book, booklet, cook, cookie, hood, look, took, wood

ELL English Language Learners

Spelling, Dictation Before you begin dictation, review the meanings of the spelling words. Hold up a book and say *book.* Have children repeat. Take a child's book and say: *I took your book.* Have the child take the book back and repeat. Point to your nose. Say *nose,* and have children repeat while doing the same.

In a Flash: High-Frequency Words

people

1. **Teacher:** Read the word.   **Children:** people
2. **Teacher:** Spell the word.   **Children:** p-e-o-p-l-e
3. **Teacher:** Write the word.   **Children write the word.**

Repeat with *ago, boy, girl, how, old* from last week.

5 mins

High-Frequency Words

MULTIMODAL

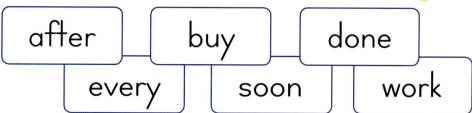

after   buy   done
every   soon   work

1 **Model** Display the **High-Frequency Word Cards** *after, buy, done, every, soon,* and *work.* Use the Read/Spell/Write routine to teach each word.

- **Read** Point to and say the word *after. This is the word* after. *Say it with me:* after. *After lunch we will go to the park.*

- **Spell** *The word* after *is spelled* a-f-t-e-r. *Spell it with me.*

- **Write** *Now write the word* after *on your Response Board as we say each letter:* a-f-t-e-r.

- Follow these steps to introduce *buy, done, every, soon, work.*

- As children spell each word with you, point out sound-spellings children have already learned as well as any irregular sound-spellings, such as /u/ spelled *o_e* in *done.*

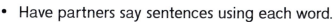
COLLABORATE

- Have partners say sentences using each word.

2 **Guided Practice** Have children read the sentences. Prompt them to identify the high-frequency words in connected text and to blend the decodable words.

1. We can play **after** school.
2. What did you **buy?**
3. When will the food be **done?**
4. **Every** kid got a book.
5. We can go home **soon.**
6. This is so much **work!**

3 **Practice** Have children build high-frequency words using letter cubes, letter cards, or magnetic letters. Have them record the words they make on a sheet of paper. Tell children to build the words without looking at the High-Frequency Word Cards and then use the cards to check their work.

For additional practice, have children do the online activities.

ELL ENGLISH LANGUAGE LEARNERS

High-Frequency Words, Model Use the High-Frequency Word Routine. Show the **High-Frequency Word Card** for *done.* Say: Done *means "finished."* Pick up a book and quickly pretend to read it. Close the book and say: *I am done reading this book. I finished reading it.* Have children think of other times they might use the word *done,* such as after eating a meal or when completing an assignment. Have partners turn and talk using the word *done.* Provide a sentence frame: I am done with this book.

FORMATIVE ASSESSMENT

› STUDENT CHECK-IN

Spelling Have partners dictate one /u/ word from the list for each other to write.

High-Frequency Words Have partners take turns reading the high-frequency words.

Have children reflect, using the Check-In routine.

✓ CHECK FOR SUCCESS

Rubric Use your online rubric to record children's progress.

Can children read and decode words with /u/ spelled *oo* and *u?*

Can children recognize and read high-frequency words?

» Small Group Instruction

If No
- **Approaching** Reteach pp. T384–T389
- **ELL** Develop pp. T384–T389

If Yes
- **On** Review pp. T392–T394
- **Beyond** Extend pp. T396–T397

We can read and understand a nonfiction text.

OBJECTIVES

Decode regularly spelled one-syllable words.

Recognize and read grade-appropriate irregularly spelled words.

With prompting and support, read informational texts appropriately complex for grade 1.

ELA ACADEMIC LANGUAGE

• *nonfiction*
• Cognate: *no ficción*

Close Reading Routine

Read DOK 1–2

• Identify important ideas and details.
• Take notes and retell.
• Use prompts as needed.

Reread DOK 2–3

• Analyze the text, craft, and structure.
• Use the Reread minilessons.

Integrate DOK 3–4

• Integrate knowledge and ideas.
• Make text-to-text connections.
• Complete the Show Your Knowledge task.
• Inspire action.

Read

"A Look at Breakfast"

Focus on Foundational Skills

• Review the high-frequency words *soon, done, every, after, buy,* and *work.*

• Review letters *oo* and *u* can stand for /ů/ sound, as in *good* and *pulled.*

• Display the words *breakfast, flour, dough, first, food, juice, oranges, wheat,* and *washed.* Spell each word and model reading it. Have children read the words as you point to them.

Read the Shared Read

Anchor Chart Review the Nonfiction anchor chart.

Genre: Informational Text: Nonfiction Tell children that "A Look at Breakfast" is a nonfiction text. It uses captions to give more information.

Reread

Explain Tell children that, as they read, they can reread parts of the text and look at the photographs to help them understand important details.

Connect to Concept: From Farm to Table

Explain that this week, children will talk about and read about how we get our food. Children can describe where food comes from.

Take Notes As children read the selection, you may wish to have them take notes in the boxes provided. Children may take notes by:

• writing the letters *oo* and *u*

• writing a word with the /ů/ sound or a high-frequency word.

Have children read each page. Then read the prompts one at a time.

Reading/Writing Companion, pp. 152–153

SET PURPOSE

Say: *Let's read to find out where some breakfast foods come from.*

CONCEPTS OF PRINT

Have children point to each word in the title as they read it aloud.

Reading/Writing Companion, pp. 154–155

Reading/Writing Companion, pp. 156–157

Reading/Writing Companion, pp. 158–159

Reading/Writing Companion, pp. 160–161

Respond to the Text

Have partners discuss where the breakfast foods in the selection come from. Use this sentence starter, as needed: *Breakfast foods come from . . .*

PHONICS

Have children circle and read aloud the words with the same vowel sound as in *look*.

REREAD

Say: *Let's make sure that we understand how flour is made. We can reread page 154.*

PHONICS

Ask children to circle and read aloud the words with the same vowel sound as in *look*.

HIGH-FREQUENCY WORDS

Have children underline and read aloud *every* and *after*.

REREAD

Say: *We can make sure that we understand what happens at a plant. Let's look at the photo and reread page 159.*

COMPREHENSION

Ask partners to talk about the steps for making orange juice.

HIGH-FREQUENCY WORDS

Have children underline and read aloud *buy* and *work*.

RETELL

Remind children that they can reread any parts of the text they do not understand before they retell the text.

SPOTLIGHT ON LANGUAGE

Page 154 Point to the word *flour*. Have children point to the word and repeat it. *Flour is a powder made from wheat. We use flour to make bread, cake, cookies, and pasta.* Explain that there is another word, *flower,* that has a different spelling and meaning. Draw a simple flower on the board, and write the word *flower* to demonstrate. Provide a sentence frame for children to use *flour:* We use flour to make <u>bread</u>.

FOCUS ON FLUENCY

Have partners reread "A Look at Breakfast" to develop fluency. Children should focus on their accuracy, trying to say each word correctly. Then have them reread the story so it sounds like speech. Remind children the goal is to keep practicing until they can read the words automatically.

DIFFERENTIATED READING

● **English Language Learners**
Before reading, have children listen to a summary of the selection, available in multiple languages.

STUDENT CHECK-IN

Have children reflect on their retelling, using the Check-In routine.

LESSON 1

- We can learn how to give reasons for an opinion.
- We can learn how to use contractions with *not*.

OBJECTIVES

Write opinion pieces in which they introduce the topic or name the book they are writing about, state an opinion, supply a reason for the opinion, and provide some sense of closure.

Demonstrate command of the conventions of standard English grammar and usage when writing or speaking.

Form contractions with *not*.

ELA ACADEMIC LANGUAGE

- *photograph*
- Cognate: *fotografía*

COLLABORATIVE CONVERSATIONS

Turn and Talk Review this routine.

Child 1: Jam is the best.

Child 2: Why do you think that?

Child 1: Jam tastes great on toast.

Have partners use the speech bubbles "What do you mean?" and "Why do you think that?" to practice collaborating.

DIFFERENTIATED WRITING

● **English Language Learners** For more writing support, see the **ELL Small Group Guide,** p. 154.

---

5 mins

Modeled Writing

Write About the Shared Read

Build Oral Language Read the prompt aloud. Ask: *Which breakfast food in the text is your favorite? Why?* Have partners use the Turn and Talk routine to discuss their favorite breakfast food from the story.

Model Writing Sentences Say: *I will write sentences about my favorite breakfast food.* Point to the text and photographs on pages 156–157. Say: *The text and the photographs tell me about grape jam.*

Sample Teacher Talk

- Listen to my sentences: *My favorite breakfast food is jam. Jam tastes great on toast.* My first word is *My*. On the Word Bank I see that *my* is spelled *m-y*. I'll write *My*. HIGH-FREQUENCY WORDS

- My next word is *favorite*. It begins with /f/. The letter *f* stands for /f/. I'll write *favorite*. PHONICS

- The next word is *breakfast*. I stretch the sounds and clap the syllables: /brrreeek/ /fffaaassst/. I hear two syllables. I'll write *breakfast*. WRITING SKILL

- Continue modeling to complete your sentences. My first sentence states my opinion about which breakfast food is my favorite. My second sentence tells the reason why this food is my favorite. TRAIT: IDEAS

> Which breakfast food in the text is your favorite? Why?
>
> My favorite breakfast food is jam. Jam tastes great on toast.

Writing Practice

Analyze and Write Sentences Have children turn to page 162 in their **Reading/Writing Companion.** Guide children to analyze the sentences using the prompts. Review the Writing Skill and Trait boxes as necessary. Then have children write and analyze their own sentences.

Reading/Writing Companion, pp. 162–163

Stephen Coburn/Shutterstock

Grammar
5 mins

Contractions with *Not*

1 **Explain** Remind children that a contraction is two words put together to form one word. Explain that some contractions are formed by putting a word together with *not*. An apostrophe takes the place of the letter *o* in *not*. Display the following:

| is not = isn't | did not = didn't | can not = can't |
| are not = aren't | does not = doesn't | do not = don't |

Read the words and contractions and have children repeat. Point out that the *o* in *not* is replaced with an apostrophe.

2 **Guided Practice/Practice** Display the sentences below and read them aloud. Have children identify the contraction in each.

Those aren't my wool socks. (aren't); I can't zip my bookbag. (can't); Mom didn't buy the book. (didn't)

Talk About It Have partners work together to orally generate sentences with contractions.

Link to Writing Review the Modeled Writing for examples of contractions with *not.* If there are no examples in the Modeled Writing, work with children to add a sentence with a contraction.

English Language Learners
ELL

Use these scaffolds with **Grammar, Guided Practice/Practice.**

Beginning

Read the first sentence. *Does this sentence have a contraction?* (yes) Circle *aren't* and have children repeat. *Name the contraction.* Provide a frame: The contraction is aren't.

Intermediate

Read the first sentence and ask: *What is the contraction?* Provide a frame: The contraction is aren't. *What words does this contraction stand for?* Aren't stands for are not.

Advanced/Advanced High

Read the sentences. *What are the two words in the contraction* aren't*?* (are not) *What letter was taken from* not? (o) *What is used in place of the* o*?* (an apostrophe)

DIGITAL TOOLS

Use this activity to practice grammar.

Grammar

FORMATIVE ASSESSMENT

❯ STUDENT CHECK-IN

Writing Have partners read each other a complete sentence that they wrote.

Grammar Have children name a contraction with *not.*

Have children reflect, using the Check-In routine.

OBJECTIVES

Identify real-life connections between words and their use.

Discuss the Essential Question.

Develop oral language.

ELA ACADEMIC LANGUAGE

• *define*

• Cognate: *definir*

▶ TEACH IN SMALL GROUP

● **ELL** See the Teacher Talk on the back of the **Visual Vocabulary Cards** for additional support.

● **Approaching** Group children with students in a higher level to practice saying the words. Then children can draw their own picture to illustrate the word.

● ● **On Level** and **Beyond Level** Have children look up each word in the online **Visual Glossary.**

FORMATIVE ASSESSMENT

❯ STUDENT CHECK-IN

Have partners use an oral vocabulary word in a sentence. Then have children reflect, using the Check-In routine.

LESSON FOCUS

READING
Revisit the Essential Question
Read Interactive Read Aloud:
"The Little Red Hen"
• Use Synonyms
Word Work
• Review /u̇/*oo, u*

Reread Shared Read:
"A Look at Breakfast"
• Review Genre
• Introduce Skill
WRITING
• Interactive Writing
• Review Grammar

Reading/Writing Companion, pp. 152–161

---

 5 mins

Oral Language

MULTIMODAL

? Essential Question

How do we get our food?

Remind children that this week you've been talking and reading about how we get our food. Remind them of the child eating corn on the cob and how wheat and fruit are made into breakfast foods.

Oral Vocabulary Words

Review the oral vocabulary words *delicious* and *nutritious* from Lesson 1. Use the Define/Example/Ask routine on the print or digital **Visual Vocabulary Cards** to introduce the oral vocabulary words *delighted, enormous,* and *responsibility*. Prompt children to use these words as they discuss the foods they eat and where they come from.

Oral Vocabulary Routine

Define: Someone who is `delighted` is full of joy and happiness.

Example: Sam was delighted to go to the baseball game.

Ask: What makes you feel delighted?

Define: `Enormous` means "very, very big."

Example: The new refrigerator came in an enormous box.

Ask: Can you name something that is enormous?

Define: A `responsibility` is something you are expected to do.

Example: It is my responsibility to wash the dishes after dinner.

Ask: What responsibilities do you have in your family?

Visual Vocabulary Cards

OPTION 10 mins

Read the Interactive Read Aloud

Connect to Concept

Tell children that you will be reading a folktale about a little red hen who works very hard to grow food. Review that a folktale often has a moral or teaches a lesson. Say: *As we read, we can think about the moral the author is trying to teach.* Display the **Interactive Read Aloud Cards**. Read the title aloud.

Set Purpose Read or play the selection. Remind children to listen carefully.

Oral Vocabulary Use the Oral Vocabulary prompts as you read the selection to provide more practice with the words in context.

Synonyms Tell children that, as you read, they can use synonyms to help them understand the meaning of unfamiliar words. Explain that synonyms are words that have almost the same meaning. Model the strategy using a sentence on Card 3.

Teacher Think Aloud I read "The pig, the duck, and the cat were all dozing in the sun..." I know that *dozing* means "taking a nap," so I thought of a word with a similar meaning. I used *sleeping* to replace *dozing*. This helped me understand that the animals were sleeping in the sun.

Continue reading the story. Model the strategy as needed.

Student Think Along After you read the first sentence on Card 4, stop and say: *The word* wonderful *means "very good." What are some synonyms for* wonderful? *How does this help you understand how the tortillas smelled?* The word *great* is a synonym for *wonderful.* Now I know how the tortillas smelled.

Moral After you finish reading, have children talk to a partner about the moral. Ask: *What lesson is the author trying to teach?*

Build Knowledge: Make Connections

Talk About the Text Have partners discuss where the little red hen's food comes from and how that might be similar to or different from where our food comes from.

Add to the Anchor Chart Record any new ideas on the Build Knowledge anchor chart.

Add to the Word Bank Then add words related to where food comes from to a separate section of the Word Bank.

"The Little Red Hen"

We can listen actively to learn about where a little hen's food comes from.

OBJECTIVES

Determine or clarify the meaning of unknown and multiple-meaning words and phrases based on *grade 1 reading and content*, choosing flexibly from an array of strategies.

ELA ACADEMIC LANGUAGE

• *synonym, sequence*
• Cognates: *sinónimo, sequencia*

DIGITAL TOOLS

MULTIMODAL

Interactive Read Aloud

ENGLISH LANGUAGE LEARNERS

Cards 1 and 3 Say *kernels*. Have children repeat. *The kernel is the small yellow part of the corn. What did Hen do with the kernels?* (She planted them.) *Dozing means "sleeping." Which character is always working? Which characters are always dozing or resting?*

▶ STUDENT CHECK-IN

Have children share one thing they learned about where food comes from. Then have them reflect, using the Check-In routine.

Display the Sound-Spelling Card *book*.

1. **Teacher:** What are the letters?   **Children:** oo
2. **Teacher:** What's the sound?   **Children:** / u̇ /
3. **Teacher:** What's the word?   **Children:** book

Continue the routine for previously taught sounds.

LEARNING GOALS

- We can blend sounds in words.
- We can read and build words with the /u̇/ sound.
- We can add the endings *-ed*, and *-ing* to make new words.

OBJECTIVES

Orally produce single-syllable words by blending sounds (phonemes), including consonant blends.

Decode regularly spelled one-syllable words.

Read words with inflectional endings.

Apply phonics when decoding words with the /u̇/ sound.

ELA ACADEMIC LANGUAGE

- *verb, ending, past, present*
- Cognates: *verbo, pasado, presente*

 TEACH IN SMALL GROUP

Word Work lessons can be taught in small groups.

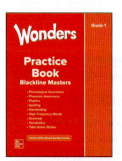

Phonemic Awareness: Page 226

OPTION
5 mins

Phonemic Awareness

Phoneme Blending

1 **Model** Say: *Listen as I say the sounds in a word: /l/ /u̇/ /k/. Now I will blend the sounds together and say the word: /lllu̇u̇u̇k/,* look.

2 **Guided Practice/Practice** Say: *Let's do some together. I am going to say some words, sound by sound. Listen as I say a word. Blend the sounds together to say the word.* Guide practice and provide corrective feedback, using the following examples:

/k/ /u̇/ /k/	/w/ /u̇/ /d/ /s/	/p/ /u̇/ /l/
/s/ /t/ /u̇/ /d/	/p/ /u̇/ /sh/	/p/ /u̇/ /t/ /s/
/f/ /u̇/ /l/	/sh/ /u̇/ /k/	/k/ /r/ /u̇/ /k/

If children need additional practice blending phonemes, see **Practice Book** page 226 or the online activity.

5 mins

Phonics

MULTIMODAL

Review /u̇/ *oo, u*

1 **Model** Display the *book* **Sound-Spelling Card.** Say: *The letters* oo *together can spell the sound /u̇/, such as in the word* cook. *The sound /u̇/ can also be spelled with the letter* u, *such as in the word* push.

Sound-Spelling Card

2 **Guided Practice/Practice** Guide children to practice connecting the letters with the sounds of the vowels, providing corrective feedback as needed. Point to the Sound-Spelling Card. *What are these letters? What sound do they stand for?*

Blend Words with /u̇/ *oo, u*

1 **Model** Display **Word-Building Cards** *t, oo, k* to form the word *took.* Model how to generate and blend the sounds to say the word. *This is the letter* t. *It stands for /t/. These are the letters* oo. *Together they stand for /u̇/. This is the letter* k. *It stands for /k/. Let's blend these sounds together: /tu̇u̇u̇k/.*
Continue by modeling the words *good, foot,* and *put.*

| t | oo | k |

2 **Guided Practice/Practice** Repeat the routine with children with the words: *book, push, hook, stood, foot, wood, shook,* and *pull,* guiding practice and providing corrective feedback as needed.

Build Words with /u̇/*oo, u*

Provide children with **Word Building Cards** *a–z.* Have children put the letters in alphabetical order as quickly as possible.

1 **Model** Display the Word-Building Cards *l, oo, k.* Blend: /l/ /u̇/ /k/, /llllu̇u̇u̇k/, *look.* Replace *l* with *b* and repeat with *book.* Replace *b* with *c* and repeat with *cook.*

2 **Guided Practice/Practice** Continue, building the words *hook, hood, had, cook, fit, pit, put, push,* and *pull.* Guide children to build each word. Then dictate the words and have children write them.

For additional practice decoding words with variant vowel spellings, see Build Words with Variant Vowel /u̇/ lessons on T387 and T394.

Structural Analysis

Inflectional Endings *-ed, -ing*

1 **Model** Write and read aloud *tag, tagged,* and *tagging.* Underline the inflectional endings *-ed* and *-ing.* Say: *We know we can add the endings* -ed *and* -ing *to verbs to change when something is happening. The ending* -ed *means the action happens in the past. The ending* -ing *means the action is happening right now, in the present.* Note the double *g* in *tagged* and *tagging.* Explain that when a word has a short vowel and ends in a consonant, you double the consonant before adding *-ed* or *-ing.*

Say *tag* and *tagged* again and have children listen for the /d/ sound at the end of *tagged.* Then write and say *stop* and *stopped.* Point out that the letters *-ed* can also stand for the /t/ sound as in *stopped.* Write and say *tag, tagging.* Point out that adding the letters *-ing* at the end of a word adds a syllable, or word part. Use each word in a sentence.

2 **Guided Practice/Practice** Write the following words on the board: *fit, tap, clap, jog.* Have children add *-ed* and *-ing* to each word and then use each word in a sentence. Guide practice and provide corrective feedback as needed.

ELL **ENGLISH LANGUAGE LEARNERS**

Blend Words with /u̇/*oo, u,* Guided Practice/Practice Review the meanings of example words that can be explained or demonstrated in a concrete way. For example, ask children to point to their foot and to a book. Model the action for *pull* or *push* by saying, *I can pull (or push) the door open,* and have children repeat. Provide sentence frames: I can fish with a <u>hook</u>. I <u>stood</u> by the window. Correct grammar and pronunciation as needed.

DIGITAL TOOLS

To differentiate instruction for key skills, use the results of this activity.

 Phonics: Practice

For more practice, use these activities.

 Phonemic Awareness Structural Analysis

❯ STUDENT CHECK-IN

Phonics Have partners build a word with the /u̇/ sound.

Structural Analysis Have partners read one word with the *-ed* or *-ing* ending and use it in a sentence.

Have children reflect, using the Check-In routine.

LESSON **2**

LEARNING GOALS

- We can sort and spell words with *oo*.
- We can read and write the words *after, buy, done, every, soon,* and *work.*

OBJECTIVES

Use conventional spelling for words with common spelling patterns and for frequently occurring irregular words.

Recognize and read grade-appropriate irregularly spelled words.

Sort words with the /ủ/ sound.

ELA ACADEMIC LANGUAGE

- *pattern*

DIGITAL TOOLS

To differentiate instruction for key skills, use the results of this activity.

High-Frequency Words: Practice

For more practice, use this activity.

Spelling

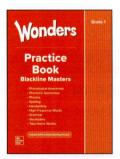

Spelling: On Level, Page 230
Approaching, Page 230A
Beyond, Page 230B
High-Frequency Words: Page 235

 5 mins

Spelling

 MULTIMODAL

Word Sort with *-ook, -ood*

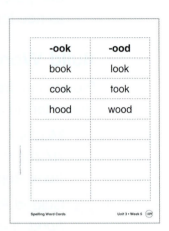

-ook	-ood
book	look
cook	took
hood	wood

Spelling Word Cards   Unit 3 • Week 5   109

1 **Model** Display the online **Spelling Word Cards** for Unit 3 Week 5, one at a time. Have children read each word, listening for /ủ/ and the ending sound.

Use cards with the endings *-ook* and *-ood* to create a two-column chart. Then model sorting the words *hook* and *good* beneath the correct word ending. Say each word and pronounce the sounds: /h/ /ủ/ /k/; /g/ /ủ/ /d/. Say each word again, emphasizing the /ủ/ plus final consonant sound. Ask children to spell each word.

2 **Guided Practice/Practice** Have children place each Spelling Word Card in the column with the words containing the same final sounds and spellings. When completed, have children read the words in each column. Then call out a word. Have a child find the word card and point to it as the class spells the word.

If children need additional practice spelling words with variant vowel spellings, see differentiated **Practice Book** pages 230–230B or the online activity.

Analyze Errors/Articulation Support

Use children's pretest errors to analyze spelling problems and provide corrective feedback. For example, some children will write only one letter for the /ủ/ sound (e.g., *o* or *u* for *oo*).

Create word sorts to analyze the vowel digraph patterns. Make index cards for *-ook* and *-ood* and display them. Also make cards for *hook, shook, brook, good,* and *stood.*

Have children sort the spelling words and the five words above and then read the words in each column.

High-Frequency Words

OPTION
5 mins

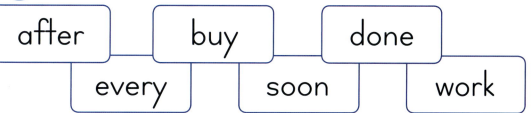

after | buy | done
every | soon | work

1 **Guided Practice** Say each word and have children Read/Spell/Write it.

- Point out irregularities in sound-spellings, such as the /ī/ sound spelled *uy* in *buy*.

2 **Practice** Add the high-frequency words *after, buy, done, every, soon,* and *work* to the cumulative word bank.

- Have children work with a partner to create sentences using the words.

- Have children look at the words and compare their sounds and spellings to words from previous weeks.

- Suggest that they write one sentence about the ways in which they get food.

Cumulative Review Review last week's words (*ago, boy, girl, how, old,* and *people)* by displaying each word and having children read it with automaticity.

Have children independently practice identifying, spelling, and reading high-frequency words using **Practice Book** page 235 or the online activity.

 ENGLISH LANGUAGE LEARNERS

Use these scaffolds with **High-Frequency Words, Practice.**

Beginning
Have children echo-read high-frequency words. Provide a sentence frame to help partners use *soon*: I can work soon.

Intermediate
Provide sentence frames such as: I can work/buy. We can go soon/after. We have every book. We are done.

Advanced/Advanced High
Model and guide children to use at least two high-frequency words in a sentence: I can work soon. I can work every day.

FORMATIVE ASSESSMENT

❯ STUDENT CHECK-IN

Spelling Have partners share one column of words they sorted.

High-Frequency Words Have partners quiz each other, using the High-Frequency Word Cards.

Have children reflect, using the Check-In routine.

✓ CHECK FOR SUCCESS

Rubric Use your online rubric to record children's progress.

Can children read and decode words with /u̇/ spelled *oo* and *u?*

Can children recognize and read high-frequency words?

❯ Small Group Instruction

If No

🔴 **Approaching** Reteach pp. T384–T389

🟣 **ELL** Develop pp. T384–T389

If Yes

🔵 **On** Review pp. T392–T394

🟢 **Beyond** Extend pp. T396–T397

OBJECTIVES

Know and use various text features to locate key facts or information in a text.

Identify the main topic and retell re;evant, or key, details of a text.

Identify time-order of events.

ELA ACADEMIC LANGUAGE

- *nonfiction, sequence*
- Cognates: *no ficción, sequencia*

TEACH IN SMALL GROUP

🔴 **Approaching** Have partners work together to complete the chart.

🔵 🟢 **On Level** and **Beyond Level** Have children write their responses independently and then discuss them.

🟣 **ELL** For specific comprehension support in reading "A Look at Breakfast," see the **ELL Small Group Guide,** pp. 148–149.

DIGITAL TOOLS

To differentiate instruction for key skills, use the results of this activity.

Details: Time-Order

"A Look at Breakfast"

Genre: Informational Text: Nonfiction

1 **Model** Tell children they will now reread the nonfiction selection "A Look at Breakfast." Have children turn to page 164 in their **Reading/Writing Companion.** Review the characteristics of informational text, or nonfiction. Nonfiction:

- tells about real people, places, things, or events.
- presents information and facts about those things.
- can use captions to give more information.

Display the text "A Look at Breakfast." Say: *On page 154, we read that flour is made from wheat.* Point to the photo and caption. Say: *The photo shows a large machine cutting the wheat. The caption tells us that the wheat is crushed to make flour. We can use captions to get more information about the text.* Model filling in the graphic organizer on page 165 by writing the information you learned from the text and the information you learned from the caption and photo.

Reading/Writing Companion, pp. 164–165

2 **Guided Practice/Practice** Guide children to copy what you wrote in the graphic organizer on page 165 in their own Reading/Writing Companion. Then have them continue by rereading pages 156–157. Have them share with a partner what they learn from the text, photos and captions. Ask: *What fact do you learn from the text about how grapes grow?* (Grapes grow on vines.)

Guide children to write this fact in the graphic organizer. Ask children to say what they learn about grapes from the photo on page 157. They can add this information to the graphic organizer. Offer help as needed.

Details: Time-Order

Anchor Chart Create a Time-Order anchor chart. Say: *Authors can give information in time-order, or in the order that events happen.* Explain that words such as *first, next, then,* and *last* can help us understand the time order. Say: *Relevant details give us information about the time order of events in a text.*

1 **Model** Display page 166 of the **Reading/Writing Companion.** Model filling in the first box on page 167, by finding what happens first in the process of making bread. Say: *On page 155, we read "First, dough is made." This is the first event.* Write this event in the first box.

Reading/Writing Companion, pp. 166–167

2 **Guided Practice/Practice** Guide children to copy what you wrote in the graphic organizer on page 167. Display page 155. Have partners reread the page and talk about the time order of events for making bread. Then say: *We know the first event. What is next?* (The dough is shaped and baked.) Guide children to write that in the second box.

Ask children to find the next two steps in the text and write them in the third and fourth boxes. Offer help as needed.

For more practice, have children complete the online activity.

 English Language Learners

Details: Time Order, Model Point to the words in the chart and have children echo-read them: *first, next, then, last.* Explain that these are words that tell the order of events. Complete a series of steps as you perform them. *First I stand. Next I clap. Then I sit. Last I smile.* Have children repeat the routine after you, naming the sequence words as they do.

BUILD KNOWLEDGE: MAKE CONNECTIONS

Talk About the Text Have partners discuss where the breakfast food discussed in the text comes from.

Write About the Text Then have children add their ideas to the Build Knowledge page of their Reader's Notebook.

Add to the Anchor Chart Record any new ideas on the Build Knowledge anchor chart.

Add to the Word Bank Then add words related to where food comes from to a separate section of the Word Bank.

FORMATIVE ASSESSMENT

STUDENT CHECK-IN

Genre Have partners take turns telling why this text is nonfiction.

Skill Have children identify one time-order event from the text.

Have children reflect, using the Check-In routine to fill in the bars.

CHECK FOR SUCCESS

Rubric Use your online rubric to record children's progress.

Can children use time order to describe the events in "A Look at Breakfast"?

Small Group Instruction

If No

🔴 **Approaching** Reteach pp. T382–T383, 390–T391

If Yes

🔵 **On** Review pp. T392–T393, T395

🟢 **Beyond** Extend pp. T396–T399

LESSON **2**

- We can read and write about a Student Model.
- We can write sentences with contractions.

OBJECTIVES

Write opinion pieces in which they introduce the topic or name the book they are writing about, state an opinion, supply a reason for the opinion, and provide some sense of closure.

Demonstrate command of the conventions of standard English grammar and usage when writing or speaking.

Form contractions with *not*.

ELA ACADEMIC LANGUAGE

- *opinion, apostrophe*
- Cognates: *opinión, apóstrofe*

COLLABORATIVE CONVERSATIONS

Circulate as partners talk about the prompt. Notice who needs help asking questions. Have them use the speech bubbles to help them generate questions. As you listen in, you may wish to write down observations about children's development.

DIFFERENTIATED WRITING

⬤ **English Language Learners**
For more writing support, see **ELL Small Group Guide**, p. 154.

⏱ **5 mins** # Interactive Writing

Write About the Shared Read

Analyze the Prompt Read aloud a new prompt: *What is the hardest breakfast food to make in the text? Why do you think so?* Have partners turn and talk about it.

Find Text Evidence Guide children to find text evidence to respond to the prompt. Ask: *What is the hardest breakfast food to make? Why do you think so?* Use a volunteer's response and the sample teacher talk below to write an answer such as: *Orange juice is the hardest breakfast food to make. It is made from trucks full of oranges.*

Sample Teacher Talk: Share the Pen

- Who knows the final sound of the word *orange*? That's right, /j/, spelled with the letter *g*. Have a volunteer write *Orange*. PHONICS

- Who can stretch the sounds in the word *juice* for me? That's right, /jūūūsss/. Have a volunteer write *juice*. WRITING SKILL

- Who can find *is* in the Word Bank and spell it? Yes, *i-s*. Have a child write *is*. HIGH-FREQUENCY WORDS

- Let's write the rest of our answer. Who can point to the reason why I think orange juice is the hardest breakfast food to make? TRAIT: IDEAS

> What is the hardest breakfast food to make in the text? Why do you think so?
>
> Orange juice is the hardest breakfast food to make. It is made from trucks full of oranges.

Analyze the Student Model

Say: *Let's read how another child responded to the prompt.* Have children turn to page 168 in the **Reading/Writing Companion.** Guide them to analyze Lisa's writing using the prompts on page 169. Then have children write what they notice. Review the Grammar box, as necessary. Use the Quick Tip box for support.

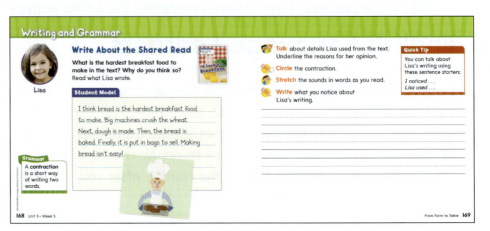

Reading/Writing Companion, pp. 168–169

Stephen Coburn/Shutterstock

Grammar

5 mins

Contractions with *Not*

1 **Review** Remind children that a contraction is a way to put two words together to make a new, shorter word.

2 **Guided Practice** Write the following sentences. Then read each sentence and guide children to identify the contraction, tell which two words make it, and tell which letter the apostrophe replaces.

Mom doesn't eat rice. (doesn't, does not, o)

They aren't going home together. (aren't, are not, o)

3 **Practice** Have partners write a sentence that tells a school rule using a contraction, such as *Children can't run in the hall; Don't cut in line.* For additional practice for contractions with *not*, see **Practice Book** page 236 or the online activity.

Talk About It

Have partners work together to orally generate sentences with contractions.

English Language Learners

Grammar, Practice Create a word bank of contractions such as *aren't, don't, isn't,* and *can't* for children to use as they write sentences about a school rule. Read each contraction and have children repeat. If necessary, review your classroom rules and help children determine how to restate them using a contraction. For example, if you have a rule to be kind, demonstrate how to make that a sentence using a contraction by saying: *Don't be unkind or mean.* Provide sentence frames: Don't be <u>unkind</u>. Children can't <u>talk</u> while others are talking.

DIGITAL TOOLS

Use this activity to practice grammar.

Grammar

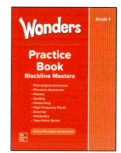

Grammar: Page 236

LESSON 3

We can learn and use vocabulary words.

OBJECTIVES

Identify real-life connections between words and their use.

Discuss the Essential Question.

Develop oral language.

ELA ACADEMIC LANGUAGE

• *information, photograph*

• Cognates: *información, fotografía*

LESSON FOCUS

READING

Revisit the Essential Question

Reread Literature Big Book:
Where Does Food Come From?
• Use Synonyms
• Analyze Author's Craft

Word Work
• Blend words with /ů/*oo, u*

Read and Reread Anchor Text:
From Cows to You
• Review Genre
• Reread Text
• Review Skill

WRITING
• Independent Writing
• Review Grammar and Introduce Mechanics

Literature Anthology, pp. 96–103

MULTIMODAL

5 mins

Oral Language

 ## Essential Question

How do we get our food?

Remind children that this week you are talking and reading about where our food comes from. Ask: *What have you learned so far about where our food comes from?* Remind children of the photograph of the person picking tomatoes, the text telling how food is produced, and the information in the food chart.

Review Oral Vocabulary

Review the oral vocabulary words *delicious, delighted, enormous, nutritious,* and *responsibility* using the Define/Example/Ask routine on the print or digital **Visual Vocabulary Cards**. Encourage children to discuss where we get the foods we eat when coming up with examples for each word.

Visual Vocabulary Cards

STUDENT CHECK-IN

Have partners use an oral vocabulary word in a sentence. Have children reflect, using the Check-In routine.

Reread

Where Does Food Come From?

As you reread *Where Does Food Come From?*, have children focus on using text evidence as they respond to questions about the author's craft. Remind children that authors often include certain features in their text to get the reader's attention or to make their writing look or sound a certain way. Point out that children can use synonyms to understand the meaning of unfamiliar words.

Author's Craft Display page 6. Why do you think the authors put some words in a different color and made them larger?

Think Aloud On page 6, all of the words that are larger and in green are the names of the foods. I think that the words in different colors emphasize what we are talking about. Without completely reading this page, I know it's mainly about apples and apple juice.

Author's Purpose Display page 9. Why do you think that the authors included the "Did you know?" features in this selection? (The features are extra information that may be interesting to the reader. The author adds these features to add interest and more information as we read.)

Continue asking questions about how the author uses the text and graphic features to help the reader understand the text.

Synonyms Model using synonyms to understand the meaning of unfamiliar words. Read page 17. Point to the word *ingredient* and review the meaning of the word.

Say: *Let's pretend that we don't know what* ingredient *means here, but we know what an ingredient usually is. We can figure out what the sentence means using words that mean the same thing, or synonyms, instead of* ingredient. *Let's use the word* part. *Milk is the main part in butter, cheese, and ice cream.* Ask children for additional synonyms. Continue to model using synonyms as needed.

Build Knowledge: Make Connections

Talk About the Text Have partners discuss where the food in the text comes from.

Add to the Anchor Chart Record any new ideas on the Build Knowledge anchor chart.

Add to the Word Bank Then add words related to where food comes from to a separate section of the Word Bank.

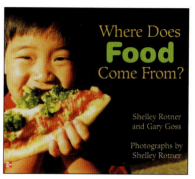

Literature Big Book

OBJECTIVES

Determine or clarify the meaning of unknown and multiple-meaning words and phrases based on *grade 1 reading and content,* choosing flexibly from an array of strategies.

ELA ACADEMIC LANGUAGE

• *synonym*

• Cognate: *sinónimo*

ELL ENGLISH LANGUAGE LEARNERS

Synonyms Point to the word *combining* on page 26. Say it and have children repeat. Read this sentence from the text: *Salads are made by combining these and other vegetables or fruits.* Can we figure out the meaning of *combining by using a word that means the same thing?* Point to the photo. *All the vegetables in the salad are mixed up.* Mixing *means the same thing as* combining. *Mixing* and *combining* are synonyms. Reread the sentence with the word *mixing.*

FORMATIVE ASSESSMENT

❯ STUDENT CHECK-IN

Have partners name one choice the author made. Have children reflect, using the Check-In routine.

LEARNING GOALS

- We can delete the first sound in a word to make a new word.
- We can read words with the /u̇/ sound.
- We can add the endings *-ed,* and *-ing* to make new words.

OBJECTIVES

Demonstrate understanding of spoken words, syllables, and sounds (phonemes).

Decode regularly spelled one-syllable words.

Read words with inflectional endings.

Delete initial phonemes in words.

Apply phonics when decoding words with the /u̇/ sound.

ELA ACADEMIC LANGUAGE

- *ending, action words, verbs*
- Cognate: *verbos*

 **TEACH IN SMALL GROUP**

Word Work lessons can be taught in small groups.

Phonics: Page 228
Structural Analysis: Page 233

Display the Sound-Spelling Card *book.*
1. **Teacher:** What are the letters? **Children:** oo
2. **Teacher:** What's the sound? **Children:** /u̇/
3. **Teacher:** What's the word? **Children:** book
Continue the routine for previously taught sounds.

book

Phonemic Awareness

(5 mins) MULTIMODAL

Phoneme Deletion

1 **Model** Say: *Listen as I say a word:* plate. *The word* plate *has four sounds /p/ /l/ /ā/ /t/. I'll take away the first sound /p/ and make a new word with three sounds: /l/ /ā/ /t/.*

Continue modeling phoneme deletion with the following word sets.

brace/race   flake/lake   swipe/wipe   slime/lime

2 **Guided Practice/Practice** Say: *Let's do some together. Listen as I say a word. The word is* bride, */b/ /r/ /ī/ /d/. Bride without /b/ is /r/ /ī/ /d/,* ride. Guide practice and provide corrective feedback.

sat	hill	plane	brake	smile
clap	grace	wedge	flick	block

 OPTION 5 mins

Phonics

Blend Words with /u̇/ *oo, u*

1 **Model** Display **Word-Building Cards** *s, t, oo, d.* Model how to blend the sounds. *This is the letter* s. *It stands for /s/. This is the letter* t. *It stands for /t/. These are the letters* oo. *Together they stand for /u̇/. This is the letter* d. *It stands for /d/. I'll blend the sounds: /stu̇u̇d/. The word is* stood. Continue by modeling the words *push, shook, crook,* and *wool.*

2 **Guided Practice/Practice** Display the Lesson 3 Phonics Practice Activity.

good	put	full	look	wood
push	cook	hood	crook	foot
book	bake	pole	pull	push
stopped	stopping	clapped	clapping	
shopped	shopping	chatted	chatting	

This bag is full of wool.

He shook his foot and waved his hand.

Lesson 3 Phonics Practice Activity

Say: *Let's blend the letter sounds to read each word: /gủủủd/. The word is* good. Have children blend each word with you. Prompt children to read the connected text, sounding out the decodable words. Provide corrective feedback as needed.

If children need additional practice blending words with variant vowel /ủ/, see **Practice Book** page 228 or the online activity.

Corrective Feedback

Sound Error Help children with any sounds they missed. Say: *My turn. This sound says* (make the correct sound). Then blend the word. Say: *Do it with me.* Blend the word aloud with children. Say: *Your turn. Blend this word.* Have children chorally blend. Say: *Let's do it again.* Follow these steps until children are confidently producing the sound.

Decodable Reader

Have children read "A Good Cook" to practice decoding words in connected text. If children need support reading words with variant vowel /ủ/, see pages T387 or T394 for instruction and support for the decodable reader.

Structural Analysis

Inflectional Endings *-ed, -ing*

1 **Model** Write the words *stop, stopped, stopping*. Remind children that we use the endings *-ed* and *-ing* to change the meanings of action words or verbs. Underline the letters *-ed* and *-ing*. Point out the letters *pp* in *stopped* and *stopping*. Remind children that you double the final consonant before adding *-ed* and *-ing* when the word ends in a short vowel and one consonant.

2 **Practice/Apply** Help children blend the words *beg, begged, begging, tip, tipped, tipping, brag, bragged,* and *bragging.* Point out that the letters *-ed* at the end of a word can stand for /d/ as in *begged* or /t/ as in *tipped*. Also point out that adding the letters *-ing* at the end of a word adds a syllable.

Have children practice decoding words with inflectional endings using Practice Book page 233 or the online activity.

DIGITAL TOOLS

For more practice, use these activities.

Word Work

Phonemic Awareness
Phonics
Structural Analysis

ELL ENGLISH LANGUAGE LEARNERS

Structural Analysis, Practice/Apply
Read *beg, begged, begging*. Have children repeat. *I'm going to read the words again. If you hear a word that ends with inflectional ending* -ed *that makes the /d/ sound, clap once. If you hear a word that ends with* -ing *that makes the /ing/ sound, clap twice.* Repeat with *brag, bragged, bragging*. Before you do *tip, tipped, tipping*, point out that the letters *-ed* can also make the sound /t/ and have children listen for that sound instead of /d/.

FORMATIVE ASSESSMENT

❯ STUDENT CHECK-IN

Phonics Have partners read a word with the /ủ/ sound to each other.

Structural Analysis Have partners use a word with the *-ed* or *-ing* ending in a sentence.

Have children reflect, using the Check-In routine.

OPTION 5 mins

MULTIMODAL

Spelling

Word Families: *-ook, -ood*

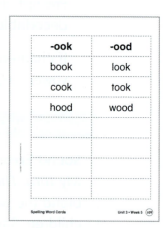

-ook	-ood
book	look
cook	took
hood	wood

Spelling Word Cards   Unit 3 • Week 5

1 **Model** Make index cards for *-ook* and *-ood* and form two columns in a pocket chart. Blend the sounds to model for children.

Hold up the online **Spelling Word Card** for *book.* Say and spell *book.* Pronounce each sound clearly: /b/ /ů/ /k/. Blend the sounds, emphasizing the vowel sound and final consonant. Repeat this step with *look, cook,* and *took.* Place the words below the *-ook* card. Read and spell each spelling word. Ask: *What do you notice about these spelling words? Yes, they have the /ů/ sound and they rhyme.*

2 **Guided Practice/Practice** Provide children with the Spelling Word Cards. Have children say and spell each word. Repeat the process with *-ood.*

Display the words *nose, cute, buy,* and *done* in a separate column. Read and spell the words together with children. Point out that these spelling words do not end with *-ook* or *-ood.*

Conclude by asking children to orally generate additional rhyming words for each word. Write the additional words on the board. Underline the common spelling patterns in the additional words. If necessary, point out the differences and explain why they are unusual.

If children need additional practice spelling words in the *-ook* or *-ood* word families, see **Practice Book** page 231 or the online activity.

English Language Learners

Spelling, Model Write *book* on the board. Have children watch you say the word *book,* emphasizing the vowel and final sounds. Have children repeat after you as you blend the sounds while pointing to the letters. Repeat with *look, cook,* and *took.*

Look at the words I wrote. What letters are the same in all of them? Provide a sentence frame: All the words end in o,o,k. What sound does *-ook* make? (/ů/ /k/)

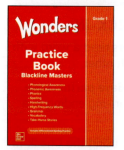

Wonders
Grade 1
Practice Book
Blackline Masters

Spelling: Page 231

High-Frequency Words

5 mins

1 **Guided Practice** Say each high-frequency word: *after, buy, done, every, soon,* and *work.* Have children Read/Spell/Write it. As children spell each word with you, point out irregular sound-spellings, such as the /u/ sound spelled *o_e* in done.

Display the print or digital **Visual Vocabulary Cards** to review this week's high-frequency words.

DIGITAL TOOLS

For more practice, use these activities.

Word Work Spelling High-Frequency Words

2 **Practice** Repeat the activity with last week's words. Children can practice reading the high-frequency words independently using the online activity.

Build Fluency: Word Automaticity

Have children read the following sentences aloud together at the same pace. Repeat several times until children can read the words automatically.

> He will be **done soon.**
>
> I will **work after** I have a snack.
>
> Do you **buy** lunch **every** day?

Word Bank

Review the current and previous words in the Word Bank. Discuss with children which words should be removed, or added back, from previous high-frequency word lists. Remind children that the word bank should change as the class needs it to.

FORMATIVE ASSESSMENT

❯ STUDENT CHECK-IN

Spelling Have partners think of another word to go with one of the word families.

High-Frequency Words Have partners point to one high-frequency word and read it aloud to each other.

Have children reflect, using the Check-In routine.

✔ CHECK FOR SUCCESS

Rubric Use your online rubric to record children's progress.

Can children read and decode words with /u̇/ spelled *oo* and *u*?

Can children recognize and read high-frequency words?

❯ Small Group Instruction

If No

● **Approaching** Reteach pp. T384–T389

● **ELL** Develop pp. T384–T389

If Yes

● **On** Review pp. T392–T393

● **Beyond** Extend pp. T396–T397

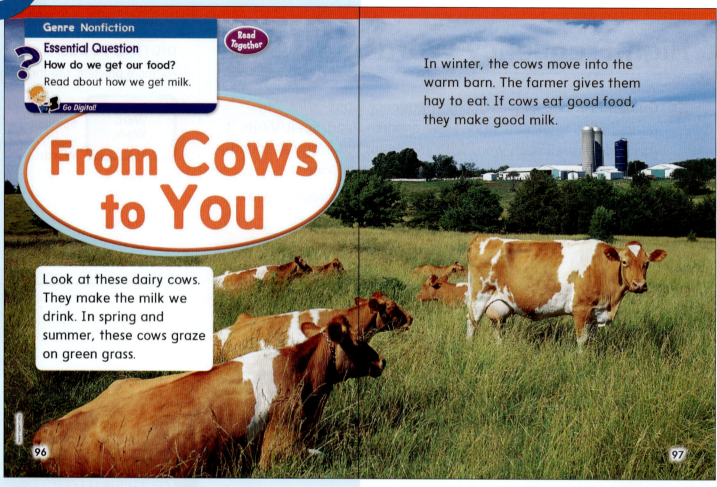

Genre Nonfiction

Essential Question
How do we get our food?
Read about how we get milk.

Go Digital!

Read Together

From Cows to You

Look at these dairy cows. They make the milk we drink. In spring and summer, these cows graze on green grass.

In winter, the cows move into the warm barn. The farmer gives them hay to eat. If cows eat good food, they make good milk.

96

97

Literature Anthology, pp. 96–97
Lexile 550L

From Cows to You

LEARNING GOAL

Read We can understand the important ideas and details in a text.

Reread We can name the choices an author made when writing a text.

Have children apply what they learned as they read.

Close Reading Routine

Read DOK 1–2

- Identify important ideas and details.
- Take notes and retell.
- Use **A C T** prompts as needed.

Reread DOK 2–3

- Analyze the text, craft, and structure.
- Use the Reread minilessons.

Integrate DOK 3–4

- Integrate knowledge and ideas.
- Make text-to-text connections.
- Complete Show Your Knowledge task.
- Inspire action.

Read

Celebratory Read You may wish to read the full selection aloud once with minimal stopping before you begin using the Read prompts.

Set Purpose

Say: *Let's read to find out how we get milk.*

DIFFERENTIATED READING

Approaching Level Have children listen to the selection summary. Use the Reread prompts during Small Group time.

On Level and **Beyond Level** Pair children or have them independently complete the prompts on **Reading/Writing Companion** pages 171–172.

English Language Learners Before reading, have children listen to a summary of the selection. For additional support, see **ELL Small Group Guide,** pp. 150–151.

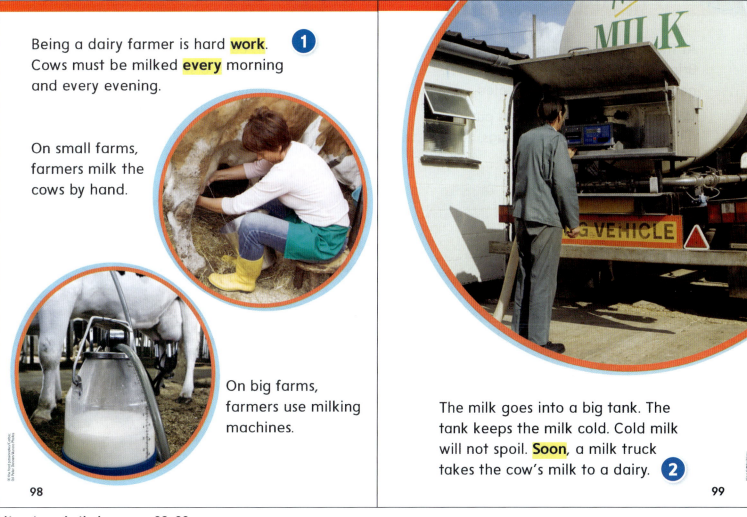

Being a dairy farmer is hard **work**. ❶ Cows must be milked **every** morning and every evening.

On small farms, farmers milk the cows by hand.

On big farms, farmers use milking machines.

The milk goes into a big tank. The tank keeps the milk cold. Cold milk will not spoil. **Soon**, a milk truck takes the cow's milk to a dairy. ❷

98

99

Literature Anthology, pp. 98–99

Story Words Read and spell the words *dairy, food, tank,* and *germs*. Explain to children that they will read these words in the selection.

Note Taking: Graphic Organizer

Have children fill in the online Time-Order Graphic Organizer 6 as they read.

❶ Reread DOK 1

Teacher Think Aloud I'm not sure I understand why being a dairy farmer is hard work. I'll reread to find out. Now I understand that farmers on small farms do the work by hand.

Build Vocabulary page 99
spoil: go bad

❷ Details: Time-Order DOK 1

The information is organized by time order, or in the order of how events happen. On page 98, what happens first? (Cows are milked.) Look at page 99. What happens next? (The milk goes into a tank and to a dairy.)

Reread

Author/Illustrator's Craft DOK 3

Reading/Writing Companion, 171

What do the photos on page 98 help you understand? (The photos help me understand the difference between milking by hand and using a machine.)

At the dairy, the milk is cooked. **3** Bringing it to a boil will kill bad germs. Then, it is quickly cooled.

When that's **done**, machines put all the milk into cartons or jugs.

After that, cartons and jugs full of milk get sent to stores. They are put in the dairy case. Look at all the kinds of milk we can **buy**.

Who will drink the milk? You!

100   101

Literature Anthology, pp. 100–101

Read

3 Details: Time-Order DOK 1

We have learned about some steps in the process of getting milk. First, cows are milked. Next, the milk goes into a tank and a truck takes it to a dairy. What happens then? Let's add that to our chart.

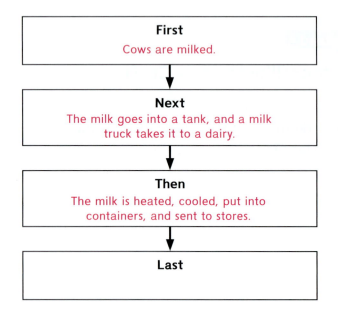

First
Cows are milked.

↓

Next
The milk goes into a tank, and a milk truck takes it to a dairy.

↓

Then
The milk is heated, cooled, put into containers, and sent to stores.

↓

Last

4 Genre DOK 1

What kind of text is this? How do we know? (It is nonfiction. It tells about real events.) What are some facts on pages 100–101? (Milk is put into cartons and sent to stores.)

Build Vocabulary page 100
boil: the hot temperature when water bubbles

ELL Spotlight on Language

Page 101 Point to the phrase *all the kinds of.* Explain this means "many different types." *What are there* all the kinds of *at the store?* (milk) Have partners turn and talk using the phrase *all the kinds of.* Provide a sentence frame: Look at all the kinds of books in the library.

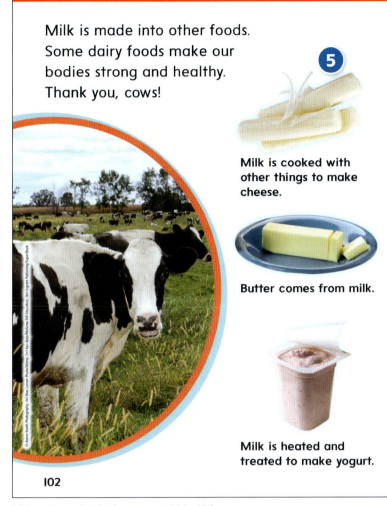

Milk is made into other foods. Some dairy foods make our bodies strong and healthy. Thank you, cows!

5

Milk is cooked with other things to make cheese.

Butter comes from milk.

Milk is heated and treated to make yogurt.

102

Fun Facts **6**

Moooo!

- Most cows give enough milk every day to fill 90 glasses.

- Some farmers say that cows give more milk when there's music playing.

Respond to the Text

1. Use details from the selection to retell the text in order. RETELL

2. Based on *From Cows to You*, which job in the milk process would you rather have? Why? WRITE

 3. What other foods do we get from a farm? TEXT TO WORLD

103

Literature Anthology, pp. 102–103

5 Genre DOK 1

Nonfiction can use captions to give more information. What is the text on page 102 about? (The text is about how milk can be made into other foods.) What does the caption about the photo at the top of the page tell us? (Milk can be cooked with other things to make cheese.)

6 Reread DOK 1

Teacher Think Aloud I'm not sure I understand why milk is heated to make yogurt. I reread page 98 and realize that in order for us to drink milk, it has to be heated first. This kills the germs. So now I understand that to make yogurt, milk has to be heated first to kill the germs.

Reread

Author's Purpose DOK 3

Reading/Writing Companion, 172

What does the author want you to understand about milk? (The author wants me to know how milk gets from cows to people.)

ELL English Language Learners

Clarifying Words and Expressions Remind children that they can use circumlocution, or paraphrasing, to help clarify words or expressions they do not understand. *What is another way of saying "comes from milk"?* ("is made from milk")

Read

Details: Time-Order

Let's review our Time-Order chart. We've read about the journey milk takes from the cow to us. What happens first? What happens next? Then what happens? Now let's fill in what happens last. Let's reread the last paragraph of page 101 to find out. Then let's add that step to our Time-Order chart.

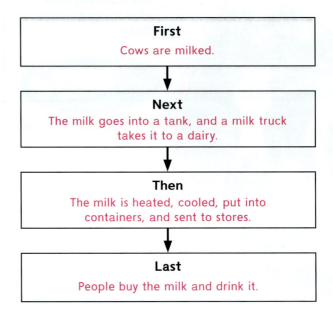

First
Cows are milked.

↓

Next
The milk goes into a tank, and a milk truck takes it to a dairy.

↓

Then
The milk is heated, cooled, put into containers, and sent to stores.

↓

Last
People buy the milk and drink it.

Return to Purposes

Have partners discuss what they learned about how we get milk. Remind them to use details from the text.

Read

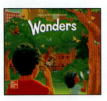
Retell

Have children turn to page 170 in their **Reading/Writing Companion.** Remind them that as they read the text, they paid attention to the order of how milk is produced. Have children use the information they recorded on their Time-Order chart to help them retell the selection.

Use Text Evidence Guide children to use text evidence to respond to the questions on page 170.

Reread

Analyze the Text

After children read and retell the selection, have them reread *From Cows to You* to develop a deeper understanding of the text by answering the questions on pages 171–172 in their **Reading/Writing Companion**. For children who need support finding text evidence to support their responses, use the scaffolded instruction from the Reread prompts on pages T359–T361.

Integrate

Build Knowledge: Make Connections

Talk About the Text Have partners discuss how we get food from cows.

Write About the Text Then have children add their ideas to the Build Knowledge page of their reader's notebook.

Add to the Anchor Chart Record any new ideas on the Build Knowledge anchor chart.

Add to the Word Bank Then add words related to where food comes from to a separate section of the Word Bank.

Compare Texts DOK 4

Guide children to compare what is different about how we get milk and how we get orange juice. Share the prompt: *What is different about how we get milk in* From Cows to You *and orange juice in* "A Look at Breakfast"*?* Say: *Think about what the author tells about milk. Does milk come from an animal? Does orange juice come from an animal?* (Milk comes from an animal, but orange juice comes from oranges.) Have partners discuss the differences in each process from both texts and then share their responses with the class. You can use a two-column chart to show the differences.

 ENGLISH LANGUAGE LEARNERS

Retell Help children use connecting words to retell the selection. Guide them to look at each page and answer a question, such as: *What is this page about? What happens first? What happens next?* Provide sentence frames to help children retell the selection, such as: First the cows <u>are milked</u>. Next the milk goes in <u>tanks</u>. Then the milk is put into <u>containers</u>. Last, people buy the <u>milk</u>.

 CONNECT TO CONTENT

Exchanging Goods and Services Remind children that this week they've been reading about how we get our food. Guide children to identify the people in the selection who are producers (the farmers and the people at the dairy), sellers (the people at the store), and buyers (the people who buy things at the store). Talk about how trading services for money allows people to get the things that they need to survive.

 STUDENT CHECK-IN

Read Have children name one important detail from the text. Have them reflect, using the Check-In routine to fill in the bars.

Reread Have partners tell one way the author used the photos to tell about milk. Have children reflect using the Check-In routine to fill in the bars.

LESSON 3

LEARNING GOALS

- We can write an opinion about a nonfiction text.
- We can write contractions with *not*.

OBJECTIVES

Write opinion pieces in which they introduce the topic or name the book they are writing about, state an opinion, supply a reason for the opinion, and provide some sense of closure.

Demonstrate command of the conventions of standard English grammar and usage when writing or speaking.

Form contractions with *not*.

ELA ACADEMIC LANGUAGE

- opinion, reason
- Cognates: *opinión, razón*

⟫ TEACH IN SMALL GROUP

Choose from these options to enable all children to complete the writing activity:

- Drawing and labeling a picture
- Completing sentence frames
- Writing one sentence
- Writing multiple sentences

Additionally, to provide differentiated support for children, see Writing Skills mini lessons on pages T420–T429. These can be used throughout the year.

⟨5 mins⟩ Independent Writing

Write About the Anchor Text DOK 3

Analyze the Prompt Read the prompt: *Based on* From Cows to You, *which job in the milk process would you rather have? Why?* Have partners turn and talk about one of the jobs in the milk process.

- Say: *The first part of this prompt is asking for your opinion. The second part of the prompt asks why you have that opinion. You will need to give reasons to support your opinion.*

Find Text Evidence Say: *We need to find information about the different jobs and make inferences about what the jobs are like. We can use that information to form an opinion about which job we would rather have. Look at page 98 in the* **Literature Anthology***.* Then ask:

- *What is the first job in the milk process?* (dairy farmer) *What does a dairy farmer do?* (feeds and cares for the cows)

- *Now look at the first photograph on page 98. The farmer is milking the cow. What clues help you know what her job is like? Where does she work? Why might she wear boots?* (She works with animals; she works outdoors. There's hay on the ground, so she is probably in a barn.)

Have children continue finding text evidence, as necessary, to respond to the prompt. You may choose to take notes on a chart or have children take notes in their writer's notebook.

Write a Response Tell children to turn to page 173 in their **Reading/Writing Companion.** Have partners talk about the text evidence they found. Guide children to use the text evidence to draft a response. Remind them to tell which job they would like and why.

- **Writing Checklist** Read the checklist aloud with children. Remind them to include reasons to support their opinion, stretch sounds in words to help them write, and spell contractions correctly.

- **Writing Support** If needed, provide sentence starters. Model completing one as necessary.

I would like _____.

It is the best job because _____.

Tell children they will finalize and present their writing the next day.

Reading/Writing Companion, p. 173

5 mins

Grammar

Contractions with *Not*

1 **Review** Remind children that a contraction is a short way of writing two words. For contractions with *not,* an apostrophe takes the place of the missing letter *o.* Have children identify the contraction in the model sentence.

Ask: *What is the contraction in the following sentence?* It isn't easy to make bread. *What two words make the contraction?* Is *and* not *make the contraction* isn't.

2 **Guided Practice/Practice** Write the sentence *I didn't know there were so many steps to making bread.* Have children identify the contraction. Have children write sentences that contain contractions with *not.*

Talk About It

 COLLABORATE

Have partners work together to orally generate sentences about a different topic. Challenge them to use contractions.

Mechanics: Apostrophes in Contractions

1 **Model** Remind children that, in contractions, an apostrophe takes the place of one or more letters. The apostrophe combines two words and makes one shorter word.

2 **Guided Practice** Write the words *isnt, arent, cant, didnt,* and *doesnt.* Ask children to correct the errors.

ELL English Language Learners

Independent Writing, Analyze the Prompt Review what is meant by *the milk process* with children. *The milk process is the way milk gets from a cow to us to drink.* Use the photographs from the **Big Book** to help children identify the jobs involved with each step. Point to the woman milking a cow on page 98. *This woman is a dairy farmer. She milks the cows. That's the first job in the milk process. What is her job?* She is a <u>dairy farmer</u>. Have children turn and talk to a partner about whether they'd like the job of dairy farmer. Have children tell a reason to support their opinion. Repeat the routine with other jobs in the milk process, such as *dairy worker* and *grocery store worker.*

For additional support, see the **ELL Small Group Guide,** p. 155.

DIGITAL TOOLS

Use these activities to practice grammar and mechanics.

Grammar

Mechanics

FORMATIVE ASSESSMENT

❯ STUDENT CHECK-IN

Writing Have partners share their responses. Have children fill in the bars.

Grammar Have children read one of their sentences.

Have children reflect, using the Check-In routine.

We can learn and use new vocabulary words.

OBJECTIVES

Identify real-life connections between words and their use.

Discuss the Essential Question.

Develop oral language.

ELA ACADEMIC LANGUAGE

• *information*
• Cognate: *información*

DIGITAL TOOLS

Visual Vocabulary Cards

LESSON FOCUS

READING

Revisit the Essential Question

Read and Reread Paired Selection:

"The Five Food Groups"
• Introduce Text Features
• Reread Text for Understanding

Word Work
• Build Words with /u̇/*oo, u*

WRITING
• Independent Writing
• Review Grammar and Mechanics

Literature Anthology, pp. 104–105

---

15 mins

Oral Language

MULTIMODAL

  Essential Question

How do we get our food?

Remind children that this week they have been learning about how we get our food. Guide children to discuss the question using information from what they have read and discussed. Use the print or digital **Visual Vocabulary Cards** and the Define/Example/Ask routine to review the oral vocabulary words *delicious, delighted, enormous, nutritious,* and *responsibility.* Then review last week's oral vocabulary words *century, entertainment, future, past,* and *present.*

Guide children to use each word as they talk about what they have read and learned about the food that we eat. Prompt children by asking questions.

• Where do *delicious* dairy products come from?

• Are you *delighted* by tasty food?

• How big does an apple have to be to be considered *enormous*?

• Do you think milk or bread is more *nutritious*?

• Who has the *responsibility* of making food where you live?

Have partners use an oral vocabulary word in a sentence. Have children reflect using the Check-In routine.

Text Features

Diagram

1 **Explain** Review that nonfiction texts have facts and details. Say: *Nonfiction texts can also have diagrams, pictures that show the parts of something. A diagram usually has labels that name the parts.*

Online Teaching Chart

2 **Model** Display **Online Teaching Chart** for Text Features: Diagrams. Say: *The diagram gives information about parts of a wasp.* Point to the feeler and say: *This label is pointing to a part of the wasp that is called a feeler.*

3 **Guided Practice/Practice** Read the rest of the labels together. Guide children to discuss the information in the diagram. *How many parts does a wasp have? What is the tip of its body called?* Have children explain how they used the diagram to get the information. Tell children to look for diagrams as they read nonfiction texts.

 ## English Language Learners

Use these scaffolds with **Text Features, Model.**

Beginning

Point to the label for feeler and slide your finger up to the feeler in the photo. Have children repeat that word. Then have a volunteer point to the label for *leg* and then to the wasp's leg in the photo.

Intermediate

What information does this diagram give? It gives information about parts of a wasp. Point to the *feeler* label. *What does this label point to?* It points to the part of the wasp called the feeler.

Advanced/Advanced High

Have partners work together to read the title of the diagram and explain how the labels and photo work together using sentence frames: The title is Parts of a Wasp. The labels show the parts of the wasp in the photo.

LEARNING GOALS

We can use text features to get more information from a text.

OBJECTIVES

Know and use various text features (e.g., headings, tables of contents, glossaries, electronic menus, icons) to locate key facts or information in a text.

ELA ACADEMIC LANGUAGE

• *information, diagram*
• Cognates: *información, diagrama*

DIGITAL TOOLS

Text Feature Activity

NEWCOMERS

Use the **Newcomer Online Visuals** and their accompanying prompts to help children expand vocabulary and language about Community (Unit 3, 15–19). Use the Conversation Starters, Speech Balloons, and Games in the **Newcomer Teacher's Guide** to continue building vocabulary and developing oral and written language.

FORMATIVE ASSESSMENT

❯ STUDENT CHECK-IN

Have partners tell one thing they learned from the diagram. Have children reflect using the Check-In routine.

LESSON 4

Genre Nonfiction

Read Together

Compare Texts
Learn how to use a food diagram.

The Five Food Groups

There are five food groups. They are dairy, grains, fruits, vegetables, and protein.

Lunch is a good time to eat food from each **1** group. Where do the foods in your lunch come from?

104

protein   vegetables   dairy   fruit   grains

2

Let's look at the diagram! This diagram shows the parts of a meal. Fruits, vegetables, and grains come from plants. Dairy comes from animals. Protein can come from plants or animals.

Make Connections
? Which food on the diagram comes from animals? Which foods come from plants? **Essential Question**

105

Literature Anthology, pp. 104–105
Lexile 450L

"The Five Food Groups"

LEARNING GOAL

Read We can understand important ideas and details in a text.

Reread We can name the choices an author made when writing a text.

Compare Texts

As children read and reread "The Five Food Groups," encourage them to think about the Essential Question. Tell children to think about which food groups the foods in "A Look at Breakfast" belong to.

Genre Focus Tell children that this is a nonfiction text. Review that a nonfiction text can tell about real things by giving facts about them. Nonfiction text can also have diagrams..

Read

1 Reread DOK 1

Teacher Think Aloud I read that lunch is a good time to eat food from every group. I'm not sure what that means, so I reread the text and the diagram. Now I understand that foods belong to different food groups and that lunch is a good time to eat a food from each group.

2 Text Feature: Diagram DOK 1

Diagrams have **labels**. What are the labels in this diagram? (protein, dairy, grains, fruits, vegetables)

Reread

Author's Craft DOK 3

Reading/Writing Companion, 174

Set Purpose Let's reread to find out about the food groups.

Which words name the five food groups? Circle the words in the text. (dairy, grains, fruits, vegetables, protein)

What is the purpose of having a question in the text? (The purpose of having a question in the text is so that you can look for the answer in the text.)

page 175

What is your favorite food in the diagram? Circle the food group it belongs to. (Answers will vary.)

Talk with a partner about how the diagram can help you understand the five food groups. (Possible answer: It shows examples of a food from each group.)

Talk About It How is a food diagram helpful for a reader? (Possible answer: A food diagram includes labels that name the foods in each group.)

Read

Retell

Guide children to use relevant details to retell the selection.

Reread

Analyze the Text

After children retell, have them reread to develop a deeper understanding of the text. Have children annotate the text and answer the questions on **Reading/Writing Companion** pages 174–175. For children who need support citing text evidence, use the Reread prompts on this page.

Integrate

BUILD KNOWLEDGE: MAKE CONNECTIONS

Talk About the Text Have partners discuss where the foods in each food group come from.

Write About the Text Then have children add their ideas to the Build Knowledge page of their reader's notebook.

Add to the Anchor Chart Record any new ideas on the Build Knowledge anchor chart.

Add to the Word Bank Then add words related to where food comes from to a separate section of the Word Bank.

FORMATIVE ASSESSMENT

STUDENT CHECK-IN

Read Have partners name one important detail from the text. Have them reflect using the Check-In routine.

Reread Have partners tell one choice the author made when creating this text. Have children reflect using the Check-In routine to fill in the bars.

In a Flash: Sound-Spellings

Display the Sound-Spelling Card *book*.
1. **Teacher:** What are the letters?   **Children:** oo
2. **Teacher:** What's the sound?   **Children:** /ů/
3. **Teacher:** What's the word?   **Children:** book
Continue the routine for previously taught sounds.

LEARNING GOALS

- We can segment sounds in words.
- We can build words with the /ů/ sound.
- We can add the endings *-ed*, and *-ing* to make new words.
- We can spell and sort words with the /ů/ sound.
- We can read the words *after, buy, done, every, soon,* and *work.*

OBJECTIVES

Segment spoken single-syllable words into their complete sequence of individual sounds (phonemes).

Use conventional spelling for words with common spelling patterns and for frequently occurring irregular words.

Read words with inflectional endings.

Recognize and read grade-appropriate irregularly spelled words.

ELA ACADEMIC LANGUAGE

- *endings, action words, verbs*
- Cognate: *verbos*

 **TEACH IN SMALL GROUP**

Word Work lessons can be taught in small groups.

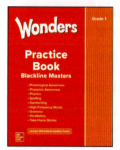

Wonders Grade 1

Practice Book
Blackline Masters

Structural Analysis: **Page 234**

OPTION 5 mins

Phonemic Awareness

Phoneme Segmentation

1 **Model** Say: *Listen as I say a word:* foot. *What sounds are in the word* foot? *Yes, /f/ /ů/ /t/. There are three sounds.*

2 **Guided Practice/Practice** Say: *I am going to say some words. Tell me which sounds you hear in the word and then say the word. Let's do the first one together.* Guide practice and provide corrective feedback, using the following examples:

book	pulls	crook	stood	put	shook
crooks	books	looks	pushed	foot	brooks
bulls	soot	nooks	hoods	wood	took

5 mins

Phonics

MULTIMODAL

Build Words with /ů/ *oo, u*

1 **Review** Provide children with **Word Building Cards** *a–z.* Have children put the letters in alphabetical order as quickly as possible. Say: *The letters* oo *and* u *can stand for the /ů/ sound.* Place the letters *f, u, l, l. Let's blend the sounds and read: /fffůůů lll/. Now change the* f *to* p. Blend the sounds and read the word.

2 **Practice** Continue with *push, put, pat, sat, set, wet, wed, wood.* Once children have finished building the words, dictate the words in the list and have children write the word-building list. Have partners exchange and check the written lists for spelling. Listen in and provide corrective feedback.

Color Coding After each dictation, reveal the secret color-coding letter(s) for children to find on their **Response Boards**. Have them say the sound(s) as they trace each letter in color. Use one or two of the phonics skills of the week for color coding.

Decodable Reader

Have children read "That Looks Good" to practice decoding words in connected text. If children need support, turn to Small Group, pages T387 or T394 for instruction for the decodable reader.

Structural Analysis

5 mins

Inflectional Endings *-ed, -ing*

1 **Review** Write the words *flip, flipped, flipping* and read them with children. Remind children that we use the endings *-ed* and *-ing* to change the meanings of action words, or verbs. Children should remember that sometimes when you add *-ed* or *-ing* to a word, the final consonant is doubled before adding the ending.

2 **Practice** Write: *grab, drip, shop.* Have partners construct words by adding *-ed* and *-ing.* Have them write sentences with each word.

If children need additional practice identifying and reading inflectional endings, see **Practice Book** page 234 or the online activity.

Spelling

5 mins

MULTIMODAL

Word Sort with *-ook, -ood*

1 **Review** Provide pairs of children with copies of the online **Spelling Word Cards.** While one partner reads each word, the other partner should orally segment the word and then write it. After reading all the words, partners should switch roles.

2 **Practice** Have children correct their own papers. Then have them sort the words by ending spelling pattern.

High-Frequency Words

OPTION 5 mins

after, buy, done, every, soon, work

Review Display the print or digital **Visual Vocabulary Cards** for high-frequency words *after, buy, done, every, soon,* and *work.* Have children Read/Spell/Write each word.

• Point to a word and call on a child to use it in a sentence.

• Review last week's words using the same procedure.

DIGITAL TOOLS

For more practice, use these activities.

Word Work

Phonemic Awareness
Phonics
Structural Analysis
Spelling
High-Frequency Words

FORMATIVE ASSESSMENT

❯ STUDENT CHECK-IN

Phonics/Spelling Have children spell words with the /u̇/ sound.

Structural Analysis Have partners read their sentences.

High-Frequency Words Have partners take turns reading the high-frequency words.

Have children reflect, using the Check-In routine.

✓ CHECK FOR SUCCESS

Rubric Use your online rubric to record children's progress.

Can children read and decode words with /u̇/ spelled *oo* and *u?*

Can children recognize and read high-frequency words?

❯ Small Group Instruction

If No

🔴 **Approaching** Reteach pp. T384–T389

🟣 **ELL** Develop pp. T384–T389

If Yes

🔵 **On** Review pp. T392–T393

🟢 **Beyond** Extend pp. T396–T397

LEARNING GOALS

• We can revise our writing.
• We can write sentences that include contractions with *not*.

OBJECTIVES

With guidance and support from adults, focus on a topic, respond to questions and suggestions from peers, and add details to strengthen writing as needed.

Ask and answer questions about key details in information presented orally.

Form contractions with *not*.

ELA ACADEMIC LANGUAGE

• *reason, revise*
• Cognates: *razón, revisar*

Independent Writing

5 mins

Write About the Anchor Text

Revise

Reread the prompt about *From Cows to You: Based on* From Cows to You, *which job in the milk process would you rather have? Why?*

• Have children read their drafts in their **Reading/Writing Companion.** Ask them to check that they responded to the prompt. Then have them review the checklist to confirm that they supported their opinions with reasons and wrote contractions correctly. Remind children to stretch sounds in words and clap syllables to help them with spelling.

Peer Review Have pairs take notes about what they liked most, questions they have for the author, and additional ideas the author could include. Have partners discuss these topics. Provide time for revisions.

Edit/Proofread

Review the online proofreading marks with children. Model how to use each mark. Then have children edit for the following:

• High-frequency words are used correctly.

• Contractions with *not* are written correctly.

Write Final Draft

Have children create their final draft in their writer's notebook by:

• writing neatly or using digital tools to produce and publish their work.

• adding reasons to support their opinions, using evidence from the text.

Teacher Conference As children work, conference with them to provide guidance. Make sure children state an opinion in their writing and support that opinion with reasons and facts from the text. Have children make changes based on your feedback.

Share and Evaluate

After children have finalized their draft, have them do the following:

• work with a partner to practice presenting their writing to each other.

• share their final draft with the class.

• ask and answer questions about each other's work.

If possible, record children as they share so that they can self-evaluate. After children share, display their final papers on a bulletin board.

Have children add their work to their writing folder. Invite them to look at their previous writing and discuss with a partner how it has improved.

Grammar

5 mins

Contractions with *Not*

1 **Review** Remind children that a contraction is a way to put two words together to form a shorter word.

2 **Practice** Write the following sentences. Read each sentence and have children repeat. Have children write the verb and the word *not* for each contraction. **The boy isn't in the race.** (is not) **Pete and Jen aren't jumping rope.** (are not) **People can't walk on the wet bridge.** (can not) **They don't want to play the game.** (do not)

Have children edit the draft in their Writer's Notebook for contractions. For additional practice with editing using contractions with not and see **Practice Book** page 237 or the online activity.

Talk About It

Have partners work together to orally generate sentences with and without contractions. Challenge them to say a sentence with a contraction, then have the partner say the sentence using the two words that were used to form the contraction.

Mechanics: Apostrophes in Contractions

1 **Review** Remind children that, in a contraction, an apostrophe takes the place of one or more letters.

2 **Practice** Prompt children to correct each sentence. **The map doesnt have our state on it.** (The map doesn't have our state on it.) **I dont like prunes.** (I don't like prunes.) **That isnt my notebook.** (That isn't my notebook.)

For additional practice with apostrophes in contractions, see **Practice Book** page 238 or the online activity.

English Language Learners

Independent Writing, Revise Display two sentences that respond to the prompt, such as: I want to be a dairy farmer. I like cows. Point to the second sentence. *This sentence tells a reason that explains why I picked the job dairy farmer. It tells why.* Have children read their drafts. *Do you have a sentence that tells why you picked that job? If not, add one.* Have children use the frame: I like _____.

For additional support, see the **ELL Small Group Guide,** p. 155.

DIGITAL TOOLS

Use these resources with the lessons.

Proofreading Marks

Grammar

Mechanics

Grammar: Page 237
Mechanics: Page 238

FORMATIVE ASSESSMENT

❯ STUDENT CHECK-IN

Writing Have children reflect on one way they revised their writing.

Grammar Have partners read each other's complete sentences.

Have children reflect, using the Check-In routine.

LESSON 4

LEARNING GOALS

We can research to learn about a food item.

OBJECTIVES

Participate in shared research and writing projects.

With guidance and support from adults, recall information from experiences or gather information from provided sources to answer a question.

Add drawings or other visual displays to descriptions when appropriate to clarify ideas, thoughts, and feelings.

Build on others' talk in conversations by responding to the comments of others through multiple exchanges.

ELA ACADEMIC LANGUAGE

• *product, sequence*
• Cognates: *producto, sequencia*

 COLLABORATIVE CONVERSATIONS

Be Open to All Ideas
Review with children that as they engage in partner, small-group, and whole-group discussions, they should:

• remember everyone's ideas are important and should be heard.

• not be afraid to ask a question if something is unclear.

• respect the opinions of others.

Integrate

Foods

10 mins

Model

Tell children that today they will research a food item. Display pages 176–177 of the **Reading/Writing Companion** and model filling them in, reviewing the steps in the research process below.

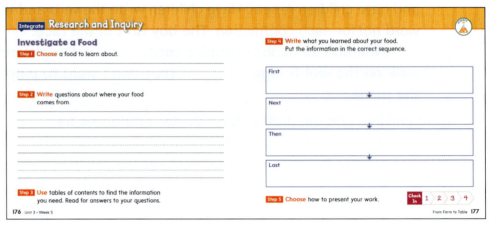

Reading/Writing Companion, pp. 176–177

STEP 1 Choose a Topic

This project is to research a food item. First I need to pick a food that I am interested in learning about. I like oranges, so I'll research oranges.

STEP 2 Write Your Questions

I need to decide what I'd like to know about how we get oranges. In what parts of the world do oranges grow? What do the people who grow oranges have to do? How do oranges get from where they grow to stores in faraway places?

STEP 3 Find Information

I can do research by looking at books or using the Internet. I can use a table of contents in the front of a book or on a website to find a chapter, section, or webpage about how oranges are transported from orange groves to markets.

STEP 4 Write What You Learned

Let's write down what we have learned about how oranges get from where they grow to our homes. I will put the steps of the process in the correct sequence.

STEP 5 Choose How to Present Your Work

I can decide the best way to present what I have learned. I will create a poster. I will draw and label each step in the process.

Apply

Have children turn to pages 176–177 in their **Reading/Writing Companion.**

Guide them as they choose a food to research and formulate their questions. If children are unsure about how to do their research, you can help them find books or websites that might be useful. Remind children to use tables of contents to help them locate information about their food.

Before children fill out the sequence chart, they can discuss their ideas with a partner. When children are ready to list the steps, have them draw pictures as well.

After children have completed their research, guide them to fill out the Research Process Checklist on the online Student Checklist. This checklist helps children decide if they've completed all of the necessary parts of the research process.

Choose the Presentation Format

Have children turn to pages 176–177 in their Reading/Writing Companion to review their research, what they learned about the food they selected, and their sequence chart. Tell them that today they are going to take the next step by creating a way to present their findings. This will be their final product. Options include:

- create a flowchart that shows the steps in the process
- draw and label a picture
- make a slideshow of photos, drawings, and text, using an interactive whiteboard

Create the Presentation

Have children develop their presentations. Remind them of the rules of working with others.

Gather Materials Have children gather the materials they'll need to create their finished product. Most of the materials should be available in the classroom or can be brought from home.

Make the Presentation Once children have gathered the materials they need, provide time for them to work. Have children review their research before they begin. Then support them as they work on their presentations.

You may wish to have children collaborate on projects.

ENGLISH LANGUAGE LEARNERS

Apply, Step 1 Create a word bank of names of foods children can research. Ask children to suggest foods they know. If children suggest foods with multiple ingredients, like *pizza* or *hamburgers*, help them pick one part of the food, such as cheese or bun, to focus on. As you add each food, read the word aloud and have children repeat.

❯ TEACH IN SMALL GROUP

You may wish to have children create their presentation during Small Group time. Group children of varying abilities together or group children who are doing similar projects.

RESEARCH AND INQUIRY: SHARING FINAL PROJECTS

As children get ready to wrap up the week, have them share their Research and Inquiry projects. Then have them self-evaluate.

 Prepare Have children gather materials they need to present their projects. Then partners can take turns practicing their presentations.

Share Guide children to present their Research and Inquiry projects. Encourage them to ask questions to clarify when something is unclear.

Evaluate Have children discuss and evaluate their own presentations. You may want to have them fill out the Presentation Checklist on the online Student Checklist.

FORMATIVE ASSESSMENT

❯ STUDENT CHECK-IN

Have children share one piece of information they learned from their research.

Have children reflect, using the Check-In routine to fill in the bars.

LESSON 5

LEARNING GOALS

- We can blend and segment sounds in words.
- We can build words with the /ủ/ sound.
- We can write words that end in -ed and -ing.
- We can write words with the /ủ/ sound.
- We can write the words *after, buy, done, every, soon,* and *work.*

OBJECTIVES

Orally produce single-syllable words by blending sounds (phonemes), including consonant blends.

Segment spoken single-syllable words into their complete sequence of individual sounds (phonemes).

Decode regularly spelled one-syllable words.

Use conventional spelling for words with common spelling patterns and for frequently occurring irregular words.

Recognize and read grade-appropriate irregularly spelled words.

ELA ACADEMIC LANGUAGE

- *verbs, endings, action words*
- Cognate: *verbos*

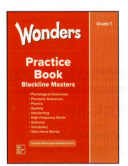

Take-Home Story:
Pages 239–240
Spelling: Posttest, Page 229

READING
Word Work
- Review /ủ/ *oo, u*

Make Connections
- Connect the painting to the Essential Question
- Show Your Knowledge

WRITING
- Self-Selected Writing
- Review Grammar and Mechanics

Reading/Writing Companion, pp. 178–179

---

⑤ mins Phonemic Awareness

Phoneme Blending

Review Guide children to blend phonemes to form words. Say: *Listen as I say a group of sounds. Then blend those sounds to form a word.*

/p/ /ủ/ /sh/	/b/ /r/ /ủ/ /k/	/b/ /ủ/ /k/ /s/	/g/ /ủ/ /d/
/b/ /ủ/ /sh/	/sh/ /ủ/ /k/	/l/ /ủ/ /k/	/s/ /t/ /ủ/ /d/

Phoneme Segmentation

Review Guide children to segment phonemes in words. Say: *I am going to say a word. I want you to say each sound in the word.*

foot	good	book	pull	put	stood
brooks	shook	crooks	full	wood	hooks

⑤ mins Phonics

 MULTIMODAL

Blend and Build Words with /ủ/ *oo, u*

Review Have children read and say the words *push, put, foot,* and *look.* Then have children follow the word-building routine with **Word-Building Cards** to build *good, wood, hood, hook, book, cook, look, took, shook, crook,* and *brook.*

Word Automaticity Help children practice word automaticity. Display decodable words and point to each one as children chorally read it. Test how many words children can read in one minute. Model blending words children miss.

Read the Decodable Reader

If children need extra practice decoding words in context, have them read one of this week's decodable readers. If children need additional support for these stories, turn to Small Group, pages T387 or T394 for instruction and support.

In a Flash: Sound-Spellings

Display the Sound-Spelling Card *book.*
1. **Teacher:** What are the letters?   **Children:** oo
2. **Teacher:** What's the sound?   **Children:** /ù/
3. **Teacher:** What's the word?   **Children:** book
Continue the routine for previously taught sounds.

DIGITAL TOOLS
For more practice, use these activities.

Word Work

Phonemic Awareness
Phonics
Structural Analysis
Spelling
High-Frequency Words

Structural Analysis

Inflectional Endings *-ed, -ing*

Review Have children explain how to add inflectional endings *-ed* and *-ing* to words that end with a short vowel followed by one consonant. Children should note that we use the endings *-ed* and *-ing* to change the meaning of action words or verbs. Have children practice writing words with *-ed* and *-ing,* such as *chatted, stopped, hopped, drumming, petting, wagged, trimmed,* and *getting.*

Spelling

Word Sort with *-ook, -ood*

Review Have children use the online **Spelling Word Cards** to sort the weekly words by vowel and ending sounds. Remind children that four of the words do not have the /ù/ sound.

Assess Test children on their abilities to spell words with /ù/oo. Say each word and provide a sentence. Allow them time to write the words. Remind children to write their answers legibly, leaving adequate space between words. As a challenge, provide more words that follow the same spelling pattern. Have children complete the spelling posttest using **Practice Book** page 229.

FORMATIVE ASSESSMENT

> **STUDENT CHECK-IN**

Phonics/Spelling Have children spell a word with the /ù/ sound.

Structural Analysis Have partners use words with *-ed* and *-ing* in sentences.

High-Frequency Words Have partners share sentences using the high-frequency words.

Have children reflect, using the Check-In routine.

✓ **CHECK FOR SUCCESS**

Rubric Use your online rubric to record children's progress.

Can children read and decode words with /ù/ spelled *oo* and *u?*

Can children recognize and read high-frequency words?

> **Small Group Instruction**

If No

● **Approaching** Reteach pp. T384–T389

● **ELL** Develop pp. T384–T389

If Yes

● **On** Review pp. T392–T393

● **Beyond** Extend pp. T396–T397

High-Frequency Words

after, buy, done, every, soon, work

Review Display the print or digital **Visual Vocabulary Cards** *after, buy, done, every, soon, work.* Have children Read/Spell/Write each word. Have children write a sentence with each word.

If children need assistance reading high-frequency words, they can practice reading independently using the Take-Home Story in the **Practice Book** on pages 239–240 or use online resources.

LESSON 5

LEARNING GOALS

- We can choose a writing activity and share it.
- We can name the two words in a contraction.

OBJECTIVES

With guidance and support from adults, focus on a topic, respond to questions and suggestions from peers, and add details to strengthen writing as needed.

Ask and answer questions about what a speaker says in order to gather additional information or clarify something that is not understood.

Use verbs to convey a sense of past, present, and future.

Self-select writing activity and topics.

ELA ACADEMIC LANGUAGE

- *presentation, evaluate*
- Cognates: *presentación, evaluar*

 **DIFFERENTIATED WRITING**

You may wish to conference with children to provide additional support for these writing activities.

- Journal Writing: Have children talk about what they have eaten that day. Have them brainstorm ideas about where the food may have come from.
- Book Review: To help children choose a topic for their review, display a list of the different texts they have read this week.

 5 mins

Self-Selected Writing

Talk About the Topic

Remind children of the Essential Question: *How do we get our food?* Have partners turn and talk about the Essential Question and encourage them to ask each other questions.

Choose a Writing Activity

Tell children they will select a type of writing they would like to do. Children may write about the theme of the week or about a different topic that is important to them. Children may choose from the following modes of writing.

 Journal Writing Remind children that a journal is a place where they can write and draw whatever they wish. Have children write about where their food comes from or about a different topic of their choice. Children may want to draw some of their ideas before or after they write.

 Picture Spark Explain to children that a picture can "spark" an idea for a writing topic. Display several photos or illustrations of different food items. Have children write and draw about what they see in the pictures.

 Book Review Explain that a book review gives a writer's opinion about a book. Have children choose a book they have read or listened to recently and write a brief review. Children's book review should tell whether or not they liked the book and why. Model as necessary.

Use Digital Tools You may wish to work with children to explore a variety of digital tools to produce or publish their writing.

Share Your Writing

 Review the speaking and listening strategies with children. Then have them share their writing with a partner or small group. You may wish to display children's work on a bulletin board or in a classroom writing area.

SPEAKING STRATEGIES	LISTENING STRATEGIES
✓ Speak slowly and clearly.	✓ Listen actively and politely.
✓ Speak at an appropriate volume.	✓ Wait until the presenter has finished to ask questions.

Grammar

OPTION
5 mins

Contractions with *Not*

1 **Review** Ask children how contractions with *not* are formed. Write these sentences and have children identify contractions.

It **isn't** time to get up. (isn't)
I **can't** walk up the big hill. (can't)
Don't nap while we take a test. (Don't)
I **didn't** get to see your new bike. (didn't)

2 **Practice** Ask: *What is a contraction? What takes the place of the letter* o *in a contraction with* not?

Have children change the contractions in each sentence to the two words each contraction stands for.

Mechanics: Apostrophes in Contractions

1 **Review** Remind children that a contraction is two words put together. An apostrophe takes the place of the letter or letters that are left out. Many contractions are made with the word *not.* The apostrophe takes the place of the *o* in *not.*

2 **Practice** Write the following sentences. Read each aloud. Have children fix the contraction in each sentence.

The cat **di'dnt** eat its snack. (didn't)
They **areno't** going to ride the bus. (aren't)
My dog **doesnt** like to take a bath. (doesn't)

ELL English Language Learners

Self-Selected Writing, Choose a Writing Activity Present the writing activities and tell the children that they will vote to select one of the activities. Then you will work on the writing as a group. Make sure to do the activity on chart paper as you will revise and publish it during small group time. Provide sentence frames and starters as you talk through the writing together. For example, if children have selected writing a book review, choose a book together. Then talk about what children like or don't like about the book. Possible sentence frames are: One thing I like/do not like about ___ is ___. I like/do not like ___ because ___.

For additional support, see the **ELL Small Group Guide,** p. 155.

DIGITAL TOOLS

Use these activities to practice grammar and mechanics.

Grammar

Mechanics

▶ TEACH IN SMALL GROUP

● **Approaching** Provide more opportunities for children to read and form contractions before they write sentences.

● ● **On Level and Beyond** Children can do the Practice sections only.

● **ELL** Use the chart in the **Language Transfers Handbook** to identify grammatical forms that may cause difficulty.

FORMATIVE ASSESSMENT

⊘ STUDENT CHECK-IN

Writing Have children share one sentence or label they wrote.

Grammar Have partners name the two words in one contraction with *not.*

Have children reflect, using the Check-In routine.

LEARNING GOALS

We can compare texts that we have read.

OBJECTIVES

Identify basic similarities in and differences between two texts on the same topic.

ELA ACADEMIC LANGUAGE

- *connections, image*
- Cognates: *conexiones, imagen*

Close Reading Routine

Read DOK 1–2

- Identify important ideas and details.
- Take notes and retell.
- Use **C T** prompts as needed.

Reread DOK 2–3

- Analyze the text, craft, and structure.
- Use the Reread minilessons.

Integrate DOK 3–4

- Integrate knowledge and ideas.
- Make text-to-text connections.
- Complete the Show Your Knowledge task.
- Inspire action.

FORMATIVE ASSESSMENT

❯ STUDENT CHECK-IN

Have partners share how they compared the painting and the text. Have children reflect, using the Check-In routine to fill in the bars.

Integrate

Make Connections

5 mins

MULTIMODAL

Connect to the Essential Question DOK 4

COLLABORATE

Turn to page 178 in the **Reading/Writing Companion.** Help partners discuss what they see in the image, using the first prompt as a guide.

Reading/Writing Companion, p. 178

Dinah Zike's
FOLDABLES
Study Organizer

Find Text Evidence Read the second prompt aloud. Guide children to discuss the connections between the painting and the photos in "A Look at Breakfast." Use the Quick Tip box for support.

Compare Texts Guide partners to compare the workers in the painting to the workers in *From Cows to You.* Children can record their notes using a Foldable® like the one shown. Guide children to record details that help them answer the Essential Question.

Build Knowledge: Make Connections

Talk About the Text Have partners discuss how we get olives.

Add to the Anchor Chart Record any new ideas on the Build Knowledge anchor chart.

Add to the Word Bank Then add words related to how we get food to a separate section of the Word Bank.

Show Your Knowledge

Write a Nonfiction Text DOK 4

Display the Build Knowledge anchor chart about how we get food. Have children lead a discussion about what they have learned. Then have children turn to page 179 in their **Reading/Writing Companion**. Guide children through the steps below to write about two workers that help us get our food.

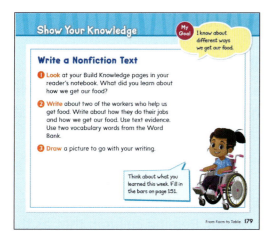

Reading/Writing Companion, p. 179

Step 1 Have children read through the Build Knowledge pages of their reader's notebook to review what they have learned about how we get food. Then have partners talk about texts they read.

Step 2 Provide a sheet of paper to each child. Have children write about two of the workers that help us get our food. Remind them to include examples from the texts. Have children use two vocabulary words from the Word Bank.

Step 3 Have children draw a picture of one of the workers they wrote about. Have them include a caption for their drawing.

Inspire Action

You may choose to extend the learning with the activities below.

Thank You Letter Have children write a Thank You letter to one of the workers they wrote about. Help children find nearby factories and, If possible, have them mail their letters.

Guessing Game Have children act out actions of one of the workers they wrote about as the class tries to guess who it is.

Choose Your Own Action Have children talk about the texts they read this week. Ask: *What do these texts inspire you to do?*

LEARNING GOALS

We can write a nonfiction text.

OBJECTIVES

Add drawings or other visual displays to descriptions when appropriate to clarify ideas, thoughts, and feelings.

Use words and phrases acquired through conversations, reading and being read to, and responding to texts.

ELA ACADEMIC LANGUAGE

• *nonfiction*

• Cognate: *no ficción*

ELL ENGLISH LANGUAGE LEARNERS

Show Your Knowledge, Step 2 Provide and model sentence frames and/or starters to help children write about two workers. Examples of sentence frames/starters are: A ___ helps by ___. The ___ makes ___. Provide sentence frames with linking or helping verbs that help children write about what the workers do and direct children to words in the Word Bank that describe the work.

DIGITAL TOOLS

RUBRIC   **Show Your Knowledge Rubric**

MY GOALS ROUTINE

What I Learned

Review Goals Have children turn back to page 150 of the Reading/Writing Companion and review the goals for the week.

Reflect Have children think about the progress they've made towards their goals. Review the key, if needed. Have children fill in the bars.

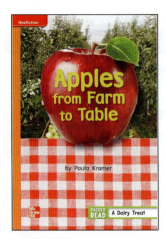

Lexile 330

OBJECTIVES

Identify the main topic and retell relevant, or key, details of a text.

Read grade-level text orally with accuracy, appropriate rate, and expression on successive readings.

Reread text for understanding.

ELA ACADEMIC LANGUAGE

• *nonfiction*
• Cognate: *no ficción*

● Approaching Level

Leveled Reader: *Apples from Farm to Table*

Preview and Predict

Have children turn to the title page. Read the title and the author's name and have children repeat. Preview the selection's photographs. Prompt children to predict what the selection might be about.

Review Genre: Informational Text: Nonfiction

Have children recall that an informational text is a selection that tells about real people, places, things, or events by presenting facts and information about them. Informational text can use captions to give more information.

Set Purpose

Remind children of the Essential Question. Set a purpose for reading: *Let's read to find out how we get the apples we eat.* Remind children that as they read a selection, they can ask questions about what they do not understand or what they want to know more about.

Guided Comprehension

As children whisper read *Apples from Farm to Table* independently or with a partner, monitor and provide guidance. Correct blending and model the key strategies and skills as needed. Provide definitions for words unfamiliar to children.

Reread

Model rereading the text: *Page 4 says there is a new way to grow apples. I must have missed the old way. I'll reread page 3 to see if that helps.* Reread page 3. *I see. The author must mean growing apple trees from seeds was the old way.* Remind children they can reread a paragraph or an earlier part of a selection if they do not understand what they are reading.

Details: Time Order

Hand out Graphic Organizer 6. Remind children that informational text can present information in time order, or in sequence. As you read, ask: *What are some things that happen to apples before they get to the store?* Display Time-Order 6 chart for children to copy.

Model recording children's answers in the boxes. Have children record the answers in their own charts.

Think Aloud On pages 3 and 4 I read that apple trees can grow from seeds or from pieces of old apple trees. I'll write that in the first box of my chart. Then I'll read on to find what happens next.

Guide children to use the text and photographs to complete the chart.

Respond to Reading Have children complete the Respond to Reading on page 12.

Retell Have children take turns retelling the selection, using the **Retelling Cards** as a guide. Help them make a personal connection by saying: *How do you eat apples? Do you eat them whole, cut up, in applesauce?*

Fluency: Accuracy and Rate

Model Model reading page 2 with accuracy and at an appropriate rate. Read aloud. Have children read along with you.

Apply Have children practice reading the text with a partner. Correct any errors as needed.

Paired Read: "A Dairy Treat"

 Analytical Writing **Make Connections: Write About It**

Before reading, ask children to note that the genre of this text is also informational text. Then discuss the Compare Texts direction in the Leveled Reader.

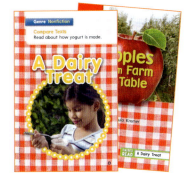

Leveled Reader

After reading, ask children to make connections between the information they learned from "A Dairy Treat" and *Apples from Farm to Table*. Provide a sentence frame, such as: *Apples and yogurt are both ____.*

Build Knowledge: Make Connections

 Talk About the Texts Have partners discuss how we get apples.

Write About the Texts Then have children add their ideas to the Build Knowledge page of their reader's notebook.

 ## LITERATURE CIRCLES

Lead children in conducting a literature circle, using the Thinkmark questions to guide the discussion. You may want to discuss what children have learned about how we get our food from both selections in the Leveled Reader.

🌎 FOCUS ON SOCIAL STUDIES

Children can extend their knowledge of goods and services by completing the social studies activity on page 16.

 # LEVEL UP

IF children can read *Apples from Farm to Table* Approaching Level with fluency and correctly answer the Respond to Reading questions,

THEN tell children that they will read a more detailed version of the selection.

- Have children read the selection, checking their comprehension by using the graphic organizer.

Approaching Level

Phonemic Awareness

PHONEME SEGMENTATION

OBJECTIVES

Segment spoken single-syllable words into their complete sequence of individual sounds (phonemes).

I Do Explain to children that they will be segmenting, or separating, the sounds in words. *Listen as I say a word:* book. *I hear three sounds in* book: /b/ /ù/ /k/.

We Do *Let's do some together. Listen as I say a word: /pùùùt/. How many sounds do you hear? That's right! The sounds in* put *are: /p/ /ùùù/ /t/. Repeat this routine with the following words:*

wood   push   pull   brook   stood

You Do *Now it's your turn. I'll say a word. Tell me what sounds you hear.*

good   cook   shook   foot   crook

Repeat the segmentation routine with other /ù/ words.

PHONEME BLENDING

OBJECTIVES

Orally produce single-syllable words by blending sounds (phonemes), including consonant blends.

I Do Tell children they will be blending sounds to say words. *Listen as I say three sounds: /h//ù//k/. I'm going to blend the sounds together: /h/ /ùùù/ /k/, /hùùùk/,* hook. *I blended the word* hook.

We Do *Let's do some together. Repeat these sounds: /w//ù//f/. Now let's blend the sounds: /wùùùf/. We made one word:* woof. *Repeat the routine:*

/sh/ /ù/ /d/   /g/ /ù/ /d/   /t/ /ù/ /k/   /s/ /t/ /ù/ /d/

You Do *It's your turn. I'll say some sounds. Blend the sounds to say the word.*

/c/ /ù/ /d/   /p/ /ù/ /sh/   /w/ /ù/ /d/   /b/ /r/ /ù/ /k/

Repeat the blending routine with other /ù/ words.

PHONEME DELETION

OBJECTIVES

Demonstrate understanding of spoken words, syllables, and sounds (phonemes).

Delete initial phonemes to make new words.

I Do Explain to children that they will be deleting beginning sounds in words. *When you delete a sound, you take a sound away. Listen as I say a word:* crib, */krib/. I will take away /k/ from* crib. *That leaves /rrr/ /iii/ /b/.* Crib *without /k/ is* rib.

We Do *Listen as I say a word:* fox. *Say the word with me:* fox. *Let's take away /f/ from* fox. *That leaves /ooo/ /ks/. Let's blend the sounds: /oooks/,* ox. Fox *without /f/ is* ox. *Repeat this routine with the following pairs of words:*

track/rack   brook/rook   shape/ape

You Do *It's your turn. Take away the initial sounds from words to form new words.*

bring/ring   cheat/eat   spoke/poke

Repeat the deletion routine with other words.

PHONEME SEGMENTATION

OBJECTIVES

Segment spoken single-syllable words into their complete sequence of individual sounds (phonemes).

I Do Explain to children that they will be segmenting the sounds in words. *Listen as I say a word:* hook. *I hear three sounds in* hook: */h/ / u̇ / /k/.*

We Do *Segment some words with me. Listen as I say a word: /shu̇u̇k/. How many sounds do you hear?* (3) *The three sounds in* shook *are: /sh/ /u̇u̇/ /k/.* Repeat this routine with the following words: *close, tame, shine, badge, page, foot.*

You Do *Now it's your turn. I'll say a word. Tell me what sounds you hear.*

cube   place   pledge   blaze   cook   tone   line

Repeat the segmentation routine with other words.

ELL You may want to review phonemic awareness, phonics, decoding, and fluency using this section. Use scaffolding methods as necessary to ensure children understand the meanings of the words. Refer to the **Language Transfers Handbook** for phonics elements that may not transfer in children's native languages.

Approaching Level

Phonics

CONNECT *oo, u* TO / u̇/

TIER 2

OBJECTIVES

Know and apply grade-level phonics and word analysis skills in decoding words.

Recognize spelling-sound correspondences for the /u̇/ sound.

I Do Display the **Word-Building Card** *oo*. *These letters are lowercase* o. *Together they can stand for /u̇/. I am going to trace the letters* oo *while I say /u̇/.* Trace the letters *oo* while saying /u̇/ five times. Repeat with *u*.

We Do *Now do it with me.* Have children take turns saying /u̇/ while using their fingers to trace lowercase *oo*. Then have them say /u̇/ as they use their fingers to trace the letters *oo* five more times. Repeat with *u*.

You Do Have children connect *oo* to /u̇/ by saying /u̇/ as they trace lowercase *oo* on paper five to ten times. Then ask them to write *oo* while saying /u̇/ five to ten times. Repeat with *u*.

Repeat, connecting *oo* and *u* with /u̇/ throughout the week.

BLEND WORDS WITH VARIANT VOWEL /u̇/

TIER 2

OBJECTIVES

Decode regularly spelled one-syllable words.

Blend and decode words with the /u̇/ sound.

I Do Display **Word-Building Cards** *g, oo, d*. *This is the letter* g. *It stands for /g/. These are the letters* o *and* o. *Together they stand for /u̇/. This is the letter* d. *It stands for /d/. I'll blend the sounds together: /gu̇u̇d/,* good.

We Do *Let's do some together.* Guide children to blend the sounds and read: *book, hood, foot, wool, push.*

You Do Have children use Word-Building Cards to blend and decode: *pull, look, woof, wood, brook.* Provide feedback as needed.

Repeat, blending additional words with variant vowel /u̇/.

You may wish to practice reading and decoding with **ELL** using this section.

BUILD WORDS WITH VARIANT VOWEL /u̇/

OBJECTIVES

Decode and encode regularly spelled one-syllable words.

Build and decode words with the /u̇/ sound.

I Do Display **Word-Building Cards** *t, oo, k. These are the letters* t, o, o, k. T *stands for* /t/. O *and* o *together stand for* /u̇/. K *stands for* /k/. I will blend /t/ /u̇/ /k/ together: /tu̇u̇u̇k/, took. The word is* took.

We Do *Let's do one together.* Change the *t* in *took* to *l. Let's blend and read this word:* /llu̇u̇u̇k/, look.

You Do Have children build and decode: *book, brook, crook, cook, hook, hood, good.*

READ WORDS WITH VARIANT VOWEL /u̇/

OBJECTIVES

Read grade-level text orally with accuracy, appropriate rate, and expression on successive readings.

Unit 3 Decodable
Reader pages 49–60

Focus on Foundational Skills

Review the high-frequency words *after, buy, done, every, soon,* and *work* with children. Review the sound /u̇/ for words with *oo* or *u*. Guide children to blend the sounds to read the words.

Read the Decodable Readers

Guide children to read "A Good Cook" and "That Looks Good." Identify the high-frequency words and words with /u̇/ *oo, u*. If children struggle sounding out words, model blending.

Focus on Fluency

Have partners reread "A Good Cook" and "That Looks Good." As children read the text, guide them to focus on their accuracy, rate, and automaticity. Children can provide feedback to their partners.

BUILD FLUENCY WITH PHONICS

Sound/Spellings Fluency

Display the following Word-Building Cards: *oo, u, o_e, u_e, e_e, dge, i_e, a_e, ch, tch, wh, ph, th, sh, ng, mp, sk, st, nt, nk, nd, e, ea, sp, sn, sl, cr.* Have children chorally say the sounds. Repeat and vary the pace.

Fluency in Connected Text

Have children review the **Decodable Reader** selections. Identify words with *oo* and *u*. Blend words as needed.

Have partners reread the selections for fluency.

• Approaching Level

Structural Analysis

REVIEW INFLECTIONAL ENDINGS *-ed, -ing*

OBJECTIVES
Read words with inflectional endings.

Identify frequently occurring root words (e.g., look) and their inflectional forms (e.g., looks, looked, looking).

I Do Write and read *hopped: /hopt/. I know* hop *and* hopped. *The -ed ending tells me the action already happened.* Underline the second *p. If the word has a short vowel and ends in a consonant, we double the consonant before adding -ed.* Use *hopped* in a sentence: *I hopped across the room.*

We Do Write and read *wagging. Is there a word you know in* wagging? *Yes,* wag. *What did I do before I added the* -ing *ending to* wag? *I doubled the* g. *Have children use* hopped *and* wagging *in sentences.*

You Do Have partners add inflectional endings to the following verbs: *stop, bat, hum, nod* and then blend and decode the words.

Repeat Ask partners to use the words they blended in sentences.

RETEACH INFLECTIONAL ENDINGS *-ed, -ing*

OBJECTIVES
Read words with inflectional endings.

Identify frequently occurring root words (e.g., look) and their inflectional forms (e.g., looks, looked, looking).

I Do Write and read *mop* and *mopped.* Circle the *-ed* ending and point out the /*t*/ sound in *mopped. The letters* -ed *at the end of a word mean something happened in the past.* Underline the double *p. For words that have a short vowel and end in a consonant. We double the consonant before adding -ed.* Repeat for *mop, mopping.*

We Do Write and read aloud *tag* and *tagged. Say* tag *and* tagged: /tag/, / tagd/. Point out the /*d*/ sound in *tagged. What did we add to* tag *to make* tagged? *We doubled the* g *and added* -ed. *Let's use each word in a sentence.* Repeat for *tag* and *tagging.* Repeat this routine with the words *bat, tip, slam.*

You Do Have children double the final consonant and add *-ed* and *-ing* to verbs. *Now it's your turn. Double the consonant and add* -ed *and* -ing *to each word. Then say each word and use it in a sentence.* Guide children as needed.

jog   snap   beg   rub   slip   tap   pin   plan

Repeat Have children add inflectional endings *-ed* and *-ing* to other words.

You may wish to review structural analysis and high-frequency words with **ELL** using this section.

High-Frequency Words

REVIEW

OBJECTIVES

Recognize and read grade-appropriate irregularly spelled words.

I Do Use **High-Frequency Word Cards** to Read/Spell/Write *after, buy, done, every, soon,* and *work.* Use each word orally in a sentence.

We Do Guide children to Read/Spell/Write each word on their **Response Boards.** Work together to generate oral sentences for the words.

You Do Have partners work together to Read/Spell/Write the words *after, buy, done, every, soon,* and *work.* Then have them use the words in sentences.

RETEACH

OBJECTIVES

Recognize and read grade-appropriate irregularly spelled words.

I Do Review the high-frequency words using the Read/Spell/Write routine. Write and read aloud a sentence for each word.

We Do Guide children to use the Read/Spell/Write routine. Ask them to complete sentence starters: *(1) After school, I ____. (2) I want to buy ____. (3) Is she done with ____? (4) Every day, we ____. (5) Soon it will be ____. (6) I work ____.*

You Do Ask children to close their eyes, picture the word, and write it as they see it. Have children self-correct.

CUMULATIVE REVIEW

OBJECTIVES

Recognize and read grade-appropriate irregularly spelled words.

I Do Display the High-Frequency Word Cards from the previous weeks. Use the Read/Spell/Write routine to review each word.

We Do Guide children as they Read/Spell/Write the words on their **Response Boards.** Complete sentences for each word, such as: *Long ago, people ____. The boy and the girl are happy when ____.*

You Do Have partners take turns reading the words and using them in sentences.

Fluency Display the High-Frequency Word Cards. Point to the words in random order. Have children chorally read. Repeat at a faster pace.

Approaching Level

Comprehension

READ FOR FLUENCY

TIER 2

OBJECTIVES
Read grade-level text orally with accuracy, appropriate rate, and expression on successive readings.

Set Purpose Tell children that they will now focus on reading *Apples from Farm to Table*. Remind them that this story is nonfiction and that they will be reading it to learn about apples. Tell children that they need to read with accuracy and at an appropriate speed.

I Do Read the first page of **Leveled Reader** *Apples from Farm to Table*. Model using an appropriate speed and reading with accuracy.

We Do Read the rest of Leveled Reader *Apples from Farm to Table* and have children echo read each sentence after you. Point out how you read so that it sounds like speech and you read each word correctly.

You Do Have children work with a partner and take turns rereading the book aloud. Remind them to read with accuracy and at an appropriate speed. Children can provide feedback to their partners as they read.

IDENTIFY RELEVANT DETAILS

TIER 2

OBJECTIVES
Identify and retell relevant, or key, details of a text.

I Do Remind children that they have been reading informational text. Point out that as they read, they should look for relevant details, or important information. *Relevant, or key, details give me information about a topic. I look for details in the pictures and words.*

We Do Read the first page of Leveled Reader *Apples from Farm to Table* aloud. Model identifying relevant details. Say: *From the picture, I can see that the girl is eating an apple. What did we learn from the words? Why are these details important?*

You Do Guide children to read the rest of the text. Prompt them to find and discuss relevant details in the text and the pictures. Provide feedback as needed.

REVIEW DETAILS: TIME ORDER

OBJECTIVES

Identify the main topic and retell relevant, or key, details of a text.

Identify the order of how events happen in a text.

I Do Remind children that they can identify relevant details when they read an informational text. *When I read, I can find relevant details in the text. Sometimes this helps me understand the order in which things happen, or the sequence. That helps me understand what I am reading.*

We Do Read pages 4 and 5 of **Leveled Reader** *Apples from Farm to Table* together. Pause to find relevant details that tell about the time order. *Where do apples grow? What happens when the flowers fall off the trees?* Help children record the information on a Time-Order chart.

You Do Have partners read the rest of the selection. Stop after each page to ask: *What happens with the apples next?* Guide children to add the information to the chart. Then help them use the chart to tell about the apples in the selection. Provide feedback as needed.

SELF-SELECTED READING

OBJECTIVES

Identify the main topic and retell relevant, or key, details of a text.

Read grade-level text with purpose and understanding.

Independent Reading

Have children select an informational text for independent reading. Children may use the **Classroom Library,** the **Leveled Reader Library,** the online **Unit Bibliography,** or other books for their independent reading. Encourage them to read for at least fifteen minutes.

Guide children to transfer what they have learned in this week as they read. Remind children that authors can give information in time-order, or in the order of how events happen. Tell children that words such as *first, next, then,* and *last* can help them understand the time order. Have children record information about time-order details on **Graphic Organizer 6.**

After reading, guide children to participate in a group discussion about the story they read. In addition, children can choose activities from the Reading **Center Activity Cards** to help them apply skills to the text as they read. Offer assistance and guidance with self-selected assignments.

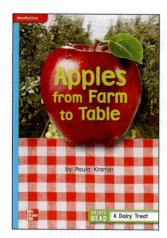

Lexile 550

OBJECTIVES

Identify the main topic and retell relevant, or key, details of a text.

Read grade-level text orally with accuracy, appropriate rate, and expression on successive readings.

Reread text for understanding.

ELA ACADEMIC LANGUAGE

• *nonfiction*

• Cognate: *no ficción*

●On Level

Leveled Reader: *Apples from Farm to Table*

Preview and Predict

Have children turn to the title page. Read the title and the author's name and have children repeat. Preview the selection's photographs. Prompt children to predict what the selection might be about.

Review Genre: Informational Text: Nonfiction

Have children recall that an informational text is a selection that tells about real people, places, things, or events by presenting facts and information about them. Informational text can use captions to give more information.

Set Purpose

Remind children of the Essential Question. Set a purpose for reading: *Let's read to find out how apples you eat get to your home.* Remind children that, as they read a selection, they can ask questions about what they do not understand or what they want to know more about.

Guided Comprehension

As children whisper read *Apples from Farm to Table* independently or with a partner, monitor and provide guidance. Correct blending and model the key strategies and skills as needed. Provide definitions for words unfamiliar to children.

Reread

Model rereading the text on page 3: *I must have missed where the seeds came from. I'll reread this page.* Reread the page. Ask: *Where did the seeds come from?* Remind children sometimes they may misread a word or miss an important point. They can reread the passage or an earlier part to help them understand.

Details: Time Order

Hand out Graphic Organizer 6. Remind children that a text can present information in time order, or in the order of how events happen. As you read, ask: *How are apples first grown? What are some of the next things that happen? What happens last?* Display Time-Order 6 chart for children to copy. Model recording answers for children. Have children copy the answers into their own charts.

Think Aloud The first part of this selection tells how apple trees can grow from seeds or from pieces of old trees. I'll write that in the first box of my chart. Then I'll read on to find the next part.

As children read, prompt them to fill in the chart.

Respond to Reading Have children complete the Respond to Reading on page 12.

Retell Have children take turns retelling the selection, using the **Retelling Cards** as a guide. Help children make a connection. *Where do you get the apples you eat? What do the apples look like? How do they taste?*

Fluency: Accuracy and Rate

Model Model reading page 2 with accuracy and at an appropriate rate. Read aloud. Have children read along with you.

Apply Have children practice reading the text with a partner. Correct any errors as needed.

Paired Read: "A Dairy Treat"

 Analytical Writing **Make Connections: Write About It**

Before reading, ask children to note that the genre of this text is also informational text. Then discuss the Compare Texts direction in the Leveled Reader.

Leveled Reader

After reading, ask children to make connections between the information they learned from "A Dairy Treat" and *Apples from Farm to Table*.

Build Knowledge: Make Connections

 Talk About the Texts Have partners discuss how we get apples.

Write About the Texts Then have children add their ideas to the Build Knowledge page of their reader's notebook.

LITERATURE CIRCLES

Lead children in conducting a literature circle, using the Thinkmark questions to guide the discussion. You may want to discuss what children have learned about how we get our food from reading the two selections in the Leveled Reader.

FOCUS ON SOCIAL STUDIES

Children can extend their knowledge of goods and services by completing the social studies activity on page 16.

 **LEVEL UP**

IF children can read *Apples from Farm to Table* On Level with fluency and correctly answer the Respond to Reading questions,

THEN tell children that they will read a more detailed version of the selection.

- Have children read the selection, checking their comprehension by using the graphic organizer.

●On Level

Phonics

READ AND BUILD WORDS WITH VARIANT VOWEL /ů/

OBJECTIVES

Decode regularly spelled one-syllable words.

Read grade-level text orally with accuracy, appropriate rate, and expression on successive readings.

Unit 3 Decodable Reader pages 49–60

I Do Display **Word-Building Cards** b, oo, k. These are the letters b, o, o, k. B stands for /b/. The letters oo together stand for /ů/. K stands for /k/. I will blend the sounds together: /bůůk/, book. The word is book.

We Do Now let's do one together. Change b to c. Let's blend and read the new word: /k/ /ůůů/ /k/, /kůůůk /, cook. The new word is cook.

You Do Have children build and blend these words: took, look, shook, hook, hood, good, wood, wool, woof. Provide feedback as needed.

Read the Decodable Readers

Guide children to read "A Good Cook" and "That Looks Good." Point out the high-frequency words and words with /ů/ oo, u. Model blending sound by sound as needed.

Focus on Fluency Have partners reread "A Good Cook" and "That Looks Good." As children read the text, guide them to focus on accuracy, rate, and automaticity. Partners can provide feedback.

High-Frequency Words

REVIEW WORDS

OBJECTIVES

Recognize and read grade-appropriate irregularly spelled words.

I Do Use the Read/Spell/Write routine to review after, buy, done, every, soon, and work. Use each word orally in a sentence.

We Do Guide children to Read/Spell/Write each word using their **Response Boards.** Work together to create oral sentences for the words.

You Do Have partners work together to use the words about this week's stories in sentences. Make sure they include at least one high-frequency word in each sentence. Provide feedback as needed.

Comprehension

REVIEW DETAILS: TIME ORDER

OBJECTIVES

Identify the main topic and retell relevant, or key, details of a text.

Identify the order of how events happen in a text.

I Do Remind children that they can identify relevant details in an informational text. *When we read nonfiction, we can look for relevant details in the text. Sometimes we can look for time order, or the order of how events happen. This helps us understand what we read.*

We Do Read the first two pages of **Leveled Reader** *Apples from Farm to Table* aloud. Discuss the relevant details that tell about the time order of events. *How do apple trees grow? How long does it take for a tree to produce fruit?*

You Do Guide partners to read the rest of *Apples from Farm to Table*. Remind them to find relevant details by discussing the time order of events.

SELF-SELECTED READING

OBJECTIVES

Identify the main topic and retell relevant, or key, details of a text.

Read grade-level text with purpose and understanding.

Independent Reading

Have children select an informational text for independent reading. Children may use the **Classroom Library,** the **Leveled Reader Library,** the online **Unit Bibliography,** or other books for their independent reading. Encourage them to read for at least fifteen minutes.

Guide children to transfer what they have learned in this week as they read. Remind children that authors can give information in time-order, or in the order of how events happen. Tell children that words such as *first, next, then,* and *last* can help them understand the time order. Have children record information about time-order details on **Graphic Organizer 6.**

After reading, guide children to participate in a group discussion about the story they read. In addition, children can choose activities from the Reading **Center Activity Cards** to help them apply skills to the text as they read. Offer assistance and guidance with self-selected assignments.

You may wish to review Comprehension with **ELL** using this section.

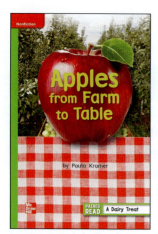

Lexile 580

OBJECTIVES

Identify the main topic and retell relevant, or key, details of a text.

Reread text for understanding.

ELA ACADEMIC LANGUAGE

• nonfiction

• Cognate: *no ficción*

●Beyond Level

Leveled Reader: *Apples from Farm to Table*

Preview and Predict

Read the title and the author's name. Have children preview the title page and the photographs. Ask: *What do you think this book will be about?* Have children ask questions about the text, based on looking at the cover and hearing the title.

Review Genre: Informational Text: Nonfiction

Have children recall that an informational text is a selection that tells about real people, places, things, or events by presenting facts and information about them. Informational texts can use captions to give more information.

Set Purpose

Remind children of the Essential Question. Set a purpose for reading: *Let's find out how we get apples. As you get ready to read this fluently, think about the purpose.*

Guided Comprehension

Have children whisper read *Apples from Farm to Table* independently or with a partner. Have them place self-stick notes next to difficult words. Monitor and provide guidance. Correct blending and model the key strategies and skills as needed.

Monitor children's reading. Stop periodically and ask open-ended questions to facilitate rich discussion, such as: *What does the author want you to know about apples in this part of the text?* Build on children's responses to develop deeper understanding of the text.

Reread

Model rereading the text: *I missed what time of year the flowers grow on the apple trees. I can go back and reread page 5 to find out.* Remind children that sometimes they may misread a word or miss an important point.

Details: Time-Order

Hand out Graphic Organizer 6. Remind children that text can present information in time order, or in a sequence. As you read, ask: *What happens to the apples first?* Display Time-Order 6 chart for children to copy. Model how to record the information. Have children fill in their charts as they read.

Think Aloud On pages 3 and 4 I read that apple trees can grow from seeds or from a process called grafting. I'll write that in the first box of my chart. Then I'll read on to find what happens next.

Respond to Reading Have children complete the Respond to Reading on page 12.

Retell Have children take turns retelling the selection. Help children make a personal connection by writing about apples. *Tell about a time you got some apples. Where did you get them? What did you do with them?*

Paired Read: "A Dairy Treat"

 Make Connections: Write About It

Before reading "A Dairy Treat," have children preview the title page and prompt them to identify the genre. Then have them discuss the Compare Texts direction in the Leveled Reader.

Leveled Reader

After reading, have children work with a partner to discuss what they learned in "A Dairy Treat" and *Apples from Farm to Table*. Prompt children to discuss how the steps they read about in each process are the same and how they are different.

Build Knowledge: Make Connections

 Talk About the Text Have partners discuss how we get apples.

Write About the Text Then have children add their ideas to the Build Knowledge page of their reader's notebook.

 LITERATURE CIRCLES

Lead children in conducting a literature circle, using the Thinkmark questions to guide the discussion. You may want to discuss what children have learned about how we get our food from reading the two selections in the Leveled Reader.

 FOCUS ON SOCIAL STUDIES

Children can extend their knowledge of goods and services by completing the social studies activity on page 16.

⭐ **GIFTED AND TALENTED**

Synthesize Challenge children to imagine they are going to do one of the jobs they read about that help get apples from the farm to the table. Encourage them to use ideas from the selection to write about the day's work.

Extend Have children use facts they learned through the week or do additional research to find out more about working on an apple farm.

● Beyond Level

Vocabulary

ORAL VOCABULARY: SUFFIXES

OBJECTIVES

Use frequently occurring affixes as a clue to the meaning of a word.

Identify and use suffix -ly.

I Do Review with children the meaning of the oral vocabulary word *delicious*. Say the sentence *This peach is delicious* and have children repeat. Discuss what *delicious* means.

Remind children that when a suffix is added to the end of a word, it changes the word's meaning. Write *-ly* on the board and say the words *delicious* and *deliciously*. Then say: *The suffix* -ly *means "in a way that is."* Deliciously *means "in a way that is delicious."*

We Do Write *nutritiously*. Nutritiously *means "in a way that is nutritious." We eat nutritiously if we want to stay healthy. Let's add* -ly *to enormous. What word do we get? What does* enormously *mean?*

You Do Ask partners to use the words *deliciously, nutritiously,* and *enormously* in oral sentences. Then challenge them to think of other words that end in the suffix *-ly.*

⭐ GIFTED and TALENTED **Extend** Have children plan and act out a skit about going on a picnic. Challenge them to use as many words that end in the suffix *-ly* as they can.

Comprehension

REVIEW DETAILS: TIME ORDER

OBJECTIVES

Identify the main topic and retell relevant, or key, details of a text.

I Do Remind children that they should identify relevant details when they read informational texts. Prompt them to explain how they can look for time order, or the order of how events happen as they read. *What are some words and phrases that can help you find the time order of events?*

We Do Guide children in reading the first two pages of **Leveled Reader** *Apples from Farm to Table* aloud. Prompt them to discuss the relevant details that tell about the time order of events. *How do the time-order words help you understand the information on these pages?*

You Do Have children read the rest of Leveled Reader *Apples from Farm to Table* independently. Remind them to find relevant details as they read.

SELF-SELECTED READING

OBJECTIVES

Identify the main topic and retell relevant, or key, details of a text.

Read grade-level text with purpose and understanding.

Independent Reading

Have children select an informational text for independent reading. Children may use the **Classroom Library,** the **Leveled Reader Library,** the online **Unit Bibliography,** or other books for their independent reading. Encourage them to read for at least fifteen minutes.

Guide children to transfer what they have learned in this week as they read by reminding them that authors can give information in time-order, or in the order of how events happen. Tell children that words such as *first, next, then,* and *last* can help them understand the time order. Have children record information about time-order details on **Graphic Organizer 6.**

After reading, guide children to participate in a group discussion about the story they read. In addition, children can choose activities from the Reading **Center Activity Cards** to help them apply skills to the text as they read. Offer assistance and guidance with self-selected assignments.

 Independent Study Have children create posters that illustrate the time order of events in their selection. Challenge them to write a few sentences within the poster telling about why they chose their selection and how the information was organized.

Notes

WRITING

Extended Writing
Expository Text

Students work through the writing process to write an expository text about something they know about.

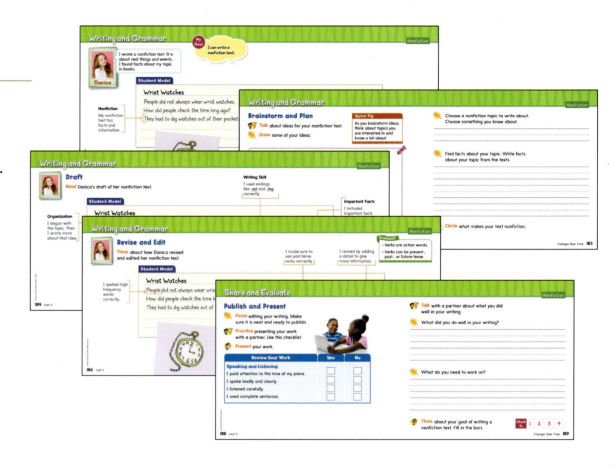

Developmental Writing:
Plan Writing Instruction

Student Writing Models help you informally assess children's progress.

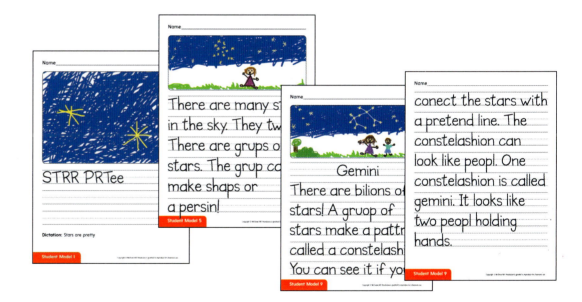

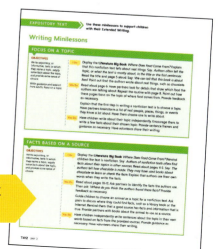

Flexible Minilessons More support for writing an expository text and developing critical writing skills

Extended Writing
Expository Text

Writing

Extended Writing Goal

- I can write a nonfiction text.

Children will engage in the writing process to write an expository text over the course of two weeks. Explicit writing instruction and flexible minilessons are provided to support children in their writing development. Children apply writing skills during independent writing time.

Suggested Pacing

	Lesson 1	Lesson 2	Lesson 3	Lesson 4	Lesson 5
Week 4	Expert and Student Models	Plan	Draft	Draft	Draft
Week 5	Revise and Edit	Revise and Edit	Revise and Edit	Publish, Present, and Evaluate	Publish, Present, and Evaluate

Writing Process Lessons

Study Expert and Student Models

The Last Train

- Analyze the Expert Model

Reading/Writing Companion, pp. 180–181

- Analyze the Student Models
- Discuss Features of a Nonfiction Text

Plan the Nonfiction Text

Reading/Writing Companion, pp. 182–183

- Brainstorm Ideas for a Nonfiction Text
- Plan, Draw, and Write Ideas

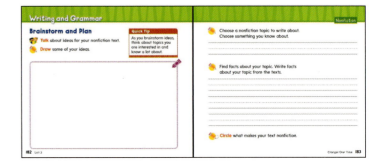

Draft the Nonfiction Text

Reading/Writing Companion, pp. 184–185

- Discuss Expert and Student Models
- Draft a Nonfiction Text

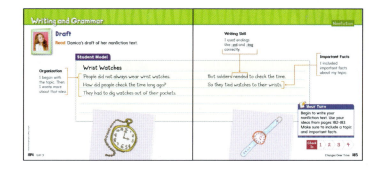

Revise and Edit

Reading/Writing Companion, pp. 186–187

- Discuss Student Model
- Revise the Draft and Edit for Mistakes

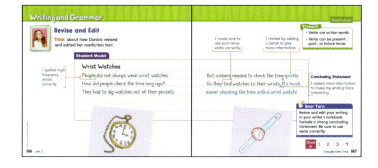

Publish, Present, and Evaluate

Reading/Writing Companion, pp. 188–189

- Prepare the Final Draft
- Share and Evaluate Writing

Flexible Minilessons

Choose from the following minilessons to focus on areas where children need support.

Expository Text Minilessons

For more support with writing an expository text, use these minilessons:

- Ideas: Focus on a Topic, T412
- Ideas: Facts Based on a Source, T412
- Ideas: Text Features, T413
- Organization: Concluding Statement, T413

Developmental Writing Support

For more support with planning your writing conferences and small-group instruction, see the Student Models, pp. T414–T419.

Writing Skills Minilesson Bank

Use these flexible minilessons to differentiate instruction and develop critical writing skills. See pages T420–T429.

- Stretch Sounds
- Sentence Capitalization
- Use Word Bank
- Left-to-Right Progression
- Spacing Between Words
- Write on the Lines
- Return Sweep
- End Punctuation
- Capitalize Proper Nouns
- Capitalize "I"

- Word Endings
- Write a Complete Sentence
- Use Correct Word Order
- Write a Question
- Use Conjunctions
- Use Facts from a Source
- Write Dialogue
- Adjust Tone and Voice
- Vary Sentence Length
- Form a Paragraph

LESSON 1

We can name the features of a nonfiction text.

OBJECTIVES

Write expository, or informative, texts in which they name a topic, supply some facts about the topic, and provide some sense of closure.

Analyze an expert model of an expository text.

ELA ACADEMIC LANGUAGE

• nonfiction, facts, information

• Cognates: *no ficción, información*

 DIFFERENTIATED WRITING

🔴🟣 **Approaching Level/ ELL** For the Plan phase, provide sentence starters to support children as they write. For the Draft phase, you may choose to have children dictate their writing or share the pen as needed.

🔵🟢 **On Level/Beyond Level** For the Plan and Draft phases, pair children and have them share their work at the end of these phases. Encourage children to ask and answer questions about their writing.

---

 10 mins

Expert Model

Features of Expository Text: Nonfiction

Explain to children that they will be writing a nonfiction text over the next two weeks. Remind children that they read the nonfiction text *The Last Train* in this unit. Then say: *Let's think about what makes a text nonfiction.*

Anchor Chart Display the Nonfiction anchor chart and review these features:

• It tells about real people, places, things, or events.

• It presents facts and information.

Analyze the Expert Model

Talk About It Display and read aloud the following sentences from page 8 of the **Literature Big Book** *The Last Train*. Ask children to listen for facts and information about real things or events that tell them this is a nonfiction text. Remind children that they should use the appropriate voice and tone when they read aloud. Model using appropriate voice and tone as you read the following text from the selection:

My Granddad was a railroad man,

he drove the trains around,

My Daddy, he sold tickets

till they closed the station down.

 Ask: *What real things does the author talk about in this text? How do you think the author feels about what he is saying?* Have children turn and talk to a partner to answer the question. Then have volunteers share their answers. Remind children to answer in complete sentences. (The author tells about trains from long ago. He talks about his dad who drove old trains and sold tickets at the station. The author sounds a little sad about what he is saying.)

As you turn the pages for the remainder of the text, ask children to share other things that tell them this is nonfiction.

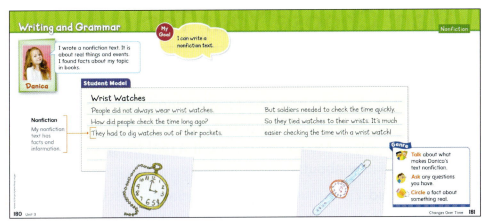

Reading/Writing Companion, pp. 180–181

Analyze the Student Model

Have children turn to pages 180–181 of the **Reading/Writing Companion.** Read the speech bubble and the student model together with children.

Read aloud the call-out on page 180. Have children discuss the text evidence that shows this text is nonfiction.

Genre Then have children complete the Genre activity on page 181. Guide children to circle a fact about something real.

Your Turn

Have children think about real things they use every day. They can draw a picture of one or more items and label them.

English Language Learners

Use the following scaffolds with **Analyze the Student Model.**

Beginning

Review the student model. *Who wrote this story? What did Danica write about?* Encourage children to point to the drawings of watches. Provide a sentence frame to help children summarize what Danica wrote about: Danica wrote about <u>watches</u>.

Intermediate

Have children tell what Danica wrote about. Provide a sentence frame to help children tell what makes this text nonfiction: Danica wrote about real <u>things</u> and <u>events</u>.

Advanced/Advanced High

Have partners identify and talk about the details in Danica's writing. *Why do you think Danica included these details?*

ELL NEWCOMER

To help children develop their writing, display pages 8–9 of the **Reading/Writing Companion** and have children identify what they see with a partner. Provide sentence frames: What do you see? I see a <u>tree</u>. Have children point to the image as they ask and answer questions. Then have them draw a picture of what they see and help them label the picture. Use the Progress Monitoring materials in the **Newcomer Teacher's Guide** to evaluate, assess, and plan instruction for your newcomers.

STUDENT CHECK-IN

Have partners share one feature of a nonfiction text. Then have children reflect, using the Check-In routine.

LESSON

2

We can choose a topic to write about.

OBJECTIVES

Write expository, or informative, texts in which they name a topic, supply some facts about the topic, and provide some sense of closure.

Brainstorm and plan an expository text.

ELA ACADEMIC LANGUAGE

• *plan, brainstorm*

• Cognate: *planear*

Plan: Choose Your Topic

10 mins

Brainstorm

Talk About It Before beginning the writing process, encourage children to turn and talk to a partner about real things, people, events, or places they know about. Model talking about a real thing, person, event, or place you know about:

Think Aloud I love music. I took music classes in school. I can play guitar.

Ask children to describe the real person, place, thing, or event they know about. Walk around the room and listen in. Remind partners to listen carefully to each other and to stay on topic as they share.

Plan Tell children they will now begin to plan and write a nonfiction text. Have children turn to page 182 in their **Reading/Writing Companion.**

Explain that the first step in writing a nonfiction text is deciding what real thing, person, place, or event to write about. Say: *Remember Danica's text? Before she wrote it, she planned by brainstorming and drawing pictures. This helped her think of real people, places, things, and events. These are ideas Danica might have had.*

Write some examples of ideas Danica might have listed:

• having a turtle for a pet

• flying to Florida

• the invention of wrist watches

Then say: *Danica chose a topic she liked.* Share Danica's plan for her text:

Think Aloud Danica's father fixes watches, so she knows a lot about them! She decided to write about the invention of the wrist watch.

Children can draw or write their ideas on page 182. Remind them to think of real people, places, things, or events. Use the Quick Tip box to support children as they work.

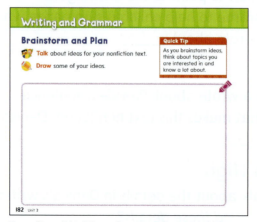

Reading/Writing Companion, p. 182

Choose Your Topic

Guide children to complete page 183 in their **Reading/Writing Companion.** Have them choose as their topic an idea they drew or wrote about on page 182. Then guide them to write facts they know about the topic. Help them circle elements of nonfiction in the text they wrote.

Reading/Writing Companion, p. 183

English Language Learners

Use the following scaffolds with **Brainstorm, Plan.**

Beginning

Help children brainstorm possible topics that they could write about. Write acceptable suggestions on the board to create a word bank. If children need help thinking of ideas, ask questions such as: *What animals do you know about? What places do you know about?* When children offer a topic, ask follow-up questions such as: *What is a fact you know about that topic?* Provide a sentence frame: A fact about <u>leopards</u> is that they are <u>fast</u>.

Intermediate

Before they complete page 182, have children discuss possible topics with a partner. Remind them to think of topics they know a lot about. Provide sentence frames to help children discuss: What topic do you know about? I know about <u>leopards</u>. I know <u>they are fast</u>.

Advanced/Advanced High

Have partners ask and answer questions to engage in an extended discussion about their topic. Examples of discussion questions include: What topic will you write about? What do you know about that topic? Where did you learn about that topic? Why is this topic important to you?

❯ STUDENT CHECK-IN

Have partners share the topic for their nonfiction text. Then have children reflect, using the Check-In routine.

LEARNING GOALS

We can write a draft of a nonfiction text.

OBJECTIVES

Write expository, or informative, texts in which they name a topic, supply some facts about the topic, and provide some sense of closure.

Draft an expository text.

ELA ACADEMIC LANGUAGE

• *source*

 **TEACH IN SMALL GROUP**

For additional mini lessons to support writing an Expository Text that include:

• focus on a topic

• facts based on a source

• text features

• concluding statements

see pages T412–T413.

Additionally, to provide differentiated support for children, see Writing Skills mini lessons on pages T420–T429. These can be used throughout the year.

 10 mins

Draft

Analyze the Expert Model

Genre Review the characteristics of the genre as you elicit from children: *Nonfiction tells about real people, places, things, or events by presenting facts and information about them.* Refer to the **Literature Anthology** selection *Long Ago and Now.* Have a volunteer tell why this is nonfiction.

Ideas: Facts Based on a Source Explain that authors often find facts about a topic from other sources. Read the following:

> Men drove trucks filled with ice to people's homes.

Explain that the author found this information in a source such as a history book. Say: *It is important to have a good source so that we can learn facts and information that is true.* Point out that when children use sources, they should make sure to write the information in their own words.

 Point out that the author tells readers right away what her one idea is: she's going to focus on how things have changed over time. Have partners turn and talk about examples of this from the text.

Analyze the Student Model

 Have children turn to pages 184–185 of their **Reading/Writing Companion.** Say: *We're going to take another look at Danica's text.*

• **Writing Skill** Danica used the endings -*ed* and -*ing* correctly.

• **Ideas: Facts Based on a Source** Danica began her text with her idea about watches and then used a source to write more about that idea. WRITING TRAIT

• **Ideas: Important Facts** Danica included the fact about soldiers tying their watches to their wrists. This helps readers have a clearer idea of the topic.

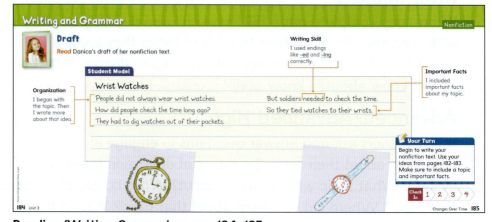

Reading/Writing Companion, pp. 184–185

Draft

Tell children that now it's their turn to start writing. Explain that you are going to use your notes to draft your own text. Model writing the beginning of a short nonfiction text: *I love music, so I'm going to write about guitars. I'm going to use a reference book about guitars as my source. Then I'm going to tell facts about two different kinds of guitars.*

Then write your text on the board and read it aloud.

A guitar is one instrument that makes music.

An acoustic guitar makes soft music. It is a big guitar.

An electric guitar makes loud music. It is smaller than an acoustic guitar.

Both kinds of guitars can make good music!

Have children tell what they noticed about your writing. Ask: *How do you know my text is nonfiction? What one idea did I focus on? What does my tone sound like?*

Your Turn

Have children use their notes to start writing their draft in their writer's notebook. Encourage children to focus on one idea and draw a picture. Remind them to think about their tone.

English Language Learners

Use the following scaffolds with **Your Turn.**

Beginning

Provide a simplified example of a topic sentence: Leopards are animals that can run very fast. Read the sentence aloud and then ask: *What will your nonfiction text be about?* Provide a sentence frame: My text will be about <u>leopards</u>. Walk around as children draft their topic sentence, providing vocabulary and spelling help.

Intermediate

Display the example topic sentence. *What is the topic of this text? Are leopards real animals?* Then have children discuss what kind of sentence would come next. (a fact about leopards) Provide an example: Leopards live in Africa and Asia.

Advanced/Advanced High

Display your example topic sentence and fact and then have children suggest another sentence that could be added that relates to the topic. As children draft, remind them to focus on one idea.

FORMATIVE ASSESSMENT

⟩ **STUDENT CHECK-IN**

Have partners read part of their draft to each other. Then have children reflect, using the Check-In routine to fill in the bars.

10 mins

Revise and Edit

Analyze the Expert Model

Reread the last sentence on page 87 of the **Literature Anthology** selection *Long Ago and Now: Which one do you like best?* Say: The author used a question for her ending because it helps the reader to think about the text. Say: *A concluding statement makes the ending of our writing stronger and more interesting.*

Analyze the Student Model

Have children review pages 186–187 in their **Reading/Writing Companion**. Say: *Danica added a detail to give more information, and she revised her ending to make it more interesting. When we revise our writing, we think about how we can make it better.*

Have children review Danica's edits. Point to *people. Danica checked the spelling of this word. She read it, spelled it, and wrote it in the air. She also made sure she used verbs correctly.* Review skills in the Grammar box.

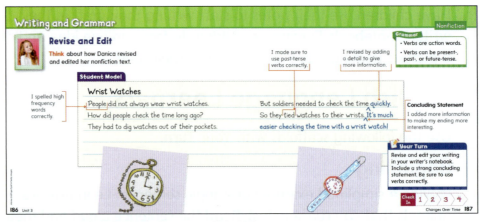

Reading/Writing Companion, pp. 186–187

Revise

Your Turn Tell children that they will now revise their draft. They can add details or rewrite parts to make their writing clearer. As children revise, remind them to check their writing for the skill and trait. Ask:

- Did you focus on one idea for the whole piece?
- Did you include a concluding statement?

Have children use the online Writer's Checklist and Proofreading Marks as they revise their work.

Peer Review Review rules for peer review, using the Peer Conferencing video if you wish. Have partners exchange drafts and note the following:

- Check that the text fits the definition of a nonfiction text.
- Tell what they like most and note any questions they have.

Edit and Proofread

Explain that once children have revised their drafts, they must edit and proofread. Remind them to focus on the following as they edit:

- Did you check your spelling? Children can use a print or online dictionary or glossary to check their spelling.

- Did you use verbs correctly?

- Did you use end punctuation?

As children proofread their draft, remind them to check that they used verbs correctly and spelled high-frequency words correctly. Have children use the Writer's Checklist as they edit and proofread.

Peer Edit Have partners exchange drafts and review them for the mistakes above. Encourage partners to discuss errors. While partners peer edit, you may choose to meet with children individually for conferencing. Follow the steps in the Teacher Conferences box.

Final Draft

Once children have finished editing, proofreading, and peer editing, have them write their final draft. Tell them to write neatly so others can read their work or guide them to explore a variety of digital tools to produce and publish their writing. You may want to have children complete the online keyboarding activity. Model finding letters on a keyboard before having children do the activity.

ELL English Language Learners

Use the following scaffolds with **Revise, Peer Review.**

Beginning

Provide sentence frames to help children express opinions about their partner's writing. I like how you tell the topic. Can you add another fact?

Intermediate

Have partners ask and answer questions about each other's writing: What is one thing you like about my draft? I like how you tell the topic. What can I add? You can add another fact.

Advanced/Advanced High

Have children identify areas where their partner could add details to their writing: I think you can add more facts about the topic. Encourage children to also tell how the added details would improve the writing.

⊙⊙⊙ TEACHER CONFERENCES

Step 1

Talk about the strengths of the writing.

You used past-tense verbs correctly.

Step 2

Focus on how the writer uses the writing trait.

In the first sentence, you stated the idea of your text, so I knew right away what the rest of the text would be about.

Step 3

Make concrete suggestions for revision.

The main idea about your topic might be clearer if you added more details about it.

▶ TEACH IN SMALL GROUP

For additional mini lessons to support writing an Expository Text, see pages T412–T413.

Additionally, to provide differentiated support for children, see Writing Skills mini lessons on pages T420–T429. These can be used throughout the year.

FORMATIVE ASSESSMENT

▶ STUDENT CHECK-IN

Have children share one edit they made to their draft. Have children reflect, using the Check-In routine to fill in the bars.

LESSONS 4-5

LEARNING GOALS

We can present and evaluate our nonfiction text.

OBJECTIVES

Write expository, or informative, texts in which they name a topic, supply some facts about the topic, and provide some sense of closure.

Ask and answer questions about what a speaker says in order to gather additional information or clarify something that is not understood.

Produce complete sentences when appropriate to task and situation.

ELA ACADEMIC LANGUAGE

• *publish, present, evaluate*

• Cognates: *publicar, presentar, evaluar*

DIGITAL TOOLS

Collaborative Conversations: How to Give Presentations

10 mins

Publish, Present, and Evaluate

Prepare to Publish

Have children review their final drafts and make any last-minute changes.

Prepare to Share Have children turn to page 188 in their **Reading/Writing Companion** and work with a partner to practice their presentation.

Speaking and Listening Review the Speaking and Listening skills on page 188.

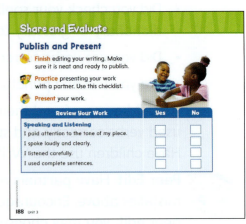

Reading/Writing Companion, p. 188

• Explain that when we give a presentation, we use more formal language. Say: *This is the kind of language we use when we speak to an adult, such as a teacher.* Then explain that when they talk to their friends, they use informal language, which is more relaxed. As needed, model the difference between formal language and informal language. Then model introducing yourself and speaking clearly at an appropriate pace, using more formal language.

• Remind children to pay attention to the tone of their piece as they present.

• Remind children to speak at the right volume.

• Remind children to listen carefully.

• Remind children to use complete sentences.

Allow children five minutes to rehearse their presentation.

Present

Before children begin presenting, you may want to show the How to Give Presentations video. Remind children that not only will they be presenters, they will also be a part of the audience for their classmates' presentations. Tell children to be respectful of their classmates. Allow time after the presentations for children to ask questions and give comments.

Evaluate

Have children discuss and evaluate their presentations. Then have them record their self-evaluations on page 189 of the **Reading/ Writing Companion.**

Publish Remind children that when writers publish their work, they put it in a place where people can read it, such as a

Reading/Writing Companion, p. 189

book. You may choose to publish children's work by hanging it on a bulletin board or placing it in the classroom library for other children to read. Provide time for children to read each other's work.

English Language Learners

Use the following scaffolds with **Evaluate.**

Beginning

Guide children to evaluate their nonfiction writing. *What did you do well? Point to it.* Have children point to a favorite part of their writing. Provide a sentence frame to help children tell what they pointed to. I did a good job telling the topic.

Intermediate

Have children ask and answer questions with a partner: What did you do well? Provide sentence frames to help children explain: I did a good job telling the topic. What do you need to work on? I need to work on adding details.

Advanced/Advanced High

Provide question and answer sentence frames to help partners discuss what they did well in their writing. Why do you think you did this part well? I think I told the topic well because I put it in the first sentence. How will your writing be better if you work on adding details? My writing will be better if I add more details because readers will understand my topic better.

FORMATIVE ASSESSMENT

❯ STUDENT CHECK-IN

Have children think about how they did on their presentation. Have children reflect using the Check-In routine to fill in the bars.

Writing Minilessons

FOCUS ON A TOPIC

OBJECTIVES

Write expository, or informative, texts in which they name a topic, supply some facts about the topic, and provide some sense of closure.

With guidance and support from adults, focus on a topic.

I Do Display the **Literature Big Book** *Where Does Food Come From?* Explain that this nonfiction text tells about real things. Say: *Authors often tell the topic, or what the text is mostly about, in the title or the first sentences.* Read the title and page 5 aloud. Say: *We can tell that this book is about food.* Point out that the authors wrote about real things, such as chocolate.

We Do Read aloud page 6. Have partners look for details that show which food the authors are talking about. Repeat the routine with page 8. Point out how these pages focus on the topic of where food comes from. Provide feedback as necessary.

Explain that the first step in writing a nonfiction text is to choose a topic. Have partners brainstorm a list of real people, places, things, or events they know a lot about. Have them choose one to write about.

You Do Have children write about their topic independently. Encourage them to write a few facts about their chosen topic. Provide sentence frames and guidance as necessary. Have volunteers share their writing.

FACTS BASED ON A SOURCE

OBJECTIVES

Write expository, or informative, texts in which they name a topic, supply some facts about the topic, and provide some sense of closure.

I Do Display the **Literature Big Book** *Where Does Food Come From?* Remind children the text is nonfiction. Say: *Authors of nonfiction texts often find facts about their topics in other sources.* Read aloud pages 4–5. Say: *The authors tell how chocolate is made. They may have used books about chocolate to learn or check the facts.* Explain that authors use their own words when they write the facts.

We Do Read aloud pages 10–11. Ask partners to identify the facts the authors use. Then ask: *Where do you think the authors found these facts?* Provide feedback as necessary.

Guide children to choose an animal as a topic for a nonfiction text. Ask pairs to discuss where they could find facts, such as a library book or the Internet. Remind them that a good source has facts and information that is true. Provide partners with books about the animal to use as a source.

You Do Have children independently write sentences about the topic in their own words based on facts from the provided sources. Provide guidance as necessary. Have volunteers share their writing.

TEXT FEATURES

OBJECTIVES

Write expository, or informative, texts in which they name a topic, supply some facts about the topic, and provide some sense of closure.

Know and use various text features to locate key facts or information in a text.

I Do Display the **Literature Big Book** *Where Does Food Come From?* Remind children the text is nonfiction. Explain that nonfiction texts often have text features such as photos, captions, labels, special print, maps, diagrams, or charts. Turn to pages 4–5. Identify the text features, including the photos, the "Did You Know" feature, and the bold print. Say: *The author put the words* cocoa beans *in large, colored print so readers notice them quickly.*

We Do Brainstorm and write a list of text features on the board with children. Then ask partners to find and discuss text features in nonfiction classroom library books. After they identify each text feature, prompt them to talk about how the text feature helps readers understand the text. Model and provide sentence frames: *This ___ shows ___. It helps readers understand ___.* Ask partners to share the text features they find. Provide feedback as necessary.

Guide children to identify a topic for a nonfiction text, such as a place they know about. Have partners brainstorm text features they could include to tell more about the topic, such as a map or a diagram with labels.

You Do Have children write or draw their text features independently. Provide guidance as necessary, and have volunteers share their work.

CONCLUDING STATEMENT

OBJECTIVES

Write expository, or informative, texts in which they name a topic, supply some facts about the topic, and provide some sense of closure.

I Do Display the **Literature Big Book** *Where Does Food Come From?* Explain that a concluding statement, or question, is the last thing your readers read. Say: *Authors use concluding statements to make their writing stronger and more interesting. The authors' concluding question helps readers think about the text in order to provide an answer.*

We Do Prompt partners to suggest other concluding statements the authors could have used. Have them look at other nonfiction texts they've read and discuss those concluding statements. Provide feedback as necessary.

Guide children to think of a topic for a nonfiction text, such as a place or event they know about. Then have children share facts about it. Ask children what they would want readers to remember about the topic. Guide children to turn these ideas into concluding statements.

You Do Have children write their concluding statement independently. Provide guidance as necessary, and have volunteers share their writing.

Developmental Writing
Plan Writing Instruction

AUTHOR INSIGHT

"Children's early writing efforts reveal what they're noticing and holding onto in their efforts to express their own words and sentences on paper. Parents and teachers may fear that young children will perseverate in these early writing "errors"— the misformed letters, ill-spelled words, and sloppy formatting— but research shows (e.g., Campbell, 2019) that growth in early writing is substantial, highly variable, and rapid. As experience with reading increases and instruction in printing and spelling are provided those short-lived errors fade away without a trace."

—Dr. Timothy Shanahan

Writing in First Grade

Overview

Children in first grade begin the year learning how to write sentences and end the year writing cohesive paragraphs. They write responses to the texts they are reading, and they learn to write informative, narrative, and opinion texts as well. In *Wonders*, children write every day.

As they progress, children learn basic Writing Skills, such as how to leave spaces between words in a sentence, as well as spelling and grammar. They also learn and use Writing Traits that help them shape and organize their ideas into recognizable pieces of writing. They learn how to write coherent sentences and at the end of the year they learn how to form a paragraph.

In this section you will see ten Student Models of writing that show a progression of writing abilities across the year. Use the models to informally assess how children are progressing with their writing development and guide their growth. Meet with children regularly to discuss their growth and writing goals. Use this routine when you meet with children.

Supporting Emergent Writers

1. Identify Strengths

Choose a piece of student writing. Think about the writing skills and traits previously taught.

- What does the writer know about writing?
- What does he or she do well?

Share your observations with the child.

2. Choose an Area for Improvement

Think about what instruction the child would benefit from. Identify a Next Step writing skill to focus on.

3. Next Steps

Share the Next Step goal with the child. You may meet individually with a child or choose to have a small group minilesson with a group of children who have the same instructional needs. You can choose from the following minilessons to focus on:

- Writing Skill Lesson Bank. (See lessons that follow these pages.)
- Writing Trait Minilesson Bank: this appears after each set of Extended Writing lessons.

In addition, see the Instructional Routines Handbook for more information on supporting children in writing about texts, the Writing Process, and Grammar and Mechanics skills.

Choose an Area for Improvement Refer to the **Language Transfers Handbook** to determine what transfer errors in speaking and writing in standard English children might need help with.

Writing Model 1

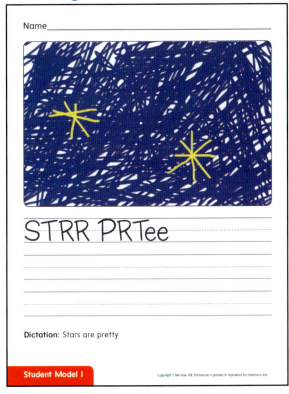

Name_____

STRR PRTee

Dictation: Stars are pretty

Student Model 1

Writing Model 2

Name_____

Strsr Prite an Ther r a lot uF Them an the Mun iz Big.

Dictation: Stars are pretty and there are a lot of them and the moon is big.

Student Model 2

STRENGTHS

- Words are connected to the image.
- Used beginning and ending sounds to write.
- Included a descriptive detail.

NEXT STEPS

- Add details.
- Put spaces between words.
- Stretch sounds to include middle sounds.

STRENGTHS

- Represented beginning, middle, and end sounds correctly.
- Included a supporting detail.
- Used Word Bank to spell some words.

NEXT STEPS

- Focus on one idea.
- Use lowercase letters appropriately.
- Fix run-ons and write complete sentences.

DEVELOPMENTAL WRITING: What to Look For

HANDWRITING

As you review children's writing, look for signs that they need some support with their fine motor development. Notice when children are:

- Writing too lightly
- Using write-on lines incorrectly
- Gripping the pencil incorrectly

See the Handwriting lessons and activities to help children develop their fine motor skills.

Developmental Writing

Writing Model 3

Name_____

There are stars in the ski there are so manee. there are sum that are clos togethr.

Student Model 3   Copyright © McGraw Hill. Permission is granted to reproduce for classroom use.

STRENGTHS

- Spelled some irregular words correctly.
- Used some end punctuation correctly.
- Focused on one idea.

NEXT STEPS

- Add supporting details.
- Vary beginnings of sentences.
- Capitalize beginning of sentences.

Writing Model 4

Name_____

There are stars in the ski it is to manee to caont They luk brit and some stars mak shaps.

Student Model 4   Copyright © McGraw Hill. Permission is granted to reproduce for classroom use.

STRENGTHS

- Used beginning, middle, and end sounds.
- Capitalized first word in some sentences.
- Added descriptive details.

NEXT STEPS

- Focus on one idea.
- Focus on word choice by adding strong verbs, specific nouns, and sensory details.
- Use end punctuation.

DEVELOPMENTAL WRITING: What to Look For

SPELLING

Review children's spelling and notice if children need more support with:

- Spelling Word Bank words correctly
- Using Word Families to help them spell words
- Writing words they frequently misspell

Children at the phonetic stage of development can benefit from instruction in Spelling Word Families, Spelling Patterns, and Phonics and Structural Analysis. In addition, you may wish to have children write words they frequently misspell in their Word Banks.

Writing Model 5

Name_____

There are many stars in the sky. They twinkl. There are grups of stars. The grup can make shaps or a persin!

Student Model 5   Copyright © McGraw Hill. Permission is granted to reproduce for classroom use.

STRENGTHS

- Focused on one idea.
- Included descriptive details.
- Added end punctuation.

NEXT STEPS

- Use word families to spell words.
- Vary beginnings of sentences.
- Add details to tell more about the topic.

Writing Model 6

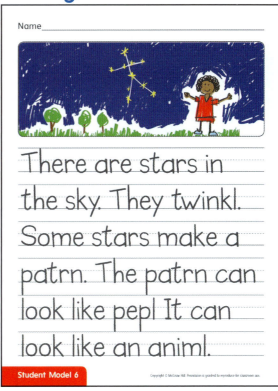

Name_____

There are stars in the sky. They twinkl. Some stars make a patrn. The patrn can look like pepl It can look like an animl.

Student Model 6   Copyright © McGraw Hill. Permission is granted to reproduce for classroom use.

STRENGTHS

- Varied beginnings of sentences.
- Used specific nouns.
- Used end punctuation correctly.

NEXT STEPS

- Write a topic sentence.
- Add details that support the topic.
- Use facts from a source.

DEVELOPMENTAL WRITING: What to Look For

SENTENCES

Review children's writing in terms of sentence composition. Notice if they can:

- Write a complete sentence.
- Use different types of sentences: statements, questions, exclamations, and commands.
- Fix run-on sentences.
- Use conjunctions to extend sentences.

For more support with writing sentences, see the Writing Skill Lesson Bank and Grammar lessons on Sentences in Unit 1.

Developmental Writing

Writing Model 7

Name_____

There are bilyons of stars in the sky! They can make a pattrn called a konslashun. The pattrn can look like peple or animals.

Student Model 7   Copyright © McGraw Hill. Permission is granted to reproduce for classroom use.

STRENGTHS

- Wrote a topic sentence.
- Included details that support the topic.
- Used facts from a source.

NEXT STEPS

- Focus on one idea.
- Include more details about the topic.
- Use Word Bank to spell words correctly.

Writing Model 8

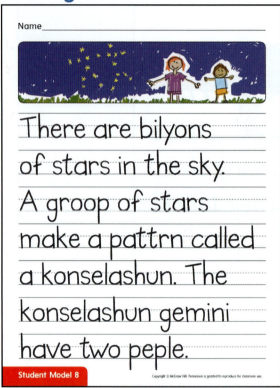

Name_____

There are bilyons of stars in the sky. A groop of stars make a pattrn called a konselashun. The konselashun gemini have two peple.

Student Model 8   Copyright © McGraw Hill. Permission is granted to reproduce for classroom use.

STRENGTHS

- Focused on one idea.
- Included more details about the topic.
- Spelled many words correctly.

NEXT STEPS

- Add more facts.
- Use describing words.
- Use the verbs *has* and *have* correctly.

DEVELOPMENTAL WRITING: What to Look For

MULTIMODAL

PARAGRAPHS

As children master writing sentences, review their beginning attempts at writing paragraphs and notice if they need support with:

- STRUCTURE: Sequencing sentences to organize them so they are clear to reader.
- CONNECTION: Connecting sentences with transition words to signal the connection of ideas.
- CONTENT: Including sentences that support the main topic of the paragraph.
- GRAMMAR & MECHANICS: Writing grammatically correct sentences that vary in length and type.

See the Writing Skills Lesson Bank for more support with writing paragraphs. Also, see Writing lessons on Sentence Structure and Grammar lessons you may wish to reteach.

Writing Model 9

Name_____

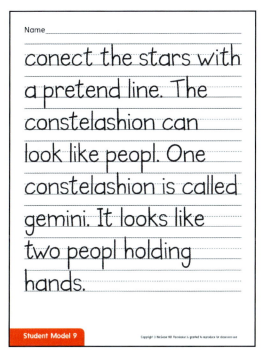

Gemini
There are bilions of
stars! A gruop of
stars make a pattrn
called a constelashion.
You can see it if you

Student Model 9   Copyright © McGraw Hill. Permission is granted to reproduce for classroom use

Name_____

conect the stars with
a pretend line. The
constelashion can
look like peopl. One
constelashion is called
gemini. It looks like
two peopl holding
hands.

Student Model 9   Copyright © McGraw Hill. Permission is granted to reproduce for classroom use

STRENGTHS

- Added a title that focuses on topic.
- Connected ideas within a paragraph.
- Used Word Bank or sources to spell words correctly.

NEXT STEPS

- Focus on writing paragraphs.
- Capitalize proper nouns.
- Add a strong conclusion.

Writing Model 10

Name_____

Gemini
There are billions
of stars! Some stars
are grouped together
in a pattern. You can
connect the stars
with an pretend line
when you look at
them. These groups

Student Model 10   Copyright © McGraw Hill. Permission is granted to reproduce for classroom use

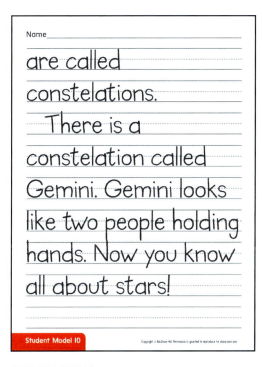

Name_____

are called
constelations.
There is a
constelation called
Gemini. Gemini looks
like two people holding
hands. Now you know
all about stars!

Student Model 10   Copyright © McGraw Hill. Permission is granted to reproduce for classroom use

STRENGTHS

- Organized ideas into clear and coherent paragraphs.
- Wrote sentences that support the main topic of the paragraph.
- Wrote grammatically correct sentences that vary in length and type.

Writing Skills

STRETCH SOUNDS TO WRITE WORDS

OBJECTIVES

Spell untaught words phonetically, drawing on phonemic awareness and spelling conventions.

I Do Use **Literature Big Book** *This School Year Will Be the Best!* to reinforce how to stretch sounds in words. Turn to page 4. Point out the rug in the illustration. Then read aloud the first sentence, pausing before the word *rug*. Explain that when the author wanted to write the word *rug*, she said each sound in the word and wrote the letter for each sound. Say each sound in the word *rug* as you point to and name its corresponding letter: /rrr/, r, /uuu/, u, /g/, g. Use this technique with any book being read.

We Do Turn to page 5, and point out the children are in a bus. Guide children to say the word *bus*, stretching the sounds and writing the corresponding letters. Then have them see how the author spelled *bus*.

Read more pages. Have partners discuss the pattern in the story. Tell children they will write a sentence about their wish for the school year. Provide the sentence frame: *I wish _____.* Tell children to stretch the sounds in words to write their wish.

You Do Have children write their sentences independently. Provide guidance as necessary, and have volunteers share their writing.

SENTENCE CAPITALIZATION

OBJECTIVES

Recognize the distinguishing features of a sentence (e.g., first word, capitalization, ending punctuation).

Use uppercase letters to start sentences.

I Do Display pages 2–3 of **Literature Big Book** *Alicia's Happy Day*. Ask children to take turns pointing to the first word in the sentence. Have partners turn and discuss what they notice about the first word. Then have volunteers share their thinking. If necessary, point out that the author begins the first word of the sentence with an uppercase letter. Explain that using an uppercase letter helps readers know a new sentence is beginning.

We Do Turn to pages 4–5 and have children identify the first word in the sentence and the uppercase letter that begins it. Read the sentence aloud.

Read more pages of the selection, asking a child to point to the uppercase letter at the beginning of each sentence. Then talk about the different wishes for Alicia's birthday. Tell children they will write a wish for a friend's birthday, using the pattern: *May you _____.* Provide examples as needed.

You Do Have children write their sentences independently. Remind them to begin each sentence with an uppercase letter. Provide guidance as necessary and have volunteers share their writing.

USE THE WORD BANK

OBJECTIVES

Use conventional spelling for words with common spelling patterns and for frequently occurring irregular words.

Use the Word Bank for help with spelling the high-frequency words.

I Do Display the cover of **Literature Big Book** *Cool Dog, School Dog.* Read the title aloud. Tell children they can use the Word Bank to help them spell words that are tricky to remember. Guide them to find the word *school* in the Word Bank. Have children spell the word aloud as you point to each letter of the word in the title. This can be done with any book the children are reading.

We Do Display page 5 and read the text. Point to the word *and.* Ask a child to find *and* in the Word Bank and spell it. Continue guiding children to use the Word Bank to spell other words from the selection, such as *go* on page 22 and *come* on page 25.

Begin a discussion about Tinka. Have children use words from the Word Bank to complete the sentence: *Tinka is a _____ dog.*

You Do Have children write their sentences independently. Encourage them to use words from the Word Bank to write another sentence about Tinka. Provide guidance as necessary and have volunteers share their writing.

LEFT-TO-RIGHT PROGRESSION

OBJECTIVES

Demonstrate understanding of the organization and basic features of print.

Write a sentence using left-to-right progression.

I Do Have children hold up their left hand and say the word *left.* Repeat the routine for the right hand. Next display page 2 of **Literature Big Book** *Friends All Around.* Read the sentence aloud as you point to each word. Ask children to point to where the author began the sentence. Have them track the print to the end of the sentence. Ask: *Does the author begin the sentence on the left or the right? Where does the author end the sentence?* Have partners turn and talk. Then have volunteers share their thinking. Note what children understand about left-to-right progression.

We Do Guide children to track the print as you read other sentences from the selection. Explain that authors begin a sentence on the left. They write one word after another, moving from the left side of the paper to the right side. This is also the order in which we read the words.

Tell children they will write a sentence about what some friends like to do. Provide the sentence frame: *Some friends like to _____.* Remind children to begin the sentence on the left side of the paper and write one word at a time, moving to the right.

You Do Have children write their sentences independently. Provide guidance as necessary and have volunteers share their writing.

Writing Skills

SPACING BETWEEN WORDS

OBJECTIVES

Recognize the distinguishing features of a sentence (e.g., first word, capitalization, ending punctuation).

Write a sentence with appropriate spacing between words.

I Do Use the **Literature Big Book** *Move!* to reinforce the importance of spacing between words. Turn to page 2. Read the sentence aloud. Then ask children to count the number of words. Have partners turn and talk. Then have volunteers identify the number of words and tell how they were able to count them. Point to each word and the spaces between. Explain authors leave a space between each word to show readers where one word ends and the next begins. Note you can use this technique with any book children are currently reading.

We Do Read the beginning of the sentence on page 3. Ask children to point to each word and count them. Make sure they identify the words correctly.

Talk about the different ways the animals move. Have partners talk about their favorite animal and how it moves. Tell children they will write a sentence about how the animal moves. Have children write their sentence, keeping space between each word. Guide children as necessary, helping them create appropriate spaces.

You Do Have children independently write a sentence about how another animal moves. Provide guidance as necessary. Have volunteers share their writing.

WRITE ON THE LINES

OBJECTIVES

Demonstrate understanding of the organization and basic features of print.

Stay on the lines when writing sentences.

I Do Display pages 2–3 of the **Literature Big Book** *Millie Waits for the Mail.* Place a piece of lined paper under the first sentence. Read the sentence aloud and ask children what they notice about the line. Invite partners to turn and talk. As needed, explain that the words appear in a straight line.

We Do Repeat with the second line. Point out how all the letters touch the bottom of the line. Some letters, such as the capital *M,* touch the top of the line. Display other sentences from the story to reinforce this concept.

Reread the story. Guide partners to talk about how Millie changes in the story. Tell children they will write a sentence describing what Millie loves to do at the beginning of the story and a sentence to tell what she loves to do at the end. Provide the sentence frames: *At the beginning, Millie loves to _____. At the end, Millie loves to _____.*

You Do Have children write their sentences about Millie independently. Remind them to use the lines to write their letters. Provide guidance and suggest corrections as necessary. Have volunteers share their writing.

RETURN SWEEP

OBJECTIVES

Demonstrate understanding of the organization and basic features of print.

Write using left-to-right and top-to-bottom progression.

I Do Turn to pages 2–3 in the **Literature Big Book** *The Three Little Dassies.* Read aloud the first paragraph as you track the print from left to right and top to bottom. Have children turn and talk about how you read the sentences. Ask volunteers to share their observations. Point out that you begin reading on the left and move across to the right. When you reach the end of the line on the right, you move down to the next line and begin reading from the left.

We Do Turn to page 4. Ask a volunteer to track the print as you read the first paragraph aloud. Have volunteers track the print as you read more sentences.

Begin a discussion about the houses each dassie builds. Have partners select one dassie and talk about its house and what happens when the eagle comes to it. Tell children they will write sentences to tell about the dassie's house. Provide a word bank with words such as *Mimbi, eagle,* and *grasses.* Remind children to write from left to right and top to bottom.

You Do Have children write their sentences independently. Provide guidance as necessary and have volunteers share their writing.

END PUNCTUATION

OBJECTIVES

Recognize the distinguishing features of a sentence (e.g., first word, capitalization, ending punctuation).

Use end punctuation for sentences.

I Do Turn to pages 4–5 in the **Literature Big Book** *The Story of Martin Luther King Jr.* Read page 4 aloud as you track the print. Ask children how many sentences are on the page. Have children turn and talk with a partner. Then have volunteers share their answer and explain how they counted the sentences. Ask: *How do you know where each sentence ends?* As needed, point out the period at the end of the first sentence and the question mark at the end of the second. Explain a period shows the end of a sentence. A question mark shows the end of a question.

We Do Continue having children count sentences as you read page 7 aloud and have a volunteer track the print. Ask children to identify each ending punctuation mark. Repeat the routine with additional pages of the story.

Tell children they will write two sentences about Martin Luther King Jr. Have partners talk about which facts they would like to write. Remind children to end each sentence with a period.

You Do Have children write their sentence independently. Provide guidance as necessary and have volunteers share their writing.

Writing Skills

CAPITALIZE PROPER NOUNS

OBJECTIVES

Capitalize dates and names of people.

Use proper nouns.

I Do Display the cover of the **Literature Big Book** *Me on the Map*. Read aloud the title and the names of the author and illustrator. Ask children what they notice about the names of the author and illustrator. Have partners turn and talk. Then have volunteers share their thinking. Point out the uppercase letters that begin each name. Explain that the names of people are special naming words called proper nouns. Proper nouns, like children's names, begin with an uppercase letter.

We Do Turn to page 12 and read the sentences aloud. Ask children what they notice. Point out the capitalization of United States of America. Explain that the name of a country is also a proper noun, so the words begin with uppercase letters. Tell children *The* is capitalized because it is the first word in the sentence. It is not a proper noun. Repeat the routine for *Earth* on page 14.

Tell children they will write sentences telling their names and where they live. Have partners talk about the proper nouns in each sentence. Provide sentence frames: *My name is _____. I live in _____.*

You Do Have children write their sentences independently. Provide guidance as necessary and have volunteers share their writing.

CAPITALIZE I

OBJECTIVES

Recognize the distinguishing features of a sentence (e.g., first word, capitalization, ending punctuation).

Capitalize the word *I*.

I Do Display pages 26–27 of the **Literature Big Book** *Mystery Vine*. Read page 27 aloud. Ask children to point to the word *I*. Ask what they notice about the word. Have partners talk about their observations and then share with the class. Explain when the letter *i* is used as a word, it should be an uppercase letter. *I* is a word you use to tell about yourself.

We Do Display pages 4–5. Read the first sentence aloud. Ask children to replace *we* with *I*. Write the new sentence aloud, pausing before writing *I*. Have children tell you how to write the word.

Talk about what the children planted and what grew in their garden. Tell children they will write a sentence to tell what they have planted or would like to plant. Have partners discuss their ideas. Provide a sentence frame: _____ *would plant* _____. Remind children to use a capital letter for the word *I*.

You Do Have children write their sentences independently. Provide guidance as necessary. Have volunteers share their writing.

WORD ENDINGS (-ed, -ing)

OBJECTIVES

Read words with inflectional endings.

Use the inflectional endings -ed and -ing.

I Do Display the cover of the **Literature Big Book** *Interrupting Chicken*. Read the title aloud. Ask children whether they know what the word *interrupt* means. Explain that it means "to begin to talking while someone else is talking." Point out the *-ing* ending. Tell children it is added to the end of a word to show the action is happening now. Turn to page 12 and point out the word *jumped.* Ask partners to turn and talk about what they notice about the word. As needed, explain that *-ed* shows an action happened in the past.

We Do Turn to page 15 and point out the word *relaxing.* Guide children to identify the word parts (*relax, -ing*) and talk about the meaning of the word. Repeat with *wished* on page 17 and *falling* on page 23.

Provide children with a list of verbs, such as *talk, pick, walk, add, wash, help,* and *fix.* Have partners take turns adding *-ed* and *-ing* to each word and discussing how the ending changes the word's meaning. If necessary, remind children what *-ed* and *-ing* mean.

You Do Have children write two sentences independently, using a verb from the list and the endings *-ed* and *-ing.* Have volunteers share their writing.

WRITE A COMPLETE SENTENCE

OBJECTIVES

Produce and expand complete simple and compound declarative, interrogative, imperative, and exclamatory sentences in response to prompts.

I Do Display the cover of the **Literature Big Book** *This School Year Will Be the Best!* Remind children the story is about what children hope will happen during the school year. Turn to pages 4–5. Read aloud the first sentence. Ask: *Is this a complete thought?* Explain that authors use complete sentences. A complete sentence is a group of words that tells a whole idea. Ask: *What is the whole idea in the sentence?*

We Do Read part of the sentence from page 5, such as *on the bus.* Ask: *Are these words a complete sentence? Do they tell a whole idea?* Have children turn and talk with a partner and then share their thinking with the class. Next, read the complete sentence aloud, and talk about what makes it a whole idea. Repeat with other sentences in the book.

Display the words *play soccer.* Ask children whether the words are an incomplete sentence or a complete sentence. Then have children suggest ways to complete the sentence, such as: *I hope to play soccer.* Repeat the routine with *my friends, in art class,* and *run in the grass.*

You Do Have children write a complete sentence about something they want to do this year. Provide guidance as necessary, and have volunteers share their writing.

Writing Skills

CORRECT WORD ORDER

OBJECTIVES

Produce and expand complete simple and compound declarative, interrogative, imperative, and exclamatory sentences in response to prompts.

Put words in the correct order when writing sentences.

I Do Display the cover of the **Literature Big Book** *Friends All Around.* Tell children that authors write sentences that are easy to understand. Authors use words in an order that makes sense and tells a whole idea. Say: *Listen to this sentence: Learn together some friends.* Ask: *Are the words in the sentence in the correct order? Does the sentence make sense?* Display pages 4–5 as partners discuss your questions. Guide children to put the words in the correct order. Read the sentence on page 5 aloud.

We Do Write the sentence from page 10 with incorrect word order. Guide children to put the words in the correct order. Repeat with the sentence on page 11.

Write the words from the sentences on pages 12–13 with incorrect word order. Have partners put the words in the correct order for each sentence. Have volunteers read the corrected sentences to the class.

You Do Give children the words for the sentence on page 14 with incorrect word order. Have children write the sentence correctly on their own. Provide guidance as necessary and have volunteers share their writing.

WRITE A QUESTION

OBJECTIVES

Produce and expand complete simple and compound declarative and interrogative sentences in response to prompts.

Turn a declarative sentence into a question.

I Do Display the cover of the **Literature Big Book** *Where Does Food Come From?* Read the title aloud. Have partners discuss what they notice about the title. As needed, point out the title is a question. Review question words, including *where, what, why,* and *how.* Show children how to turn a sentence into a question. Turn to page 5 and read the first sentence aloud. Model turning the sentence into a question: *Where do cocoa beans grow?*

We Do Read aloud the second sentence on page 5 and guide children to turn it into a question. Ask: *Which word can we begin the question with?*

Tell children they will read a sentence and turn it into a question. Display page 6 and read the last sentence aloud. Have partners discuss their ideas for turning the sentence into a question. Remind children to begin with a question word and end with a question mark.

You Do Give children another sentence from the selection and have them turn it into a question independently. Provide guidance as necessary. Have volunteers share their writing.

PUT SENTENCES TOGETHER: WRITING WITH CONJUNCTIONS

OBJECTIVES

Use frequently occurring conjunctions.

Produce and expand complete simple and compound declarative, interrogative, imperative, and exclamatory sentences in response to prompts.

I Do Display pages 20–21 of the **Literature Big Book** *Millie Waits for the Mail.* Read aloud the next to last sentence on page 20. Ask partners to turn and talk about what they notice about the sentence. Have them share their observations. As needed, point out that the author used the word *and* to join two ideas. Tell children the two ideas are *box bounced right past her* and *box landed under the wheels of the farmer's tractor.*

We Do Review that *and, or,* and *but* are words that join ideas. Read the last sentence on page 20. Ask children to identify the word the author uses to join two ideas. (but) Discuss the two ideas being joined.

Write these sentences on the board and read them aloud: *I could go here. I could go there.* Have partners put the sentences together with a conjunction. Have volunteers share their work.

You Do Provide children two new sentences to combine independently: *Millie might hide in the barn. Millie might hide behind a tree.* Provide guidance as necessary, and have volunteers share their writing.

FACTS FROM A SOURCE

OBJECTIVES

With guidance and support from adults, gather information from provided sources to answer a question.

Use sources to find facts and information.

I Do Display the cover of the **Literature Big Book** *Where Does Food Come From?* Remind children the text is nonfiction. It gives facts and information about where food comes from. Turn to pages 4–5 and read the text aloud. Ask: *What facts and information does the author give?* Explain that authors of nonfiction texts find facts about their topic in sources, such as another nonfiction book and the Internet. Authors make sure the source's information is true. Then they use their own words to write the facts.

We Do Turn to pages 8–9 and read the text aloud. Ask: *What facts and information does the author give? Where might the author have found the facts and information?* Have children turn and talk with a partner and then share their thinking with the class.

Guide children to identify a food. Brainstorm questions about the food. Provide sources, such as nonfiction texts and the Internet. Locate a relevant fact and read it aloud. Have partners work together to restate the fact in their own words. Have children write the fact and share it aloud.

You Do Read another fact and have children independently write it in their own words. Provide guidance as necessary and have volunteers share their writing.

Writing Skills

WRITE DIALOGUE

OBJECTIVES

Demonstrate command of the conventions of standard English capitalization, punctuation, and spelling when writing.

Write dialogue.

I Do Use **Literature Big Book** *The Three Little Dassies* to help children write dialogue. Turn to pages 6–7 and read the text aloud. Then ask children to identify the words Mimbi speaks. Have partners turn and talk. Then have them share their ideas. Note what children understand about dialogue.

We Do Read page 8 aloud. Say: *The words characters speak are called dialogue.* Ask children to identify the dialogue and the character speaking. Point out the quotation marks. The words the character says appear inside these marks. Guide children to recognize the importance of the words "she said" after the dialogue. Repeat the routine with Timbi's dialogue on page 10.

Write an example of simple dialogue on the board: *"I see you," the eagle said.* Have partners discuss the dialogue and then work together to write another line of dialogue for the eagle or for Mimbi, Timbi, or Pimbi, using the example on the board as a model. Have volunteers share their dialogue.

You Do Have children independently write another sentence with dialogue for the eagle or one of the dassies. Have volunteers share their writing.

USE APPROPRIATE TONE AND VOICE: FORMAL AND INFORMAL LANGUAGE

OBJECTIVES

Produce and expand complete simple and compound declarative, interrogative, imperative, and exclamatory sentences in response to prompts.

Write sentences using formal and informal language.

I Do Display page 10 of the **Literature Big Book** *Friends All Around.* Read the text aloud and show children the photograph. Ask children to imagine what these children might be saying to each other. Tell children that, when we talk to our friends, we speak one way, but when we talk to adults, such as teachers, we talk another way. Say: *We can use informal language with our friends. With teachers, we speak more formally.* Have partners turn and talk about ways they talk to friends and ways they talk to adults.

We Do Write and read aloud: *yes, yep.* Tell children these words mean the same thing but one is more formal than the other. Ask children how they would use these words. Repeat with *You are welcome* and *No problem!*

Display and read aloud: *What is going on? What's up?* Have partners discuss which question is formal. Then give partners the example: *I'll see you tomorrow.* Have them suggest ways to say the same thing informally.

You Do Have each child write a sentence with formal language. Then have them write the same idea with informal language. Provide guidance as necessary and have volunteers share their writing.

VARY SENTENCE LENGTH

OBJECTIVES

Produce and expand complete simple and compound declarative, interrogative, imperative, and exclamatory sentences in response to prompts.

I Do Turn to pages 6–7 in the **Literature Big Book** *Me on the Map.* Read the text aloud. Then have children turn and discuss what they notice about the length of sentences. As needed, point out the varying length of sentences. Explain that authors write some short sentences and some long sentences to make their writing flow like speech and sound more interesting.

We Do Read aloud pages 14–16. Have children identify short and long sentences. Ask how the sentences would sound if they were all short or all long.

Tell children they will write sentences about their home or a place on a map. Have partners work together to discuss ideas and write sentences. Remind them to use different lengths of sentences. Provide guidance and suggestions as needed. Have partners share their sentences aloud.

You Do Have children reread the sentences they wrote with their partner. Ask them to rewrite sentences to include long and short ones. Provide guidance as necessary, and have volunteers share their work.

FORMING A PARAGRAPH

OBJECTIVES

Write informative/explanatory texts in which they name a topic, supply some facts about the topic, and provide some sense of closure.

Write a paragraph.

I Do Display pages 6–7 in the **Literature Big Book** *The Three Little Dassies.* Read aloud the sentences in the second paragraph on page 7. Begin a discussion about paragraphs by asking: *What do we learn in the opening sentence of this paragraph? What details tell us more about how Mimbi uses the long grasses? How does the paragraph conclude, or end?*

We Do Explain how a paragraph often has an opening sentence, detail sentences, and a concluding statement. Guide children to discuss the paragraph on page 15. Have them identify the opening sentence, details sentences, and the concluding statement. Repeat with the first paragraph on page 17.

Guide partners to think of a topic for a paragraph, such as an animal or sport they both know about. Before writing, have them discuss what they would say about their topic in an opening sentence, which details they could include, and how they would wrap up or conclude their paragraph. Provide sentence frames and examples as necessary.

You Do Have partners work together to write a paragraph with four to five sentences. Provide guidance as necessary, and have volunteers share their writing.

Notes

EXTEND, CONNECT, AND ASSESS

Extend

Reading Digitally

Reader's Theater

Level Up with Leveled Readers

Connect

Connect to Science

Assess

Reflect on Learning

Unit Assessments

Fluency Assessment

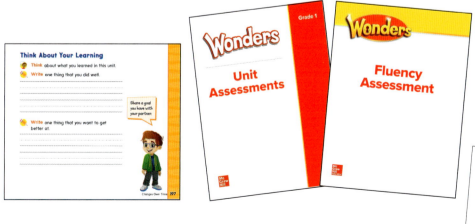

Content Area Reading Options

Student Outcomes

FOUNDATIONAL SKILLS

Fluency

- Read grade-level texts with accuracy, appropriate rate or expression

READING

Reading Informational Text

- Use text features including titles, headings, captions, graphs, maps, glossaries, and/or illustrations to locate key facts or information
- Read informational texts appropriately complex for grade 1

Compare Texts

- Read and comprehend grade-level complex texts proficiently

ELL Scaffolded supports for English Language Learners are embedded throughout the lessons, enabling children to communicate information, ideas, and concepts in English Language Arts and for social and instructional purposes within the school setting.

COMMUNICATION

Writing

- Write expository texts about a topic, using a source, providing facts and a sense of closure

Communicating Orally

- Retell a text to enhance comprehension
- Use appropriate collaborative techniques and active listening skills when engaging in discussions in a variety of situations

Researching

- Participate in shared research and writing projects

Creating and Collaborating

- Add drawings and visual displays to descriptions
- Use digital tools to produce and publish writing

VOCABULARY

Academic Vocabulary

- Acquire and use grade-appropriate academic vocabulary

Extend, Connect, and Assess

Extend

TIME KiDS

Reading Digitally

"Seasons Bring Change"
Genre: Online Article

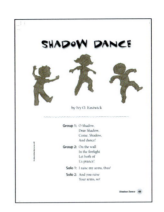

Reader's Theater

Shadow Dance
Genre: Play

Connect

Science

Genre Read-Aloud, pp. 54–57

"Twinsies"

Reading/Writing Companion, pp. 190–191

Respond to the Text

Assess

Unit Assessments

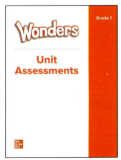

Unit 3 Test

Unit 3 Test Online

Fluency

EVALUATE STUDENT PROGRESS

Use the *Wonders* online assessment reports to evaluate children's progress and help you make decisions about small-group instruction and assignments.

Self-Assess Have children complete Reflect on Your Learning and note any areas where they need improvement.

Planner

Customize your own lesson plans at
my.mheducation.com

 LESSON 1

 **LESSON 2**

 60+ mins

Reading/Writing Suggested Daily Time

LESSON GOALS

- I can listen to and understand a science text.
- I can write a letter about my science project.

▶▶ SMALL GROUP OPTIONS
The designated lessons can be taught in small groups. To determine how to differentiate instruction for small groups, use Formative Assessment and Data Dashboard.

Reading/Writing

Lesson 1

⊳ **Reading Digitally, T432–T433**
Read "Seasons Bring Change" TIME **KiDS**

⊳ **Reader's Theater, T434–T435**
Shadow Dance
Read the Play and Model Fluency

Lesson 2

⊳ **Reader's Theater, T434–T435**
Shadow Dance
Assign Roles and Practice the Play

⊳ **Connect to Content: Science, T436–T437**
Read Aloud: "Twinsies"

Teacher-Led Instruction

SMALL GROUP

Level Up with Leveled Readers
⬤⬤ **Approaching Level to On Level, T444**
Apples from Farm to Table

Level Up with Leveled Readers
⬤⬤ **On Level to Beyond Level, T445**
Apples from Farm to Table

Level Up with Leveled Readers
⬤⬤ **ELL Level to On Level, T446**
Apples from Farm to Table

Independent/Collaborative Work

Reading

Comprehension
- Make Inferences

Fluency
- Reader's Theater

Independent Reading

Make Inferences Card 40

Reader's Theater Card 39

Writing

Self-Selected Writing

Writing Process Card 42

LESSON 3

 LESSON 4

 LESSON 5

Reading/Writing

▶ Reader's Theater, T434–T435
Shadow Dance
Practice the Play and Extend

Connect to Content: Science, T438–T439
Observe a Plant

▶ Reader's Theater, T434–T435
Shadow Dance
Perform and Reread the Play

Connect to Content: Science, T440
Write a Friendly Letter

Choose Your Own Book, T441

Wrap Up the Unit, T442
Connect to the Big idea

Think About Your Learning, T443

Summative Assessment and Next Steps, T448–T450

Level Up with Leveled Readers
● **Beyond Level to Self-Selected**
Trade Book, T447
Apples from Farm to Table

Student's CHOICE

Content Area Connections

Content Area Reading
• Science, Social Studies, and the Arts

We can use interactive features to read an online text.

OBJECTIVES

Know and use various text features (e.g., headings, tables of contents, glossaries, electronic menus, icons) to locate key facts or information in a text.

Add drawings or other visual displays to descriptions when appropriate to clarify ideas, thoughts, and feelings.

With guidance and support from adults, use a variety of digital tools to produce and publish writing, including in collaboration with peers.

ELA ACADEMIC LANGUAGE

• *sidebar*

DIFFERENTIATED READING

🔴🟣 **Approaching Level** and **ELL** Read the text aloud to children. Have partners work together to complete the Sequence Graphic Organizer.

🔵🟢 **On Level** and **Beyond Level** Have partners read the text and access the interactive features independently, as they are able. Complete the Reread activities during Small Group time.

TIME for **KiDS**

"Seasons Bring Change"

Before Reading

Introduce the Genre Display the online article "Seasons Bring Change" at my.mheducation.com. Review that online articles are digital texts we access on a computer or a personal device. Remind children that digital texts have special characteristics, such as links and sidebar features we can click on. These links and features provide more information about the topic. Tell children that you will read the article together and then use the features.

Close Reading Online

Read

Take Notes Scroll back to the top and read the article aloud. As you read, ask questions about the seasons. Model taking notes, using the Sequence Graphic Organizer #6. After each section, have partners use text evidence to discuss what they learned. Help children use context clues to discuss antonyms, such as *warm/cool, days/nights*.

Access Interactive Features Help children click on or roll over each sidebar feature. Discuss the information these features add to the text.

Retell Review your Sequence Graphic Organizer with children. Model using the information to begin retelling "Seasons Bring Change." Then encourage children to continue retelling the rest of the selection.

Reread

Craft and Structure Tell children they will reread parts of the article to help them answer specific questions:

• What do plants and animals do during each season?

• Why is "Seasons Bring Change" a good title for this article?

Integrate

Make Connections

Text Connections Have children compare what they learned about the seasons with what they learned about changes in other texts they read in this unit.

Research Online

Search Results Model conducting an Internet search about the life cycle of a plant. Use a child-friendly search engine and type in the key words. Then discuss the results page. Point out that the most relevant results are usually listed first. Demonstrate clicking on the link at the top of a result to jump to that page and then using the back button to return to the results.

Inspire Action

Plants Are Living Things Remind children that plants are living things that change with the seasons. Have children name parts of a plant. Then discuss how plants change during their lifetime. Ask children to tell facts from the article that help them understand that plants are living things.

- How do plants change from season to season?
- How do plants change as they get older?

Independent Study

Investigate

Choose a Topic Have children brainstorm questions related to how plants change during the seasons. Then have them choose a question to research. For example: What is a plant's life cycle? What happens in each season?

Conduct Internet Research Have children conduct an Internet search. Type in the URL for a child-friendly search engine. Enter key words and click Search. Click on a link on the results page to go to a site.

Present Help children use their research to make a diagram of a plant's life cycle or use presentation software to share it with others.

 ENGLISH LANGUAGE LEARNERS

Craft and Structure Read the second question with children. *What are the four seasons?* Have children answer by chorally reading the headings from the article. *When something changes, does it stay the same, or is it different?* (different) Then have children use the four images at the beginning of the article to explain how one tree changes through the seasons. Provide sentence frames: In winter, there is snow/it's snowy. The tree has no leaves.

FORMATIVE ASSESSMENT

⊙ STUDENT CHECK-IN

Have partners share what they learned about seasons from the online text.

Have children reflect, using the Check-In routine.

LESSON 1-4

Shadow Dance

Introduce the Genre

Explain to children that *Shadow Dance* is a play in which a shadow speaks and dances. Before reading the play, make sure children know what a shadow is. Distribute scripts and the Elements of Drama handout from the online Reader's Theater PDF.

- Review the features of a play.
- Review the cast of characters.
- Explain that the setting of the play isn't specified, but it is probably somewhere indoors where firelight can cast a shadow on a wall.

Read the Play

Model reading the play as children follow along in their scripts.

Model Fluency As you come to each part, state the name of each character and read the part, emphasizing the appropriate phrasing and expression. Provide an example of the tone a character may use and demonstrate reading with it.

Focus on Vocabulary Stop and discuss any vocabulary words that children may not know. You may wish to teach *shadow, firelight, prance, raise,* and *thus.*

Discuss Each Role After reading the play, ask children to identify the difference between each character's part and the part everyone reads. Check that children understand the characters, setting, and plot.

Assign Roles

Depending on the number of children, you may choose to have more than one cast. To more evenly distribute the lines, you might assign the role of Solo 1 to a child who is part of Group 1 and the role of Solo 2 to a child who is part of Group 2. Remind children that everyone reads the part at the end labeled *All.*

Practice the Play

Practice Fluency Have children use highlighters to mark their part in the script. Each day, allow children time to practice. For each part, pair fluent readers with less fluent readers. Have children chorally read their part, focusing on accuracy and rate. As needed, work with less fluent readers to help them read with emotion.

Throughout the week, have children work on **Reader's Theater Center Activity Card 39.**

Once children have practiced reading their parts several times, allow time to practice performing.

LEARNING GOALS

We can read fluently to perform a play.

OBJECTIVES

Use context to confirm or self-correct word recognition and understanding, rereading as necessary.

Participate in collaborative conversations with diverse partners about grade 1 topics and texts with peers and adults in small and larger groups.

Read, practice, and perform a play.

ELA ACADEMIC LANGUAGE

- *script, gestures, expression*
- Cognates: *gestos, expresión*

▶ TEACH IN SMALL GROUP

You may want to teach the Reader's Theater lesson during Small Group time and then have groups present their work to the class.

Extend: Dress the Part

Explain that costumes and props can add to a performance and make it more interesting for the audience. Have children work in small groups to create a prop or costume for each character.

Add Actions

Help children create their own shadows, like those in *Shadow Dance,* to enhance their performances.

- Hang a sheet and put a light behind it.
- Darken the room and stand between the sheet and the light to demonstrate how a shadow is cast.
- Then have children act out the play between the sheet and the light.

Children might enjoy performing the play in small groups for the rest of the class or for a kindergarten class.

Perform the Play

- Invite children to act out their parts and face the audience as much as possible. Encourage them to bring the text to life by using their voice, facial expressions, and/or gestures.
- Remind children to focus on their scripts as the play is being performed and to read along, even when it is not their turn to speak.
- Remind children to speak at an appropriate pace and say each word loudly so their voices can be heard.
- Explain how performing a play aloud is different from reading it silently. Have partners discuss what they liked about performing and what they didn't.

Extension

In *Shadow Dance,* a shadow speaks and dances. Have children pretend to be something else and dance and talk like their new character.

1. Tell children to pretend they are flowers. Ask: *How can you dance? How can you speak? What will you say?*

2. Have partners act out being different things. Provide examples, such as a chair, dog, tree, or raindrop. Invite children to think about their own character and how the character might act.

3. Have partners create a play with their new characters and perform for classmates.

ELL ENGLISH LANGUAGE LEARNERS

Practice the Play Review the features of a play: character, setting, dialogue, stage directions. Have children read their lines aloud. Record them, and with each child, listen to the recording as you trace the dialogue with your finger. To help children monitor their own language production, ask: *Which words or phrases do you find difficult to pronounce?* Model pronouncing the words and phrases slowly and record them for children to use for practice. Encourage children to use appropriate pacing and intonation, speaking as naturally as possible. For the part at the end labeled *All,* have children practice speaking together. Record children's dialogue for them to use for practice.

FORMATIVE ASSESSMENT

◆ STUDENT CHECK-IN

Have partners talk about how well they read their lines.

Have children reflect, using the Check-In routine.

LEARNING GOALS

We can listen to and understand a science text.

OBJECTIVES

Use words and phrases acquired through conversations, reading and being read to, and responding to texts, including using frequently occurring conjunctions to signal simple relationships.

Build on others' talk in conversations by responding to the comments of others through multiple exchanges.

ELA ACADEMIC LANGUAGE

• drama, details

• Cognates: drama, detalles

DIGITAL TOOLS

Genre Read-Aloud

DIFFERENTIATED READING

🔶🟣 **Approaching Level** and **English Language Learners** After reading, have children listen to the selection to develop comprehension.

Genre Read-Aloud, pp. 54–57

Read Aloud: "Twinsies"

Build Knowledge Remind children that in this unit they read about how things change over time. Encourage children to share what they have learned about how plants grow. Tell them that now they will listen to a play about how two trees are alike and different. Explain that sometimes we call a play a *drama*.

Set Purpose *Let's read this play to find out what happens to two trees as they grow and change.*

Read the Selection

Read "Twinsies" aloud. Pause from time to time to have children discuss story events or to point out details in the illustrations. Ask volunteers to talk about how Birch Seed and Pine Seed change as they grow.

You may wish to use the prompts in the **Genre Read-Aloud.** Pause after each page and have children answer the questions.

Oral Vocabulary As needed, define these words as you encounter them in the text.

• **meadow:** flat, grassy land

• **suddenly:** very quickly

• **lovely:** beautiful

• **miserable:** very unhappy

• **discovered:** found out

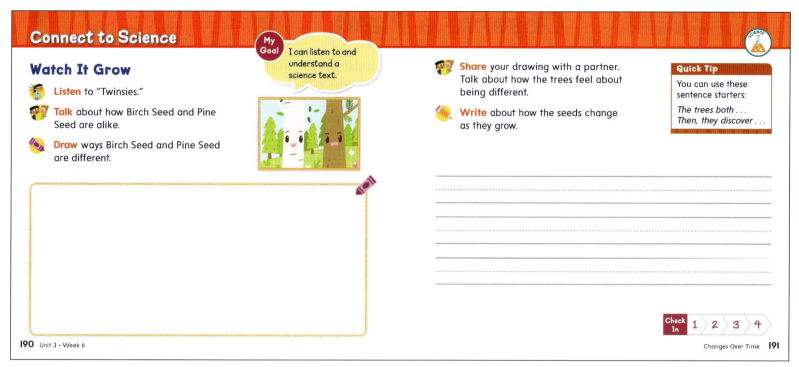

Reading/Writing Companion, pp. 190–191

Respond to the Text

Tell children that now they will respond to the text. Have them turn to page 190 in the **Reading/Writing Companion.** Read the prompts aloud and guide children in responding to them.

Turn and Talk Have partners talk about ways Birch Seed and Pine Seed are alike. *What do Birch Seed and Pine Seed both like to do? How do they both start to grow?* Encourage children to use the oral vocabulary words *meadow, suddenly, lovely, miserable,* and *discovered* in their discussion if possible.

Draw Ask children to draw two ways Birch Seed and Pine Seed are different. Children should draw leaves on the branches of Birch Seed and needles on the branches of Pine Seed. They should also show that Birch Seed's bark is white and Pine Seed's bark is brown. Encourage children to add details.

Share Have children share their drawings with a partner. Encourage partners to talk about how the trees are different and how the trees feel about being different. Model as necessary.

Write Guide children to respond to the prompt. Have them talk with a partner about how the trees change as they grow. Ask: *How are the trees the same as they begin to grow?* (Both trees grow roots; then they grow branches.) *What do the trees discover as they grow?* (They discover that they look different: Birch Seed grows leaves, and Pine Seed grows needles. Birch Seed grows white bark, and Pine Seed grows brown bark.) Remind children they can use the sentence starters in the Quick Tip box for support. Then have children complete page 191.

ENGLISH LANGUAGE LEARNERS

Respond to the Text Provide vocabulary support as partners discuss how Birch Seed and Pine Seed are alike. Before children complete the writing activity, create a word bank of the vocabulary needed to complete the sentence starters in the Quick Tip box. Include challenging vocabulary such as *roots, branches, bark,* and *needles.* Model completing the sentence starters. *Both trees grow roots and branches. Then they discover they are different.* Provide sentence frames to help children say how each tree changes: Birch Seed grows white bark, and Pine Tree grows brown bark.

FORMATIVE ASSESSMENT

❯ STUDENT CHECK-IN

Have partners share what they learned about trees.

Have children reflect, using the Check-In routine.

OBJECTIVES

Add drawings or other visual displays to descriptions when appropriate to clarify ideas, thoughts, and feelings.

Participate in collaborative conversations with diverse partners about grade 1 topics and texts with peers and adults in small and larger groups.

ELA ACADEMIC LANGUAGE

• *observe, compare*
• Cognates: *observar, comparar*

Observe a Plant

Discuss Have a discussion about plants that children might observe. Ask: *What trees, bushes, and other plants can we see around our school?* Make a list of the plants near or in school that children might study.

Explain and Model Tell children they will observe a plant and draw a picture of it. Explain that the purpose is to practice looking at plants closely and recognizing features that plants have in common. Tell children to label the different parts of the plant in their drawing. Model identifying and drawing a plant's different parts. Remind children that they might not be able to see a plant's roots because roots grow underground. In addition, explain that many flowers appear only at certain times of the year.

leaves

stem

roots

Shutterstock/ifong

Talk About It Have partners discuss plants they would like to observe and identify the parts of the plant they will include and label. Then have children gather the materials they will need to do the activity.

What to Do

Read aloud the steps for doing the activity on **Reading/Writing Companion** page 192.

STEP 1 **Observe** Instruct children to observe a plant they can find near or in the school.

STEP 2 **Draw** On page 193, have children draw a picture of the plant they observed.

STEP 3 **Add** Have children add important details to their drawings. Remind them to draw the different parts of the plant and label them. Ask: *Did you include a stem and leaves? Can you see the roots of your plant? Does your plant have a flower?* Encourage children to draw what they see.

STEP 4 **Compare** Have children compare their plant to a partner's plant. Ask:

• *How are your plants the same?*

• *How are your plants different?*

Have children discuss their answers.

STEP 5 **Write** At the bottom of page 193, have children write about what they observed. Remind them to begin each sentence with a capital letter and end it with the correct punctuation mark.

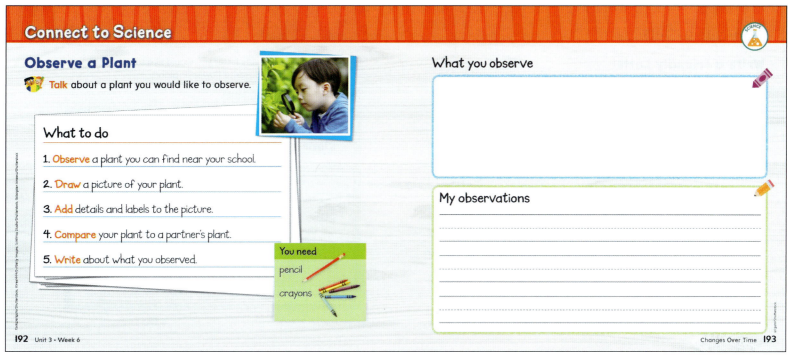

Connect to Science

Observe a Plant

 Talk about a plant you would like to observe.

What to do

1. **Observe** a plant you can find near your school.
2. **Draw** a picture of your plant.
3. **Add** details and labels to the picture.
4. **Compare** your plant to a partner's plant.
5. **Write** about what you observed.

You need
pencil
crayons

What you observe

My observations

192 Unit 3 · Week 6

Changes Over Time 193

Reading/Writing Companion, pp. 192–193

English Language Learners

Use the following scaffolds with **What to Do, Step 5.**

Beginning

Display page 57 of the **Genre Read Aloud,** "Twinsies." Remind children that they talked about how the trees are alike and different. *What is one way the trees are alike?* Provide a sentence frame: Both trees have branches. *What is one way the trees are different?* Birch Seed has leaves, and Pine Seed has needles. Then provide sentence frames to help partners: Both our plants have _____. My plant has _____, and (partner's name's) plant has _____. Provide vocabulary support.

Intermediate

Have children look at the text and illustrations in "Twinsies" to get ideas for comparing their plant with their partner's plants Then ask questions and provide sentence frames: *In what two ways are your plants alike?* Both plants have _____ and _____. *In what two ways are your plants different?* My plant has _____ and _____, but (partner's name's) plant has _____ and _____.

Advanced/Advanced High

Have partners discuss all the ways they observed their plants to be alike and different and then write sentences describing at least two similarities and two differences between their plants. Provide vocabulary support or a model for writing about two plants as needed.

FORMATIVE ASSESSMENT

❯ **STUDENT CHECK-IN**

Have children share what they observed in their experiment.

Have children reflect, using the Check-In routine.

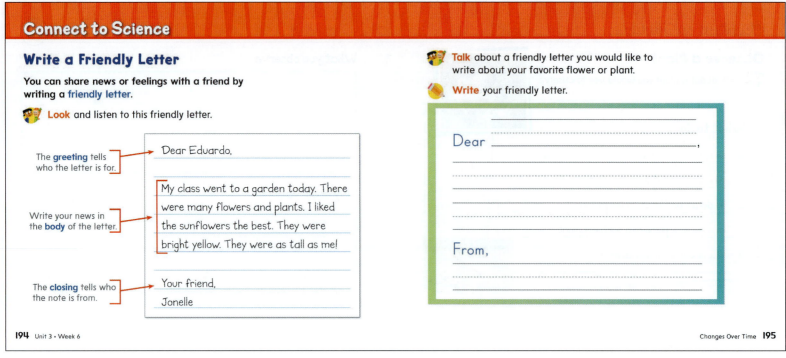

Connect to Science

Write a Friendly Letter

You can share news or feelings with a friend by writing a **friendly letter**.

Look and listen to this friendly letter.

The **greeting** tells who the letter is for. → Dear Eduardo,

Write your news in the **body** of the letter. → My class went to a garden today. There were many flowers and plants. I liked the sunflowers the best. They were bright yellow. They were as tall as me!

The **closing** tells who the note is from. → Your friend,
Jonelle

Talk about a friendly letter you would like to write about your favorite flower or plant.

Write your friendly letter.

Dear _____,

From,

194 Unit 3 · Week 6   Changes Over Time 195

Reading/Writing Companion, pp. 194–195

Focus on Writing

Explain Have children turn to page 194 of the **Reading/Writing Companion.** Tell them that you will read a friendly letter about news that a girl named Jonelle shares with her friend Eduardo. Point out that a friendly letter has the following features:

- a greeting that tells who the letter is addressed to;
- the body of the letter, or the main message;
- and a closing that tells who the letter is from.

Have children listen as you read the friendly letter aloud. Then go back and review the different features of a friendly letter as you read it aloud again. Point out that Jonelle shares her feelings with Eduardo when she says, "I liked the sunflowers the best." Tell children they can share their opinions in their own friendly letter. Model coming up with your own idea for a friendly letter. Then write a brief friendly letter and read it aloud.

Guided Practice Guide children to identify the different parts of the letter that you wrote. Then have partners discuss what they would like to include in a friendly letter about a favorite flower or plant.

 Apply Have children write their friendly letter neatly on page 195 of the Reading/Writing Companion. Remind them to look at page 194 if they need help with the different features of a letter.

Extend Your Learning

Choose Your Own Book

Minutes I Read

Tell a partner about a book you want to read. Say why you want to read it.

Write the title.

Write about the book. What was it about? Did you like it? Why or why not?

196   Unit 3 · Week 6

Reading/Writing Companion, p. 196

Choose Your Own Book

Explain Tell children that choosing books they like and reading on their own is one of the pleasures of being a reader. Set up a specific time each day for children to choose their own reading material. For more guidance on helping children choose their own books, see the Self-Selected Reading Routine on page S97 of Start Smart and the online Instructional Routines Handbook.

Model giving your opinion about a book you have read recently. Be sure to include reasons for your opinion about whether you like the book.

Guided Practice Have children turn to page 196 in the **Reading/Writing Companion.** Tell children about a book you would like to read and explain why you are excited to read it. Remind them that books that tell stories and books that give information have major differences. Have children discuss a few characteristics of fiction and nonfiction. Then have partners trade information about their chosen book. Be sure that partners tell each other why they would like to read the book. Guide children to write the name of the book on the line. Provide time for children to read for fifteen minutes during class. Encourage them to read a little longer the next time they read at school or at home.

Apply After children have had a chance to read a book of their choice, have them come back to page 196. Guide them to fill in the box with the number of minutes they read. Then have them write what the book was about and whether they liked it. Remind children to give reasons to support their opinion.

LEARNING GOALS

We can choose a book to read and share our thoughts about it.

OBJECTIVES

Read grade-level text with purpose and understanding.

Explain major differences between books that tell stories and books that give information, drawing on a wide reading of a range of text types.

ELA ACADEMIC LANGUAGE

- *specific*
- Cognate: *específico/a*

ENGLISH LANGUAGE LEARNERS

Choose Your Own Book, Apply Provide sentence frames to help children answer the questions: The book was about a cat and a dog. I liked/didn't like it. It was funny/not interesting. Encourage children to add more information using connecting words, such as *and*. Help them write sentences with more details about what happened in the story.

FORMATIVE ASSESSMENT

❯ STUDENT CHECK-IN

Have partners share what they liked or disliked about the book they read.

Then have children reflect, using the Check-In routine.

LEARNING GOALS

We can make connections across texts to gain information.

OBJECTIVES

Use words and phrases acquired through conversations, reading and being read to, and responding to texts, including using frequently occurring conjunctions to signal simple relationships.

Build on others' talk in conversations by responding to the comments of others through multiple exchanges.

ELA ACADEMIC LANGUAGE

• *graphic organizers, notes*
• Cognate: *notas*

The Big Idea:
What can happen over time?

Connect to the Big Idea

Text to Text Write the Unit Big Idea on the board: *What can happen over time?* Remind children they have been reading selections about how people, animals, and other things can change over time. Divide the class into small groups. Tell children that each group will compare what they learned about how things can change over time to answer the Big Idea question. Model how to compare this information by using examples from the Shared Reads.

Review Oral Vocabulary Remind children they have been learning different vocabulary words over the course of this unit. Use the Define/Example/Ask routine with the **Visual Vocabulary Cards** to review ten of the oral vocabulary words children learned in Unit 3. As you review each word, prompt children to turn to a partner and use the word in a sentence.

Collaborative Conversations Have children work together to discuss what they learned about the Big Idea from the Shared Reads. Explain that each group will use an Accordion Foldable® to record their ideas. Model how to use an Accordion Foldable® to record comparisons of texts. Guide children to focus their conversations on what they learned about the way things can change over time. Encourage children to include some of the oral vocabulary words they learned in this unit within their writing.

Present Ideas and Synthesize Information When children finish their discussions, ask for volunteers from each group to share their ideas aloud. After each group has presented, ask: *What have we learned about the way different things can change over time?* Lead a class discussion and list children's ideas on the board.

Building Knowledge Have children continue to build knowledge about the Unit Big Idea. Display classroom or library sources and have children search for articles, books, and other resources related to the Big Idea. After each group has presented ideas, ask: *What can happen over time?* Lead a class discussion asking children to use information from their chart to answer the question.

FORMATIVE ASSESSMENT

❯ STUDENT CHECK-IN

Have children reflect on how well they compared information across texts.

Have children reflect using the Check-In routine.

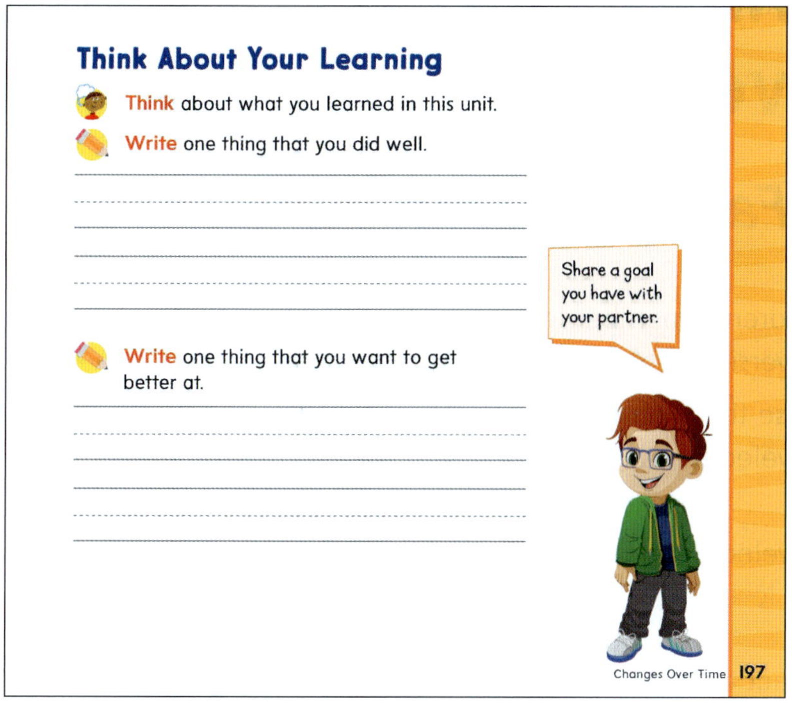

Think About Your Learning

Think about what you learned in this unit.

Write one thing that you did well.

_____

_____

_____

_____

Share a goal you have with your partner.

Write one thing that you want to get better at.

_____

_____

_____

_____

Changes Over Time 197

Reading/Writing Companion, p. 197

LEARNING GOALS

We can reflect on our learning.

OBJECTIVES

Participate in collaborative conversations with diverse partners about grade 1 topics and texts with peers and adults in small and larger groups

Reflect on what they learned in the unit.

What Did You Learn?

Guide children in thinking about and discussing some of the skills, concepts, and content they learned during this unit. If necessary, remind children of the various Word Work, Comprehension, Fluency, Writing, and Grammar topics that were covered in this unit. You may also tell them to recall how they rated themselves in the **Reading/Writing Companion.**

Have children turn to page 197 in the Reading/Writing Companion.

- Have children look at the first pencil icon. Tell them they should write on the first set of blank lines something they think they did well in this unit.

- Once each child has identified one of his or her strengths, have partners discuss their strengths with each other.

- After partners have finished sharing, tell children to fill in the second set of blank lines, writing one thing they hope to improve as the year continues.

FORMATIVE ASSESSMENT

❯ STUDENT CHECK-IN

Have children share one thing they are proud of learning.

Leveled Reader

OBJECTIVES

With prompting and support, read informational texts appropriately complex for grade 1.

ELA ACADEMIC LANGUAGE

• *flowchart, retell, events*
• Cognate: *eventos*

Approaching Level to On Level

Apples from Farm to Table

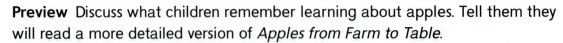

Preview Discuss what children remember learning about apples. Tell them they will read a more detailed version of *Apples from Farm to Table*.

High-Frequency Words Use the **High-Frequency Word Cards** to review the high-frequency words in the Leveled Reader. Use the Read/Spell/Write routine for the high-frequency words.

Have children read the Leveled Reader. Monitor their progress to determine whether they are ready to level up.

 Help children access complex text, using the following information as needed.

▶ **Specific Vocabulary** Review the following science words that are new for this title. Model how to use the photographs, sentences, and what children already know about apples to determine their meaning. *growers   sweet   planted   ripe*

▶ **Connection of Ideas** Children may need support connecting the new information in the On Level text to the production process. Help them connect ideas by creating a flowchart that shows each stage of apple growth and production. Ask children to retell several events in order before reading the next event. Also help children understand the additional information provided in the captions.

▶ **Sentence Structure** Some sentences at this level are more complex than in the Approaching Level text. To help children understand the information, follow this routine when reading complex or compound sentences, such as the third sentence on page 3:

Read aloud: *A long time ago growers took the seeds and planted them.*

Break it down: *Long ago growers took seeds. Then they planted them.*

Have children then read the sentence aloud.

Ask children to complete the Respond to Reading on page 12, using the new information from the On Level text. Once children have finished reading, have them discuss how well they could read and comprehend the Leveled Reader.

On Level to Beyond Level

Apples from Farm to Table

Leveled Reader

Preview Discuss what children remember about apples and how they get to people's tables. Tell them they will be reading a more detailed version of *Apples from Farm to Table*.

High-Frequency Words Use the **High-Frequency Word Cards** to review the high-frequency words in the Leveled Reader. Use the Read/Spell/Write routine for the high-frequency words.

Have children read the Leveled Reader. Monitor their progress to determine whether they are ready to level up.

 **Help children access complex text, using the following information as needed.**

▶ **Specific Vocabulary** Review the following science words that are new for this title. Model how to use the glossary at the end of the book to determine their meaning. *bruise   harvest   mature   nurseries   tricky*

▶ **Connection of Ideas** Children may need help connecting ideas from chapter to chapter. Have children chorally read each title from the table of contents. Point out that both chapters are about apples. Help children to see how the information in the two chapters will differ. As you read, have children retell each chapter.

▶ **Sentence Structure** The sentence structure at this level is more complex than in the On Level text. To help children understand the information, follow this routine when reading complex or compound sentences, such as the third sentence on page 3:

Read the sentence aloud.

Break down the information into simpler sentences.

Have children then read the sentence aloud.

Ask children to complete the Respond to Reading on page 12, using the new information from the Beyond Level text. Once children have finished reading, have them discuss how well they could read and comprehend the Leveled Reader.

OBJECTIVES

With prompting and support, read informational texts appropriately complex for grade 1.

ELA ACADEMIC LANGUAGE

• *chapters, information*

• Cognate: *información*

Leveled Reader

OBJECTIVES

With prompting and support, read informational texts appropriately complex for grade 1.

ELA ACADEMIC LANGUAGE

• *nonfiction, facts, information*

• Cognates: *no ficción, información*

English Language Learners to On Level

Apples from Farm to Table

Preview Remind children that nonfiction tells about real people, places, things, and events by presenting facts and information about them. Nonfiction texts can be organized by description. Ask what facts children remember about apples. Tell them they will be reading a more detailed version of *Apples from Farm to Table*.

High-Frequency Words Use the **High-Frequency Word Cards** to review the high-frequency words in the **Leveled Reader.** Use the Read/Spell/Write routine for the high-frequency words.

Have children read the Leveled Reader. Monitor their progress to determine whether they are ready to level up.

A C T **Help children access complex text, using the following information as needed.**

▶ **Specific Vocabulary** Help children name elements in each photograph now that there are no labels. Then review the following science words that are new for this title. Model how to use the photographs and what children know about apples to determine their meaning. Review any cognates.

▶ **Connection of Ideas** Children may need support connecting the new information in the On Level text to the production process. Help them connect ideas by creating a flowchart that shows each stage of apple growth and production. Ask children to retell several events in order before reading the next event. Also help children understand the additional information provided in the captions.

▶ **Sentence Structure** Help children understand information when reading complex sentences:

Read the sentence aloud.

Break down the information into simpler sentences.

Have children then read the sentence aloud.

Ask children to complete the Respond to Reading on page 12, using the new information from the On Level text. Once children have finished reading, have them discuss how well they could read and comprehend the Leveled Reader.

Beyond Level
to Self-Selected Trade Book

Leveled Reader

Independent Reading

Together with children identify the particular focus of their reading, based on the text they choose. Children who have chosen the same title can work together to closely read the selection.

Set Purpose As children select a text to read for themselves, they should establish a purpose for reading. Provide assistance as needed.

Taking Notes Assign a graphic organizer for children to use to take notes and cite text evidence as they read. Reinforce a specific comprehension focus from the unit by choosing one of the graphic organizers that best fits the book.

EXAMPLES	
Fiction	**Nonfiction**
Character, Setting, Events	Sequence of Events
Graphic Organizer #2	Graphic Organizer #6

Reread Remind children that as they read, if they do not understand what happened or a piece of information, they can go back and reread. Point out that rereading can also help them remember important information from a selection. Encourage them to write the events or information from the sections they reread.

Write About Text Have children use their notes, graphic organizers, and information from any discussions they had to write a response to the reading.

EXAMPLES	
Fiction	**Nonfiction**
How did identifying the characters, setting, or plot help you understand the story?	How did understanding the order of events help you understand the information in this book?

Literature Circles Suggest that children hold literature circles and share interesting facts or favorite parts from the books they read.

OBJECTIVES
With prompting and support, read informational texts appropriately complex for grade 1.

Build on others' talk in conversations by responding to the comments of others through multiple exchanges.

ELA ACADEMIC LANGUAGE
• *purpose, reread, events*
• Cognate: *eventos*

UNIT 3

Summative Assessment

Online Assessment Center

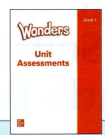

Wonders Unit Assessments — Grade 1

Unit 3 Tested Skills

COMPREHENSION	PHONEMIC AWARENESS	PHONICS STRUCTURAL ANALYSIS HIGH-FREQUENCY WORDS	GRAMMAR
• Events: Beginning, Middle, End • Sequence of Events • Moral • Folktale: Descriptive Words and Phrases • Details: Compare and Contrast • Details: Time-Order • Text Features: Diagrams	• Phoneme Blending • Phoneme Isolation • Phoneme Segmentation • Phoneme Substitution	• Long *a: a_e* • Long *i: i_e* • Long *o: o_e* • Long *u: u_e* • Soft *c* • Inflectional Endings *-ed, -ing* • Contractions with *Not* • High-Frequency Words	• Verbs • Present-Tense Verbs • Past- and Future-Tense Verbs • Irregular Verbs *Is, Are* • Contractions with *Not*

Additional Assessment Options

Fluency

Access fluency using the Letter Naming Fluency (LNF), Phoneme Segmentation Fluency (PSF), and Sight Word Fluency (SWF) assessments in **Fluency Assessment**.

Wonders Fluency Assessment

ELL Assessment

Assess English Language Learner proficiency and track children's progress by using the **English Language Development Assessment**. This resource provides unit assessments and rubrics to evaluate children's progress in the areas of listening and reading comprehension, vocabulary, grammar, speaking, and writing. These assessments can also be used to determine the language proficiency levels for subsequent set of instructions.

Wonders Unit Assessments — English Language Learners

Making the Most of Assessment Results

Make data-based grouping decisions by using the following reports to verify assessment results. For additional support options for children, refer to the reteaching and enrichment opportunities.

ONLINE ASSESSMENT CENTER

- *Gradebook*

DATA DASHBOARD

- *Recommendations Report*
- *Activity Report*
- *Skills Report*
- *Progress Report*
- *Grade Card Report*

TIER 2

Reteaching Opportunities with Intervention Online PDFs

IF CHILDREN . . .	THEN RETEACH . . .
answer 0–7 **comprehension** items correctly	tested skills using the **Comprehension PDF.**
answer 0–3 **phonemic awareness** items correctly	tested skills using the **Phonemic Awareness PDF.**
answer 0–8 **phonics/structural analysis/HFW** items correctly	tested skills using the **Phonics/Word Study PDF** and the **Fluency PDF.**
score below the benchmark score on the **constructed-response** items	tested skills using the Write About Reading lessons in the **Comprehension PDF.**
name 0–33 letters correctly in **LNF** or have 0–22 phonemes correct in **PSF** or have an accuracy rate less than 50% in **SWF**	tested skills using the **Phonemic Awareness PDF** and/or the **Phonics/Word Study PDF.**

GIFTED and TALENTED

Enrichment Opportunities

Beyond Level small-group lessons include suggestions for additional activities in the following areas to extend learning opportunities for gifted and talented children:

- *Leveled Readers*
- *Vocabulary*
- *Comprehension*
- *Leveled Reader Library Online*
- *Center Activity Cards*

Next Steps

NEXT STEPS FOR YOUR CHILDREN'S PROGRESS . . .

Interpret the data you have collected from multiple sources throughout this unit, including formal and informal assessments.

Data Dashboard

Who

Regrouping Decisions

- Check children's progress against your interpretation of the data. Consider whether children are ready to Level Up or accelerate.
- Use the English Learner Benchmark Assessment to determine the progress of English language learners.

What

Target Instruction

- Decide whether to review and reinforce or reteach particular skills or concepts.
- Target instruction to meet children's strengths/needs.
- Use Data Dashboard recommendations to help determine which lessons to provide to different groups of children.

Coach and Classroom Videos

Methodology

How

Modify Instruction

- Vary materials and/or instructional strategies.
- Attend to children's social and emotional development.
- Provide children with opportunities for self-reflection and self-assessment.

AUTHOR INSIGHT

"As you re-group children, think about their learning gaps as well as opportunities to validate and extend their thinking. Form groups focused on specific instructional and learning goals. And remember, some children need to be part of a few groups, and some children only need to be in one group."
—Dr. Doug Fisher

Courtesy of Douglas Fisher

PROFESSIONAL DEVELOPMENT

NEXT STEPS FOR YOU . . .

As you prepare children to move on to the next unit, don't forget to take advantage of the many online opportunities available for self-evaluation and professional development.

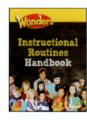

Instructional Routines

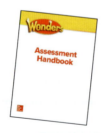

Manage Assessments

Program Author Whitepapers

Research Base Alignment

Contents

Additional Digital Resources

my.mheducation.com

- Unit Bibliography

- Word Lists

- More Resources

Start Smart Scope and Sequence

	Read Alouds	Comprehension	Print Concepts
Week 1 **All About Me** **Essential Question:** Who Am I? **Genre Focus:** Nursery Rhyme	**Genre Read Aloud:** "1, 2, Buckle My Shoe" **Teacher's Edition:** "Mary Had a Little Lamb" **Genre:** Nursery Rhyme	Ask and Answer Questions Character	Directionality Concept of a Sentence Concept of a Word Parts of a Book, Capitalization, End Punctuation, Word Spaces Parts of a Book, Periods, Pronoun *I*
Week 2 **Let's Pretend** **Essential Question:** What can you imagine? **Genre Focus:** Fairy Tale	**Genre Read Aloud:** "Jack and the Beanstalk" **Teacher's Edition:** "The Three Billy Goats Gruff" **Genre:** Fairy Tale	Reread, Ask and Answer Questions Character	Return Sweep, Capitalization Word Spaces, Punctuation, Pronoun *I*, Title Page Match Print to Speech, Word Length, Sentence Boundaries Sentences, Quotation Marks, Title Page Sentences, Italics, Repeated Letters
Week 3 **Let's Do Things Together** **Essential Question:** What happens during my day? **Genre Focus:** Informational Text	**Genre Read Aloud:** "Work, Play, and Learn Together" **Teacher's Edition:** "How Do We Get Around Today?" **Genre:** Informational Text	Visualize, Ask and Answer Questions Topic and Relevant Details	Capitalize *I*, Punctuation Sentence Boundaries Sentences, Directionality, Return Sweep Sound-Letter Correspondence, Directionality Sound-Letter Correspondence, Sentence Lengths

Phonological/Phonemic Awareness	Phonics/Handwriting	High-Frequency Words	Writing
Phonological Awareness: Onset and Rime, Syllable Segmentation, Rhyme **Phonemic Awareness:** Phoneme Isolation, Phoneme Identity	**Phonics:** Identify and Blend: *m, s, a, p, t, n, r, i* **Handwriting:** Writing position, pencil grip, *m, s, a, p, t, n, r, i*	**Review:** *a, can, do, go, has, he, I, like, to, you*	**Write About the Text:** Nursery Rhyme
Phonological Awareness: Onset and Rime, Syllable Segmentation, Rhyme **Phonemic Awareness:** Phoneme Isolation, Phoneme Blending	**Phonics:** Identify and Blend: *c, f, o, d, h, s, e, b, l, ll* **Handwriting:** *c, f, o, d, h, e, b, l*	**Review:** *this, is, my, look, little, where, here, play, the, we*	**Write About the Text:** Fairy Tale
Phonological Awareness: Rhyme **Phonemic Awareness:** Phoneme Blending, Phoneme Segmentation	**Phonics:** Identify and Blend: *k, ck, u, g, w, x, v, qu, j, y, z* **Handwriting:** *k, u, g, w, x, v, q, j, y, z*	**Review:** *are, me, she, with, for, and, have, said, see, was*	**Write About the Text:** Informational Text

Scope and Sequence

Getting to Know Us Big Idea: What makes you special?	Literature Big Book	Interactive Read Aloud	Shared Read	Literature Anthology	Leveled Readers	Vocabulary	
Week 1 **At School** **Essential Question:** What do you do at your school? **Genre Focus:** Realistic Fiction	*This School Year Will Be the Best!* **Genre:** Realistic Fiction	"School Around the World" **Genre:** Informational Text	"Jack Can" **Genre:** Realistic Fiction **Lexile:** BR	**Anchor Text:** *Nat and Sam* **Genre:** Realistic Fiction **Lexile:** BR **Paired Selection:** "Rules at School" **Genre:** Informational Text **Lexile:** 180L	**Main Selections:** **Genre:** Realistic Fiction 🟠 *A Fun Day* **Lexile:** BR 🔵 *We Like to Share* **Lexile:** 60L 🟣 *We Like to Share* **Lexile:** 100L 🟢 *Class Party* **Lexile:** 360L **Paired Selections:** **Genre:** Informational Text 🟠 "We Share" 🔵 "Look at Signs" 🟣 "Look at Signs" 🟢 "Our Classroom Rules"	**Oral Vocabulary Words:** *learn* *subjects* *common* *object* *recognize* **Oral Vocabulary:** Context Clues: Sentence Clues	
Week 2 **Where I Live** **Essential Question:** What is it like where you live? **Genre Focus:** Fantasy	*Alicia's Happy Day* **Genre:** Realistic Fiction	"City Mouse, Country Mouse" **Genre:** Fable	"Six Kids" **Genre:** Fantasy **Lexile:** 250L	**Anchor Text:** *Go, Pip!* **Genre:** Fantasy **Lexile:** 30L **Paired Selection:** "A Surprise in the City" **Genre:** Personal Narrative **Lexile:** 50L	**Main Selections:** **Genre:** Fantasy 🟠 *What Can We See?* **Lexile:** BR 🔵 *A Trip to the City* **Lexile:** 30L 🟣 *A Trip to the City* **Lexile:** BR 🟢 *Harvest Time* **Lexile:** 330L **Paired Selections:** **Genre:** Informational Text 🟠 "My Home" 🔵 "Where I Live" 🟣 "Where I Live" 🟢 "Where We Live"	**Oral Vocabulary Words:** *city* *country* *bored* *feast* *scurried* **Oral Vocabulary:** Context Clues: Sentence Clues	
Week 3 **Our Pets** **Essential Question:** What makes a pet special? **Genre Focus:** Fantasy	*Cool Dog, School Dog* **Genre:** Fantasy	"Our Pets" **Genre:** Informational Text	"A Pig for Cliff" **Genre:** Fantasy **Lexile:** 280L	**Anchor Text:** *Flip* **Genre:** Fantasy **Lexile:** 30L **Paired Selection:** "What Pets Need" **Genre:** Nonfiction **Lexile:** 370L	**Main Selections:** **Genre:** Fantasy 🟠 *Mouse's Moon Party* **Lexile:** 120L 🔵 *Pet Show* **Lexile:** 200L 🟣 *Pet Show* **Lexile:** 20L 🟢 *Polly the Circus Star* **Lexile:** 280L **Paired Selections:** **Genre:** Informational Text 🟠 "A Mouse in the House" 🔵 "Love That Llama!" 🟣 "Love That Llama!" 🟢 "Birds That Talk"	**Oral Vocabulary Words:** *care* *train* *groom* *companion* *popular* **Oral Vocabulary:** Use a Dictionary	

Comprehension	Print Concepts	Phonological/ Phonemic Awareness	Phonics/Spelling/ Handwriting/ Structural Analysis	High-Frequency Words	Fluency	Writing and Grammar	Research and Inquiry
Visualize Main Story Elements: Character Photographs	Book Handling ELA.1.F.1.1	**Phonological Awareness:** Identify Rhyme **Phonemic Awareness:** Phoneme Isolation, Phoneme Blending, Phoneme Segmentation	**Phonics/Spelling:** Short *a* *Differentiated Spelling Lists available* **Handwriting:** Upper- and Lowercase *Aa* **Structural Analysis:** Inflectional Ending -*s* **Decodable Readers:** *Pam Can; Pack a Bag!*	*does* *not* *school* *what*	Accuracy and Rate	**Write About the Text:** Informational Text **Writing Skill:** Stretch Sounds to Write Words **Writing Trait:** Focus on a Topic **Grammar:** Sentences **Mechanics:** Sentence Capitalization	**Project:** Take a Poll about School
Visualize Main Story Elements: Character Bold Print	Book Handling	**Phonological Awareness:** Alliteration **Phonemic Awareness:** Phoneme Blending, Phoneme Categorization, Phoneme Segmentation	**Phonics/Spelling:** Short *i* *Differentiated Spelling Lists available* **Handwriting:** Upper- and Lowercase *Ii* **Structural Analysis:** Double Final Consonants **Decodable Readers:** *Kim and Nick Zip!; Jill and Jim*	*down* *out* *up* *very*	Accuracy and Rate	**Write About the Text:** Informational Text **Writing Skill:** Sentence Capitalization **Writing Trait:** Descriptive Details **Grammar:** Word Order **Mechanics:** Sentence Punctuation (periods)	**Project:** Interview About a Neighborhood
Visualize Main Story Elements: Character, Setting and Events Labels	Track Print and Return Sweep, Title, Author, Illustrator	**Phonological Awareness:** Contrast Vowel Sounds **Phonemic Awareness:** Phoneme Blending, Phoneme Substitution, Phoneme Segmentation	**Phonics/Spelling:** Beginning Consonant Blends: *l*-blends *Differentiated Spelling Lists available* **Handwriting:** Upper and Lowercase *Ll* **Structural Analysis:** -*s* (plural nouns) **Decodable Readers:** *Cliff Has a Plan; A Good Black Cat*	*be* *come* *good* *pull*	Accuracy and Rate	**Write About the Text:** Narrative **Writing Skill:** Use Word Bank **Writing Trait:** Descriptive Details **Grammar:** Statements and Questions **Mechanics:** Capitalization and Punctuation (periods and question marks)	**Project:** Plan for a Pet's Home

Scope and Sequence

Getting to Know Us	Literature Big Book	Interactive Read Aloud	Shared Read	Literature Anthology	Leveled Readers	Vocabulary
Week 4 **Let's Be Friends** **Essential Question:** What do friends do together? **Genre Focus:** Informational Text	*Friends All Around* **Genre:** Informational Text	"Games Long Ago" **Genre:** Informational Text	**"Toss! Kick! Hop!"** **Genre:** Informational Text **Lexile: 290L**	**Anchor Text:** *Friends* **Genre:** Informational Text **Lexile:** 60L **Paired Selection:** "There Are Days and There Are Days" **Genre:** Poetry **Lexile:** NP	**Main Selections:** **Genre:** Informational Text 🔴 *Friends Are Fun* **Lexile:** 130L 🔵 *Friends Are Fun* **Lexile:** 110L 🟣 *Friends Are Fun* **Lexile:** 100L 🟢 *Friends Are Fun* **Lexile:** 350L **Paired Selections:** **Genre:** Poetry 🔴 "I Like to Play" 🔵 "I Like to Play" 🟣 "I Like to Play" 🟢 "I Like to Play"	**Oral Vocabulary Words:** *cooperate* *relationship* *deliver* *chore* *collect* **Oral Vocabulary:** Word Categories
Week 5 **Let's Move!** **Essential Question:** How does your body move? **Genre Focus:** Informational Text	*Move!* **Genre:** Informational Text	"The Monkey's Fiddle" **Genre:** Folktale	"Move and Grin!" **Genre:** Informational Text **Lexile:** 370L	**Anchor Text:** *Move It!* **Genre:** Informational Text **Lexile:** 60L **Paired Selection:** "My Family Hike" **Genre:** Personal Narrative **Lexile:** 210L	**Main Selections:** **Genre:** Informational Text 🔴 *We Can Move!* **Lexile:** 170L 🔵 *We Can Move!* **Lexile:** 200L 🟣 *We Can Move!* **Lexile:** 190L 🟢 *We Can Move!* **Lexile:** 390L **Paired Selections:** **Genre:** Poetry 🔴 "What's Under Your Skin?" 🔵 "What's Under Your Skin?" 🟣 "What's Under Your Skin?" 🟢 "What's Under Your Skin?"	**Oral Vocabulary Words:** *physical* *exercise* *agree* *exhausted* *difficult* **Oral Vocabulary:** Context Clues: Sentence Clues

Week 6	Reading Digitally	Fluency	Connect to Science	Extend Your Learning
Extend, Connect, and Assess	"Time for Kids: World Games" **Genre:** Online Article	**Reader's Theater:** *Look at Me Now*	**Genre Read-Aloud:** "Playground Pushes and Pulls" **Activities:** Experiment with Motion Write a Letter	Choose Your Own Book

Comprehension	Print Concepts	Phonological/ Phonemic Awareness	Phonics/Spelling/ Handwriting/ Structural Analysis	High-Frequency Words	Fluency	Writing and Grammar	Research and Inquiry
Ask and Answer Questions Topic and Relevant Details Rhyme	Book Handling and Labels, Title, Author	**Phonological Awareness:** Identify and Produce Rhyme **Phonemic Awareness:** Phoneme Categorization, Phoneme Segmentation, Phoneme Deletion, Phoneme Blending	**Phonics/Spelling:** Short o *Differentiated Spelling Lists available* **Handwriting:** Upper- and Lowercase *Oo* **Structural Analysis:** Alphabetical Order (one letter) **Decodable Readers:** *Bob Is a Fun Pal; Dog and Fox*	*fun* *make* *they* *too*	Accuracy and Rate	**Write About the Text:** Informational Text **Extended Writing:** Personal Narrative **Writing Process:** Expert and Student Models; Plan; Draft **Writing Skill:** Left-to-right progression **Writing Trait:** Supporting Details **Grammar:** Exclamations and Interjections **Mechanics:** Exclamation Marks (in exclamations and interjections)	**Project:** Take a Poll about Friends
Ask and Answer Questions Topic and Relevant Details Bold Print	Special Text Treatments, Title, Author	**Phonemic Awareness:** Phoneme Categorization, Phoneme Segmentation, Phoneme Deletion, Phoneme Blending	**Phonics/Spelling:** Beginning Consonant Blends: *r*-blends and *s*-blends *Differentiated Spelling Lists available* **Handwriting:** Upper- and Lowercase *Ss* **Structural Analysis:** Possessives **Decodable Readers:** *Snap, Skip, Trot!; Snip and Trip Can Move*	*jump* *move* *run* *two*	Accuracy and Rate	**Write About the Text:** Informational Text **Extended Writing:** Personal Narrative **Writing Process:** Revise; Edit and Proofread; Publish, Present, and Evaluate **Writing Skill:** Spacing between Words **Writing Trait:** Supporting Details **Grammar:** Writing Sentences **Mechanics:** Capitalization and Punctuation (periods, question and exclamation marks)	**Project:** How We Move in Sports

Scope and Sequence

Getting to Know Us **Big Idea:** What makes a community?	Literature Big Book	Interactive Read Aloud	Shared Read	Literature Anthology	Leveled Readers	Vocabulary	
Week 1 **Jobs Around Town** **Essential Question:** What jobs need to be done in a community? **Genre Focus:** Realistic Fiction	*Millie Waits for the Mail* **Genre:** Fantasy	"Jobs Around Town" **Genre:** Nonfiction	"Good Job, Ben!" **Genre:** Realistic Fiction **Lexile:** 130L	**Anchor Text:** *The Red Hat* **Genre:** Realistic Fiction **Lexile:** BR **Paired Selection:** "Firefighters at Work" **Genre:** Nonfiction **Lexile:** 290L	**Main Selections:** **Genre:** Realistic Fiction 🔴 *Pick Up Day* **Lexile:** 70L 🔵 *Ben Brings the Mail* **Lexile:** 200L 🟣 *Ben Brings the Mail* **Lexile:** 70L 🟢 *At Work with Mom* **Lexile:** 330L **Paired Selections:** **Genre:** Informational Text 🔴 "The Recycling Center" 🔵 "At the Post Office" 🟣 "At the Post Office" 🟢 "Tools for the School Nurse"	**Oral Vocabulary Words:** *occupation* *community* *equipment* *fortunately* *astonishing* **Oral Vocabulary:** Morphology: Suffixes	
Week 2 **Buildings All Around** **Essential Question:** What buildings do you know? What are they made of? **Genre Focus:** Fantasy	*Three Little Dassies* **Genre:** Fantasy	"Three Little Pigs" **Genre:** Folktale	"Cubs in a Hut" **Genre:** Fantasy **Lexile:** 390L	**Anchor Text:** *The Pigs, the Wolf, and the Mud* **Genre:** Fantasy **Lexile:** 320L **Paired Selection:** "Homes Around the World" **Genre:** Informational Text **Lexile:** 370L	**Main Selections:** **Genre:** Fantasy 🔴 *What a Nest!* **Lexile:** 170L 🔵 *Staying Afloat* **Lexile:** 150L 🟣 *Staying Afloat* **Lexile:** 10L 🟢 *City Armadillo, Country Armadillo* **Lexile:** 330L **Paired Selections:** **Genre:** Informational Text 🔴 "Stone Castles" 🔵 "A Day on a Houseboat" 🟣 "A Day on a Houseboat" 🟢 "City or Country?"	**Oral Vocabulary Words:** *shelter* *materials* *collapsed* *furious* *refused* **Oral Vocabulary:** Shades of Meaning/Intensity	
Week 3 **A Community in Nature** **Essential Question:** Where do animals live together? **Genre Focus:** Informational Text	*Babies in the Bayou* **Genre:** Informational Text	"Animals in the Desert" **Genre:** Informational Text	"The Best Spot" **Genre:** Informational Text **Lexile:** 160L	**Anchor Text:** *At a Pond* **Genre:** Informational Text **Lexile:** 190L **Paired Selection:** "Way Down Deep" **Genre:** Poetry **Lexile:** NP	**Main Selections:** **Genre:** Informational Text 🔴 *Meerkat Family* **Lexile:** 170L 🔵 *Meerkat Family* **Lexile:** 210L 🟣 *Meerkat Family* **Lexile:** 170L 🟢 *Meerkat Family* **Lexile:** 370L **Paired Selections:** **Genre:** Poetry 🔴 "I Live in a House!" 🔵 "I Live in a House!" 🟣 "I Live in a House!" 🟢 "I Live in a House!"	**Oral Vocabulary Words:** *habitat* *depend* *hibernate* *tranquil* *tolerate* **Oral Vocabulary:** Multiple Meanings	

Comprehension	Print Concepts	Phonological/ Phonemic Awareness	Phonics/Spelling/ Handwriting/ Structural Analysis	High-Frequency Words	Fluency	Writing and Grammar	Research and Inquiry
Make and Confirm Predictions Main Story Elements: Character, Setting, Events Labels	Ellipses and Dashes, Title, Author	**Phonemic Awareness:** Phoneme Blending, Phoneme Isolation, Phoneme Segmentation	**Phonics/Spelling:** Short e spelled e and ea *Differentiated Spelling Lists available* **Handwriting:** Upper- and Lowercase *Ee* **Structural Analysis:** Inflectional Ending -ed (no spelling change) **Decodable Readers:** *Ted Gets a Job; I Sell Crabs*	*again help new there use*	Accuracy and Rate	**Write About the Text:** Opinion **Writing Skill:** Write on the Lines **Writing Trait:** Ideas: Focus on an Idea **Grammar:** Nouns **Mechanics:** Commas in a Series	**Project:** Interview a Community Worker
Make and Confirm Predictions Main Story Elements: Character, Setting, Events Captions	Quotations, Title, Author	**Phonological Awareness:** Identify and Produce Rhyme **Phonemic Awareness:** Phoneme Identity, Phoneme Blending, Phoneme Segmentation	**Phonics/Spelling:** Short u *Differentiated Spelling Lists available* **Handwriting:** Upper- and Lowercase *Uu* **Structural Analysis:** Contractions with 's **Decodable Readers:** *Can Bud Stop Bug?; It's Up to Us*	*could live one then three*	Accuracy and Rate	**Write About the Text:** Informational Text **Writing Skill:** Return Sweep **Writing Trait:** Ideas: Descriptive Details **Grammar:** Singular and Plural Nouns **Mechanics:** Apostrophes with Contractions	**Project:** Choose a Building
Reread Author's Purpose Poetry: Repetition and Alliteration	Distinguish Sentences, Title, Author	**Phonemic Awareness:** Phoneme Blending, Phoneme Substitution, Phoneme Categorization, Phoneme Segmentation	**Phonics/Spelling:** Ending Consonant Blends *Differentiated Spelling Lists available* **Handwriting:** Upper- and Lowercase *Tt* **Structural Analysis:** Inflectional Ending -ing (no spelling change) **Decodable Readers:** *In a Land of Grass; Stomp and Romp*	*eat no of under who*	Accuracy and Rate	**Write About the Text:** Informational Text **Writing Skill:** Sentence Capitalization **Writing Trait:** Ideas: Focus on a Topic **Grammar:** Singular and Plural Possessive Nouns **Mechanics:** Apostrophe with Possessive Nouns (singular and plural possessives)	**Project:** Where Animals Live

Scope and Sequence

Our Community	Literature Big Book	Interactive Read Aloud	Shared Read	Literature Anthology	Leveled Readers	Vocabulary	
Week 4 **Let's Help** **Essential Question:** How do people help out in the community? **Genre Focus:** Fantasy	*The Story of Martin Luther King Jr.* **Genre:** Biography	"Luis's Library" **Genre:** Biography	"Thump Thump Helps Out" **Genre:** Fantasy **Lexile:** 510L	**Anchor Text:** *Nell's Books* **Genre:** Fantasy **Lexile:** 200L **Paired Selection:** "Kids Can Help!" **Genre:** Informational Text **Lexile:** 350L	**Main Selections:** **Genre:** Fantasy 🔴 *The Sick Tree* **Lexile:** 40L 🔵 *Squirrels Help* **Lexile:** 200L 🟣 *Squirrels Help* **Lexile:** 190L 🟢 *Wow, Kitty!* **Lexile:** 390L **Paired Selections:** **Genre:** Nonfiction 🔴 "Beach Clean-Up" 🔵 "Food Drive" 🟣 "Food Drive" 🟢 "Sharing Skills"	**Oral Vocabulary Words:** *leadership* *admire* *enjoy* *rely* *connections* **Oral Vocabulary:** Inflectional Endings	
Week 5 **Follow the Map** **Essential Question:** How can you find your way around? **Genre Focus:** Informational Text	*Me on the Map* **Genre:** Realistic Fiction	"Map It!" **Genre:** Informational Text	"Which Way on the Map?" **Genre:** Informational Text **Lexile:** 160L	**Anchor Text:** *Fun with Maps* **Genre:** Informational Text **Lexile:** NP **Paired Selection:** "North, East, South, or West?" **Genre:** Informational Text **Lexile:** 360L	**Main Selections:** **Genre:** Informational Text 🔴 *How Maps Help* **Lexile:** 130L 🔵 *How Maps Help* **Lexile:** 230L 🟣 *How Maps Help* **Lexile:** 60L 🟢 *How Maps Help* **Lexile:** 420L **Paired Selections:** **Genre:** Informational Text 🔴 "On the Map" 🔵 "On the Map" 🟣 "On the Map" 🟢 "On the Map"	**Oral Vocabulary Words:** *locate* *route* *height* *model* *separate* **Oral Vocabulary:** Prefixes	

Week 6	Reading Digitally	Fluency	Connect to Social Studies	Extend Your Learning
Extend, Connect, and Assess	"Time for Kids: Help Your Community!" **Genre:** Online Article	**Reader's Theater:** *I Speak, I Say, I Talk*	**Genre Read-Aloud:** "Follow the Map" **Activities:** Make a Community Map Write a Letter	Choose Your Own Book

Comprehension	Print Concepts	Phonological/ Phonemic Awareness	Phonics/Spelling/ Handwriting/ Structural Analysis	High-Frequency Words	Fluency	Writing and Grammar	Research and Inquiry
Reread Main Story Elements: Character, Setting, Events List	Special Text Treatments, Title, Author, Illustrator	**Phonemic Awareness:** Phoneme Isolation, Phoneme Categorization, Phoneme Blending, Phoneme Segmentation	**Phonics/Spelling:** Consonant Digraphs *sh, th, -ng* *Differentiated Spelling Lists available* **Handwriting:** Upper- and Lowercase *Ff* **Structural Analysis:** Closed Syllables **Decodable Readers:** *Dash Has a Wish; Help in a Flash; The Helping Gang; Send a Big Thanks!*	*all* *call* *day* *her* *want*	Accuracy and Rate	**Write About the Text:** Narrative **Extended Writing:** Fantasy **Writing Skill:** End Punctuation **Writing Trait:** Organization: Beginning, Middle, End **Writing Process:** Expert and Student Models; Plan; Draft **Grammar:** Common and Proper Nouns **Mechanics:** Capitalize Proper Nouns (people, pets, places, and things)	**Project:** Interview a Helper
Reread Topic and Relevant Details Maps	Reading Sentences Across Pages, Title, Author, Illustrator	**Phonemic Awareness:** Phoneme Segmentation, Phoneme Addition, Phoneme Blending	**Phonics/Spelling:** Consonant Digraphs *ch, -tch, wh, ph* *Differentiated Spelling Lists available* **Handwriting:** Upper- and Lowercase *Cc* **Structural Analysis:** *-es* (plural nouns) **Decodable Readers:** *A Map Match; A Fun Chest; Phil and Steph Get Lost; Maps and Graphs*	*around* *by* *many* *place* *walk*	Accuracy and Rate	**Write About the Text:** Informational Text **Extended Writing:** Fantasy **Writing Skill:** Capitalize Proper Nouns **Writing Trait:** Ideas: Supporting Details **Writing Process:** Revise; Edit and Proofread; Publish, Present, and Evaluate **Grammar:** Irregular Plural Nouns **Mechanics:** Capital Letters and Periods (in sentences)	**Project:** Make a School Map

Scope and Sequence

Changes Over Time **Big Idea:** What can happen over time?	Literature Big Book	Interactive Read Aloud	Shared Read	Literature Anthology	Leveled Readers	Vocabulary	
Week 1 **What Time Is It?** **Essential Question:** How do we measure time? **Genre Focus:** Fantasy	*A Second Is a Hiccup* **Genre:** Poetry	"Measuring Time" **Genre:** Informational Text	"Nate the Snake Is Late" **Genre:** Fantasy **Lexile:** 460L	**Anchor Text:** *On My Way to School* **Genre:** Fantasy **Lexile:** 330L **Paired Selection:** "It's About Time!" **Genre:** Informational Text **Lexile:** 270L	**Main Selections:** **Genre:** Fantasy 🟠 *Busy's Watch* **Lexile:** 40L 🔵 *Kate Saves the Date!* **Lexile:** 220L 🟣 *Kate Saves the Date!* **Lexile:** 330L 🟢 *Uncle George Is Coming* **Lexile:** 320L **Paired Selections:** **Genre:** Informational Text 🟠 "Make a Clock" 🔵 "Use a Calendar" 🟣 "Use a Calendar" 🟢 "So Many Clocks!"	**Oral Vocabulary Words:** *schedule* *immediately* *weekend* *calendar* *occasion* **Oral Vocabulary:** Antonyms	
Week 2 **Watch It Grow!** **Essential Question:** How do plants change as they grow? **Genre Focus:** Drama	*Mystery Vine* **Genre:** Realistic Fiction	"The Great Big Gigantic Turnip" **Genre:** Folktale (Russian)	"Time to Plant!" **Genre:** Drama **Lexile:** NP	**Anchor Text:** *The Big Yuca Plant* **Genre:** Drama **Lexile:** NP **Paired Selection:** "How Plants Grow" **Genre:** Informational Text **Lexile:** 400L	**Main Selections:** **Genre:** Drama 🟠 *Corn Fun* **Lexile:** NP 🔵 *Yum, Strawberries!* **Lexile:** NP 🟣 *Yum, Strawberries!* **Lexile:** NP 🟢 *A Tree's Life* **Lexile:** NP **Paired Selections:** **Genre:** Informational Text 🟠 "Ear of Corn" 🔵 "Strawberry Plant" 🟣 "Strawberry Plant" 🟢 "Inside Trees"	**Oral Vocabulary Words:** *assist* *bloom* *grasped* *spied* *sprout* **Oral Vocabulary:** Context Clues: Sentence Clues	
Week 3 **Tales Over Time** **Essential Question:** What is a folktale? **Genre Focus:** Folktale	*Interrupting Chicken* **Genre:** Fantasy	"The Foolish, Timid Rabbit" **Genre:** Folktale (India)	"The Nice Mitten" **Genre:** Folktale **Lexile:** 460L	**Anchor Text:** *The Gingerbread Man* **Genre:** Folktale **Lexile:** 320L **Paired Selection:** "Drakestail" **Genre:** Folktale **Lexile:** 450L	**Main Selections:** **Genre:** Folktale 🟠 *How Coquí Got Her Voice* (Puerto Rico) **Lexile:** 300L 🔵 *The Magic Paintbrush* (China) **Lexile:** 230L 🟣 *The Magic Paintbrush* (China) **Lexile:** 240L 🟢 *Rabbit Tricks Crocodile* (Japan) **Lexile:** 420L **Paired Selections:** **Genre:** Poetry/Song 🟠 "El Coquí/The Coquí" 🔵 "Make New Friends" 🟣 "Wanted: A Friend" 🟢 "Fish School"	**Oral Vocabulary Words:** *eventually* *foolish* *hero* *tale* *timid* **Oral Vocabulary:** Compound Words	

Comprehension	Print Concepts	Phonological/ Phonemic Awareness	Phonics/Spelling/ Handwriting/ Structural Analysis	High- Frequency Words	Fluency	Writing and Grammar	Research and Inquiry
Make and Confirm Predictions Events: Beginning, Middle, End Bold Print	Capitalization and Punctuation, Title, Author, Illustrator	**Phonemic Awareness:** Phoneme Identity, Phoneme Addition, Phoneme Substitution, Phoneme Blending, Phoneme Segmentation	**Phonics/Spelling:** Long *a* spelled *a_e* *Differentiated Spelling Lists available* **Handwriting:** Upper- and Lowercase *Dd* **Structural Analysis:** Contractions with *not* **Decodable Readers:** *Dave Was Late; Is It Late?*	*away now some today way why*	Accuracy and Rate	**Write About the Text:** Narrative **Writing Skill:** Return Sweep **Writing Trait:** Word Choice: Strong Verbs **Grammar:** Verbs **Mechanics:** Commas in a Series	**Project:** Interview About Your Day
Make and Confirm Predictions Main Story Elements: Sequence of Events Diagram	Punctuation within Sentences, Title, Author	**Phonological Awareness:** Alliteration **Phonemic Awareness:** Phoneme Deletion, Phoneme Segmentation Phoneme Blending	**Phonics/Spelling:** Long *i* spelled *i_e* *Differentiated Spelling Lists available* **Handwriting:** Upper- and Lowercase *Vv* **Structural Analysis:** Plurals (with CVCe words) **Decodable Readers:** *A Fine Plant; Plants Take Time to Grow*	*green grow pretty should together water*	Accuracy and Rate	**Write About the Text:** Narrative **Writing Skill:** Capitalize "I" **Writing Trait:** Word Choice: Sensory Details **Grammar:** Present-Tense Verbs **Mechanics:** Capitalize and Underline Titles of Plays	**Project:** From Seed to Plant
Make and Confirm Predictions Moral Descriptive Words and Phrases	Quotation Marks/Text Styles, Title, Author	**Phonological Awareness:** Identify and Produce Rhyme **Phonemic Awareness:** Phoneme Segmentation Phoneme Blending	**Phonics/Spelling:** Soft *c*, *g/dge* *Differentiated Spelling Lists available* **Handwriting:** Upper- and Lowercase *Yy* **Structural Analysis:** Inflectional Endings: *-ed* and *-ing* (drop final e) **Decodable Readers:** *The King and Five Mice; Tales from a Past Age*	*any from happy once so upon*	Accuracy and Rate	**Write About the Text:** Narrative **Writing Skill:** Word endings: *-ed* and *-ing* **Writing Trait:** Word Choice: Specific Words **Grammar:** Past- and Future-Tense Verbs **Mechanics:** Commas in a Series	**Project:** All About a Folktale

Scope and Sequence

Changes Over Time	Literature Big Book	Interactive Read Aloud	Shared Read	Literature Anthology	Leveled Readers	Vocabulary	
Week 4 **Now and Then** **Essential Question:** How is life different than it was long ago? **Genre Focus:** Informational Text	*The Last Train* **Genre:** Song	"Let's Look at Video Games!" **Genre:** Informational Text	"Life at Home" **Genre:** Informational Text **Lexile:** 490L	**Anchor Text:** *Long Ago and Now* **Genre:** Informational Text **Lexile:** 480L **Paired Selection:** "From Horse to Plane" **Genre:** Informational Text **Lexile:** 370L	**Main Selections:** **Genre:** Informational Text 🟠 *Schools Then and Now* **Lexile:** 170L 🔵 *Schools Then and Now* **Lexile:** 220L 🟣 *Schools Then and Now* **Lexile:** 270L 🟢 *Schools Then and Now* **Lexile:** 380L **Paired Selections:** **Genre:** Informational Text 🟠 "School Days" 🔵 "School Days" 🟣 "School Days" 🟢 "School Days"	**Oral Vocabulary Words:** *century* *past* *present* *future* *entertainment* **Oral Vocabulary:** Base Words	
Week 5 **From Farm to Table** **Essential Question:** How do we get our food? **Genre Focus:** Informational Text	*Where Does Food Come From?* **Genre:** Informational Text	"The Little Red Hen" **Genre:** Folktale	"A Look at Breakfast" **Genre:** Informational Text **Lexile:** 340L	**Anchor Text:** *From Cows to You* **Genre:** Informational Text **Lexile:** 500L **Paired Selection:** "The Five Food Groups" **Genre:** Informational Text **Lexile:** 450L	**Main Selections:** **Genre:** Informational Text 🟠 *Apples from Farm to Table* **Lexile:** 330L 🔵 *Apples from Farm to Table* **Lexile:** 550L 🟣 *Apples from Farm to Table* **Lexile:** 430L 🟢 *Apples from Farm to Table* **Lexile:** 580L **Paired Selections:** **Genre:** Informational Text 🟠 "A Dairy Treat" 🔵 "A Dairy Treat" 🟣 "A Dairy Treat" 🟢 "A Dairy Treat"	**Oral Vocabulary Words:** *delicious* *nutritious* *responsibility* *enormous* *delighted* **Oral Vocabulary:** Synonyms	

Week 6	Reading Digitally	Fluency	Connect to Science	Extend Your Learning
Extend, Connect, and Assess	"Time for Kids: Seasons Bring Change" **Genre:** Online Article	**Reader's Theater:** *Shadow Dance*	**Genre Read-Aloud:** "Twinsies" **Activities:** Observe a Plant Write a Letter	Choose Your Own Book

Comprehension	Print Concepts	Phonological/ Phonemic Awareness	Phonics/Spelling/ Handwriting/ Structural Analysis	High-Frequency Words	Fluency	Writing and Grammar	Research and Inquiry
Reread Details: Compare and Contrast Captions	Reading Sentences Across Pages, Title, Author, Illustrator	**Phonemic Awareness:** Phoneme Segmentation, Phoneme Isolation, Phoneme Blending	**Phonics/Spelling:** Long *o* spelled *o_e;* Long *u* spelled *u_e;* Long *e* spelled *e_e* *Differentiated Spelling Lists available* **Handwriting:** Upper- and Lowercase *Ww* **Structural Analysis:** CVCe Syllables **Decodable Readers:** *Those Old Classes; That Old Globe*	*ago* *boy* *girl* *how* *old* *people*	Accuracy and Rate	**Write About the Text:** Opinion **Extended Writing:** Expository Text **Writing Skill:** Use Word Bank **Writing Trait:** Ideas: Focus on an Idea **Writing Process:** Expert and Student Models; Plan; Draft **Grammar:** Irregular Verbs: *Is* and *Are* **Mechanics:** Commas in Dates	**Project:** Interview About Long Ago
Reread Details: Time-Order Diagram	Special Text Treatments, Title, Author	**Phonemic Awareness:** Phoneme Segmentation, Phoneme Blending, Phoneme Deletion	**Phonics/Spelling:** Variant Vowel Spellings with Digraphs: *oo, u* *Differentiated Spelling Lists available* **Handwriting:** Upper- and Lowercase *Bb* **Structural Analysis:** Inflectional Endings: *-ed* and *-ing* (double final consonant) **Decodable Readers:** *A Good Cook; That Looks Good*	*after* *buy* *done* *every* *soon* *work*	Accuracy and Rate	**Write About the Text:** Opinion **Extended Writing:** Expository Text **Writing Skill:** Stretch Sounds to Write Words **Writing Trait:** Ideas: Give Reasons for an Opinion **Writing Process:** Revise; Edit and Proofread; Publish, Present, and Evaluate **Grammar:** Contractions with *not* **Mechanics:** Apostrophes in Contractions	**Project:** Investigate a Food

Scope and Sequence

Animals Everywhere Big Idea: What animals do you know about? What are they like?	Interactive Read Aloud	Shared Read	Literature Anthology	Leveled Readers	Vocabulary	
Week 1 **Animal Features** **Essential Question:** How do animals' bodies help them? **Genre Focus:** Folktale	"The Elephant's Child" **Genre:** Folktale	"Snail and Frog Race" **Genre:** Folktale **Lexile:** 270L	**Anchor Text:** *Little Rabbit* **Genre:** Folktale **Lexile:** 180L **Paired Selection:** "Animals Can Go Fast!" **Genre:** Informational Text **Lexile:** 300L	**Main Selections:** **Genre:** Folktale 🟠 *The King of the Animals* (Africa) **Lexile:** 350L 🔵 *Snail's Clever Idea* **Lexile:** 450L 🟣 *Snail's Clever Idea* **Lexile:** 400L 🟢 *Plop!* **Lexile:** 540L **Paired Selections:** **Genre:** Informational Text 🟠 "Lions and Elephants" 🔵 "Snails: Small, Slow, and Slimy" 🟣 "Snails: Small, Slow, and Slimy" 🟢 "Animal Traits"	**Oral Vocabulary Words:** *feature* *appearance* *determined* *predicament* *relief* **Academic Vocabulary:** *special* *splendid* **Vocabulary:** Use a Dictionary	
Week 2 **Animals Together** **Essential Question:** How do animals help each other? **Genre Focus:** Informational Text	"Animals Working Together" **Genre:** Informational Text	"A Team of Fish" **Genre:** Informational Text **Lexile:** 340L	**Anchor Text:** *Animal Teams* **Genre:** Informational Text **Lexile:** 480L **Paired Selection:** "Busy as a Bee" **Genre:** Informational Text **Lexile:** 500L	**Main Selections:** **Genre:** Informational Text 🟠 *Penguins All Around* **Lexile:** 340L 🔵 *Penguins All Around* **Lexile:** 450L 🟣 *Penguins All Around* **Lexile:** 340L 🟢 *Penguins All Around* **Lexile:** 610L **Paired Selections:** **Genre:** Informational Text 🟠 "Animals Work Together!" 🔵 "Animals Work Together!" 🟣 "Animals Work Together!" 🟢 "Animals Work Together!"	**Oral Vocabulary Words:** *behavior* *beneficial* *dominant* *instinct* *endangered* **Academic Vocabulary:** *partner* *danger* **Vocabulary:** Context Clues/Sentence Clues	
Week 3 **In the Wild** **Essential Question:** How do animals survive in nature? **Genre Focus:** Informational Text	"Animals in Winter" **Genre:** Informational Text	"Go Wild!" **Genre:** Informational Text **Lexile:** 540L	**Anchor Text:** *Vulture View* **Genre:** Informational Text **Lexile:** 70L **Paired Selection:** "When It's Snowing" **Genre:** Poetry **Lexile:** NP	**Main Selections:** **Genre:** Informational Text 🟠 *Go, Gator!* **Lexile:** 320L 🔵 *Go, Gator!* **Lexile:** 510L 🟣 *Go, Gator!* **Lexile:** 270L 🟢 *Go, Gator!* **Lexile:** 590L **Paired Selections:** **Genre:** Poetry 🟠 "Ducklings" 🔵 "Ducklings" 🟣 "Ducklings" 🟢 "Ducklings"	**Oral Vocabulary Words:** *communicate* *provide* *superior* *survive* *wilderness* **Academic Vocabulary:** *search* *seek* **Vocabulary:** Word Categories	

Comprehension	Print Concepts	Phonological/ Phonemic Awareness	Phonics/Spelling/ Handwriting/ Structural Analysis	High-Frequency Words	Fluency	Writing and Grammar	Research and Inquiry
Ask and Answer Questions Main Story Elements: Sequence of Events Chart	Glossary Title	**Phonological Awareness:** Identify and Produce Rhyme **Phonemic Awareness:** Phoneme Categorization, Phoneme Blending, Phoneme Segmentation	**Phonics/Spelling:** Long *a* spelled *a, ai, ay* *Differentiated Spelling Lists available* **Handwriting:** Upper- and Lowercase *Nn* **Structural Analysis:** Alphabetical Order (two letters) **Decodable Readers:** *April the Agent; A Basic Dog; Snail Mail; Tails*	*about animal carry eight give our*	Accuracy	**Write About the Text:** Informational Text **Writing Trait:** Word Choice: Descriptive Words **Review Trait:** Ideas: Focus on a Topic **Grammar:** Irregular Verbs: *Was* and *Were* **Mechanics:** Apostrophe with Contractions	**Project:** Animal Bodies
Ask and Answer Questions Topic and Relevant Details Captions	Glossary Title	**Phonological Awareness:** Identify and Produce Rhyme **Phonemic Awareness:** Phoneme Identity, Phoneme Segmentation, Phoneme Blending	**Phonics/Spelling:** Long *e* spelled *e, ee, ea, ie* *Differentiated Spelling Lists available* **Handwriting:** Upper- and Lowercase *Gg* **Structural Analysis:** Prefixes *re-, un-, pre-* **Decodable Readers:** *The Green Eel; Clean Up the Team*	*because blue into or other small*	Appropriate Phrasing	**Write About the Text:** Opinion **Writing Trait:** Organization: Introduce the Topic **Review Trait:** Ideas: Give Reasons for an Opinion **Grammar:** Irregular Verbs: *Has* and *Have* **Mechanics:** Capitalization and End Punctuation	**Project:** Animal Teams
Ask and Answer Questions Topic and Relevant Details Poetry: Stanzas and Line Breaks	Author Illustrator	**Phonological Awareness:** Contrast Vowel Sounds **Phonemic Awareness:** Phoneme Categorization, Phoneme Blending, Phoneme Substitution	**Phonics/Spelling:** Long *o* spelled *o, oa, ow, oe* *Differentiated Spelling Lists available* **Handwriting:** Upper- and Lowercase *Pp* **Structural Analysis:** Open Syllables **Decodable Readers:** *Toads; Joan and Elmo Swim; A Doe and a Buck; Joe Goes Slow*	*find food more over start warm*	Rate	**Write About the Text:** Informational Text **Extended Writing:** Poetry **Writing Trait:** Ideas: Main Ideas **Review Trait:** Ideas: Supporting Details **Writing Process:** Expert and Student Models; Plan; Draft **Grammar:** Irregular Verbs: *Go* and *Do* **Mechanics:** Capitalize Proper Nouns	**Project:** Animal Life Cycles

Scope and Sequence

Animals Everywhere!	Interactive Read Aloud	Shared Read	Literature Anthology	Leveled Readers	Vocabulary	
Week 4 **Insects!** **Essential Question:** What insects do you know about? How are they alike and different? **Genre Focus:** Fantasy	"Insect Hide and Seek" **Genre:** Informational Text	"Creep Low, Fly High" **Genre:** Fantasy **Lexile:** 290L	**Anchor Text:** *Hi! Fly Guy* **Genre:** Fantasy **Lexile:** 200L **Paired Selection:** "Meet the Insects" **Genre:** Informational Text **Lexile:** 400L	**Main Selections:** **Genre:** Fantasy 🟠 *Where Is My Home?* **Lexile:** 170L 🔵 *The Hat* **Lexile:** 290L 🟣 *The Hat* **Lexile:** 230L 🟢 *Come One, Come All* **Lexile:** 330L **Paired Selections:** **Genre:** Informational Text 🟠 "Wings" 🔵 "Let's Look at Insects!" 🟣 "Let's Look at Insects!" 🟢 "Compare Insects"	**Oral Vocabulary Words:** *different* *flutter* *imitate* *resemble* *protect* **Academic Vocabulary:** *beautiful* *fancy* **Vocabulary:** Context Clues/Sentence Clues	
Week 5 **Working with Animals** **Essential Question:** How do people work with animals? **Genre Focus:** Informational Text	"Ming's Teacher" **Genre:** Folktale (China)	"Time for Kids: From Puppy to Guide Dog" **Genre:** Informational Text **Lexile:** 680L	**Anchor Text:** *Time for Kids: Koko and Penny* **Genre:** Informational Text **Lexile:** 370L **Paired Selection:** "Save Our Bees!" **Genre:** Opinion Text **Lexile:** 450L	**Main Selections:** **Genre:** Informational Text 🟠 *Teach a Dog!* **Lexile:** 270L 🔵 *Teach a Dog!* **Lexile:** 330L 🟣 *Teach a Dog!* **Lexile:** 220L 🟢 *Teach a Dog!* **Lexile:** 440L **Paired Selections:** **Genre:** Informational Text 🟠 "Working with Dolphins" 🔵 "Working with Dolphins" 🟣 "Working with Dolphins" 🟢 "Working with Dolphins"	**Oral Vocabulary Words:** *advice* *career* *remarkable* *soothe* *trust* **Academic Vocabulary:** *clever* *signal* **Vocabulary:** Base Words	

Week 6	Reading Digitally	Fluency	Connect to Science	Extend Your Learning
Extend, Connect, and Assess	"Time for Kids: Teeth at Work" **Genre:** Online Article	**Reader's Theater:** *Fooba Wooba John*	**Passages:** "Crocodiles" "Sloths" **Activities** Two-Column Chart Observe Animal Needs	Choose Your Own Book

Comprehension	Print Concepts	Phonological/ Phonemic Awareness	Phonics/Spelling/ Handwriting/ Structural Analysis	High- Frequency Words	Fluency	Writing and Grammar	Research and Inquiry
Visualize Narrator Headings	Table of Contents	**Phonemic Awareness:** Phoneme Categorization, Phoneme Identity, Phoneme Segmentation, Phoneme Substitution	**Phonics/Spelling:** Long *i* spelled *i, igh, y, ie* *Differentiated Spelling Lists available* **Handwriting:** Upper- and Lowercase *Zz* **Structural Analysis:** Inflectional Endings (change *y* to *i*) **Decodable Readers:** *Jay Takes Flight; Be Kind to Bugs; Why Hope Flies; Glowing Bugs Fly By*	*caught flew know laugh listen were*	Appropriate Phrasing	**Write About the Text:** Informational Text **Extended Writing:** Poetry **Writing Trait:** Organization: Concluding Statement **Review Trait**: Ideas: Descriptive Details **Writing Process:** Revise; Edit and Proofread; Publish, Present, and Evaluate **Grammar:** Irregular Verbs: *See* and *Saw* **Mechanics:** Underline Titles of Books	**Project:** Compare Two Insects
Visualize Details: Time-Order Graph	Table of Contents	**Phonemic Awareness:** Phoneme Categorization, Phoneme Deletion, Phoneme Blending, Phoneme Addition	**Phonics/Spelling:** Long *e* spelled *y, ey* *Differentiated Spelling Lists available* **Handwriting:** Upper- and Lowercase *Mm* **Structural Analysis:** Compound Words **Decodable Readers:** *Race Pony!; Study with Animals*	*found hard near woman would write*	Intonation	**Write About the Text:** Informational Text **Writing Trait:** Organization: Introduce the Topic **Review Trait:** Word Choice: Specific Words **Grammar:** Adverbs That Tell When **Mechanics:** Commas in a Series	**Project:** Caring for Animals

Scope and Sequence

Figure It Out Big Idea: How can we make sense of the world around us?	Interactive Read Aloud	Shared Read	Literature Anthology	Leveled Readers	Vocabulary	
Week 1 **See It, Sort It** **Essential Question:** How can we classify and categorize things? **Genre Focus:** Fantasy	"Goldilocks" **Genre:** Folktale	"A Barn Full of Hats" **Genre:** Fantasy **Lexile:** 320L	**Anchor Text:** *A Lost Button* (from *Frog and Toad Are Friends*) **Genre:** Fantasy **Lexile:** 340L **Paired Selection:** "Sort It Out" **Genre:** Informational Text **Lexile:** 210L	**Main Selections:** **Genre:** Fantasy 🟠 *Nuts for Winter* **Lexile:** 170L 🔵 *Dog Bones* **Lexile:** 360L 🟣 *Dog Bones* **Lexile:** 260L 🟢 *Spark's Toys* **Lexile:** 390L **Paired Selections:** **Genre:** Informational Text 🟠 "Sort by Color!" 🔵 "Sorting Balls" 🟣 "Sorting Balls" 🟢 "Sorting Fruit"	**Oral Vocabulary Words:** *distinguish* *classify* *organize* *entire* *startled* **Academic Vocabulary:** *trouble* *whole* **Vocabulary:** Context Clues: Multiple Meanings	
Week 2 **Up in the Sky** **Essential Question:** What can you see in the sky? **Genre Focus:** Fantasy	"Why the Sun and Moon Are in the Sky" **Genre:** Folktale: Pourquoi (Nigerian)	"A Bird Named Fern" **Genre:** Fantasy **Lexile:** 360L	**Anchor Text:** *Kitten's First Full Moon* **Genre:** Fantasy **Lexile:** 550L **Paired Selection:** "The Moon" **Genre:** Informational Text **Lexile:** 440L	**Main Selections:** **Genre:** Fantasy 🟠 *Little Blue's Dream* **Lexile:** 280L 🔵 *Hide and Seek* **Lexile:** 310L 🟣 *Hide and Seek* **Lexile:** 310L 🟢 *The Foxes Build a Home* **Lexile:** 420L **Paired Selections:** **Genre:** Informational Text 🟠 "Hello, Little Dipper!" 🔵 "Our Sun Is a Star!" 🟣 "Our Sun Is a Star!" 🟢 "Sunrise and Sunset"	**Oral Vocabulary Words:** *certain* *observe* *remained* *thoughtful* *vast* **Academic Vocabulary:** *leaped* *stretched* **Vocabulary:** Shades of Meaning/Intensity	
Week 3 **Great Inventions** **Essential Question:** What inventions do you know about? **Genre Focus:** Biography	"Great Inventions" **Genre:** Informational Text	"The Story of a Robot Inventor" **Genre:** Biography **Lexile:** 420L	**Anchor Text:** *Thomas Edison, Inventor* **Genre:** Biography **Lexile:** 510L **Paired Selection:** "Windshield Wipers" and "Scissors" **Genre:** Poetry **Lexile:** NP	**Main Selections:** **Genre:** Biography 🟠 *The Wright Brothers* **Lexile:** 410L 🔵 *The Wright Brothers* **Lexile:** 500L 🟣 *The Wright Brothers* **Lexile:** 430L 🟢 *The Wright Brothers* **Lexile:** 660L **Paired Selections:** **Genre:** Poetry 🟠 "Fly Away, Butterfly" 🔵 "Fly Away, Butterfly" 🟣 "Fly Away, Butterfly" 🟢 "Fly Away, Butterfly"	**Oral Vocabulary Words:** *complicated* *curious* *device* *imagine* *improve* **Academic Vocabulary:** *idea* *unusual* **Vocabulary:** Prefixes	

Comprehension	Print Concepts	Phonological/ Phonemic Awareness	Phonics/Spelling/ Handwriting/ Structural Analysis	High-Frequency Words	Fluency	Writing and Grammar	Research and Inquiry
Make and Confirm Predictions Narrator Photographs and Illustrations	Glossary	**Phonological Awareness:** Contrast Vowel Sounds **Phonemic Awareness:** Phoneme Categorization, Phoneme Blending, Phoneme Segmentation	**Phonics/Spelling:** *r*-Controlled Vowel *ar* *Differentiated Spelling Lists available* **Handwriting:** Upper- and Lowercase *Hh* **Structural Analysis:** Plurals: Change *-y* to *-ies* **Decodable Readers:** *Charm Scarves; Car Parts*	four large none only put round	Automaticity	**Write About the Text:** Opinion **Writing Trait:** Sentence Fluency: Vary Sentence Length **Review Trait:** Word Choice: Descriptive Words **Grammar:** Words That Join **Mechanics:** Capitalize Proper Nouns (places)	**Project:** Sort a Collection
Make and Confirm Predictions Events: Cause and Effect Descriptive Words and Phrases	Table of Contents	**Phonological Awareness:** Identify and Produce Rhyme **Phonemic Awareness:** Phoneme Substitution, Phoneme Blending, Phoneme Deletion	**Phonics/Spelling:** *r*-Controlled Vowels *or, ir, ur, er* *Differentiated Spelling Lists available* **Handwriting:** Upper- and Lowercase *Kk* **Structural Analysis:** Suffix *-er* **Decodable Readers:** *Sir Worm and Bird Girl; Bird in the Sky; Ginger and the Stars; Bats Under the Dark Sky*	another climb full great poor through	Intonation	**Write About the Text:** Informational Text **Writing Trait:** Word Choice: Strong Verbs **Review Trait:** Ideas: Focus on an Idea **Grammar:** Adjectives **Mechanics:** Capitalization and End Marks	**Project:** The Sun Helps Us
Ask and Answer Questions Details: Problem and Solution Descriptive Words and Phrases	Author	**Phonemic Awareness:** Phoneme Categorization, Phoneme Substitution, Phoneme Blending, Phoneme Addition	**Phonics/Spelling:** *r*-Controlled Vowels *or, ore, oar* *Differentiated Spelling Lists available* **Handwriting:** Upper- and Lowercase *Rr* **Structural Analysis:** Abbreviations **Decodable Readers:** *Born to Learn; Sport Stars; A Board That Can Soar; Hard Chores*	began better guess learn right sure	Automaticity	**Write About the Text:** Informational Text **Writing Trait:** Organization: Order of Events **Review Trait:** Fluency: Varying Sentence Length **Grammar:** Adjectives That Compare (*-er* and *-est*) **Mechanics:** Capitalize Days, Months, and Holidays	**Project:** Find out About an Inventor

Scope and Sequence

Figure It Out	Interactive Read Aloud	Shared Read	Literature Anthology	Leveled Readers	Vocabulary	
Week 4 **Sounds All Around** **Essential Question:** What sounds can you hear? How are they made? **Genre Focus:** Realistic Fiction	"The Squeaky Bed" **Genre:** Folktale (Puerto Rico)	"Now, What's That Sound?" **Genre:** Realistic Fiction **Lexile:** 240L	**Anchor Text:** *Whistle for Willie* **Genre:** Realistic Fiction **Lexile:** 520L **Paired Selection:** "Shake! Strike! Strum!" **Genre:** How-To Text **Lexile:** 290L	**Main Selections:** **Genre:** Realistic Fiction 🟠 *Thump, Jangle, Crash* **Lexile:** 180L 🔵 *Down on the Farm* **Lexile:** 390L 🟣 *Down on the Farm* **Lexile:** 170L 🟢 *Going on a Bird Walk* **Lexile:** 420L **Paired Selections:** **Genre:** How-To (Procedural) 🟠 "How to Make Maracas" 🔵 "How to Make a Rain Stick" 🟣 "How to Make a Rain Stick" 🟢 "How to Make a Wind Chime"	**Oral Vocabulary Words:** *distract* *nervous* *senses* *squeaky* *volume* **Academic Vocabulary:** *suddenly* *scrambled* **Vocabulary:** Suffixes	
Week 5 **Build It!** **Essential Question:** How do things get built? **Genre Focus:** Informational Text	"The Sheep, the Pig, and the Goose Who Set Up House" **Genre:** Folktale (Norway)	"Time for Kids: The Joy of a Ship" **Genre:** Informational Text **Lexile:** 560L	**Anchor Text:** *Time for Kids: Building Bridges* **Genre:** Informational Text **Lexile:** 550L **Paired Selection:** "Small Joy" **Genre:** Informational Text **Lexile:** 490L	**Main Selections:** **Genre:** Informational Text 🟠 *What Is a Yurt?* **Lexile:** 430L 🔵 *What Is a Yurt?* **Lexile:** 440L 🟣 *What Is a Yurt?* **Lexile:** 390L 🟢 *What Is a Yurt?* **Lexile:** 620L **Paired Selections:** **Genre:** Informational Text 🟠 "Treehouses" 🔵 "Treehouses" 🟣 "Treehouses" 🟢 "Treehouses"	**Oral Vocabulary Words:** *contented* *intend* *marvelous* *project* *structure* **Academic Vocabulary:** *balance* *section* **Vocabulary:** Inflectional Endings	

Week 6	Reading Digitally	Fluency	Connect to Science	Extend Your Learning
Extend, Connect, and Assess	"Time for Kids: Great Ideas!" **Genre:** Online Article	**Reader's Theater:** *Supper with the Queen*	**Passages:** "The Night Sky" "Billions of Stars" **Activities:** Venn Diagram Observe the Sky	Choose Your Own Book

Comprehension	Print Concepts	Phonological/ Phonemic Awareness	Phonics/Spelling/ Handwriting/ Structural Analysis	High- Frequency Words	Fluency	Writing and Grammar	Research and Inquiry
Ask and Answer Questions Events: Problem and Solution Directions	Title	**Phonemic Awareness:** Phoneme Substitution, Phoneme Isolation, Phoneme Blending	**Phonics/Spelling:** Diphthongs *ou, ow* *Differentiated Spelling Lists available* **Handwriting:** Upper and Lowercase *Xx* **Structural Analysis:** Comparative Inflectional Endings *-er, -est* **Decodable Readers:** *Up or Down Sounds; Sounds Around Us*	*color* *early* *instead* *nothing* *oh* *thought*	Expression	**Write About the Text:** Narrative **Extended Writing:** How-To Article **Writing Trait:** Sentence Fluency: Vary Sentence Beginnings **Review Trait:** Organization: Beginning/ Middle/End **Writing Process:** Expert and Student Models; Plan; Draft **Grammar:** Using *a, an, this,* and *that* **Mechanics:** Capitalize/ Underline Book Titles	**Project:** Experiment with Sounds
Ask and Answer Questions Details: Cause and Effect Captions	Table of Contents Title	**Phonemic Awareness:** Phoneme Blending, Phoneme Segmentation, Phoneme Categorization	**Phonics/Spelling:** Diphthongs *oi, oy* *Differentiated Spelling Lists available* **Handwriting:** Upper- and Lowercase *Jj* **Structural Analysis:** Final Stable Syllables **Decodable Readers:** *Joy's Birdhouse; Beavers Make Noise*	*above* *build* *fall* *knew* *money* *toward*	Intonation and Phrasing	**Write About the Text:** Opinion **Extended Writing:** How-To Article **Writing Trait:** Ideas: Give Reasons for an Opinion **Review Trait:** Organization: Concluding Statement **Writing Process:** Revise; Edit and Proofread; Publish, Present, and Evaluate **Grammar:** Prepositions/ Prepositional Phrases **Mechanics:** Abbreviations (capitals and periods with *Mr., Mrs., Ms., Dr.*)	**Project:** How to Build a(n) _____

Scope and Sequence

Together We Can! Big Idea: How does teamwork help us?	Interactive Read Aloud	Shared Read	Literature Anthology	Leveled Readers	Vocabulary	
Week 1 **Taking Action** **Essential Question:** How can we work together to make our lives better? **Genre Focus:** Fantasy	"The Cat's Bell" **Genre:** Fable	"Super Tools" **Genre:** Fantasy **Lexile:** 430L	**Anchor Text:** *Click, Clack, Moo: Cows That Type* **Genre:** Fantasy **Lexile:** 380L **Paired Selection:** "Be a Volunteer!" **Genre:** Opinion Text **Lexile:** 520L	**Main Selections:** **Genre:** Fantasy 🔴 *Two Hungry Elephants* **Lexile:** 290L **O:** *What a Feast!* **Lexile:** 500L **ELL:** *What a Feast!* **Lexile:** 350L **B:** *Beware of the Lion!* **Lexile:** 480L **Paired Selections:** **Genre:** Informational Text 🔴 "Dogs Helping People" 🔵 "Helpers Bring Food" 🟣 "Helpers Bring Food" 🟢 "Pete Seeger"	**Oral Vocabulary Words:** *fair* *conflict* *shift* *risk* *argument* **Academic Vocabulary:** *demand* *emergency* **Vocabulary:** Synonyms	
Week 2 **My Team** **Essential Question:** Who helps you? **Genre Focus:** Informational Text	"Anansi's Sons" **Genre:** Folktale (Trickster Tale)	"All kinds of Helpers" **Genre:** Informational Text **Lexile:** 530L	**Anchor Text:** *Meet Rosina* **Genre:** Informational Text **Lexile:** 420L **Paired Selection:** "Abuelita's Lap" **Genre:** Poetry **Lexile:** NP	**Main Selections:** **Genre:** Informational Text 🔴 *Helping Me, Helping You!* **Lexile:** 310L 🔵 *Helping Me, Helping You!* **Lexile:** 400L 🟣 *Helping Me, Helping You!* **Lexile:** 290L 🟢 *Helping Me, Helping You!* **Lexile:** 540L **Paired Selections:** **Genre:** Informational Text 🔴 "Fire!" 🔵 "Fire!" 🟣 "Fire!" 🟢 "Fire!"	**Oral Vocabulary Words:** *decision* *distance* *inspire* *respect* *swiftly* **Academic Vocabulary:** *accept* *often* **Vocabulary:** Antonyms	
Week 3 **Weather Together** **Essential Question:** How can weather affect us? **Genre Focus:** Realistic Fiction	"Paul Bunyan and the Popcorn Blizzard" **Genre:** Folktale (Tall Tale)	"Wrapped in Ice" **Genre:** Realistic Fiction **Lexile:** 320L	**Anchor Text:** *Rain School* **Genre:** Realistic Fiction **Lexile:** 440L **Paired Selection:** "Rainy Weather" **Genre:** Informational Text **Lexile:** 470L	**Main Selections:** **Genre:** Realistic Fiction 🔴 *Snow Day* **Lexile:** 390L 🔵 *Heat Wave* **Lexile:** 460L 🟣 *Heat Wave* **Lexile:** 370L 🟢 *Rainy Day Fun* **Lexile:** 420L **Paired Selections:** **Genre:** Informational Text 🔴 "A Mountain of Snow" 🔵 "Stay Safe When It's Hot" 🟣 "Stay Safe When It's Hot" 🟢 "Let's Stay Dry!"	**Oral Vocabulary Words:** *creative* *cycle* *frigid* *predict* *scorching* **Academic Vocabulary:** *country* *gathers* **Vocabulary:** Similes	

Comprehension	Print Concepts	Phonological/ Phonemic Awareness	Phonics/Spelling/ Handwriting/ Structural Analysis	High-Frequency Words	Fluency	Writing and Grammar	Research and Inquiry
Reread Theme Captions	Glossary	**Phonological Awareness** Identify and Produce Rhyme, Syllable Deletion **Phonemic Awareness:** Phoneme Identity, Phoneme Segmentation, Phoneme Substitution	**Phonics/Spelling:** Variant Vowel Spellings *oo, ou, u_e, ew, ui, ue, u* *Differentiated Spelling Lists available* **Handwriting:** Upper- and Lowercase *Qq* **Structural Analysis:** Suffixes *-full* and *-less* **Decodable Readers:** *Rooster and Goose;* *Choose a Room;* *The Flute Youth;* *Group Rules;* *Lewis and His New Suit;* *A Cruise Crew;* *Sue and Lucy; A True Team*	*answer* *brought* *busy* *door* *enough* *eyes*	Expression	**Write About the Text:** Write a Letter **Writing Trait:** Organization: Paragraph **Review Trait:** Word Choice: Strong Verbs **Grammar:** Pronouns *I, you, he, she, it, we, they* **Mechanics:** Capitalize *I*	**Project:** Poll about Taking Action
Reread Author's Purpose Stanzas and Line Breaks	Author	**Phonemic Awareness:** Phoneme Categorization, Phoneme Reversal, Phoneme Blending, Phoneme Segmentation, Phoneme Substitution	**Phonics/Spelling:** Variant Vowel Spellings *au, aw, a, augh, al* *Differentiated Spelling Lists available* **Handwriting:** A Story **Structural Analysis:** Vowel-Team Syllables **Decodable Readers:** *Paul's Paw;* *Thank You Authors!;* *Not Too Small;* *My Baseball Coach;* *A Walk with Mayor Moose;* *Teacher Talk*	*brother* *father* *friend* *love* *mother* *picture*	Intonation	**Write About the Text:** Informational Text **Writing Trait:** Voice: Use Own Voice **Review Trait:** Organization: Introduce the Topic **Grammar:** Possessive Pronouns **Mechanics:** Capitalize Days, Months, and Holidays	**Project:** Interview a Helper
Visualize Events: Cause and Effect Headings	Table of Contents	**Phonemic Awareness:** Phoneme Categorization, Phoneme Segmentation, Phoneme Substitution	**Phonics/Spelling:** Silent Letter Consonant Digraphs: *wr, kn, gn* *Differentiated Spelling Lists available* **Handwriting:** A Story **Structural Analysis:** Compound Words **Decodable Readers:** *Miss Wright's Job;* *A Lighthouse Stops Wrecks;* *Know About Snowstorms;* *The Rusty Knight*	*been* *children* *month* *question* *their* *year*	Intonation	**Write About the Text:** Write to Sources **Extended Writing:** Opinion **Writing Trait:** Ideas: Main Idea **Review Trait:** Ideas: Descriptive Details **Writing Process:** Expert and Student Models; Plan; Draft **Grammar:** Special Pronouns (*anyone, everyone, anything, everything, nothing*) **Mechanics:** Commas in Dates and Letters	**Project:** The Weather in My State

Scope and Sequence

Together We Can!	Interactive Read Aloud	Shared Read	Literature Anthology	Leveled Readers	Vocabulary	
Week 4 **Sharing Traditions** **Essential Question:** What traditions do you know about? **Genre Focus:** Realistic Fiction	"Let's Dance!" **Genre:** Informational Text	"A Spring Birthday" **Genre:** Realistic Fiction **Lexile:** 380L	**Anchor Text:** *Lissy's Friends* **Genre:** Realistic Fiction **Lexile:** 460L **Paired Selection:** "Making Paper Shapes" **Genre:** How-To Text **Lexile:** 520L	**Main Selections:** **Genre:** Realistic Fiction 🔴 *The Quilt* **Lexile:** 380L 🔵 *Latkes for Sam* **Lexile:** 410L 🟣 *Latkes for Sam* **Lexile:** 290L 🟢 *Patty Jumps!* **Lexile:** 440L **Paired Selections:** **Genre:** How-To (Procedural) 🔴 "Making a Quilt Square" 🔵 "What Is a Taco?" 🟣 "What Is a Taco?" 🟢 "How to Play Four Square"	**Oral Vocabulary Words:** *ancient* *drama* *effort* *movement* *tradition* **Academic Vocabulary:** *difficult* *nobody* **Vocabulary:** Compound Words	
Week 5 **Celebrate America!** **Essential Question:** Why do we celebrate holidays? **Genre Focus:** Informational Text	"Celebrate the Flag" **Genre:** Informational Text	"Share the Harvest and Give Thanks" **Genre:** Informational Text **Lexile:** 650L	**Anchor Text:** *Time for Kids: Happy Birthday, U.S.A.!* **Genre:** Informational Text **Lexile:** 490L **Paired Selection:** "Time for Kids: Martin Luther King, Jr. Day" **Genre:** Informational Text **Lexile:** 510L	**Main Selections:** **Genre:** Informational Text 🔴 *It's Labor Day!* **Lexile:** 440L 🔵 *It's Labor Day!* **Lexile:** 620L 🟣 *It's Labor Day!* **Lexile:** 360L 🟢 *It's Labor Day!* **Lexile:** 660L **Paired Selections:** **Genre:** Informational Text 🔴 "A Celebration of Trees" 🔵 "A Celebration of Trees" 🟣 "A Celebration of Trees" 🟢 "A Celebration of Trees"	**Oral Vocabulary Words:** *design* *display* *pride* *purpose* *represent* **Academic Vocabulary:** *nation* *unite* **Vocabulary:** Metaphors	

Week 6	Reading Digitally	Fluency	Connect to Social Studies	Extend Your Learning
Extend, Connect, and Assess	"Time for Kids: This Land Is Our Land" **Genre:** Online Article	**Reader's Theater:** *That Goat Has GOT to Go!*	**Passages:** "Max's Plan" "Let's Recycle!" **Activities:** Venn Diagram Take Action Poster	Choose Your Own Book

Comprehension	Print Concepts	Phonological/ Phonemic Awareness	Phonics/Spelling/ Handwriting/ Structural Analysis	High-Frequency Words	Fluency	Writing and Grammar	Research and Inquiry
Visualize Theme Directions	Author	**Phonological Awareness** Syllable Addition **Phonemic Awareness:** Phoneme Segmentation, Phoneme Blending, Phoneme Substitution	**Phonics/Spelling:** Three-Letter Consonant Blends: *scr, spl, spr, str, thr, shr* *Differentiated Spelling Lists available* **Handwriting:** Dates **Structural Analysis:** Inflectional Endings *-ed* and *-ing* **Decodable Readers:** *Three Shrimp; A Thrilling Dance*	*before front heard push tomorrow your*	Phrasing	**Write About the Text:** Write a Letter **Extended Writing:** Opinion **Writing Trait:** Sentence Fluency: Varying Sentence Types **Review Trait:** Organization: Beginning/ Middle/End **Writing Process:** Revise; Edit and Proofread; Publish, Present, and Evaluate **Grammar:** Subjective and Objective Pronouns **Mechanics:** Commas in Dates and Letters	**Project:** Interview about Traditions
Reread Author's Purpose Captions	Table of Contents	**Phonological Awareness** Syllable Deletion, Syllable Addition **Phonemic Awareness:** Phoneme Reversal, Phoneme Blending, Phoneme Deletion, Phoneme Addition	**Phonics/Spelling:** *r*-Controlled Vowels *air, are, ear* *Differentiated Spelling Lists available* **Handwriting:** Letter **Structural Analysis:** *r*-Controlled Vowel Syllables **Decodable Readers:** *A Pair at the Fair; Lights in the Air; The Bears Prepare a Feast; Leaders Care*	*favorite few gone surprise wonder young*	Phrasing	**Write About the Text:** Opinion **Writing Trait:** Voice: Author's Voice **Review Trait:** Ideas: Give Reasons for Opinion **Grammar:** Adverbs That Tell How **Mechanics:** Abbreviations (capitals and periods with *Mr., Mrs., Ms., Dr.*)	**Project:** Find Out About a Holiday

Social Emotional Development

Emotional Self Regulation
Manages feelings, emotions, and words with decreasing support from adults

As the child collaborates with a partner, the child uses appropriate words calmly when disagreeing.

Behavioral Self Regulation
Manages actions, behaviors, and words with decreasing support from adults

Rules and Routines
Follows classroom rules and routines with increasing independence

Transitioning from one activity to the next, the child follows established routines, such as putting away materials, without disrupting the class.

Working Memory
Maintains and manipulates distinct pieces of information over short periods of time

Focus Attention
Maintains focus and sustains attention with minimal adult supports

During Center Time, the child stays focused on the activity assigned and is able to stop working on the activity when it is time to move on to a different task.

Relationships and Prosocial Behaviors
Engages in and maintains positive relationships and interactions with familiar adults and children

Social Problem Solving
Uses basic problem solving skills to resolve conflicts with other children

Self Awareness
Recognizes self as a unique individual as well as belonging to a family, community, or other groups; expresses confidence in own skills

Creativity
Expresses creativity in thinking and communication

Initiative
Demonstrates initiative and independence

When working independently, the child understands when to ask for help and gets the help needed.

Task Persistence
Sets reasonable goals and persists to complete the task

Logic and Reasoning
Thinks critically to effectively solve a problem or make a decision

Planning and Problem Solving
Uses planning and problem solving strategies to achieve goals

Flexible Thinking
Demonstrates flexibility in thinking and behavior

Throughout the grades, students continue to progress in each aspect of their social emotional growth. See the Social Emotional Development checklists for each grade span to monitor students' progress.

GRADE 2 ⟫	GRADE 3 ⟫	GRADE 4 ⟫	GRADE 5

During class discussions, the child can wait until called upon to provide a response, without shouting out.

When responding to a text, the child can identify text evidence from notes previously recorded.

The child willingly works with any other child in the class on partner or group activities that are assigned.

When working on a project in a small group, the child negotiates roles and cooperates with others to complete the task.

In class discussion, the child is not fearful of sharing a unique perspective while respecting the opinions of others.

The child finds a creative way to gather information needed for a writing assignment.

When assigned to read a difficult text, the child applies routines or strategies learned to complete the reading.

Through logic and reasoning, the child is able to figure out how the author's choices of words and structures affect the communication of ideas.

When working on a long-term research project, the student can think through how to complete the different parts of the assignment over a period of time.

As the child struggles with an activity, he or she can determine a different way to complete the activity successfully.

(t) Radius Images/Image Source; (b) Patrick Foto/Shutterstock

Text Complexity Rubric

In *Wonders*, children are asked to read or listen to a range of texts within a text set to build knowledge. The various texts include:

- Literature Big Books
- Shared Reads
- Anchor Texts
- Paired Selections
- Leveled Readers
- Differentiated Genre Passages

Understanding the various factors that contribute to the complexity of a text, as well as considering what each child brings to the text, will help you determine the appropriate levels of scaffolds for children. Quantitative measures, such as Lexile scores, are only one element of text complexity. Understanding qualitative factors and reader and task considerations is also important to fully evaluate the complexity of a text.

At the beginning of each text set in the *Wonders* Teacher's Edition, information on the three components of text complexity for the texts is provided.

Qualitative		
The qualitative features of a text relate to its content or meaning. They include meaning/purpose, structure, language, and knowledge demands.		
Low Complexity	**Moderate Complexity**	**High Complexity**
Meaning/Purpose The text has a single layer of meaning explicitly stated. The author's purpose or central idea of the text is immediately obvious and clear.	**Meaning/Purpose** The text has a blend of explicit and implicit details, few uses of multiple meanings and isolated instances of metaphor. The author's purpose may not be explicitly stated but is readily inferred from a reading of the text.	**Meaning/Purpose** The text has multiple levels of meaning and there may be intentional ambiguity. The author's purpose may not be clear and/or is subject to interpretation.
Structure The text is organized in a straightforward manner, with explicit transitions to guide the reader.	**Structure** The text is largely organized in a straightforward manner, but may contain isolated incidences of shifts in time/place, focus, or pacing.	**Structure** The text is organized in a way that initially obscures meaning and has the reader build to an understanding.
Language The language of the text is literal, although there may be some rhetorical devices.	**Language** Figurative language is used to build on what has already been stated plainly in the text.	**Language** Figurative language is used throughout the text; multiple interpretations may be possible.
Knowledge Demands The text does not require extensive knowledge of the topic.	**Knowledge Demands** The text requires some knowledge of the topic.	**Knowledge Demands** The text requires significant knowledge of the topic.

Quantitative

Wonders provides the Lexile score for each text in the text set.

Low Complexity	Moderate Complexity	High Complexity
Lexile Score Text is below or at the lower end of the grade-level band according to a quantitative reading measure.	**Lexile Score** Text is in the midrange of the grade-level band according to a quantitative reading measure.	**Lexile Score** Text is at the higher end of or above the grade-level band according to a quantitative reading measure.

Reader and Task Considerations

This component of text complexity considers the motivation, knowledge, and experiences a child brings to the text. Task considerations take into account the complexity generated by the tasks children are asked to complete and the questions they are expected to answer.

In *Wonders*, children are asked to interact with the texts in many different ways. Texts such as the Shared Reads and Anchor Texts are read over multiple days and include tasks that increase in difficulty. The complexity level provided for each text considers the highest-level tasks students are asked to complete with the texts.

Low Complexity	Moderate Complexity	High Complexity
Reader The text is well within the student's developmental level of understanding and does not require extensive background knowledge.	**Reader** The text is within the student's developmental level of understanding, but some levels of meaning may be impeded by lack of prior exposure.	**Reader** The text is at the upper boundary of the student's developmental level of understanding and will require that the student has background knowledge of the topic.

Task

The questions and tasks provided for all texts are at various levels of complexity, ensuring that all students can interact with the text in meaningful ways.

Index

B

C

Key 1 = Unit 1

Key **1** = Unit 1

E

F

Folktale. *See* **Genre: literature/fiction/ prose and poetry.**

G

Key **1** = Unit 1

H

I

M

Main Story Elements. *See* Comprehension.

N

O

P

Key **1** = Unit 1

Key **1** = Unit 1

S

Science, 1: T205, T227, T237, T241, T383, T393, T397, T436–T440, **2:** T201, T231, T234, **3:** T116, T123, T145, T155, T159, T436–T440, **4:** T39, T135, T157, T169, T175, T247, T259, T265, T315, T321, T343, T355, T361, T482–T488, **5:** T43, T127, T139, T163, T175, T181, T251, T263, T269, T320, T345, T357, T364, T405, T437, T443, T484–T488, **6:** T251, T263, T269

   informational text, 1: T210–T213, T356–T361, **2:** T194–T201, **3:** T128–T131, T369, **4:** T50–55, T124–T135, T140–T143, T212–T227, T326–T329, **5:** T48–T53, T144–T149, T328–T331, T400–T405, T410, **6:** T234–237

Science of Reading, Units 1–6: xviii–xix

Self-Selected Reading, 1: T73, T77, T81, T155, T159, T163, T235, T239, T315, T319, T323, T391, T395, T399, **3:** T73, T77, T81, T153, T157, T161, T235, T239, T317, T321, T325, T391, T395, T399, **4:** T79, T85, T91, T167, T173, T179, T257, T263, T269, T353, T359, T365, T433, T439, T445, **5:** T77, T83, T89, T173, T179, T185, T261, T267, T273, T355, T361, T367, T435, T441, T447, **6:** T81, T87, T93, T167, T173, T179, T261, T267, T273, T357, T363, T369, T437, T443, T449

Sensory Words. *See* **Vocabulary.**

Shared Reading, 1: T14–T15, T94–T95, T176–T177, T258–T259, T336–T337, **3:** T14–T15, T94–T95, T174–T175, T258–T259, T338–T339

Show Your Knowledge, 1: T145, T305, T381, **2:** T63, T143, T219, T301, T375, **3:** T63, T143, T225, T307, T381, **4:** T67, T155, T245, T341, T421, **5:** T65, T161, T249, T343, T423, **6:** T69, T155, T249, T345, T425

Sight words. *See* **High-Frequency Words.**

Small Group Options. *See* **Approaching Level Options; Beyond Level Options; On Level Options.**

Social-Emotional Learning, 1: T4–T5, T248–T249, **2:** T242–T243, **3:** T4–T5, T248–T249, **4:** T4–T5, T274–T275, **5:** T4–T5, T278–T279, **6:** T4–T5, T280–T281, **Units 1–6:** xvi–xvii, T4–T5

Social Studies, 1: T65, T75, T79, T157, T161, T287, T307, T317, T321, **2:** T43, T145, T155, T159, T281, T387, T391, T430–T434, **3:** T65, T75, T79, T287, T309, T319, T323, T363, T397, **4:** T403, T423, T435, T441, **6:** T169, T325, T407, T427, T439, T445, T486–T490

   informational text, 1: T48–T51, T278–T287, **2:** T48–T51, T128–T131, T286–T289, T352–T357, T363, **3:** T48–51, T278–T287, T292–T295, T358–T363, **4:** T398–T403, T409, **5:** T218–T229, T410, **6:** T52–T57, T126–T137, T330–T333, T402–T408, T413

   personal narrative, 1: T128–T133, T147

Speaking. *See also* **Collaborative Conversations; Research and Inquiry; Writing Process: publish and present.**

   appropriate facts/relevant details, 1: T60, T142, T222, T302, T378, **2:** T60, T140, T216, T298, T372, **3:** T60, T222, T304, T378, **4:** T64, T154, T242, T338, T418, **5:** T62, T160, T246, T340, T420, **6:** T66, T154, T246, T342, T422

   complete sentences, 1: T60, T142, T222, T302, T378, **2:** T60, T140, T216, T298, T372, **3:** T60, T222, T304, T378, **4:** T64, T154, T244, T338, T418, **5:** T62, T160, T246, T340, T420, **6:** T66, T154, T246, T342, T422

   create recordings, 1: T60, T142, T222, T302, T378, **3:** T60, T140, T222, T304, T378, **4:** T64, T154, T242, T338, T418, **5:** T62, T160, T200, T246, T340, T420, **6:** T66, T154, T246, T342, T422

   descriptive words, using, 5: T104, T114, T140–T141, T152–T153, T160, T200, T210, T230–T231, T240–T241, T246

   retelling. *See* **Retelling.**

Spelling

   analyze errors, 1: T22, T102, T184, T266, T344, **2:** T22, T102, T182, T260, T340, **3:** T22, T102, T182, T266, T346, **4:** T22, T112, T200, T292, T386, **5:** T22, T110, T206, T296, T388, **6:** T22, T114, T200, T296, T390

   assess, 1: T59, T141, T221, T301, T377, **2:** T59, T139, T215, T297, T371, **3:** T59, T139, T221, T303, T377, **4:** T63, T151, T241, T337, T417, **5:** T61, T157, T245, T339, T419, **6:** T65, T151, T245, T341, T421

   dictation, 1: T12, T92, T174, T256, T334, **2:** T12, T92, T172, T250, T330, **3:** T12, T92, T172, T256, T336, **4:** T12, T102, T190, T282, T376, **5:** T12, T100, T196, T286, T378, **6:** T12, T104, T190, T286, T380

   pretest, 1: T12, T92, T174, T256, T334, **2:** T12, T92, T172, T250, T330, **3:** T12, T92, T172, T256, T336, **4:** T12, T102, T190, T282, T376, **5:** T12, T100, T196, T286, T378, **6:** T12, T104, T190, T286, T380

   review, 1: T53, T59, T103, T135, T141, T215, T221, T295, T301, T371, T377, **2:** T53, T59, T133, T139, T209, T215, T291, T297, T365, T371, **3:** T53, T59, T133, T139, T215, T221, T297, T303, T371, T377, **4:** T57, T63, T145, T151, T235, T241, T331, T337, T411, T417, **5:** T55, T61, T151, T157, T239, T245, T333, T339, T413, T419, **6:** T59, T65, T145, T151, T239, T245, T335, T341, T415, T421

   spelling words, 1: T12, T92, T174, T256, T334, **2:** T12, T92, T172, T250, T330, **3:** T12, T92, T172, T256, T336, **4:** T12, T102, T190, T282, T376, **5:** T12, T100, T196, T286, T378, **6:** T12, T104, T190, T286, T380

Spelling Patterns

   word sort, 1: T22, T32, T53, T59, T102, T135, T141, T184, T194, T215, T221, T266, T276, T295, T301, T334, T344, T354, T371, **3:** T22, T32, T53, T59, T102, T133, T139, T182, T192, T215, T221, T266, T276, T297, T303, T336, T346, T356, T371, **4:** T22, T32, T57, T63, T112, T145, T151, T200, T210, T235, T241, T292, T302, T331, T337, T376, T386, T396, T411, **5:** T22, T32, T55, T61, T110, T151, T157, T206, T216, T239, T245, T296, T306, T333, T339, T378, T388, T398, T413, **6:** T22, T32, T59, T65, T114, T145, T151, T200, T210, T239, T245, T296, T306, T335, T341, T380, T390, T400, T415

   words with /ā/a, ai, ay, 4: T12, T22, T32, T57, T63

   words with air, are, ear, 6: T380, T390, T400, T415, T421

   words with ch, -tch, wh, ph, 2: T330, T340, T350, T365, T371

   words with diphthongs

     oi, oy, **5:** T378, T388, T398–T399, T413, T419

     ou, ow, **5:** T286, T296, T306, T333, T339

   words with /ē/e, ee, ea, 4: T102, T112, T122, T145, T151

   words with end blends, 2: T172, T182, T192, T209, T215

   words with /ī/i, y, igh, ie, 4: T282, T292, T302, T331, T337

   words with l-blends, 1: T174, T184, T194, T215, T221

   words with long a: a_e, 3: T12, T15, T16, T22, T32, T53, T59

   words with long e: y, ey, 4: T376, T386, T396, T411, T417

   words with long i: i_e, 3: T92, T102, T112, T133, T139

   words with o_e, u_e, 3: T256, T266, T276, T297, T303

   words with /ō/o, oa, ow, oe, 4: T190, T200, T210, T235, T241

   words with -ook, -ood, 3: T336, T346, T356, T371, T377

   words with r- and s-blends, 1: T334, T344, T354, T371, T377

   words with r-controlled vowels

     /är/ar, **5:** T12, T14, T15, T22, T32, T55, T61

     /ôr/or, ore, oar, **5:** T196, T206, T216, T239, T245

     /ûr/er, ir, ur, or, **5:** T100, T110, T120, T151, T157

   words with short a, 1: T12, T22, T32, T53, T59

   words with short e, 2: T12, T22, T32, T53, T59

   words with short i, 1: T92, T102, T112, T135, T141

Key **1** = Unit 1

Key **1** = Unit 1